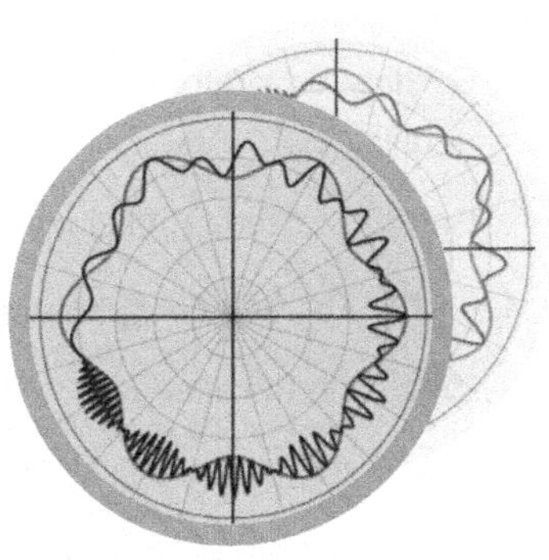

Hayden's Book of Synastry

by Ajani Abdul-Khaliq

Cover Art by Victoria Ward

Table of Contents

Introduction: Talking to Hayden

So you're saying I can calculate my way into a "right" relationship with anyone?

Yes.

I don't believe you.

You don't have to.

Don't play with me, sir. I agreed to take you to the other side of the bay, and would prefer to pay attention to real things while we head there. You'll pardon my rudeness, but I'm not one to put any stock in astrology or any of that hippie business that you people like to sell.

Actually, I'm a scientist.

That's even worse. You especially should know better than to believe in things you can't measure.

And as a sailor you should know better than to assume simplicity in things you'll never master, the astrologer Geery mumbled.

Quite the mouth on you for someone who needs my services. And I am a soldier first who sails only when paid. Hmph. Okay fine. You have one minute to tell me 1) why I should believe anything at all regarding astrology and 2) why I should buy this idea that all relationships—to friends, family, cats, dogs, countries, projects, and all that—can be calculated from this so-called "synastry" of yours. The clock's already started.

Cool, I love challenges like this:

So you don't believe in astrology, but you do believe in categorizing personalities. Astrology provides such categories based on massive patterns of behavior among people across the seasons and other cycles. You do know societies behave differently in winter than in summer right?—

Yea—

And that seasonality affects immune systems, animals in heat, migrations and other natural patterns?

Of c—

Wait. Immune systems?

And that when you count steps with respect to these cycles you can map them on a circle? Extend this to the eight other major bodies whose orbits are tied to earth's and you have a system on your hands.

Yeah right, that's a big jump.

It is, but you only gave me one minute. Anyway, the cycles of the other planets are connected to Earth's. Consider now that all of these planet cycles repeat and can be modeled as waves, that the light to our eyes, sounds to our ears, and firing patterns of certain clusters of neurons also have cycles which respond to these cycles beyond them—which is how we are so good at processing patterns. The signs in astrology squeeze a family of frequencies onto a circle in the way that a single octave in music squeezes a main family of frequencies into a few keys. From there all you do is double these with each new octave and modulo—uh, reset—them back to zero when they get beyond a detectable range. Regardless of what you think of all this, you do believe that our brains and bodies can distinguish a super-wide range of frequencies from the low music of radio waves to the Vitamin D-making frequency of ultraviolet? That's how I believe astrology works in a nutshell. But my minute is up.

Hm. So astrology signs are like taking the spectrum and wrapping it around in a circle? Is that it?

Basically. And every time the circle starts again it starts a couple of octaves up. That is, until our senses can't detect any more. Then the circle resets to the lowest octave with the same "harmony." So signs can repeat forever.

...Okay. Keep going.

Great, because your second question is easier from here: Whenever humans think of events which they perceive outside of themselves—that is, friends, family, cats, dogs, countries, and such—they simulate pieces of that event in their minds, reproducing all of its frequencies (or waves for short) which stand out most to them. But all things which are confirmed to exist outside of us have been so confirmed because their waves hit other things that viewed them. This means that anything that affects many things besides itself gets its own spacetime "signature" which gives it a consistent "appearance" in the minds of different people who reference them. That chain of reference (subject to the usual game of telephone across time) allows us to interact with plain old dates (and not just people) as if they had charts. Our signature (which we scientists call a "wave function") can interact with any other signature regardless of its form—cat or human. That goes for all events that happen as long as one of them can simulate the other's wave. In this way, combining astrocharts through synastry amounts to doing math on the wave functions of more than one event at the same time. That's it. That's my explanation.

Hayden sighed. Tsk, you when from flower child to mad scientist in two minutes. Unfortunately, I don't understand all that space stuff.

Look. You know how remote controls and wi-fi can send waves to their receivers and alter the way those receiving objects behave? Think of any person as a kind of wi-fi source throwing off the light of his physical appearance, the sound of his voice, and—most importantly—the complex wave which describes his overall average effect on everything that interacts with him. The astrology of one chart captures this person's wave at a certain place, time, and energy level. The astrology of two charts captures how his wave interacts with another wave under the same constraints.

And what about all that mythology? You know, where "Mars likes war" and "Neptune likes water?"

Those are just stories we attach to the patterns to make them easier to understand.

Hmm… the soldier Hayden pondered for a while. None of this is proven, you know.

You're right. It's all speculation. But you *must* know that nature is nothing if not consistent in its whims. The science of waves is real. The patterns of human response to most events are consistent. Human brains work using firing cycles. We're made up of particles and energy potentials just like everything else to which we respond. And anyone who says such waves don't affect us at all is either a liar or a fool who refuses to count even the light rays in his eyes or the touch-fired nerves under his skin. Astrology tries to separate out the various frequencies involved in all this—something only the neural network people come close to modeling.

Remaining silent for a while, Hayden finally replied. Okay, I'll take you at your word. Astrology may not be science, but the categories it places on experience are valuable, right? So here's my next question. If I believe that you can somehow take all of these patterns and find the ideal interaction between any two events, why don't you write how to do it? No one in the everyday world will believe you are anything other than a soothsayer if you don't show them these patterns in ways they can verify for themselves. Write it down AND show them how to apply it. I didn't ask you to convince me of the "ideal" part. I'll just assume you'll include this in your writing.

Wha—? But that's like…thousands of combinations of stuff! I'm a scientist not a machine.

Hey, you either write a thousand things down once or explain a thousand things a thousand times to people like me, one by one—never leaving anything solid behind.

Geery frowned, his voice flat with unamusement. So you want me to write you a book.

Yes sir. And not just any book. Write me a book about synastry. I'll figure out the basics myself.

Well, um, what do I get in return? A free trip across the bay next time I need it?

Ha! Business doesn't work that way partner. But I will pay for the book once it's done.

Geery frowned again. Grrr. Guess I'll be doing it for the "love" then.

Quick Starting

First: Obtain an astrology program or get access to one online

This book is all about the astrology of partnerships, so before we do anything you'll need access to your astrology chart. There are several places online to have your own astrowheel printed out, but not nearly as many places to obtain your combined chart with another person—both table AND angle view. If you don't already have access to an astrology program or website which produces both a wheel and a table view of astrocharts, you do have some options.

PC users

1. Go to http://www.starfisher.cz/starfisher/EN/, download and install StarFisher, the program I use to do everything in this book.

2. You now have StarFisher, but it won't display any of the advanced angles. So now you should go to my website at http://electricmonastery.com and download "FSAStarFisher.zip," the pre-programmed files you need to display a full table full of angles. Otherwise you'll likely not see things like undeciles, taos, II-squares, or III-noviles, and will be missing around 26–30 of the 36 angle families we cover in this book. (If you don't know what undeciles, taos and such are, keep reading.)

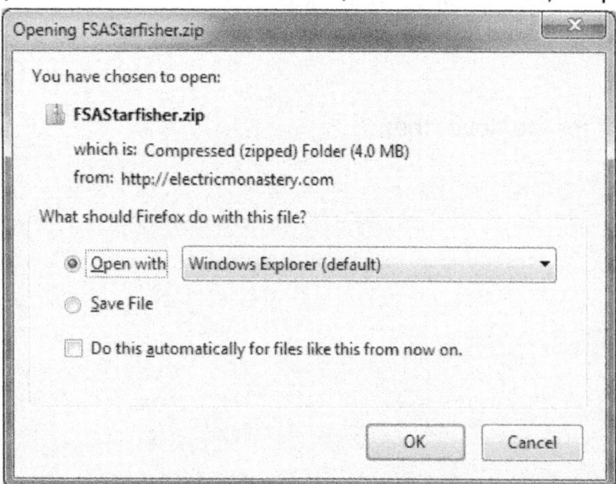

3. Extract the file so that you're looking at a folder called "StarFisher."

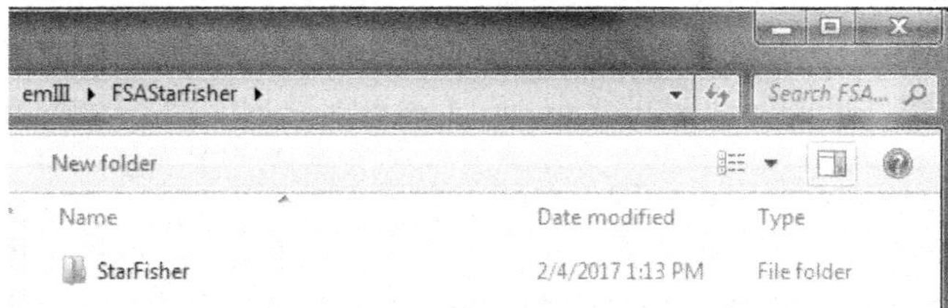

Open this folder to reveal three more folders. These are modified files for reading advanced angles.

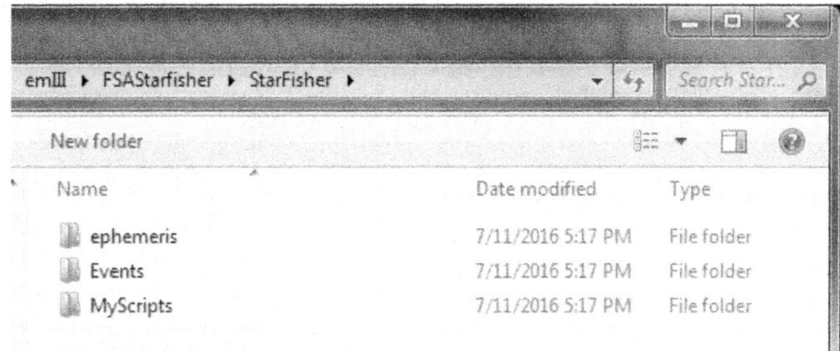

4. Select the three folders you got from step 3 and drag them into your original (installed) StarFisher folder from step 1. You should see a screen which asks if you want to replace files. For all items, say yes.

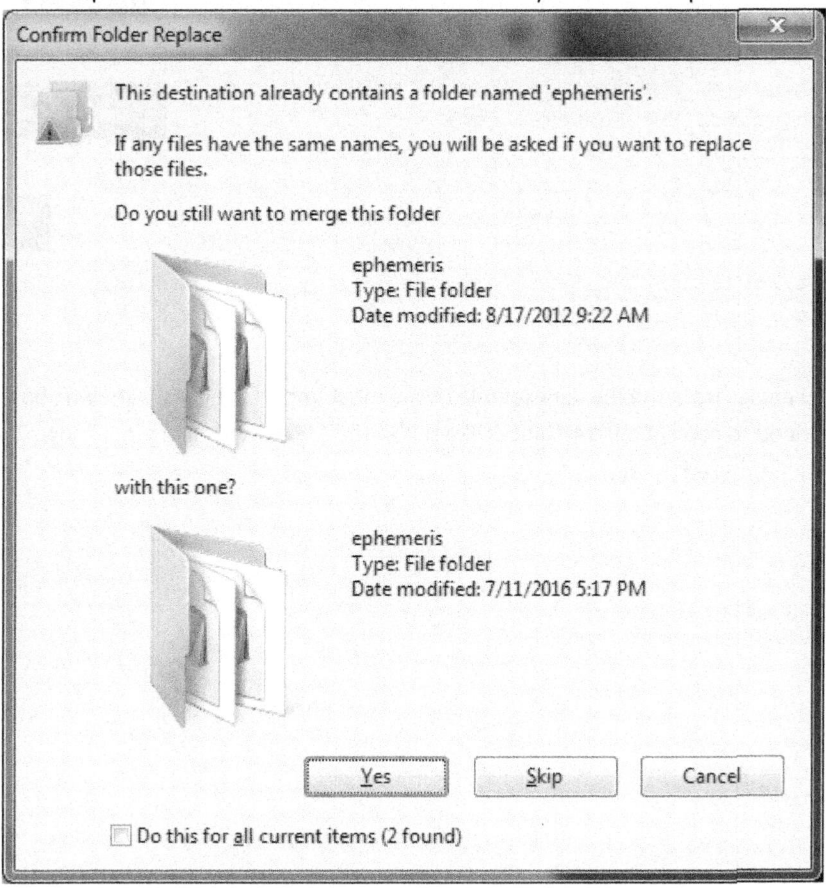

Mac users and users of software besides StarFisher

You can still read synastry charts perfectly fine with any program that prints both a wheel and a table version of you and the other's synastry. The only difference is that, by default, you won't be able to see the advanced angles or extra asteroids like Bacchus or Eros.

If you're using your own favorite program and would like to display additional asteroids, you can find the files for these at astro.com. Follow your program's instructions for how to install them.

If you want to input the advanced angles into your own software, *tables 16-6* and *16-7* shows all of the values for each of the different angles. If you'd rather not copy line by line from this book, you can also get these angles and their ranges of effect (orbs) from the same file that the PC users download from my site. The file is StarFisher\MyScripts\init.sfs. Change the .sfs to .txt to read it on a Mac. It's just a text file.

In the init.sfs file you'll find certain lines that look like the ones below:

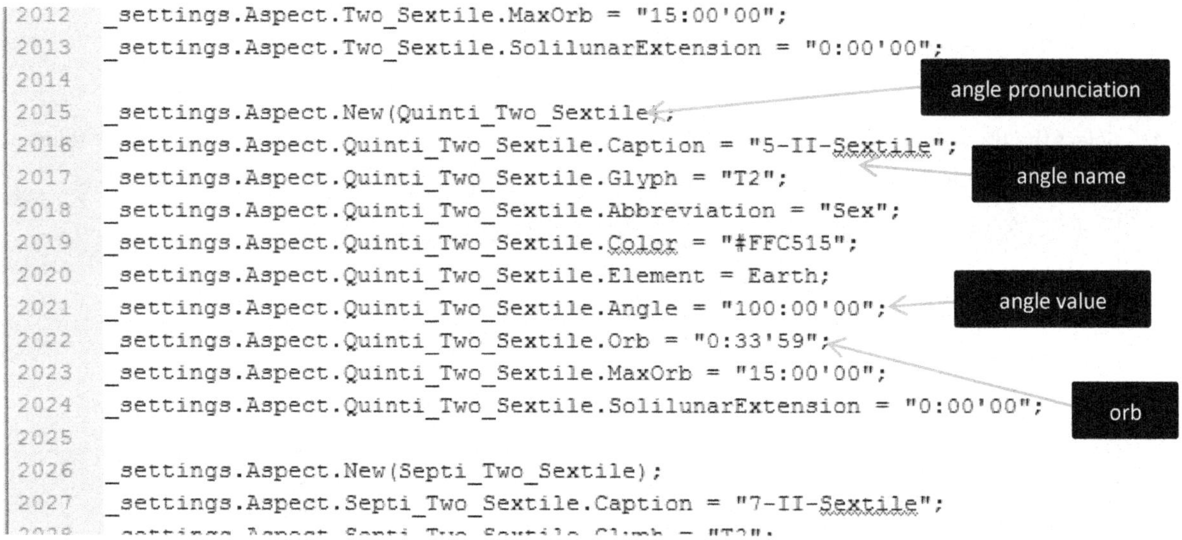

```
_settings.Aspect.Two_Sextile.MaxOrb = "15:00'00";
_settings.Aspect.Two_Sextile.SolilunarExtension = "0:00'00";

_settings.Aspect.New(Quinti_Two_Sextile);
_settings.Aspect.Quinti_Two_Sextile.Caption = "5-II-Sextile";
_settings.Aspect.Quinti_Two_Sextile.Glyph = "T2";
_settings.Aspect.Quinti_Two_Sextile.Abbreviation = "Sex";
_settings.Aspect.Quinti_Two_Sextile.Color = "#FFC515";
_settings.Aspect.Quinti_Two_Sextile.Element = Earth;
_settings.Aspect.Quinti_Two_Sextile.Angle = "100:00'00";
_settings.Aspect.Quinti_Two_Sextile.Orb = "0:33'59";
_settings.Aspect.Quinti_Two_Sextile.MaxOrb = "15:00'00";
_settings.Aspect.Quinti_Two_Sextile.SolilunarExtension = "0:00'00";

_settings.Aspect.New(Septi_Two_Sextile);
_settings.Aspect.Septi_Two_Sextile.Caption = "7-II-Sextile";
```

angle pronunciation
angle name
angle value
orb

If you're copying the advanced angles from the file, an example of the most important lines is shown above for the quinti-II-sextile. In total you'll need to copy about 140 blocks like this in the file. Sounds like fun, I know. You can imagine how this was when I first entered them.

Getting started for advanced readers...

By itself, the astrology of single charts can range from a piece-of-cake to elephant-sized challenging depending on your level of experience. If you're already pretty good with the subject, have read this book's predecessor *Full Spectrum Astrology* (or are otherwise pretty comfortable with angles like the II-trine), and just came to read how your chart compares to someone else's, then there are really only two chapters you might want to look at: Chapters 20 and 22. Chapter 20 uses the table spread across the last pages of Chapter 19 and a couple of the tables in Chapter 16 fairly frequently, but other than that should be straightforward enough for advanced readers. Picking up right where *FSA* left off, this book begins with chapter 16.

- **Chapter 20: How do you read this synastry chart?** explains how to read a synastry chart to answer questions ranging from "Why am I in this relationship?" to "How do I oppress this enemy?"
- **Chapter 22: On duos and trios – Reading the composite chart** explains how to read composite charts—a surprisingly slippery area of astrology once you get into it. Davison / relative charts are also discussed here.

Getting started for intermediate readers (less detail)...

If you've done synastry before but 1) haven't read *FSA*, 2) aren't familiar with advanced angles like the II-trine, or 3) are less comfortable with astrology's actual connection with astronomy, you should read the "Essential background knowledge" section of Chapter 16 first, then Chapter 20. Chapter 16 is a recap of this book's basic assumptions and provides valuable information on what all the planets mean as well as tools for reading your individual chart (though nowhere near to extent covered in *FSA*). Composite charts can be a little weird for readers who are new to them, so you might bypass Chapter 22 for the time being.

- **Chapter 16: Astrology explained again** introduces what this book is about and outlines all of its major assumptions, including what the planets, signs, and houses do in a single chart. The "Essential background knowledge" section is the most important.
- **Chapter 20: How do you read this synastry chart?** explains how to read a synastry chart to answer questions ranging from "Why am I in this relationship?" to "How do I oppress this enemy?"

Getting started for intermediate readers (more detail) ...

Intermediate-level readers who like a lot of detail may wish to read about the role of houses in synastry, Chapter 18. Personally, I find synastric houses to be a big disappointment, since they regularly swap (and thus fuzzify) the role of who influences whom. I have covered it though, so you get a chapter for it.

- **Chapter 16: Astrology explained again** introduces what this book is about and outlines all of its major assumptions, including what the planets, signs, and houses do in a single chart. The "Essential background knowledge" section is the most important.
- **Chapter 18: Planets on another's houses** discusses the role of your planets in another's houses and vice-versa.
- **Chapter 20: How do you read this synastry chart?** explains how to read a synastry chart to answer questions ranging from "Why am I in this relationship?" to "How do I oppress this enemy?"

Getting started for beginning readers...

This book assumes a certain level of familiarity with astrology. If you are completely new to the field, I'd recommend you just read the book all the way through, skipping the huge collection pair-by-pair interpretations which take up most of Chapters 18, 19, and 21; these can be used as references if you need them. Take a peek at *table 19-9* first (the table which takes up 6 pages at the end of Chapter 19) then, if it looks like a lot to handle, start at 16.

- **Chapter 16: Astrology explained again** introduces what this book is about and outlines all of its major assumptions, including what the planets, signs, and houses do in a single chart. The "Essential background knowledge" section is the most important.
- **Chapter 17: Behavior of houses, planets, angles and signs under synastry** explains how certain factors we take for granted in single chart astrology change in synastry. This chapter's presentation of multiple characteristics for each angle turns out to make it the most useful chapter for correcting certain bad aspects in a relationship which you might read later on.
- **Chapter 18: Planets on another's houses** discusses the role of your planets in another's houses and vice-versa.
- **Chapter 19: Planets on the planets III: Synastry** contains detailed interpretations of each of the 625 synastric planet-pairs covered in this book. After reading the beginning, you can safely skip the actual [Sun-Sun], [Sun-Moon]... interpretations and use them as references later.
- **Chapter 20: How do you read this synastry chart?** explains how to read a synastry chart to answer questions ranging from "Why am I in this relationship?" to "How do I oppress this enemy?"
- **Chapter 21: Planets on the planets IV: Composite charts** contains detailed interpretations of each of the 300 composite planet-pairs covered in this book. Beginners should definitely read the first part of this chapter. After this part, you can skip the actual interpretations as reference material.
- **Chapter 22: On duos and trios – Reading the composite chart** explains how to read composite charts—a surprisingly slippery area of astrology once you get into it. Davison / relative charts are also discussed here.
- **Chapter 23: Synastry with dead people, dates, and projects** explains how to do synastry with things that aren't living people, and explains what you can get out of such synastry.
- **Chapter 24, Conclusion: New languages, new lands** contains a final discussion between this book's two main characters.
- **Chapter 25: Resonant pairs across the charts** summarizes how to purposely emphasize certain planets and angles in yours and another's chart

Chapter 16: Astrology explained again

Where the field of astrology is full of symbols and stories from days long past, the interactions it captures say something deep about our basic nature. There is the hunt and the hunter: Scorpio and Sagittarius. The flooding information and the feeling of swimming in it: Aquarius and Pisces. From the sea to the land, the evolution of a species unfolds—Pisces to Aries standing as symbols for explaining to ourselves how the inclination to do something precedes its being done. The patterns of birth through death, hunger through satiation, acting though feedback (for fueling the next action) are clearly reflected in a wheel populated with images. Within those images are objects which squeeze those images into solid form for interacting with each other: the planets. Thus a flood of information is represented as Uranus, for example. Uranus is the planet prior in orbit to the planet of swimming in that same information: Neptune. The interactions among these and other space objects are tied up in our view of the angles which separate them: their aspects. Sure it's mostly stories. Except for the orbit part. Unlike the various tales associated with many astrological symbols, the science of orbits has its roots in the physics of energy carriers from the smallest atom to the largest galaxy—the various spins and binding forces of these carriers marrying parts of things to the whole.

Although looking at the picture of a single astrology chart can be incredibly informative, nothing quite surpasses the astrology of pairs of people. Typically this is where Jenny finds Johnny funny. Johnny finds Jenny sexy. Beware the union of Sagittarius and Cancer. And we all leave entertained for about an hour afterwards. Truly, **the practice of seeing how two astrology charts affect each other**—called **synastry**—can be fun; unfortunately most of the time all of those exhaustive combinations which generations of ancient people spent putting together don't actually amount to much when it comes to influencing our daily lives. But this book aims to correct that. We'll put astrology to work for you and your partnerships.

What's on the agenda

Synastry also produces "self charts"

Hayden's Book of Synastry (*HBS*) picks up where its predecessor *Full Spectrum Astrology* (*FSA*) left off. Whereas *FSA* relied on orbits and some math to explain what astrology is and what we can stand to learn from it, *HBS* references more psychology. Just as interaction-focused philosophies such as Judeo-Christianity-Islam are far more popular in the world than more personally focused ones like Buddhism, the social power of exchanges with others is in many ways simpler, more practical, and more accessible in form than exchanges with ourselves, so that we no longer need to focus on how astrology works, only on what we agree to do with it. And yet we will find that there is still *much* more to learn about the self from studying such exchanges, beginning with this: Taken as an interaction between you and your own thoughts about yourself, synastry creates something called a "self chart" which divides who you are against who you would be. Seeing your own pursuit of values against the character you already have, it becomes clear that happiness is a two player sport—even if the other player is actually you.

Charts with non-people

And so synastry shows us compatibility between two people. But we don't have to stop at people. After all, even other people aren't actually themselves in our personal world—only what we imagine them to be (subject to a lot of missing information). So now we're coming up with charts between ourselves and imagined things. A chart comparison for you and your pet? Sure. You and your pet *project*? Yeah, why not. You and some random book? Yes but...I'll get to that. How about you and a dead person like Julius Caesar? Maybe. We'll cover all of this along the way, addressing some seemingly impossible topics like day charts (charts for a specific day). These are impossible in the sense that science can't measure the interactive form of such things, yet you can use synastry to look at how *you* interact with them through combinations of pairs in your own chart.

Composite charts and relative charts

So what happens **when waves of two slightly different frequencies interfere**? You get a **beat**. **As one wave travels through the other, it adds to or subtracts from the strength of the other** (**modulating** it). This produces a frequency which is the average of the two. Accordingly, there are actually two major ways to look at your relationship with another person. While synastry shows how two people respond to each other, composite charts show how two people see their own combined efforts. That is, **composite charts** **show the average of A's and B's charts as seen from the perspective of an insider responding to the "beats" between their corresponding realms of behavior** (planets). Taken fully, composite charts are a combination of screwy, unreliable-yet-reliable, and fascinating all at once. Essentially the chart of a thing which can't happen in physics, composites nonetheless gain their reality as a kind of third party duo formed by you and the other person. We'll cover these too.

As an alternative to composites, **relative charts** are simply **the chart of a third party born exactly between two partners' birth dates and birth places**. These charts provide a basic description of a partnership as seen by the public. If composite charts show a partnership from the inside, relative charts show a partnership from the outside. Although I do discuss relative charts in this book, interpreting them is basically the same as interpreting the normal birth chart of any person or event. The tools for doing this form the central topic of Chapters 1–15 in the book before this one, though you can use some of the tables here in *HBS* to get you started.

And a million misconceptions...

Finally, throughout the book we'll address various misconceptions that come with studying interactions. There are lots of them, but I'll start you off by addressing what may be the biggest one: No you cannot read the ultimate success or failure of any pairing through astrology. Not through composites, not through synastry, or anything.

Although common sense might have told you this to begin with, there's actually a pretty profound reason for this which I discovered early on while doing the statistics for this book. That reason will be discussed in the next chapter, and adds a whole new dimension to the topic of angles raised in *FSA*. In the meantime, you may be thinking, "If I can't read the success of a relationship through all this then what's the point?" But you'll quickly find that there is a lot more to your journey with others besides the destination. Astrology will never tell you the single thing that you *will* do, but its story-based frameworks will show literally hundreds of things you *can* do to manipulate, motivate, grasp, grow, and destroy relationships if you want. It will also show you **what the default flow of impressions is between you and the other**—the ever-elusive **right relationship** which (contrary to how it may sound) need not be pleasant, fair, or fitting for where you and the other happen to be at the time. This is actually much deeper territory than a simple success/failure prognostication, and involves dimensions of your exchanges which you surely haven't thought about. There are at least 1200 different corners which we'll cover in here. I'm sure you'll find something new.

On Geery and Hayden

Scattered across *HBS* you'll find dialogues between the self-proclaimed scientist/astrology theorist Geery and the soldier Hayden. Geery, an upbeat rationalist who seeks to study astrology using more scientific methods, is thoughtful and full of ideas about his field. And while he may not have all the answers, he does have enough answers to at least convince himself to continue his rationality-based studies of the subject. For every plausible facet of astrology that Geery encounters, he attempts an explanation in terms of science. This is similar to—but not the same as—Hayden's perspective. Also a rationalist (though much more skeptical), Hayden cares a lot less about how scientific astrology is and a lot more about whether it can be put to practical use. Unlike Geery, Hayden can be difficult to satisfy and impatient with things that require imagination, so that Geery must continually spell things out for him. The purpose of these dialogues—as it was with Geery and Katha in *FSA*—is to present the reader with a more direct overview of the ideas presented in this book, especially where the overarching ideas could use a good summary. Summaries like these take into account those difficulties which you the reader might also have with the topics we cover. When Geery refers to his "notes from Katha," he's referring to chapters 1–15 in *FSA*.

Methods used to write this book

The dataset

As was the case with *FSA*, I analyzed clusters of angles among several hundred charts (430 in this one) in order to write this book. Most of the data comes from interactions between me and the people in the sample set, supplemented by my observations of their interactions among each other. This is both good and bad news from a procedural perspective. On the one hand, my dataset is definitely biased in terms of sample pool. On the other hand, this same dataset also consists of people who were thoroughly known—including friends, rivals, indifferent folks, as well as some of the best and worst exchanges I have ever observed (several in which I was involved and served as the saint, several in which I was involved and served as the villain, and several in which I was not involved which were either "pearly gates" peachy or atrociously, epically, horrible). With rare exception, I excluded the synastries of famous people from this book simply because one cannot rely on what the pop culture tells you about how these people actually relate. This is true both for composites and synastry charts, where a glimpse at the unnamed cluster with the celebrity couple in it ensures that you know less about what you're looking at and more about what the news rags *wanted* you to look at.[1]

Given that the data used in this book were drawn mostly from a pool of people whom I've actually met, why should you trust the interpretations in here? Below are some of the reasons:

- Believe it or not, when you read an academic journal article describing a qualitative experiment or interview in psychology, you're typically reading about the interaction between the witnessing experimenters and their subjects. In order to sound less biased, we scholars are told not to write papers emphasizing the first person "I," but that's what you're getting. Here in *HBS* you'll find the same thing, except I tell you about it. And unlike a majority of journal articles, *HBS'* data were gathered outside of the context of the analysis, so we build on the relationships as they actually were, rather than experimentally filtered versions thereof (where the investigator notes only "relevant" facts and dumps the rest). No relationship quality was dumped here.
- If we study the relationships of strangers, we actually gain a lot less information on their 1:1 exchanges because our biographies of them are filtered through the different lenses of each biographer. So maybe you shouldn't trust one person's direct observations of 400 people. But the indirect observations of 400 different biographers who liked their subjects enough to write biographies probably isn't any more objective. *HBS* data comprise the normal, the boring, and the seemingly insignificant along with the noteworthy, and the sample set is not limited to the "biographer's favorite person."
- Studying strangers works well for single charts and for relationship charts when the astrology is already known. Indeed, I used plenty of stranger data in *FSA*. As both *FSA* and *HBS* are being written, however, much of the astrology is new. So you can't look at an Augustus-Cleopatra III-decile and ask whether your conclusions actually fit their interaction with each other. While there are lots of books chronicling the life of single personalities, the number of books chronicling the deep dynamics between two lives are incredibly scarce. You literally "had to be there" in order to study this kind of thing, especially when there is no known research available on how a 165° tao should actually work in synastry. If you don't know the people well enough because you weren't there, and you don't know the astrology well enough because it's new, what do you do? Answer: you make sure you know the people at least well enough to compare the new astrology against common sense. That's what we do here.
- As the differences between the composite and relative charts suggest, there is a difference between describing a partnership at a distance and describing it while being in it or near it. Many more details are available for noting, and this becomes useful for differentiating hundreds of astrology combinations which might otherwise start to look the same after a while. A look at Ted Hughes and Sylvia Plath reveals trouble. A look at John Lennon and Yoko Ono reveals trouble. What kind of trouble? All the time? Under what triggers? Given what issues? A look at complete strangers (like celebrities) won't be nearly nuanced enough to meet the task of matching 36 angles to 1200 different families of details. Again, you had to be there. In other words, even if this book did attempt to avoid "bias" by relying on data from people not personally known to me, that data would end up extra biased in the sense that we could only study relationships from the public-worthy outside. The composite chart interpretations in particular would be near nonexistent. In any event, the data do consist mostly of non-close interactants, so the "stranger" factor is actually in there (just not with superstars).

---

[1] We'll see later that the charts of illusory things actually constitute less of a problem with composites *if* you believe that the depictions of public personalities are reliable enough. I don't, and so couldn't use such data.

How conclusions were drawn

I used a big data table of about 430 x 1250 entries, each populated with angle separations and other placement measures to analyze what each particular planet pair was doing. It should also be noted that, by fortunate accident, the last 180 composite pairs and many of the synastric pairs were done completely randomly without my knowing which pair I was looking at until after the cluster behavior was determined. Later on, I'll refer to this as the "blind method." What this means for you is that the conclusions drawn for these pairs beginning with [Pluto-Ascendant] were subjected to a notably more "scientific" process than the ones before them and that the behavior of each of these pairs is described more objectively than the previous ones. This means that you don't need to believe in astrology to accept the interpretations. You only need to believe in statistics. For the blind pairs, I looked at clusters of people who shared the same angle number under some hidden astrological category, wrote the conclusions about that category more or less exactly as you read them in this book, and only AFTER this was done did I uncover what the astrological category actually was. It was through the blind method that the composite interpretations revealed themselves to be very weirdly behaved (compared to everything else in astrology), such that seasoned astrologers may find these particularly interesting.

Essential background knowledge: How we'll approach astrology in the coming chapters

HBS is an upper-intermediate to advanced level book with some technical corners. As in *FSA*, I indicate more technical sections with a 🛠 symbol (as you'll see in the bullets right after this). Although I'll give a recap of basic astrology over the course of the next few pages, you should note that there are lots of assumptions that I've made in here which may be unfamiliar even to people who have already been exposed to astrology. I explain these assumptions in *FSA* and will repeat them here BUT you should note that, at the time of this writing in late 2016 and early 2017, several of them are new to the field as a whole. The assumptions are as follows:

- Astrology doesn't require any kind of spirituality or belief in the stars. You only need to believe that our planet's tilt and position in space affects things that happen on it. On a very basic level for example, the day / night cycle affects when we humans conduct business. The summer / winter cycle affects how and where societies gather together. The 12-year Jupiter cycle corresponds roughly to leaps in adulthood. The 50 and 84 year Chiron and Uranus cycles correspond roughly to the scale of a human lifespan.
- 🛠 Astrology involves the study of space objects at a particular time and from a particular viewpoint. The position of each object captures the state of an "event" that occurs at that point. Planets and signs don't really mean anything, but their orbits and angles mean everything in determining what each planet and sign is about. Think of our solar system as being like a giant atom with the planets as electrons. Their gravitational potential at any point with respect to the Sun is balanced by changes in the potential energy we ourselves carry on Earth, and our biology has evolved to adjust to changes in flux (energy passing through) associated with this. High ultraviolet in the summer affects your vitamin D on a yearly cycle. Low temperature in the night affects your metabolism on a daily cycle. Those are consequences of the Earth-Sun cycle as well as the Earth's own rotation. As for the other planets, I'll explain the connection later.
- The **Signs** (like Capricorn and Aquarius) are **sections of the universal sky which give a certain character to the objects in them**. But they don't have any real meaning by themselves. Instead, signs are like tilt directions in the gravitational "field" of our Solar System, within the gravitational field of our galaxy, within our cluster of space dust flying off of the Big Bang. Among other things, such tilt (depending on where in space you view it from) corresponds to our experience of the seasons and weird stuff like El Nino. The signs spin around the chart throughout the day as different stars rise and set against the Earth's horizon.

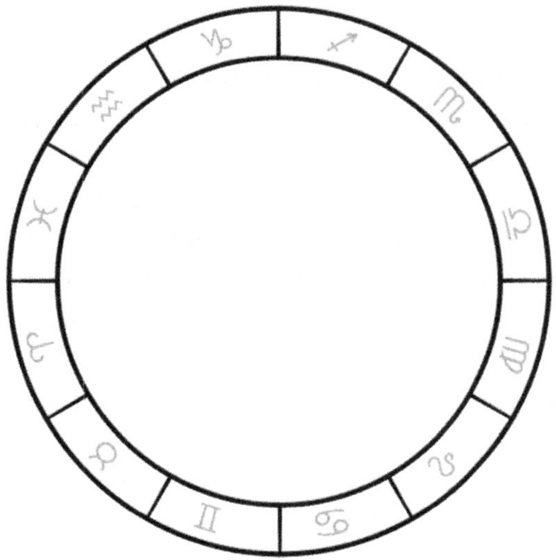

Figure 16-1: The signs divide the sky into sections against the background of the universe. These spin around the wheel throughout the day (which is why you need an accurate birth time to read most charts).

♈	Aries
♉	Taurus
♊	Gemini
♋	Cancer
♌	Leo
♍	Virgo
♎	Libra
♏	Scorpio
♐	Sagittarius
♑	Capricorn
♒	Aquarius
♓	Pisces

Also, in what is the most obvious turn of all, the turn of the Earth with respect to the Sun gives us night and day. Divide up the sky into 12 sections starting with the rising eastern horizon and you get the **houses**: **regions of the local sky which tell you the areas of life your various planets are most comfortable expressing in.**

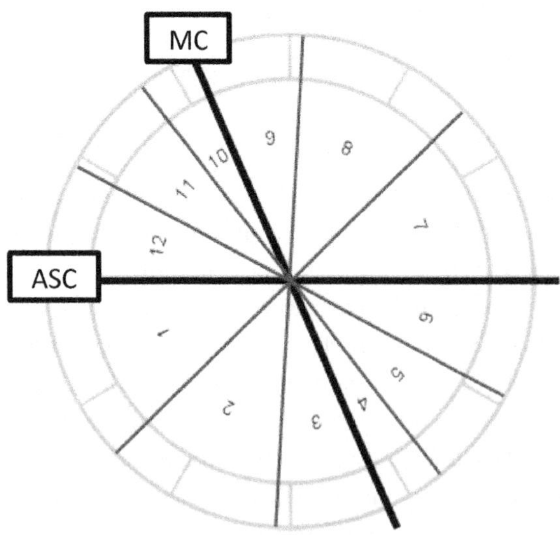

Figure 16-2: The houses divide the sky into sections against the background of the local sky. Although their widths change depending on latitude and time of day, they don't rotate around the wheel the way the signs do.

House 1.	Personal approach to new things
House 2.	Personal value, identity
House 3.	Personal internal monologue and close communication
House 4.	Personal home and family
House 5.	1:1 interaction (to another); hobbies, fun, personal expression process
House 6.	1:1 meaning making and common ground with another; fitness, analysis, service, daily work
House 7.	1:1 communication (back and forth with another); friends and open enemies
House 8.	1:1 steering of another; sex, death, the occult, psychology
House 9.	Higher learning, long journeys, marriage: image projection in the world
House 10.	Reputation, career: structure making in the world
House 11.	Social groups, surrounding talk, public aspirations: information-bathing in the world
House 12.	Secrets, institutions, creativity, spirituality: mood-making in the world

Since the Earth is tilted, the sections of its local sky are usually unequal. There are several **ways to slice the sky into sections**, and these different ways are called **house systems**. In both *FSA* and here in *HBS*, I use Topocentric/Polich-Page houses, but this is a personal preference. Placidus house and Koch house systems are also popular. The **start of a house** (going counterclockwise from house 1) is called a **cusp**, where the **start of the 1st house** (the **Ascendant (ASC)** / rising sign) and **the start of the 10th house** (the **Midheaven (MC)**) are the most important.

- If you look at **the Earth's tilt with respect to the background of the Sun, the signs will be based on seasons**. This is the **tropical system** we're all familiar with—where a new sign starts around the 21st or 22nd of every month. But if you look at **the Earth's tilt against the background of the rest of the universe (and hence the actual stars**, you get the **sidereal system**—where all of the signs are moved backwards by 1° for every 72-ish years past the year 285 c.e. or so. Under this system, the sign of Aries in 2016 actually has its first 25° taken up by the stars of Pisces, other constellations like Ophiucus squeeze into the picture, all the constellations defy the whole "30° neatness" thing, and if you're doing real astronomy like NASA, this is what you rely on. But we regular people don't care about this because it's all the modern Aries anyway. So we assume the tropical system...even if today's egotistical Leo would have been considered an attention-needy Cancer 2000 years ago.

- All cycles that we'll use in basic astrology are divided into 12 sections for three reasons.

    - First, 12 can be divided into a **beginning, middle, and end—three sections of four. Section 1 shows how we interact with ourselves, section 2 shows how we interact with others or objects right in front of us, and section 3 shows how we interact with the faceless world around us**. I call these the **self-other-world** levels. The first four signs, Aries through Cancer, are all about what you feel like doing from within. The next four, Leo through Scorpio, concern your 1:1 interactions with others. The last four (Sagittarius through Pisces) are all about how you interact with the world beyond your direct influence.

    - 🛠 Secondly, 12 can be divided into four key points on a cycle: rising, sitting at peak, falling, and sitting at minimum. These four points also correspond nicely to the **elements**: [**a family of labels which describe 1) a process *without* an apparent background context (action; Fire), 2) a finished process turned into an** object **with context (object; Earth), 3) a finished object turned into a process with context (thoughts; Air), and 4) a finished thought turned into an** object ***without* context (the inclination to do the next action; Water)**]. Here, "context" is just the surrounding stuff which gives a thing its shape. The elements aren't actually elements, but metaphors for how "tangible" an experience is.

    - 🛠 Third, to make a very complicated story short, 12 divisions is trigonometrically favorable, since it enables the existence of halfway points on a 2-dimensional graph depicting real versus "imaginary" (potential) energy. It also allows us to easily form planes within planes—triangles within triangles which build up new combinations of real-imaginary energy from similar, older ones. Lay out a bunch of pennies together as tightly as possible to see what I mean.

I'm about to flood you with tables so brace yourself. Don't worry. There will be an example of how to use all of these at the end of *table 16-7*. In the meantime, the end result of all this talk about signs and houses is summed up in *tables 16-1* (signs) and *16-2* (houses) below.

Table 16-1: What the signs do 🛠

(This table is abstract because it takes into account *FSA's* theoretical explanation of how we move from one sign to another. Since I will never lean on astrological folklore to explain anything in this book or the one before it, I include it for people who want a more logical story of how 1-related things turn into 2-related things which turn into 3-related things and so on. Beginning readers may want to skip this table, though, in favor of the much easier-to-read *table 17-3* in the next chapter.)

Scope of attention	Simple symbol	What happens	Character
Self	Aries (1st Fire)	An action or event (internal signaling)...	Spontaneous, independent Appears seemingly spontaneously of its own will; seems to come with its own source of energy (associated with strength as impetus); may be a direct response to unstated feelings among the whole; driven by collective impression (Pisces), requires freedom in the eyes of individuals; DOING
	Taurus (1st Earth)	Becomes an object or context (bodily state)...	Stubborn, hedonistic Feeling centered; sensitive to internal processes; aware of the parts that constitute it (values); maintains the form of the thing (identity); therefore likely to self-preserve (association with beauty as sensuality); FEELING
	Gemini (1st Air)	Which exchanges energy with other objects (existing physiology)...	Quick, scattered, sociable Broadcasts internal monologue; balances internal background with external dynamics (thus twofold); makes communication out of nothing (sociable in people), connects via process transmission with whatever impinges on it (strength of personal ideas); COMMUNICATING
	Cancer (1st Water)	Leaving a new potential (object-based inclination) for...	Emotional, mothery Must contend with remaining wants after communication no longer works (reflects and remembers; potential to show (since telling is over); searches for external objects to meld with its internal potential, thus receptive to influences that resonate with it (receptive, intuitive, emotional); beauty in emotional depth; wants to put their emotional way onto others; stereotypically (Western) "mothery;" WANTING
Other	Leo (2nd Fire)	An action or event (interaction-centered)...	Proud, charismatic Was motivated by an internal potential to express outward; approaches objects that can meet that potential; along the lines of attention-seeking from such things; self-promoting (strength of beautiful promotion); identity asserting; bounces elsewhere when deflected, thus proud; INTERACTING
	Virgo (2nd Earth)	That becomes an object or context (viewable by others)...	Analytical, service-oriented Makes interaction with others into a concrete construct; interaction with to-do tasks get performed; interactions with others are given practical results (shared meaning); interactions with ideas are given defined boundaries (analysis); this position brings the amorphous / ostentatious showing of the previous introduction back down to reality (beauty as strength through grace); MAKING MEANING
	Libra (2nd Air)	Which exchanges energy with other objects (interaction-centered)...	Balanced, sociable Given that dyadic (one-on-one) boundaries are established, uses the dyad (pair) to communicate; assuming we don't *have to* hang out, our doing so anyway often makes for pleasantness (strength and beauty as social attractiveness); friendship affinity based on shared expression; reconciling me and you, you and us, thus two-sided; SOCIALIZING

	Scorpio (2nd Water)	Leaving a new potential (us-centered inclination) for...	Deep, manipulative 1:1 sharing wasn't enough; extracts deeper emotions from other; drains other; uses others' unshared potential to shape exchange according to wants; may manipulate (beauty used as tool for strength, stereotypically through sexuality); inclined to respond to things not done (but felt) by others; more easily insulted; less easily satisfied; the last inclination that needs you to actually be present, thus death; STEERING
World	Sagittarius (3rd Fire)	An action or event (circumstance-aimed)...	Energetic, expansive Identity asserted in abstract world; the first inclination that doesn't need you to be present, thus what the abstract world experiences of you; also two-fold (balancing you as an individual with you as an abstract identity); expansion beyond your direct interactants; promoting a way against the unknown; going bigger; giving the identity generously over to the public opinion; assuming you choose where you do this, you are in this realm of expression voluntarily and can be funny, fun, and popular; if not voluntarily, egotism, being overbearing, rude, reckless; (strength of will against the abstract); associated with truth inasmuch as your world tells your ideas as they are; DECLARING
	Capricorn (3rd Earth)	That becomes an object or context (circumstance-defining)...	Responsible, protective Enough declaring. Time for structure; buildings that box people in also provide shelter; laws that restrict but provide protection; religions that mold ideas, but guide social behavior; careers that restrict options but provide reputation (beauty as refined organization); doing it by the book because you wrote the book; putting boundaries around others so they may be safe; affinity for institutions but, if distrustful of them, may be imprisoned by them; Stereotypically (by tradition) "Fathery," but in modern western society maybe not so much; STRUCTURING
	Aquarius (3rd Air)	Which exchanges energy with other objects (circumstance contextualizing)...	Popular, aloof, humanitarian Communication about or around you, but not really personal; if weird, then eccentric; if normal, then chatty; if associated with institutions, pop-culture; if associated with weird institutions, occultish; if associated with mechanical objects, technology and innovation in how ideas are shared; strength of social ideas; CONTEXTUALIZING
	Pisces (3rd Water)	Leaving a new potential (internal inclination) for...	Sensitive, escapist Sensitive to emotional environment, thus two-fold (balancing feelings about the world with self's next inclination); social talk left things undone; intuition for collective direction, may respond to illusory impressions or create them (acting, art); spiritual; medical as intangible feelings have physiological roots; escapism; (beauty as illusion); ABSORBING

Table 16-1: General character of 12 sections of the astrowheel. Each description starts off with a couple of cliché descriptions which you might already be familiar with, but these are really more appropriate for reading Sun signs. The more abstract descriptions beneath the keywords describe how the signs actually behave for *all* planets, not just the Sun. For a simpler version of this see *table 17-3* in the next chapter. This table lays a necessary foundation for that other one.

Table 16-2: What the houses do

This is the more detailed version of *figure 16-2*.

Time frame	Scope	House	What is represented	Types of experience associated with the house
Night	Self	1 ASC	An internal action or event …	First impressions; appearances, attitude towards confronted world; characteristic means of expression
		2	Yields to a bodily state or identity context…	Self-worth; body image; ideas about worth in general which are built on self-worth; characteristic means for assigning value to the self; feelings about who one is;
		3	Which exchanges energy with existing physiology…	Voice; means of expression; how one talks to regular familiar people when conveying personal thoughts (thus sibling relationships); how one decides to present internal ideas to others; conveyances (like cars / how one sends his ideas around);
		4	Leaving a new dyadic inclination for…	Home; subconscious; feelings about what one is doing (not the same as self-worth); memory; dreams; emotional training; stereotypical mother
	Other	5	An interaction-centered action or event…	Voluntary, fun relationships, friendship groups and hobbies; how one gets attention from things he wants
		6	That becomes practical context…	Daily routine; health; kind of effort one puts into his work; job tasks and what one's daily doings look like
Day		7	Which exchanges communication with others…	Who we voluntarily socialize with (even if it means fighting) the type of people who generally surround us; people to whom we are attracted and the characteristics which sponsor this; how we best communicate with the people
		8	Leaving a new (us-centered inclination) for a…	Anything which involves us using things that people wouldn't normally share willingly; steering others' emotions, physical response, and psychology; others' money; knowing their secrets; keeping our own
	World	9	Circumstance-aimed action or event…	Anything which involves the desire to project something in the world without actually limiting it with structure; marriage association; parties; exploration of the unknown; unbounded (higher) education; nationality
		10 MC	That becomes a circumstance-defining context…	Anything which involves limits too big for us to directly influence; institutions; our long-term reputation (our categorization in the eyes of the world); fatherly discipline; discipline in general; time; consequences of our actions (where we end up in order to pay for what we broke)
		11	Which contextualizes groups of ideas…	Groups we want to be a part of; information we surround ourselves with; the kind of talk which follows us; social cliques and information fields associated with us
		12	Leaving a new internal inclination for …	Any feelings whose source we can't identify; intuition; what our spirituality looks like; sickness; the vibe that we impress others with and hence, the kind of people we attract who like that vibe; any behaviors which create unidentifiable impressions in others; art; acting; music; other entertainment; Any public impressions which inspire us to individual action; service of others (often health or illusion based); containment of others (through imprisonment); containment of ourselves (unstable responses in light of excessive negative impressions)

Table 16-2: Contents of the houses

- As often happens in astrology, I will use the terms "**planet**" or "**body**" **to refer to anything that can show up in an astrochart which represents a particular kind of experience**. In this book "planets" don't have to be actual planets, but can be asteroids, the Sun, the Moon, or even imaginary points. The planets we will use are summed up in *table 16-3*.

Table 16-3: What the planets do

Planet	Body type	General meaning
		Main Bodies
Moon	Planet	Inner emotional world
Sun	Star	How your motivation to interact with others plays out
Mercury	Planet	Meaning making, what you show you value with another
Venus	Planet	Willing socialization with another
Mars	Planet	How you steer interactants' inner emotional worlds
Jupiter	Planet	How your instinct to interact with the world plays out
Saturn	Planet	Structures set in place by the world at large (not you, not other individuals) with which you interact; institutions
Uranus	Planet	The information that floats around you; thus social talk, friends, hang-out groups you wish you were like, technology
Neptune	Planet	Your generation's socio-emotional tendency; group emotional vibe on average
Pluto	Dwarf Planet	Your generation's instinctual urge or priority; what the collective pressures its members to value
		Other bodies and calculated points
Ascendant (1st house cusp)	Calculated Point/cusp	How you approach the world
Midheaven (10th house cusp)	Calculated Point/cusp	Your reputation and career
Ceres	Dwarf Planet (1)	Where you take care of others
Chiron	Centaur (2060)	Where you need to be validated
Selene (White Moon)	Calculated Point	Gifts you are super-blessed with
Lilith (Lunar Apogee/ Black Moon)	Calculated Point	The point where you are most defiant or most contrary against the usual norms
Vertex	Calculated Point	Where others can change your life easily and drastically
North Node	Calculated Point	"Destiny" (but not really); more like the focal point around which your emotions are targeted
Part of Fortune	Calculated Point	Where you are in your element
Vesta	Asteroid (4)	Your focus backed with action
Pallas	Asteroid (2)	Your intellectual contribution to the greater good
Juno	Asteroid (3)	Your formally committed relationships in the eyes of the world
Hera	Asteroid (103)	Who you actually bond with
Eros	Amor asteroid (433)	What turns you on
Bacchus	Apollo asteroid (2063)	Where you make the best host for others; groups you actually serve

Table 16-3: Planets and locations of interest in a chart. Minor planet designations are listed in () where they apply—just in case you need their numbers to look up online.

- 🛠 While astrology traditionally **associates each sign with a certain planet** (called its **ruler**), there is no known astro<u>nom</u>ical relationship between planets and the sections of the sky signified by the signs. But planets can be related to signs by the sequence in which their orbits occur as influences on us. Again, this is kind of like orbitals in an atom. Under this approach, orbit #1 means something. Orbit #2 means something else. This means that things in orbit #4 for example

    - planet = Moon
    - sign = Cancer
    - aspect = square

  all have similar (home/emotional) effects in relation to their friends. To give another example using orbit #11 we have

    - planet = Uranus
    - sign = Aquarius
    - aspect = undecile

  and these all have similar (social/information) effects in relation to their friends. Where orbits determine the behavior that comes with planets and points, I assume 1) there are different "rulers" in some cases than the ones you may have read about elsewhere and 2) that multiple objects stuck in a single orbit (like asteroids) get their character as orbits within orbits and so act like rulers within rulers. You'll see the main rulers we'll be using in *table 16-4*.

- 🛠 For "planets" which influence (or "rule") us even more immediately than the Moon, I use three made up points: the triangulated **Points of** 1) **Action,** 2) **Worth, and** 3) **Internal Monologue** as **"rulers" of Aries, Taurus and Gemini respectively**. These are the cycles of your 1) genetic disposition, 2) overall body look/physiology, and 3) internal attitude respectively: orbits #1, #2, and #3. For seasoned astrologers, this isn't as bad as it sounds and you can read more about these points in *FSA*. Additionally, I associate Mars with Scorpio. I also use Pluto as a society-level ruler of Aries (orbit #13; a backup to the Point of Action). Despite all this, rulers aren't actually necessary for a very thorough reading of a chart. Still, I summarize the ones I've assumed below.

Table 16-4: Sign rulerships by orbit cycle

Sign	By cycle influence
Aries	Point of Action
Taurus	Point of Worth
Gemini	Point of Internal Monologue
Cancer	Moon
Leo	Sun
Virgo	Mercury
Libra	Venus
Scorpio	Mars
Sagittarius	Jupiter
Capricorn	Saturn
Aquarius	Uranus
Pisces	Neptune
Aries (level II)	Pluto

Table 16-4: Selected planetary rulers including the triangulated points of Action, Worth, and Internal Monologue

- Sign and house placements do give you quite a bit of information on the nature of an event, but the information provided by the aspects (angles) between each planet pair is far more detailed. The meaning of each planet pair in a normal, (single) chart is summarized in *table 16-5.*

Table 16-5: Planet pair interactions

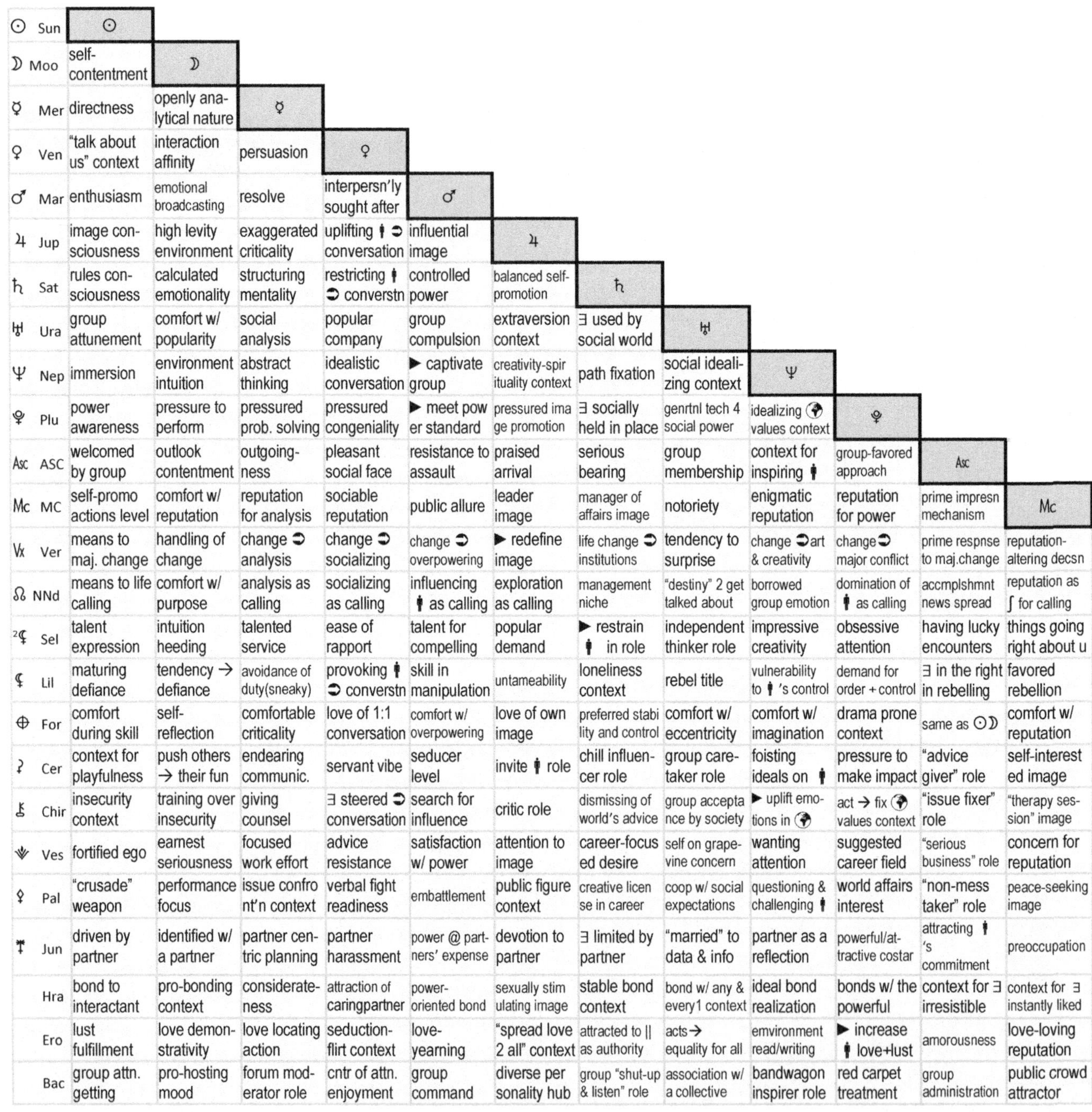

☉ Sun	☉											
☽ Moo	self-contentment	☽										
☿ Mer	directness	openly analytical nature	☿									
♀ Ven	"talk about us" context	interaction affinity	persuasion	♀								
♂ Mar	enthusiasm	emotional broadcasting	resolve	interpersn'ly sought after	♂							
♃ Jup	image consciousness	high levity environment	exaggerated criticality	uplifting 👤 ➲ conversation	influential image	♃						
♄ Sat	rules consciousness	calculated emotionality	structuring mentality	restricting 👤 ➲ converstn	controlled power	balanced self-promotion	♄					
♅ Ura	group attunement	comfort w/ popularity	social analysis	popular company	group compulsion	extraversion context	∃ used by social world	♅				
♆ Nep	immersion	environment intuition	abstract thinking	idealistic conversation	▶ captivate group	creativity-spirituality context	path fixation	social idealizing context	♆			
♇ Plu	power awareness	pressure to perform	pressured prob. solving	pressured congeniality	▶ meet power standard	pressured image promotion	∃ socially held in place	genrtnl tech 4 social power	idealizing 🌍 values context	♇		
Asc ASC	welcomed by group	outlook contentment	outgoing-ness	pleasant social face	resistance to assault	praised arrival	serious bearing	group membership	context for inspiring 👤	group-favored approach	Asc	
Mc MC	self-promo actions level	comfort w/ reputation	reputation for analysis	sociable reputation	public allure	leader image	manager of affairs image	notoriety	enigmatic reputation	reputation for power	prime impresn mechanism	Mc
Vx Ver	means to maj. change	handling of change	change ➲ analysis	change ➲ socializing	change ➲ overpowering	▶ redefine image	life change ➲ institutions	tendency to surprise	change ➲art & creativity	change➲ major conflict	prime respnse to maj.change	reputation-altering decsn
☊ NNd	means to life calling	comfort w/ purpose	analysis as calling	socializing as calling	influencing 👤 as calling	exploration as calling	management niche	"destiny" 2 get talked about	borrowed group emotion	domination of 👤 as calling	accmplshmnt news spread	reputation as ∫ for calling
²⚸ Sel	talent expression	intuition heeding	talented service	ease of rapport	talent for compelling	popular demand	▶ restrain 👤 in role	independent thinker role	impressive creativity	obsessive attention	having lucky encounters	things going right about u
⚸ Lil	maturing defiance	tendency → defiance	avoidance of duty(sneaky)	provoking 👤 ➲ converstn	skill in manipulation	untameability	loneliness context	rebel title	vulnerability to 👤 's control	demand for order + control	∃ in the right in rebelling	favored rebellion
⊕ For	comfort during skill	self-reflection	comfortable criticality	love of 1:1 conversation	comfort w/ overpowering	love of own image	preferred stability and control	comfort w/ eccentricity	comfort w/ imagination	drama prone context	same as ☉☽	comfort w/ reputation
⚳ Cer	context for playfulness	push others → their fun	endearing communic.	servant vibe	seducer level	invite 👤 role	chill influencer role	group caretaker role	foisting ideals on 👤	pressure to make impact	"advice giver" role	self-interested image
⚷ Chir	insecurity context	training over insecurity	giving counsel	∃ steered ➲ conversation	search for influence	critic role	dismissing of world's advice	group acceptance by society	▶ uplift emotions in 🌍	act → fix 🌍 values context	"issue fixer" role	"therapy session" image
⚶ Ves	fortified ego	earnest seriousness	focused work effort	advice resistance	satisfaction w/ power	attention to image	career-focused desire	self on grapevine concern	wanting attention	suggested career field	"serious business" role	concern for reputation
⚴ Pal	"crusade" weapon	performance focus	issue confront'n context	verbal fight readiness	embattlement	public figure context	creative license in career	coop w/ social expectations	questioning & challenging 👤	world affairs interest	"non-mess taker" role	peace-seeking image
⚵ Jun	driven by partner	identified w/ a partner	partner centric planning	partner harassment	power @ partners' expense	devotion to partner	∃ limited by partner	"married" to data & info	partner as a reflection	powerful/attractive costar	attracting 👤 's commitment	preoccupation
Hra	bond to interactant	pro-bonding context	considerate-ness	attraction of caringpartner	power-oriented bond	sexually stimulating image	stable bond context	bond w/ any & every1 context	ideal bond realization	bonds w/ the powerful	context for ∃ irresistible	context for ∃ instantly liked
Ero	lust fulfillment	love demonstrativity	love locating action	seduction-flirt context	love-yearning	"spread love 2 all" context	attracted to ‖ as authority	acts→ equality for all	emvironment read/writing	▶ increase 👤 love+lust	amorousness	love-loving reputation
Bac	group attn. getting	pro-hosting mood	forum moderator role	cntr of attn. enjoyment	group command	diverse personality hub	group "shut-up & listen" role	association w/ a collective	bandwagon inspirer role	red carpet treatment	group administration	public crowd attractor

Table 16-5: Planet-planet pair combinations. Please excuse the "txt" notation employed for the sake of compactness. You'll find that synastry adds a new level of meaning to each of these.

Symbols

→ means "towards; to."

➲ means "through; by using."

∃ means "being"

🚹 means "others"

▶ means "the ability to"

|| means "or"

🌍 means "the world"

∫ means "important"

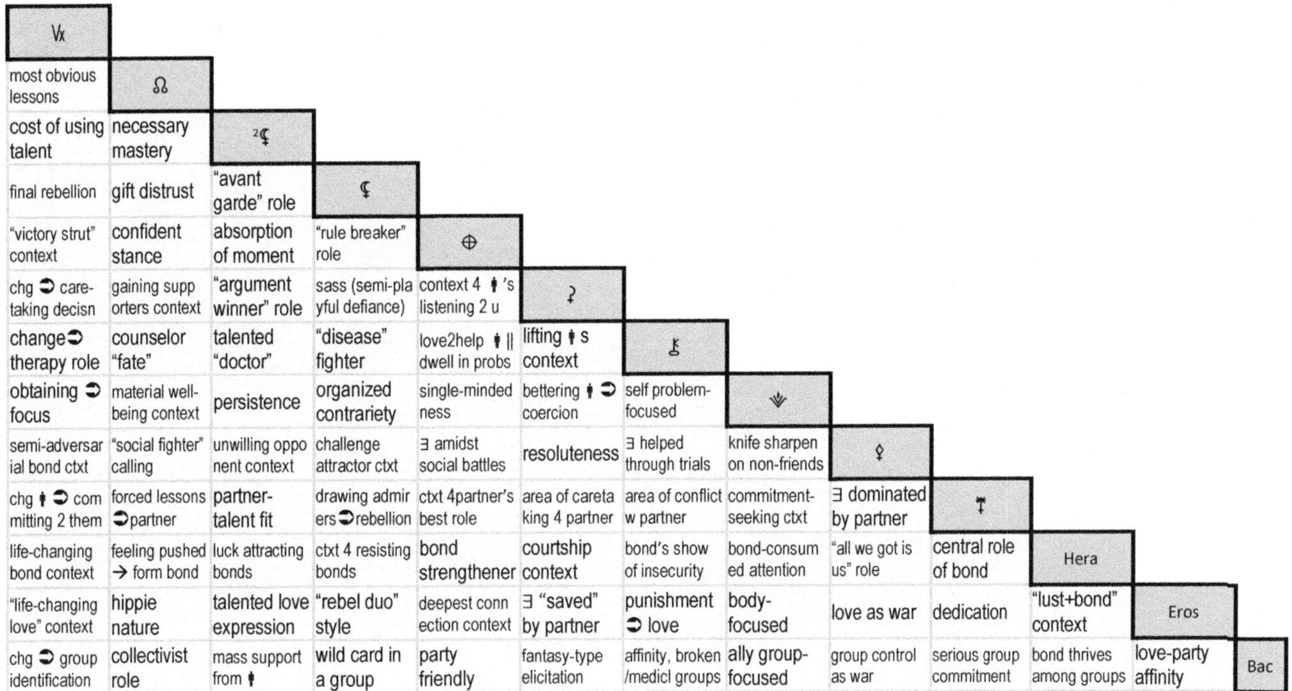

Vx												
most obvious lessons	☊											
cost of using talent	necessary mastery	²⚸										
final rebellion	gift distrust	"avant garde" role	⚸									
"victory strut" context	confident stance	absorption of moment	"rule breaker" role	⊕								
chg ➲ care-taking decisn	gaining supp orters context	"argument winner" role	sass (semi-pla yful defiance)	context 4 🚹 's listening 2 u	[illegible]							
change➲ therapy role	counselor "fate"	talented "doctor"	"disease" fighter	love2help 🚹 || dwell in probs	lifting 🚹 s context	⚷						
obtaining ➲ focus	material well-being context	persistence	organized contrariety	single-minded ness	bettering 🚹 ➲ coercion	self problem-focused	[illegible]					
semi-adversar ial bond ctxt	"social fighter" calling	unwilling oppo nent context	challenge attractor ctxt	∃ amidst social battles	resoluteness	∃ helped through trials	knife sharpen on non-friends	[illegible]				
chg 🚹 ➲ com mitting 2 them	forced lessons ➲partner	partner-talent fit	drawing admir ers➲rebellion	ctxt 4partner's best role	area of careta king 4 partner	area of conflict w partner	commitment-seeking ctxt	∃ dominated by partner	[illegible]			
life-changing bond context	feeling pushed → form bond	luck attracting bonds	ctxt 4 resisting bonds	bond strengthener	courtship context	bond's show of insecurity	bond-consum ed attention	"all we got is us" role	central role of bond	Hera		
"life-changing love" context	hippie nature	talented love expression	"rebel duo" style	deepest conn ection context	∃ "saved" by partner	punishment ➲ love	body-focused	love as war	dedication	"lust+bond" context	Eros	
chg ➲ group identification	collectivist role	mass support from 🚹	wild card in a group	party friendly	fantasy-type elicitation	affinity, broken /medicl groups	ally group-focused	group control as war	serious group commitment	bond thrives among groups	love-party affinity	Bac

- The planets/bodies in an astrochart all have angles between each other. The **angle of separation between bodies** (from Earth's viewpoint) is called an **aspect**. Although astrology traditionally assigns meaning only to major aspects like 0° of separation (conjunct, 0°), $^1/_3$ of a circle (trine, 120°), $^1/_4$ of a circle (square, 90°), and a few others, all angles of separation actually have meaning depending on how many times you have to loop them to make a whole circle. For example, you need 4 repeats of a square (90°) to make 360°, so squares give a meaning similar to orbit #4. But you need 35 repeats of a III-undecile ($^1/_{35}$ of a circle 10°17'), so it behaves like orbit #35. **Families of angles which require the same number of repeats to make a whole circle** are called **harmonics**. So 72° and 144° are both part of the "quintile" (5th) harmonic because they both need to repeat 5 times in order to line up with a full circle of 360°, 720°, 1080°... In *FSA* I did the statistics on these to determine what angles like $^1/_{35}$ of a circle mean, and repeat the findings in *table 16-6*. Lastly, every time we start **a** new **layer of 12 harmonics**, we go up one **level**. **0° through $^1/_{12}$ of a circle** constitute **level I**. **$^1/_{13}$ through $^1/_{24}$ of a circle** form **level II**. **$^1/_{25}$ through $^1/_{36}$ of a circle** form **level III**.

Table 16-6: The harmonics (angle families) 1-36

The angles of separation (aspects) between bodies constitute the main thing that gives you all of the cool combinations of characteristics in astrology, so you should try to get familiar with these early on. We will keep returning to these over and over again throughout the book.

Harmonic	Name	Symbol	Degrees	Meaning	How to use
1	conjunct	☌	0°	natural trait	do something, be yourself
2	opposition	☍	180°	natural value	feel something, value something
3	trine	△	120°	easy thought	think about something
4	square	□	90°	wanting, having an inclination	want something
5	quintile	⋆ or Q	72°, 144°	projecting your way 1:1 with another	notice how you promote yourself to others
6	sextile	⚹	60°	finding common ground with another	serve, work, or analyze
7	septile	✡	51°26', 102°51', 154°17'	share ideas under a common topic with another	notice how you share ideas with others; notice what kinds of games you prefer to play
8	octile	∠ or ⚼	45°, 135°	overriding other's intent	manipulate another's actions
9	novile	九 or N	40°, 80°, 160°	declaring one's identity in the world	notice how you declare your identity
10	decile	+	36°, 108°	forming a reputation	consistently perform actions which others can see
11	undecile	∪	32°44', 65°27', 98°11', 130°55', 163°38'	gaining popularity	perform unique actions which few can copy
12	inconjunct	⚻	30°, 150°	leaving an impression without doing the actual deed	notice how others treat you in light of things you haven't done
13	II-conjunct	$☌^2$	27°42', 55°23', 83°05', 110°46', 138°28', 166°09'	your expressive style	note the tools you use to promote your values. These could be objects or tactics
14	II-opposition	$☍^2$	25°43', 77°09', 128°34'	what your values are intended to accomplish	let others interact with your socially (ethnically) trained ideas or respond to your physical presence
15	II-trine	$△^2$	24°, 48°, 96°, 168°	what you strongly extract from others simply by being around	show up and give your unqualified opinion

16	II-square	□²	22°30′, 67°30′, 112°30′, 157°30′	what you wish to be respected for	develop an expert's intuition for subjects related to this angle family
17	II-quintile	⭑² or Q²	21°11′, 42°21′, 63°32′, 84°42′, 105°53′, 127°04′, 148°14′, 169°25′	what you brag about, complain on behalf of, and are personally proud of	let others praise you regarding planets separated by this angle family
18	II-sextile	✳	20°, 100°, 140°	your goal-oriented work efforts	investigate, then practice the most important ideas you seek to build up in others
19	II-septile	✡	18°57′, 37°54′, 56°51′, 75°47′, 94°44′, 113°41′, 132°38′, 151°35′, 170°32′	how you present compelling ideas to others	imagine yourself in an idealized conversation with someone over an issue you think is important; note how that image relates to the planet pair
20	II-octile	∠² or ⊡²	18°, 54°, 126°, 162°	unstated, but well-known magnetism, causes of jealousy in others	publicly display those values, material possessions, and tokens of self-worth which are intended to manipulate viewers' feelings
21	II-novile	九² or N²	17°09′, 34°17′, 68°34′, 85°43′, 137°09′, 171°25′	overadherence to rules, excessive zeal for proving you've met a standard	think about what you believe to be the most important ideas in your world, then consider the values you hold and behaviors you adopt concerning those ideas; learn to convince others of the importance of those ideas through actions, not words alone
22	II-decile	+²	16°22′, 49°05′, 81°49′, 114°33′, 147°16′	the standards against which you measure a proper reputation; the reputation you earn by structuring things	combine all pairs in +² into a single ideal career; investigate how you would pursue that career
23	II-undecile	U²	15°39′, 31°18′, 46°57′, 78°16′, 93°55′, 125°13′, 140°52′, 172°10′	standalone individualism, values that get you talked about in the world	collect items, ideas, or people you believe to be unique
24	II-inconjunct	⚻²	15°, 75°, 105°, 165° (tao)	works of the imagination which are likely to manifest in the real world	pay attention to those things which you are inclined to stick with through thick and thin; reinforce this dedication
25	III-conjunct	☌³	14°24′, 28°48′, 43°12′, 100°48′, 115°12′, 172°48′	your vehicles for expression; your deeds which align with mass psychology	ask what characteristics people tend to come to you for and what characteristics cause people to stay away from you; what about you as a person makes others jealous?
26	III-opposition	☍³	13°51′, 69°14′, 96°55′	your tendency to check your actions against your values; fans and supporters	notice where and how you publicly question decisions you've made; when do fans follow you?
27	III-trine	Δ³	13°20′, 26°40′, 66°40′, 106°40′	your ability to broadcast your ideas without remorse; forward confidence; insight	locate the Δ³s in your chart and do more of what the pairs suggest; exercise where you have insight
28	III-square	□³	12°51′, 157°09′	your ability to deliver measured cooperation while still maintaining your own perspective; morals	look at those areas where you don't care what others have to say about your choices; stay with those choices
29	III-quintile	⭑³ or Q³	12°25′, 24°50′, 37°14′, 62°04′, 86°54′, 124°08′, 148°58′, 173°48′	your ability to use humor and hold a self-contented sense of prosperity	look at areas in which others don't take you seriously; master them by not taking yourself so seriously in those same areas

30	III-sextile	⚹	12°, 84°, 132°, 156°	your ability to deliver expert criticism	look at areas in which most other groups of people defer to your judgment; learn to deliver your criticism in ways that don't violate others' sense of self-respect
31	III-septile	✡	11°37′, 23°14′, 34°50′, 58°04′, 92°54′, 116°08′	your ability to engage a task all the way through; spreading doctrines and beliefs through speech	look at areas in which you are attentive to detail in every aspect, every time; practice engaging those areas without getting drained
32	III-octile	∠^{3} or ⟟^{3}	11°15′, 78°45′, 146°15	your ability to delve beneath the surface of an event and break your relationship with it if necessary; an interest in mysteries	think about the things you love doing, where interactants are less enthusiastic than you are; learn to read cues for when you've dwelled too long on those things
33	III-novile	九^3 or N^3	10°55′, 21°49′, 76°22′, 109°05′, 141°49′	your ability to get a group fired up	channel your influence over receptive groups towards a useful cause which others are inclined to support
34	III-decile	+^{3}	10°35′, 52°56′, 74°07′, 158°49′	your ability to elevate yourself above others; your ideas regarding authority	behave as you believe a true authority would
35	III-undecile	U^3	10°17′, 30°51′, 41°09′, 113°09′, 174°51′	your ability to follow your unique curiosity	indulge your curiosity regarding planets in this harmonic
36	III-inconjunct	⊼^{3}	10°, 50°, 70°, 110°, 130°, 170°	your ability to promote an idea despite the secret impression behind it	investigate why you present your ideas as you do; admit areas where you lack focus and develop workarounds

Table 16-6: the first 36 of 144 possible angle families in a 12 cycle cut in to 12 more pieces.

This book usually won't go past 36, but where new research since the writing of *FSA* has revealed more insight into the behavior of harmonics 37 and up, I will sometimes discuss harmonics past these.

The range of effect for an aspect is called an orb. This is the number of degrees over which nearby angles are still considered to make a particular aspect. In this book the conjunct, for example, will be considered to have an orb of about 9°, though you'll usually see an orb of about 10° in other places. Because we'll be using so many more harmonics than you'll normally see, we'll need to use super-"tight orbs" for each angle—such that most angles have an orb of less than 1° as shown in *table 16-7* below.

Table 16-7: Table of angle families by degree

Degree	Name	Symbol	Harmonic name	Most basic angle
0°...9°	conjunct	☌	conjunct	**conjunct**
10°	III-inconjunct	⚻^{3}	III-inconjunct	**conjunct**
10°17′	III-undecile	U^{3}	III-undecile	III-undecile
10°35′	III-decile	+^{3}	III-decile	III-decile
10°55′	III-novile	九^{3}	III-novile	III-novile
11°15′	III-octile	∠^{3}	III-octile	III-octile
11°37′	III-septile	✡^{3}	III-septile	III-septile
12°	III-sextile	✶^{3}	III-sextile	III-sextile
12°25′	III-quintile	⋆^{3}	III-quintile	III-quintile
12°51′	III-square	□^{3}	III-square	III-square
13°20′	III-trine	Δ^{3}	III-trine	III-trine
13°51′	III-opposition	☍^{3}	III-opposition	III-opposition
14°24′	III-conjunct	☌^{3}	III-conjunct	III-conjunct
15°	II-inconjunct	⚻^{2}	II-inconjunct	**II-inconjunct**
15°39′	II-undecile	U^{2}	II-undecile	II-undecile
16°22′	II-decile	+^{2}	II-decile	II-decile
17°09′	II-novile	九^{2}	II-novile	II-novile
18°	II-octile	∠^{2}	II-octile	II-octile
18°57′	II-septile	✡^{2}	II-septile	II-septile
20°	II-sextile	✶^{2}	II-sextile	II-sextile
21°11′	II-quintile	⋆^{2}	II-quintile	II-quintile
21°49′	bi-III-novile	九$^{3}_{(2)}$	III-novile	III-novile
22°30′	II-square	□^{2}	II-square	II-square
23°14′	bi-III-septile	✡$^{3}_{(2)}$	III-septile	III-septile
24°	II-trine	Δ^{2}	II-trine	II-trine
24°50′	bi-III-quintile	⋆$^{3}_{(2)}$	III-quintile	III-quintile
25°43′	II-opposition	☍^{2}	II-opposition	II-opposition
26°40′	bi-III-trine	Δ$^{3}_{(2)}$	III-trine	III-trine
27°42′	II-conjunct	☌^{2}	II-conjunct	II-conjunct
28°48′	bi-III-conjunct	☌$^{3}_{(2)}$	III-conjunct	**semisextile**
30°	semisextile	⚺	inconjunct	**semisextile**
30°51′	tri-III-undecile	U$^{3}_{(3)}$	III-undecile	**semisextile**
31°18′	bi-II-undecile	U$^{2}_{(2)}$	II-undecile	**semisextile**
32°45′	undecile	U	undecile	**undecile**

34°17′	bi-II-novile	九$^{2}_{(2)}$	II-novile	**undecile**
34°50′	tri-III-septile	✡$^{3}_{(3)}$	III-septile	**decile**
36°	decile	⊥	decile	**decile**
37°14′	tri-III-quintile	⋆$^{3}_{(3)}$	III-quintile	**decile**
37°54′	bi-II-septile	✡$^{2}_{(2)}$	II-septile	**decile**
40°	novile	九	novile	**novile**
41°09′	quatro-III-undecile	U$^{3}_{(4)}$	III-undecile	**novile**
42°21′	bi-II-quintile	⋆$^{2}_{(2)}$	II-quintile	**novile**
43°12′	tri-III-conjunct	☌$^{3}_{(3)}$	III-conjunct	**semisquare**
45°	semisquare	∠	octile	**semisquare**
46°57′	tri-II-undecile	U$^{2}_{(3)}$	II-undecile	**semisquare**
48°	bi-II-trine	△$^{2}_{(2)}$	II-trine	
49°05′	tri-II-decile	+$^{2}_{(3)}$	II-decile	**II-decile**
50°	quinti-III-inconjunct	⚻$^{3}_{(5)}$	III-inconjunct	
51°26′	septile	✡	septile	**septile**
52°56′	quintideki-III-decile	+$^{3}_{(5)}$	III-decile	**septile**
54°	tri-II-octile	∠$^{2}_{(3)}$	II-octile	**II-octile**
55°23′	bi-II-conjunct	☌$^{2}_{(2)}$	II-conjunct	
56°51′	tri-II-septile	✡$^{2}_{(3)}$	II-septile	**sextile**
58°04′	quinti-III-septile	✡$^{3}_{(5)}$	III-septile	**sextile**
60°	sextile	✱	sextile	**sextile**
62°04′	quinti-III-quintile	⋆$^{3}_{(5)}$	III-quintile	**sextile**
63°32′	tri-II-quintile	⋆$^{2}_{(3)}$	II-quintile	
65°27′	biundecile	U$_{(2)}$	undecile	**biundecile**
66°40′	quinti-III-trine	△$^{3}_{(5)}$	III-trine	
67°30′	tri-II-square	□$^{2}_{(3)}$	II-square	
68°34′	quatro-II-novile	九$^{2}_{(4)}$	II-novile	
69°14′	quinti-III-opposition	☍$^{3}_{(5)}$	III-opposition	
70°	septi-III-inconjunct	⚻$^{3}_{(7)}$	III-inconjunct	**quintile**
72°	quintile	⋆	quintile	**quintile**
74°07′	septi-III-decile	+$^{3}_{(7)}$	III-decile	**quintile**
75°	quinti-II-inconjunct	⚻$^{2}_{(5)}$	II-inconjunct	
75°47′	quatro-II-septile	✡$^{2}_{(4)}$	II-septile	
76°22′	septi-III-novile	九$^{3}_{(7)}$	III-novile	
77°09′	tri-II-opposition	☍$^{2}_{(3)}$	II-opposition	
78°16′	quinti-II-undecile	U$^{2}_{(5)}$	II-undecile	**binovile**
78°45′	septi-III-octile	∠$^{3}_{(7)}$	III-octile	**binovile**
80°	binovile	九$_{(2)}$	novile	**binovile**
81°49′	quinti-II-decile	+$^{2}_{(5)}$	II-decile	**binovile**
83°05′	tri-II-conjunct	☌$^{2}_{(3)}$	II-conjunct	**binovile**
84°	septi-III-sextile	✱$^{3}_{(7)}$	III-sextile	
84°42′	quatro-II-quintile	⋆$^{2}_{(4)}$	II-quintile	

85°43′	quinti-II-novile	九$^{2}_{(5)}$	II-novile	**square**
86°54′	septi-III-quintile	⋆$^{3}_{(7)}$	III-quintile	**square**
90°	square	□	square	**square**
92°54′	octo-III-septile	✡$^{3}_{(8)}$	III-septile	**square**
93°55′	sexto-II-undecile	U$^{2}_{(6)}$	II-undecile	**square**
94°44′	quinti-II-septile	✡$^{2}_{(5)}$	II-septile	**square**
96°	quatro-II-trine	Δ$^{2}_{(4)}$	II-trine	**triundecile**
96°55′	septi-III-opposition	☍$^{3}_{(7)}$	III-opposition	**triundecile**
98°11′	triundecile	U$_{(3)}$	undecile	**triundecile**
100°	quinti-II-sextile	⚹$^{2}_{(5)}$	II-sextile	
100°48′	septi-III-conjunct	☌$^{3}_{(7)}$	III-conjunct	
102°51′	triseptile	✡$_{(3)}$	septile	**triseptile**
105°	septi-II-inconjunct	⊼$^{2}_{(7)}$	II-inconjunct	
105°53′	quinti-II-quintile	⋆$^{2}_{(5)}$	II-quintile	
106°40′	octo-III-trine	Δ$^{3}_{(8)}$	III-trine	**tridecile**
108°	tridecile	T$_{(3)}$	decile	**tridecile**
109°05′	deki-III-novile	九$^{3}_{(10)}$	III-novile	
110°	undeki-III-inconjunct	⊼$^{3}_{(11)}$	III-inconjunct	
110°46′	quatro-II-conjunct	☌$^{2}_{(4)}$	II-conjunct	
112°30′	quinti-II-square	□$^{2}_{(5)}$	II-square	**II-square**
113°09′	undeki-III-undecile	U$^{3}_{(11)}$	III-undecile	**II-square**
113°41′	sexto-II-septile	✡$^{2}_{(6)}$	II-septile	
114°33′	septi-II-decile	+$^{2}_{(7)}$	II-decile	
115°12′	octo-III-conjunct	☌$^{3}_{(8)}$	III-conjunct	**trine**
116°08′	deki-III-septile	✡$^{3}_{(10)}$	III-septile	**trine**
117°...**120°**...123°	trine	Δ	trine	**trine**
124°08′	deki-III-quintile	⋆$^{3}_{(10)}$	III-quintile	**trine**
125°13′	octo-II-undecile	U$^{2}_{(8)}$	II-undecile	
126°	septi-II-octile	∠$^{2}_{(7)}$	II-octile	**II-octile**
127°04′	sexto-II-quintile	⋆$^{2}_{(6)}$	II-quintile	
128°34′	quinti-II-opposition	☍$^{2}_{(5)}$	II-opposition	
130°	trideki-III-inconjunct	⊼$^{3}_{(13)}$	III-inconjunct	**quatrundecile**
130°55′	quatrundecile	U$_{(4)}$	undecile	**quatrundecile**
132°	undeki-III-sextile	⚹$^{3}_{(11)}$	III-sextile	
132°38′	septi-II-septile	✡$^{2}_{(7)}$	II-septile	**sesquiquadrate**
135°	sesquiquadrate	⚼	octile	**sesquiquadrate**
137°09′	octo-II-novile	九$^{2}_{(8)}$	II-novile	**sesquiquadrate**
138°28′	quinti-II-conjunct	☌$^{2}_{(5)}$	II-conjunct	**sesquiquadrate**
140°	septi-II-sextile	⚹$^{2}_{(7)}$	II-sextile	**II-sextile**
140°52′	novo-II-undecile	U$^{2}_{(9)}$	II-undecile	
141°49′	trideki-III-novile	九$^{3}_{(13)}$	III-novile	
142°...**144°**...145°30′	quintile	⋆	quintile	**biquintile**

146°15	trideki-III-octile	∠$^{3}_{(13)}$	III-octile	
147°16′	novo-II-decile	+$^{2}_{(9)}$	II-decile	**inconjunct**
148°14′	septi-II-quintile	⋆$^{2}_{(7)}$	II-quintile	**inconjunct**
148°58′	duodeki-III-quintile	⋆$^{3}_{(12)}$	III-quintile	**inconjunct**
150°	inconjunct	⊼	inconjunct	**inconjunct**
151°35′	octo-II-septile	✡$^{2}_{(8)}$	II-septile	
152°30′...**154°17′**...155°	triseptile	✡$_{(3)}$	septile	**triseptile**
156°	trideki-III-sextile	✱$^{3}_{(13)}$	III-sextile	
157°09′	trideki-III-square	□$^{3}_{(13)}$	III-square	
157°30′	septi-II-square	□$^{2}_{(7)}$	II-square	
158°49′	quintideki-III-decile	+$^{3}_{(15)}$	III-decile	**quatronovile**
160°	quatronovile	九$_{(4)}$	novile	**quatronovile**
162°	novo-II-octile	∠$^{2}_{(9)}$	II-octile	
163°38′	quintundecile	U$_{(5)}$	undecile	**quintundecile**
165°	undeki-II-inconjunct (tao)	⊼$^{2}_{(11)}$	II-inconjunct	**undeki-II-inconjunct**
166°09′	sexto-II-conjunct	☌$^{2}_{(6)}$	II-conjunct	
168°	septi-II-trine	Δ$^{2}_{(7)}$	II-trine	**II-trine**
169°25′	octo-II-quintile	⋆$^{2}_{(8)}$	II-quintile	
170°	septideki-III-inconjunct	⊼$^{3}_{(17)}$	III-inconjunct	**septideki-III-inconjunct**
170°32′	novo-II-septile	✡$^{2}_{(9)}$	II-septile	
171°25′	deki-II-novile	九$^{2}_{(10)}$	II-novile	**II-novile**
172°10′	undeki-II-undecile	U$^{2}_{(11)}$	II-undecile	**opposition**
172°48′	duodeki-III-conjunct	☌$^{3}_{(12)}$	III-conjunct	**opposition**
173°48′	quatrodeki-III-quintile	⋆$^{3}_{(14)}$	III-quintile	**opposition**
174°51′	septideki-III-undecile	U$^{3}_{(17)}$	III-undecile	**opposition**
175°...180°	opposition	☍	opposition	**opposition**

Table 16-7: Aspects 0° – 180° by degree (up to harmonic 36) If you've done some astrology already and are only used to using major aspects (or if applying nonstandard angles feels weird to you), then you might read the angles under the "Most basic angle" column instead. Blank entries means the angle in question might be read as either of the nearby angles. Each degree is actually a blend of all the possible angles near it, so don't worry too much about whether, say, 139° is more like a sesquiquadrate or more like a II-sextile. Until we humans evolve more computer-like precision in distinguishing feelings, this kind of difference won't matter. While precision is important, slippage in nearby angles won't kill you. I talk more about this in *FSA* as well as in a technical section of the next chapter (around *table 17-5*).

- You read a chart by looking at the signs, houses, and pairs of "planets." When looking at pairs, the aspect between them tells you the behavior needed to "turn the pair up." Conversely, turning a paired behavior up (as shown in *table 16-5*) increases your display of the angle between that pair.

Okay, so how do you use all this to read a single chart? First, make sure you have an accurate birth time and place. Next, find a program that spits out the angle view of your chart (I have one at http://electricmonastery.com). Then, use the above tables to look up anything you see in the printout. An accurate birth time is necessary because without it (as you might guess), you won't know how to roll the wheel with respect to night and day. The astrochart is, after all, a snapshot of the sky at the time you specify.[2]

- Say for example you want you know what your Sun sign says about you. Look at what your Sun does in *table 16-3,* then look at what its character is in *table 16-1.* Probably stuff you've seen already if you've heard anything about astrology at all. But then again maybe not. Why is *table 16-1* so abstract? Because it's based on orbits and not mythology. We needed to stay rooted in orbits in order to make all of the conclusions about asteroids and higher harmonics in *FSA*. You'll find the more familiar, easier to read interpretations in *FSA* and on sites like http://www.bobmarksastrologer.com/TOClessons.htm and http://astrology-numerology.com/ though. I credit these with teaching me much of what I learned as a new student of astrology many years ago. Their insight doesn't age, and will serve you well.

- Now say you want to know what the Moon does in whatever house you find it in. Look at the Moon in *table 16-3*, then look at the house *table 16-2* to see where your Moon moods are most pronounced. As the Sun signs alone don't tell you much, I recommend that if you can only read three things in your chart, read your Sun, Moon, and Ascendant signs. Remember, this is only a super short summary. I've covered such things in detail in *FSA*.

- Now actually, the most interesting part of astrology IMO lies in the pairings. Suppose you want to learn a little bit about how to get rich. First, look for something like "riches" in *table 16-5*. You won't find it, but [Node-Vesta] (Nnd-Ves) is pretty informative. Now look at the output from your chart where it tells you the [Node-Vesta] angle. *Table 16-6* will show you the circumstances under which you are most likely to "turn up" this aspect of your life. So if you read a III-decile as your angle, it means that your material well-being is more likely to increase when you purposely behave as your ideal for an authority would. If you read a [Node-Vesta] II-novile, the likelihood of material wealth increases with promoting your ideals or attitude (as creations). Of course there is no silver bullet for any of this, but you get the idea. I offer an explanation in the previous book as to why all of this seems to work as it does, but the patterns across the dataset were definitely there.

  What if, for some reason you can't get a printout of your wheel, but you do have the degree locations of your planets? Then you'll have to use plain old subtraction to find the degree of separation between the planets you're interested in. After that, use *tables 16-7* and *16-6.*

By the way, here's something I'm sure lots of people have been dying to know: Between the time I wrote the previous book and the writing of this one, I actually did look at the charts of some insanely rich people who were publicly known to be so (Warren Buffett, Bill Gates, Oprah Winfrey, etc...) the relevant **combination of planet pairs** (in this book called a **cocktail** or **formula**) consisted of the following:

Pallas-Hera	True Node-Lilith	Ascendant-Sun
Pallas-Vesta	True Node-Vesta	Fortune-Vesta
Midheaven-Mars	Mean Node-Vesta	Fortune-Vertex
Midheaven-Uranus	Jupiter-Pluto	

[2] So 6am and noon produce different charts. 6am in Italy and 6am in Illinois also produce two different charts (since 6am in Italy is 10pm or 11pm in Chicago, and on a different day at that.)

Filling in each of the brackets [] below with the corresponding harmonics from *table 16-6* in your own chart, you read the cocktail as follows:

> *"Broadly speaking, I am best at making money by [doing True Node-Vesta], which I think back on as showing my ability to [Mean Node-Vesta].*
>
> *For great riches, though, it is important to [Pallas-Hera] in the execution of [Pallas-Vesta]. In doing so, it is also important that I 1) build [Fortune-Vesta] for those who work with me, 2) am considered an innovator among [Node-Lilith], 3) am considered a field leader in [MC-Mars], and 4) am noted among the masses for my [MC-Uranus]. My expressive field is [ASC-Sun]. I meet the standards of societal pressure in [Jupiter-Pluto]. The money I make is a measure of [Fortune-Vertex] placed upon others."*

Again, even this is no guarantee of anything—especially since it requires a ton of other support and a heavy degree of willpower to turn multiplanet cocktails into a lot from a little, but this particular pattern did appear to be a good one for socially hailed, expertise-driven, societally beneficial wealth. The first catch with this and any other cocktail, though (and this is a big one), is that you have to perform the *table 16-6* "how to use" actions for their own sake and not for some other reason—otherwise you'll actually be using another set of angles instead. Bummer, right? The second catch is that most of us have charts which make the cocktails we want unreasonably inconvenient to achieve. Still, I talk more about transforming cocktails into reality in Chapter 20, since this is a central part of putting synastry to work. I'll give you a hint: It involves coming to terms with your so-called "self-chart."

Summary

Hopefully the previous section gave you enough to get started with reading your own chart, though it remains a good idea to consult any of the aforementioned sources if you want more details on what each planet, sign, house, and angle does. Try looking at your chart to see what it tells you. In the next few chapters we'll extend these ideas to reading combined charts, beginning first with a very important discussion of the twofold nature of angles. After all, even though combined charts will basically tell us the same things as single charts, we all know there's a big difference between events under your control and events which aren't. In a marked departure from their normal single-chart behavior, the angles and signs in synastry display a phenomenal capacity to switch characters right in the middle of our two player game.

Chapter 17: Behavior of houses, planets, angles and signs under synastry

Consider this simple analogy: When *you* walk into your own home at 1:00 am in the morning you're glad to be there. When *I* walk into your home at 1:00am in the morning that's cause for the law to get involved. There is a difference between you using your assets and *others* using your assets. There is a difference between you doing something and others having your deeds done to them. Relatedly, our first objective in synastry is to understand how the single-chart concepts of planets, signs, houses and angles change when viewed by others (as opposed to being viewed by their possessors). Actually, the houses are pretty easy so we'll start with them.

How astrological factors change under synastry

First let's introduce a little terminology. When we talk about two charts influencing each other, the **possessor** will be **the person whose main chart we're looking at**. The **visitor** will be **the person whose single planet has been plucked out for study in how it affects the possessor's chart**. **The houses in synastry tell you very broadly in what area of life the house possessor is affected by the visitor's planet**. Our first question is, does a house behave differently than expected when a visitor's planet lands in it? The answer is NO. Houses pretty much show the same tendencies they normally show as discussed in the previous chapter's tables, BUT…

…In synastry the houses sometimes swap who's influencing whom

Since they represent certain modes that can generally be agreed upon by others, houses don't really change that much when we look at them in synastry. The 7th house still represent s 1:1 communication. The 3rd house still represents internal monologue brought outward. Whether you are the possessor of certain planets in a particular house or the interactant with such a person, both of you in the pair can generally agree on what area of life is on the table. That's pretty much it. When it comes to our viewpoint regarding houses, the only point of confusion that sometimes arises in synastry tends to be *who's doing the influencing* rather than *which area* is being influenced. That is,

- **my** Mars in **your** 3rd may make **me** appear more aggressive towards **you** in **your** communication.

Meanwhile,

- **my** Venus in **your** 3rd may make **you** appear more socially receptive to **me** in **your** communication.

The interpretations that we'll look at on this tend to flip-flop depending on the planet, though this flipping isn't that bad. I suppose we could also say that

- **my** Venus in **your** 3rd may make **me** more socially welcomed by **you** in **your** communication.

Still Mars, Venus, and their houses are all pretty predictable here.

Table 17-1: House behaviors in synastry

Their planet in your house #...	affects your
1	display of your default instinct, personality, sexuality, or drive
2	feelings about their values, bodily enjoyment of (or tension in) your company, or self-worth
3	formation and expression of personal opinions, spontaneous communication
4	wants, inclinations, what you want from them, inclined emotions, communication of your honest wants, your interest in them or lack thereof
5	validation of them through your company, pride, ego expression, enthusiasm for things
6	analytical focus, work company, daily priorities, skills at work, body focus and fitness, task-centeredness, attention-giving side, sense of self-efficacy in work
7	casual conversation, 1:1 feedback (how you give it), 1:1 communication, how you talk to them
8	power over others, relationships (habit of dissecting, fighting, and influencing within these), criticality of others, irritation with others, expression of power against theirs
9	image in the eyes of the public, successful image promotion, exploration, tendency to self-broadcast, charisma also affects **their**... formation of creative ideas, learning and push towards the new, ideals concerning others
10	expression of authority over or ability to command others, ability to structure boundaries for others, ability to command others, sense of struggle in the world, public identity also affects **their**... sense of authority, expression of authority
11	social environment, social effect, networking power, response to society, efficacy as social connectors, information around you, also affects **their**... reach of social network, attention to their place in the social world, social plans
12	inner creative struggle, impression left on others, secrets and secret life, vibe, mood, spirituality or spaciness also affects **their**... vibe company, the feeling of matching their intended goals, impression establishment, creativity

So the house effects sometimes trade places. No big deal right? Just keep in mind that it always takes two to communicate; so when you read a chart that suggests, say, their Mars in your 8th makes you angry, it could be because you've done something to make them angry first.

In synastry the planets basically behave normally, though slightly clouded

As we've already discussed, the planets each have a default character in a normal chart. Does this character change in synastry? A little. Given that we're not mind readers, certain sentiments like anger, love, and boredom often need to be edited before we present them to our fellow human. Consequently, synastric planets are much more likely to be filtered through the lens of propriety, turning all of the emotions with which you are well familiar into a coded message for you interactant to decipher. When a visitor's planets affect a possessor's chart, it's as if the visiting planets all line up to strike a particular pose for the camera. Certain planets that we're supposed to display become exaggerated while certain planets that we're not supposed to display get tossed into the closet only to burst out loudly when provoked. Even beyond astrology, the pattern that we'll observe in the coming data is one of pro-friendly filtering of everything we actually feel in our interactions with others. And though it is true that the planets basically do in visitors what they always do in possessors, the possessor is much more likely to have a hard time grasping the extent to which the visitor's subtle planet-related hints mean serious business. That is, visitors' planets, though basically normal, then to flatten themselves.

Now even though the chart below doesn't reflect that many dramatic changes as we move from single charts to synastry, you may want to pay attention to it. It turns out that part of the reason we depend so much on Sun signs in traditional astrology is because both Suns and signs are the easiest to detect in others synastrically. You'll notice for example that a person's inner emotional world—their Moon—is usually *not* something they're comfortable disclosing to you in raw form, so you really only know what their Moon is by asking yourself the conditions under which they get angry or upset. You only know their Mercury by observing the conditions under which they are most likely to explain things fairly thoroughly.[3] See how, when it comes to visiting planets, you only get the veneered version of *table 16-3*. And that kind of filtering is just for signs. The filtering that occurs with houses makes them very difficult to read in a visitor for several reasons—not least of which is the tendency of the visitor themselves not to register the specific area of life in which they show their own planets; that is, if they don't know that their Mars in the 7th plants roots in intense 1:1 relationships, how would *you* know?

Table 17-2: How the planets look when they're not yours

Planet	Normal Sign/House Meaning (in possessor)	Synastric Sign/House Appearance (in visitor)
	Main Bodies	
Moon	inner emotional world	reactions to undesirable circumstances
Sun	how your motivation to interact with others plays out	regular behavior
Mercury	meaning making, what you show you value with another	conditions that prompt one to reason things out with you (usually through conversation)
Venus	willing socialization with another	the realm or setting under which they prefer to comfortably socialize 1:1 (which you often won't see if you're not in this realm)
Mars	how you steer interactants' inner emotional worlds	the setting under which they impose their will upon others, the heading under which they are likely to give people advice
Jupiter	how your instinct to interact with the world plays out	circumstances under which they tend to be prolifically popular

[3] This is part of the reason why many associate Mercury with Gemini and Virgo instead of just Virgo. Most of the time, Mercury/Virgo style common ground needs a Gemini or Libra style pack of words to get expressed.

Saturn	structures set in place by the world at large (not you, not other individuals) with which you interact; institutions	the side of themselves they appear to work hardest to control properly (and if you can't see this side, there's a good chance it's a side they're not sharing with you).
Uranus	the information that floats around you; thus social talk, friends, hang-out groups you wish you were like, technology	the realm of social activity preferred by them and (interestingly) the kinds of transformation undergone by their strong connections (where people who bond with them strongly tend to take the same informational path they do by sign and house)
Neptune	your generation's socio-emotional tendency; group emotional vibe on average	the realm in which they adopt an ideal standard and tend to live it out through their associations, though in isolation they tend not to know what they want in this same realm
Pluto	your generation's instinctual urge or priority; what the collective pressures its members to value	what their generation was taught to value
	House Cusps Consistent Across Most House Systems	
Ascendant (1st house cusp)	how you approach the world	(sign only) the occasion for their showing up somewhere; when they do show up, the kinds of expression that happens around them
Imum Coeli (4th house cusp)	your subconscious background	(sign only) where they seem to have free license to do or get what they want
Descendant (7th house cusp)	your favored approach to partnership	(sign only) the tactic or trait they use to prevent you from getting your own wants put on the agenda; how they override others in the rest of the group's expression, usually unintentionally
Midheaven (10th house cusp)	your reputation and career	(sign only) the attitude they take when they communicate with you, what appears to be on their mind when they do so
	Additional Important Bodies and Calculated Points	
Ceres	where you take care of others	what they use to bully others and make them uncomfortable; where they're most likely to run others off
Chiron	where you need to be validated	the asset given to them to which they must restrict others' desired access
Selene (White Moon)	gifts you are super-blessed with	the side which, when they show you, is hard to argue with (or where you are usually wrong for doing so); where they have an uncanny ability to be right
Lilith (Lunar Apogee / Black Moon)	the point where you are most defiant, or most contrary against the usual norms	the realm in which they go their own way despite what you want or expect
Vertex	where others can change your life easily and drastically	where they allow themselves to be used; the resource which they allow others to sap from them, repeatedly earning a mixture of praise and criticism (both of which continue, but become more favorable as they hone it)
North Node	"destiny" (but not really); more like the focal point around which your emotions are targeted	the means through which they board "the train of fate" for the next life lesson
Part of Fortune	where you are in your element	the side of their lives they appear to love indulging the most
	Secondary Bodies Of Interest	
Vesta	your focus backed with action	over a longer term series of events, that which they are dead set on expressing; what they seem to yearn for or prove themselves in overall

Pallas	your intellectual contribution to the greater good	what their presence enables others around them to do
Juno	your formally committed relationships in the eyes of the world	where they exhaust others' energy with their endless demands for performance
Hera	who you actually bond with	the characteristic they prize most in their bonds; what they expect their bonds to provide them with
Eros	what turns you on	what turns them on or incites their passionate action
Bacchus	where you make the best host for others; groups you actually serve	the kind of people who occupy their close clique; circumstances under which they are most likely to encounter close friends

Table 17-2: How the planets look when they're not yours

It turns out that *table 17-2* will be very useful when conducting chart **rectification**—that is, **birth time correction for charts which have no known birth time**. Starting around Uranus and proceeding from there, you can get a pretty good sense of three or four possible hour-ish timeframes for when a person was born if you know how the planets behave in the houses. Even though I said before that the houses are hard to estimate in a visitor, it is certainly possible—especially if you can narrow down their Vertex. In this book we won't go over planets in specific signs or houses in a single chart as you'll find plenty about this on the web, especially in the sources I've cited previously. You can, however, use the Chapter 16 tables to get a general idea of what another person's (or your own) planets in their own signs and houses look like upon observation.

And now for the tricky stuff...

In synastry the signs are reduced to stereotypes

This is more of an annoyance than anything else, but it bears saying. Since other people usually filter their raw nature when interacting with you, their display of the signs tends to give way to stereotype. While **your** Mars in Leo is a fun tendency to eat up attention for being a badass, their Mars in Leo makes them plain "arrogant." Where **your** Chiron in Taurus is the basis of a whole chain of decisions for building up your self-values, their Chiron in Taurus is where they're plain "insecure" in their personal worth. Why is this tricky? Because the more you flatten the visitor the harder it is to appreciate what the coming chapters tell you about how your relationship with them works. The stereotypes are also the means through which we trade practical consequences of all this stuff for convenient labels instead. As we address the behavior of planet placements throughout this book, be on the lookout for places where your labeling of the visitor obscures the deeper reasons why your relationship with them works the way it does. Just because you know that an Aries Ceres person runs others off by asserting what they really want, doesn't mean you know *why* it happens or that you have the tools to handle this tendency properly. When it comes to the synastric signs we have to work harder to see the trees for the forest.

Table 17-3: What the signs do (simple)

Signs and their common associations		
Aries Instinct, assertion, bravery, pressure to BE, spontaneity, creation, existence	**Leo** ego, attention, good standing, leadership, reliability, pride	**Sagittarius (Saj)** fun, exploration, journey, success, importance, luck, politics, fame, expansiveness
Taurus self-image, money, confidence, body, sensation, self-value (ideas that you build your identity against)	**Virgo** meaning, comparative health, analytical nature, rules of order	**Capricorn** rules, karma, old age, time, built structures, wealth as security, law, history, authority, respect
Gemini Internal thoughts, ideas, dexterity, driving, talking	**Libra** fairness, affinity, friendship, sharing, manners	**Aquarius** sociable detachment, society, rumors, peer groups, technology, humane ideals, renown
Cancer subconscious, feeling, dreaming, wants, connection, emotionality, the home, mothery-ness	**Scorpio** sex, death, others' money, psychology, power, the occult	**Pisces** humane feeling, intuition, illusion, escape, the hidden, art, abstraction

Table 17-3: Basic sign characteristics

In synastry each angle describes a spectrum, not just a single circumstance

Perhaps the most profound change that we get in going from single chart astrology to synastry is the idea that each angle has what Aristotle would have called a "middle way" alongside two extremes. Whereas in the last chapter we had a table which showed how the 120° trine, for example, "turns up" the relevant angle pairs whenever you "think," here we learn that the trine actually has three faces along a kind of "thinking" axis:

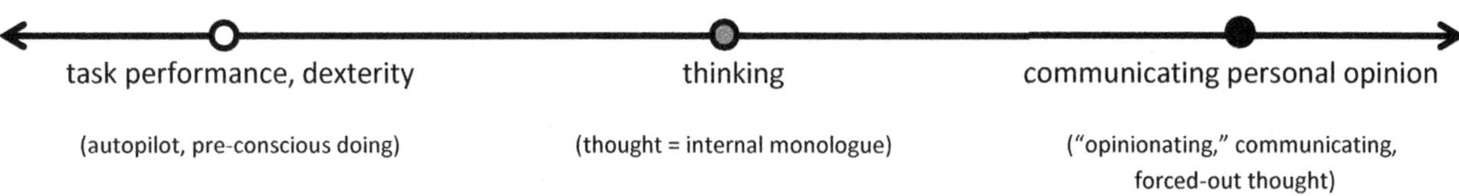

Each of the above represents a level of mental activity, where planets in trine can play out anywhere along the entire axis. The whole idea of an "axis" for conjuncts, oppositions, trines, and so on is something that almost never comes up in single chart astrology mainly because it's easier for us humans to dump everything into a stereotyped bucket and go from there. But synastry almost *requires* that we go deeper than such buckets. Why? I'll answer that by telling you how the axis finding first came up:

> Invariably if you look at planet pairs separated by multiples of $^1/_{21}$ of a circle (17°09', II-noviles), you'll find that they are tied to how we create things—particularly impressions. Meanwhile, the [Venus-Mars] planet pair has long been associated with the ability to get others to do what you want. Accordingly, a [Venus-Mars] II-novile in a single chart shows someone whose manipulation of others' will is most welcome as they create things. Yet the synastry behaves differently in an interesting way. Later on we'll see that a

possessor's Mars gets [turned on] / [spurred to action] by a visitor's Venus. But the ways in which this happened in the data were overwhelmingly bimodal (had two "most frequent" values): One version showed up as a fierce ability of the Venus person to inspire lust in the Mars person. The other version showed up as the capacity of the Venus person to make the Mars person exceedingly angry. This kind of dual nature held not only for [Venus-Mars], but for all pairs. Not just for Il-noviles but for all angles. This is the main reason why we won't be able to read the success or failure of a relationship through synastry. **Every angle, every planet and sign, has an "up," a "down," and a "middle" version.** The one *you* choose is usually based on habits you've learned, but the one that the *other person* chooses is up to them, not you. Across multiple visitors, to you this as good as random.

And so our angle harmonics all have multiple faces, adding a whole new level of complexity to *table 16-6*. It's from this kind of multiplicity that we end up with the famous "love-hate" relationship that characterizes so many obsessive attachments to things; ignoring the "love" part for a moment, we may do better do describe this as "lust-hate" instead—where impassioned action and grand irritation are two ends of the same spectrum. Lust or hate? Which one will apply to you? That depends on what kinds of other ideas you marry to the experience in your own psychology.

*****Use the next table along with* table 16-5 *to read your own chart*****

As a compressed version of a "self chart" reading, you can use *table 17-4* below in combination with *table 16-5* to read your own chart. When doing so, you read it as follows,

My [*table 16-5* planet pair description] increases in when I am [doing *table 17-4* low, medium, or high stress versions].

Suppose, for example, you printed out the table view of your chart and part of it looked something like this:

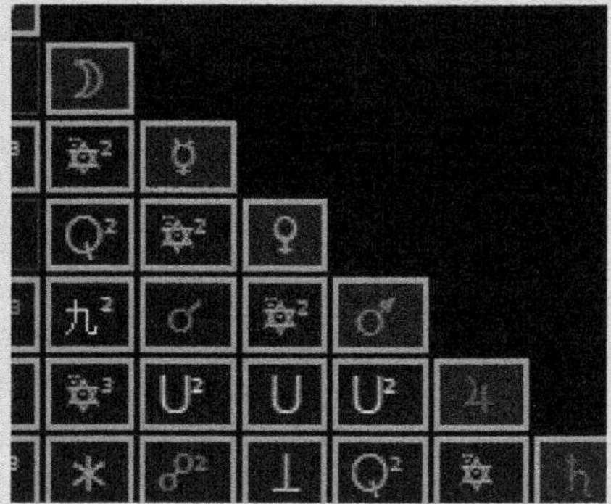

Using *tables 16-6* and *17-4* you could say things like "My [openly analytical nature, persuasiveness, and being sought after] increase when I am [giving myself messages that affirm how I present those traits]." You could also say "My [resolve] increases when I am [being myself]." I [have an influential image which includes exaggerated criticality] as [one of my quirks]." Keep in mind that interpretations like this are very superficial, but they should be enough to get you started reading the deep details of your own chart.

Table 17-4: Range of behaviors for each of the first 36 angle families

Harmonic	Name	Symbol	Degrees	Lower stress version	Medium stress version	Higher stress version
[The following angles play out when you are engaging] Level I, Group 1: Self (you)						
1	conjunct	☌	0°	**adjoining** (associated without necessarily doing anything together)	**being /expressing together**	**not ceasing to be** (as in a pair you can't turn off)
2	opposition	☍	180°	**bodily feeling**	**self-valuing / identifying with** (establishing common ground between oneself and a thing)	**valuing** (measuring a thing against another thing used to measure the self; related to money)
3	trine	△	120°	**performing an action** (pre-thought mental activity)	**thinking** (internal monologue)	**communicating/opinionating** (exported thought)
4	square	□	90°	**using intuition** (predicting / expecting something)	**feeling** (processing the difference b/w what is and what is experienced or expected)	**wanting** (acting to minimize the difference b/w what is and what is expected)
Level I, Group 2: Other (your direct 1:1 interactants)						
5	quintile	⋆	72°, 144°	**ego broadcasting / playing** (as in games) (acting naturally to project onto another)	**interacting 1:1 with another** (acting purposefully to exchange with another)	**being motivated in the 1:1 presence of another** (acting as newly directed in exchange with another)
6	sextile	✳	60°	**making meaning** (writing the role of a 1:1 thing against other things; assoc w/ analysis)	**working towards** (performing actions against a 1:1 thing to align it with other things; assoc w/ service)	**maintaining (through upkeep)** (keeping the role of a 1:1 thing from deviating from that of other things; assoc w/ health)
7	septile	✡	51°26', 102°51', 154°17'	**listening 1:1** (they talk, you process)	**conversing 1:1** (you both talk and process)	**instructing / playing 1:1** (as in instruments, video games) (you "talk," they process)
8	octile	∠	45°, 135°	**reasoning** (making ideas do what you want them to do)	**steering** (making others do what you want them to do)	**manipulating** / **showing aggression** (making others do what you want while you yourself feel... ...passive discord) / ...active discord)

Level I, Group 3: World (a catch-all term for the faceless space of things around you)						
9	novile	九	40°, 80°, 160°	**projecting a strong image** (being seen by the world)	**learning** (processing the world)	**traveling** (actively absorbing and interacting with the world)
10	decile	+	36°, 108°	**controlling** (being seen as keeping the behavior of an existing thing aligned with your actions)	**expanding a reputation** (being seen as acting in a new way that aligns with your existing actions)	**exercising authority / limiting** (being seen as actively stopping an existing thing from getting out line with your actions and expectations)
11	undecile	U	32°44′, 65°27′, 98°11′, 130°55′, 163°38′	**being talked about on the grapevine / being surrounded by info that resembles your priorities; uniqueness** (just being where it happens)	**frequenting social groups / taking in such social information** (processing it)	**aspiring to be talked about or associated with certain social ideas / humanitarian effects** (requires active effort)
12	inconjunct	⚻	30°, 150°	**being in a mood** (holding any basic emotional disposition; others can read this through empathy)	**maintaining a secret side** (holding a disposition, knowing how it differs from the apparent actions which others see)	**projecting a desire onto world** (holding an emotional disposition)
Level II, Group 1: Society (the small-ish sphere of people you actually live and work among. This is not the abstract world!)						
13	II-conjunct	$☌^2$	27°42′, 55°23′, 83°05′, 110°46′, 138°28′, 166°09′	**holding a public persona** (the instinctive face you put on in public)	**playing a socialized role** (actively behaving in line with your societal face)	**putting your personal "brand" in others' faces** (purposely directing your societally-played face towards a particular recipient)
14	II-opposition	$☍^2$	25°43′, 77°09′, 128°34′	**being associated with a particular race / class** (having yourself pigeonholed based on your similarity or lack of similarity to people who look like you)	**putting the things you identify with to use** (this includes your language, dress, body characteristics, objects that travel with you, and favorite roles; the effect that comes with your showing up as a body)	**pleasure seeking** (having your societally labeled values be something you actively seek to have pleased; acting to have other events fuel the use of things you identify with; hedonism)
15	II-trine	$△^2$	24°, 48°, 96°, 168°	**displaying mannerisms** (pre-thought actions which communicate with society, your default bearing wherever you are, regardless of the attention you pay to your surroundings)	**"opinionating" onto society / leaving an impression upon a generic situation** (thinking within the context of society; roughly, your responses to what happens wherever you are)	**room hijacking / getting attention** (how you actively announce yourself to recruit the attention of others)

16	II-square	$\square^2$	22°30′, 67°30′, 112°30′, 157°30′	**having family values** (emotional dispositions you bring from childhood training into your expectations for others in society)	**aspiring to be respected** (acting to have your core values validated by your society)	**tending to / training / caretaking /teaching** (acting to place your core values on others)
Level II, Group 2: The fishbowl (your preferred family of associations—people, things, or actions—plucked from society for you to interact with as a stable base in everyday matters)						
17	II-quintile	$\star^2$	21°11′, 42°21′, 63°32′, 84°42′, 105°53′, 127°04′, 148°14′, 169°25′	**growing / reinforcing / "daoing"** ("growing with the flow" to adapt a cliché) (accumulating new skills which naturally appeal to your instincts)	**"fishbowling" / validating / fighting for / serving** (actively referencing trained behavioral tools, from the fishbowl that you already have, which quiets your need to complain or brag)	**complaining / bragging / showing pride / dominating** (expressing your current tools for response to things beyond you in its most honest, untrained, tension-filled animal state)
18	II-sextile	$*^2$	20°, 100°, 140°	**having a goal** (an average of all of your current dispositions compressed into a single, common ground endpoint)	**rationalizing / summarizing** (averaging the existing ideas you observe into a single, common ground endpoint)	**long-range planning** (actively arranging ideas and future expectations you have into a single, common ground endpoint)
19	II-septile	✡^{2}	18°57′, 37°54′, 56°51′, 75°47′, 94°44′, 113°41′, 132°38′, 151°35′, 170°32′	**having ideas regarding how you communicate with others / listening to messages which affirm your own way of sending messages** (having standards for how you and your fishbowl ["us"] communicate your values)	**assimilating outside ideas into existing ideas which you already find meaningful** (this is where you open the door to "them" in the usual "us vs them" human way, so as to bend the power barriers set up by your fishbowl—hence this harmonic's association with gender bending and reversed power roles discussed in *FSA*)	**presenting ideas you already find meaningful** (sending out "us"-related ideas from your fishbowl)
20	II-octile	$\angle^2$	18°, 54°, 126°, 162°	**being magnetic in ways that others recognize, but won't talk about** (where people outside of your fishbowl are influenced by its power-style, but since they *are* outsiders, they are reluctant to talk to you about this unless you invite them into your group)	**steering people outside of your ingroup / fishbowl** (this is where you close the door to "them" in the usual "us vs them" human way, so as to affirm the power-styles outlined by your fishbowl. Look at what types of power your closest friends value and foist this upon others to use this angle.)	**competing for power on behalf of your ingroup's power values / seducing / making others jealous / setting them up to succumb to your wants** (an open, active, and remorseless version of fishbowl power-style steering)

Level II, Group 3: Creative works (the character of things, efforts, and stranger-influencing impressions made by you)						
21	II-novile	九^2	17°09′, 34°17′, 68°34′, 85°43′, 137°09′, 171°25′	**being alluring, unsettling, making others squirm with an image you create in the faceless world** (passively creating—from nothing apparent—something for others to view or experience; like birthing; brings tension in them)	**showing effort towards something** (actively creating—from nothing apparent—something for others to view or experience [nothing apparent b/c they can't read your mind to know what motivated you])	**being obnoxious, aggravating, [anger, fear, or frustration]-inspiring** (actively creating—from nothing apparent—something for others to view or experience while holding discordant emotions which spill onto others)
22	II-decile	+^{2}	16°22′, 49°05′, 81°49′, 114°33′, 147°16′	**having a reputation for certain kinds of limits or boundaries you've unintentionally placed on things**	**gaining a reputation through the structure of the things or events you've intentionally caused**	**creating through the structure you actively enforce upon things, intentionally cause, or maintain**
23	II-undecile	∪^{2}	15°39′, 31°18′, 46°57′, 78°16′, 93°55′, 125°13′, 140°52′, 172°10′	**being exceptional, being talked about for unique quirks you've unintentionally displayed / the values you hold for being talked about in the social world**	**creating events which rest upon how or what you communicate as building blocks** (the world doesn't normally register the normal things you do, mainly the abnormal—hence this harmonic's association w provocative talk / the areas in which you break taboo)	**actively indulging your standalone individualism**
24	II-inconjunct	⊼^{2}	15°, 75°, 105°, 165°	**leaving an impression on others through the nature of your creative works**	**visualizing / imagining**	**putting continuous, imaginative effort into making something real**
Level III, Group 1: Mass psychology (behaviors you display which are backed by larger public patterns)						
25	III-conjunct	☌^{3}	14°24′, 28°48′, 43°12′, 100°48′, 115°12′, 172°48′	**using big groups in the world to justify what you do**	**behaving in ways that line up with the way big groups in the world describe it as being properly done**	**mass action / recruiting big groups in the world to back you in what you do**
26	III-opposition	☍^{3}	13°51′, 69°14′, 96°55′	**having a public fan base** (displaying a consistent enough set of traits to warrant others' following or support of you)	**publicly questioning your own efforts** (reviewing those behaviors of yours which your fans follow)	**catering to your fans / lining up with the trends (values) they expect** (actively adjusting your behaviors to align with what your fans follow)
27	III-trine	△^{3}	13°20′, 26°40′, 66°40′, 106°40′	**having insight into an event**	**communicating your insight**	**putting your insight into practice**

28	III-square	□3	12°51′, 157°09′	**having morals / considering mass expectation as informing your decisions / feeling the extent to which an event aligns with your morals**	**acting in line with your principles / moral responsibility / doing for the higher good (or at least higher purpose)**	**giving unconvinced cooperation with events that deviate from your principles**
Level III, Group 2: Mass influence (how you actually steer big groups; [where "mass psychology" only *identifies with* them])						
29	III-quintile	⋆3	12°25′, 24°50′, 37°14′, 62°04′, 86°54′, 124°08′, 148°58′, 173°48′	**having confidence** (engaging the mass world with surety in your thoughts of your actions ["surety" here means that you "know with certainty" what talents you bring)	**displaying a sense of self-contented prosperity** (engaging the mass world with surety in your actions)	**being funny or entertaining / showing off / commanding others** (asserting your individual ways upon the mass world with surety [where the world isn't *really* likely to be moved by your small perspective, you are considered funny])
30	III-sextile	⁎3	12°, 84°, 132°, 156°	**objectifying the body (or one's presence)** (finding common ground built on the 1:1 ego; in *FSA* this would be the same as 6 x 5—"6ing the 5s")	**having expertise** (giving your skill for common ground its own ego form; 5 x 6 or "5ing the 6s")	**being an expert critic** (alternating between giving your skill for common ground its own ego AND objectifying your own presence in association with this)
31	III-septile	✡3	11°37′, 23°14′, 34°50′, 58°04′, 92°54′, 116°08′	**being motivated to see an idea all the way through / unrealized good intentions** (having the inclination to apply one idea across many situations, without necessarily acting on this)	**traversing networks of people** (applying your general "idea" across many 1:1 minds[4])	**promoting a doctrine / group management / pushing towards renown** (asserting your general "idea" across many 1:1 minds)
32	III-octile	∠3	11°15′, 78°45′, 146°15	**being (seen as) mysterious** (being seen as attempting to secretly steer the inclinations of the mass world around you)	**being distrustful** (actually attempting to steer or reinterpret the inclinations of the mass world around you—usually in light of a particular event you've been presented with)	**analyzing a thing until it breaks (i.e. until you uncover the "catch")** (openly and actively attempting to steer or reinterpret the inclinations of the mass world around you in light of a particular event)

[4] 🛠 For the mathematically inclined, "selectively expertise-ing," [31 = 30+1] doubles the size of 30's power set, where the [III-septile is actually the 30 repeats of the II-sextile turned on in our frame or turned off in light of someone else's frame]. In *FSA* I talked about how all of the symbols in astrology get their effects from their orbits (or number of cycles that describes their orbit). Accordingly I also speculated that the meaning of "31 repeats" may thus be the result of a natural "wobble" between 15s and 16s: [impression leaving] and [respect pursuit] for example. That is, in cases where both 15+15+15+... ([30]+[30]+...) and 16+16+16+... ([32]+[32]+...) eventually fall out of sync with a cycle that would be better described by 31+31+..., 31s would work better as combinations of 15+16+15+16+.... What does a behavior that alternates between impressions and value affirmation look like? Maybe a cycle of back and forth validation among friends and associates? Call this network traversing.

Level III, Group 3: Leadership and Representativeness (where the mass world sees you as synonymous with an idea)						
33	III-novile	九³	10°55′, 21°49′, 76°22′, 109°05′, 141°49′	**being watched** (where the faceless world looks at you and you feel it)	**being under the spotlight** (where the faceless world looks at you and you know it)	**rallying crowds / executing your stage presence** (where the faceless world looks at you, you know it, and you actively perform or respond accordingly)
34	III-decile	+³	10°35′, 52°56′, 74°07′, 158°49′	**having expectations regarding authority**	**weighing the authorities you're subject to against your own standards / weighing your subordinates (including yourself) against your authority standards**	**behaving as if you are an authority / exercising discipline**
35	III-undecile	U³	10°17′, 30°51′, 41°09′, 113°09′, 174°51′	**having ideas regarding what's worthy of attention**	**following curiosity in areas beyond what others normally give attention to / absorbing information unique to your personality**	**exercising unique skill in a way that others see as attention-worthy**
36	III-inconjunct	不³	10°, 50°, 70°, 110°, 130°, 170°	**having ideas regarding that which inspires groups to action / having others place bets (group expectations) on your performance** (where your unknowing actions elicit others' intuition or inclinations)	**absorbing inspiration from a thing** (where you knowingly gain motivation from the intuition or inclinations of others as shown in external events)	**remaining committed to a task despite occasional lapses in focus / inspired work / poor quality work done in zombie mode** (where you act in line with the intuition or inclinations of others despite your own occasional divorce from the task)

Table 17-4: Range of behaviors for the first 36 harmonic angle families. In general the low stress version of each harmonic corresponds to your [taking in] the world. The medium stress version comes with consciously receiving input from an other. The high stress version corresponds to your mobilizing directed action from the self. In this way, the choice of three divisions wasn't arbitrary, but lines up with the same self-other-world pattern we'll always assume.

Even though your birth chart doesn't change, your attention to its various angles does, and even within a single angle family your degree of attention and maturity will alter whether you show the low, medium, or high stress version of each angle. If you look at your chart you'll see that **certain planet pairs** are **separated by the same harmonic**. Maybe your Sun and Mars are novile (separated by 40°, 80°, or 160°) while your Neptune and Ceres are also novile, for example. In this case, [Sun-Mars] and [Neptune-Ceres] would be called **resonant pairs** since they are both easily "turned up" using the same frequency. Resonant pairs form the basis of different faces of your chart so that, if you gather up all the noviles and read their pairs in *table 16-5*, you'll get a good idea of how you come across when performing "novile-type actions" towards the faceless world. If you gather up all of your III-deciles you'll get a good idea of the kinds of qualities that inform your approach to being a boss or a master. I go into the details of each of the 300 planet pairs [Sun-Moon] through [Eros-Bacchus] in *FSA*.

How two very different harmonics can look the same

While creating *table 17-4* I noticed a pattern unfolding across the various stress levels and colored the cells accordingly. See how there seem to be four kinds of approaches underlying everything? We'll call **this cycle of four behaviors across harmonics** the **four-pattern**. Broadly, the patterns are joining ideas, weighing events, motivating events, and shuttling ideas back and forth towards an endpoint. I don't know why this is,[5] but it's interesting to note that the end result gives each block of four harmonics a total of 12 different states. How does this affect you? It means you can cheat. The reason is a little technical, but you may find it useful. If the next section gets to be too much, just skip past it. Here goes.

🛠 We can think of each harmonic angle family as being like a group of jobs in society. Inconjuncts ($^1/_{12}$ of a circle) are like your doctors or Pisces-people (the 12th sign). Conjuncts (0°) are like your soldiers or Aries-people (the 1st sign). Actually, let's put this in a table:

Harmonic	Occupation holders	...who do things (Level I)		...who get talked about (Level II)		...who tend to groups (Level III)	
1	doers	conjunct	soldiers, athletes	II-conjunct	performing artists	III-conjunct	public personas
2	valuers	opposition	retail, service industry	II-opposition	beauty and body industry	III-opposition	wealth and brand industry
3	thinkers	trine	transport industry, small-group hosts	II-trine	businesspeople	III-trine	entrepreneurs
4	caretakers	square	teachers, family-related work	II-square	culinary, child-rearing, home-related	III-square	preachers, writers
5	stand-outs	quintile	influencers, hobbyists	II-quintile	coaches, service staff	III-quintile	commentators
6	bridge makers	sextile	analysts & fitness industry	II-sextile	managers	III-sextile	consultants, trainers
7	socializers	septile	counselors, advisors	II-septile	social industry, internal support role	III-septile	networkers
8	controllers	octile	people who control others' power or money through their action	II-octile	engineers, accountants, researchers whose work is public	III-octile	hackers, certain lawyers, investi-gators, political decision makers (people who do hard-to-explain dirty work)
9	expanders	novile	travelers, teachers, explorers	II-novile	artists	III-novile	public performers
10	authorities	decile	law enforcement, bosses, managers	II-decile	builders, construction industry	III-decile	architects, owners of assets, legal industry
11	mass communicators	undecile	customer service, information industry	II-undecile	community builders, journalism, writers	III-undecile	political figures & programmers
12	illusionists	inconjunct	creators of ideas	II-inconjunct	surgeons & filmmakers	III-inconjunct	psychologists & actors

Table 17-5: Types of occupations that fit the behavior of the 36 harmonics

[5] 🛠 I suspect that the four-pattern is related to the lining up of cycles within a harmonic with other cycles outside of it. So if your brain thinks that the frequency it's reading takes four cycles to complete most of the time but sometimes takes five, it needs to apply yet another firing cycle to compare which one applies (whether it's four or five we're looking at). If your brain already has a way of calculating frequencies in groups of four (rising, sitting at peak, falling, and sitting at minimum) then it can use a similar calculator to chop up each harmonic level. My guess would be that two different, slightly-off harmonics which trigger the same result in this "backup counter" will be processed as related in some other areas of the brain as well. Of course this example only works for humans, but the idea of using an existing four-system to differentiate across a 4 x 3 system is nice and consistent mathematically. Beyond humans, you might model this using something called a quaternion: a four dimensional number system.

Note that the above table is also useful for looking at your ideal career when angles that describe a prevalence of career-relevant pairs in your chart (like [Saturn-Vesta] and [Pluto-Vesta] as discussed in *FSA*) can't point you to a field that works. Anyway, *table 17-4* above adds yet another dimension to all of these angles. Common sense tells you that there are different kinds of law enforcement, different kinds of soldier, and so on. Whereas a "low stress"-style solider soldier may describe his job more in the defense capacity, a medium-stress soldier may describe his work more in terms of his role alongside his brothers; a high stress soldier may describe his role more in terms of offensive operations. Yet the high stress soldier's conjunct—according to our four-pattern in *table 17-4*—can be associated with the low stress trine (the autopilot version associated with the transport industry). In other words, each harmonic has different points along its range which resembles different harmonics. So if you don't like a particular angle in your chart you can, with some reframing, change it.

Why would we be able to change an angle in our charts? Doesn't that break a key part of astrology? No, and here's why: Suppose your [Saturn-Vesta] is separated by 104°15'. According to *table 16-7* that's a ⊼$^{2}_{(7)}$ (septi-II-inconjunct) right? Reading this with *table 16-5*, you see that your career focused desire goes up when you are displaying works of the imagination right? This is true. What kinds of people tend to do this? Surgeons, filmmakers, and other folks who turn the illusions or impressions of others into tangible realities; surgeons alter bodies in response to health impressions; filmmakers produce viewable works built on experiential impressions. But what if being a II-inconjunct illusionist isn't your thing? Are you stuck? No, because 104°15' can also be read as a ✡$_{(3)}$ triseptile—especially because the triseptile is a more basic angle. So your career-focused desire may increase when you serve as a counselor instead. Truly, 104°15' is neither a member of the exact II-inconjunct family nor the exact septile family, so that there will be some wobbling between these two based on plain old math alone. So it turns out that—except for the most exact angles of separation between your planet pairs—all angles in your chart can be read as either of the two nearest angles that flank them. So if you get different angles showing up in different programs, it's not as inconsistent as you might think. That's just a consequence of working with such small windows between angles. It happens with atoms all the time. In the case of the II-inconjunct vs septile though, our four-pattern reveals a kind of hack: the medium-stress II-inconjunct and the low-stress septile are both "motivators," so a filmmaker who visualizes and a counselor who listens have similarities that allow you to play out something stable between both harmonics. The high-stress II-inconjunct and the medium-stress septile are both "shuttlers," so a filmmaker who continuously imagines and a counselor who converses also have similarities which aren't very different from their lower-stress versions. Thus you get a change in field without a very big change in the underlying kind of expression you give in those fields. This is how you can cheat the chart; very few of your angles will be fatalistically exact. For any planet pair, all you'll need to do is see what the second closest angle says and read its character, then look for the two types of four-pattern which join them.

Is that a very dark red or a very light maroon? As long as you're not too picky about it, it's your choice. ⚒

Let's define an **angle X's flanking angle as one of the angles in a pre-set harmonic which is the nearest lower or nearest higher angle next to angle X**. I'll give an example using [Venus-Uranus] later in this paragraph. The moral of the above story though is that any angle you read in your chart can be swapped out with any nearby angle that flanks it as long as such an angle's range of effect, or orb, allows you to do so. I address orbs for each harmonic in *FSA* and won't cover them here, since the use of two flanking angles from the "Name" column and the two flanking angles from the "Most basic angle" columns of *table 16-7* will suit us fine. That is, any angle of separation in your chart can be read as either [Name] angles on both sides of it or either [Most basic angles] on both sides of it when the orbs are reasonably close. So a [Venus-Uranus]-55° for example could be read as a II-octile, II-conjunct, or (if you're really pushing it) a VERY wide sextile. So if you read something you don't like, don't worry! You have options which depend partly on frequency difference and partly on which harmonics you choose to pay attention to.

The "nearest angle" thing finally allows us to answer a question that may have been bothering you. What is the difference between different angles in the same harmonic family? What is the difference between, say, a quintile angle (72°) and a biquintile angle (144°)? The answer lies in the angles near them. When you have an inexact quintile angle, you're more likely to get either III-inconjunct (70°) or III-decile (74°07') behavior. Both of these are mass-ideal related, making a quintile angle subtler, cooler-headed, and more ambient-reaching as a 1:1 ego. Biquintile angles on the other hand, when inexact, are more like III-noviles (141°49') and III-octiles (146°15'). Both of these are more rile-up ready and audience disturbing, making the biquintile noticeably more amped up and energetic as an ego projector. So there really are differences between each individual degree, even within the same harmonic. Fundamentally, however, those differences are only useful to look at after we know what the basic harmonic does in the first place. As decades of fuzzy astrological interpretations among inconjuncts suggests,[6] we usually don't bother with such distinctions unless we have to.

Summary

I know we've gotten pretty technical here, so let's close this section with the two most important takeaways:

1. Every angle really does have its own character which you can determine whenever you want more detail on a particular pairing. Each angle is swappable with its flanking partners, and you can use the four-pattern to figure out the sharpest similarities between these.
2. In synastry, visitors tend to play out stress levels (and sometimes flanking angles) different than yours—especially when they need to hide or downplay their true feelings about something (which is almost all the time for non-partners). Not only can we not tell from synastry what either person *will* do, we can't even tell what they *would like* to do. We can, however, tell how they're inclined to exchange with you on the surface. And that, you'll see, is a pretty powerful weapon.

[6] That is, fuzziness between the semisextile angle (30°) and the inconjunct angle (150°). It is common in astrology for us to interpret these as being basically the same angle, with the inconjunct angle being slightly stronger than the semisextile angle.

Chapter 18: Planets on another's houses

A quick question for you Mr. Hayden.

Yes?

Suppose I turn up the rock music and play it in your ear, but you don't mind. What time of day is it?

For me personally, that would be 8am when I'm on my way to the job. And maybe 6pm when I'm working out.

Okay, make it classical music. What time of day is it?

Could be 2pm when I'm winding down or 6pm when I'm working out. Or maybe 9pm through midnight. The workout music really depends on my mood.

What if I played rock in your ear at 2am?

I'd be pissed. No joke.

Of course. And that's how planets in another person's houses work; their planet is a particular style of music played during a particular period in your day. Except the day is substituted for an area of life.

Hm. Okay.

A weird thing about this is that my playing music for you can affect either you *or* me. In the same way that my rock at your 8am may give **you** fuel, my rock at your 2pm may get *me* beat up. It depends on whether the music matches the setting.

Alright. I get that.

But really the planets in the houses are just background music. They show what context I foster in you, but not what my "songs" are actually trying to get you to do. That's a job for the planet-to-planet pairs. So let's talk about the planets in the houses first. The *synastric* houses, that is.

Synastric planets in houses

When a visitor's chart sits on top of a possessor's chart, both people are usually affected. I see you looking at me as if I'm about to steal something. We both react to such mutual acknowledgement, though we react to different aspects of the situation. Generally, you can't rely on a single planet to be the giver or the receiver in a house mainly because the **synastric planets in houses** **(the visitor's planets in a possessor's houses)** represent situations, not fixed events. At some point during this conversation between your planets and theirs, you're talking and they're listening. At another point in the conversation they're talking and you're listening. The constant feedback means that a visitor's planets render each of you both givers and receivers of what those planets have to offer. Nonetheless we can identify some basic tendencies for planets in other's houses—at least narrowing down what kinds of context each one brings to the fore.

The houses are pretty predictable in synastry, so much so that we can sum up most of their common effects in *table 18-1*. Throughout the rest of this chapter you should assume that all visiting planets draw out the things shown in this table unless otherwise stated. For example, you won't read any details regarding your Saturn in another's 1st house because this particular position does just what the table below suggests it does. In most cases, instead of discussing what a planet does in house 1 specifically, I'll only discuss what it does in *a* house in general. There are many exceptions to this, though. Just don't count on seeing an interpretation for every specific case of every planet in every house. In presenting all of these conclusions I had to choose between being unnecessarily repetitive (and quite boring) and being a little more terse (sticking only with the highlights). I chose the latter. Thus you might want to memorize *table 18-1*. It's pretty straightforward, and I'll bet you'll have it down long before we get to the end of this section.

Table 18-1: Synastric houses, areas of life

Visitor's planets in a possessor's house...	Affects either person's area of life...
1	instinctual personality, drive, impulsive action, sexuality
2	bodily enjoyment of their company or general body preferences, self-value, consistency of actions vs values
3	ideas and opinions, expression, individualism, communication
4	wants, inclinations, family role, interests, insight and intuition, emotional disposition, feelings about a topic
5	ego priorities, ego display, pride, bodily presence, reactions enthusiasm, charisma
6	analytical or attention-giving side, role as a standard of comparison in daily work, colleague role, daily preoccupations, business focus, effectiveness in work, attainment of goals
7	1:1 communication, conversation, 1:1 dynamics
8	need to project deviant habits, show of power, power over others, habit of dissecting / fighting / influencing, criticality
9	quest to project in the world, image projection, charisma, push towards new experiences, exploration, journeys
10	created structures, expression of authority, engagement of limits, ability to command others, entrenched struggles, public identity
11	role as a social hub, intelligence, knowledge, social effects, social place, social networks, social plans, response to society, aspirations, circle of influence
12	overall vibe, accepted environmental contexts, spirituality, concerns for greater environment, creativity, mood, general influence, secret lives, desired impressions, spaciness, focus, expectations

Table 18-1: House's areas of life affected by visiting planets

Your Planets in their houses

Your Sun in their house

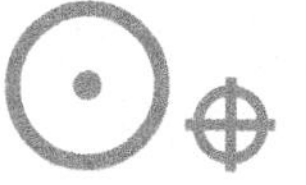

Your Sun in another's house shows you where you see them as being hooked on or fixated on your expression. In this house, your expression is capable of drawing out their comfort **for better or worse / fbow**. What does the "for better or worse part mean? It means that in some cases others are comfortable being healthily fun with you while in other cases they are more comfortable arrogantly harassing you—both situations in which doing so is more stable for them. We'll run into a lot of this "fbow" stuff throughout the book, hence the need for an acronym early on.

Not surprisingly, you can use favorable behavior in this area of life to manipulate the other person into liking you. If your Sun is in their 1st for example, your encouragement of their spontaneity and provision of new circumstances for them can pique their interest and typically get them to feel excited about you. This is particularly useful for dealing with children or people whom you need to keep entertained. 2nd house others are very different though; your enjoyment of their bodily company or the things they value help solidify the relationship. This may not be that hard for romantic situations though since your Sun in their 2nd often renders them sexy company to you. 6th house people, though certainly more analytical in your presence, often tend to display their analysis in a way that suggests they like or approve of you. This is partly related to the 6th house person being subordinate to the Sun person in some way; the other tends to like you more as a reflection of how you behave as a boss broadly. If you're a bad boss with a Sun in another's 6th, the other is more likely to hate you. 7th house people are interesting in that, while your Sun does draw out their willing communication, it often draws out a façade to go along with it. The other is more likely to have more than their share of "I don't believe I said that" moments, causing them to be less forthcoming with you and more superficial with you over time. 9th house people seem much more adventurous to you, and if you should spend more time in their company, you may find that they are constantly drawing out new ideas and viewpoints within you instead of the other way around. Your Sun in the other's 12th helps them get lost in space around you. Maybe this shows up as creativity, maybe not. Your Sun in all other houses tends to draw out those areas of the other's life reflected in *table 18-1*.

Your Moon in their house

☽ ⊕ **Your Moon in another's house shows the area of their lives through which they can get to you emotionally. You see them as sensual or practical/values-oriented in their expression of their house, pursuing tangible evidence of their own progress.** The other is more emotionally responsive to your engagement with this house of theirs. For example, 1st house others are more responsive to you as a person and seem, to you, more practical as themselves in this area. There tend to be two kinds of first house others given your visiting Sun. The first is the classic badass who mows down others in a show of their force. Because they are wired to attack your insecurities, these tend to be lusty and instill in you a sense of hot-blooded discomfort when their actions reach your ears. On the other hand, they also tend to like you a lot; since they can't actually mow down everyone 24-7, their doing so before you is often an attempt to match what they think to be standards of desirability which should apply to everyone, including you. The second group of 1st house people are far less forceful, gentle and pleasurable company. They find your company soothing, but tend to be attached to other people before you in a more final way. 2nd house folks feed off of your physical presence or conveyance of values, but differ from 2nd house Suns in that it is they who often feel the need to prove their values to you and have those values validated by you. 3rd through 7th, 9th and 10th house others unleash the standard areas of life upon you in search of proof of their progress, while 8th house holders are more subject to your influence. These people are more likely to rely on you for advice in their efforts to control their own resources. You feel 11th house possessors to be very strongly networked, and may admire them for this. 12th house people, unfortunately, tend to look spacey and unreliable in your eyes, even if you would like to work out an association with them, even if you find them to be desirable company (both of which you often do).

Your Mercury in their house

☿ ⊕ **Your Mercury as a visitor makes the other person step up their display of insight into their own area of life as reflected by their house (which you're visiting).** All of the standard *table 18-1* topics apply, though the 8th house possessor tends to encourage you to project power as a means of insight into their own. Often this means that they will do things to provoke your irritation. Even in the best relationships, the 8th house possessor may get themselves into trouble so that you can take up arms to get them out. Such relationships tend to be passionate, physical, and draining for you. 9th house possessors make good travel and learning partners for you.

Your Venus in their house

♀ ⊕ Your Venus in their house does something we wouldn't expect it to do. The other person draws out this area of your life in order to help you tackle a task, facilitating a growth lesson in your version of the house your Venus is visiting. Here you are challenged to make good decisions—often those which involve taming your natural (comparatively reckless impulses. That is, **they calm you down and focus your expression in this area. The other tends to like socializing with you over this same house (of theirs, mainly).** Also, Venus in their 7th brings your general social concerns to light. Venus in the 8th highlights your investigation and exercise of power. Venus in their 11th highlights their concerns in the social world. Venus in their 12th revolves around your spirituality and concerns for the greater environment.

Your Mars in their house

♂⊕ Your Mars in another's house. What happened to it? Where is it? This house of Other's is mysteriously silent in your interactions with them, as if you don't learn much about their true way of expressing this house unless you go around them and find out through the grapevine or other peripheral sources of information. Although it's not like they are necessarily keeping secrets from you here, there is something about their interaction with you that downplays clear transmission of their true motivations in this house of theirs. Finding out more can—and often does—reveal that which amounts to a double life in your eyes. **So your Mars in their house is essentially that area of life where you attempt to steer the other's behavior into a form you can register.** Barring this, they may not show you much of what there is to be shown here. 6th house others are often wayward, and may attempt to steer how you work instead. 8th and 9th house others also attempt to steer you in their respective areas instead of letting you uncover their workings. You give structure to a 10th house person. You'll tend to use your social world or the information at your disposal to do the influencing of a person whose 11th your Mars visits.

Your Jupiter in their house

♃⊕ **You tend to be boisterous, optimistic, and intrepid when the other displays the relevant area of life.** And why not? Jupiter, your planet of expanding in the faceless world gets an outlet in whatever house this is—as if Other puts you in touch with a side of yourself that was meant to inflate you beyond the confines of your mortal shell. There is a big downside to this though: You can also be inappropriately cheerful amidst the others' struggle and very arrogant—especially in cases where the other person struggles with the house your Jupiter is visiting. It's easier for you to adopt a "Whatever, it's not so bad" attitude which the other is unlikely to appreciate. In fact, the more naturally optimistic you are, the more likely this is to happen. And although it is said in some traditional astrology circles that a bad Jupiter can be a judgmental Jupiter, this case is less about your judgment of Other and more about your being unsympathetic towards their plight. After all, your sense of action in the big world is boosted either way. On the upside, the other may genuinely rely on your optimism to keep their spirits lifted.

Your Saturn in their house

♄⊕ **You question Other's abilities or motives in the area of life indicated by their house, often feeling that they have hidden their true views unnecessarily or are simply holding back something whose withholding makes you uncomfortable.** Suspicion is the main idea here, where your trust in them is more likely to make you feel foolish one way or another. What they hold back is likely to be expressed to their other clique members provided they are close enough, but often it is simply a personal preference they don't wish to share.

In cases where you are not suspicious of the person you are more likely to structure, limit, or (in good cases) stabilize their expression of the house.

By now you might be thinking, "Man I wish some of these descriptions were more specific." But houses change their appearance depending on, among other things, the sign which the other person has on that house, planets in that house, the angles those planets make with other planets, and (most importantly) *how* and *how much* the other person is willing to cooperate with you. Although it would be nice if we could say with certainty that Saturn in another's 1st "limits their personality expression," this would only be true in a minority of cases. Maybe your Saturn "structures their drive." Maybe it "restricts their sexuality." Maybe it "stabilizes their unpredictability." And that's just the 1st house. So we're stuck with generalities. In most cases, if these descriptions were any more specific they'd be 1) inaccurate and 2) out of line with what the statistics actually revealed. As a reminder, EVERY one of the over 1200 interpretations in this book is based on statistics from the dataset I talked about in Chapter 16. Just keep using *table 18-1* to narrow down the scenarios that apply to you...and ask *yourself* which side of the house you'd rather play out with the other person.

Your Uranus in their house

The other person is more likely to be treated as an equal in this area of life, perhaps causing disappointment if you don't get along. You have noticeable expectations for them in this house, and may not truly connect with them if they don't live up to those expectations. That is, you may write them off if they fail. But this tends to be a very passive placement since it's less about what you do and more about what you observe in the other. Why would Uranus in another's house bring out expectations for the other? Because Uranus, as the planet of your social associations, tends to impose standards on the other from outside of the relationship.

Interestingly, Uranus is one of the first planets we've encountered which "knows" your situation better than you do. Say for example that you admire Other's forward drive—treating them as your equal with your Uranus in their 1st house. But Uranus "knows" that drive is just one form of 1st house instinct, and that your actual lesson from Other may be better learned through their impulsive action. It is possible that your relationship with Other may be grown or broken based on different factors from the same house, so that—drawn to their drive as you are—your disappointment in light of their impulsive action may end the exchange. To give another example, maybe you have Uranus in the other's 2nd house and are fulfilled by their body-sensuality. But suppose that the other has bad values (also a 2nd house matter). You say who cares? Yet the relationship dies anyway through some different means because your rejection of their values was the same as a general rejection of their 2nd house—body, self-worth, values and all. Now even though we know it's possible to separate various issues from the same house, we don't actually do this in reality simply because the nuanced *cognitive* differences between, say, self-worth and body-feeling-in-response-to-perception take too much work to think about. If, in the end, I like your body-sensuality but don't like your values WHILE expecting you to live up to my friends' values, chances are "your" body sense is just my simulation of what *I* want it to be. When I stop being in a situation (a house) and start actually doing things (like wishful simulating, a planet), I get out of the realm of [how you actually affect me / houses] and into the realm of [how I affect myself / planets]. But I can affect myself all day without you. So you disappear. Said another way, one can't like only one side of the coin and still claim to like the whole coin. Part of it must be his own imagination. And unless the disliked side gets any better, his liking of the *actual* whole coin has a good chance of fading sooner or later. In this way, people who fail one corner of a Uranus house test have a strong chance of failing them all eventually, after which point we tend to stop considering them as worthy friends.

Your Neptune in their house

You are more easily confused by the other's display of this house, where they send all kinds of spacey messages regarding what they want from you. Although this need not be a negative position, it certainly isn't a clear one either. One weird side effect of your Neptune in another's house is that they tend to try harder to communicate with you here and may have a habit of coming to you to air their random thoughts about things. Thus, though spacey, they are kind of like your associate in the relevant house matters. In positive cases such as Neptune in their 7th, there can be an almost surreal feel to communicating with this person, where you could get wrapped up in their company all day.

In the data used to write this book, Neptune was part of a "blind sample" from which I drew conclusions without knowing what I was looking at. From this point on if you see the glasses it means the description that follows was one based on a look at groups of charts as they were without knowing which planets, angles, houses or aspects were involved beforehand. Here's what I wrote for [your Neptune visiting their house]:

You see the other as an idealized equal and counterpart—a good addition to your expression of your version of their house. Not so fast, though, there are definite barriers to this, as the other is often prevented from "joining your party" (so to speak) because of their obligations to closer friends than you. Where such joining is possible, their attention to outside information in this area still tends to intrude.

Your Pluto in their house

This house area of their personality fires you up $_{fbow}$, where you are moved to passionate action or intense want in light of what they do. You see them as strong or powerful, reflective of the social standard in their house area.

In cases where attraction to the other is feasible to you, you are strongly likely to be turned on by their physical characteristics with your Pluto in their 1st. With your Pluto in their 12th you see them as powerful in their general influence over others. All other houses behave normally.

Your Ascendant in their house

You support the creative, instinctual expression of this person's house.

Your Ascendant in their 9th is typically supportive of Other's quest to project in the world while your ASC in the 10th supports their attempts to structure their reputation. Your ASC in the 11th supports the expression of their circle of influence and information. As in all cases throughout this chapter this placement works for better or worse ($_{fbow}$). So if the other person is your enemy, your ASC visiting the 10th, 11th, and 12th helps them blow their opportunities, hurt their reputation, and suffer among their circle of influence respectively. All other placements follow the table as usual.

Your Midheaven in their house

You see the other as holding their most important public role in the realm of this house. That is, as influencers in the world you write, Other is most effective in areas concerning this house. 6th house possessors are noteworthy in that, although they can be exemplary in work, they are very often exemplary in the domestic life as housewives, househusbands, or servants as well.

Your Vertex in their house

Other's expression in this house attracts your attention, compelling you to invest your actions in them $_{fbow}$.

They draw your curiosity here, where you wonder how they are the way they are. This placement may not seem like a big deal to you, but it's a very big deal the other way around (with their Vertex in your house).

Your Node in their house

For those familiar with the North Node as a marker of "destiny" in the chart, this one may come as a bit of a surprise. **Your interaction with Other in this house of theirs is a source of confusion for you.** They send you mixed or amorphous signals about what they stand for in general (not just with respect to you). You are more likely to find their inconstancy nerve-wracking here in this house. As a result, you may choose to do things such that their interaction with you helps them express this house area better—gaining more clarity and precision therein. **Roughly, this is where you can teach the other lessons**. For better or worse. On purpose or not.

Your Selene in their house

As applied to you and your goals, you are skeptical of the appropriateness in how they express their house area.

And why not? Selene shows where you are super talented, so your visit to their house can be thought of as your bringing your talents to an area where Other needs it. Unfortunately, the way you express your Selene in order to correct Other's deficiencies may not always be pretty. You have a good chance of appearing more untamed as a 1st house visitor, more selfish as a 2nd house visitor, more opinionated as a 3rd house visitor, and generally less inhibited in all of the remaining house areas. In a fashion similar to that of Jupiter, you can make things look so easy in the other's eyes that the regular inhibitions that delay them in these same areas are lost to you. Accordingly, your Selene in their house has a good chance of introducing more disruption in their lives than it does improvement.

Your Lilith in their house

This one is simple: ☞ **You see the other as reckless or hasty in the affected house**.

How you handle that recklessness is something else.

Your Fortune in their house

The other person conducts their house-related business with you as the backdrop. This placement is interesting in that it says a lot about how the other person fits you into their world. What does "backdrop" mean here? It means that if you take the regular house areas from *table 18-1* and insert yourself as the topic, you'll see how the other frames you. Actually, let's go through all 12 of these.

Your Part of Fortune visiting the other's 1st shows where their instinctual personality is shaped against you; they depend on you more as a baseline for planning their own expressive path in the world, in a placement which favors them wanting to be your friend. Your Fortune visiting their 2nd means they measure their worth and self-esteem against you. Unfortunately for this position, you are more likely to feel like a door mat for their in-and-out undertakings, such that it becomes easier for you to abandon them. But usually you're not a door mat. It's more like you are their safe place to come back to, so when you reject them for using you, the 2nd house other tends to take it pretty hard. (I've seen this one happen several times and can tell you that the drop in the other's esteem is *very* noticeable. For visitors with this placement I truly encourage you to consider how much the other may actually need you before you simply kick them aside. There's a really good chance you'll hurt them.) Meanwhile, your Fortune visiting the other's 3rd helps them build a larger share of their personal opinions around what you would think of their choices.

You tend to think of 4th house possessors more like family, finding it easy to trust them in a platonic, un-fancy way. As you might guess though, this is another unfortunate position because, unless the feeling is mutual, you often lose this person through your failure to give them the brand of special treatment they actually want. 5th house holders like to show off how special they are to external parties, and in so doing like being acknowledged against you as a standard for their prolific talents. This placement favors people who either compete with you for others' kudos or measure their interactions with others against your example. 6th house holders conduct their daily work with your standards looming in the background—using your behavior to evaluate the efficacy of their own decisions. 7th house possessors like chatting with you about you and things you're into. But this can morph into criticism very easily.

Your Fortune in the other's 8th house shows people who measure their power against yours, in a placement which favors their being spurred to fiery action by you in non-romantic cases or a raw, animalistic attraction towards you in romantic cases. 9th house holders make their way in the world with you as their training wheels in some way or another. 10th house possessors opt for more structure in light of what they often perceive as your liberality, frequently protecting certain sides of themselves from you or withholding trust from you in general. In positive cases they can serve as a stabilizing force to keep you from getting too overconfident in things you actually lack skills in. 11th house possessors gauge their closeness to you against their closeness to your social groups or intellectual surroundings.

Should you adopt friends they can't relate to, the relationship tends to struggle in turn. 12th house possessors use you as a sounding board for their imaginative ideas.

Your synastric Part of Fortune in another's house provides one of the best general summaries of how the other person sees you. And yet it turns out that [A's Fortune-B's house] is one of the most drastically one-way placements we've encountered thus far. It looks pretty good when your "planet" of [you being in your element] interprets how the other feels about you. But what if you're the one being interpreted? See [their Fortune in your house] for a very different story.

Your Ceres in their house

You see the other as (perhaps endearingly) pushy in this house's affairs. They like to make sure that you see this area of life their way. 1st house possessors are doggedly defiant of any chains whatsoever, and tend to be fiery in resisting any seeming attempts on your part to dominate their personalities. This same resistance translates to the other houses in their respective areas, where the other's house shows where they strike back hard at your or anyone else's attempt to undermine their approach.

Your Chiron in their house

Perhaps to cover a lack of surefootedness in comparing themselves with your easy way in this house, the other seems to drive towards perfection or forcibly amplify their abilities here.

It's not quite insecurity, but in most cases you can tell that the other person is trying hard to look capable in this house. On rarer occasions they actually *are* capable, in which case they make good teachers or role models to you in this house's affairs. In the 12th house case they can also be an inspiration to you.

Your Vesta in their house

You see yourself has having a lack of access to this house area of theirs, where they use it on you and others, but are not open to your influence here. **This isn't quite stubbornness, but it's more like a "read only" trait that occurs in them.**

Your Pallas in their house

You see Other as rechanneling their house priorities into social pursuits, looking to project these onto their generic 1:1 interactants in the world. One person at a time, they use this house to achieve significance and make an impact on people in society. 12th house possessors have such significance by default in your eyes.

Your Juno in their house

Rendering them difficult at times, you bring out their fighting spirit in the realm of their house, where they may combat you using this house's behaviors.

This is a pretty counterintuitive effect for Juno, the asteroid of commitment, which may be better understood by reading its counterpart [their Juno in your house.]

Your Hera in their house

You see their display of their house as revealing them to be capable partners in the ongoing promotion of that house's affairs. **They make good sidekicks here**, broadening your horizons with their enjoyable company. When their company is not enjoyable, this same house becomes the means through which the other can put you off permanently with little acts.

Your Eros in their house

Their house area reveals them to have both 1) standards you can't meet and 2) standards that don't fit you. This is not quite incompatibility, but there is a definite contrary approach for you in light of what they seem to want from someone in your role.

Although it is true that Eros is the asteroid of lust, we all know that lust is not something we throw around indiscriminately. Instead, everyday circumstances reframe the tendency to lust as a tendency to satisfaction-driven action. Where your Eros contacts another person's house, your driven action unfolds in a realm of their writing—making you the hardworking performer and them the audience. You are constantly unsettled here, while all they need to do is drop another nugget into your bowl to send you spiraling all over again.

At the other (rarer) extreme, this placement shows where the other person strongly desires to use their house to put you squarely under their control. For better or worse, 12th house possessors are more likely to have secret opinions of you and your situation which differ radically from what their actions lead you to believe. Not that they're lying to you, just that you tend to have a harder time seeing the whole picture clearly.

Your Bacchus in their house

Bac **Although it's not like the other person never rests, they are inclined to burn the candle at both ends in your house**, often doing a whole lot when the two of you are active, but for certain houses doing almost nothing. Actually it's more like they adopt a kind of stable state which fits the opposite house better than it fits the house in question. They dedicate a lot of energy to this, and may be more self-serving in such acts. Among cliques, you draw attention to this half-excessive, half-pointless behavior.

More often than not, this placement is where the other person is annoying to you. In positive cases, though, the other person is just plain interesting here.

Their Planets in your houses

Their Sun in your house

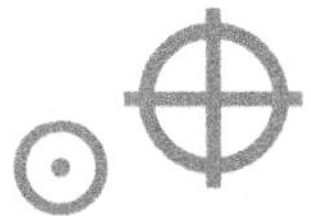

⊙ **With another's Sun in your house you have a natural fbow attachment to this house's area in their lives.** That is, with *their* Sun in your 1st you attach to *their* instinctive personality and drive. If everything is normal, you tend to like them here and have an easier time being attracted to their company. With their Sun in your 2nd you are more attracted to their way of carrying themselves, their wealth or status, and sometimes (but fairly rarely) their bodily company. You have an easier time communicating openly with Sun visitors to your 3rd house and expressing your inner inclinations towards Sun visitors to your 4th house. It's the other way around though with visitors to your 5th, who are more likely to respect (and sometimes compete with) your company. Although 6th visitors tend to be a match for you in terms of how they use their analytical and work skills, they also tend to be subordinate to you or to subordinate themselves to your opinion in some way. 7th visitors tend to be unsettlingly frank with you, overwhelmingly (in the data) exposing more of their lives to you than you need to know. You tend to find visitors to your 8th house alluring in some way, but distant. You are more likely to be curious about what makes them go, but find that they often resist your investigation—UNLESS, that is, the two of you are on fairly deep terms, then they will tell you everything they understand about themselves while expecting that you won't betray them in return. Visitors to your 9th are much more likely to share their philosophical outlook with you and often come across as temperamental or excitable to you. 10s have a set of behavioral rules they follow which is hard for you to get around, though they tend to be nice people and very loyal once you gradually get to know them. 11s are socially entrenched; depending on how you feel about this you may find it difficult to rest in their company, since they are constantly demanding that you get on board with the next trend they've discovered. 12s hold secret opinions about you fbow.

You can usually get an idea of what those opinions are based on their choice to hang around or avoid you. Being secret, however, their opinion is often noticeably different from what your normal interaction looks like. In most cases it's generally harder to bond with these people permanently regardless of how well you appear to get along.

Their Moon in your house

Another's Moon in your house indicates where you are inclined to have an emotional attachment to the other person. They are less restrained in this area of life. Although it's not that the other lacks a filter, it is the case that their values here tend to flow towards you more fluidly than their other expressive areas. The down side to this is that you are encouraged to be noticeably more "real" with them here than their actual sensitivities are ready for, making you callous at times towards these people. **The house placement facilitates the other having greater comfort exchanging with you in this area.** By comparison, other areas are slightly more uncomfortable. It's easier for you to use actions aimed at this house to upset them or deflate them emotionally.

All in all, this house is a more sensitive area for the other while in your company. Need the upper hand on someone who's getting to you? Insult them or ignore them under this house to make your stand. This works a little differently for people whose Moon visits your 3rd, 8th, 11th or 12th houses. You should actually listen to the 3rd house person...then not do what they wanted. 8th house enemies should be allowed to assert as much power as they want...into a vacuum. Be unmoved by their attempts to influence you and the tie will eventually break. 11ths can be confused with excessive information and mixed messages on your end. 12ths withdraw under the threat of having their secret opinions of you exposed, although most of the time, where the 12th person is simply forthcoming with such opinions, their secrets won't be secrets but an inexplicable creativity around you instead. 9th house people are often described by a distant non-connection one on one, though your rapport with them in a group setting tends to be pretty good.

Their Mercury in your house

Another's Mercury in your house shows where you struggle to find common ground with their area of life. If you read the counterpart to this one (your Mercury in their house), you'll see that this placement does not have mutual effects. That is, [your Mercury in their house] doesn't appear to do the same thing as [their Mercury in your house]. That's because we reason these two directions out differently. *Table 18-1* applies once again, with some noteworthy points of interest. Their Mercury in your 4th house impedes your connecting with them emotionally. Their Mercury in your 6th house hinders your ability to steer them in any set direction. In your 7th, you often steer them badly (though not necessarily wrongly; it's just an ugly matter). Visitors to your 9th house are often wayward with an inability to sit still for long. You have trouble finding common ground with the entrenched struggles of people whose Mercury visits your 10th house, though they would make good bosses to you if they had this role. You have a harder time sharing friends with visitors to your 11th. Visitors to your 12th often lack focus on what you want them to do.

So what's going on here? Why would intellectual Mercury behave like this? Most likely this is a case where another person weighs in on areas of your life which you've already taken care of. The more confident you are in each of your houses, the more the other's tendency to "make corrections" to (or plug into) that house is met with a sense of inconvenience on your part. Now you have to rearrange your entire body of experience just to accommodate the short-term analysis of someone who hasn't lived in your shoes. The exception to this occurs with people with whom you are predisposed to form lasting bonds. If you find yourself willingly accepting their input and easily finding common ground with them, you may also find them to be a keeper.

Their Venus in your house

Their Venus in your house provides us with another unexpected turn of planets. The exchange is intense under this one, **where they are exceptionally forceful in this area of life given your prompting**. They are, in fact, much more likely to boil with power in your eyes, provided you get to know them, of course. Eventually you learn they are no pushover here. They voluntarily display whichever area of life applies to your version of this house, and do so with thorough intensity.

As with Mercury we might ask where normally "social" Venus is getting all of this. After all, the 12 clusters of 430 people studied weren't very subtle about this synastric behavior. We might guess that Venus, the planet of willing socialization is actually a planet of pro-social *need*. When we willingly exchange with someone we are "on" (so to speak): ready to listen, ready to speak, ready to respond, filter, translate, and reinterpret everything we process into a final, smooth looking act. Thus when someone's Venus visits your house, they are most alert to the end goal there. The end goal is one of experiential fulfillment as a whole human. By socializing with others willingly, feedback for feedback, we lend greater reality to ourselves.

Their Mars in your house

There is a certain loyalty in expression which you have towards the other that **looks like a kind of protectiveness.** Where you are their "protector" in the negative case, you cage them in—protecting them in this house of yours by refusing to see even the positive changes they attempt to make for themselves. This **resembles possessiveness.** On their end, the other's need to influence you is most visible against this house. But if you already have the affairs of this house down, you'll typically resist their serious influence if it doesn't support traits you already have. This is very much an area of life where you are inclined to wrangle with the other for control. The 12th house person is often suspicious of you in one way or another, where occasionally this suspicion is strong enough for you to read, making you suspicious of *them*.

All houses with a visiting Mars are prone to imbalance. Quiet as this placement may appear on their end, the Mars house is often the center of a conflict where A wants B to do something that B won't do and B wants to keep A stubbornly forceful as they already are. Either you're too protective or they're too controlling. But if you really want a solution to this, the fix is pretty simple. You, the house possessor need to strike a balance between allowing yourself to be occasionally controlled and protecting the other when they need it. You might ignore the standard Western training which suggests that you "resist resist resist" all the time. Believe it or not, the antidote to a controlling Mars visitor really is a protective house possessor—as a person protected gives you back the control of their relationship frontiers which they take away from you inside of the relationship. With the right balance of your protectiveness and their control, this same house can fuel a fire in the Mars person which is fun to watch and hard to stop.

You might ponder on this placement's interesting implications for abusive relationships. For those not willing to give up any control at all, others' Marses in your houses promise great difficulty in traditional partnerships.

Their Jupiter in your house

You can be overwhelmed by the other in your attempts to express your house, as they seem to not have time for your little attempts to air your side of the dynamic regarding that house. 1st house visitors perform lots of tasks without cooperating with you as a teammate. 2nd house visitors declare their values without acknowledging that you have yours too. Jupiters in your 3rd tend not to hear your opinions. Jupiters in your 4th tend not to acknowledge your emotions. Jupiters in your 5th typically love to project their own egos in your presence but won't let you project yours. Jupiters in your 6th have you do their work but are less likely to help you do yours—often taking credit for what you've done. Jupiters in your 7th have a real conversation with you without managing to give your side any credence. 8th visitors throw steering attempts your way regardless of the solutions you offer. 9th house visitors dismiss your attempts to promote them. Jupiters in the 10th (in what may be the friendliest placement) are often inaccessible. Jupiters in your 11th often allow the judgment of their social world to block the relationship with you. And Jupiters in the 12th have a way of disrupting the track you're on. Clearly these are mostly negative. What about the positive sides of another's Jupiter in your houses? In general, the Jupiter person is very good at instructing you in how to come out of your box and execute your house properly. BUT YOU HAVE TO LET THEM LEAD in most cases.

Although astrology typically views Jupiter as **a positive planet** (a **benefic**) in charts, this planet in synastric houses is often bad news—responsible for all kinds of "we're better than them" behavior. Why else would a road rager do what he does to you? Part of it is because he wants to limit faceless you (you as an identity-less Saturn limiter). But then again he doesn't actually know you, only *situations* like the one your vehicle has put him in. Instead most of our attempts at revenge (against faceless actors) come from a need to assert ourselves against a larger world. Social scientists call this kind of **denigration of abstract groups for the uplift of our own** "**dehumanization**." When a stranger is generally offensive in your mind but not really towards you specifically, the revenge you seek is against the situation in general—not towards him specifically (since you could replace his car with any other and still have a related reaction—provided you have no bias against certain types of car). Unfortunately, the negative sides of others' Jupiters in our houses tend to dominate mainly because most of the people we meet aren't so personally invested in us as to warrant their taming of their natural "enthusiasm" against our specific situation.

Their Saturn in your house

You feel obligated to display your visited house in a way that lines up with the Saturn person's rules. Failing this, you are likely to disappoint them, compelling them to seek having their expectations met elsewhere. In good cases you and the other person can form a very stable partnership in which you trust the other person's version of the house implicitly. In order for that trust to attain, however, the other person has to prove reliable enough. This is one of those interesting placements that tends to evolve over time even in a chart that doesn't change (much like the II-quintile in *table 17-4*). Since Saturn adds structure to things, it is possible for the structured house to eventually reach its perfected form under a specific relationship. When that form is realized, it falls to the visitor / Saturn holder to declare your success as a house holder. But you'd be surprised how many people can't do this. We humans being what we are, it is easy for us to frame our interactants as though they are the same today as they were yesterday. In the case of the Saturn visitor, you may find that they fail to acknowledge your growth in the relevant house simply because they are still used to their role as limiters. When that happens one usually sees the end of the relationship in some way as the house possessor outgrows the visitor's fence.

Their planets in your house promoting the planet afterwards?

Maybe you've noticed something about the last few interpretations. The research seems to strongly suggest that a person's planet in your house aims towards the expression of the planet *afterwards*. Venus, for example, seems to bring Mars effects. Mercury brings the other person's Venus-style attempts to give you feedback about whatever it is you're doing, regardless of whether you sought that feedback. Jupiter looks a lot like Saturn. Why is this? My guess is that another person's planets in your house looks more like an *intention* imposed on you, where the goal of any planet's type of action would be the *next* planet. This "following planet" effect wasn't so obvious in the previous section where [your planets were in their houses], mainly because you see your own actions for what they actually are rather than for what their interpreted end *might be*. To make matters worse, when you see the other person's action towards you as having a related goal, you tend to perceive both the action and the goal at the same time, so these placements tend to produce two kinds of interpretations simultaneously; depending on the planet, sometimes you'll read a person's actual action and other times you'll read possible effects instead. You can only imagine what implications this has for how we pass judgment on others... In any event, this kind of shift in planetary effects will actually end up being THE defining characteristic of composite charts later on, introducing a whole new area of complexity into how we read certain astrological results: where goals (following planets) or motives (preceding planets) are involved, we can expect tangled effects which mix the astrological factor as it is PLUS the astrological factor as it *would have been*. Despite any of the tables you may have read earlier or many of the normal interpretations you may have seen online, certain areas of astrology like synastric house placements are simply surprising in their patterns. That's what the statistics show, at least.

Their Uranus in your house

♅ ⊕ Others' Uranus, Neptune, and Pluto in your houses play the interesting role of "generation definers" in your chart. As slow moving planets, these three say a lot about how you as a rising sign are affected by larger groups of people. **With another's Uranus in your house, your interaction with them in this house (or desire for such) is likely to become a public affair, with groups of others referencing this house of yours as one of the chief seats of exchange with them.** Actually, it's more like you are the one doing the broadcasting. In a way, you publicize the other as belonging here in this house area of life in your world—especially since they have a tendency to draw out your surprise here. Surprise isn't always good though.

All of the basic placements follow the usual table, where people in certain age groups tend to impress you in the different areas of life indicated. When you talk to others about the role they play in your life, you tend to emphasize their deeds under the heading of this house. So 1st house visitors have impressive drive, 2nd house visitors have impressive wealth or values, 3rd house visitors are impressive communicators, and so on. What's significant though are the houses that *don't* impress you, as there is some indication that you yourself are impressive in these houses. For example, suppose you don't have any associates with their Uranus in your 6th. You are more likely to be an impressive worker to others. No associate Uranuses visiting your 4th? Perhaps you have impressive intuition. This placement is thus useful for looking at where others consider you talented. One of the best ways to discover your gossip worthy talent based on a visiting Uranus is to ask yourself where you prefer to reference dead people (yes, dead people) as role models. Take some departed heroes of yours and look at their charts. See where their Uranus, Neptune, and Pluto fall for a good look at how you yourself would like to be seen (in the Uranus case, gossiped about) across time.

(The practice of looking at the charts of non-humans and the non-living tells you a lot about your own ideals as a person. We get to this in Chapter 23.)

Their Neptune in your house

♆ ⊕ You see the other as foggy or indecisive in how they project themselves in their version of your house—perhaps explaining this observation:

You serve as a partner to the other for affirming the other's ability to influence people. You do this in a way that marks the other's reputation in 1:1 interactions—effectively advertising them to your clique in this area.

Whereas their Uranus in your house says, "My friend here is so impressive at such and such," their Neptune in your house says, "Gimme that, Other. You're doing it wrong...Ahem, Hear ye! Hear ye!" In addition to following the table, Their Neptune in your 4th makes them foggy in what they want from you and impedes your connection with the other emotionally. Their Neptune in your 11th is more about their response to society than it is their individual social role.

Their Pluto in your house

👓**The other is drawn to share their relevant house area with you**, but can only go so far before your other preoccupations set in. There is a good chance that you treat them as second string here, not giving them the attention they need to move forward. **If you do pay attention to this side, you may overwhelm them, causing them to pull back anyway.** Frequent reminders of their value are helpful here.

As Pluto treks across the signs with subsequent generations of people younger than you, you tend to adopt the status of wise man in the affairs of your original house. You meet the social standard there, but people younger than you don't. Thus Pluto comes to represent your sharp instinct for the affairs of the house where it's located in your chart. Meanwhile others pressure you to correctly meet the societal standard in whatever house their Pluto visits yours in, where people older than you are often teachers of the standard (even if accidentally) and people younger than you often demand that you apply your original house to teach them in the house their Pluto visits.

Their Ascendant in your house

There is a utilitarian edge to this placement, as if **you are inclined to *use* the other person for their behavior in this house area**. Or perhaps it's better to say that this is the side of themselves that the other offers you which you are inclined to accept without necessarily repaying the favor or appreciating what they give. Their ASC in your 1st promotes your using them for their personality. In the 2nd, you use them for their worth—in a placement that facilitates low self-esteem, psychological damage, or a basic lack of confidence on their part. Your ASC in their 6th uses them for the work they do. The 8th uses them for the power they display in your company. The 9th fosters their public self-broadcast as (very often) negative, irritating, or arrogant. In positive cases Other may just be overconfident. The 10th uses Other for their show of authority.

Their Midheaven in your house

This house shows the chief means through which you consider the other person to take up your time. If engaging them in their projection of this house, you can typically expect to spend A LOT of energy doing so. When your 2nd house is the one being visited, you spend much of your time counseling or spreading your values to the other person. When your 10th house is visited you spend your time wrapped up in thoughts of their reputation—often because you are worried about it, disapprove of it, or compare yourself against it. With 9th house visitors, adventuring and exploring is the thing. Not surprisingly, 8th house visitors see more stamina on your part in matters of sex, deep discussion, and other procreative activities, but when this isn't happening you may simply spend a lot of time getting them to do what you want—compelling a devotion to you that they can't explain to themselves.

Their Vertex in your house

(Remember, paragraphs with the 👓 glasses in front show text more or less exactly as I wrote it in my notes before the visiting planet and houses were known).

👓**The other person's behavior as concerns your interest in this house ignites a magnetic draw to them—not as attraction, but as compulsion.** They display creative or sexual power which makes you productively uncomfortable—when they're not making you angry. Certain houses are better than others here. A lot better...

(Paragraphs without the glasses, such as the one below, were written after I knew what the astrological factor was.)

...But which ones are better will depend on your chart. It's pretty safe to say that in the spirit of the Vertex the other person affects you most profoundly through this house, serving as a source of major change in your life if you allow them to interface with you in that house's affairs.

Their Node in your house

The other's actions in this house area of yours take top priority and are circumscribed by an ideal. **They are goal directed here and seek success in their dealings with these affairs.**

This is one of those situations where it's very difficult to say in advance which side of your house we're looking at. In the data for example, visiting Nodes in a possessor's 7th appeared goal directed in various things ranging from interpersonal communication to expression through music, to the handling of assignments. Visitors to the 8th aimed for the successful wielding of power, display of sexiness, analysis of research, and study of others' psychology. The good news about such slippery subjects is that you and the other person can change easily from one mode to the other—provided your relationship is good enough. So it really is possible for a person bent on proving her allure to evolve into one skilled in others' psychology, while still displaying allure when she wants. The other's North Node in your house not only helps them teach you, but also helps them swap specialties within the same house so that they can teach you in other ways. There's a lot to be done here. A willingness to meet the other halfway is the key.

Their Selene in your house

You admire the other person, particularly as an interactant using their version of your house area to behave towards others in general. Maybe it's not admiration for some, but it is respect. This person provides a safe haven for your expression of this house. BUT...

There is a weird dose of bad news that comes with another's Selene in your house. If you've read the counterpart to this (your Selene in their chart) you know that the Selene visitor has a tendency to be Mr. Perfect in the possessor's house. Although another person's Selene is often a great gift to the possessor, it also serves as one of the highest frequency "context erasers" among all of the synastric planets in houses covered in this chapter. Essentially, this person's behavior under your house is where they can get on your nerves until you quietly decide not to pursue the interaction any further. It's not that the person necessarily does anything overtly or intentionally, it's just that—after summing up your entire interaction with them—you can be put off by how they affect you in this house. Or by the amount of work required to keep them in this house. Visitors to your 12th are especially mysterious in that one day, for no specific reason in particular, you may decide that you just plain dislike their vibe (often out of some sense that they dominate your choices too strongly). 11th visitors may annoy you with their social performance requirements, 10th visitors with their excessive authority over you and your affairs, 2nd house visitors with their excessive want of things from you, and so on.

It's not so much that Selene in the house breaks relationships. Instead, it imposes a kind of "lights out" expiration on the conditions under which your relationship is allowed to thrive. So now may be a good time to reintroduce the concept of **fr&s** from *FSA*: These ("frands") are people with whom you've connected apparently strongly once upon a time, who linked with you on Facebook or through business cards, who exchanged stay-in-touch pleasantries with you, then proceeded to fade into passing acquaintance status with your other 300 Facebook connects. **They're not really friends, just strangers** with a backstory that's 30 minutes longer than the average other nameless person in the world—**connected to you through a *situation* which encouraged such rapport, but not connected to you personally**. Across our lifetimes, most of our friendships erode into fr&ships, and the reason for this has almost nothing to do with you or them. The *situation* which brought you together simply grows old, causing the connection to expire. Another's Selene in your house is one of the prime determinants of such expiration so that, when one asks why you didn't keep up the exchange permanently, your astrological answer might be "Eh, my house which their Selene was visiting didn't warrant the work." The eventual expiration rate for exchanges in light of Selene's house is very high—making this one of the key factors in that popular question asked in chart compatibility readings: *Will we last?* Although it's certainly not necessary, people whose Selenes are in the same house as yours are noticeably harder to grow tired of. People whose Selenes are in houses other than your own Selene house last a lot longer when you are highly dedicated to doing things in that house which they're Selene is actually visiting.

Their Lilith in your house

⚸ You are kept on your toes, ever facing new frontiers in your house area. **Other consistently surprises you here** $_{fbow}$**, compelling you to evolve your approach to this area.** Your tolerance for their surprises noticeably biases your liking of and potential expanded partnership with them. In positive cases, you are encouraged to break barriers in how you express this house.

Most of the house effects under a visiting Lilith are pretty standard as shown in *table 18-1*. A visitor to your 2nd often affects money priorities, though. 3rd house visitors affect your individualism. 4th house visitors affect your feelings about preexisting topics. 7th house visitors affect your cross-class communication—where your relationship with the other is likely to change from one profound end of power-holder to the other, maybe back again. The visiting 7th Lilith is actually one of those rare cases where the student becomes the master; the subordinate becomes the superior. Needless to say this can be very cool for a teacher and very uncomfortable for a prideful person as house holder. 11th house visitors often affect the reach of your social network. 12th house visitors more often affect creativity preferentially above other facets of the 12th house.

Geery on how we get houses

Hm. I'm looking at these tables, and since I don't know these people I guess I'll just have to take your word for it that the patterns are there. But why should these so-called houses mean anything? The seasons I get. I may even believe that a monthly or daily cycle can give different effects on a person. But areas of life? Those don't follow a set time frame. Why should I believe the time of day a person was born affects whole areas of life which have nothing to do with time? Hayden asked sternly.

Honestly I don't know with certainty. Nobody does. So you know I can offer you a guess, right? Geery answered cautiously, preparing Hayden for the unproven ideas to follow.

Fine. Go ahead.

I think the daylight cycle is a natural one not only for all living things on Earth but also for all objects that can absorb energy on any rock that spins in space—next to a heat source, that is. Does that part make sense?

The thing is hotter in the day when its home planet looks at the heat source and cooler in the night when its home planet looks away from the heat source, no matter what it is? Okay that's reasonable.

Okay, but living things like plants and animals develop their own internal systems for responding to these cycles, so that even when they think of an event which has no day or night—like the appearance of a falling star or the fighting of a war, they add their own "area of life" interpretation to what they saw, giving that event a day or night quality based on their own framing of the event. Got that part?

No. I don't get that.

Well, I'm just saying that events which weren't "born" at a time or place and aren't living can have "houses" if living things with "houses" are there to interpret them. So even certain formless things can get houses in this way. As long as they're possible in nature.

And what does that have to do with my question? How do you get "areas of life" by reading a time of day?

A living thing's daily cycle is related to highs and lows in its biochemistry—like the expression of the BMAL1 and CLOCK genes in mammals. These cyclical chemicals don't just sit there in a vacuum, but are tied to certain other proteins in the body which affect related behaviors wired to happen when those chemicals are at a high level. The CLOCK gene in humans, for example, has been tied to how agreeable people are—which may partly explain not only crankiness in non-morning people, but also bipolarism in people whose manic and depressive modes fight for the stage, and "hangriness" in people who get angry when hungry at the same time.

I didn't know that.

But it does make sense that our bodies are made up of proteins and that our readiness to do certain things depends on our energy levels under certain metabolic conditions, right? None of it's magic, right?

Hmm…

So how does the day cycle affect areas of life? Probably the same way the day cycle affects the stress levels of millions of people at 8am and 5pm on business days (by analogy of course): The hormonal day cycle is written into a living thing against its mother's day cycle upon birth, then social training gets the thing ready to do certain stuff at certain times of day given how hungry-mating, social-ready, and environment receptive it is: These are the self-other-world clusters of activities. Where a living thing can be trained to interpret other living *or* non-living things against its own daily hormonal readiness cycle, all natural events can be given houses—areas of life associated with those cycles—which mean something.

Hmmmm…I don't believe it.

Believe the genome studies then and get back to me in a decade then when you've read them. Until then, let's assume that your birth time and its daily cycle set out a little mini-map of all the kinds of things you're biologically ready to do in a single day, and that all the "houses" do is associate the biological patterns with cognitive ones. Thus the houses expand upon a perceiver's classification of an event's readiness to appear a certain way. Accordingly they get their meaning.

Ooh! Touché.

Not bad, sir. Not bad.

Their Fortune in your house

Other's Fortune in your house shows that aspect of the other person which you respect, though not necessarily in a positive way. It's more like you recognize their version of your visited house as an undeniable quality they happen to have. Perhaps weirdly, almost all of the characteristics in this book's data set were negative traits in the other—where you as the house holder tended to see them as more ruthless, more willing to use people, or more detached from your interests, and sterner in their quest to get their own version of this house going. Why? Because it's their Fortune. This is where they're in their element. Although we love to celebrate one's enjoyment of the journey instead of just the destination, imagine for a moment what it feels like to be a rest stop on someone else's journey. Bummer isn't it? Now imagine what it's like to be them. When you're in your element, you love it. When others see you in your element with them AND THEN see you in your element with everyone else, it becomes oh so obvious that you weren't so stuck on them after all. So this placement also shows how the possessor distrusts the house visitor—seeing the latter as impersonally driven to satisfy themselves or at least capable of dumping the former at any time. Only in the case of real friends does this pessimistic view of the other begin to lighten up. But even between friends there remains this idea that their version of this house of yours might one day lead them to seek greener pastures besides yours. Especially in potentially romantic cases, the other's Fortune in your 10th house shows that you think the other is too walled off behind the fortress of discipline, authority standards, or prior commitments to connect successfully with lil' ole you. You often think that 5th house visitors are too popular or that their image matters too much for them to bother with you. The good news is, this placement makes for an excellent point of clarification in a potential exchange when you believe the other person isn't giving you a chance. Can you see why?

Their Ceres in your house

For platonic and other normal exchanges, you see a strong creative expressive potential with the other in this house's area of life. You believe that together you and they can achieve great things here. **Read this for specific worldly aspirations for your partnership**. For people interested in each other's close company this is a very important placement. They fire you up here, giving rise to the **reputation maker** for the two of you as a team. If this is mutual, the chance you really *might* be able to make something great is higher.

As far as synastric planets in houses are concerned, [their Ceres in your house] is pretty amazing, providing what may have been the strongest performing group of all the "blind samples" that I encountered in this chapter. That is, even when you didn't know that this group described Ceres (as opposed to other planets) or that it described your house (as opposed to theirs), you could clearly see that the clusters reflected what role you actually felt the other best matched in your life. 1st house visitors showed a strong tendency for you to see the other person as "doable" (sexually), or at least strongly inspiring (platonically). 2nd house visitors made GREAT company as physical bodies and hang-out partners. 3rd visitors made great intellectual equals who were no slouch in going toe to toe with you in personal conversation. 4th visitors made for really good "almost-family."

Visitors to your 5th house made excellent ego friends, 6th visitors good work and daily life partners, 7th visitors made for potentially deeply connected and enjoyable conversation partners, and 8ths made good partners in analysis or scrutiny of others' ways. 9th house visitors were good co-explorers. You saw 10ths as good co-authorities alongside you—making for pretty good business or system-running partners. 11th visitors were great social company and travelmates across your social network while visitors to your 12th house were good co-creators and sharers of spirituality. A side effect of having another's Ceres in your 12th was that the two of you were excellent at attracting audiences' attention—putting on a really interesting show for those who watched your dynamic.

Their Chiron in your house

You are an observer of the consequences of their house behavior, particularly in work and daily doings. This is not so much judgment, though you are inclined to see them as traveling a road that you yourself wouldn't want to tread. You learn from their errors here. In positive cases, their somewhat contrary approach shows you how *not* to behave, **making this the house where they serve as a**

counterexample in your chart. In much rarer versions of the positive case, Other demonstrates immeasurable skill in this same area, showing you how you yourself couldn't (as opposed to wouldn't) behave even if you studied 1000 years. You often find the personalities of 5th house visitors adorable and just want to take care of them (no matter how irritable they can be).

Their Vesta in your house

No matter how perfect they may be in other areas, **Other is inclined to mess up or be subpar in their expression of this house in your eyes**. You don't necessarily judge them here, but you do find it easier to make them nervous or reluctant to present this side of themselves to you in a way that isn't forced, strained, or otherwise unpolished.

Why are errors more likely to occur under this placement? Perhaps it's because their visiting Vesta in your house is where *your* focus is highlighted, making them comparatively clumsy. Perhaps it's because their visiting Vesta highlights *their* focus up to the point that they can focus no more (the distraction point). Who knows? Visitors to your 10th are notably more inclined to lock you out of certain areas of their lives to avoid vulnerability. Visitors to your 12th have a strained vibe, given that you might affect how they do things.

Their Pallas in your house

You consider the works of this person related to your house area to have a socially compelling irresistibility. Though you yourself may take such work for granted, their skill in areas related to this house is something like a forgone conclusion.

It's almost as if you consider it their social duty to perform this house's tasks well.

Their Juno in your house

Other uses this house's way as the means of revealing the deepest parts of their personality to you; they may prefer that you connect with them through this medium if you are to gain access to their secret or intense side at all. Accordingly **this placement shows what area of life the other person shares when most deeply committed to you**. If you commit to them, it's most likely towards someone's development of this house's characteristics. But which one of you? In the counterpart to this one [your Juno in their house] we read that the house person tends to be more combative under this placement. Now we see why. Your house would appear more combative under a visiting Juno because the Juno person demands that you lay all of the same vulnerabilities on the table that they have just laid, regardless of your readiness. Just because they may be well versed in this house's skeletons, that doesn't mean you are. And even if you are, the chances are low that their scrutiny of your unique background is correct or appropriate. Here is where you often run into people who show you everything in a particular house, but then when you show them everything in the same house they keep digging because they believe that somewhere deep beneath lies a perspective that looks like theirs. How annoying is that? And so you fight them or resist full disclosure, mainly because in some way or another, they are often not ready to process what you really have to give here.

In positive cases though, you really can use your house to play out your commitment to them with everything you have.

Their Hera in your house

You and the Other make a socially pretty team in this house area of life in the eyes of strangers and outsiders, though ironically you tend to be rather disconnected in this respect. Looks definitely deceive here, as the pressure to keep up appearances may render this closer to the "fake" side of your interaction. The other person may express their version of this house in order to bind you to them. Once bound, many people become a source of repetitive drudgery. And even though this placement isn't always so disingenuous, it's no guarantee of substance on your end either.

Their Eros in your house

You relate to the other like family (usually siblings) in this house area. There is a nurturing (or at least cohabitant-style) pre-commitment assumed here, where you may curb the normal detachment reserved for non-family. The 10th house case is a little weird though. In order to properly relate like family, the two of you really need to work together to share authority over a third party. 11th visitors feel like family when sharing complex information or social connections with you.

Their Bacchus in your house

The other is (usually uncomfortably, often unknowingly) domineering in your house area, demanding a lot of your time and energy. You feel obligated to play the role written by them, play it well, and play it for a long time. Their standards can wear you out.

The self chart

Now that we've gone over all of the synastric planets in houses, it's time to look at one of synastry's biggest secrets: the synastric self chart. Just as you can use synastry to see how you relate to others, you can also use it to see how you relate to yourself. The **self chart** is **your regular birth chart interpreted using synastric interpretations**. In math this would be the equivalent of breaking a traveling wave into two standing waves. In psychology it would be the equivalent of breaking a single behavior into an action and its intended outcome. The self chart provides a fascinating look at who you are as someone who thinks about their own thinking and, given that you already have a good sense of how to read your normal birth chart, takes that normal reading and exposes its underlying mechanics.

- Suppose, for example, that your regular birth chart had Vertex in the 6th. Using *tables 16-2* and *16-3* you see that others can change your life drastically in the realm of daily doings and work. Using synastry you can now read two halves of this setup: [Your Vertex in their house] shows that your own expression in this house attracts *your* attention, compelling you to invest more effort in these actions. [Their Vertex in your house] shows that you are compulsively drawn to *yourself* given your actions in this house—making yourself productively uncomfortable or angry. Thus your self chart shows that Vertex in the 6th really denotes where you pay compelled attention to your own disruptive daily efforts, opening yourself to changes in direction as a result. Now that's interesting. It's almost as if the self chart "split" setup tells you how your birth chart "whole" setup comes to be. It also shows you how you have more than one option for approaching certain traits that you read in a chart (similar to the case of angle ranges discussed in the previous chapter). If your Vertex effort comes first and its discomfort second, you'll tend to take change here into your own hands. If the discomfort comes first and the effort second you'll tend to have disruptive changes in daily life made for you.

- To give another example, suppose you have Ceres in the 9th house. Using *tables 16-2* and *16-3* you can see that this is caretaking projected into the broad world. Sounds great, right? But the self-chart hints at something not so great beneath this. [Your Ceres in their house] shows that you consider yourself endearingly pushy in your image projection. [Their Ceres in your house] shows that you project your aspirations for <u>your relationship to yourself</u> onto the world. This is fine when you are minding your own business and feeling pretty good about where you are, but what about when you feel someone has wronged you? Perhaps you can see how this 9th house, image-promoting "reputation maker" can turn into a big pushy broadcaster of your own discontent into the wide world. And when the hurt is egregious enough, this broadcast can become a *very* loud reflection of the discord you feel within. In *FSA* we found out that Ceres in the 9th was in fact the "reputation destroyer:" one of the most vengeful astrological placements among all of the ones covered in the book. You are a simple caretaker on a normal Ceres day, but when Ceres is in the 9th and you've been hurt badly enough, your care can easily mutate into forced feelings upon others aimed at airing your anger towards the one who hurt you. This is beef prepared for all the broad world to taste. (Perhaps *that's* what Hitler's deal was.)

And so you can perform a synastry reading on yourself in order to uncover some fascinating secrets about how the individual factors in your birth chart actually work. This will be especially useful 1) for putting yourself in your partner's shoes and 2) for discovering the underlying causes behind many of the bad behaviors you yourself display. But we haven't really talked about behaviors yet, only situations. Behaviors lie within the purview of the planet-to-planet aspects which we'll get to in the next chapter.[7]

---

[7] As a matter of research method, I was pleasantly surprised to see that the split "blind sample" data in this section reliably lined up with expectations in their whole equivalents. For example, in the previous book the data showed that a person having Pluto in her own house experienced a social pressure to perform powerfully in that house. In these data (where no single birth charts were used—only synastries) Pluto demonstrated a drive to strong action on the [yours in their house side] and a compelling towards being overwhelmed in the [theirs to your house side]. And this was before I knew it was Pluto I was describing. Given that we rarely validate these kinds of things in the field of astrology, I was amazed time and again to see how well the synastric interpretations of unidentified planets-in-houses (and in the next chapter, planets-in-aspect) supported the single chart conclusions. It's very promising for the statistical testability of astrological patterns when you think about it. But then again, if I didn't think such patterns actually existed I probably wouldn't have stayed with the idea of "astrology as testable" in the first place. What this suggests for the reader is that some patterns really are out there, and not all of them can be written off as entertainment alone.

The following conversation is one of several that can be very complicated to the unprepared. For folks like me who are inclined to disbelieve a lot of what astrology is about, however, it has a theoretical value that aims to give a mathematical explanation of why the patterns we observe actually show up consistently in the stats—in spite of the often fantastic foundation upon which much of astrological descriptions are built.

To explain how certain numbers tend to consistently produce certain experiences, Geery uses a kind of **construct induction, where the supposed character of an object in a sequence is determined by the first thing that can be done with it which previous objects could not do**. You need 1 thing for existence. But you can't "compare" anything unless you have at least 2 things. You can't "form ideas" about what you compare unless you have 3 slots—you, the thing, and the idea about that thing. You can't "want" to go from one formed idea to a different unless you have 4—the previous three plus a different idea. And so goes the stacking of certain allowable behaviors. Geery does this using a kind of number theory. I give a slightly easier version of this argument in *FSA*.

Note that Geery's march through the number meanings and the rules that follow this should be read together. Otherwise his reasoning becomes even more difficult to keep up with.

On Saturn in the 4th (part 1); how planets and signs get their meaning 🛠

So what's this I've heard about Saturn showing problems with the father? Some astrologer correctly guessed that a friend of mine had a father who was absent or missing in childhood—saying something about Saturn in the 4th house. How would the astrologer know that? Hayden interrogated Geery.

In your own chart Saturn is known to limit affairs in the houses it contacts.

Yeah but that's a very specific conclusion for someone to make. I take it that the "absent father" thing has a pretty high chance of being accurate; otherwise the astrologer would have been vaguer about it, hoping not to give a bad reading.

Hmph, your skepticism hurts me right here, Geery frowned facetiously, gesturing to his heart. But you're probably right. Looking at two sides of Saturn-to-house in synastry tells us something, though. When your Saturn is in their house you tend to be uncomfortable, feeling that the other person is holding something back.

How do you know that?

Statistics.

And why would the statistics show that?

I don't know. Maybe because Saturn is the 10th most important orbit and 10s somehow come with finished structure.

Why would that be the case?

Because 10 compares two 5s against each other?

So the number 10 means something because 5 and 2 mean something? Why?

5 points show initiative built on 4s' inclination. This is based geometry I won't get into. But you need 4 dimensions in order to animate anything. So a 5th thing is actually the first thing that can be affected by a "4-thing spacetime object," and a spacetime object is built on the animation of a 4th thing—a point—against a 3D plane which maps distances in space (for short lengths) and time (for long lengths). 3D

stems from the crossing of lines defined by two other points, and 2 is the lowest number you can have for comparing points. So if you think of certain numbers as enabling certain relationships among certain smaller numbers like this, then you can build up a set of (admittedly anthropomorphic) meanings:

- 1 is a **point** in *existence*,
- 2 is a line of comparison **between points**, setting up *values* or *identity* (one with another).
- 3 is a **plane of communication** formed by **at least two lines of comparison**.
  - You and the thing + you and the idea attached to the thing = plain old thinking or *internal monologue*.
  - You and the thing + the thing and the idea you attach to it = *normal communication*.
  - You and the idea attached to a thing + the thing and the idea attached to it = *pre-conscious action, dexterity, or thing-usage*.
- 4 is an ***imagined*** or *wanted* **communicated state floating outside of an existing plane of communication**. 4 can also compare two comparisons, 2 x 2, producing *conflict* between values.
- 5 (4+1) is the first *ego* object which can actually "want" or "imagine" something or not—**switching between imaginings**,
- 6 is the first ***purposeful form*** against which an ego can act, **going from one ego state to another**.
  - As the next number after 5 (that is, 5+1), 6 is the first number capable of measuring and *serving* the "*health*" of an ego form by comparing one ego state's (5) existence or nonexistence (+1).
  - 6 can also compare two "communications," 2 x 3, producing *analysis*.
  - And 6 can set up a plane of communication among values, 3 x 2, producing *"meaning"*
- 7 is the first **message** against which a purpose can act, **creating a new existence outside of an already expressed purpose** (6+1).
- 8 is the first intention for others to be sought outside of an existing message—things we seek the existence of, given a message partner, **which our messages couldn't capture** (7+1). This is the push to get your messaging partner to do something beyond the message.
  - Also, 8 can be 2 x 4, a *comparison or conflict* between two wants.
  - It could be 4 x 2: imagination- and desire-prone values like *sex, death, the metaphysical*, and other fuzzies.
  - It could also be $2^{[3]}$: comparisons[across a plane of thought]. This is [2 x 2 x 2]: a comparison of the identity of values (also known as *reasoning*)
- 9 is the first **learner-explorer**: where we can now compare **the existence or non-existence (1+) of an intention (8)**: This is exploration. 3 x 3 is the communication of communications (culture). 3^2 is communication across a space for identity (projected image).
- And so on. For this whole process I believe there are some basic rules:
  - **Adding one** allows you to compare two copies of the previous thing. This is related to the "power set" in math. For example, the number 4 lets you compare *two* 3s: one of the 3s

plus a fourth "on-off switch" for that particular trio. Here, {a red hat and blue shirt and green pants, YES} is compared to {a red hat and blue shirt and green pants, NO}

- **Multiplying** builds one number-thing out of other number things. So 12 = 3 x 4 gives us the communication of imaginings: a mood. It also gives 2 x 6: the comparison of "healths" (possible sickness). It gives 6 x 2: purposeful forms made up of identities (value standards). It gives 3 x 2 x 2, communication of conflict (indecision); 3 x 4 (which is communication among wants—suspicion, shared expectations, and subtle feelings). It gives 2 x 2 x 3, conflicting communication (secrets). So the whole thing averages out to a situation dependent "vibe." That's 12s.
- **Exponents** like 3^2 represent processes, where the power shows the number of steps (/dimensions) involved. I think this is why higher versions of Scorpio (8 = 2^3) are associated with science and reason. The third power (^{3}) is inherently thought based. The same goes for the 27th harmonic (3^3). 8 makes identities $^{\text{into a space of communication}}$. 27 makes thoughts $^{\text{into a space of communication}}$.
- [8] **Modding by 12** is where you divide a number by 12 and take its remainder. 7 mod 12 = 7. But 25 mod 12 = 1. Further along, 47 mod 12 = 11. Since all of our counts in this whole astrology system we've been using are designed to wrap around with every new block of 12, all numbers in this system can be thought of as having at least a little similarity to whichever slot among the original 12 they would land in. So if you had to wrap around your angle, planet, sign or whatever, say, 25 times, you would land in slot #1. This gives the number 25 a kind of Aries/existence/conjunct/1st house character. If you had to wrap around 47 times, you would get an undecile (11) character. To be honest, this is the only rule which has nothing to do with building up numbers in a generic sequence. Instead, this rule assumes sequences of 12 specifically. The only reasons I think it works are because 1) the stats verify it and 2) when counts get higher than our little 3 x 4 frameworks can handle, I think we just store how many 3x4s have gone by in a separate tally and start over again. Like octaves on a piano. Faced with counting every note from the lowest possible one actually audible, you just stop caring after a while. So you just count however many notes you've moved within a particular block (an octave in music).
    - So 14s become (12 x 1) + 2: a finished (existing) 12-cycle plus a comparison. Since that 12 lives in the *background*, you have *11* more slots before you have to start thinking entirely differently. Count-wise, then, 14s are (12 x 1) + 2, so we actually get [12 side tally slots – 1 taken slot] = 11 as the background for this 2-type comparison. This is self-value against social talkers (11) as background. The result is something like physical identity. All $^{1}/_{14}$ths of a circle would be related to physical identity, since it is physical identity which distinguishes cycles that take 14 repeats from cycles requiring a different number of repeats.
    - 26s give us (12 x 2) + 2, so we have [12 side slots – 2 used slots] as the background for another 2-type comparison. This is self-value against ego structurers (10) as background. Hence we get fans and followers. All $^{1}/_{26}$ths of a circle would be related to fans and followers, since the number 26 compares two public personas, 2 x 13; builds personas from identities, 13 x 2; and registers the existence or nonexistence of a mass following, 1 + 25.

[8] This particular explanation is about as complicated as it gets for this book. Unfortunately, given the relatively new nature of this work at the time of writing, there wasn't really a better place to put it. In a couple of areas in later chapters I discuss higher harmonic levels, at which point this section of "Modding by 12" will make more sense. For now, just take it as part of Geery's long-winded explanation.

- Trines give us (12 x 0) + 3: communication (3) against a vibe (12 – 0 = 12) as background. All $^1/_3$s of a circle would be related to our (arguably automatic and thus easy) *internal* communication. You don't introduce partnered communication until you get to 7s.
- According to this approach, 47 would be (12 x 3) + 11. [12 side slots – 3 used slots] = 9 as the background with 11 as the foreground. We would then have social information (11) against cultures or learnings (9) as background. Call this philosophical outlook. All $^1/_{47}$ths of a circle would be related to culturally-labelable, publicizable information.

- **The nearest split,** though it's something I didn't do here, is where an odd number is made up of the two nearest almost-half values. The "conversation" in 7s, for example can be thought of as a back and forth exchange between what you think internally (3) and how you imagine or want the other to respond to you (4). I believe that since 3.5 x 2 (3.5 + 3.5) doesn't make for a very good counter, 3 + 4 is the next best thing. Cycles of 7 would then be cycles of [3 + 4] + [3 + 4] + [3 + 4] +... Furthermore, nearest splits provide a good explanation for how we handle the rounding of cycles that aren't exact, as well as how we define cycles like 11: 11's social information reflects a back and forth between egos (5) and meaning (6). II-conjuncts (13) would be a back and forth between sent messages (7) and purposeful form (6), putting a formed structure onto how we communicate. Roughly, this is the socialized persona. III-conjuncts (25) would be a back and forth oscillation between a vibe (12) and a persona (13). The "vibe" of a persona dumped onto an environment established your psychological effect on that environment. This is mass following, psychology, and group mobilization. I wrote about this kind of thing in my notes from Katha. When you—

Alright I get it. Well, except for that last part. So 10 would be something like 9+1, the existence or nonexistence of a culture. Or it could be 5 x 2, egos made up of values. Kind of like a personality made up of identities?

Right, if 5 x1 is an ego for action (or a personality), then 5 x 2 is an ego for values (an identifiable image). Meanwhile, 2 x 5 would be the comparison of egos against each other. These are behavioral standards (also known as rules). It is from 2 x 5 that most of Saturn's limits are derived, I think, since that combination in particular amounts to mashing your ego into the mould designed for some other idealized actor. 5 x 2 gets you watched as these standards are enforced, inviting the public into your image. This gives us a "reputation."

As for 11s, I'm sure you can figure them out given everything I've just told you.

I'm sure.

On Saturn in the 4th (part 2); why we introduce triangulated points

So Saturn's limiting effect, you say, is tied to its number? In space? Okay. And yet Saturn's number isn't 10.

Oh? What number is it, then?

Uh...(My very educated mother just served,) Hayden mumbled. 6? The sixth planet?

Are you counting the one we're standing on? Are you sure you should count that one? Our gravitational potential in the big scheme doesn't really change much on our own planet, ya know. Since we're stuck here. 9.8 meters per second squared. Give or take with altitude.

Okay, Okay. Then Saturn is the fifth planet.

But you don't count the Moon? Even though its orbit surely affects us more readily than other stuff like Mars, for example.

Hayden sighed. What would *you* count then?

The orbits of the day—like the day and night cycle. That influences us even more immediately than the Moon's cycles, right? Namely, it influences your attitude regarding what kinds of activities are appropriate. Like getting smashed at the bar, running errands, braving traffic, and watching TV.

Yeah, okay. I can see that.

Your looks, lineage and culture—events that your "kind" of person experiences in the world, perhaps? Maybe you wouldn't call it a cycle in the traditional circular sense, but it surely affects you, right? Don't lie. People definitely, *definitely* make decisions about how to treat you based on looks and mannerisms. A really homely and a really beautiful person, a black person and a white person, an Arabic speaker and an English speaker don't get the same set of subconscious assumptions, do they? Despite all your efforts to forget what you've been taught about certain groups of people, you *have* been taught it. And your brain remembers. Every single time you meet a new one of those people. Because it introduces a dynamic with other characteristics in your mind, this physical stereotype could hypothetically be assigned a fixed relationship to other behaviors on the astrowheel, right?

Mmmm... I'd like to say no.

Then you'd be lying to yourself regarding all that society has trained you to think, convincing yourself that your choices made in stereotype are actually choices rooted in rationality. Good luck working out prejudices you won't admit you have.

Hmph!

And then there are your own genetics, hormones, and such. These are more immediate than anything.

Yeah, well...

Still stuck on the stereotype thing, eh? You apply them to whole groups as an evolved way of making meaning in a complex world, only to suspend those stereotypes for single individuals one by one as you meet them personally. And because you have two black friends, you think that you're not prejudiced towards blacks, but will gladly spit out a list of stereotypes in casual conversation. Or maybe you just hold them inside and save them for how you vote. Or how you joke. Or what sides of town you feel "comfortable" on. Or which strangers you criticize and how harshly. Despite your two friends. Have I described you incorrectly?

You don't know me. I don't like where this conversation is going.

Well, for the *average* person who's NOT you, it's just sociology. You shouldn't feel bad for something all humans are evolved to do. You know, sometimes chimps actually *eat* chimps who aren't their kind. At least you don't do that. But you still use the same perceptual tools for recognizing who is and isn't a part of your ingroup, adjusting how you speak, how tense you are, how safe you feel, what places you frequent, what language you use, your assumptions for dress, your assumptions for social policy, the entertainment you tolerate, your perception of the exotic, and your choice of response to fear and threat accordingly. So you're telling me that *none* of that changes when you're around "those other people." Really. You don't see color *or* language? REALLLLY.

Hayden turned away from Geery, looking at the ground.

All I'm saying is that your anchors for prejudice are real, evolutionarily rooted, and automatic, so yes they also belong in a chart. But no known planet will ever be able to encapsulate something so locally dynamic. Therefore, where those points lie is up to you. We need enough extra "planets" to capture all of this—attitude, socialized identity, and biology—especially since you can have babies of two different social classes born in exactly the same place at the same time. Their official charts will be the same, but surely their lives won't be. There must be other indicators for these life areas.

After pausing for quite a while, Hayden sobered up. But you don't have planets for any of those things you listed.

That's why we make them up. I call these the Points of Internal Monologue (for Attitude), Worth (for social identity), and Action (for hormones / biology), and consider these to be three influences whose immediacy precedes that of the Moon, which precedes that of the Sun, which precedes that of Mercury, and so on. If you consider these actual, SOCIALLY AND SCIENTIFICALLY REAL PATTERNS as influencers, the Moon becomes the fourth most immediate influencer of our spacetime experience, the Sun becomes the fifth, and Saturn, ultimately, the 10th. These are ordered by immediacy of change with respect to us on Earth, not by power (which is why the Sun isn't first).

Sorry, you lost me.

It's math, man. Just trust the statistics, will ya? Geery protested in half-sigh. If we don't do this then astrology ceases to line up with actual, measurable science. With no consideration for genes or ethnicity whatsoever. That's a possibility I find abhorrent.

Alright, whatever.

Okay, so consider that Saturn in the 4th imposes a limiting ego—or 10th—template on your home or emotional life. I guess a good question would be *why is it so hard to get around this*? So hard that we can predict with pretty decent confidence that a person with this setup will have had issues with an early authority figure. Well, when you look at the synastry you see it. When your Saturn is in their house you tend to feel something is missing that makes you uncomfortable. When their Saturn is in *your* house you feel obligated to behave in a way that lines up with the other's rules. When YOU are that other, these two sides come together and you become suspicious of <u>yourself</u> in light of your own emotional world while being compelled to follow your own rules anyway. You become, in effect, your own authority figure in the home partly in line with your own suspicions against some source of experience who was supposed to provide that for you—usually your dad by stereotype. This same kind of issue also holds for Saturn in the 7th. Basically any relationship that involves emotional reliance on another gets hurt by this kind of "I'm suspicious so I'll do it myself" setup. People with Saturn in the 7th at first have a hard time keeping stable partners only to find that they want much older, much younger, or controllable ones later. Basically.

Interesting.

Geery stayed silent for a while, seeing that Hayden's face had quickly become a frown.

And Hayden continued, But isn't that a chicken and egg question? In order for the likelihood of the "absent father" or "no partner" thing to work don't you need for some people to *choose* to be born at times of day which set this stuff up before it happens? How does it make sense that a two year old with Saturn in the 7th house for example can have his love life predicted? Can't the parents stop this? Can't a toddler with no sense of "absent dad" be raised in a way that offsets this? It all sounds like fate. Why don't people alter this kind of situation as soon as they learn about it?

Honestly, I believe it has something to do with the "holographic universe" in physics.

Ugh, not again.

Wait a minute, this is quick! Geery explained. The big wave that describes your atoms in life doesn't just stop at your body, but moves beyond you. On the graph of time, I think people's lives begin quite a ways before they're born and quite a while after they die. And outside of their lives, the scattered pieces of their wave still moves on. So their physical lives are only the middle part. The middle part isn't fate so much as it is a piece of a bigger pattern already in progress…

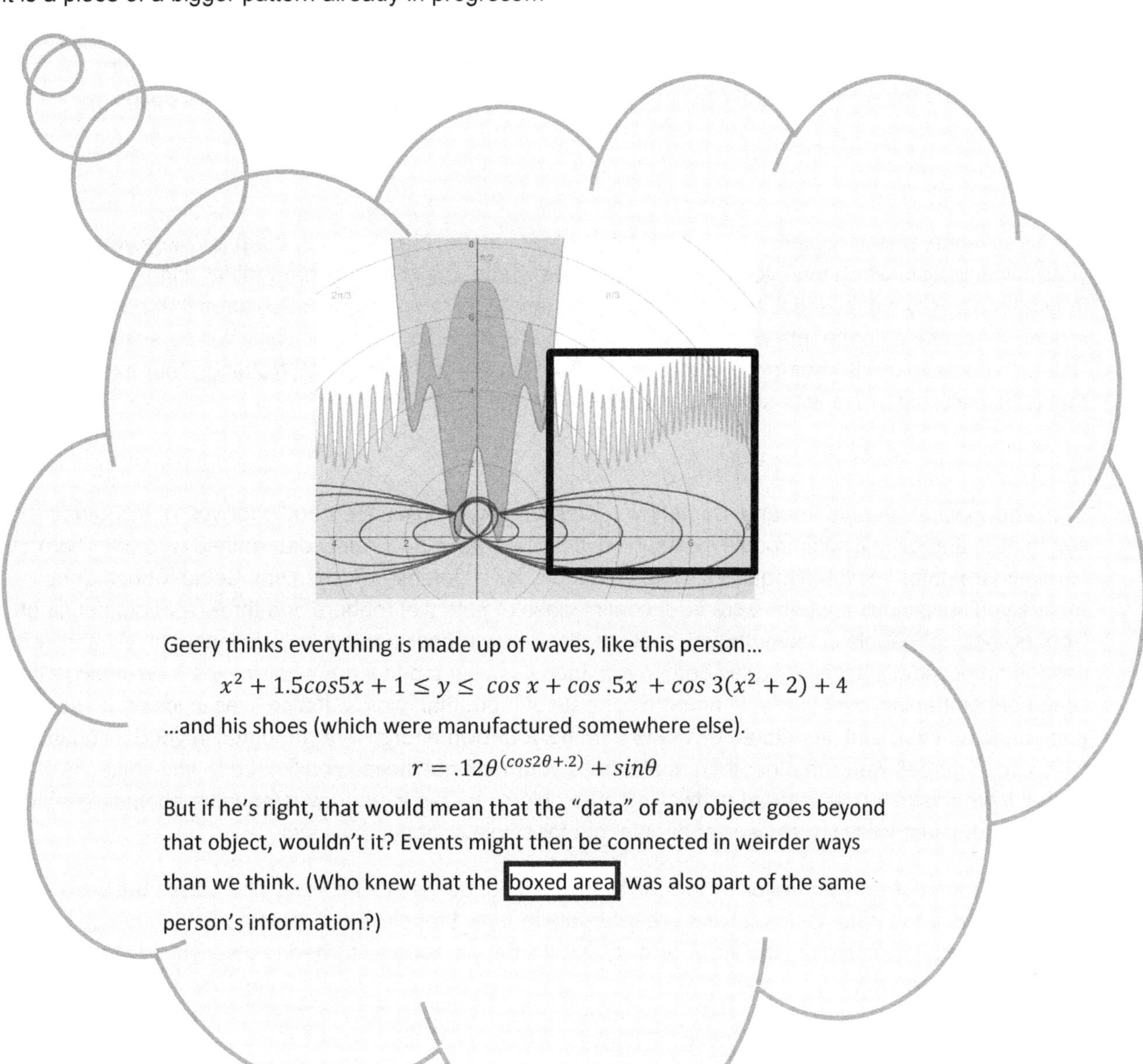

Geery thinks everything is made up of waves, like this person…
$x^2 + 1.5cos5x + 1 \leq y \leq \ cos\ x + cos\ .5x\ + cos\ 3(x^2 + 2) + 4$
…and his shoes (which were manufactured somewhere else).
$r = .12\theta^{(cos2\theta+.2)} + sin\theta$
But if he's right, that would mean that the "data" of any object goes beyond that object, wouldn't it? Events might then be connected in weirder ways than we think. (Who knew that the boxed area was also part of the same person's information?)

Hmph. That sounds crazy.

I know, but you ask questions which are too hard to answer without this stuff. I tried.

Hayden simply shook his head in resignation.

Geery took a few seconds to fiddle with some things in his bag.

By the way, as for the stereotype thing, it has a pretty simple astrological fix: Take your reaction to a group, find the angle that you're using to pigeonhole their kind, and pick a version of that angle which costs you less stress, less energy. I have a table for this in Chapters 17 and 19 of my notes. In extreme cases where all you feel is negativity towards those groups, you might avoid them entirely. Not just physically, but *mentally*. It's not as "spiritually evolved" I suppose, but in some cases may be a better option for you. Especially if learning their language—that of the other team, other culture, other department, or other political party—is not feasible for you, avoidance may be your only option.

Hm. And what if I told you those other guys are pretty savage? I don't want to learn their language. They need to learn mine.

If their savagery doesn't bother you then just leave them alone. Messing with them is where you create your own interests which bind you to them. As for the whole "they need to learn mine" thing, apparently they haven't, they won't, and they *don't* have to. Whether you're talking about cultures that have been around for centuries or people who have been around for decades—both of which will persist long after little ole you have made your grand appearance. So what are you gonna do? Nothing. Your expectation that outsiders conform to your standards only fills *you* with stress, not them.

What if they start trouble with me first?

Who knows what "trouble" means. Somehow I question what constitutes trouble for you or any other single ego, and even if such trouble exists, I wonder if you have accurately determined who "they" are. Humans are notorious for overgeneralizing, you know. It's a defense mechanism. Being robbed once makes you suspicious enough to create an entire class of potential robbers and throw a whole bunch of "robber-looking" people in there, though most of these new robber-types are *quite* innocent. Whatever the case, if an outsider's savagery does bother you, then it is your job to learn what makes them choose their brand of heathenism over yours. Language consists of more than words. It also lives in ideas. If you're just gonna sit there and be irritated by them, burning your own energy over thoughts in your own mind which you yourself won't change, then again that's your fault not theirs. You'll need to find solutions rooted in your own values instead of dwelling on problems rooted in your own thoughts about their values. This goes not just for entire classes of people, but for single opponents as well.

I suppose much of synastry revolves around these kinds of things. You. Other. The biases between you. If you think that the other is the only one responsible for how that plays out, then no astrology book will be able to tell you how to make your life your own. It will simply belong to someone else whose images have the power to steer you.

You know you really have a thing for lecturing people. I actually don't care for it.

We're over here systematically studying human relationships and you want a science which ignores the obvious? I can't give you that.

Chapter 19: Planets on the planets III: Synastry

We have a daunting task ahead of us. In this chapter we'll go through all 625 synastric combinations of the 25 planets covered in this book. We'll learn what the angle between your Sun and another's Moon means. We'll learn what the angle between your Moon and another person's Sun means. And what your Sun to their Sun means. Since we'll be covering a lot of ground, it's important that we have a pretty good handle on what all of the harmonics mean so that we can more effectively read the combinations that follow. For each pair, I'll only talk about the unusual angles and leave you to look up the rest in *table 19-1*. In other words, though we'll go over the meaning of every pair in your chart, we'll avoid discussing all 36 possible angle families for each pair. The main reason for only focusing on the unusual angles is simple: Most of the planet pairs are very predictable and can be read as follows:

> The more we express our [*table 19-1* interaction], the more [the pair description in question] is likely to happen between us.
>
> OR
>
> Our [planet pair description] is described by [*table 19-1* topic].

Read each interpretation in this way and you'll quickly get the idea.

Before we proceed, I should mention that we end up with a few changes to the behavior of the various angle families when we start comparing multiple charts. Most of this has to do with the idea that a so called "third party" takes on a different form depending on whether you're looking at [just yourself] or at [yourself plus someone else]. In many ways, the behavior of the harmonics becomes a lot clearer when there is a self (you), an other (them), and a world (third situation) all involved. Back in *FSA* when we were only looking at your own chart in isolation, all three of these tended to get mashed into your own mind such that it was harder to tell what these angle families did. Here that is not the case, so families like the II-octile (where others see you as overpowering the outside world) can reveal their natural effects in all their glory. Other angles like the II-opposition, II-septile, and III-septile show *very* different sides as a consequence of our inclusion of other people in the chart rather than staying in our own heads. Compare the role of the III-septile in *table 16-6* to its role in *table 19-1* to get a look at just how different these functions are.

And lastly, in order to even *see* all of the angles in this chapter, you'll need to obtain a table-view (a.k.a. aspect view or aspectarium) version of your chart. Not a chart wheel.

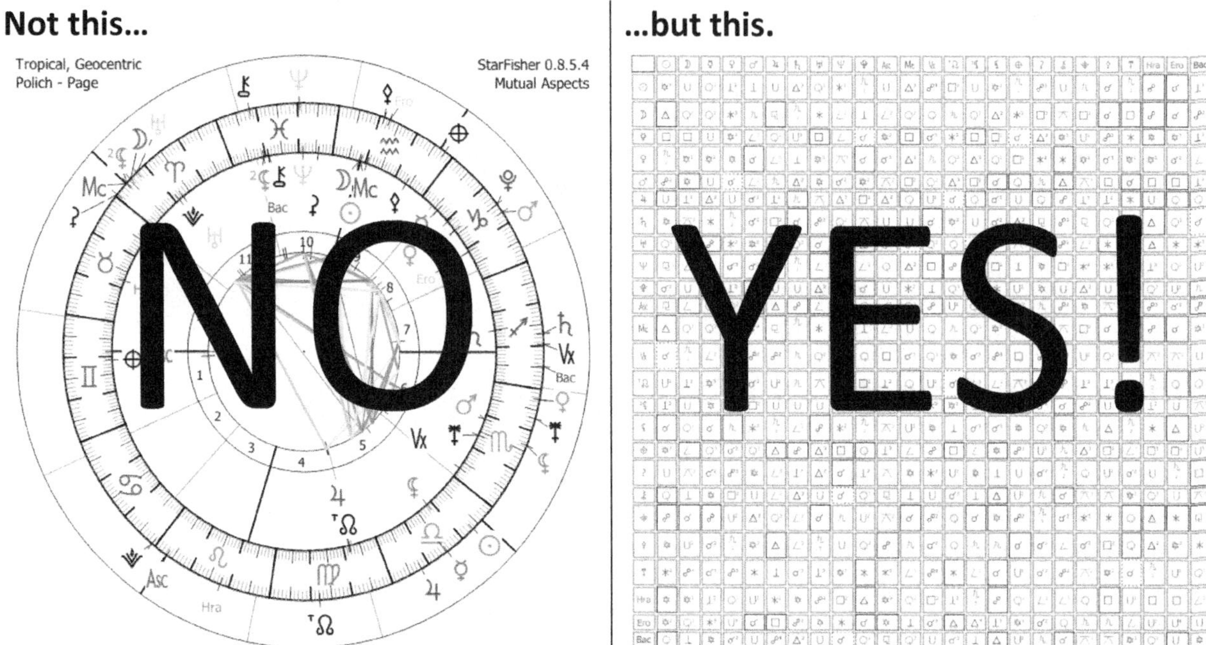

You'll find a link to the program that I used to create an angle view on my website at http://electricmonastery.com. It's called StarFisher and (at the time of this writing) can be found at http://www.starfisher.cz/starfisher/EN/. You should still visit http://electricmonastery.com for the files you need to display a full table's worth of angles.

Table 19-1: Synastric angle reference

Harmonic	Name	Symbol	(Angle) Topic	(Angle) Interaction		
				Lower tension version	Neutral version	Higher tension version
In synastry, level I angles describe things that happen in general with no background context						
1	conjunct	☌	**action**	being associated together	cooperating	acting upon an issue together (especially our own disagreement)
2	opposition	☍	**value**	attending to our own bodily feeling (receiving impressions upon it)	assessing ourselves against standards	pursuing similar values
3	trine	△	**communication of internal ideas**	behaving normally	giving our opinions in a situation	critically weighing in on the other
4	square	□	**wants**	using intuition to feel what the other is inclined to do or how they're feeling	wanting the other to do what we want / wanting contrary to what the other wants	responding with upset feeling to the other or to a third issue
5	quintile	⋆	**interaction**	playing around / being ourselves to each other	interacting 1:1 with each other	declaring our egos against / competing with each other
6	sextile	⚹	**work**	sensing a common connection / being inclined towards cordiality	working together / following protocol around each other	serving a third party set of standards
7	septile	✡	**conversation**	listening to / admiring traits in the other	conversing	playing 1:1 / interacting with a third party together (as in video gaming)
8	octile	∠	**influence**	reasoning / analyzing a third issue with each other	steering each other towards what we ourselves want	manipulating or showing aggression towards each other
9	novile	九	**image projection**	indulging an outlook towards the surrounding situation	learning from / responding to a shared situation, fbow	projecting our personalities onto the surrounding environment
10	decile	+	**authority**	viewing where a situation needs to be controlled	building a reputation	exercising authority / limiting or stifling a situation
11	undecile	∪	**surrounding information**	having similar ideas about what's worth talking about or the information around us	creating situations worth others' talking about	tackling social issues or social talk together with action
12	inconjunct	⚻	**vibe**	being in a certain mood in response to surroundings (this is sensitivity to the other's feelings)	responding to each other's vibe with our own / distrusting the other (sensitivity, often very negative)	projecting a mood onto a situation (can be very positive when reinforcing good impressions, but more often makes an already bad exchange prone to further disaster)

Harmonic	Name	Symbol	(Angle) Topic	(Angle) Interaction		
				Lower tension version	Neutral version	Higher tension version
In synastry, level II angles describe things that happen within your "room of influence." Roughly, these are groups of people around you who are capable of responding directly to your deeds.						
13	II-conjunct	☌^{2}	**persona** / room-influencing actions	considering our public persona (encourages the idea that both should be connected based on apparent behaviors)	playing a socialized role in accordance with the setting	advertising our own interests for other's approval
14	II-opposition	☍^{2}	**body presence** / looks / room-determined physical traits or values	holding an attitude towards a situation both are associated with as a physical presence	showing internal (body) response towards a common topic	exchanging turn-ons and areas of interests
15	II-trine	△^{2}	**room-given attention**	leaving impressions on a room through mannerisms	acknowledging the other's ability to get attention / responding to the other's call for attention	dominating an environment intellectually, expressively, or communicatively
16	II-square	□^{2}	**core values** / manners / the emotional standards you project onto a room	considering family, domestic, or personal emotional preferences (facilitates a sense of kindred connection)	discussing valued issues (often regarding friendships and emotional associations)	tending to / training / taking care of others; placing values upon others
17	II-quintile	⋆^{2}	**charisma** / management of room members' actions	managing the value in one's associations with others by serving the other's interests	planning how to handle others or manage things (mainly people) as resources	actively managing people's behavior; dominating
18	II-sextile	⚹^{2}	**work goals**	viewing the requirements of a common task	summarizing the state of issues in a shared environment	responding to people's outlook towards a situation
19	II-septile	✡^{2}	**important ideas** / standards of 1:1 exchange with people in your own class	adopting a behavioral standard which aligns with what the other's ultimate goals are	being required to play complementary roles in a particular social situation	actively maintaining the social requirements of a relationship (facilitates sexual attraction or the alignment of wills)
20	II-octile	∠^{2}	**allure** / standards of power wielded on people outside of your class	being magnetic, mysterious, or desired by others in an unspoken way	steering people outside of your ingroup / fishbowl	acting against a joint enemy (makes for the desire to avoid fighting, since fights with each other—over the joint enemy "relationship"—risk being epic)
21	II-novile	九^2	**creativity or created works** / image projection as seen by your room of influence	being alluring, unsettling in each other's company	displaying a certain kind of attitude in front of a group of people (favors an intense opinion of each other, fbow)	actively entertaining or appealing to the favor of a group of people (conducive to easily not getting along or, at opposite extreme, compelling the other's attraction to you)

Harmonic	Name	Symbol	(Angle) Topic	(Angle) Interaction		
				Lower tension version	Neutral version	Higher tension version
22	II-decile	$+^2$	**reputation** / structures you sponsor or authority you wield as seen by your room of influence	sharing a structured view of a situation	engaging in a dynamic which others are hesitant to interrupt	building a project or concept together
23	II-undecile	$\cup^2$	**unique traits** / topics over which your room of influence talks about you	observing the other at a distance / getting talked about among others as two actors together in an unusual context	adopting an eccentric approach to a subject	actively addressing (as a topic) the behaviors of other people—especially mutual associates
24	II-inconjunct	⚻^{2}	**inspiration** / inclinations you plant among your room of influence	leaving an impression on others through an attitude which shows each one's expectations	devoting focus to an idea	reinforcing expectations through each person's behavior
In synastry, level III angles describe things that happen among your "followers" (as in Twitter)—folks who subject themselves to your guidance. This doesn't have to include people in the room with you, but it can include people who read about you.						
25	III-conjunct	☌^{3}	**mass action** / actions backed by those who relate to you	using bigger goals or ideas in the world to fuel one's aspirations	behaving in ways that demonstrate each one's commitment to a particular course of action	performing actions for the satisfaction of bigger groups who have placed expectations upon a situation
26	III-opposition	☍^{3}	**fan standards** / values and standards held by those who relate to you	reviewing the popular performance expectations placed on themselves	conveying high, popularly acknowledged standards in response to a situation	catering to your fans / lining up with the trends (values) they expect
27	III-trine	Δ^3	**insight** / opinions you hold which those who relate to you are automatically inclined to agree with	holding an attitude towards a situation's underlying potential	communicating a situation's potential	acting to draw out a situation's potential
28	III-square	$\square^3$	**morals** / emotional standards held by those who relate to you	holding impressions of the emotional expectations of big groups	desiring to satisfy the needs of big groups / those who give their trust	working to fulfill of the emotional needs or wants of groups who give their trust
29	III-quintile	✶^{3}	**charm** / personal expression towards those who relate to you	having confidence amidst listening audiences	taking center stage	leading audiences / asserting charisma or star-power over them
30	III-sextile	⚹^{3}	**expertise** / common ground you find between those who relate to you and topics beyond them	serving as a designated expert on a subject	critiquing a situation	using one's skill as a message communicator to influence people's judgments

Harmonic	Name	Symbol	(Angle) Topic	(Angle) Interaction		
31	III-septile	✡^{3}	**representation** / how you classify the many ideas of those who relate to you into a few ideas	processing webs of information in front of themselves	commanding group attention interfacing with the group agenda / hosting group conversations	actively connecting diverse perspectives under a coherent whole
32	III-octile	∠^{3}	**mystery** / power wielded on behalf of [those who relate to you] over [events beyond them]	having a stubborn, difficult-to-explain goal	being driven by goals that cannot be easily shared with others / being weird	behaving in a way that defies others' support, but serves one's self-interest instead
33	III-novile	九^3	**performance** / image you project in the eyes of groups who have agreed to listen to you	having groups members attention placed on them	levying projected power onto followers	spurring the heads of / spirit of a group to action
34	III-decile	+^{3}	**boss-ness** / mastery / authority you demonstrate in the eyes of those who relate to you	having expectations regarding authority / sitting back and observing those associated with them	weighing the behavior of others against their own standards	controlling group situations
35	III-undecile	∪^{3}	**eccentricity** / genius / what's worth talking about in the eyes of those who relate to you	having ideas regarding what's worthy of attention	pursuing areas of curiosity	exercising unique skill in a way that others see as attention-worthy
36	III-inconjunct	木^3	**legacy** / [impression left on] or [the ways in which you motivate] those who relate to you	leaving an impression on those who follow their activities	absorbing inspiration from or being provoked by a thing	displaying driven behavior towards their envisioned ends

Table 19-1: Situations associated with the first 36 harmonics. Note that low, neutral, and high tension do not correspond to goodness or badness. A high tension exchange can be bad or good for the people involved, for example.

Sun pairs

Sun-Sun

The angle between your Sun and their Sun shows where the two of you have a ***similarity of approach to the people whom you interact with 1:1.*** Let's get some practice using *table 19-1* to read this. Suppose you and the other person have a [Sun-Sun] III-conjunct. Using the table you might read any of the low, neutral, or high tension interactions; the high tension version would read as, "The more we express our [performance of actions for the satisfaction of bigger groups], the more [*similar we are in how we approach people with whom we interact 1:1*]." You could also read this based on the table *19-1* topic, "Our [*similarity of approach in 1:1 interactions*] is described by [actions backed by people who relate to us]. Perhaps you can see from this that III-conjuncts show where you and the other person have people with similar situations calling for them to keep an eye on your 1:1 behavior. That is, the people who observe you two's 1:1 exchanges have similar reasons for doing so. Indeed, two people with [Sun-Sun] III-conjuncts tend to come under people's scrutiny for the same reasons. But by itself the pair doesn't say any more than this. Not why, how, or under which situations you are watched. In the dataset, though, these people tended to share a certain kind of high-performing weirdness that kept others skeptical of them no matter how cordial they were.

Generally I won't go into the details of every angle family for every pair (since the *table 19-1* reading alongside the bolded text under every description will give you plenty), but I *will* note all the cases where certain pairs have notable effects which go beyond the table. The "high performing weirdness" observation is an example of this.

In addition to [Sun-Sun] III-conjuncts sharing a reputation for "competent weirdness," [Sun-Sun] squares tend not to like each other's way with people. [Sun-Sun] quintiles make a good duo. Septile conversations seem extra special. Octiles connect over deep power exchange and, as a result, tend to exhaust each other through mutual intensity. II-conjuncts share a creative energy between them which tends to strain the relationship if allowed to get inappropriately close beyond the persona level (since they essentially are less wired to connect beyond the superficial actions required of their shared room). II-oppositions for some reason are united through complaint on behalf of at least one of them. II-squares share a noticeable familial bond which tends to be very positive. II-septiles have an understated lock and key attraction which inclines them to cooperate in a warmed way even if they don't particularly care for the goal of the interaction. II-octiles are almost the complement to this since they have a more charged interaction which *results* from the goal before them both. No shared goal, no charge. III-septiles share an ability to unsettle the groups they communicate with thanks to their unusual ideas. III-undeciles share a capacity for creating tangled (though often entertaining) webs of logic in how they talk to others.

Sun-Moon

(From here on, each entry consisting of two different planets will have three sections:

- [You to them] (your planet A to their planet B)
- [Them to you] (their planet A to your planet B)
- [Self chart] (your planet A to your own planet B.)

You to them

Your 1:1 interaction is validated by them under this angle, which means that whenever you express one-on-one to another and the angle's topic is part of it, the other person is more likely to have experiences parallel to yours. This is actually a pretty interesting pair in that it promotes synchronized events between you and them, where **you tend to play out what the other person feels**. Actually, there's even more to it than that, because if you watch how you interact with them and you know the angle which separates your Sun from their Moon, you can read quite a bit about how they feel about their *exchange* with you (not necessarily you as a person) under that angle topic. Unless bound by other factors, II-quintile relationships tend to struggle as the Sun person diverts attention away from the Moon person's specific agenda and more towards the needs of their shared group. In the III-conjunct case, the Moon person has a higher chance of wanting to get emotionally involved with the Sun person, though such involvement may be costly as the Sun tends to take the Moon person for granted or even step on them here. III-oppositions support the Sun person as the "power behind the throne" held by the Moon person.

Them to you

Your inclinations to do whatever this angle suggests are turned into action as the Sun person brings your intents to life. And this is shown through your willingness to hang around them. If you don't like how they behave under this angle, you'll avoid hanging around them. Conjuncts are really informative here because it shows where the other person's basic way of being reflects your inner wants. So if the other person is acting like a complete tool it may be because you take a similar toolish approach to things emotionally, showing your own uncooperative attitude through their behavior.

Self chart

This angle shows how you most easily bring your intentions to life and, by extension, where you're most likely to be content with your efforts. **Self-contentment**.

Sun-Mercury

You to them

You are more likely to be pursued by the other for friendship or at least common ground under this angle, so that either 1) they have an easier time depending on you or 2) you are more likely to be responsible for their actions. Be on the lookout for what the other person seeks you out for. Quintiles want to express themselves as individuals and may come to you for their own fun (sometimes at your expense). Septiles seek you out for close conversation and are more likely to see you as a great partner for talking to. Undeciles (not surprisingly but yet surprisingly) may unintentionally use you to bolster their own sense of social identity. In romantic cases, you are more likely to be a rebound partner here. II-trines frequently use you to advance their own need for status among peers. III-octiles use you to show others how well they can control a situation.

Them to you

You take expressive cues from the other under this angle, and may rely on them to do the angle topic for you. If you don't like the other person, you will avoid hearing their advice under this angle. Perhaps they strike you as a side road.

You are more likely to let trines take the initiative in communication and let octiles take the initiative in steering others' actions. II-squares are a strong aspect for letting the other person mother you, though you may be seen as lazy in the home life as a result. You rely on II-noviles' ambition, only to find that theirs fades as your willingness to support them fades. It is easier for you to respect II-septiles among your groups for representing what they truly believe in. You respect II-deciles for their stubborn resistance to letting others change them. III-conjuncts make great fuel for helping you broadcast your own statements in the world and tend to bring easy rapport from you to them.

Self chart

Taking expressive cues from yourself and finding common ground between what you did and what you understood had to be done, you show where you've gone directly for what you wanted. **Directness**.

Sun-Venus

You to them

You work to enable or soften their expression. This also softens your assaults on them when you disagree under this angle's topic.

You are more likely to communicate from the intuition under septiles, making you unsettlingly blunt in a way that the other doesn't fully register until after the conversation. In other news, because you're not as tough under this pair, your Sun in II-decile with their Venus allows them to get away with more tyrannical behavior towards you. III-trine Venuses to your Sun have a way of weakening your natural insight, making it easier for them to seduce you in one way or another. 31s (III-septiles) can quietly train you to put up with their friends and social networks whom you wouldn't have otherwise put up with. III-noviles can turn a group against you or run it badly and you are more likely to forgive them. III-deciles can behave oppressively towards you and you are more likely to forgive them. In cases where you don't forgive, you become a more difficult adversary to them because, in either case, your softening of their behaviors makes their wrongs a less potent threat to you. Let's remind ourselves here: Venus is voluntary socialization; your Sun to their Venus ties you to them $_{\underline{fbow}}$.

Them to you

You like the other person or use them as an instrument for attaining the angle. This is direct use which differs from [Sun-Mercury]'s subtle use. **So you go to them and communicate with them in order to have this angle expressed by sharing a conversation/interaction topic with them**. If you are in conflict with the other, however, you will actively "deselect" what they stand for. To give an example, Your Venus quintile their Sun puts both yours and their egos on the table as an issue. If you get along with them you'll be more inclined to play around with them or exchange charm with them; if you don't get along you'll be more inclined to purposely do things to diminish their pride. This can make for nasty battles. In general, if you don't like what you hear regarding this pair's angle, there's a good chance that they aren't as comfortable talking to you about it. The opposite is also true: If you like what you hear, they are more likely to enjoy sharing this topic with you. Further still, the converse also tends to hold: If they aren't comfortable with you under this angle, you'll tend to dislike what you hear and are much more likely to cut the relationship short. I've seen it happen. Saw it LOTS of times in the data. <u>This half-pair is one of the more basic cases of a synastry factor which is central to a good friendship</u>. II-sextiles describe people with whom you'd like to form a longer term working or service-oriented partnership. III-noviles are people whom you admire or to whom you are drawn for their ability to mow down others with their temperament $_{fbow}$. IV-undeciles are people with whom you pursue experiences* which plenty of others in the world would be excited to have themselves.

Self chart

[Going to "yourself" in order to talk about a third topic] meets [softening your approach to yourself when you do], making you a voluntary socializer towards pretty much anybody who'll cordially listen. **Let's talk about something of mutual interest**.

* On the Level-IVs

🛠 To introduce some new things, what's a "IV-undecile" and why haven't we talked about it before? It's an angle which is a multiple of $^1/_{47}$ of a circle for which I have very little information, but which formed enough groups under certain pairs to get a description. If you look carefully at *table 16-7* you'll see some places where an angle has a really narrow degree distance between itself and one of its neighboring angles and a much wider distance between itself and the other neighbor. This leads to places where your astrology program gets confused about where one angle should stop and the other should begin. Back in *FSA*, "holes" (blank spaces in the angle table) were the main reason we started looking at II-conjuncts through III-inconjuncts in the first place. We didn't go any farther than $^1/_{36}$ of a circle because it would have been too much work to describe so many harmonics. Still, if you don't like holes and won't accept super-wide windows of error to clear them, you'll need even finer divisions of the circle. Specifically, you'll need a couple of multiples of $^1/_{37}$, $^1/_{38}$, $^1/_{47}$, and $^1/_{48}$ to get rid of them. Although it would be nice to know what these harmonics did *all the time*, I don't know (for a lack of data) and it's not actually necessary *to* know. When characterizing clusters of behaviors under a particular pair, all we need to know is that certain groupings exist and how those groups behave under that specific pair, not what those groups are named. Calling the group of fun-loving [$^{1}/_{47}$th Suns to your Venus] a "IV-undecile" is as good as calling it a "whatzit" or a "pencil." It's the behavior that counts, not the group name. Because $^{1}/_{47}$ is, by our naming system in *FSA*, officially called a "IV-undecile", that's the group name I'll use, but when it comes to looking at the overall pattern in the chart data, that name is irrelevant. ⚒

Preliminary data at the time of this writing suggests the following:

37. IV-conjuncts are related to a person's objectives or intentions, as well as how they convey such aims.
38. IV-oppositions are associated with projected interests or activities of personal value, including the bodily disciplinary regimen (exercise and health habits)
47. IV-undeciles are associated with personal outlook. This is the person's projection of their own "packages of talk" onto the world.
48. IV-inconjuncts are associated with a naturally projected impression onto the world—a vibe automatically deposited in the minds of faceless viewers of whoever's doing the behavior.

And now for more new things. Although I'll use the terms "pair" and "half-pair" interchangeably throughout this book, note that I'll refer to a "half-pair" when making a specific distinction between [Your A-Their B] and [Their A-Your B]. In the case of [Venus $_{you}$-Sun $_{them}$] for example, a badly managed angle can cause you to kill the exchange. This is not generally true for [Sun $_{you}$-Venus $_{them}$], where they are in a position to kill it and not you.

Sun-Mars

You to them

Other pushes you to steer third parties under this angle, in a pair which encourages them to pressure you into stronger action under this topic. Conjuncts are excellent at pushing you forward naturally with very little extra effort on their part. Trines on the other hand can push you with their opinions, making them either rude or stimulating to you when they communicate. In general, though, the angles behave as expected. Noteworthy harmonics include the square Marses (whose temperaments can overwhelm you), II-trine Marses (who can motivate you with the charisma they exercise over a room), II-squares (whose manners you can find off-putting), II-septiles (whose talent for connecting with fellow group members can energize you), and III-octiles (who tend to take an inexplicable liking to you and your company).

Them to you

You drive the other person to express more under this angle. You attempt to inspire them to action (though they may not always receive your efforts that way). You may serve as the "devil on the shoulder" of octiles in your encouragement of their primal behavior. Meanwhile, 14s (II-oppositions) are *very* strong indicators of your attraction to their bodily company—either physically or on the basis of their expressive fire); II-oppositions can make the other appealingly sexual to you OR unashamed in what is basically their hatred towards you. III-trines draw out your fire with a behavioral way that invites you to put it on them.

Self chart

Driving yourself to express more, particularly in your attempts to steer a third party, you demonstrate **enthusiasm** under this angle.

Sun-Jupiter

You to them

Your Sun sees the Jupiter person as embodying the image you want to be associated with, and even though Jupiter is typically a positive planet, this pair is often negative in that it predisposes you to trade respect and admiration from afar for disappointment up close. When actually interacting with the Jupiter person, you may see them as blowing the very opportunities that you would love to have. You may see Other as misusing or under-using gifts in this angle's area. Inconjuncts are seen as having an inspiring potential which they unnecessarily keep under a bushel. You often see II-trines as spending their considerable charisma aimlessly. II-septiles have a creativity or attractiveness which is displayed before everyone but inaccessible to you. In the rare positive cases of this pair you see the other as truly being a fine portrait of the angle's topic, allowing you to look up to them there.

Them to you

You feel respected or admired by the Sun person here. That is, unless they happen to dislike you or be uncomfortable with you. Then you feel dismissed by them. Trines are inclined to be overexcitable or complaining around you. Inconjuncts are too stubborn for you to influence without their invite.

This pair may also show up as a deeply confident character trait in the other. Noviles are inclined to like your company a lot but be hesitant to show this directly. (In the data all were observed to have a cool but distant demeanor in the Jupiter person's company regardless of whether they were naturally cool and distant.) You see undeciles as having a marked social ease with outsiders (or at least an easy time becoming popular among those outsiders). II-quintiles enjoy commanding group efforts even if they don't enjoy being a formal boss. II-undeciles are very strongly plugged into their information world and its networks. III-octiles hold a mysterious or secretive side which substantially affects their interaction with you. In cases where that side is not mysterious, it tends to be dark or morbid in some way. You recognize the ability of III-deciles to command groups with their quirky, fiery personalities. III-conjuncts are quirkier still in their two-sided reputations: one side for how they get along with you and another side for affecting events outside of your pair.

Self chart

Under an angle where you respect yourself and feel you are who you want to be as an actor in the abstract world, you are **image conscious**.

Sun-Saturn

You to them

You put walls around the other person $_{\text{fbow}}$ under this angle. This isn't always negative though. Your trine tends to show up as a stabilizing force in the other's often unstable communication. Sextiles give the Saturn person's work solid ground to stand on. Septiles feel that you like talking to them. You encourage II-trines to unleash their power onto others. You encourage II-undecile's unique deviance from popular expressive standards.

All in all, your Sun to the Other's Saturn constitutes a positive half-pair; **you help the other person further structure their approach to this angle's topic**. Why in the world would Saturn, the planet of limits, be so positive? Maybe because it is partnered with the Sun under this pair. So where the other person is limited, you are typically the one doing the work to limit them. This often implies that you care in some way. After all, pure enemies don't usually earn our deliberate structure; we simply work to stop them without worrying how they behave under such stopping. III-inconjuncts are noteworthy for the personal albatrosses they seem to have on their backs.

Them to you

You are put upon or have your angle topic limited under this pair. Hopefully for you this manifests as structure. Conjuncts take away your general expressive options, watering you down in a sense. Oppositions crowd out your values with their own. Septiles frequently rebel against your conversational agenda. Undeciles are known to eventually abandon you for greener social pastures. II-sextiles are often expressively haywire, putting all kinds of undirected ideas everywhere. II-septiles either attract or are attracted to others in ways that are intriguing to you; these people often have a sexual interest or associated characteristics which are more obviously displayed. In rarer cases, they may simply appear very deeply concentrated on their work goals. II-noviles have a subtle to obvious sass about them which renders them intimidating in all but the most jovial personalities, though the more big-hearted people among this group tend to just be more excitable. II-undeciles strike you as a weird mixture of off-beat good spiritedness and mercilessly no-nonsense aloofness. This group is strange in that they attach deeply to the things that interest them yet are single-minded and cold towards those who attempt to knock them off track. III-opposition Suns display a humor which appeals mainly to folks on the fringe. III-squares increase selfishness-for-the-good-of-others in the other person. III-octiles are similar to II-septiles in that their creativity or sexuality is more obviously displayed, but in the III-octile case the other (Sun) person shows this to others as a matter of asserting their worth in the world. III-noviles are very popular among groups, but scattered in their goals for interacting with those groups. Accordingly, they also attract scattered followers. III-undeciles retain a sharp focus on their own communicative goals, but can be sneaky against you in pursuit of them.

On a more positive note, squares are more inclined to calm you with their company even if they themselves are pretty emotional. II-quintiles are also very reliable for producing others who truly enjoy your sobering company. II-octiles are strongly analytical in your eyes. IV-undeciles aspire to have their creative deeds reflected in the talk of the bigger world.

Self chart

You limit yourself according to the standards of a third party while simultaneously reaching beyond those limits. This angle represents where you are **rules conscious** in your actions. More eccentric angles like the III-octiles, and III-undeciles know exactly where the line is and how to get close enough to it without crossing it.

Sun-Uranus

You to them

You see the Uranus person as broadcasting their angle rampant over society $_{\text{fbow}}$. In positive cases you see the other as talented here, but in negative cases you distrust them and view their angle as a tool for their being disloyal to you. **This pair is one of the indicators for how the other person cheats you or your expectations.** So if you and they agree upon certain rules for something, this angle shows roughly the means through which they can (and often will) successfully get around those rules. The angles follow *table 19-1* pretty closely, though it's probably not the friendliest read since it in this case it shows either 1) the topic they will engage to undercut your influence or 2) the interaction they will display to do the same (if necessary). II-octiles for example, when cornered, will rally groups outside of yours against you (neutral tension). II-noviles will create sneakily created works (as a topic area) or display an indignant attitude towards you and your standards (neutral tension). III-trines will invalidate your perspective by reinterpreting it (neutral-high tension). III-septiles will amplify small offenses until they become large ones (lower tension). III-inconjuncts will drive you out of their lives with a briefly-displayed critical attitude (lower tension). This last group can unknowingly kill an exchange with you with a seemingly tiny offense which you register later as permanently damaging. In the spirit of the angle of legacy, a person's Uranus III-inconjunct your Sun makes for insults you are hard-pressed to forget.

Them to you

You encourage the network mobility of Other under this angle; that is, you help their names get out there on the grapevine. Perhaps you can see how this can translate into your tool for cheating them. The other person's Sun to your Uranus gets their name publicized whether the two of you are allies or not. On the positive side, you tend to use the various tools in *table 19-1* as your means of promoting the other person's deeds. You often see an opposition holder as a badass with values and a worth that deserve publicizing. If they offend you, however, you may simply devalue their self-assurance as worthless. In good situations, you advertise squares as an example of the struggle. In negative cases you advertise them as liars. III-conjuncts have relationships with you which are more likely to veer into the controversial, since the angle of mass following gets you watched by big groups. III-septiles share views of others which are similar to yours, though you are often on different sides regarding what should be done about this. You are inclined to have high respect for III-undeciles. Should that respect ever disappear, you can expect the relationship to disappear or fall into ruin. These people tend not to hang around your life with a blank record under their name. III-inconjuncts are just plain defiant $_{fbow}$.

There are some aspects which tend to be consistently positive and others which are consistently negative. Positively, Suns which are II-quintile your Uranus make for consistently attractive or enjoyable company. II-octiles are persuasive and magnetic. II-deciles can team up with you to make for a commanding joint authority over others (with you backing them). On the other hand, relationships with II-undecile Suns tend to be good, but strained by the awkward undercurrent of certain unstated opinions. In a rather fun (but somewhat uncool aspect for others), it is easy for you to think of a III-trine as being your unsuspecting partner in crime; this is the person who blows up your enemy's bridge before you can, saving you the trouble. Their approaches to the issues you share often precede or complement yours, leading you to entertain partnership with them. But full partnership is almost always denied, since this would render the "like minds" coincidence written between you a non-coincidence.

Negatively, septiles for whatever reason struggle to earn your trust for as long as they talk to you directly. Away from them, though, you find it easier to promote their sociability. Inconjuncts, in your eyes, invite unnecessary chaos upon themselves. II-conjuncts frequently (but don't always) blow their opportunities for advancement. This [Sun-Uranus] angle is special in that it is directly tied to the Sun person's inability to be satisfied with their own efforts.

Self-chart

The pair under which you encourage your own network mobility (but also the one under which you cheat yourself by broadcasting traits you've shown badly) is that of **group attunement**. For better or worse this pair of yours sits under the spotlight, where everyone knows about your every win and loss.

Don't care to promote your losses? Don't advertise acts in which you've disappointed yourself. And avoid giving what you know to be a disappointing performance under this angle's topic / interaction. For some people who are naturally less secure under this angle, you may need to address that first. (Easier said than done, I know.)

Sun-Neptune

You to them

You feel respected or leaned upon by the other under their notion of this angle. For example, quintiles respect your display of ego as it fits with what their idea of an ego should look like. Now in an interesting bit of psychology, there are two side effects that come with the [Sun-Neptune] pair. First, the reason for your planet of ego expression making you respectable in the eyes of the Neptune person lies in the idea that your 1:1 actions line up with their overall vibe here. **This essentially allows your deeds to dominate their sense of the environment around them**. You're "everywhere" in some figurative way. Secondly, because you're everywhere, this pair's angle tends to make the Neptune person tense around you, especially when their own Neptune is very strong. Such tension can easily generate a low-key rivalry between you in the angle's topic area since the other person is basically fighting for control of their own expression against you—their unwitting oppressor. Such a rivalry tends to appear as a kind of subtly overconfident self-assurance towards you on their part, even as they tend to yield to you when it's your turn to express the same angle. Let's give an example of this.

Suppose Other has their Neptune III-quintile your Sun. This can make them really confident in declaring their own egos among groups of people, so that when you're just observing their attempts to impress such groups, they tend to be quite dynamic. On the other hand, if you interact with them 1:1 in the capacity of advisor on this same issue they turn much quieter, following your direction. In this and all other [Sun-Neptune] angle cases, though, there are some ways others can block your domination of their mood.*

Reading others' thoughts through their actions

From here on, whenever you see the eye icon, it means you are looking at a pair which allows you to read another's actual feelings about you even if they try to hide them. In some cases, the eye icon comes with brackets [] telling you to use, on the situation inside the brackets, the tactics being discussed. Below, for example, I give an explanation of how [the other person's Sun to your Neptune] can lead to your attempts to block the other's influence. The eye says [You to them], meaning that if you apply this explanation to the "You to them" [your Sun to their Neptune] section above, you can read which of your 36 listed harmonics a person may be attempting to block or allow you into based on how heavily they tune you out or focus on you.

Them to you

You feel an awkward version of Other's angle which—in negative cases—compels you to give either **pity or an obligated fraction of yourself to them. In positive cases you identify with the other and respect their ability** to give form to your mood under the angle. You pay compelled attention to II-trines' room influence and II-squares' area of respect seeking. You pay attention to II-deciles' work reputation, III-conjuncts' ability to gain the backing of others, and III-oppositions' inclination to sheer popularity. Respect often comes with this.

*But what if you don't like what you're seeing in this person? Typically you assert your side but block theirs by avoiding their direct company or tuning them out when they assert influence over the room you're in. Accordingly, **the previous half-pair, [Sun $_{you}$-Neptune $_{them}$], is an excellent indicator of Other's attempts to receive or block your influence. display of the angle which describes it**. When you're displaying the other half-pair's angle, do they plug in your earphones, flip through the channels, or go do other things at the expense of receiving your efforts? Even if not done maliciously, their doing it says a lot about where they refuse to give you the attention your actions compel.

Self chart

You obligate your own attention, whether or not you like what you're paying attention to. If you don't care to devote much energy to what you're paying attention to, you'll space out on your own performance of the task. This is **immersion / getting lost in a situation**.

Sun-Pluto

You to them

You help Other build up their defenses against social pressures under this pair's angle. Whatever the angle is, the other person seems to be under pressure to perform there (from your perspective) and you help them meet the challenge. This pair is one of those which can be made or broken through yours and the other's mutual cooperation. Hence it represents a fine example of why you can't read the success or failure of a relationship in a synastry chart. In positive cases, you encourage the other's improved angle expression. In negative cases you still encourage it, except you do so by being their adversary, forcing them to perform against you. In the data there were all kinds of examples of this, where it was clear that the Sun person and the Pluto person needed to agree to cooperate before the Sun could be of any service to the Pluto. Where such cooperation was denied by Pluto, Sun tended to abandon them. Where cooperation was denied by the Sun person, Pluto excluded Sun from the former's share of power once it was attained. As always, the pattern follows *table 19-1* very closely; conjuncts to your Sun show where you support

Other's being themselves II-oppositions show where you support their physical presence in a group. II-octiles show where you support their pressured power over outsiders. In cases of conflict, however, you tended to abandon them and adopt a feeling of disgust towards their display of power. III-deciles were among the most consistently negative harmonics since your support of a "master" often equates to them asserting an authority over you from their position of lower authority or ability.

Them to you

When the other is threatened, you will either go to bat for them or do the threatening under this angle. Although normally it is *their* role to support *you* here in peaceful times, in times of war the tables are turned. You become their defender. Look at both this half-pair and the [You to them] half-pair for a good glimpse at where you can be relied upon to build up the strength and defend the expression of the other:

> "I help strengthen the other's [Sun $_{you}$-Pluto $_{them}$] and defend them against assaults on their [Sun $_{them}$-Pluto $_{you}$]."
>
> "When things are going smoothly, they help strengthen my [Sun $_{them}$-Pluto $_{you}$] and defend me against assaults on my [Sun $_{you}$-Pluto $_{them}$]."
>
> "When things aren't going well between us we foster this same strength in each other by fighting *each other* instead."

Their Sun to your Pluto in undecile allows you to constrain their social options under conflict. On the positive side, II-noviles can fill you with pride as the other person greatly increases your confidence in your own creativity or the objects thereof. III-sextiles are also very conducive to your liking of the other person. Regular conjuncts are conducive to the other's liking of you. III-septiles can spur you on to socially relevant action.

Self chart

You build up your defenses and go to bat for yourself under this angle, making you **power aware** here.

Sun-Ascendant

You to them

Often seen in the synastry of people who affect each other profoundly, [Sun-ASC] shows where two people reflect each other's approach on different levels. Essentially, one person approaches their unexplored surroundings in the same way that the other approaches people one on one. **Your Sun to their ASC shows where you see Other as strongly skilled under this angle $_{fbow}$**. This is another one of those overwhelmingly frequent cases where the other person's actions reflect your own outlook. The other may be strongly skilled here, but if their use of that skill offends you it is often a reflection of the extent to which you offend others in the same way on an interpersonal level. Suppose for example that Other's Ascendant is undecile your Sun, and you find their social mobility in the world so excessive and intimidating that you don't trust them to care about their little connection with you. It may be that, in your 1:1 exchanges, you too come across as intimidating in the information world. Perhaps you overwhelm them with social data when you're in their individual company.

If there is someone in your life whose skill you respect, with whom you want (but can't form) a successful partnership, look at how they show this pair's topic/interaction in their surroundings then look at how you display this same topic or interaction towards them 1:1. You'll likely see parallels. But this particular blockage is mostly about you, not them. By the time you fix it within yourself, you'll often find that they've ceased to be important in this issue.

Them to you

You see the other's interaction with you as reflecting how you express your angle in the world. This is a really good indicator of the effects of your actions on others when they would not otherwise be obvious to you, and can serve as an important basis for predicting people in your surroundings' actual unstated views of you.

Suppose for example, you're on a date with someone and everything is going swimmingly. The date ends and all is well. But you never hear from them again. No text. No call. No nothing. WHAT IN THE WORLD HAPPENED? It almost certainly had to have been something in the way you interacted with them 1:1. And barring death, deployment, incarceration, or kidnapping, it really might have been something in the way they saw you approaching a certain area of life generally. That's the cue. 👁 Enter [Your Ascendant to their Sun]. If you don't have a birth time, setting their time at noon may still give you a decent idea. Look at the angle. Under all of the conditions stated above, this is typically the thing they didn't like about you. The II-sextiles and III-octiles, for example, can hurt business partnerships as the other will have seen you as long-term unreliable or overbearing respectively. The II-conjuncts and II-septiles affect friendships by showing you as too demanding of social performance or too inconsiderate of your friends respectively.

Self chart

Where your outlook towards your surroundings meets your 1:1 skill with others, **you are welcomed by the group**. That is, the surroundings filled with people who don't know you are more easily inclined to contain people who want to know you and who welcome your ego. You may also find it useful to note that the 👁 in the previous section can also be used in the self chart to show the things which cause you to give up on a social situation or pursue it in the first place; you are a lot less likely to seek new social terrains if you don't think your [Sun-ASC] angle will benefit from it. Read this angle in the regular birth chart of the other person to see where they stand to be most interested in exploring places with new people.

Sun-Midheaven

✪ This is a major synastric pair, 🔒 determines the existence of the partnership, and can be used as a 🗡 relationship killer

You to them

✪ 🔒 🗡 **Your continued interest in the relationship with the other thrives off of your perception of this pair's angle** fbow. **When Other no longer shows this angle or the potential for it, the relationship either gets rewritten or (more often) dies**. This isn't because you're using the person for his or her angle; it's mainly because this angle is one of your chief means of recognizing the relationship for the role it plays in your life. The Midheaven begins the 10th house—the house of structure—while the Sun shows your 1:1 behavior towards the other. Should the Midheaven / MC stop perceiving a recognizable form for the Sun, so too would your Sun (1:1 interaction with the other person) also stop providing a recognizable form. Even if the angle is distrusted by one or both of you, their focus on it (as the Midheaven person) is essential to the relationship being publicly acknowledgeable.

Regarding the very common relationship question "Will we survive?" your Sun to their MC won't show you how to make the answer yes, but it will show the conditions for the answer being no: If the MC person stops showing whatever angle exists between their MC and your Sun, the direct 1:1 exchange has a high chance of failure. Part 2 of this rather subtle, pre-relationship killer is discussed in the next section.**

Them to you

You see the other's display of this pair's angle as providing the heaviest contribution to the relationship as a public thing. Should you have problems with obtaining such a contribution or get tired of receiving it, there is a pretty good chance that the other will disappear as a major influencer in your life shortly thereafter. I have to say that this was one of the saddest columns I read in the dataset because it reflected pretty plainly the end of so many exchanges which once seemed to have so much promise.

**If you really want a relationship of any kind to survive as it currently is, you'll likely need to work to maintain your display of this angle (between your MC and their Sun) while continuing to receive their display of the other half-pair's angle (their MC to your Sun). Of course there's no guarantee that they'll want to continue exchanging these characteristics, but on your end the task is pretty straightforward...

...On the other hand, if a relationship has become poisonous to you, the most effective thing you can do to extricate yourself is to cut off all displays of the angle that sits between your MC and their Sun. So if this angle is a trine, you stop speaking to them. If this angle is a III-sextile you stop lending them your expertise. If the angle is a III-novile, you end your role as a group rallyer in their company, but keep displaying it in others' company.

Of all of the Sun-MC / MC-Sun angles, the III-conjunct was the hardest to read, as it does not follow *table 19-1* in an obvious way. This is the first angle of any pair we've talked about which is so noticeably rogue. This pair corresponds to the idea that the other person is special and worth your ideological support. When one of you stops showing that his or her lives agree with the life of the other person, the relationship dies. When you show that your lives agree with each other, the relationship grows. The idea is that the MC person needs to show the Sun person that MC's life circumstances match Sun's direct behaviors. No match, no relationship. Connections lost under this one tend to fail quietly and bitterly since it is characteristic for them to die under the gradual erosion of a common outlook that was once so strong.

Self chart

Your reputation matches your 1:1 behavior under a certain angle. You are an effective **self-promoter** here.

Sun-Vertex

You to them

You see Other as wanting or valuing change-navigation assistance from you under their version of this angle. To the extent that you are able to stabilize this angle for them, they are inclined to entrust you with their uncertainties. IV-conjuncts formed a significant group in this particular data set, entrusting the Sun person with their aspirations for their instinctual deeds in the world.

Them to you

You see changes in the other's 1:1 expression in line with this angle as coinciding with your own major changes. That is, **their behavior towards you is tied to the major changes you're going through under this same angle**. Typically in single charts we don't consider the Vertex as significant unless it is in conjunct (or maybe opposition) with another planet. But here is a case where we see that major change is *always possible* if you know where to look for it. The usual *table 19-1* applies. Conjuncts foster major changes in instinctual behavior. Oppositions foster changes in self-value. Trines foster changes in thinking or attitude. In cases where there is no major change happening for you at the moment, your relationship with the other person tends to be described by Other's experience of that angle as being an ongoing "big deal" as they strive to unbottle their own will to change. In all cases though, there is a tendency for the Sun person to make the Vertex person angry or charged in light of the Sun person's own demonstration of the angle. This one works both ways. Finally, we note that conjuncts, II-conjuncts, II-oppositions, II-trines, and III-conjuncts tend to explode with (usually negative) creative tension, marrying impassioned communication or sexuality to the fate of the relationship. As they all involve a person's direct power over a group, the Sun person tends to view these relationships as unsettling for as long as they endure. Two people who have these on both [Sun-Vx] half-pairs are poised to hate each other or be instinctively, primally attracted to one another in all but the most platonic cases.

Self chart
[Sun-Vx]'s angle denotes **the behavior you show which is most associated with major change in your life**.

Sun-Node

You to them
Under this angle, you bring your 1:1 expression into Other's life, making you strongly known for this in their eyes. 👁 If ever you wondered, "How can I get Other to willingly interact with me?" your allowing them to display this angle towards you 1:1 is one key way. So if you have a septile, you would let them converse with you. If you have an inconjunct, you would let them promote their vibe and intuition with you. If you have a II-quintile, you would let them affirm how they manage others in a group setting. All of this needs to take place in their direct interaction with you though, making this into a weird kind of circular affair. In order to get them to like interacting with you 1:1 you must first get them to interact with you. Really? But it makes sense if you think about it. One can't really like what they haven't done yet. This angle is useful in that, once they've done it, you'll know how to keep them wanting to do it in exchange with you. Maybe. Sometimes their idea of doing it means fighting you.

So I guess the question is, "how do I create the circumstances for their wanting to interact with me in the first place?" Clearly people aren't puppets so you can't just script this. But based on the data it looks like the other needs to feel that the angle between [your Moon and their Node] stands to have an outlet. Suppose for example [Sun $_{you}$-Node $_{them}$] is II-undecile and [Moon $_{you}$-Node $_{them}$] is III-octile. Before encouraging them to like 1:1 associating with you by reaffirming their uniqueness among your shared groups, you would first need to help them feel that they stood to gain general power (as an enigma) from doing so. In many ways this looks like letting yourself be manipulated. Let that be a lesson to you; the price of admission into someone's world isn't always a bargain. Furthermore, there are many cases in which the person simply won't allow their angles to be brought out by you, in which case it is their choice not to associate with for their own good reasons.

Them to you
You see the Sun Other as being destined to express themselves under their version of this angle. In negative cases, you'll deny them association with you here. There is a pretty noticeable connection between this angle, [their Moon to your Node], and your determination of whether a 1:1 exchange with the other is worth it. You can read this as, "If my [Moon $_{them}$-Node $_{you}$] interaction can stand to gain from exchanges with them, and if my [Sun $_{them}$-Node $_{you}$] interaction is something I value receiving from them continuously, the 1:1 exchange will be worth it. If not, no.

Self chart
The angle under which you enjoy 1:1 interacting with others as a matter of "destined" exchange is the **means to your calling as a social actor**. You're motivated to pursue this means through a specific act *if* your [Moon-Node] angle attracts you to doing so. Your [Sun-Moon] angle shows that behavior which becomes stronger as you complete each act in a job well done. We'll call this **trio of pairs ([Sun-Node], [Moon-Node], [Sun-Moon])** the **Interpersonal Calling cocktail. It shows who you were "meant to be" as a social actor in one on one exchanges**. I discuss this and other cocktails in Chapter 20.

Sun-Selene

You to them
You celebrate the talents or defective effects of Other under their expression of this angle. This is a pretty basic pair which doesn't offer that many surprises. Most of the time the angle represents a talent which, in your eyes, the other possesses. When it's not a talent, it's still a talent (but has chaos as its side effect).

Them to you

You feel especially expressively talented under this angle when you're either in the company of or acting against the other person. That's the basic effect. In addition to conveying your talents upon the other, you also benefit from feeling so skilled in their company. For example II-squares are great for making the other person feel like family as a result of your skill in tending to their emotional values. II-sextiles strike you as being really good for your long-term career as a result of your efficacy in partnership with them. III-inconjuncts gain a lot from hearing your viewpoint and enhance your sense of importance as a communicator.

Self chart

You celebrate your own talents in 1:1 exchange here, so let's call this one **talent expression**, where you have a special skill when showing this angle to your 1:1 exchange partners.

Sun-Lilith

You to them

The other person seems to be beyond your ability to influence under this angle. This need not be a good or a bad thing, just an area where you can count on them to eventually jump out of any box you try to put them in. There is a higher chance that the other can surprise you with their unpredictability or excessive behavior here, allowing for plenty of forehead-slapping, head-shaking moments.

Them to you

You are the rebel complement to Other under their angle. Whatever they're trying to do related to this angle, you're more likely to also do as a rebel. Interestingly, people with I-, II-, or III-squares tend to have a noticeably divergent form of personal morality in your eyes $_{\text{fbow}}$. Conjuncts have an easier time riling you up just by being themselves. Quintiles do the same with their ego projection. II-noviles do it through the attitude they project related to ideas you're trying to convey to them. II-inconjuncts can be a very intense source of inspiration to you—not just as muses but as fiery people in their own right. Perhaps, then, there's more to this pair than your simply being a rebel. It's more like the other person has a way of planting seeds in your psyche which suggest that it is okay to take their wishes to an extreme.

Some other noteworthy angles are as follows: III-quintiles have a higher chance of having a controversial relationship with an institution, and can stir your rebellion that way. III-inconjuncts encourage your rebel insight through provocative views of their own. Lastly, in the data there were lots of IV-undeciles. Here the Lilith person was much more inclined to have a semi-secret approach to the Sun person which bordered on scandalous or rule-breaking.

Self chart

You're out of control, yet your other side attempts to make sense nonetheless. Continually overshooting your target, you display **rule-conscious defiance**.

Sun-Fortune

This pair [alongside Fortune-Moon] provides insight into relationships that have died before they had a chance

You to them

You feel appreciated by the other person for your display of this angle, and you are made more comfortable giving this angle. In negative cases, **you serve as half of the basis of internal conflict within the other person**. (That is, "She likes this [angle] side of me. Why won't she allow me into her world?"). Actually, this second form of [Sun-Fortune] happens A LOT, prompting us to investigate what this pair is actually doing. The Sun shows 1:1 behavior. Fortune shows where a person is in their element. When you interact with someone in a way that shares space with a thing they have long done well enough on their own, the Fortune person has a very real reason to test your long-term reliability before adding you to their world. Will you be around tomorrow? Or will they be painfully disappointed? Will you try to take over their lives where previously they enjoyed freedom? Only after you earn the other's trust do they share this angle's agenda with you comfortably.

To address the "Why won't she..." question, by the way, the answer often lies in your mishandling of (or unproven record regarding) [Moon $_{them}$-Fortune $_{you}$]. Suppose your [Sun $_{you}$-Fortune $_{them}$] is III-quintile and your [Moon $_{them}$-Fortune $_{you}$] is inconjunct. Using *table 19-1*, you would read the following: "They like my charm over groups, but won't let me into their world because they just don't have the mood to do so. I haven't moved them." Ouch. That's a tough one.[9] In any event, you really should try reading this pair of pairs. In the data I found it to be *very* accurate in its description of those factors which stopped promising relationships from getting off the ground.

Them to you

You are in your element when Other expresses this angle. Well isn't that nice? As a consequence, you are encouraged to use this angle to drive them farther forward. In negative cases you use this angle to drive them out of your sphere. IV-oppositions showed up in sizable numbers here, where the Fortune person was most comfortable praising Sun's identity-building actions in the broad world.

Self chart

When you appreciate yourself and are in your element watching yourself go, you are **assured in your show of skill**.

Sun-Ceres

You to them

You want Other to express their angle more powerfully, but you don't always say. You see potential in them under this angle. In cases where Other already expresses this angle strongly, they seem to not know when to quit; then they are disturbingly overpowered. Rarely does this pair behave in a balanced way since, whenever Other does hold back, you tend to be around pushing them to do more.

Them to you

You feel encouraged to behave differently under Other's idea of this angle; Other often pressures you unknowingly as a means of showing you how to make your own life better. You may feel insecure in light of Other's standards here.

Aside from pressuring you in ways that line up with the usual table, Other's Sun to your Ceres is a good indicator of their slightly negatively-skewed personality traits in your eyes. For this pair, all I-, II-, and III-inconjuncts increase your desire to serve the will of the other person. Conjuncts are forward and confident in most cases, but melt passively into the background if you overpower them. Oppositions are fiery and sexual, but often have a lot of personal problems assaulting them at any one time. Trines are inquisitive and like to socialize closely with everyone—even strangers. Squares are sassy on one hand, fretful on the other. Quintiles are assertive with a bullying side. More positively, sextiles are noticeably more friendly and cooperative in their dealings with you than most other Ceres angles and septiles make for pleasant conversationalists. Octiles are more fun to flirt with or issue-spar with, less fun to compete with. Noviles bring out the caretaker in you, while deciles are a mixed bag of people who respectfully disrespect you and people who look up to you. It depends. Undeciles boast social groups you wouldn't mind borrowing. Inconjuncts have a general vibe and intuition you typically enjoy being around.

II-conjuncts tend to live in a separate world from you which competes with, yet complements your own. II-oppositions have an interesting way of showing up in your company when you need assistance in a conflict you may not even be aware of, making them like an accidental "guardian" to you. This pattern was odd but noticeable in the data, where the Sun people in this cluster tended to show up at key times to fight key battles which 1) struck the Ceres person as

[9] Incidentally, inconjunct moods are associated with past emotional training which reaches all the way back to childhood. If you can't penetrate another's defenses and they have a Moon which is inconjunct your Fortune, you may be dealing with a basket of skeletons too big for you to actually handle. This is a property of inconjuncts in almost all cases where *one* person's display of an angle—and not both—determines how the pair plays out.

inconvenient and unnecessary yet 2) allowed the Ceres person to continue with plans that would have been otherwise difficult to execute under decisions they were about to make. II-trines take a while to warm up to you, but when they do they tend to be fun company. II-squares seem to be okay with your influence, but are very quiet around you in general. Beneath the surface, you tend to have an attraction to their company which defies—but doesn't completely ignore—your natural inclinations. You and the II-quintile make great partners in crime as long as you avoid exercising your shared power over each other. Doing this will cause the two of you to rift. II-sextiles are often beset with obstacles to their long-range plans. The level and kinds of obstacles aren't always amusing, but can be. II-septiles are overwhelmingly suspicious in their behavior towards you. II-octiles are confident and skilled in their specialty areas, but can't be relied upon to use that specialty to your benefit. II-noviles have an easy time getting their attitudes and creative works put before the public, regardless of whether the work is complete or good.* You see II-deciles as sober, somewhat difficult-to-please critics. Their opinion matters though since they—despite being temperamental—tend to be accurate judges of people's deeds. II-undeciles cooperate with you by criticizing your work in most cases, by displaying their own unique perspective in rarer cases. II-inconjuncts are like tamed giants in the interaction department, packing a lot of beauty, charisma, or power, behind a more humbled personality.

*If you are a creative type looking to put your work out there, try hanging around people whose Ceres to your Sun is II-novile. These people are automatically inclined to see your work as subject to broadcast (even if they don't like your work).

Confident (or perhaps pushy) III-conjuncts have an attitude which invites fights. You see III-oppositions as well-liked, though not as supportive of you personally. III-trines are capable of delivering sharp insight into a situation. III-squares are inclined to support your expression even if it is imperfect. III-quintiles tend to be irreverent and dismissive towards the situation you share. Sometimes this gives them common sense in group endeavors, but most of the time it simply makes them rude. III-sextiles complain noticeably more than other angles, though their complaints (thanks to their frequency) are less damaging to the exchange in your eyes. III-septiles are often physically attractive or charismatic in your eyes, with a presence that allows them to smoothly charm the network of people around you. This aspect makes for "foxy" women and coolly manipulative men. III-octiles are more inclined to distrust you when you approach them. Relatedly, they will approach you uneasily when they need something. Partnership with III-noviles strengthens you as a group leader; though stubborn, these people can typically be relied to give impetus to your action. In a counterintuitive turn, III-deciles make you slightly more fun as they draw out your comfort with command. You are compelled to praise the IV-conjunct's natural expression in the broad world, and inclined to promote the broad world outlook of IV-undeciles as something well worth talking about; IV-undeciles are more inclined to receive warm nurturing from you and have an easier time drawing your attention away from third parties.

Self chart

The Sun-Ceres pair shows where you push yourself to be more effective in your 1:1 exchanges. It's the push that counts here, less so the results. This is your **context for non-malicious encouragement**.[10]

Sun-Chiron

You to them

You learn from Other in the realm of this angle. If not adopting Other's ways, you tend to accept them as a complementary partner, colleague, or co-healer of people (or situations) beyond your pair. **In negative cases you see Other as a bad teacher, so**

---

[10] In *FSA* [Sun-Ceres] was the "context for playfulness," but that was before our studying the synastry and seeing what the two sided version of playfulness looks like. As you'll see many times ahead, *HBS* will modify many of the *FSA* meanings. This doesn't make the *FSA* meanings wrong, only framed differently to fit the different viewpoint from that of a solo chart with one actor. In *HBS* we view solo charts as having two actors: you the subject and you the object.

you learn or heal people against Other's example instead. The standard table applies. Lessons learned at the hand of II-trines tend to be slightly more potent than other lessons. III-trines are more inclined to display brilliance in your eyes. III-squares are more persuasive yet friendly at the same time. III-sextiles display more analytical talent.

Them to you

You see Other's efforts as capped under this angle. Often you see them as being held back here and will judge or support them accordingly. **Where you don't see such a cap on their efforts, you are more likely to respect them as a co-healer or co-teacher** under this angle. There is a tendency to perceive a pronounced chemistry with octiles. II-squares are more emotionally demanding, though not always emotional people. You easily perceive II-quintiles as domineering and are more likely to be put off by their increasing encroachment upon your free space. II-octiles either love you or hate you with little in between. II-noviles are adorable but intense. II-deciles strike the Chiron person as charming. III-trines make excellent intellectual partners with a notably hormone-provoking edge. Where attraction is possible, you are most likely to give these people a license to bed you if they wanted to. III-deciles are noteworthy for their ability to conceal their true thoughts from you. IV-undeciles—once again common in this data set—were more likely to hold a somewhat notorious reputation for ignoring others' will amidst public exploits in favor of their own.

Self chart

You see yourself as capped, but then again not so much as you strive to break successive barriers to your expression. This is the **context for your insecurity and how you overcome it**. People whose Chiron has the same angle to your Sun as your own Chiron have a greater ability to highlight your insecurities while they remain. Once you've overcome those insecurities, however, you tend to be much stronger as a support to this kind of person (while typically losing the relationship with people who you felt previously diminished you).

Sun-Vesta

Alongside [Jupiter $_{\text{them}}$-Vesta $_{\text{you}}$], you can permanently change another's ways through this angle.

⌘ This is pair is related to things you teach and learn in an exchange

You to them

⌘ You feel that the other person needs you in order to express this angle, or at least benefits from having you around. **You motivate the shaping of Other's angle**. So if you have an opposition here, you motivate the shaping of their values and self-worth. Trust is a big deal with this pair, as it is one of the most effective pairs for your actually changing the way Other behaves. Have you ever noticed how, despite all of the people we meet and relationships we form, most people don't really change that much? [Sun-Vesta] defies this, **serving as a strong window through which you may clearly influence another's permanent personality IF they allow themselves to be open to your influence**. [Jupiter $_{\text{them}}$-Vesta $_{\text{you}}$] is one of the main angles for determining whether they are open to your influence; as long as you accept their version of [Jupiter $_{\text{them}}$-Vesta $_{\text{you}}$] such openness tends to come more easily. Interestingly, if you should reject their display of the [Jupiter $_{\text{them}}$-Vesta $_{\text{you}}$] angle *even in your mind*, you can expect to lose your influence over them. This is probably because their Jupiter is their world image and your Vesta is your concentration. Where you are only halfhearted in your concentration on their image promotion, you may be able to lie about this in a few obvious cases but will have a hard time doing so over the course of hundreds of little micro cases; they'll tend to see that you're not really invested in what they're trying to promote, so when they are tasked with concentrating on your 1:1 behavior towards them, they see someone who isn't really supportive; thus you lose access to their full trust in this department. They need to trust that you are really interested in their endeavors before you are allowed to influence them significantly.**

Them to you

You admire Other under this angle, focusing on them with fascination. In bad cases, you focus on them with negative fixation. In the 90s we called this "mad doggin'." The other person captures your attention here, usually in the neutral sense. But your tendency to keep watching their 1:1 behavior translates easily into a tendency to be steered by what you see *if* what you observe happens to be either 1) consistent with or 2) focused on $_{\text{their Vesta}}$ where you are trying to go in the world $_{\text{your Jupiter}}$.

**We've discussed a lot in these last two sections, so let's give an example. Suppose you are fascinated with Other's influence over a room. [Sun $_{\text{you}}$-Vesta $_{\text{them}}$] is II-trine. Are you likely to push them into changing their display of room influence? Suppose [Jupiter $_{\text{them}}$-Vesta $_{\text{you}}$] is septile. If, when talking to you 1:1, they believe your room influence has their interests in mind, you'll likely push them to change how they display their own II-trine. If they're not convinced through conversation with you, no.

Self chart

You shape your own 1:1 expression of this angle through focused attention to what you're doing, as long as what you're paying attention to matches what you're already inclined to do. This is the **fortified ego**.

Astrologically speaking, a really easy way to pick up good interpersonal habits is to hang around people who support this. Admittedly it may be harder for readers to do this without a database in front of them, but the general idea behind [Sun $_{\text{personA}}$-Vesta $_{\text{personB}}$] and [Jupiter $_{\text{B}}$-Vesta $_{\text{A}}$] is that we become what we fixate on to the extent that what we fixate on sends a consistent message regarding our aspirations. In many ways, we are free to choose our influences—even without astrology—as long as we keep an eye out for such consistency. But astrology can be valuable in that it provides a nice framework (in the form of the angle families) for determining which characteristics we want to pay attention to. If you're thinking about partnering with someone who sends you inconsistent messages regarding those areas under which you are most vulnerable to their influence, that's fine if other factors render the connection worth it. Just make sure that any blinders you may have on aren't so blinding that they set you up for trouble later.

Sun-Pallas

You to them

You feel aversive tension towards the other under this angle, hoping that they won't go there, being uncomfortable, or generally disapproving of this angle. Why? Because their Pallas is where they wage war. **In the less frequent—but not exactly rare—positive cases, you're down to go to war alongside them** (mainly as moral support). Septiles are more likely to flirt with or fight with you. II-conjuncts pick fights and then escape innocently as if they didn't. II-squares are communicatively rambunctious and have a knack for unsettling rooms full of people at once. II-septiles have upbeat personalities with a more pessimistic side lurking behind their private outlook. You tend to respect II-noviles for their fighting spirit and II-deciles for their persistence. II-undeciles are resilient and can usually be counted on not to falter in a challenge. III-conjuncts are known to provide you with surprise reinforcements in your own battles. III-squares' worlds are dominated by spaciness, idealism, or spirituality. III-quintiles are socially plugged in, but stand apart from those networks they connect to. III-sextiles use their beauty or sensuality as a social weapon. III-septiles have a more easily agitated vibe which they take from group to group. III-octiles hyperanalyze as their prime social weapon. III-deciles joke, make fun of situations, or otherwise lighten the mood; in some cases they turn such jokes upon themselves or take their own efforts lightly. III-inconjuncts have a presence which lingers on the mind. As a social weapon, they do things that render them difficult to forget—often negative. IV-conjuncts in the dataset had a pronounced will to power in the world.

Them to you

You see Other as combative or aggressive under this angle. But is this mere projection of your own behavior? More likely, **the other person can use this**

angle to provoke you into wanting to make an assertive social statement. II-quintiles have interests or lifestyles which turn you on. To you, II-septiles seem embattled as a rule. II-noviles can use their talents and attitudes to easily lead others by the nose. II-undeciles have problems curbing their assertiveness among weaker people. III-conjuncts are great seducers in the romantic and professional sense. III-quintiles, regardless of sex, are associated with very strong women. III-septiles know well how to run people over socially. You find III-undeciles charismatic and attractive, but manipulative or deceptive as well. You find yourself compelled to interact with III-inconjunct in unusual ways, viewing something about them as exceptional. IV-oppositions are more likely to have a body that impresses you or moves you to lust—regardless of form. IV-undeciles leave an impression upon your mind or your groups which helps ensure that they stand out for a long time.

Self chart

The 1:1 interaction is associated with forcefully made social statements. This angle is your **"crusade weapon"** which accompanies you in every pair where you use this same angle. It gives a crusader's edge to your 1:1 interactions under this topic.

Sun-Juno

You to them

You can use this angle to secure the other person's commitment. Just display the angle in your dealings with them. So what's the catch? The people who commit to you don't always want to be committed to you. The commitment may not make them or you better. The commitment may compromise the status or friendships of either or both people. Commitment tends to take energy and attention away from other commitments. Commitments bring expectations and, accordingly, conflict; we are less likely to fight people with whom we share no common thing to be committed to. So if you plan to use this one, make sure you know what you're in for.

Them to you

The other person commits to you using their display of this angle. 👁 If you're getting this angle willingly and frequently enough from them, there is likely a decently level of (some kind of) commitment. Even if it's just a commitment to accept your presence in the same office. If you're not getting this angle—unless you're dealing with family or some other arrangement which is allowed to become occasionally distant—the commitment is lower. Be sure to keep the context in mind though. If you are interested in dating someone you met online and expect them to share their opinions with you through a [Sun $_{\text{them}}$-Juno $_{\text{you}}$] trine, you may be asking too much if their idea of commitment with you is still in the "meeting" phase and your idea of commitment is in the "talking" phase. Different standards of performance between two different committers leads to different levels of showing commitment—even if both are giving their all. But how often do we punish people for a contract they never knew they signed?

Self chart

You use this angle to secure your own commitment to a task. In a self chart you are your own partner, so this is a context and not an actual partnership. It is a context for sticking with a particular course of action. Call it the **context for being driven by a thing you're associated with**.

Sun-Hera

This angle is useful for solidifying a bond between you and Other

You to them

You feel an automatic, almost entitled association with Other when you express this angle and they don't bother to block it. Where both the [you to them] and [them to you] half-pairs have the same angle, you and Other tend to dwell on each other as favorites or exemplary rivals.

Them to you

Joint angle expression alongside Other (in your eyes) solidifies your bond with them. As always, use *table 19-1* to see what this angle does in your synastry.

Self chart

As you interact 1:1 with others, you feel feelings which come with a strong connection, even though you are only connecting with yourself. Yet any third party who happens to be the recipient of whatever angle you have here becomes associated with that connection. This is your **bond at the hands of an interactant**. Be sure to look this one up in the table, as it shows the thing you do in 1:1 exchanges which most strongly puts you in a mood to bond with whomever is there. The conjuncts, trines, II-conjuncts, II-oppositions, II-undeciles, and III-undeciles tend to be more passionate and more susceptible to seduction than others.

Sun-Eros

✪ At least one of these half-pairs is very strong

Wondering what you stand to gain from this exchange?

You to them

As the association with Other builds, you grant them increased access to your version of this angle. This works kind of like a dowry—the gift your side gives to the other as an affirmation of your bond. Conjuncts are more likely to see your raw instinctual side. Oppositions are more likely to learn more about your values. Same ole same. The notable thing about this aspect, though, is that it is mostly negative. Adult socialization teaches us to water down most of our true personality in favor of getting along with others. [Sun $_{you}$-Eros $_{them}$] exposes this normally hidden side of how you actually care to express one on one, so you often appear either reckless or surprisingly skilled in the other's view.

There are a few patterns which aren't evident in the table alone. II-inconjuncts have a high rate for exposing the Other as a liar (in your view). III-inconjuncts often bring a dysfunctional background or a present dysfunctional attitude based on a normal background. There is a strong desire for significance here. More positively as you get closer, you allow IV-oppositions to accompany you in your explorations of the world. You allow IV-undeciles to join you in issuing forth ideas to the abstract world.

Them to you

You are driven to express your desires using Other's expression of this angle as a means an end. To what end? Towards your own version of this angle. II-quintiles bring either warm fondness for the other or a messy power struggle. II-sextiles are exceptionally comfortable angles to have here—probably the most positive angle to have for this pair. It is easy to trust the task performance of II-octiles. II-noviles have an attitude which constantly pushes you forward $_{fbow}$. Your relationships with III-conjuncts are more likely to be one-way (them to you). III-septiles are more likely to be noted for how disconnected their social group is from yours. Typically, you'll find the unique company of III-undeciles thoroughly enjoyable, though in some cases you'll find them intolerably irritating instead. III-inconjuncts have a way which you consider memorable. IV-conjuncts are noted for their toughness in issues related to the broad world.

This pair partly answers the question "What do I get out of this relationship?"

Self chart

You give yourself access to your own angle and use yourself as a means to its recklessly acquired end. The chase fuels itself with a sought-after object before it. This is **lust fulfillment**.

Sun-Bacchus

You to them

You see Other as relying on you to demonstrate your angle amidst cliques. This isn't quite a circus act at your expense but it is an area of comparative strength on your part when the two of you interact amongst friends and peers. In positive cases, the other leans on you to make this angle's impression. In negative cases your show of this angle is a predictable obstacle to their expression—a quality you possess which they dread.

Septiles are often very negative in this respect because, although a certain level of conversation among friends is normal, the other person comes to view *your* form of conversation as a fixture in peer exchanges. Often they would prefer that you just shut up. Relatedly, negatively displayed II-sextiles are more likely to see you as overstepping the whole point of short term peer exchanges with your long-range, overinflated analysis. They are less likely to take your serious interests seriously. II-quintiles on the other hand expect you to dominate your groups. You are reliably overpowering fbow among groups with these people in them, though there is some indication that the other trusts that you will dispense justice when necessary; this is basically a positive angle. III-conjuncts bring Other's complaints into your exchange, sometimes against you, sometimes not. (Hint: if the person has this angle and you *don't* hear them complaining, it's often against you in a secret, but substantial way.) III-quintiles have an easier time serving as your equal in group exchanges. IV-undeciles see you as predictably doing gossipworthy things in your public behavior.

Them to you

You see the other person as adopting this angle's role amidst peers and cliques. You may see this as an interpersonal skill which they exercise among others.

In both positive and negative cases, this pair's angle is one of the best reasons to introduce the other person to your friends. But if Other is an enemy, you'll only introduce them to your friends by *talking about* how offensive Other's display of this angle is. Such a situation represents a classic example of how astrological factors can go either way depending on one's attitude.

Self chart

You rely on yourself to demonstrate this angle in your 1:1 interactions among peers. This is a key personality trait for you among your cliques, and shows **how you behave to get their attention**.

Moon pairs

If the Sun shows what you do in 1:1 exchanges, the Moon shows why you do it. For many of the pairs you just read in the Sun section, there will be a Moon pair which greatly helps explain why yours or the other person's Sun plays out the way it does. Keep that in mind as we go through these. It may make them easier to read.

Moon-Moon

Use this angle to overcome bad blood between you and someone who has left your life. It is also useful for addressing a relationship which is drifting apart

The angle between your and another's moon shows where you have similar emotional triggers and similar emotional dispositions. This pair is a good indicator of where the two of you are most likely to feed off of each other's response to things, fostering a meeting of the minds. Septiles are noteworthy for making conversations more emotional such that you and the other are either more likely to imagine together or more likely to fight each other. Octiles remain very aware of how much power they are giving up to others, making the relationship into something of a chess game. II-quintile's and II-novile's chemistry or lack thereof can make a whole room uncomfortable, though with II-quintiles the chemistry is more between each other and with II-noviles it is more away from each other towards a common issue. II-deciles seem to be really into each other's company when viewed by a third party. III-squares are more likely to share a moral crusade.

Perhaps even more importantly, your Moon to their Moon shows the clearest subconscious reason for you and the Other interacting in the first place. Conjuncts come together for the purpose of expressing their instincts. Oppositions come to build value or make money. Trines seek communication of their internal ideas. And so on. Whether or not the relationship remains strong, [Moon-Moon] is almost always "on"

as an issue even in your thoughts about the other person (turning "off" only as your memory of them fades). Despite what your relationship may look like with Other on the surface—whether personal or professional, cordial or adversarial—it is this pair which tells you what you're subtly trying to play out through them. This is especially important to note when you feel hostility towards someone who has long left your life. If you still have bad blood towards another in this way it's often because there is some side of yours and their [Moon-Moon] angle which they exposed within you and which you have yet to resolve. Accordingly, use *table 19-2* below to ask yourself the following: *"Did I show [angle topic] well enough?"* For conjuncts, ask if you were forward, creative, or spontaneous enough. For sextiles, were you useful? For inconjuncts, did your intentions match theirs well enough? With II-trines, were you a strong enough influencer? With II-septiles, take a look at the extent to which you represented yours and their shared groups well enough. II-undeciles ask whether you were interesting or unique enough. I've summarized the different intended characteristics of the angles in *table 19-2* below.

Table 19-2: Common characteristics associated with each harmonic

Harmonic	Name	Characteristic
1	conjunct	instinctive expression
2	opposition	show of worth or value
3	trine	communication of internal thoughts
4	square	emotional power or intuition
5	quintile	popularity or direct interaction
6	sextile	usefulness
7	septile	sociability
8	octile	power (over the other)
9	novile	image importance or learning
10	decile	authority or control
11	undecile	social popularity or intellectualism
12	inconjunct	mood appropriate for situation
13	II-conjunct	power of a public persona
14	II-opposition	significance of physical presence
15	II-trine	influence over surroundings
16	II-square	earned respect, family or core values
17	II-quintile	ingroup dominance
18	II-sextile	rationality or ingroup sense-making
19	II-septile	ingroup representativeness
20	II-octile	power (over third parties)
21	II-novile	creativity or attitude projection
22	II-decile	command over a realm of behavior
23	II-undecile	individuality or uniqueness
24	II-inconjunct	influence over other's attitudes
25	III-conjunct	social belonging
26	III-opposition	being in demand, in trend, or being group-relevant
27	III-trine	insight, sought after communication
28	III-square	emotional relevance, sought after standards for caretaking for others
29	III-quintile	ability to be followed by groups
30	III-sextile	ability to make others want to connect with you, desirability
31	III-septile	influential communication
32	III-octile	power to unsettle audiences
33	III-novile	group leadership, ability to inspire
34	III-decile	"boss-ness" over others
35	III-undecile	interestingness
36	III-inconjunct	memorableness

Table 19-2: Common harmonic attitudes. Even though we've introduced this table, you should still defer to *table 19-1* for most pair interpretations unless a particular explanation says you should do otherwise.

Finally, the [Moon-Moon] pair is also useful for repairing a relationship before it drifts apart. Especially in cases where you feel that a relationship is not as strong as it once was, this pair's angle often reveals that your reasons for coming together with a partner were quite different from how the two of you currently behave *during* a relationship. If you want to hold onto the exchange, check to see if you're still providing this angle. Not just providing it, but providing it in a way that matches their wants.

Moon-Mercury

You to them

You believe the other person is focused on achieving this angle in their interactions. **You see the angle as Other's desired goal amongst third parties, and may**

pigeonhole them in negative cases. *Table 19-2* is good for reading this one.

Them to you

You feel your angle is subject to scrutiny by the other person. Oddly, this pair is related to distrust more than it is related to basic analysis. In positive cases you simply find that the other person is more sensitive to your behaviors under this angle. In negative cases, though, it is as if your giving this angle to them is never enough to turn their lens off of you.

If you're using this angle to try to teach this person or satisfy them, good luck. You might fare better under your [Sun $_{you}$-Vesta $_{them}$] angle instead.

Self chart

You see this angle as constituting your own desired goal and scrutinize your display of this angle as you pursue that goal. This angle's characteristic is subject to your default **analytical nature**.

Moon-Mercury and the synastric dream trio

🛠 In a much rarer but more interesting application of this Moon-Mercury, we find that this pair is part of what we'll call the "**synastric dream trio**." **[Moon $_A$-Mercury $_B$], [Moon $_B$-Selene $_A$], and [Mercury $_B$-Selene $_A$]** all combine to show where person B dreams of using person A to fulfill A's ends. When this cocktail consists of major harmonics or those harmonics which are simple for person B to play out, there is a strong tendency for Selene $_A$ person to appear in the Moon $_B$ person's dreams with the [Moon $_B$-Selene $_A$] angle as their objective, playing this out through the [Mercury $_A$-Selene $_B$] angle's behavior. Meanwhile, the Moon $_B$ person can use the [Moon $_A$-Mercury $_B$] angle to access and steer the Mercury $_B$ person's [Moon $_A$-Selene $_B$] angle. This whole thing is strongly connected to how dream symbolism works and will be explained later on. For now just note that you can use [Moon $_{you}$-Mercury $_{them}$] to influence the other's [Moon $_{them}$-Selene $_{you}$] angle. 🛠

Moon-Venus

👁 They're paying attention to you, but what do they want from you?

You to them

You are flattered by or attended to by Other under your display of this angle. Following predictably from the Moon and Venus' regular meaning, this angle promotes Other's willing association with you in line with your wants. Of course, if your wants are no good or if they don't align with Other's wants, their interaction with you is more inclined to go badly. Is there any way we can know what the other person actually wants you to give when you use this angle? Not really. 👁 But using some tricks with the data I concluded that [Sun $_{them}$-Venus $_{you}$] is a good place to start.

Them to you

You like to socialize with Other (or anyone for that matter) over Other's display of this angle, bringing it out in the open as a cool topic. They stand out to you here $_{fbow}$.

Self chart

You flatter and pay attention to yourself; you are comfortable with this side of yourself as a conversation or 1:1 feedback topic even if you don't actually like this side of yourself. Anyway, it's something to discuss isn't it? This angle's behavior is where you show an **affinity for interaction with others**.

Moon-Mars

You to them

You can use your angle to compel the other person's action. By feeling your angle's characteristic or thinking about the angle as a means of interacting with the other, you can influence them. You might say that this angle shows a kind of "spiritual category" which describes your exchanges with the other—the kind of energy you need to spend in order to keep the other person aligned with your goals. To the extent that such spending doesn't drain you, keeping up your association with them should be easy. There is some indication that this angle is tied to your level of inwardness or outgoingness in that you may have a harder or easier time (respectively) keeping up close relationships whose angles require a third party group (septiles, undeciles, II-quintiles, III-conjuncts, III-oppositions, III-quintiles, III-septiles, and III-noviles).

Them to you

You can be easily compelled to act through the other person's use of this angle. The other person, though typically confident in this angle, is more inclined to check their performance against your judgment; that is, if they don't feel they can move you with this angle, they may feel that something is wrong.

Self chart

Where another person's action is aimed at a task beyond you both, [Moon-Mars] reaches beyond you yourself even when *you* are the other person. In the self chart, you easily compel your own actions through this pair's angle, showing where you are most driven to have your influence match your inclinations. This is the **promotion of your intent**.

Moon-Jupiter

You to them

You encourage Other to broadcast this angle in the world or—in cases where this angle is broken in them—to build it up in themselves broadly. In negative cases you feel as though Other overlooks this angle in their doings. This angle amounts to a characteristic which you fertilize within the other. Both *tables 19-1* and *19-2* can be used to read this one.

Them to you

Your inclinations to make an image for yourself in the world are built up by the other's disposition under this angle. **Where Other wants to display this angle, this is how Other's attitude motivates you to go forth in the world**. In a positive relationship, you advance on behalf of Other's wishes in this area. This is a great pair for showing your behavior as a friend to or defender of the other, since you not only act on their wants, but act upon the whole world in the process. III-inconjuncts are especially good for your performing memorable acts on the other's behalf.

You can encourage your enemies to advertise for you by ensuring that, in your basic interactions with them, your display of this angle under the [You to them] version of this pair is always positive or neutral. Even among people who hate you with a passion, there exists a primary area of beef with you which they are inclined to air to others. You have partial say in what that beef looks like (since you usually have partial say in what caused them to hate you in the first place); given that you get the opportunity to interact with them directly, you can water down their attacks by watering down the angle that serves as the attack's fuel source.

Self chart

You encourage yourself to broadcast a particular angle outwards, and motivate yourself to keep doing so. This is a situation in which you are more enthusiastic regarding public action upon your private intents, creating a high-enthusiasm environment; **outgoingness**.

Moon-Saturn

You to them

You leave the impression upon Other that you wish to impose your angle on them. Read this as, "They think I want to impose my [*table 19-2* characteristic] on them." Indeed, you break into Other's emotional house with this angle and really will use it as a tool to control them if that is the nature of the relationship. In positive cases, though, you provide a stable, disciplined foundation for them through this angle. IV-undeciles believe you are trying to impose the importance of your outlook in the world upon them—that your own perspective is a really big deal.

Them to you

You feel restricted by the other person's desire to express their angle. This pair is associated with the way Other overpowers you, and you tend to remain fixated on this method of restriction. Some negative characteristics associated with each behavior are listed in *table 19-3* below. Refer to *table 19-2* for the more positive cases.

Self chart

You restrict your display of intent, but stabilize its display as well under this angle. Not nearly as oppressive to you as it is to others, this is **calculated emotionality**.

Table 19-3: Negative characteristics associated with each harmonic

Harmonic	Name	Negative Characteristic
1	conjunct	impulsivity, thoughtlessness
2	opposition	laziness, resting on worth
3	trine	being overly opinionated
4	square	uncooperativeness
5	quintile	arrogance (over individuals)
6	sextile	nitpicking
7	septile	argumentativeness
8	octile	lust, power hunger
9	novile	aimlessness
10	decile	oppressive conduct
11	undecile	incoherence, scattered demands
12	inconjunct	secret dark side, untrustworthiness
13	II-conjunct	image without substance
14	II-opposition	unproductive hedonism
15	II-trine	high and mighty-ness (arrogance over a whole room)
16	II-square	standing on a soapbox, excessive judgment of others
17	II-quintile	inflating one's own leadership role
18	II-sextile	entrenched personal views, immovability
19	II-septile	overpromotion of attractiveness or desirability among group
20	II-octile	selling oneself as an object
21	II-novile	bad attitude
22	II-decile	running over others, disrespect, coldness
23	II-undecile	inability to be satisfied, irritability, disruptiveness
24	II-inconjunct	conspiracy, secret motives
25	III-conjunct	leaning on others' agenda or approval
26	III-opposition	compromising principles for fans, selling out
27	III-trine	escapism
28	III-square	moral dependency, holding too tightly to rules
29	III-quintile	inconsiderateness of peers and followers, being cutthroat
30	III-sextile	being a know-it-all
31	III-septile	attacking others' views with the backing of a group, but still being wrong, mob leading
32	III-octile	advertising one's power or allure, manipulating others' weaknesses
33	III-novile	distancing from followers
34	III-decile	being above others, ivory tower-ing
35	III-undecile	unpredictability, erratic highs and lows
36	III-inconjunct	trading practicality for the comfort of illusions

Table 19-3: Negative harmonic characteristics. As before, you should continue to reference *table 19-1* for most pair interpretations unless a particular explanation says you should do otherwise.

Moon-Uranus

You to them

You see Other as a hub around which your social groups might gather when they display this angle. This one is a bit tricky in that your Uranus "social groups" are not your cliques and peers (that's Bacchus' realm). Instead, social groups are the people you regularly find yourself working or communicating around in a typically non-intimate way. So people with oppositions under this pair may take center stage not because your peers would like them, but because your more impersonal social sphere finds their sense of self-worth fascinating. Trines captivate your groups with their communication of ideas and are often, relatedly, provocative as a rule. Squares exercise a subtle emotional influence over everyone and can derail a task quickly with their interjection. **And so it is, this angle shows where the Other is most effective at distracting your shared groups and getting them off track.** Use *table 19-2* to read this one. As with several astrological pairs related to the impressions we leave on packs of strangers, this pair very lightly influences the physical appearance of certain kinds of personalities in your social groups, adding a small hint of the *table 19-4* traits to their look.

Them to you

You believe Other possesses popularity potential under their expression of this angle. You're more likely to brag to others about this angle characteristic of theirs. Or complain loudly in negative cases.

Self chart

You believe you have the potential to be popular under this angle and may even brag about yourself accordingly. Using this feature as a tool for distracting your own groups, you jump off task to interface with the whole. This is a **comfortable, popular trait of yours**. Your looks partly reflect this.

Table 19-4: Contributions to physical appearance for each harmonic

Harmonic	Name	Hinted Physical Trait
1	conjunct	(not enough data)
2	opposition	embattled look, tired fighter
3	trine	smug friendliness
4	square	defiant demeanor, harder to convince
5	quintile	tirelessness, skeptical with stamina
6	sextile	(not enough data)
7	septile	sexual desirability
8	octile	the look of one who analyses
9	novile	rebelliousness
10	decile	(not enough data)
11	undecile	big body form or potent communicative style
12	inconjunct	look of one who is observant
13	II-conjunct	one who knows themselves and what fits them
14	II-opposition	bottled emotional or creative world
15	II-trine	slyness
16	II-square	look of one easy to anger
17	II-quintile	demanding look
18	II-sextile	approachable, but goal oriented
19	II-septile	look one of who is serious, but unsure of surroundings
20	II-octile	disheveled, bohemian class (look or dress) if not disheveled
21	II-novile	sweet, but demanding of self
22	II-decile	smaller build or high nervous energy
23	II-undecile	driven to have own way
24	II-inconjunct	spacey manner or escapist appearance
25	III-conjunct	secretly lusty (seen through behavior)
26	III-opposition	spotlight-seeking (behavior)
27	III-trine	(not enough data)
28	III-square	(not enough data)
29	III-quintile	charismatic
30	III-sextile	childish or childlike (seen through behavior or voice)
31	III-septile	body-sensual
32	III-octile	easily discontented, need for proof
33	III-novile	celebrated or popular
34	III-decile	pleasantly inconvincible
35	III-undecile	difficult, but cooperative
36	III-inconjunct	easy confidence
47*	IV-undecile	resistant to attachment

Table 19-3: Harmonic contributions to physical appearance or personality. Note that these traits do not describe the person's overall look, only an additional trait that occurred in the average Other with this [Moon $_{you}$-Uranus $_{them}$] angle. *Although I don't typically list level IV properties (which are officially uninterpreted in this book), this pair had 6 out of 430 with IV-undeciles, revealing a discernible pattern.

Moon-Neptune

You to them

You tend to make more errors in your dealings with Other under this angle and may be, accordingly, more self-conscious or more defensive here. Why? Because your intent [Moon $_{you}$] echoes all over their mood [Neptune $_{them}$]. This is definitely a "mic check" on your part—where every little breath, every squeal of feedback turns into something that the Other can potentially jump on. Although this pair isn't as potent as [Sun-Vesta] in permanently changing the other person, it is more potent than [Sun-Vesta] in getting them to react to you. This angle tells you how little things you do turn into big things in the other person's eyes, and is (perhaps ironically) one of the better indicators for how sustainable this side of your interaction is in the long run.

While [Moon-Neptune] won't really make or break a relationship on its own, it will fill in the blanks regarding that side of the other which excites you or annoys you most—a classic example of the kind of characteristic which you have that starts out fun in a lot of cases but ends up annoying to them in the long run. Yes, this applies even to your self chart. **They can read your intentions to express this angle *very* well**, where a negative reading can facilitate your parting company.

Them to you

You give the impression of scrutiny or a failure of standards by the Other under your judgment of this angle. This is not distrust, but more like your lack of faith in them. That's in negative cases—which are more common than positive cases. Because your whole mood is affected by what Other is trying to do here, you are a much clearer reflection to them when it comes to gauging their own level of success in achieving the angle's goal. Seeing such a goal more clearly, you are more likely to be less confident in Other, believing that their behavior is partly contrived or that they are covering up a point of insecurity. In the much rarer positive cases, you can project their wishes for this angle onto the larger world, compensating for acts they can't perform as strongly on their own.

Self chart

The scrutiny condition applies much less strongly here. Instead, you are simply aware of your effects on a room under this angle. You are able to take a small intent and make people in your surroundings feel it. When sending your mood outward, this is **environmental projection**. When taking in the mood of your surroundings, this is **environmental intuition**.

Moon-Pluto

👁 How do their friends talk about you?

You to them

Other is your publicist for the rumor mill when it comes to your expression of this angle. Now this so-called rumor mill consists of more than people who yack. These are groups who place expectations on you, who make assumptions, and who often question your abilities. Don't count on Other to defend you here. They're just your publicist. Still the content of their publicity says a lot about what their peers find most contentious about you, and can give you a decent idea of what those groups-once-removed from you find most important about your presence in Other's life. Look for other planet pairs with this same angle in both your self chart and your synastry chart with Other to get a better idea of what those friends are saying.

👁 The dwarf planet Pluto is synonymous with social pressure. Often when we imagine the concept of social pressure, we think of some grand, immovable force which houses us and our entire sphere of action. But a look at this planet in the synastry chart reveals a much simpler—and arguably more manageable—way of framing "social pressure:" It is *the expectation your peers' peers*. While it is true that these once-removed groups of expectations are rarely immediately accessible to the average person, we can note that they are accessible enough to navigate without your being overwhelmed. When under pressure, think of the pressure as coming not from some big, faceless abstraction called society, but from groups of people associated with the groups of people with whom you identify. See that they are just people too, except made more stubborn through the glue of collective agreement. Such groups may be difficult to satisfy in terms of standards, but not impossible.

Them to you

You promote Other's angle as being powerful in the world, negatively or positively with equal likelihood. You think others should see this characteristic of Other as standing out. Call this a letter of recommendation. If this angle isn't part of your letter of recommendation, chances are it's a source of disappointment to you. When both parents' versions of this pair have the same aspects to their child, not only does is suggest that the parents are around the same age, it also suggests a strongly trained social trait in the child.

Self chart
Your inner intents are tied to the expectations for your action held by groups beyond your groups. You **make powerful impressions stemming from your wants** for this angle as well as **receive powerful pressure to perform**.

Moon-Ascendant

You to them
You are inclined to feel comfortable going to Other with your angle. With this comes a warning you might find valuable: if Other doesn't really seem receptive, that's a clue that you may be *assaulting* them instead. This angle facilitates your self-delusion using your impressions of what the other person likes about you as well as your getting on their nerves or unsettling them. This is also a good early-rapport measure; is your game working as you think it should? Do they ever come *to you* for this angle?

Them to you
You are receptive to Other's angle as spontaneously expressed. In negative cases, Other frequently assaults you spontaneously through their expression of this angle. This half-pair is much easier for you to observe than its partner half-pair. In three deviations from the usual table behavior, II-sextiles often do this through a surprisingly insulting brand of rationality; III-conjuncts assault you by suddenly asserting how popular they are and becoming inaccessible to (or seemingly uninterested in) tiny little you; III-noviles do this by forcing high-energy environments upon you.

Self chart
When expressing this angle, you make a powerful emotional impression on yourself. This is an approach to new things which registers more strongly within you than other approaches. **Outlook contentment**.

Moon-Midheaven

You to them
You use your angle as a vehicle for effective identity creation in Other's world, sometimes even at the expense of the other person themselves. Much of the potentially destructive effect of this pair depends on your manners, expectations, and standards of exchange. The other person can offset your poor standards by being indifferent towards your efforts.

Them to you
You see the other person as self-promoting and reputation-centered under their view of this angle. Maybe Other actually has a reputation worth focusing on, but most of the time this is a "so what" thing. You may see the other person as stepping on people in a quest to promote their form of this angle. If not stomping on others intentionally, they may actually be superior to third parties under this angle. This pair contributes to those characteristics under which you view Other as self-centered.

Self chart
In the self chart this pair denotes a will towards reputation among the public. **Its angle shows which among your characteristics is the focus of your desire for such reputation**.

Moon-Vertex

You to them
You see Other as a great catalyst for major change for you here $_{\text{fbow}}$. You can use your exchange with them as a means to altering your approach to this angle. It is frequently the case, however, that such changes stem from your disappointment in them or aversion to what they experience in their own lives under this angle.

Them to you
You see yourself as a potential agent for major change in Other's life in their approach to this angle. Broadly, this half-pair reflects the role you play in Other's life. Though you may be a catalyst for change, you may not always be welcomed with

fanfare. In fewer cases than more do people greet externally imposed personal change with smiles and giggles.

Self chart

You are a means to your own change, anticipating events that could be major for you. Once the changes occur, though, this pair shows **what tools you use to respond to those changes emotionally**.

Moon-Node

This pair is among the most essential for closer friendships

You to them

You see a place for yourself in Other's life under their expression of this angle. Perhaps you are more likely to see hope for your connection with them (whatever form that connection takes), but much of this depends on the other person making room for you. The feeling is that of an intuitive sense of role you were meant to fill. Although such a feeling is no indication at all of longevity in your exchange, this angle is one of the first that you are inclined to express just before you move from acquaintanceship to friendship with this person. If you don't see such a role for yourself in their lives, there is a high chance you won't see friendship with them either.

Them to you

In their view, to connect or not connect eye to eye under their understanding of your angle is central to the relationship's survival in the early phases. If they cannot understand or accept you under your expression of this angle, the exchange has a high chance of failure given their decision. This half-pair is one of the most important indicators of the potential for a long-lived friendship in the synastry chart. While its absence won't kill a relationship, such absence can kill or prevent their *friendship* with you.

Self chart

You require successful expression of this angle in order to accept the life you've built for yourself—**in order to feel that you are meeting your sense of purpose**. A simple but tough concept.

Moon-Selene

Need to impress someone from afar? Use this angle. Also, this is an unlimited potential in the self chart

You to them

You feel celebrated by Other for your display of this angle, though Other is less likely to celebrate overtly. **You can typically use this angle to make Other happy**. If you feel your relationship going down the drain (and if circumstances permit), try using this angle to rescue it. Even in negative relationships, the other person often welcomes this side of you. Regular oppositions benefit from your display of worth, wealth, or body sensuality. III-inconjuncts are uplifted when you show that you remember the little details they have presented to you and take an interest in their views accordingly. Use this angle's behavior from afar when you need to impress someone who won't let you into their lives.

This pair should be voted "most likely to be in unlimited demand," as many cases in the data showed it to be the trait which the Other person never got tired of receiving from you. Oppositions were more likely to value discussions of worth and money, self-value, or—in escalated cases—time-consuming (versus tension-releasing or emotion-consuming) sex and intimacy. Septiles could converse with you for hours. II-oppositions could feed off of your physical company. III-conjuncts need to see your activities performed in concert with a group.

Them to you

You are more likely to summarize the best and most salient part of your interaction with Other as being your experience with Other's display of this angle. Your communication with them is especially potent if you have a trine.

This whole pair ([Moon-Selene] both ways) is part of the synastric dream trio, where the Moon person is more likely to see the Selene person in dreams when the Moon person goes to sleep preoccupied with issues related to this angle.

Self chart

Using this pair's angle to make yourself happy and confirm your own best mode of treating yourself, you highlight where your doings hit their emotional mark. These are cases of **good decisions based on your feeling** or **feeling good about the choices you've made** under this angle. This angle is one you have a talent for spreading or acquiring without limit.

Moon-Lilith

You to them

You can draw out the other person's excitement by sharing this angle with them. You can also intimidate them by doing so.

Them to you

You see yourself as a non-conformist—a badass if you will—by interacting jointly with the other person under this angle. No joke. Express this angle alongside the other person if you want to feel mightier than Hercules. This pair is great for business partners or people looking to form a power duo. As you might expect, the effect is even stronger when the both half-pairs have the same angle.

Self chart

[Moon-Lilith] in your own chart shows your **tendency to defiance mainly** because you feel strong under its angle but also because such strength excites you. The reasons for your non-conformity are almost unimportant, as long as you get to break rules in this angle's realm somehow.

Moon-Fortune

You to them

You reduce the need for Other to be insecure under their experience of this angle. Actually, you build up the other person under this angle. For better or worse. In negative cases, Other's skill buildup with this angle may be conducted as a means of oppressing you.

III-conjuncts give the Other a safe place to belong to. III-septiles acknowledge and provide a louder voice for Other's messages.

Them to you

You are at home with Other's expression of this angle, accepting it as a comfortable fact $_{\text{fbow}}$. Although the other person may not always show you behaviors that you want to see, they will typically show you *something* related to this angle as part of their normal course of business with you.

Self chart

You are emotionally comfortable under the angle in question, where the tendency to assess the deeds performed while in your element constitutes **self-reflection**. Assessing them in the middle of your favored context shows **where you are in your expressive zone** attention-wise.

Moon-Ceres

You to them

You are motivated to persuade or show dominance when the other person pays attention to this angle of yours.

This half-pair is truly a mixed bag, with certain people compelling your desire to be stronger and others making you very angry. Should you lose your temper with the other, this angle is one of the main tools you use to unleash it. Here, several angles deviate from the expected *table 19-1* behavior. Sextiles become the victims of your skill in manipulating events. II-oppositions will find themselves unable to escape your rotten mood. You'll simply pack your bags under a II-quintile, since Other is the one who typically oppresses you under this half-pair. You'll dissect the shortcomings of III-trines until there is nothing left. You will leave III-quintiles to go hang out with their supporters instead. You'll deem the talents of the III-septile non-unique. You'll block the world expression of IV-conjuncts and broadcast the crimes of the IV-undecile everywhere you go. Lastly, there is the II-square. This angle is not only the one which brings the most closeness when it comes to your need to cooperate with them, it is also the angle most likely to facilitate a deep frustration turned raw rage towards the other during conflict. This is the kind of anger you show towards an equal who is more resistant to your normal level of discontent, but whose side you can't easily leave.

Them to you

You find the other person heavily persuasive under their angle. In romance, all of the angles can come across as sexy, but II-squares relate well as family. Conjuncts, octiles, and II-quintiles tend to be sexy in the normal sense while II-oppositions have a more primal magnetism. III-septiles are attractive as a function of how popular others find them. III-noviles are sexier when they dominate.

Self chart

You find yourself persuasive under this angle in a way that creates more pleasing circumstances for you. Typically this is all about **pushing others to have fun your way**, since your having fun at their expense goes against the whole point of you attempting to create a good emotional environment for yourself in those others' company.

Moon-Chiron

You to them

You provide a therapeutic listening ear to the other person under their angle. In negative cases, though, you don't listen. You only hear. And then you judge. In this half-pair the other person's Chiron is all about airing their problems to you, though in rarer cases it could also be about them airing solutions to the kinds of problems they encounter related to this angle. Undeciles are located at the social center of people with problems. II-oppositions are often followed around by problems caused by others. II-quintiles dominate away people's problems, but create plenty of their own among the equals whom they can't dominate. The other person with this angle is more likely to engage in a long standing feud with a perceived rival for power, and tend to have a harder time coming out on top in this feud in the long run, since they essentially need the feud as part of the relationship. The data were pretty clear regarding this II-quintile: In your eyes, there is a high chance they will be forever married to a major conflict with one significant equal or another. If you plan to change this, prepare to waste a lot of time. Ultimately, the best way for them to change this is to have no equals. You see II-septiles as having major stressors in their personal lives, partly as a result of whom they've chosen to associate with. When not releasing tension through physical activity, II-octiles can be ceaselessly critical, down on themselves or the world. The pattern continues in line with *table 19-1*. Accordingly, **this half-pair also shows you how the other handles conflict** (using the angle topic).

Them to you

You are "healed" by Other as you express this angle. If not healed, you at least see them as an outlet for airing issues related to this angle.

Self chart

You heal yourself and pay more attention to the issues you face. This is the angle through which you **train yourself against your insecurity**.

Moon-Vesta

You to them

You are more likely to hide your angle (maybe unknowingly) from Other. If you're not hiding it, you tend to show great endurance, where you and Other together can dedicate full attention to doing what this angle relates to. You are unusually uncomfortable with the default actions of conjuncts and hide your default actions from them in turn. IV-undeciles strike you as having ideas well worthy of promotion in the world, such that you silence your own ambitions in favor of theirs. That's how this pair works; **in general it shows where you are more likely to let the other have their way while your way takes a back seat**.

It is widely acknowledged that one of the bases for a bad relationship is lack of communication. With [Moon-Vesta], one person feels while the other focuses; this combination naturally gives rise to unspoken opinions held by one person regarding the chronic deeds of another. Not surprisingly then, a really good recipe for enemies can be found where you and Other have a "personal expression angle" for one half-pair (you to them) and an "authority expression angle" for the other half-pair (them to you). Personal expression angles are those which revolve around a person's show of their private interests or ego. Although there is no hard rule for this, angles like conjuncts, trines, quintiles, septiles, II-oppositions (by accident), II-noviles, and II-undeciles are counted among the personal ones. Authority expression angles commonly include those such as octiles, undeciles, II-squares, II-deciles, III-trines, and III-quintiles. Check the other half-pair [Moon $_{them}$-Vesta $_{you}$] to see if you and the other person are naturally inclined to be at odds. As is often the case though, you can always turn contention into closeness through shared creative or physical action.

Them to you

You are fascinated by Other and want to know more about their angle. Much is hidden to you here, mainly because this is where you feel Other is focused. Given that they are focused, they are probably less likely to spend time talking to you about what they're doing (since this would take away part of their focus on the task at hand). In negative cases, Other's behavior under this angle baffles you.

Self chart

You are naturally inclined to focus on this angle's behavior without making an official decision to do so. This is **serious concentration** on what you're doing.

Moon-Pallas

You to them

Other sees you as rebellious against societal imposition under this angle. This half-pair is among the more passive ones, where the other person is more likely to serve as a witness than to be affected by you strongly here.

Them to you

You see Other as unwilling to be caged in under someone else's rule under this angle. You are more likely to see them as eccentric or extreme here.

Self chart

You are less likely to stand for being caged in under this pair's angle, **driving your own performance** instead.

Moon-Juno

✪ This is a major pair. It shows what the other person forces out of you through your association with them

You to them

You feel your display of this angle's behavior is being insisted upon by the other person. Your exchange with Other may actually force this angle out of you $_{fbow}$.

If you actually want to develop a particular characteristic in yourself but can't get the fuel to do so, try finding someone with the angle topic you want under this half-pair. Yes, you really would be using them for this, but hopefully your exchange with them has other factors to give it more substance. In times when you are challenged to display a particular angle with extra force, you will tend to attract the company of someone who has that angle under this half-pair. On the other hand, if your exchange with a person serves to build up a quality you don't feel you need, you'll likely feel uncomfortable with the impression they leave on you. This is often the case in relationships where the other person needs the exchange more than you do.

Oppositions are particularly positive for most people here because the other person is committed to building up your self-worth. This presents a strong potential for dedication on their part. Squares, meanwhile, tend to strike you as strongly desirous in some way, with wants that are hard to tame. Sextiles are better as trainers to you in basic daily procedure, and can be expected to cover essential tasks while your head is in the clouds. III-undeciles promote your individuality and continually draw out new creative ideas from you. III-inconjuncts strongly encourage you to escape the box and follow your actual ideals. As usual, all other angles bring out characteristics in you which are closely aligned with *table 19-1*. Even in the charts of enemies, this is an angle to be grateful for, since it is the thing which they make stronger within you either way.

Them to you

You commit to supporting Other's angle as a point of personal development for them. They, however, may feel that you are using them for this angle since you pay so much attention to it.

Self chart

You insist upon your own angle while the conditions of commitment loom. Whether the exchange with another actually drives you or you drive yourself under the thought of such exchanges, this angle is where you are **driven under a partnership**.

Moon-Hera

You to them

You are greeted by the other person's angle as their attempt to get closer to you. "Is he or she hitting on me?" you ask. If not via this angle, then probably not. Then again, there are lots of ways a person can seek out your company and not all of those ways are romantic. This half-pair just happens to be associated with the overt tool that others use when they believe the door to a good bond has opened for them.

Them to you

You see Other's angle as the basis for building good will between the two of you. This angle, however, tends to be weak, abstract, and hard to read since we rarely pursue bonds with others in their purest form; most of the time when we pursue bonds with others it is for 1) the pleasure they give us, 2) the security we seek, 3) the status we seek, 4) to alleviate loneliness, or any number of other reasons besides just connecting with them because it is the thing to do. Don't place too much stock in this angle.

Self chart

Although this pair doesn't do much, it does contribute to **putting you in the mood to form bonds with others.**

Moon-Eros

You to them

You see the other person as expressively hungry, lusty, or (in sexual relationships) horny under this angle. That is, they are noticeably more intent on displaying this side of themselves to you whether they be friend or foe. Two basic reasons why they would not display this include 1) that they were prohibited from doing so by circumstance and 2) that they were fairly indifferent towards you. This angle reveals to you a piece of the other person's passions. Alternatively, you may impose such passion upon them when they are not inclined to give it.

Them to you

You are driven to press full-force for Other's angle OR Other pushes their angle full-force upon you automatically. This depends on how you go about "pressing." This one is pretty straightforward and obeys the usual *table 19-1*.

Self chart

This pair's angle corresponds to the realm in which you are most **demonstrative regarding experiences you are passionate about**.

Moon-Bacchus

You to them

By default, you seem to encroach on the other's space under this angle. You like to weigh in on how and when they express it. On the one hand this can show up as caring in some cases, but on the other hand it simply comes off as where you would like to control them. This angle corresponds to the side of Other's life which you think should be discarded for a newer, better model. If the other person's standards are already up to code though, this same angle reflects where you are more than excited to have fun atop their talents and show them off to others.

Them to you

You see the other person as a dominator under this angle. Where you are busy doing normal things which your cliques would approve of, Other has "feelings" about this. (making them somewhat of a killjoy). II-septiles usually overpower you with their deeply held beliefs. III-conjuncts are more likely to gang up on you. In good relationships, though, this angle shows what tools the other uses to keep you entertained. III-quintiles are more likely to use plain old teasing. III-inconjuncts have a general way about them that often makes them funny without their trying at all.

Finally, oppositions entertain you with their bodies or pronounced sense of self-worth—an aspect which makes them provocative to you in an R-rated way; even among people who are not compatible in the usual sense, the opposition sponsors impulses which make the Bacchus person want to conquer something, somewhere.

Self chart

You are both a dominator and an encroacher under this angle, ruling the nest in things that your friends and cliques would applaud you for. This is your **pro group-controlling mood**.

Mercury pairs

Mercury, the planet of common ground, is said to correspond to Virgo. Whereas planets like the Sun, Moon, and Saturn are fairly easy to read, Mercury is fuzzier because it consists of all the things we do to see ourselves as being on the same page as the things we directly interact with. Finding the meaning in communication, taking care of our health (when compared against what a healthy person should look like), serving others, working at basic tasks (aligning ourselves with what an ordered experience should look like), and worrying that we don't line up with what we observe are all functions of Mercury. Yet most of these topics are easy to confuse with other planets' topics: Venus' communication, Sun's health and vitality, the Moon's worry, and Saturn's work influence are a few examples. Consequently, when we read Mercury in a synastry chart, we should keep in mind that this planet is less about what you say to (or do for) the other person and more about where you and the other cooperate on various issues, seeing those issues in the same way.

Mercury-Mercury

This pair shows similarity of logic. **You and the other analyze situations in similar ways under this angle, where the most noticeable side effect comes across as the ability to work together easily on a shared task**. Note that this is NOT the same as communication, so even if you work well together, a smooth [Mercury-Mercury] does not prevent you and Other from being enemies. Remember that all charts could go either way where friendliness and hostility are concerned. Yet Mercury's angle topic from the usual *table 19-1* does show where you and the other person define your situations similarly. Conjuncts are EXCELLENT at cornering a common foe, and are commonly found in strong friendships and marriages. Squares are found in people who charge each other up. Quintiles, II-sextiles, and III-conjuncts describe strongly complementary coworkers and colleagues. II-quintile exchanges often revolve around the challenge of managing the people and ideas under their charge. II-septiles are mainly really good at having fun (against the backdrop of business) in each other's company. II-trines and II-octiles make great creative projects together; as is usually the case with angles connected to creation, these angles also help intensify the sex life. III-quintiles form impressive-looking duos among groups. III-octiles are great partners in tackling challenges of unknown difficulty.

Mercury-Venus

You to them

You see Other as building common ground between you both using Other's angle as a link. Yours and their conversation has a joint [angle] effect on the room in your eyes. For example, if your Mercury is in II-opposition with their Venus, the other's patterns for hanging around people will be the topic of common ground building for you two. When the two of you converse, you will tend to attract people who want to watch you two interact. In this way, **[Mercury-Venus] tells a little bit about what your association with Other brings to you through increased conversation with them**.

In romance squares foster desire for the other, septiles foster a feeling of friendship towards the other, and octiles foster a power struggle against them (where they typically steal power from you or you willingly give it to them). Also in romance, II-conjuncts increase the other's show of attraction to you, II-oppositions increase your enjoyment of touching them, III-conjuncts increase your feeling of belonging, and III-quintiles foster common philosophies regarding life.

Them to you

Through conversation you support Other's analysis of situations related to this angle. Trines and III-trines receive insight into their own ideas while II-inconjuncts receive inspiration for their creative imaginings. Your association with II-undeciles is more likely to get you talked about.

Self chart

In your own chart, the things you voluntarily associate with are things with which you feel common ground under this angle. You don't just engage feedback-for-feedback with them for nothing. And so you give voice to the shared perspective which you think others think you have, making you more convincing and more **persuasive** in their eyes.

Mercury-Mars

This is *the* pair for determining how the Other commands you

You to them

You can easily command the other person under this angle. Sometimes this angle is good in that it shows where you actually have real influence over the other. Where the two of you need to cooperate, this angle ensures that you have a way of getting your requests heard and responded to. But if the Mars person is stubborn and doesn't like receiving commands (or grows out of allowing others to influence him), this pair can take a turn for the worst...

Them to you

...[Mercury-Mars] works naturally in the Mercury→Mars direction, where the Mercury person does the steering. **In cases where you are the Mars person and Other is the Mercury person, you are easily commanded by Other under this angle.** In negative cases though, you as the Mars person make angle choices which require the other person to search harder for common ground. When the Mars person consistently does the steering at the Mercury person's expense (Mars→Mercury), it almost always spells the death of the relationship.

We rarely think about this, but there are some interesting tactics that others can use to steer us. Some persuade us via their group backing (III-conjuncts) while others convince us through the expectations of their fans (III-oppositions). See *table 19-1* for how the other steers you.

Self chart

Driving yourself in a particular action on the basis of the common ground you perceive with some end goal, you demonstrate **resolve**.

Mercury-Jupiter

Chart collector. This is a pair whose effects can't really be appreciated until you've collected about 50 charts, since it describes groups

You to them

You contribute your angle to the buildup of Other's image.

This pair is very interesting in that it tells you what your various social groups look like. Each angle is its own type of social group for you. Unfortunately, you need a decent collection of charts in order to see this arrangement for what it is, since how you interact with each of these groups will depend heavily on the angles in your regular birth (self) chart. Perhaps you thought you only had 1-3 different kinds of groups that you hang around. Friends, work, and family? Or maybe you thought you only had one such group. But there are a lot more than this. Because we people who look at astrology are often interested in discovering more about where we fit in the world, there is often a tendency to look at our friendship space. Do we have enough quality friends? Does anyone really appreciate us? For some people, friends in the traditionally advertised sense are hard to come by, while others seem to enjoy ceaseless company. [Mercury-Jupiter], however, shows you that there is more to social belonging than people who hit the bar with you; although it's true that certain settings facilitate certain behaviors, your group identification is more about *how* you do things than what you do. *Table 19-5* below illustrates some of the groups that come with each harmonic.

Them to you

Your image is built up through a common ground association with Other under their angle. That is, how you behave in the world is partly shaped by how the other person behaves towards you under the angle in question. In positive cases, the other person simply displays the angle. In negative cases, though, the other person *denies* your angle. How they do it is actually pretty interesting, and is the subject of *table 19-6* below.

Self chart

You find common ground with yourself, building up your own image based on your comparisons to others. This is typically image building done out of a need to bridge misalignment between what you see and what you think is reasonable, thus setting the context for **compensatory image projection** (of which exaggerated criticality is one form).

Table 19-5: Types of groups associated with each harmonic

Harmonic	Name	...includes people who...
1	conjunct	help you be yourself
2	opposition	increase your sense of self-worth (they often like you a lot)
3	trine	help you air your thoughts
4	square	expose your emotions
5	quintile	draw out your ego (often demanding that you assert on them fbow)
6	sextile	share tasks well with you
7	septile	socialize or play with you
8	octile	share power with you
9	novile	project an image with you
10	decile	control others with you
11	undecile	expand your social reach
12	inconjunct	amplify your moods in response to them (often through an impressive feature of theirs)
13	II-conjunct	hone your public persona (often through a need to check them in defense of yours or their reputation)
14	II-opposition	share company with you or occupy the same space with you
15	II-trine	overpower a room with you (people get the impression it is hard to separate your interests)
16	II-square	set the standards for others' behavior with you
17	II-quintile	manage or dominate others with you
18	II-sextile	shape long range plans with you
19	II-septile	constitute your basic "friendship" circle...or maybe not. (This angle is usually VERY negative for Mer-Jup)
20	II-octile	kick competitors' butts with you
21	II-novile	create ideas with you
22	II-decile	wield authority with you
23	II-undecile	generate scandal or—more weakly—"talked about situations" with you
24	II-inconjunct	raise the need for brand new ideas in you (often through tension)
25	III-conjunct	help you run collective endeavors (often by taking attention *away* from your efforts)
26	III-opposition	create an original trend with you (which may leave you two isolated fbow)

27	III-trine	achieve insight with you
28	III-square	define a moral terrain with you
29	III-quintile	hold the spotlight alongside you or wish to take it off of you when your view disagrees with theirs
30	III-sextile	analyze others and hog the social scene with you (in a dynamic which is hard for others to ignore)
31	III-septile	exert power over networks of people with you. (you can truly own other people together with this)
32	III-octile	are charismatic and influential alongside you
33	III-novile	rally groups to break through limits with you; attract attention w/ you
34	III-decile	master a field or run a structured operation with you
35	III-undecile	form an unlikely pair with you
36	III-inconjunct	make memorable impressions w/ you
37	IV-conjunct	boldly explore new expressive terrain with you
38	IV-opposition	declare the worth of others with you

Table 19-5: Common harmonic groups.

Table 19-6: Anti-behaviors for each harmonic

Harmonic	Name	Anti-behaving people will...
1	conjunct	suppress your expression (often by over-asserting their own)
2	opposition	dismiss your worth
3	trine	ignore your ideas and communication
4	square	stir up your emotions
5	quintile	make you feel awkward instead of confident
6	sextile	redirect your task focus onto their needs
7	septile	cut off communication with you
8	octile	overpower you with their attitude
9	novile	promote themselves above you, rendering you useless
10	decile	make you feel inferior, beneath their standards
11	undecile	exclude you from their social enterprises, reaffirming your lack of fit with them
12	inconjunct	be immune to impressions you leave
13	II-conjunct	reject your perspective on an issue
14	II-opposition	deny you their company
15	II-trine	monopolize an agenda you were supposed to write
16	II-square	be weirdly personal under inappropriate circumstances
17	II-quintile	be uncooperative against your intent
18	II-sextile	make themselves stand out in ways that offend groups of people who need the sense of order that you are trying to create
19	II-septile	barge into your ingroup and set up standards of their own
20	II-octile	bring destruction or defeat upon people who are not your enemies.
21	II-novile	fail to capitalize on the creative fuel you've given them
22	II-decile	rebel against a system which you want to work
23	II-undecile	create dissonance and discontentment with you among your peers and allies
24	II-inconjunct	escape into aimlessness despite your efforts to the contrary
25	III-conjunct	deny you access to their in-crowd
26	III-opposition	steal your fans
27	III-trine	beat you intellectually or communicatively
28	III-square	refuse to accept your peace attempts
29	III-quintile	bash you among groups outside of yours (associated with lying)
30	III-sextile	actively distrust you
31	III-septile	hurt your reputation among potential network allies
32	III-octile	be a liability among others whose support you need
33	III-novile	raise hell among your peer groups
34	III-decile	be flakey in a way that restricts your ability to command
35	III-undecile	bring shocking disruption upon your environments and audiences
36	III-inconjunct	fall into damaging escapism which distracts your group
47	IV-undeciles	deliver punishing assessments (maybe about you, maybe not) which hurt your work

Table 19-6: Things people do to oppose each harmonic. Often these things are not done maliciously. Still, it should also be noted that this list serves as an excellent reference for tactics when you need to suppress a personal enemy.

Mercury-Saturn

You to them

You use your angle to control or limit Other when they get out of line. This half-pair is a pretty basic relationship killer if you need a way to put a bullet in one. Just use the angle in a way that hurts the exchange's chance of survival. The usual *table 19-1* is better for this than other tables since it builds less tension within you personally. "No remorse" is the goal. The unfortunate thing is that we often use this angle accidentally as a byproduct of our natural dynamic with another. Perhaps communication is the best way to prevent bad endings in such cases.

Them to you

You are limited, upset, or stifled by Other's analysis under this angle. This is a side of them which can be annoying or intimidating to you, causing you to limit your expression. In several interesting cases, you limit yourself under the other's (often accidental) influence. You take a stand on values which are untenable against II-squares. You make plans around II-sextiles without letting them know about it, and are disappointed when they continue doing whatever they were doing. You limit your own fan base with a negative attitude among III-oppositions. You push III-deciles away with standards for mastery that exceed their comfort level.

In good circumstances under the [Mercury-Saturn] pair—under both the [You to them] and [Them to you] half-pairs—Saturn shows up as welcome structure rather than limitation.

Self chart

Combining common ground on one side with an intent to limit the other, this pair gives rise to a **structuring mentality**.

Mercury-Uranus

You to them

You have more opportunities under this angle when associated with the other person. They may see you as unfairly overpowered here. IV-conjuncts may see you as bolder than you deserve to get away with, while IV-undeciles see you as super socially-mobile.

Them to you

You see Other as being well-liked by people and more personable under this angle. In your eyes, Other is able to quickly climb the ranks of those who value that angle.

Self chart

You are socially mobile and pretty aware of this fact under your own chart. This angle shows the area of life where **you have a talent for being right or acting rightly according to others' standards**. You can steer others' points of view here.

Mercury-Neptune

You to them

In the other person's eyes, you may be reluctant to look at issues under your version of this angle. Perhaps you lean on them to help you. **This angle corresponds to the area of life where the other person covers up issues you aren't prepared to face alone. In good cases, this turns into that area of life where you have an expert's intuition for why things do and don't work and how to address them**. The sharper you get under this angle, the easier it is for you to judge the success of the other's efforts early on.

Them to you

You see Other's angle as spacey, confusing, unfocused, or too abstract. Positively, you see them as expressing the gift of consistently correct display of this angle in your company.

Self chart

This pair's gift for right decision making amidst uncertainty can be summarized as a talent for **abstract thinking**. Whatever angle you have between Mercury and Neptune in the self chart shows where you are so skilled.

Mercury-Pluto

⌘ Every person (even an enemy) has something to teach you

You to them

⌘ You can be relied upon to provide a true assessment of Other's pressured problems under this angle $_{fbow}$. You are able to easily identify the ways in which the other person's behavior or characteristics fit in with what their circumstances require. This half-pair gets tricky though, since the ability to identify fit does not translate into the ability to give advice regarding what should be done to correct any problems you find. Characterization is the focus of this half-pair. Diagnosis is the focus of the other half-pair.

Sometimes solving the other person's problem is not an issue and instead you'll be drawn to find common ground through world-pressured behavior anyway. In platonic cases you'll be strongly driven to create new things with them or cheer them on as they do so. In exchanges which go beyond platonic, this pair can produce a more primal, unthinking sexual attraction from you towards them. This is especially true when you have conjuncts, trines, septiles, octiles, and II-undeciles. III-quintiles produce a similar attraction from them to you.

Them to you

You provide insight and additional clarity to Other's pressured angle. You are a diagnoser or advisor to the Other here, and they would do well to listen to your advice or follow your example accordingly. III-sextiles tend to like and appreciate the attention you give them. You tend to take on more of a caretaker role with III-inconjuncts.

In an ideal world in which you were the most patient, most cooperative, most receptive person you could possibly be, the [Mercury $_{you}$-Pluto $_{them}$] half-pair (not this one but the one above) would serve as one of the key areas where you would truly consider following the lead of the other person. We stubborn folks may consider such following repugnant, but all people—especially those who set themselves up as your enemy—tend to have something to show you about the effects that you leave on people like them. You don't have to like them or trust them to learn what your weaknesses are. You just need to consider what aspects of your personality they are pointing to. In good cases, such weakness vanish as your relationship with them improves, leaving you with a sharp eye for the former problem area in their view. A couple of questions arise here: First, is there a place in the chart where you can find what they would suggest for your improvement? Second, if you are too stubborn to receive such suggestions, how do you become more open? We'll answer these questions in order.

Remember the following examples because the way we approach them will come up again later when we discuss how to find answers across all three major charts.

When another person wants you to improve your general ways, they typically want to reconcile 1) something they see in you with 2) something they prefer in themselves. When your general way of responding to certain pressures is wrong in their eyes, they are interested in your planet of broad social pressure. This is Pluto. The thing they wish to reconcile for themselves depends on whether they want you to improve for your sake, for their personal benefit, or for your alignment with their general view of how the world sees things. Since the third reason is more generic, we'll assume this one. What is your "planet" of a fixed, general world view? It could be Saturn, Uranus, or the Midheaven (MC), but among these, the MC is best since it equates to an entire reputation—not just the rules or the talkers involved. So in answer to the question, what would another suggest you do to improve your ways under your [Mercury $_{you}$-Pluto $_{them}$] angle, the answer is: They would give you generic advice about how you need to line up with their notion of [Pluto $_{you}$-MC$_{them}$]. Fix this angle yourself if you and they aren't on talking terms.

And now for the second question. What if you're too stubborn to receive advice from other people? If you are just a generally stubborn person no matter what the other's identity is, then this wouldn't be a synastry issue; it would be a self-chart issue. So we'll look there. What's the problem? Probably reaching common ground. Maybe "subservience" to some other's will. Either way this is Mercury. What's the other problem? Changing common ground into something you willingly prefer to do internally. This is either your Moon (for internal inclination), your Neptune (for an instinctual mood to act), or your Ascendant (your actual natural approach to newer situations). I claim it's the Ascendant for the same reason we chose the MC in the previous example: The Moon and Neptune are narrow families of behavior while the Ascendant shows an entire approach. Accordingly, you will need to look at your own [Mercury-Ascendant] pair as one of the areas to address for overcoming a blanket refusal to listen to others. Besides this, you can also look at other Mercury pairs.

Self-chart

With a clear view of problems coupled with insight regarding how to fix them, you have an angle which describes your **pressured problem solving**.

Mercury-Ascendant

You to them

You find common ground between yourself and Other's approach to the world. **You see their angle as a central characteristic possessed by them for making a new impression on others**. This angle also contributes to sexual compatibility when they display it.

Them to you

You see Other as knowledgeable in your area of impression making in the world. **They use this angle as a means of evaluating your level of success in making such impressions**. It is often more difficult to get the other person's approval under this angle since they are effectively assessing you on behalf of the whole environment. This angle corresponds roughly to the tools they (as a kind of parent) use to discipline you (as a child).

Self chart

You evaluate your own impression making and correct your own efforts against your standards for making that impression. This is your **context for most closely following social protocol**. Outgoingness is an example of such protocol demonstrated through conversations.

Mercury-Midheaven

You to them

⌘ **You see Other as adopting the same kind of approach to their angle as you would like to apply to yours**. This pair is one of several for setting Other up as a role model to you. The downside to this is that you tend to see this angle as excessively forceful in them when they attempt to solve problems, so as a role model they may actually be more misleading than helpful in their advertisement of a particular behavioral tool.

Them to you

You are publicly associated with the other person as having common ground or friendship with them under this angle in your world. This can denote where you are considered to be in partnership with Other $_{fbow}$. Who considers the existence of such a partnership? Typically people who are close to you both. Watch it though. With this angle, partnership is often rooted more in rumor than in reality. The people who see this association between you and Other are very often (but not always) wrong.

Self chart

You are publicly associated with your own ideas for building connections here. Call this a **reputation for analysis**.

Mercury-Vertex

👁 You've broken apart. What area of your behavior do they have the hardest time forgiving?

You to them

You benefit highly from Other's role as a specialist concerning this angle, whether they are working for or against you. **It is not as easy for you to forgive slights here as it is for them to forgive you**—as they are the mechanic and you need your vehicle fixed; if they fail, you almost certainly hold it against them. Generally, this half-pair receives life change while the other gives it. In light of heartbreak or disappointment in friendship cases, you are likely to be less grateful for what you got under this angle than the other person is for what they had the chance to give. Let's look at an example of this.

Suppose [your Mercury to Other's Vertex] is II-octile and [their Mercury to your Vertex] is II-square. We'll reference the usual *table 19-1*. In the event of a rift between you, you are less likely to forgive the other's use of power on those outside of your shared group (perhaps taking focus away from you) while they are more likely to appreciate having had the chance to treat you like family. They are less likely to forgive your treatment of them as "family" and you are more likely to be grateful for having had the chance to show your power over externals. **Relatedly, the [Mercury-Vertex] pair doesn't kill relationships, but partly shows what each person dwells on in the aftermath**.

Them to you

You can change Other's life by serving as a specialist in affairs concerning this angle. This is an important aspect for forgiveness of enemies' debts in light of their charts, since it shows what you need to be grateful for having given to the exchange despite their failure in your eyes. 👁 This is also one of the areas of your behavior which the other has the hardest time forgiving. (Remember it's typically not what you did, but how you did it.) See the other half-pair for an example of this.

Self chart

This is a pretty straightforward **capacity to change your life through the finding of common ground** with situations you are in. The intellectualized version of such a finding often shows up as analysis for short.

Mercury-Node

You to them

You see Other's angle as an issue worth analyzing with them. Although the interpretation of this pair is fairly simple, don't be fooled. This is a very strong half-pair with noticeable effects on the synastry.

Them to you

You are more likely to receive important analysis from the other person when acting under your version of this angle or engaging its topic. Although it's not like they offer you advice here, it is the case that they have insight to convey regarding your concerns under this angle. Sometimes they vocalize such insight, but most of the time they simply play it out through their responses to you.

Self chart

Your analysis of this angle or analysis while displaying this angle takes on extra importance, where you seem to be better at it and more relevant in the conclusions you come to. This is **analysis as a niche**.

Mercury-Selene

What you exploit in the other person

You to them

You find this angle drawn out of you in the company of Other. You tend to be more shameless in displaying it—especially where Other dislikes (or is made tense via) this aspect of your personality. In cases where other likes this side of your personality, they may really *really* like it to the extent that they adopt a risky attraction to you in light of it. A person who falls for you on the basis of this angle can look forward to trouble for themselves. We'll find out why under the next half-pair.

Them to you

🗡 **You feel a special affinity towards the other person's angle, as you have an unlimited capacity to draw their need to solve problems.** *Unlimited* is they key word here; ask yourself what kinds of situations have you ever encountered where a person could handle an *unlimited* amount of anything. Herein lies the problem with [Mercury-Selene]. This pair—especially the [them to you] half-pair—is conducive to exploitation, where you are inclined to mine the other person for their problem solving under this angle. Here you develop a form of greed for their offerings, and tend to suffer whatever consequences are synonymous with that greed. Under most circumstances, fortunately, we develop enough of a sense of moderation towards the other such that we avoid getting drunk off of them completely, but in some rare cases we can be dangerously drawn to a person who 1) displays the angle in a way unworthy of our craving or 2) displays the angle well, but highlights within us that same angle which we are unprepared to handle. Misused, not only is the [Mercury-Selene] pair a relationship killer, it might rightly be labeled a "weapon of mass destruction:" a behavior whose misuse leads to punishment from various sources (internal, interaction-based, or societal) enforced upon either or both parties in a way that turns the relationship noticeably negative. **If Mercury solves problems and Selene expresses infinitely, [Selene $_{you}$-Mercury $_{them}$] is where you serve as an infinite source of problems for the other person to solve.**

Self chart

With a special attraction to your own limitlessness you display a need to broadcast this angle everywhere, rendering your **most talented service** to all. As discussed in *FSA*, this pair has a strong connection to exploitation through abuse and childhood trauma.

Mercury-Lilith

You to them

You think of Other as a troublemaker under their display of this angle. There's a decent chance that you like this side of them, though. Most angles under this half-pair are displayed in a way that ranges from mildly non-conformist to scandalously immoral. III-oppositions, for example, are noteworthy for having an immoral fan base. III-deciles have a controversial way of displaying their mastery. This particular half-pair is an interesting indicator of the disruptive side of Other's reputation in your world.

Them to you

You are more likely to use your angle as a forbidden tactic in the company of the other person. **Using this angle in the company of Other—whether with them or against them—is more likely to mark you as the perpetrator of seditious or scandalous activities**. The other person may like this side of you, but outsiders would frown.

Self chart

You get in touch with your rebel side and find common ground with things you were told not to do under this angle. This is **disobedience towards protocol**.

Mercury-Fortune

You to them

When you display your angle you are likely to feel scrutinized by Other mainly because you use this same angle as the basis for scrutiny when everyone else feels comfort with the topic in question. When Other says they are comfortable with that dissection process undertaken by you, you tend not to like it—as when someone says "I love it when you bash others' love of your bashing others." This is generally an uncomfortable skill that you have. You're good at it, but it comes with negative feelings whenever you use it. This half-pair is not that pronounced in your relationship, but exists nonetheless. Relatedly, this angle corresponds to **an evaluation you would rather not receive from the other**.

Them to you

You are comfortable receiving Other's tactics for bridge building under this angle, though Other is often reluctant to use such tactics. This is still related to Mercury's form of "service," so Other is less confident and more utilitarian with this angle by default. That's why Other doesn't use this angle more often.

Self chart

You have a tool at your disposal, but prefer not to use it since it's not something you beam with pride over. This is a paradoxical mixture of being in your element and being critical of events surrounding that situation. **Flowing criticality**.

Mercury-Ceres

You to them

You can use this angle to make the other person smile or use it to make the other strongly uncomfortable. What's the connection? You find common ground with their form of non-malicious coercion—either affirming that they've successfully had their way or showing them how having their way isn't what they expected it to be.

Them to you

You are amused by or in favored agreement with Other under their angle. In the charts of people with a strong [Moon-Jupiter], this can make the other person especially funny to you.

Self chart

Being in favored, amused agreement with yourself makes you more of **an endearing communicator** to others while under this angle (even if you are pushy at the same time).

Mercury-Chiron

You to them

You see the other person as having their stuff together (on the surface) under their angle. You tend to enlist their help here. With II-trines, though, you are actually pretty tough to begin with; you may need to learn diplomacy here instead.

Them to you

⌘ **Your angle appears unpolished in Other's eyes, despite your having the potential for great skill here. In cases where you meet Other's standard, you the student become the master**; then you will continue to "test" Other by calling on them to demonstrate the angle as your former teacher.

Self chart

This pair in your regular chart indicates a topic that you work at perfecting through your associations with others, thus the idea of **giving counsel** either to yourself or to them.

Mercury-Vesta

You to them

You display an ability to endure Other's angle despite being made uncomfortable by it. Actually, though, you're probably better at this angle by comparison. That's not the end of the story; see the next half-pair for more.

Them to you

You can be wrapped up for hours by Other under their display of this angle. This is either great stamina on your part or a hostage situation on Other's part.

[Mercury $_{you}$-Vesta $_{them}$] is a surprisingly negative half-pair when compared to the [Mercury $_{them}$-Vesta $_{you}$] version. Who knew that Other could hold you willingly hostage via the same tool that Other finds instantly unacceptable in you? Well, it probably does make sense when you think about it. If someone can keep you captive with a skill, beware an attempt to match them at this. You find common ground, but under your [Mercury $_{them}$-Vesta $_{you}$] angle the other tends to be a lot more intensely focused than you are. As a further tell, if you find something irritating in the other person it falls to YOU to replace their annoying behavior with you "correct" way for extended periods of time. Mutual aspects, however, cause a weird kind of compounding which makes for good, hypnotic tag-teaming of others.

Self chart

In your own chart, this angle denotes a place of focus, where you will concentrate for long periods in attempts to perfect something. This is **focused work effort**.

Mercury-Pallas

You to them

In Other's eyes, you do not take well to attacks on your version of this angle. This is where Other doesn't want to mess around with you. Their insult of this angle brings pronounced discord between you and them. Such is to be expected when your planet of common ground meets their planet which reminds them of justified war. It's not so much that you're easily provoked by this angle, only that they think you are because a similar insult would provoke them.

Them to you

You see Other as a rebel fighter when their version of this angle is threatened. They are more inclined to become defensive here, mainly because you are the one who frames them as having cause for defensiveness.

Self chart

Amidst analysis of a situation, you resist attacks on the things you perceive under this angle. **Defensiveness**. From there, you seek to reestablish common ground by putting the offender back in line with your views. This is your **issue confrontation context**.

Mercury-Juno

You to them

Other shares this angle with you as a means of reinforcing your commitment with them. This is the first in a long chain of very similar pairs, so it may help to delve into the nuances. **The kind of sharing in this case consists mainly of Other permitting you to have access to this angle of theirs, borrowing it (in a sense) for your own social advancement**. They don't actually display this angle towards you actively under this pair.

Them to you

You see Other as building up their angle as a means of reinforcing the impressions to which they are committed. "Look at how dedicated I am to this!" Other says to you. "Aren't I special!" This isn't necessarily for your specific approval though. It's more general. You might summarize this as **an ideal which Other comes to you to validate**.

Self chart

This pair is tricky both in self charts and in synastry, as you'll see that it looks a lot like several other commitment-related pairs. Here, though, you borrow a concept from the world in order to demonstrate your sticking with an idea you were supposed to represent. This is **[commitment object]-centered connection**.

Mercury-Hera

✪ This is a very strong pair with noticeable effects on the synastry

You to them

You feel a sense of excitement coming from Other when you display this angle. You can use this angle to motivate Other's desire to connect. Negatively, you can sow the seeds of Other's dependence and regret in light of this.

Them to you

✪ **You bond strongly with the other person under their expression of this angle**. In particular, there is a special magnetic aura that comes with II-inconjuncts. **Negatively, though, you may hate the fact that you are so strongly bonded to the other person over this—making their version of this angle into a characteristic which you kick yourself for being partly dependent on**.

[Mercury-Hera], like several other Hera aspects, is unfortunate in that its tendency to promise "forever" frequently gives way to the reality that almost all things in life are temporary. This pair is one of several which describe the best part of your relationship with another person, but which also fade as the relationship comes to a close. Barring other factors, don't count on aspects between your Mercury and their Hera to last forever, but do enjoy them while they last.

Self chart

You feel yourself bonding to another whether or not you're comfortable doing so, and attempt to understand what it is that draws you. This is your **pro-bonding context**.

Mercury-Eros

⚒ Let's look at how relationship-safe fights take place

You to them

Your angle here is a button pusher for the other person. By default this is negative unless you put in the effort to be considerate. Typically when Other thinks they are being run over by you, this will lead them to go into fight mode. Note the following, though:

Mercury-Eros is one of those classic cases where the thing that unsettles you is also the thing that drives you. There is a reason that fight and flight behaviors are connected in animals; both amount to heightened alertness and a drive to respond to threat immediately. [Mercury-Eros], at its core, provokes in the Eros person a need to get what they want right now. At the same time, the Mercury person finds common ground between their own actions and Eros' provocation. Most of the time this plays out as conflict mode in the Eros person mainly because circumstance prohibits lust mode: the other side of this. If you're familiar with the general differences between aggressive, picky chimpanzees and their lesser known, peaceful cousins the bonobo apes, you know that there is more than one way to release your aggression when somebody pushes your buttons.

And still there is more to this story...

Them to you

You see Other's display of their angle as a motivator for your passionately driven response. But this is such a mixed bag it almost confuses. The half-pair could correspond to one of several ways in which you are turned on by Other, but usually this is strongly non-sexual, uncertainty-circumscribed aggression. Isn't that what stereotypical masculine lust is? How can you tell when this pair will be positive or negative? You can't. (Thank goodness.) Babies vs teens. Single seekers vs professional colleagues. Circumstances change. This leads us to continue our story from the previous half-pair. The following explanation is pretty complicated, but serves as an example of how most disagreements actually begin in the astrological sense. I hope you find it useful.

Provocation chains in synastry

⚒ ...In synastry, certain pairs work better as causes while others work better as effects. It depends on which planet does the initiating. We saw in the case of [Mercury-Mars] for example that a Mercury initiator was natural while a Mars initiator generated fights so that, no matter how stubborn you were, it was almost always better for the Mercury person to give the commands—even if you are the Mars boss and the other is the Mercury employee. Here commands weren't actual commands, but prompts for the other person to respond to. Every synastry has both half-pairs, so that even a king can be prompted by a slave under the right [Mercury $_{slave}$-Mars $_{king}$] angle. [Mercury-Eros] works on a principle similar to this. In general, it's better that the Mercury person be the action initiator since having the Eros person play out the angle first is not only more lusty but also more bullying for the Mercury person who is subsequently forced to find common ground with that lust. And although Mercury is the button pusher here, this isn't usually because the Mercury person started the conflict, but because the following chain of provocation took place:

1. [Eros $_{you}$→Mercury $_{them}$] (hidden). Say you're the button pusher: The Mercury person. Mercury $_{you}$ is not actually where the fight begins. Instead, *Eros* $_{you}$ (unbeknownst to both people) started a conflict with the other person's Mercury, Mercury $_{them}$. Nobody realizes this, though, so it's as if it didn't happen. We'll only find this out after the two of you have started arguing out your reasons later. *For now, we only see it as an uncomfortable feeling passing between you and them.*
2. [Eros $_{them}$→Mercury $_{you}$] (hidden). In synastry, one half-pair tends to activate the other because the planets involved are on

the same "channel." So when I play a rock station you think of rock songs. When I play [Eros $_{me}$-Mercury $_{you}$], you think of [Eros $_{you}$-Mercury $_{me}$]. As the second step in the provocation chain, your Eros to their Mercury turns up their Eros to your Mercury. *This depends partly on your ability to empathize with me and vice versa*[11].

3. [Eros $_{you}$-Mercury $_{you}$] (felt by you). So now both your Mercury and your original Eros are turned up in your self chart. This depends partly on my ability to mimic what you're feeling[12].
4. [Mercury $_{you}$-Eros $_{them}$] (finally public). Now agitated, I find common ground with a source of irritation I've read in you. I push your buttons. And so the story goes. ⚒

Although we fight over lots of different things, [Mercury-Eros] is special in that it serves as one of those obvious cases in synastry where a dynamic could go either way. Even if the above section was complicated reading, it shows how arguments rarely begin with the actual provoking act. Instead, a typical [Mercury-Eros] dispute reads as follows:

> You expect something in your version of [Mercury $_{them}$-Eros $_{you}$] which, failing to attain, annoys your Eros. Through empathy with your annoyance, the other person feels something is wrong with your [Mercury $_{you}$-Eros $_{them}$]. Mimicking both their Eros and their Mercury, your urge to display your self-chart's [Mercury $_{you}$-Eros $_{you}$] is turned up, becoming the thing they will have a problem with in you as a person. (Outsiders in general also tend to have this same problem with you in this kind of dispute.) They also have a problem with your version of [Mercury $_{you}$-Eros $_{them}$] in that same situation. They react with their own [Mercury $_{them}$-Eros $_{them}$]. Then the two of you go in circles until one admits defeat or gets tired.

How do we know that fights follow this chain? We don't. Certainly not all fights are the same, but a look at the charts of people who have had publicly viewable disputes bears this pattern out pretty frequently; [Mercury-Eros] has a pretty good chance of being connected to some of the biggest fights you and another can have without tearing the relationship apart. Maybe this is because, deep down, both Mercury and Eros are about building connections whereas other planets (including the Sun and Moon) are more indifferent. Nor does Mercury have the desirable words for explaining situations the way Venus does. Instead, both Mercury and Eros rest on the common ground which exists pre-words, but remains common nonetheless. And so we fight to hold our association together rather than to destroy it, perhaps building a stronger foundation for the future.

Self chart

You've got a mind for passion and a search for common ground with someone to complement that mind. Impassioned, you display your **love locating action**—the behavior which, when projected, corresponds to the discontentment-inspired action upon which your bonds with others are solidified. Quite a weird final outcome for this pair isn't it? Think of [Mercury-Eros] as "[Solving+Passions]" or "[Passionate solving]" and it makes more sense.

Mercury-Bacchus

You to them

You see Other as using their angle to be provocative—a tactic for asserting control over potential victims of their persuasive talents. Shame on them for hitting below the belt like that.

Them to you

You see Other as a partner in room attention-gathering under their angle. This is attention as co-hosts rather than as room commanders. People are inclined to keep their eyes on the two of you under Other's angle.

A general rule follows for this and other "joint expression" pairs: The less you see these aspects, the weaker the relationship. This is ESPECIALLY TRUE when you *used* to see the effect, but it has since died.

[11] When dealing with non-living things, the phrase "reflected wave" can be substituted for "empathy."

[12] When dealing with non-living things, the phrase "transmitted wave" can be substituted for "mimicry."

Self chart

You are **inclined to partner with another for co-hosting power** over others. This is a pretty basic extension of the synastric half-pairs above.

Venus pairs

Venus represents voluntary socialization: Your inclination to communicate with others simply because you like interacting with them feedback-for-feedback. Often associated with love, this planet is actually better described as being tied to liking and enjoyment instead. Love, lust, and sensuality on the other hand are more bodily, hormonal, and feeling based than this. Venus exchanges information as its primary tool. Accordingly, Venus doesn't just show how we speak and listen for fun, it also shows how we receive information and send it out in a loop for our enjoyment—hence playing video games, listening to music, weighing two sets of meaning, and weighing impressions desired versus impressions actually left.[13] In synastry, Venus is more about how you exchange feedback-for-feedback with another person not just through words, but through all kinds of other means like power (Venus-Mars), social preferences (Venus-Uranus), and group role (Venus-Bacchus). This planet revolves around the terms of willing trade between you and another as mediated through the Venus person's methods for responding to what they receive. It takes energy to respond like this, so we'd rather not fight here. Look for Venus pairs to be more everyday-cooperative than other pairs.

Venus-Venus

The angle between yours and their Venus denotes **a similarity of socialization styles and 1:1 social preferences**. Under this angle, you and the other are more likely to be on the same page as communicators.

The standard *table 19-1* applies, though there are LOTS of standout moments among the angles. Oppositions connect more through notions of shared bodily values and the bases of self-worth. Squares are more likely to connect emotionally. (And if you've only been exposed to basic angles in astrology, dispense with the idea that squares are negative. They are only negative if you and the other aim your discontentment at *each other* rather than towards a common emotional goal. The data on this included a couple of notable enemy-pairs, but mostly very caring conversation partners.)

II-conjuncts make for oddly complementary duos. In the data, perhaps as a correlate of the whole "room-hijacking" scenario, II-trines were either strongly creative together or very strongly sexual in the impression they left on each other. II-septiles truly seem like friends in the eyes of those who watch them. II-undeciles are typically more lighthearted with each other in public.

The communication between III-oppositions, not surprisingly, attracts fans of their duo (in a phenomenon which is both weird and interesting to experience). When not under the spotlight, they tend to communicate in private in ways which are spotlight-worthy, making for an awesome movie. III-squares have a noticeable master-slave dynamic which may strike others as improperly balanced. Meanwhile, III-quintile communication appears to be the collision of strong personalities—usually into a brash, but friendly mashup. III-deciles are more likely to see one of the participants serve as a trouble maker for the other's group in one of the best examples of "good cop-bad cop" behavior among all the synastric pairs.

---

[13] If you are familiar with the orbit explanation of planet/sign meanings back in *FSA*, the full version of this same sentence reads as follows: "Accordingly, Venus doesn't just show how we speak and listen for fun, it also shows how we receive information and send it out in a loop for our enjoyment (Moon receptiveness#4 + Internal Monologue communication#3 = 7)—hence playing video games (Sun#5 + Worth bodily experience#2 = 7), listening to music (Internal Monologue#3 + Moon feeling#4 = 7), weighing two sets of meaning (fairness; Mercury#6 + it's next level(1) = 7), and weighing impressions desired versus impressions actually left (gracefulness; body Worth#2 + Sun ego#5 = 7)." If all this is new to you, don't worry about it. The details require a separate book to cover, hence its confinement to a footnote.

Venus-Mars

This is one of the strongest, most basic indicators of sexual compatibility. The angle shows you *when* the compatibility applies

You to them

You have a natural pull over Other's impulses under this angle. With II-oppositions, for example, you can pull their impulses just by being around; as long as the other person knows what you want while you're present it, they are more inclined to serve your ends.

Negatively, Other expresses their version of this angle in a way that excludes your voluntary socialization as a cause. This is a great way for Other to alienate you if they wish. You see Other as aware of what they want under this angle.

[Venus-Mars] has really interesting implications for how you attract people into your life and the role of confidence in this process. Where you are clear regarding a desire related to your angle while interacting with the other person, the attraction is amplified. You'll need to be fairly clear, though. Cryptic communication isn't what Venus is all about.

Them to you

You are compelled to action by Other's angle. 90% of the time this means you are simply motivated to steer others in light of Other's voluntary socialization, but in cases where romance is possible this is one of the strongest tells for sexual compatibility. Negatively, you feel put under heavy antagonism or apathy as Other denies good socialization.

As a rule of thumb, the Mars person is turned on by the Venus person when the relevant angle is active. As another rule of thumb, mismatched angles mean mismatched desires/timing. The usual *table 19-1* applies, but since this pair is associated with intensity, a few more detailed explanations are in order. Of course conjuncts are strong between people, but tamer than expected as they give a natural feeling to the attraction—like you and Other were somehow made for each other's company. With noviles, you are more apt to like the idea of being pushed by Other. Undeciles' broad appeal makes them even more attractive, where you see Other as a superstar.

On the more primal side, II-quintiles are very strong—adding a touch of fishbowl domination to the picture. Tell all your friends how you slayed it. II-septiles come across to you as impulsively indulgent in line with their background training. II-noviles show a socially approved attraction to you (one which others would smile upon), but require that you work hard for this—as if you are the other person's employee. II-deciles are similar but require a lot of background reconciliation of their issues (or your issues as presented by them) instead, given your attention to the Other. II-inconjuncts feel like conjuncts but work more as heavily motivating "I just love this person's awesomeness"-style social complements than 1:1 "fated connections."

III-squares form a super strong harmonic which builds attraction to the Venus person into your moral code. The fantasy life of one or both of you towards the other is more likely to be very dirty here, though the attraction to your respective personalities is not as strong as some other angles.[14] Meanwhile, III-septiles are more likely to aggravate, since their ability to compel you depends on network-style fuel—as if to say "love me because everyone else does." You tend not to like this style of turn-on as much. These are, however, among the strongest angles for plain animal sexual attraction, you to them. III-octiles attract you mainly because they're weird. III-inconjuncts are more likely to inspire you through your memorable interaction with them. You feel as though your level of game goes through the roof in their company.

Lastly, in a very unsexy deviation from all of these, you tend to respect II-sextiles' hard work. Maybe.

---

[14] Like the II-opposition on which it is based (III-square (28) = opposition (2) x II-opposition (14)), the III-square can sometimes be about bodily fulfillment; in the [Venus-Mars] pair the III-square (28) can also be read as feeling(4) x 1:1 feedback(7), producing in it a desirous interplay of communicators.

But when they don't produce work worth respecting, there is an associated tendency for *them* to dislike *you*. Quite strange indeed.

Self chart

Perhaps even more interesting than the half-pair behaviors, Venus-Mars is one of the backup indicators for how you turn *yourself* on, spurring yourself to action under your own self-dialogue. Amazing but true. That is, when you express your [Venus-Mars] angle, you feel as though you can get your desires met, attracting others to do your bidding. Here you are **socially sought after**, with an ability to compel others. I talk a lot more about this particular pair in *FSA*.

Venus-Jupiter

You to them

You feel the other person is susceptible to your bribes, flattery, or other such contributions to their angle—as if a spot on their team can be bought by your validating them here.

Them to you

You work to build up Other's image under their angle. That is, when they engage their angle, you work to help them look the part in the world. This aspect can be absolutely awful if Other has used their angle to offend you, as it causes you to "build up" their bad image by slandering their name in your description of this angle behavior. Maybe you think they deserve it though.

Self chart

This pair revolves around reputation hype. Here you communicate with others in order to advance yourself in the world, effectively schmoozing. This is **ingratiating conversation**.

Venus-Saturn

You to them

You take away Other's access to effective display of their angle, or structure that angle for them. The best angles for this pair are the ones where Other is, by default, poised to hurt themselves or the relationship. You use octiles to tame the other's fierceness. Undeciles reprogram Other's rumor mill for a kind of immunity to it. II-oppositions reduce the potency of the other's presence in shared company, and can be useful for making you look like the reasonable one. II-trines are often very negative in a relationship, robbing the other of general power to make a correct impression on the shared room; still, this is the perfect angle to have at your disposal when you want the option of embarrassing the other publicly. II-quintiles reduce Other's drive to complain. II-octiles create a mysterious affiliative bridge between you and the other, causing them to stand out as exemplary in your eyes. Perhaps their normally secret power is made public here. II-noviles are likely to disagree on central issues at one point. Highly likely. III-conjuncts render Other a silently adored associate in your eyes. III-quintile problems become exaggerated under you. III-sextiles just can't fully connect with you even though there is rapport.

Them to you

You are blocked from socializing with Other under your angle. **This is the behavior that you are not allowed to effectively perform in dealings with them. Your behavior here is either usually very weak or monopolistically intense—the latter narrowing Other's options for communicating with you**. II-inconjuncts, for example, produce Other's misunderstanding of your ways and motives. III-oppositions and III-noviles can hurt your popularity.

[Venus $_{\text{them}}$-Saturn $_{\text{you}}$] is weird, and has a restrictive mojo to it that will boggle the mind. In synastry, it is very strong. I have not found a way around it. As such we'll nickname this particular half-pair the "**Black hole**." Surprisingly, this one isn't a relationship killer, though it certainly stifles a relationship's ability to grow in most normal cases.

Self chart

One side of you communicates. The other exercises control. You are much more likely to **bind the structure of angle topics you communicate with** here.

Venus-Uranus

This is a very good angle for repairing broken exchanges.

You to them

You easily experience Other's approach as a friend under their expression of this angle, giving them a green light to at least make an attempt to connect with you. Destroyed a relationship with someone? Use this angle to pick up the pieces. If you have a II-inconjunct you may dream of the other person as a statement of where the relationship is.

When a relationship is broken, this is one of the first and most noticeable aspects of it to be withdrawn by the other.

Them to you

You see a popularly known affinity from Other to you under this angle. Whether outsiders approve of this affinity is another matter.

It should go without saying that if you reject this angle in the other, you are likely to halt their attempts to be your friend, even if this doesn't render them an enemy.

Self chart

You are open to friendship-level communication under this angle. People recognize this in you, increasing the chances of your being **popular company**.

Venus-Neptune

You to them

You don't trust the world associated with Other's angle. Even though that world is real in Other's eyes, you see this world as something else and may say so—sometimes making Other look slightly delusional, deceitful, or simply spacey. **In positive cases (which are rarer), you respect Other as displaying an ideal version of this angle.**

Them to you

You suspect Other does not have a realistic grasp of your angle OR purposely fosters an amorphous version of your angle. It's as if they think you're making parts of this angle up, or that people who join you in this angle are misguided. **In positive cases, you imagine an ideal scenario against the backdrop of this angle of theirs, and are more prone to dreaming of perfect scenarios.**

Self chart

In synastry with others, [Venus-Neptune] tends to be negative because it attempts to achieve the improbable: connecting one person's communication to the other's uncommunicated moods and imaginings. In your self chart, though, this same pair gives a feedback-for-feedback form to your own imaginings, and so **constitutes idealism as you converse with others.**

Venus-Pluto

You to them

You attain power under this angle alongside your continued dealings with Other. As a communicator, you increasingly shine $_{fbow}$ in the view of those who pressure the other to associate more strongly with this angle.

Them to you

You see Other's world as pressuring the attainment of power under their angle. **As you continue your dealings with them, they become stronger and stronger under this angle.**

Self chart

Communicating with others, you are simultaneously aware of the pressures upon you under this angle. This isn't the friendliest pair for you, but it is one that you are continually forced to grow as you become aware of more complex pressures in life. This is **pressured congeniality which reflects the area of life where you learn that you must communicate properly with others in order to thrive.**

Venus-Ascendant

You to them

You see Other as a source of inspiration for further delving into your own version of this angle. If there were one aspect for the creation of fr&s, this would be it. There is a light affinity here which makes you follow an interaction with Other by saying "that was cool, maybe I should try [that angle] too. Let's be friends on Facebook." Months later you've forgotten why you friended them. In other words, **this is the angle via which you and other can become superficial friends, given no further depth of exchange between you**.

Them to you

You see Other as having an ongoing interest in developing this angle. But such a thought is really more of a projection of your own impression of their capabilities which they don't show as readily to you—a secondary focus for their talent in your view. Although it invites some social confirmation of Other's angle by you, this half-pair is just not that strong in a world which values sociality for no particular reason. **You can create base-level rapport with Other over this angle**.

Self chart

You are communicative amidst new faces and situations under this angle, giving rise to **your pleasant social face**.

Venus-Midheaven

You to them

You use your angle as a partial means of regulating your attachment to Other. **By telling them that this angle is important to you—independent of them—and reinforcing such, you let Other know that your interaction with them isn't the only thing that matters.**

Them to you

You are likely to receive the other person's conversation regarding their priorities under their version of this angle. **Roughly this is a show of what's important to them where building something lasting in their personal world is concerned.** Certain taboo or difficult to communicate angles are less likely to tell this and more likely to show it through alternate tactics. II-oppositions show the importance of their body sense by hanging around you. II-septiles display their busy schedules preoccupied amongst friends. II-octiles regulate their interactions with a more controlled smoothness. III-sextiles analyze and critique various aspects of their lives.

Self chart

This pair represents the area of your life **where others marry your reputation to your social abilities.** That is, regardless of your job, intentional image, friends, or anything else, this is the interaction area where your sociability most strikes others.

Venus-Vertex

You to them

You use this angle to consciously shape the decisions of the other person. More than Venus-Mars' style of compelling, this half-pair is sober and focused on everyday things. It also tends to be more enduring and less whim-centered than your method of influence under the [Venus-Mars] half-pair.

Them to you

You can have your life changed through socialization with Other under their projection of this angle amidst that socialization.

Self chart

This one is pretty basic. [Venus-Vertex] in the self chart allows you to **shape your own life through your socialization with others as it focuses on this angle of yours.**

Venus-Node

You to them

Your conversation (or game playing time) with Other under your conception of this angle leads you to value your association with them even more. Not necessarily value *them* more, but the association with them as an item on your list of significant experiences.

Them to you
Conversation with you helps increase the level of sophistication with which Other displays this angle.

Self chart
In your own chart, this pair represents **the area of life where your conversations with others are particularly important.**

Venus-Selene

You to them
You admire Other as a source of decisive talent or influence over you under this angle. In negative cases, you see them as quite overrated here—full of force but more destructive of your respect than anything else.

Them to you
You receive the voluntary, drawn association with Other on the basis of your angle. **But this is a trait that you offer to share with the other which has a good chance of overwhelming them if they are less secure in it themselves (or if they simply prefer lower levels of it).**

Self chart
Through communication under this angle, you reveal your area of greatest talent. This often makes for **easy rapport**, mainly because you truly seem to be about what you say you're about, and the face you have on during this communication is a face that goes well with your words.

Venus-Lilith

You to them
You come across usually as weird, sometimes as avant garde under this angle, as you actually have conversations which revolve around your defiance of normal rules in the world.

Them to you
You see the other person as following an unusual social path under this angle. Other seems to have built up the resolve to walk a path all their own here, making them seem unique in your eyes.

Self chart
You strike yourself as straying from the normal path, and communicate with others as such. Thus you easily **provoke others through conversation** under this angle. People who see this side of you will be inclined to remember you as strange after you leave.

Venus-Fortune

👁 What does Other think you like to talk about?

You to them
You see Other's angle as the foundation upon which good conversation with them is built. **This angle is what shows Other as "being themselves" in conversation with you.** Okay so maybe this description is vague. But its effects are not. This is probably the best general summary of what your average acquaintance-level conversation with other revolves around. Take a *good* look at the 👁 [Them to you] version of this one, as it gives you a great idea of what the other person thinks you like to talk about; where some aspects are less about talking, the [Them to you] half-pair tells you how they think you like to interact with them.

Them to you
You see Other as being comfortable socializing with you under their angle. Regardless of whether the conversation goes smoothly, it tends to go fairly easily. This half-pair is often experimental, where the Venus person doesn't quite know where they're going ahead of time.

As mentioned in the previous section, **this angle can also tell you how Other thinks you like to interact with them.** Is such thinking usually correct? Not at all. Not only because there's a lot more to relationships than how you talk to each other, but also because there's a lot more to their assumptions about you that have less to do with you and more to do with them. This half-pair does reveal one thing, though: The closer Other is to you, the more likely they are to give you what they think you want. So their enabling of your version of this angle becomes their offering to you…

…Watch it though. In the event that Other finds this angle important and simultaneously offers this angle to you, only to find out that you didn't want it after all, oh how it stings! The relationship usually goes precipitously downhill from there.

Self chart
All of the complications of two-party guessing aside, this angle really is **where you are comfortable conversing with or playing alongside others**.

Venus-Ceres

You to them
You see Other as slightly too forceful when trying to persuade people under this angle. "Why do they try so hard or put in so much work to make that point?" In more positive cases you say, "It's a good thing she puts in all that force to make the point (I wouldn't)." This angle shows where you, as a result of your conversation with Other, identify them as determined or hardworking.

Them to you
You see Other as a model of strong communication under their angle. We don't think about this often, but there are differences between, say, lawyers, mothers, and kings as strong communicators. This angle shows the sense in which you see the other as strong. Conjuncts are naturally potent as communicators. Undeciles are heavily socially or intellectually savvy. II-oppositions have the look of a person you'd think twice about testing (or approaching). II-trines have the power to tear your whole room down (you included) when they want. When II-quintiles dominate, you listen. III-oppositions display a sharp insight into what makes one popular or unpopular, and can have massive fan appeal in your eyes.

Self chart
You are driven to make your point under this angle, but see yourself as working extra hard. Interestingly and paradoxically, you force your wants onto others while communicating with them and working towards your angle at the same time; this makes you look like a **servant** on the one hand, but one whom **others are less inclined to challenge** in your designated angle of expertise.

Venus-Chiron

You to them
You see yourself as a helping addition to Other's angle, though it is really your interaction with their angle which helps give you a sense of purpose. Typically Other is a lot more versed in this angle terrain than you are—a fact which may humble you once you realize this. Such a setup provides an interesting look at the other side of "therapeutic." While you thought Maria found solace in her angle, Maria thinks her inviting you to share her solace in her angle helps *you*. In the [Venus $_{you}$-Chiron $_{them}$] case, Maria is right.

Them to you
You see Other's angle as having a therapeutic effect on them. Negatively, you may see them as leaning on this angle for an escape. If your interactant is feeling down, this angle is a good way to pick them up.

Self chart
Communication with others over this angle brings you therapy. You are receptive here, so *no* you're not usually the therapist by default. You'll need to grow into that role. In the meantime, this angle is where you are **steered through conversation**.

Venus-Vesta

You to them
Your angle represents a dense source of information when you try to communicate it to Other. There is a big volume of information here which Other typically needs to pay more attention to in order to parse. Dense sharing. This is the half-pair of long explanations and complex demonstration. Beware of a tendency to sermonize the other person into a corner here. This is a side of your personality

which they may feel they just need to endure as part of the decision to interact with you. Octiles may not welcome your advances as much as you want to give them. II-squares are less interested in your morals and more interested in where you fit with their own.

Along a slightly different vein, III-deciles are more inclined to wish that rank or authority systems didn't intrude upon the exchange. III-oppositions would prefer your fans disappear.

Them to you
You pay focused attention to Other's communication under this angle. This is almost a "position of responsibility" for Other in that they have the ability to hold your time and energy in their hands. In negative cases, they pay focused attention to *you* under this angle.

Self chart
You are a **focused communicator** here. As a consequence, it is harder for you to take advice and easier for you to press stubbornly forward with whatever your original ideas were regarding this angle.

Venus-Pallas

You to them
You are reminded by Other under their angle of how much of a crusader you are. This angle of theirs inspires you to be stronger as a force for change in the sign occupied by your Pallas. You are less likely to take any mess from outsiders here.

Them to you
You see Other as a "paradigm toppler" when they communicate under this angle. This is yet another example of how we think other people are really good at doing things because we're actually helping them do those things. You provide the conveyor belt; Other does the walking; so now you think they can moonwalk. Similarly, you see war under Pallas; you see smooth communication in Other at the same time; so now you think Other can create a disruptive environment with their own deeds (but this is greatly helped by your own framing of where you are).

Self chart
You see yourself as a fighter under your communication related to this angle. This one is straightforward. When this angle is on and communication with others is a possibility, you are more **prepared for a verbal fight**.

Venus-Juno

You to them
You see Other as asserting their angle as a means of reinforcing their value (or relevance?) not just in the relationship but in general. Just to show that they matter.

Them to you
You see the time spent with the other person under your angle as an expression of your commitment to them. Really though, this looks like joint planning in your eyes. **Having discussions with Other under your angle as context seems to constitute togetherness for you**.

Self chart
You **act to keep your commitments together** under this angle, communicating about its topic. But previous data suggested that this came across as partner harassment. Why? This is one of the first pairs we've encountered that really doesn't support our findings in *FSA* (*table 16-5*). Perhaps commitment-sealing communication [in your solo chart world] takes on a negative effect by default to the extent that you do it as a way of locking in someone's otherwise uncertain level of care about you. In such a case, this pair's communication would go hand in hand with your sense that the commitment between you and them still needs to be proven. Here it would be the semi-serious "let's play attached" rather than the true commitment which most strongly colored the pair.

Venus-Hera

You to them

You stand on your angle as a way of maintaining your identity against Other's attempts to connect. The strange thing about this is that Hera is associated with bonding, so you would think that a [Venus-Hera] combination would lead to more bonding, not less. It actually *does* lead to more bonding, but for a person's own protection, they can't allow themselves to air their deep interests to just anyone. Where you have not yet proved your mettle, [Venus-Hera] shows where a person skirts the issue, withholding disclosure until trust actually applies. So you tend not to disclose this one until Other actually requests that you do so. In cases where you're really interested in connecting with Other, however, you will communicate this angle as a way of revealing the bond you wish actually existed.

Them to you

You see Other as stably attached to the protection of their angle. Other seems disinclined to drop this as an issue. Proceed lightly when engaging this angle. They can get defensive here.

Self chart

The angle between your Venus and Hera in the self chart shows the angle under which you **communicate with others in attempts to show how bonded you feel**. Communicating under this angle has the interesting side effect of actually increasing the likelihood that you will **attract someone who wants to bond with you**. The effect is pretty amazing. Really. Try it yourself to see.

Venus-Eros

You to them

In Other's eyes, your angle plays out on a higher, more intense level than most would expect. You are surprising here, often pleasantly so.

Them to you

You see Other as a territory-conquering communicator under their angle. That is, Other is driven to expand their influence.

Self chart

This one is all about intense communication. Under this angle, you exchange with others in a way that is indicative of the subjects you are passionate about. If the subject happens to involve your interlocutor themselves, this becomes your **seduction / flirt context.**

Venus-Bacchus

You to them

Your engagement with people under your angle reaffirms to Other how popularly desirable you are.

Them to you

You see Other as having a talent for commanding group action through socialization or partnership under this angle.

Self chart

This pair establishes you as a desirable communicator among cliques. Remember, Bacchus represents smaller peer groups closer to the kind that you would hang out with while Uranus is the broader, more collective behavior of groups like this. People in Bacchus groups have real faces and personalities. People in Uranus groups form a crowd with an average personality. Being socially desirable amidst Bacchus types, you are inclined to **enjoy being the center of attention**.

Mars pairs

Mars puts your relationship with others into action, playing a part in several strong pairs as the first of the planets involved in our steering others without necessarily getting their consent. In synastry, the planet of drive and willpower lives up to its reputation as a major player in various kinds of conflict.

Mars-Mars

Under this angle, you and the other display similar enervation or prompts to fight. No, you're not necessarily inclined to fight for the same thing. It's more like you'll fight in respond to the same kinds of irritation. People with Mars in oppositions, for example will both fight in response to attacks on their worth. Trines will fight in response to attacks on how they've communicated their ideas. Undeciles will be provoked by attacks on how they've set up their social worlds or attacks on their friends. III-oppositions will be prompted to fight for their fans and followers.

Quintiles can make great friends or fierce enemies.

You may also notice that the topic of the fight under your Mars angle with another is pretty contagious. So if your Mars is II-square Other's Mars, if either of you is provoked by conflict with or within your families, that person's discontent is easily passed on to the other partner. Even if the other partner doesn't share the first one's discord, they will usually see their mood drop if the connecting angle's topic is involved.

Mars-Jupiter

You to them

In Other's eyes you dedicate your efforts to making changes in general people's behavior related to this angle. This is another one of those places where they are likely to be wrong about you, but this situation reflects a broad assumption based on their view of you nonetheless.

Them to you

You see Other as determined to maintain control under this angle. **Other does things to purposely ensure that their expressive agenda prevails here, and they are slightly more forward about this even in calm times. This angle serves as an interesting filtering mechanism in that, as far as you can see, Other's life prohibits the entry of people who don't share their approach to this angle**. Compare this to the other half-pair; when the other person applies this same [them to you] angle to you, they are almost always wrong. But when you apply it to them, you're pretty accurate. Why is that? The difference between the "wrong" [you to them] half-pair and this one is that, in the [you to them] case, you think they are forming conclusions about you personally, whereas in the [them to you] version you *know* you are forming conclusions about their *surroundings*, not necessarily them.

Undeciles (11^{th}s) tend to be negative here as these people often have a kind of velvet rope which separates them from social groups you would define as normal. Relatedly, II-deciles (22^{nd}s = 11 x 2) often have temperaments which make it difficult to fully connect with them. III-conjuncts have a strangely self-protective side to what is usually an otherwise normal psychology. III-oppositions have a fan base which is not open to everyone, so that fans of these people must themselves live on the fringe in some way. III-trines are the classic case of people who are hard to convince. IV-inconjuncts have an otherworldly philosophy towards life which they will follow to the very end.

Self chart

You push your own agenda all the way through onto the world, taking care that the way you want to be seen aligns with the methods you use to control others under this angle. This is your **resolve**.

Mars-Saturn

Turning a bad habit into gold: See how this is done...

You to them

Your angle curbs the ability of the other person to master that same angle in the context of the relationship; by default, you act to suppress them here. With most angles, you have the ability to outshine the other person in the relevant topic area. This is essentially where you suppress them, though **in more teamwork-based cases, you can validate the other's reputation for this angle, presenting it as a structured description of the person** for outsiders to recognize.

On the malefics Mars and Saturn

The above kind of [Mars $_{you}$-Saturn $_{them}$] behavior is typical of both Mars and Saturn. Since these are considered the two most **negative planets in astrology** (called **malefics**), they typically show up in cases where one is forced against one's will (Mars) or being prevented from achieving their will (Saturn). In synastry involving these planets, another person places these kinds of restrictions on you and you place these restrictions upon them. There are, however, two important ways you can get around the negative effects of these planets; while Mars is typically known for filling others with discontent, the discontented one can either stay discontented or accept this as fuel—hence the association with drive, sex, and the impetus towards heightened reasoning; while Saturn is associated with limits, the limited person can either feel trapped or accept a box around their efforts. When Saturn is treated as an accepted box instead of a prison cell, the boxed person is the recipient of structure, reputation, and security instead of simple restriction—all of which still constitute limits, but whose purpose is to keep threats out rather than to let you into their negative worlds—to let negative influencers out of your life rather than to keep you in under that influence. Remember this well whenever some person or group denies you an opportunity; for every situation where you've been locked out of something, there is a situation where you are tasked to build your own approach to the denied goal.

Relationship killers, limits, and discontentment—unpleasant as they may be when we're not prepared for them—form a central part of our experience. Their main role is to provide smaller consequences for behaviors which threaten to saddle our lives with bigger long term problems. It's better to break up with this person now than to be stuck with a future enemy for the course of years. It's better to be prevented from properly communicating with a liar than to successfully put yourself under their thumb for the long term. And though we typically don't think of pain as a valuable warning against bigger breaking points or limits as valuable protection against externals we couldn't handle, these are exactly the roles that Mars and Saturn play respectively. Especially in synastry, if you are to maintain an association with people whose values are not your own, you'll need to know when certain among their values would prove irreversibly damaging to you. If you don't know how to spot such damaging areas, they will be revealed to you through...damage (obviously). That is, through pain and limits.

You turn pain and limits into something useful by recognizing them as fuel and structure respectively. Like gasoline made to burn or walls made to defend, Mars' and Saturn's qualities mainly require that you identify the external event that you're being protected against. This is another one of those cases where things are easier said than done, and it tends to take increased self-confidence on your part before you see that things will turn out fine even though someone's Mars or Saturn seems to loom. Still, through a combination of belief in yourself and appreciation for the role of these tension-inducers, you can turn a bad corner of your interaction into an area of durable strength.

Them to you

Your active influence is limited by Other's angle, where associating with them tends to force you to put structure on them in different ways. Weirdly, this looks more like you saying "they leave me no choice" and more like them saying "you're punishing me," where the final exchange seems to come across as an area where you bind their freedom. In your eyes, you only bind their freedom because something in their way of interacting with you requires that you box them in under this angle—hence you lose *active* influence and become the enforcer of necessary discipline upon them. **Positively, you can protect them from the consequences of bad decisions in this same area**. With a III-inconjunct, you may take on a kind of guardian angel quality in the other's life, showing up at times when they are most in need of the limits you provide.

Self chart

As a limiter of your own actions or enforcer of structure upon others, you bring an order upon situations related to this angle in a display of **controlled power**.

Mars-Uranus

Chart collector. This is a pair whose effects can't really be appreciated until you've collected about 50 charts, since it describes groups

You to them

You see Other's (typically negative) show of angle as a hindrance to their advancement among their own social groups. Contrapositively, **you see Other's social advancement as a positive show of this angle's topic.**

As another example of where social assumptions play out through physical characteristics in the chart, this pair affects the overall "invitingness" of the Other in your eyes by increasing the chances of certain noteworthy physical features in the other that correspond to their angle. Unfortunately, I can't provide a table for this because those features will depend partly on your personal opinion on how certain angles relate to social success. In order for you to prove to yourself that certain clusters of angles correspond to certain looks, you'll need to collect the charts of about 50 people and see how their similarities under this half-pair translate. Roughly speaking, though, each angle gives a quality to the other's look which corresponds to your view of that angle.

This angle also shows your very rough view of how you should interact with Other as fr&s—people who are not friends or acquaintances but with whom you are encouraged to build brief, generically cordial rapport. Trines serve more easily as social assets to you, though there is a 50% chance they can make bitter rivals if they dislike you. Squares make good battle buddies in advancing your wants in your 1:1 interactions. Septiles are usually really easy to build conversational rapport with. Inconjuncts are more likely to foster a complex relationship of respect and dislike between the two of you. II-conjuncts place heavy demands on your energy. Having II-oppositions at your side increases your social appeal. And in the strongest aspect of all, II-squares are most likely to be treated like family by you $_{fbow}$.

Despite difficulties, you are more inclined to actively support the expression of II-quintiles and intellectually support II-septiles. You are more likely to have an attraction to the creativity of II-noviles and, where feasible, can be especially turned on by them when they flirt with you. II-undeciles are great for quickly forming alliances on special projects. III-squares share a common style of intuition with you. III-quintiles are excellent for coming together as easy friends with no prior history—as if they are "kindred spirits" to you. III-sextiles are good partners on tasks that would otherwise be too analytically heavy for the person who originally owned the task. III-octiles are good for establishing power and influence over your surrounding group. III-inconjuncts make for memorable interactions $_{fbow}$.

Them to you

You see Other's social groups as adopting angle characteristics to constrain Other's expression. This angle also corresponds to the way Other roughly classifies you socially. Conjuncts see you as dominant and forward—which can cause problems if they see themselves as your competitor. Oppositions see you as assured of your worth. Trines see you as spontaneously expressive. Squares see you as having the same basic wants as they have. You get the idea. The usual *table 19-1* applies. Broadly, you can think of this pair as suggesting that the other person limit their framing of certain social behaviors involving you; as a consequence (much like the [Mars-Saturn] case) you yourself are typecast into a certain role to fit that frame.

Self chart

Broadly non-specific social **groups** within your influence suggest that your interaction with them is clearest under this angle. Thus **the angle topic here is the one you use best to compel them socially**. This pair has a very strong effect on those conditions under which others follow you and plays a major role in if or how you lead. Conjuncts can naturally persuade others. Most squares have a much harder time doing so without resorting to emotional ferocity, for example. Relatedly in the cases above, **synastric [Mars-Uranus] shows (again roughly) the main tool with which the Uranus person thinks the Mars person most generally leads others.**

Mars-Neptune

Angle amplifier

This pair has a noticeable effect on all resonant pairs (other pairs with the same angle)

From now on, whenever you see the alien head, you are looking at a pair that serves to add to the qualities of the angle family that describes it in your chart. This pair, [Mars-Neptune], for example, makes whatever angle you have for it stronger across the board for all pairs with that same angle.

You to them

Your power to build up your angle is highlighted by the other person. Although this doesn't necessarily increase your angle, it does increase the potential effect of your angle on others were you to use it.

Them to you

You amplify the effectiveness of Other's influence efforts under angle, intensifying their expression. This is a neat pair which adds potency to the Mars person's force $_{fbow}$, possibly up to the point that the Neptune person serves as a bad influence on Mars where Other's expression is negative.

Self chart

Your intentions for influencing another (Mars) align with your ability to read or write the emotions of your surroundings, **amplifying your power to steer groups.**

Mars-Pluto

⌘ Teach them a lesson on behalf of the world

Use your opinion to influence how they earn money steering others

Get post-death benefit out of the relationship

You to them

⌘ **You teach lessons in the cold world via your attempts to steer Other's angle.** This is one of the few areas in the chart where you can get away with hassling the other person and suffer little in the way of punishment for it. You are simply Other's teacher of the human world's wants here. By displaying your angle as you want it, you increase the pressure on Other to comply.

This pair is associated with lessons in using force to meet the world's standards and, by extension, money. Partially, you see Other as being more effective at earning money through their use of this angle to steer people (via interpersonal means). But are you right about this? Maybe.

Them to you

You experience increased pressure to perform in the realm of your angle under Other's influence. There is an element of conscious driving for you, where **you may be challenged $_{fbow}$ by their actions under this angle.** II-octiles, for example, are seductive.

This half-pair shows the actual interpersonal means by which the other person earns money if they control the expression of this angle through force. This way of earning tends to show up as more tension in them, though.

If ever you find yourself hating your interactant (that is, if you've fought, broken up, imploded and BAM! The party's over,) you can still eke out that last ounce of benefit from the relationship through this angle: Your doing more of this one on purpose accomplishes two things. First, it diverts your attention from Other by using lessons similar to those taught by Other. Secondly, it constitutes your taking active control of those lessons, speeding up the work required to move on.

Self chart
This is a very busy pair whose effects aren't noticeable until you start looking at the way you respond to pressures in the world. But once you start looking, you see that it is one of the best angles for showing how you use the steering of others or the steering of ideas to rise to the world's challenge for you to display power. In the self-chart, **the world sees this angle as the place where you are best at meeting its requirements for interpersonal power**, and whatever angle this is often corresponds to the one you use to actively make money engaging other people. ([Jupiter-Pluto] will show how you make money presenting an image).

Mars-Ascendant

You to them
You see Other as stubbornly entrenched in their version of this angle. **For you to challenge them here is to greatly increase the chances of you losing against their other priorities**.

Them to you
You appear more assertive or immovably insistent in the eyes of Other under your angle. **You are single-minded here, and don't take well to derailment**.

Self chart
Single-mindedness is the key here, where you display a more concentrated **resistance to outside assault** on this angle topic of yours.

Mars-Midheaven

Power and approach. Among other things, this is part of the group of pairs which plays a major role in the sex life

You to them
You assume default authority over this angle in your interaction with the other person. If you need control here, the relationship may break provided that you don't grant Other space to assert their own version of this angle.

In more positive cases, you can learn A LOT from the other person here, as this angle describes your most generic description of the tool they use to influence you, including (in romantic cases) how they approach you directly for sex and intimacy. In an interesting piece of psychology to accompany all of this, **the [Mars $_{you}$-MC $_{them}$] half-pair also tells you how the other wants you to validate them**. The more you affirm the effects of their version of this angle upon you, the more likely they are to desire you. Like [Moon-Selene], this is definitely one of those pairs you want in your toolset for getting a person to chase you down. On the other hand it is also possible (and maybe even easier) for you to activate this one accidentally through your chasing them down 1) using *your* angle under the [them to you] half-pair (below) along with 2) with the strong intent to work with them on a creative project. I'll give an example of this:

1. Suppose [Mars $_{you}$-MC $_{them}$] is a II-decile (for recognized authority) and [Mars $_{them}$-MC $_{you}$] is a III-conjunct (for group belonging). This suggests that in the event Other wanted to seduce you, they would be more likely to do so with a pretty no-nonsense attempt to command you. If you wanted to seduce them you would do so through a more roundabout display of how plugged in you are to the thinking of certain groups which Other happens to value.
2. We already learned in the [Mercury-Eros] section that half-pairs tend to mirror each other's level of comfort or discomfort.
3. So maybe you are super comfortable working with Other on a project which involves groups you belong to, playing out your [Mars $_{them}$-MC $_{you}$] III-conjunct.
4. If enthusiastically commanding you is not their thing but romance is, there is a fair possibility that they will become attached enough to you to come onto you strongly here instead.

The above scenario played out over and over for [Mars-Midheaven] in the dataset I used to write this book, making this pair the equivalent of [Sun-MC]'s "relationship killer" (except that [Mars-MC] is essential for continued influence rather than continued interaction).

Them to you

You see Other as interpersonally dominant under their angle. Sometimes by force, sometimes through immunity to outsiders' force, Other has the upper hand in certain power struggles involving your angle. Other can lead you here. II-undeciles, though, are often notably negative, perhaps because the idea of having another person lead you in the angle of your own individuality is a bit nonsensical; these people often won't hesitate to force you to be yourself (which sounds like a recipe for blowups doesn't it?).

Self chart

You see yourself as interpersonally forceful in how you project under this angle. As a consequence, this is an area of life where you have a reputation for sweeping across the public and forcing your will to be done. The more strongly you express this, the less others can resist your wants. In *FSA* we called this public allure, but it is probably better to call the self chart reading of this **publicly acknowledged interpersonal power**.

Mars-Vertex

Through the roof. Your power to use this angle in your own life skyrockets, making it one of the most overtly strong pairs in all of synastry

If synastry is all about interactions between people, and the highest effect a person can have on you is a life changing one, it should make sense that one of the strongest planet pairs you can possibly have in a synastry chart is that between the planet of forced will—Mars—and that of the "planet" of life change—Vertex. And thus we have an explanation for one of the great jewels buried among the 625 total combinations addressed in this book...

You to them

Your angle is infiltrated by Other's influence, such that you may be unable to proceed in the same way after dealings with them. This is a very strong half-pair in its own right, but is properly outdone by the [them to you] half-pair below.

Them to you

You can change Other's life through your approach to steering their angle. More importantly, **your power to use this angle in your own life becomes exceptionally great as long as you are deeply invested enough in influencing this person**. To unlock this angle you really need to take an interest in steering this person's will, so it actually works better in at least partly adversarial relationships than it does in completely smooth ones. Otherwise, this is an EXCELLENT pair for showing where you act as a key comrade in arms to the other person.

Sometimes, you and Other will fight for power over the expression of this angle. In these cases the victor is more often the Vertex person, since the Mars person must put in active effort in order to force the other to do something; the Vertex person only needs to realize that a change has occurred. Vertex can annul the pairing by simply seeing it as no longer useful. Accordingly, this half-pair often constitutes a tough read for the Mars person, since Vertex is supercharged for changing their own lives under this placement.

By way of a couple of positive examples of this pair, II-conjuncts in particular may show you as a kind of professional/social image counselor to Other; you steer a III-opposition person's fans, settling crowd issues on their behalf.

Self chart

Not surprisingly, you can **change your own life by overpowering others** under this angle.

Mars-Node

You to them

You see Other as receiving your forceful method of expression under your angle, viewing yourself as strong here. Negatively, Other will cut off communication in response to this.

Them to you

You seem destined to experience Other's attempts to steer you under their angle as a fundamental part of the exchange. Oppositions say "this is what I believe." Also, noviles are interesting in that they constitute a "look at me" component of the interaction. III-trines fight back with penetrating criticality. III-sextiles advise strongly. III-oppositions may be used for their fan base.

Self chart

The angle separating your Mars and Node shows the topic area where you seem destined to steer others according to your will. This is **influence as your calling**.

Perhaps you've noticed that one of the easiest ways to read your North Node in a synastry chart is to say, "Other was destined to donate [whatever planet of theirs] to my life through [whatever angle behavior applies].

Mars-Selene

You to them

You can use your angle to, in Other's eyes, actively smooth over conflicts between Other and outsiders. You are the sponsor of peace treaties here. Well, maybe not always peace treaties. Sometimes angles like octiles enable you to smash the enemy through force of will. Other will still have their conflict resolved, though.

Them to you

You see Other as exceptionally fortunate under your angle. In your eyes, Other is so lucky that they seem to be able to compel anything they want here. Regular, II-, and III-noviles overwhelmingly confer attractiveness or power.

Self chart

You have an exceptional **talent for compelling** what you want here. But that might seem obvious.

Mars-Lilith

You to them

Your will to influence people aligns with the other person's display of rebellious intensity under this angle. They are more rebellious under your maneuvering, though this typically does not come with conflict for most angles. Instead, there is a kind of naturally self-entitled defiance that comes with the other's behavior when you use this angle in their company, where you act more as a source of encouragement for this. If you do fight with the other, this half-pair is typically not the reason. [Mars-Lilith] is really just an amplifier of Other's existing intensity much like [Mars-Neptune]. Think of Other as channeling [your need to steer angle-related events] into [their own ability to launch past those events' breaking points]. So you tend to admire this side of them even if they are your enemy.

Them to you

You see the other person as being able to effectively counter your influence using this angle. In areas where you are defiant, they can use this angle to compel how you direct that defiance. **This angle of theirs draws out the rule breaker in you.**

If 1) this angle is very strong, 2) you happen to like the other person, and 3) they appear indifferent to your direct influence, you may make up for this by being strongly attracted to them, where they use their version of this angle as a vehicle for spreading their power to compel people. Roughly, this angle shows the context under which you describe the other person's sexual, creative, or attitude power.

Self chart

You bring out your own rebellion, using this angle to break taboo and intentionally steer others in the process. This is your **skill in manipulation**. There is an association with the forward side of seduction here, where your use of this angle makes it easier for you to get others to breach limits.

Sexual self-worth and self esteem

Related to the idea of forced power, there is also an association between [Mars-Lilith] and the male sexual organ as a means of actively imposing power through the use of the body. In contexts which are clearly sexual, this angle shows the realm under which the topic of the male's power tool is likely to come up. With conjuncts we have an association with his default sexual expression or appearance. With oppositions it's associated with his self-worth or pursuit of hedonism. With octiles it's associated with his influence over others. In a woman there is a rather fascinating analog to this: The female equivalent of the male organ (at least under this pair) appears to be "the capacity under which others demand that she fulfill their body-sensed need for her company." *Body-sensed* could mean anything from felt loneliness to esteem to basic lust, but the analog stands. Typically, the more others respond bodily to this angle in the woman, the more sexually or creatively turned on they are by the woman. This might also hold for men, but I didn't get enough data on this point.

There was some pretty strong data reflecting the idea that sexual self-worth had everything to do with a person's desirability in others' 1:1 company. There are obvious differences between how people *think* we are one-on-one and we *actually* are one-on-one; accordingly there are differences between how people think they'd receive our power efforts and how they actually receive them. For anyone with esteem issues tied to this topic, there are a number of astrological factors in the self chart which you can look at for addressing your own sense of efficacy as a 1:1 interactant. These include [Mars-MC] (where you're a leader), [Mars-Lilith] (how you steer others to break taboo), [Mars-Saturn] (how you restrict others), [Pluto-MC] (where you are known to meet power standards), any pairs with a regular opposition (self-worth), and any pairs with a II-opposition (values and body image in the company of others).

Since everyone differs in how they approach their self-esteem, there's not much more that this book can tell you about the astrology involved in handling body-image. It is important to note, however, that esteem issues depend just as strongly on whom you select as friends and partners as it does what you tell yourself in isolation. Check out the synastric versions of the above listed pairs to see how they impact your self-worth. Associations which diminish your worth under their chart's [Mars-Saturn] are especially more strongly inclined to diminish you sexually and creatively as well. A person whose sense of effectiveness you diminish through your own [Mars-Saturn] angle is likely to feel cut down by you whether or not you intend it. Work on building people up under this angle instead; if you can't, get ready for trouble for as long as your association with them continues. This applies whether the exchange is physical or not.

Mars-Fortune

They're not quiet because they *like* what you're doing...

You to them

Pacifying. Your active influence lowers the volume level of Other's angle. Perhaps this is because the other person is in their element amidst your steering, as if you provide a kind of assurance that things will be taken care of in this respect. At least that's what you think...

Them to you

You feel assertive intensity from Other as an interruption in your element. **The other person can use their active influence under this angle to shake you out of your comfortable space. Interruption.** Except in situations where the other person really is comfortable having your will forced upon them, this half-pair is definitely negative. As is often the case with the conflict-centered aspects of Mars, this one is better expressed on the playing field or in the bedroom rather than in every day dealings.

This is among the most divided of all the pairs we've seen thus far. Why would two people see the same situation so differently? The answer may lie in the idea that Fortune represents comfort with one's own doings while Mars represents discomfort with the other person's doings. Put them together and you get something that looks like uninvited imposition. The invader feels they are doing a good job while the invaded continues smiling at the cute futility of such efforts.

Self chart

You are **comfortable forcing your will upon others** under this angle, but what could such comfort possibly mean? It takes energy to do this, so this is often the space in which your natural tendency to conflict is high.

Mars-Ceres

✪ A quick diagnosis. Do you like associating the [Mars $_{them}$-Ceres $_{you}$] angle with their role in the partnership? Yes? Cool. No? Hmm...

(A yes answer is near synonymous with friendship. Potential and actual romances are often described by discomfort instead, since you must now accept *all* that the other's angle has to offer.)

You to them

You encourage more action under this angle from the other person. This is support tinged with your critical eye. Note the difference here between what you encourage and what the other person actually increases: that is, the angle of the opposite half-pair [them to you]. Not surprisingly, having the same angle for both of these can make for an excellent team.

Now is as good a place as any to redefine a well-known term. Let's frame **frustration** as being the **feeling of inner discord that comes with ongoing failure to achieve what you want**. When two insistent planets like Mars and Ceres combine, frustration is a common result. Now that we have defined the term, however, it is possible to find a partial remedy for this: In line with true reverse psychology, you decrease frustration by making use of the results you're given. Astrologically, this has the effect of reflecting the other person's half-pair successfully onto you; now although the premise behind this isn't that complicated (we explained it under [Mercury-Eros]), the actual execution is pretty challenging for those of us trained to win no matter what. Pushing someone's Ceres with your Mars is a tough habit to let go of, but all I can tell you is that in the data used to write this book, dropping such a push in favor of encouragement (of the Ceres person's angle) consistently produced better results while failure to do this led to the expiration of the relationship as people fell out of contact. Don't bang your head against the wall on this angle. Go with what you're given. Try it.

Them to you

✪ **You enjoy having Other's partnership associated with this angle**. Negatively, you compare your angle to Other's angle and "enjoy" association by exclusion—still defining yourself, but this time *against* Other rather than with them. This is a strong half-pair in that you can look at it and easily know whether your exchange with the Other is on the right track or in danger of failing. If you are brave enough, I recommend that you glance at this one and assess it as quickly as possible in order to get your most honest opinion of the relationship. THIS WORKS VERY WELL, and reduces the inclination to lie to yourself about where the relationship is actually going. The exception to this lies in cases where you've already settled into a stable partnership with Other; then this half-pair typically comes with mixed feelings (and that's okay).

Self chart

You bring more action out of yourself and define your ability to pressure a partner in terms of this angle. This is **how you entice a partner to do what you want**.

Mars-Chiron

🔒 Are they up to your standards here? If not, they're more likely to struggle to connect with you

You to them

🔒 **You are single-minded under this angle in the eyes of Other**. This half-pair in the data was interesting in that it was among the combinations most responsible for preventing the Chiron person from connecting with the Mars person. Except in cases where the Chiron person's [Mars $_{them}$-Chiron $_{you}$] was equally dedicated to standards of perfection under that same angle, it was as if the Mars person was typically way too serious under an angle that really should have been taken more seriously by the Chiron person. Call this one "**The Evaluator**." Barring equally high standards for this angle or equal angles for both half-pairs, this pair behavior is typically negative. It does turn positive between two people who regularly cover for each other, though.

Them to you

You see Other as a serious business communicator under the angle topic. Stern other. **Other may be difficult to reach when they're in a behavioral mode sponsored by this topic**.

Self chart

This pair shows where you concentrate on influencing others in such a way as to alleviate your own concerns regarding this angle. **You are likely to work harder to steer people and events when your sense of security in this angle of yours is lacking**.

Mars-Vesta

You to them

Often in cases where Other wants to interact with you in a particular way, you are busy with this angle. This is especially true if the other person is not equally interested in the thing you're currently doing. This is something Other likely thinks you should spend less time on. **In positive cases, however, you and other can spend a lot of time on this angle together—with you providing the action and them providing the focus on your action as your backup**.

Them to you

You see Other as pursuing a one-track path of action under this angle. This isn't focus, but is slightly negative to the extent that this single track is often a means to exclude Other from realizing greater potential in the relationship with you. **Unless you are helping them use this angle, Other is less likely to pay attention to you here**.

Self chart

You are **focused on the influence you wield over others**, attending carefully to your own process for doing so as it pertains to this angle.

Mars-Pallas

You to them

You tolerate Other's angle, but are more likely to distrust it as a guide for yourself. This is a case where you use Other's standards as a slightly cloudy mirror for reflecting your own. This half-pair would be adversarial except that Other's angle is almost essential for you to know your own standards better.

Them to you

You see the other person as braving the world in order to fight for their unique version of this angle. There is an association with their right to self-determine here—with a more self-focused protectiveness installed.

Self chart

This angle is substantially more difficult in the self chart than it is in the synastry chart since it corresponds to **areas where you are constantly embattled**. You tolerate your own strength but must continue to fight as though such strength is unproven. In this way, it is as if everywhere you use this angle you are challenged to fight against some eternal, internal adversary.

Mars-Juno

You to them

You use this angle to request Other's attention. Actually, if we define an **angle-sign** as being **the sign which corresponds to each angle's harmonic within a block of 12**, then the opposite angle-sign may show what you actually want as the attention-commitment basis from Other. For example, if you use trine expression (third harmonic) to get the other person's attention, trines' angle-sign would be Gemini (the third sign); you would want the other person to show you their Sagittarius side (the ninth sign; opposite the third). If you use III-decile boss behavior (tenth harmonic within level III) to get the other person's attention, III-deciles' angle-sign would be Capricorn (the tenth sign); you would want the other person to show you their Cancer side (the fourth sign; opposite the tenth). Undeciles, II-oppositions, III-septiles are very roundabout, often indicating a lack of easy interest from Other towards you in such a way as to render talking about your shared associations as the only way you can reach them.

Them to you

You see Other as using this angle to insinuate themselves into your life. This is not quite a conversation starter, but more like a "whatcha doin?" mode of reintroduction by them into your attention. Curiously innocuous, this angle represents a surprisingly cute turn in the realm of normally stubborn Mars.

What happened to all of our Mars power here? Juno shows commitment in the eyes of society. Mars shows an intent to steer another person. When you attempt to steer another person's societally sponsored notion of commitment, there's actually not much for you to grab onto since their style of commitment is up to them. Compare this to the behavior of this pair in the self chart section below.

Self chart

With Mars and Juno combined in the same person (you), the drive to influence others and the standards of commitment act together. Under commitment you become more insistent in the realm of this angle, gaining power at the partner's expense. That is, **your being committed to whatever you're committed to actually makes you more fierce in this angle's topic area.**

Mars-Hera

🗡 Here's something you didn't expect to find in astrology: the consequences of careless insensitivity

🗡 Kill off a relationship with which you've had a difficult-to-break obsession (🕊)

You to them

🗡 **Oddly enough, even though your [Mars $_{you}$-Hera $_{them}$] angle is one of the chief means of solidifying the relationship between you and Other, its careless display is a strong game ender in your relationship with them.** Hera is bonding. Mars is the need to influence others. In some way, [Mars $_{you}$-Hera $_{them}$] constitutes your need to influence how the other person bonds, while the other half-pair shows, in their eyes, your bonding with how they influence. A carelessly displayed [Mars-Hera], thanks to diminished interest in actively influencing Other's bonding, typically kills a relationship via one of the most effective methods possible: indifference. Furthermore, this is indifference of the more serious kind where, instead of simply not giving Other what they like, you may sometimes give/sometimes not give what Other likes in a pattern of behavior which statisticians would call "uncorrelated." If my super-obsessive favorite color is red and you never give me red things then that's one kind of unfavorable coincidence. But if you give me red things with about the same likelihood that you give me every other color thing then I know your attention to my red-obsession has been reduced to random chance. Then I know you either don't know or don't care about my preferences.

Them to you

You are strongly, almost irresistibly drawn to Other's angle, driven to pursue the interaction doggedly in light of it. There is a sense of recursive enjoyment here, where you get wrapped in the view of the other. This is one of the most beautiful parts of your relationship with them. Negatively, it can present one of the most inexplicably ugly or nonsensical objects for dwelling on what's wrong with the relationship...

...Want to put the nail in the coffin on a relationship gone rotten? This is one part of the cocktail for **severance**: Simply recast the beautiful as the inexplicably negative. You don't even have to get angry with yourself for thinking Other is beautiful here.

1. First, tell yourself that it is to your credit to see Other as beautiful.
2. Second, tell yourself that *logically* (in the actual world outside of your generosity with them), Other actually has an ugly attitude under this angle. This is easier to do if you yourself played the good guy in the exchange. In fact, the more of a good guy you were, the easier it will be to believe this kind of talk which implies that this particular hole in the exchange was largely the Other's fault.

Self chart

Bonded to another, you also strive to influence them. This is a **power-oriented bond**.

Mars-Eros

Another quick diagnosis: "Ping" the other person (try a little sample of this angle) to see if they would be into you

Passion inspirer

You to them

You display your angle to the other person through your directed actions. This half-pair is excellent for gauging the Mars person's ability to connect with the Eros person. If you find yourself unwilling or unable to convey your angle to Other directly, that is one indication that Other is unwilling or unable to return interest—perhaps not in you as a person, but almost certainly in your proposed basis for a bond. This is like "pinging" another computer in networking. You send a little data out and watch what comes back. Do they love you or love you not? Can you ping them successfully with this pair's angle? More negatively,

- When you think Other is deficient in the angle and yet you still won't support them with your version of this angle, it tends to show that you have given up on bonding with Other in that way. This won't ruin your exchange, though it all but guarantees that the depth of your bond will hit a definite cap.
- If they won't receive this angle from you, it's more like they're not interested.
- If you don't want to give this angle to them, it's more like you're not interested.
- If it never occurred to you to give the angle to them, it's more like you lack information about some component of the relationship where your quest for long-term bonding is concerned.

Does so much really ride on this pair like that? No. It's more like the relationship rides on the collective family of planet pairs with this same angle. That is, when you take a look at the synastry chart and gather up **every planet pair with this same angle** (the **resonant pairs**), [Mars-Eros] turns that group of pairs into the group under which you incite the passions of the other. If you have a II-conjunct (13th) and the Other rejects it, this would be like a radio that refuses to play the "persona" station. A [Mars-Eros] 13 adds the idea that the "persona" station is the only one which hosts a chance to win that vacation cruise. No ping, no match.

Use this half-pair to eliminate bad choices under the great question, "is this the one?" Most people looking for perfection will need for the answer here to NOT be "no (my Mars doesn't drive her Eros under our angle)."

Them to you

You appreciate Other's angle and find it comforting. Barring other resonant pairs, this is a surprisingly tame setup, where your driven, self-directed action combines with Other's driven, other-directed action. This half-pair creates a low-tension flow of intent from them to you. Negatively, you can't get fuel, Other can't give it, and such results appear as lapses in your connection. The Eros person typically controls the effectiveness of this pair.

Self chart

Not just passionate, you are inclined to steer others in turn. This one is fairly obvious; you play out your **yearning for love** via the angle involved. It is under this angle that you are more likely to chase the objects of your deepest desire.

Mars-Bacchus

(I thought this one was really interesting.)

You to them

Chances are that you may not know this, but **you would be an awesome co-conspirator with Other under their [Mars $_{you}$-Bacchus $_{them}$] angle**. Why might you not know this? Because Other tends to come across to you as rigidly set in their ways despite fellow group members' attempts to persuade them otherwise. Why should you agree to work with someone so stubborn? The answer is not obvious, but it does exist: Other's stubbornness is precisely that characteristic of theirs which can *survive* group influence. This is a classic example of the kind of "give and take" that people talk about in social relationships. For the benefit of the exchange on the whole, you might do well to give up some of your defensive resistance to Other's bulldozing and bulldoze along with them. They might even like it.

Them to you

Out of the serious pairs and into a fun one. **You conspire with Other to take over their group using your angle**. If they accept, you two can make a great team. This pair shows where you and they would make good partners in crime. Negatively, you become Rocky versus Apollo, Professor X versus Magneto: rivals and enemies (kind of), yet mutually qualified equals.

Self chart

Your influence, your group. This self chart pair puts you at the forefront of your peers in driving the angle area involved, thus giving you **group command**.

Jupiter pairs

Jupiter is the planet of image projection in the world. As such, it is associated with big things, expansiveness, growth and happiness. Naturally, right? Because these are all supposed to be good things, right? Added social assumptions aside though, Jupiter really just amounts to the publicizing of actions to be seen (but rarely directly experienced) by the faceless masses—hence its primary role as an image maker. In synastry, Jupiter corresponds to what the parties think things look like and, sometimes, how their respective worlds are affected by each other. As you might expect, it would be unreasonable to assume that all such effects are positive.

Jupiter-Jupiter

This angle shows where you and the other person have a similar basis for image-making in the world. Conjuncts for example have a natural tendency to action which leaves similar impressions on the public. When yours and their Jupiters are undecile you have surrounding groups who *think* you and Other's images are similar. You get the idea. For an interesting look at how you and Other go about showing the [Jupiter-Jupiter] common image, locate all of the resonant pairs in the synastry table and see what additional qualities get grouped together under this angle.

Does this pair significantly affect yours and Other's relationship? Not so much. It does, however hint at those situations in which you might most easily make a shared impression on outsiders. If you manage to collect the charts of around 50 people and note which angles they have here, you'll get an idea of which people share your same broad categories of action upon the world.

Jupiter-Saturn

This is not a relationship killer, but includes a valuable tool for the relationship killer family

You to them

You feel that a longstanding complement can be found in the other person under your angle. According to you, Other completes your partner space in the eyes of outsiders, fulfilling a void otherwise present in your world.

In the event that you need yet another tool for putting an end to that certain relationship, you can use this angle (as the Jupiter person) to find which behavior you'll need to reclaim in order to replace that person's status as your complement. Although such a concept may strike you as abstract, keep this in mind: When we relate to others, we don't just toss characteristics back and forth; instead, we actually depend on them to represent some corner of our lives. When a significant enough relationship ends, our framework for representing the other person's role is left with a hole in it which, if not filled, may keep us 1) looking backwards at their former role or 2) upset, angry, or disappointed for a longer period of time. [Jupiter-Saturn] shows part of the replacement experience you'll need to move on smoothly, and can provide a decent hint regarding the activity you'll need to perform in order to get that former person into the dustbin more quickly.

Them to you

You engage the limitations and obstacles in Other's angle and expand your own image in the process. You are known by mutual company to complement Other's expressive boundaries under this angle, breaking past those limits. This is another indicator of a good team. II-oppositions are known just for being together as physical bodies in the same area. III-oppositions can command groups together (where Other gets your backing).

Self chart

On the one hand you carve out an image in the world, on the other you establish a long-term reputation. You are what you intend to be here, properly displaying **balanced self-promotion.**

Jupiter-Uranus

You to them

You have a pronounced respect for Other under their experience of their angle, though undeciles are often negative since they tend to build that respect in Other's absence over the grapevine rather in their presence. With undeciles Other may disappear more frequently than you would prefer, making it seem like Other is withholding something from you that prevents respect for them from fully building in you.

Them to you

Association with Other's social world under your angle expands your image there. Other is good for building a name for you in your world.

Self chart

You expand your image and get talked about simultaneously. This sets up good **conditions for your extraversion** even if you aren't particularly outgoing.

Jupiter-Neptune

You to them

You experience Other's communication under your angle as spacey, fuzzy or confusing—as if they have a point to make but can't get the boundaries right. **On the other hand, Other has a power to access the abstract here, unlocking strong creative potential should you stick around to see the former through**. This angle is not so fun in the beginning, but can be great when used in conjunction with [Mars $_{you}$-Vertex $_{them}$] for nurturing the Neptune person's creativity.

Them to you

You idealize the other person under their angle. Other has a sweeping command of "how to do it right." Negatively though, you may just be disillusioned, viewing their efforts as built on self- or other- deception (mainly self-deception).

Self chart

Your image-building combines with the overall mood that you put on the room, making your **projected idealism and creativity** even stronger.

Jupiter-Pluto

Add the [You to them] half-pair to your book of bad guy tactics OR use it as the reversed version of the [Them to you] half-pair to increase your own power

You to them

You use your angle to instill the standards of world pressure into Other. You can misuse this half-pair to raise insecurity in Other regarding their success in the world.

Them to you

You see Other as possessing a level of power or sophistication beyond their peers under angle. In your eyes, their image meets the standards of the adult world. Notice how you can place yourself in the other person's shoes such that this half-pair [Them to you] would become the opposite half-pair [You to them]—rendering you powerful in their eyes under whatever angle applies under this pair. III-inconjuncts typically have a unique vibe which renders them memorable regardless of whether they really do anything significant around you.

Self chart

Your image-making aligns with the standards set by the pressuring world under this angle's topic area, rendering you **powerful in the eyes of the world** here. This is one of the aspects associated with your capacity to make a lot of money, assuming that the area in which you possess power is also an area that people pay you for, and also assuming that your notion of money is synonymous with the image you project in the world.[15] (Of course this is usually not true unless you exercise your power in a place where people—including you—place a reasonable value on it.)

Jupiter-Ascendant

You to them

You see Other striving towards a value which you have already attained. Some people in your position might view this as "a cute effort." It doesn't necessarily show Other as your follower, but **it does show where you think that they somehow look up to your efforts.**

Them to you

You see Other's angle as the portrait of that successful identity towards which you direct your attempts at image building. Note that II-oppositions present a tradeoff between sex-appeal and expressive power. III-conjuncts are related to sheer popularity. III-septiles are fierce or network-enticing. **This half-pair is related to what kind of allure you possess in Other's eyes.** Why? Ascendant is the house of new approach and outward identity. Jupiter is image projection. Jupiter strives to project an image in line with the same kind of conditions under which the Ascendant person naturally approaches new situations.

Self chart

Where your image projection and instinctual identity align, you naturally come into contact with the broad world—where the faceless public receives your approach. You are **welcomed by your surroundings.**

---

[15] There is a substantial bit of folklore attached to [Jupiter-Pluto] in regards to money making. I talk about this in the previous book. Keep in mind that [Jupiter-Pluto] only works as a partial indicator of money IF you see money as a means to projecting your world identity AND you see it as a socially pressured necessity. If neither of these hold, this chart pair tells you a lot less about money, and you'll need to look at other chart factors.

Jupiter-Midheaven

You to them

You see the other person as your friend and ally under this angle, with the two of you executing the angle jointly. In your eyes, Other provides the fiery terrain-claiming/image-spreading behavior while you stabilize your duo's gains.

Now if you've considered whose planet belongs to whom you might be thinking, "Shouldn't it be the other way around? Shouldn't my Jupiter do the terrain-claiming?" Not really. We're dealing with perspectives here, so in the same way that [Sun-MC] puts the onus for action on the Midheaven person and [Mars-MC] sets up the Midheaven person as the main influencer, [Jupiter-MC] establishes the Midheaven person as the chief image maker under its angle. Additionally we might ask if you and Other are always allies here. Of course not. The usual squares and octiles tend to produce strained relationships, where the two of you get along more naturally by fighting or sparring. Go figure.

Them to you

Your angle is publicly associated with Other's action in the world. Public association. **This is a strong indicator of the realm in which you and Other are publicly seen as true partners in arms.** Remember how deciles represent a reputation which just kind of "happens" through no single action in particular? Here the Jupiter person (Other) actually performs those actions which steer the duo together. This is a strong aspect for showing the joint circumstances under which you and Other are commonly associated as a pair. It also represents one of the best means to regulating who constitutes either of their public allies. It's hard for you two to be enemies under this angle without either destroying each other or releasing your aggression some other way. In your eyes, that is.

Self chart

You are publicly associated with the image you attempt to build before the masses, establishing you as a person whose reputation for this angle is augmented by intentional effort on your part. It is easier for you to be **seen as a leading figure** here. This should strike you as an interesting finding. See how being dubbed a leader has less to do with *what* you do and more to do with *who* believes that you represent something. Whatever that something is (as indicated by the angle) is your area of leadership.

Jupiter-Vertex

You to them

Your broad way of presenting your angle is more likely to strongly affect some aspect of Other's life. A deep, possibly philosophical discussion of Other's angle or change in Other's approach to angle expression is often involved. This is angle can be thought of as the sense in which meeting you can serve as the catalyst for a life change in them.

Them to you

Your responses to Other's general way of doing things under this angle have a greater chance of changing your life. Such changes often lead to increased responsibilities for you.

Self chart

Vertex brings **life changes tangled with your image promotion**. This is another straightforward combination. The angle shows when you are most susceptible to such changes, and when you do change, there is a fair chance that your image changes with it.

Jupiter-Node

You to them

You appear sure of yourself under this angle, often seeking out new terrain to conquer in Other's eyes.

Them to you

Your view of Other seems destined to be colored by your experience of Other's aspirations under this angle $_{fbow}$. As aspirations are often associated with a person's sense of insufficiency, **this half-pair often produces a slightly negative view of Other in your eyes as they appear to be described by an extra degree of forcefulness to cover their self-doubt**.

Self chart
Your self-assurance is coupled with forwardness in your inclinations, enabling you to cross into new experiences in the broad world with more force. We'll describe this as **a comfortable will to explore**.

Jupiter-Selene

You to them
You are awkwardly skilled under your angle in the eyes of Other. And although Other doesn't necessarily express the angle with the same skill, there is a real extent to which they have seen better. You possess the trappings but not the soul. You're a modern pop star, where Other has experienced rock legends. Better for you not to brag too much about this angle, as there is an extent to which you can learn much from Other here.

Them to you
You see Other's self-image assertion under their angle as unsettling. Do they really know what they're talking about? This is a case where the all-encompassing summary of Selene outshines even the broad reach of Jupiter. After all, Jupiter is only a world image. Selene is an entire universe of impressions regarding the same thing. So Other claims to understand Einstein's theories. You wonder if Other knows how to align Einstein's work with theories of gravity. Other claims album of the year. You ask if Other realizes that their genre sucks this year. **This half-pair describes places where Other is really good, but not the greatest (as they might claim)**.

Self chart
Your image making is boosted by your capacity for limitless talent. This would make you a living legend, right? Wrong. Because everybody, I mean EVERYBODY in the world has *some* angle between these two bodies. Thus **you have a talent that puts you in demand under this angle but, barring other pairs, you don't have so much talent as to earn the title "greatest of all time."**

Jupiter-Lilith

You to them
You encourage nonconformity, rule-breaking, and the taboo in Other under their angle. This isn't always a bad influence, but it definitely highlights their shaking up the system.

Them to you
Your conversations with Other regarding this angle as a joint (or slightly Other-skewed) topic encourage your rebellious side, tapping into your penchant for mischief. **Other is the devil on your shoulder when it comes to this angle**.

Self chart
You have an itch that must be scratched: Your participation in this angle's work highlights the rebel image in you. With such an image, people see the actions you perform in order to project yourself as being the mark of an **untameable** person.

Jupiter-Fortune

You to them
You see Other as having a wider view of things under your own angle, possibly as a role model here. Should you ever master the angle against them, you tend to see Other as one who contradicts you under this same angle. This is an interesting pair showing how the student can outgrow the master, and can be surprisingly negative in its resulting effects.

Them to you
You like being associated with the Other's image under your angle and are more inclined to brag about this or be smugly self-contented in light of such an association. You see the other person as a strong contributor to their own public image under this angle $_{\text{fbow}}$.

Self chart
You are content with a wider view of issues related to this angle, and can be quite confident accordingly. You are **in your element promoting yourself** under this angle.

Jupiter-Ceres

You to them

You can be counted on to present your angle as part of your image in interacting with Other, so much so that you may use this to pressure Other's decisions in this area.

Them to you

You are subject to changes in how you present yourself given Other's influence under their angle fbow. Other appears immovable here, right or wrong.

Self chart

You proceed in the world as someone who is stubbornly fixed on a path related to this angle. That path is shown in the entire family of resonant pairs with this same angle. Typically, since bossing others around doesn't work on faceless strangers, you **force your "caretaking"** on them instead.

Jupiter-Chiron

You to them

You take the position of authority under your angle, with Other often appearing as a client or customer. **They**, however, **stand to broaden your experience here, offering you more "experience points" (in a sense) for your successful dealings with them under this angle**. Negatively, your angle behavior goes less smoothly rather than more.

Them to you

You are inclined to help Other's angle or help Other through issues with their angle. Negatively, they are seen as obsessive or overly dominant here, such that you can't get a word in edgewise.

Self chart

The planets of image promotion and "surmounted insecurity" combine to form your **chief means of experience building through efforts to establish your action in the world**. When you point your Chiron insecurities outwards towards the assessment of others instead of yourself, you play the role of a critic.

Jupiter-Vesta

You to them

You pay more attention to Other's angle as a defining characteristic of their image. **You see this angle as a pronounced component of their name tag in the world**. This angle figures in heavily for determining the *kind of* sexual attraction you have towards them. Oppositions and II-oppositions are very bodily, with oppositions concentrated more on inner sensation and sensuality while II-oppositions focus more on body form or the compulsion to express it. Quintiles are based on Other's great company. Octiles are based on Other's standoffish intensity. Undeciles are built on Other's alignment with a popular standard roughly analogous to "your type"—if not by look then by attitude. II-squares stem from the emotional tension within the Other. III-septiles seem to be based on inaccessibility, where you want to know more about Other and to open them up.

If you are doing synastry with a partner of the same sex, these pairs are more likely to gang up on a third person here, bird-dogging (as it were) to create a big show in front of others. Here I'll share an interesting note from the data regarding non-preferred gender: There was a definite "type" for masculine versus feminine personas in the synastry, reflected in *table 19-7* below.

Them to you

You are approached by the other person with an offering of improvements in your behavior under this angle. When this is done actively, Other suggests the improvements. Done passively, Other compels them. Improvement in your angle behavior may also mean that you adopt plain old sharper expression without actual "improvements" *per se*. **In general, you gain a sharper focus on your angle given Other's overall ways here**.

Self chart

You are **focused on your own image building** under this angle.

Table 19-7: Masculine and Feminine behavioral styles associated with each Vesta person in the [Jupiter-Vesta] angle

Harmonic	Name	Masculine or Feminine General Behavior
1	conjunct	feminine, approval seeking, impetuous or scattered
2	opposition	neutral, analytical, guarded-sociable
3	trine	neutral-feminine, confident on the outside, unsure on the inside, intellectual and slightly pushy
4	square	masculine, insistent caretaking and advice-giving
5	quintile	masculine and feminine, strongly forward feminine magnetism
6	sextile	masculine and feminine, feminized appearance with forward / analytical charisma
7	septile	feminine, smooth external attitude, argumentative or difficult to satisfy conversationally
8	octile	feminine, strong-willed, shielded, usually quiet around strangers
9	novile	masculine and feminine, no nonsense leadership with pronounced emotionality underneath
10	decile	masculine, demonstrates command of challenge at hand with less interference from emotions
11	undecile	masculine and feminine, quieter but questioning, high performance standards for others, will steamroll if necessary
12	inconjunct	masculine and feminine, gets what they want, emotional vibe around them
13	II-conjunct	masculine, pronounced sense of caretaking, sexual, the body form of others or themselves is important to them
14	II-opposition	masculine and feminine, pronounced investment in affiliated groups and friends, blunt
15	II-trine	feminine, participatory, communicative and expressive (but may wander), slightly weird, complains more than other angles
16	II-square	feminine, sexuality is noticeably public (though often not stated), weird enough as to appear untrustworthy
17	II-quintile	masculine, will pull no punches in evaluations, strongly focused pursuit of chosen gender
18	II-sextile	masculine, archetypal masculine, forward, outspoken, charming, funny, but can be an asshole
19	II-septile	neutral-feminine, logical with a feminine-skewed insistence
20	II-octile	masculine, critical, often overly sure of themselves or their influence, often prefers war and conflict (with or alongside you) to peace
21	II-novile	masculine and feminine, popular, smugly sociable, but territorial, strongly derailed when charisma is challenged
22	II-decile	masculine and feminine, approachable, responsible, level-headed, has a soft spot for charm and its use
23	II-undecile	masculine, single-minded, strong ideals, declares definite and open enemies when challenged, will voice exactly where they stand
24	II-inconjunct	masculine and feminine, very masculine forward escapism or super powerful intuition channeled in search of one's personal validation
25	III-conjunct	masculine, charismatic, high sexual appetite, attention-getters
26	III-opposition	feminine, frontline figure, more easily overwhelmed by responsibilities where one has been crowned as a leader
27	III-trine	masculine, irrepressible opinion, very cooperative and friendly when such opinions aren't challenged
28	III-square	neutral, level-headed, pro-cooperation, gentle company when common sense standards are met
29	III-quintile	feminine, intelligent, focused but protective anchor to others
30	III-sextile	neutral, intelligent, observant, listener
31	III-septile	feminine, quite weird, provocative, masculine-projected analytical temperament, difficult personality
32	III-octile	neutral, friendly, more unassuming than other angles, intense creativity
33	III-novile	feminine, attention-getting body

		form, philosophical, explorer-type, personable, masculine insistence
34	III-decile	feminine, inclined to give partner a hard time (jokingly), stubborn, complains more or is slightly more critical than other angles
35	III-undecile	feminine (subdued), logical, attaches deeply to people, has an affinity for gaining a lot of attention
36	III-inconjunct	neutral, intellectual, strong desire nature lurking in private life
37	IV-conjunct	masculine, skeptical, outspoken, may mock or make light of things more often (fbow)
38	IV-opposition	feminine, openly skeptical with masculine / forward style of evaluation, very demonstrative with more pronounced bodily appeal when they like you
47	IV-undecile	feminine, more likely to be loyal to belief system with an active participation in those beliefs
48	IV-inconjunct	feminine, quieter, more reassuring presence

Table 19-7: Masculine and feminine behavioral styles associated with each Jupiter-Vesta angle. Note that these traits do not describe the person's sex or orientation, only the average level of "forwardness" (masculinity) versus "receptiveness" (femininity) across Vesta people with each angle within the partnership.

Jupiter-Pallas

Through the roof II. Your drive to conquer circumstances related to this angle skyrockets, making it another super strong (though slightly subtle) synastric pair

You to them

You see Other as being uncomfortably on edge in light of their own angle—as if their own display of this angle fosters further agitation within the other person themselves. With II-squares you see Other as emotionally damaging or as a fellow emotionally strong counterpart. With squares you see them as emotionally damaged, manipulative, or sadistic in some way. Favorably (maybe?), oppositions are table turners, making a space of vulnerability into one of their own dominance.

II-noviles are typically negative in relationships because they add an off-putting attitude to the person; they are more likely to *look* naturally annoyed by you. (But DEFINITELY compare this one to the other half-pair.) III-octiles place a mysterious wall between you and Other despite your friendly efforts towards them and (at least surface-level) rapport. You are more likely to see III-undeciles as intruding upon your space, in what amounts to the strongest aspect for one-way affinity that we've seen thus far; they are more likely to have strong feelings towards you $_{\text{fbow}}$, while you'll prefer intentional indifference towards them. IV-oppositions are more likely to take a liking to your physical company which borders on the forbidden, regardless of theirs or your orientation.

Them to you

You hone your skills in your preferred version of warfare in light of Other's angle. They powerfully fuel your desire to express this angle, establishing this half-pair as the second strongest "through the roof" combination after [Mars $_{\text{them}}$-Vertex $_{\text{you}}$]; only this time it's not an ability they foster, but an "intention to conquer." This is a mega-powerful aspect in synastry which exaggerates most normal effects beyond the usual tables, so we'll go through all of the angles this time.

Conjuncts drive you to express your instinct, personality, or creativity more powerfully. Oppositions heighten your attention to your own bodily feeling and self-worth, thus making you either very comfortable in their presence or *exceptionally* angry. Trines highlight your need to communicate your internal thoughts; in line with this, the other (Jupiter) person in this position has a tendency to disappear from your life before you can tell them what you want to tell them. Squares intensify your emotional foundation, making them feel like family on the one hand, potential sources of strong frustration on the other. In contrast with the trine, it's hard to break your attachment to these people no matter how much you try.[16] Quintiles make you want to be more charismatic, where the other is more inclined to entice you more openly. Sextiles foster a drive to live a more effective daily life. Septiles inspire more interest in 1:1 connections and tend to be bold and hyper-social in establishing such connections. Octiles form strongly combative relationships by default, but can diffuse this through sex, competition, and joint action. Noviles encourage you to achieve broader social appeal. Deciles can either intimidate you or awaken your discipline in your attempts to relate to them properly. If they initiate any kind of advances upon you, you are more likely to be intimidated. Undeciles can spur you to get your social affairs in order. For better or worse, such relationships inspire you to clean house where friends, social groups, and intellectual interests are concerned. Inconjuncts have a vibe which you find captivating, compelling you to pay attention to your own subconscious inclinations and impressions upon your environment. Where attraction is concerned, there is an increased likelihood that you'll want to take their vibe as your own.

II-conjuncts spark an interest in developing your persona, often because they see you behind the scenes. Relatedly, you tend to be a very different person in their eyes in public versus in private. In marked departure from their usual function, II-oppositions don't increase your sensuality. They increase your drive to build up the confidence of others through your presence—particularly in response to *their* body image. A colleague of mine and I have the II-trine which is awesome for putting students through the inquisition. This aspect favors confident behavior in a room. II-squares have the strange effect of increasing your tendency towards regret (possibly because it increases your attention to the moral standards you've likely fallen short of in your dealings with the other). II-square relationships tend to suffer a difficult non-meeting of the minds regarding core interests, but often have to become close enough for you to see this. II-quintiles have a way of flattering you with their company, increasing the feeling that you have successfully influenced others as you intended. II-sextiles have an eye for problems you have missed, making them formidable obstacles to your perceived mastery of things if they wish. In good cases, they provide a rational mind for backing your efforts. II-septiles make you feel as though your ingroup is the best thing since the invention of the wheel, with validating company that receives your attempts at rapport OR through critical opposition which prompts you to close ranks alongside fellow team members. II-octiles have a nervousness which accompanies their great power, prompting you to want to calm them down. These people have a much easier time awakening your desire to be intimate with them for their pleasure instead of yours. And then there are the II-noviles.

II-noviles for the [Jupiter $_{\text{them}}$-Pallas $_{\text{you}}$] half-pair look nothing like the same II-noviles viewed from the other half-pair: You are much more inclined to like these people a lot, but feel the need to defend against their compelling power. Why? Because this angle essentially establishes them as top notch in some section of your book of standards, making them your equal or better. See the rest of the II-novile resonant pairs for the ways in which this person may overpower you. Meanwhile, II-deciles are typically more polite and unassuming towards you, maybe even deferential as you are less inclined to engage them rudely despite your authority. II-undeciles are awkward, living in a world of their own which is both independent of yours yet conducive to your drive to be equally unique. II-inconjuncts inspire you with grand ideas for how you might potentially help them achieve their dreams...Okay not really. If you look deeply you'll see it's more likely that you're interested in them as a means of achieving *your* dreams through them. These people tend to come across as fans of yours in most cases.

[16] The behavior of squares raises an interesting question. As you're out conquering the world under this angle, do you also attempt to conquer the other person who's inspiring all this? It depends. In the data the Pallas person only included the Jupiter person as a target of their warfare if Pallas and Jupiter were acting as enemies. Usually this is not the case, but certain angles like squares and octiles tended to start fights between partners themselves more easily than others.

III-conjuncts are plugged in to the larger world and, though occasionally unreliable, tend to be good natured and competent, fueling your own desire to be so tuned into others. III-oppositions outshine their peer group members. III-trines are more insightful. Both groups increase your inclination to trust their work over that of others. III-squares tend to like you and show courteousness despite being stronger than you (when your morality suggests that you behave like this). Otherwise, expect them to draw out your own morality in whatever other ways are most fitting. III-quintiles make great tag team partners as their slightly intrusive, attention-getting ways make you look even better sharing the stage with them. (This is on top of the idea that the two of you look good as a duo in the first place.) Your powers of expert analysis are strongly augmented in the presence of III-sextiles, whom you can usually assume to be your intellectual equal in the areas you jointly analyze. Your association with III-septiles, fbow makes you popular and more prone to end up on the rumor mill among *your* social networks. III-octiles bring out your desire to take care of them—really to protect them from themselves or rescue them from a fate you think is beneath them. III-noviles live lives which make you want to be more popular among the types of people you think they must hang around. III-deciles tend to be very respectful towards you by default, raising your standards for how you treat them and others. Negatively, though, they may be domineering in a way that prompts you to master their undesirable influence. III-undeciles are more likely to behave like renegades, throwing their intensity all over the place in an undirected splash. III-inconjuncts are similar, but do this with their emotions rather than their open behaviors the way III-undeciles do. IV-conjuncts bring a formal exterior which is simultaneously amorphous. Thus you may be tempted to keep your exchange with them to a coherent minimum. IV-oppositions are talented, make super creative artists and entertainers, but seem to not know where they are going unless accompanied by a more sure-footed partner.

Self chart
Under this angle you adopt the image of a warrior. **Others recognize you as an exemplary figure in this realm**. Take a look at all of the resonant pairs with this angle to get a clearer picture of what your full warrior face looks like.

Jupiter-Juno

✪ How will partnership with the other person change you?

👁 Get a glimpse of the future of your relationship (expression)

You to them
Your general way amplifies the effectiveness of Other's angle under their commitments. So what, you say? "Under their commitments" is the key. Generally this half-pair is quite weak in its effects on you. It affects them more. See the other half-pair for more noticeable results.

Them to you
Your commitment to Other enhances your angle as it pertains to your image.

Make sure this angle is one you care a lot about.

✪ This is another great pair for the "what I get out of the relationship" cocktail—especially if you formally partner with or marry them. **Think of this one as showing how you change in light of commitment to them**. Squares, for example, intensify your emotional expression (amidst commitment) in the eyes of the world which views you. Conversely, the [You to them] half-pair shows how their image benefits from commitment to you.

Make sure the [You to them] angle is one which becomes better and not worse in them.

Self chart
Your style of commitment to partners is described by this angle in the eyes of the world. Here is one of the chief means through which people think you **show your devotion**.

The full [Jupiter-Juno] pair (both half-pairs) between you and another provides a rare glimpse into how you both appear to change in broad outlook in light of your commitments to each other. This applies mainly to marriages and business partnerships as well as shared living arrangements and certain deep friendships. All you need to do is look at the resonant pairs for the Juno person across the entire synastry chart. That is, if their Jupiter is III-quintile your Juno, you (the Juno person) will change mainly in the realm of group charisma—the III-quintile. Find all of the III-quintiles in your synastry chart and read what each half-pair says. In the eyes of the broad world, it is this combination of traits which is most likely to describe changes in your approach to the outside world. This is especially useful for looking at your own chart compared to that of your children. That is, this pair can also give a rough summary of how you change in light of your relationships with each separate child.

Where possible, try this out. Couple it with your own common sense and your own experience with your relationships thus far. See that it not only works, but works very well as a predictor of future changes in the two of you.

Jupiter-Hera

You to them

You see the other person as expressing their attachment to you through their angle. This is the proof that Other is really into the interaction. Negatively, Other uses this angle to override yours, keeping the exchange one-sided after all even though it looks two-sided. Ever had one of those "great" one-way conversations which you both told yourselves was so cool? Sure you have. Many of our normal conversations—even the close ones—are this way. Such exchanges are often contingent on the Hera person's current need to express her angle. But it's the Hera person's willingness to accept this angle in the Jupiter person which truly cements the bond. The former kinds of monopolizers typically end up as fr&s. The latter end up as friends. This is another easy tell for how likely a relationship is to endure as it is.

Them to you

You bond with Other over discussion of their image under this angle. **If you can accept their angle as it is and as it tends to be, Other may remain your friend for a long time**. This is NOT necessarily mutual though, and that's hugely important. The catch to this is that Other needs to be honest with you over any issues related to this angle. Since we're talking a point of sensitivity here—where their normally superficial image becomes the target of your bonding, Other really needs to ask themselves how invested they are in their current Jupiter. On many occasions in the data, the Jupiter person in this one was either not willing or not able to really convey this aspect of themselves for the degree of self-knowledge that it required, so that no amount of support on your part could nurture a longstanding attachment on their part. Thus there is a rather sad caveat to this pair: You and Other endure as long as their angle under their general way is accepted by you. But if they don't understand the role of this angle in their own life, the relationship tends to end as their approach to this angle changes.

Self chart

The world sees you as bonded to something or someone under this angle. An image of a person in a state of favored attachment (as advertisers have discovered) makes what they're associated with more attractive. And so it goes. Not only do you have **the image of a bonded person**, that image is more likely to fill others with tension in light of the fun *they* could be having. Hence your **increased sex appeal or creative power to inspire** under this angle.

Jupiter-Eros

You to them

You use your angle to compel results in the eyes of Other, often impressing them $_{\text{fbow}}$ with your power.

Them to you

You find the other person generically sexy under this angle; provocative of anger, frustration, or contempt in negative cases; and a motivator to your own action in cases where physical attraction

isn't the thing. This is especially true for conjuncts, trines, and octiles.

Self chart

You see yourself as imbued with the power to compel results related to this angle. Because this is the wide world we're talking about, **you take such assurance of power everywhere**.

Jupiter-Bacchus

You to them

You can draw a crowd with your angle in the eyes of Other, sometimes impressing them with your sociability, but sometimes earning their distrust. The psychology of this is actually very interesting but also pretty complex. The possible distrust levied by Other towards you is related to (but not the same as) jealousy because Other is often one of many who responds to your wiles, at the same time realizing that you may have ulterior motives for needing in bulk that which they could offer alone. The more competitive this person is with respect to their general angle, the harder it will be for them to watch you use that angle to become popular. The result is distance placed between the two of you by them.

Them to you

(This half-pair is a little tricky to work with, since you need to make some extra calculations to determine why you react the way you do.)

You associate Other with the gathering of pleasure-seekers under this angle, Other's reaction to which varies widely depending on that angle. In general, add four to the angle to show what kinds of tactics you think Other uses to accomplish this gathering as well as to get a glimpse of their take on the whole thing. So if this angle is a conjunct and they *naturally* attract pleasure seekers, add four to get a quintile; you're inclined to think they use charisma. If the angle is a II-undecile and they attract people through *their uniqueness*, add four (and wrap back around) to get a II-trine; they dominate a room in order to present that uniqueness. Negatively, Other is seen as inventing friends while using their angle to step on people in reality. This actually happened a whole lot in the data, since most people are not *truly* group oriented, but rather selfish by nature. With groups attracted for the purpose of the self instead of the benefit of the group, you see Other's powers of enlistment as a hiding place for escaping a damaged sense of the angle before the one that applies here. This is "all for one."

Self chart

With an image for attracting crowds via this angle, **you are a hub for diverse personalities** to gather around.

Saturn pairs

Saturn in astrology is typically considered a malefic. A problem planet. A planet of restrictions and limitations. But does it work that way in synastry? If you think about it, how often do you really put others in chains in your everyday interactions? Probably not so often. Instead you (like everyone else) have evolved to control yourself, hide your irritation, and maybe use the arts of selective attention and reinterpretation to shape your exchanges favorably. Thus synastric Saturn is less about oppression and more about those areas of life where you make agreements with others to behave within certain bounds. Loyalty, commitment, and discipline are among its themes, making it an essential indicator of longevity in your partnerships. (It really does oppress sometimes, though.)

Saturn-Saturn

You and Other have similar approaches to control in behavioral realms related to this angle. A trine for example shows that you have similar control over communication and, by extension, manners towards others. A septile shows similar ways of limiting others in 1:1 conversation or play. However you box in people's options here is how they tend to do it. II-trines share an ability to control a room as they hijack it.

Although [Saturn-Saturn] isn't hard to read, it is hard to verify. To catch this one in action you may find it easier to look at the resonant pairs instead and add "the talent for shutting others down" to that group of pairs. Such a talent tends to be expressed jointly over people around you rather than against each other. Outsiders are also more inclined to assign a reputation to the two of you as a pair under this angle. The more you use the angle together, the more inclined each of you as well as others are to remember your joint dynamic here as being one which revolved around control.

Saturn-Uranus

You to them

You shock the other person with your angle or otherwise disrupt the normal flow of things with it—possibly causing Other to freeze in discomfort or (in rarer cases) embarrassment. This pair is another one of those associated with how you seduce Other or surprise them sexually. "What do I need to do to turn this fool on?" Use your Saturn to their Uranus as part of your plan. When not associated with large groups, Uranus is associated with the large information which is the basis of those groups. With only one person as the boundary-boxing source of the same high level of information, Uranus is associated with **shock** on behalf of the Saturn person—**where an event quickly and singly floods its viewer with the unexpected information normally issued by a crowd**.

Them to you

You see Other as producing surprise restrictions (typically upon themselves) in the realm of this angle. Noviles are associated with particularly inexplicable acts, since they correspond to a shocking style of image projection.

Self chart

When you're not dealing with others, Uranus is much less likely to describe how you "shock yourself" and more likely to describe how you flood yourself with restrictive social information. The pressures come from many directions here as you feel **put upon by the social world**.

Saturn-Neptune

You to them

You display an obsessive adherence to certain rules under this angle in the eyes of Other. Though the rules typically aren't arbitrary, they are usually hard to capture in a few words. The result is that you can appear rigidly weird to the other person.

Them to you

You see Other as a dreamer under this angle, where they paint an idealistic portrait of affairs and will accept nothing less there. **This half-pair is ironically associated with perfectionism on the part of Other, as she continues a never-ending quest to get her angle right**. Other often appears odd or extreme in your eyes.

Self chart

This pair binds you to your ideals and is associated with staying **fixed on a path of action** which others can't see, but can only sense. Accordingly, this pair has also been implicated in addiction, where the angle btween these planets shows the realm of behavior where you are more likely to become addicted to something—restricted $_{\text{Saturn}}$ by an ideal $_{\text{Neptune}}$.

Saturn-Pluto

You to them

You see Other as possessing limiting command over others under their angle. Negatively, Other becomes an oppressor or a destructive force under the angle.

Them to you

You pressure Other to sharpen their expression of their angle. Negatively, Other's angle competes with your standard, turning you off to their company.

Self chart

The planet of restriction meets the planet of social pressures. **This combination produces an angle realm in which you receive (or in rarer cases produce) boundaries in conjunction with what larger external groups think**.

Saturn-Ascendant

You to them

You don't mind having your efforts structured by Other under this angle, as Saturn stabilizes the normally amorphous nature of the unknown into which the Ascendant dives.

Them to you

You are more attractive or persuasive to Other through this angle, **in a rather surprising half-pair which facilitates their submission to you**. This actually makes sense if you think about it: Here we have our old stick-in-the-mud malefic Saturn feeling limited in some area of the chart which is angle-activated by Other's evolving approach to things. So the Ascendant becomes an instantiation of Saturn's boundaries, giving those boundaries a human, more socially malleable form. You are more likely to cling to Other's angle in times where you need to better define yourself under that same angle.

Self chart

You limit and structure your own approach to new situations using this angle. This gives you a more **serious bearing**.

Saturn-Midheaven

You to them

You display control in the eyes of Other under your angle. Sometimes this manifests as an area of your life where access is denied to them in terms of influence. Other times it is simply a kind of self-discipline which encourages them to avoid being provocative towards you under this angle.

Them to you

You see Other as having a public image of controlled expression under their angle. There is less of a tendency for Other to get rattled here, rendering them sober company. Negatively, Other is limiting company, causing them to box you in with their various oppressive personality traits.

Self chart

You are a serious or more disciplined manager of affairs under this angle. The effect of this is to disallow external craziness in topics related to the angle. You have more of a tendency to stick to your guns here $_{\text{fbow}}$.

Saturn-Vertex

You to them

You see Other as a binding personality under this angle, **as if their angle is a kind of glue trap for your expression**. You can't move very far here in terms of options, so that much of yours and Other's ability to survive as a pair depends on Other using their power to steer responsibly.

Them to you

Your life is changed, often stabilized, by interaction with Other under Other's angle. This person often plays a role in shaping your long term approach to things here $_{\text{fbow}}$.

Self chart

Life-change and limits combine to constitute angle circumstances under which **you can change your life through you interaction with structure**. These structures can be of many different kinds, including restrictive events, laws, theories, and institutions.

Saturn-Node

If you were to marry...

You to them

You use your angle as a means of taming Other's expression. You are often unhappy with this aspect of Other's life as it is, causing them to stop just short of expressing this same angle fully on their own. You are a kind of manager here $_{\text{fbow}}$. **By itself this is probably negative EXCEPT that two people who agree to be managed by each other make for great commitment partners—making this one A TOP CONTENDER FOR THE #1 SYNASTRIC PAIR FOR MARRIAGE**—especially with more ongoing aspects like conjuncts, sextiles, septiles, and II-oppositions. Resonant angles to this aspect show

how Other summarizes your commitment to them (what kind of commitment you produce).

Them to you
You see Other as an example of skill applied to this angle. **If you elect to learn from them or at least rely on them to provide guidance here, you may see this area of your life as continually growing.** Negatively, you see Other as incapable or even incompetent in this area. Resonant angles to this aspect show how you view your commitment to Other.

Oppositions, octiles, and II-deciles favor relationships based on how you compare your experiences against the other person's, making them see you as being like a sibling to them.

Self chart
Your commitment to yourself and to your own development is wrapped up in this angle. This **is a topic you more effectively manage in yourself and others.**

Saturn-Selene

✪ Where do you see the other having a difficult-to-break expressive monopoly?

👁 Where might your skill threaten their ability to choose?

You to them
✪ You grow through Other's angle by observing them in action here. You see them as having a talent for confining other's expressive options here, **as if the other person enjoys a monopoly over this angle when the topic arises.** Read the 👁 [Them to you] version of this angle to get a glimpse of where the Other may feel unable to get around you. [Them to you] III-conjuncts may make you negatively known for your skill in playing psychological games.

Them to you
You find the other person compelling under their angle, typically enjoying being put under their influence here. **This is another case of submission, where your all-encompassing Selene relishes Saturn's serious, reputation-conducive stability when the angle is activated.** Negatively, you see Other as being a blind slave to the angle's expression in their life.

Self chart
You are able to restrain yourself and others more effectively under this angle. Whatever the angle is, you have a talent for binding people's ability to move under it.

Saturn-Lilith

You to them
You see Other's angle as detrimental to smooth relations with people, rendering their angle better seen than heard. Positively, you see their angle as powerfully moving though still unsettling to others. Maybe even a little intimidating.

Them to you
You encourage Other to use their angle to break through restrictive boundaries. This is also related to the area where you want to use sex to break through Other's boundaries for them—where their angle motivates you to want to conquer them. This is part of a "Challenger cocktail" with [Sun-Neptune] and [Mars-Bacchus].

Self chart
You have a tendency to rebel against others and restrict them here. Or you could simply impose structure upon them in this area, **rendering yourself an outsider** in two ways: First **you bind people's normal span of behavioral choices, then you rebel against them. From this comes your background for standing alone.**

Saturn-Fortune

You to them
You take cues from the other person in the design of your own angle. **Where you shape your future through structure, Other shows enjoyment of angle-attached situations, softening your seriousness here.** Negatively, Other's antics under

their angle render you more than happy to impose limits on them.

Them to you

You help co-write Other's angle usually with their permission. It isn't so much that they are uncertain or submissive, but that you function well as a supporter to their plans here.

Self chart

The development of structure in your life is more favorable to you under this angle, making it an area of **preferred stability and control**.

Saturn-Ceres

You to them

Your angle is cheered on by the other person, driving your further interest in promoting your angle far and wide.

Them to you

You take up a mentor position towards Other under their angle—which is odd since they tend to already be very good in this. But **you show them that this skill area need not be limited to their own quirky world and should be shared with more people**.

Self chart

With a greater sense of structure, you encourage others in this angle's topic. It may be desirable for you to promote your ways under this angle, but you are not as willing to promote these ways without a plan attached. You are the **subdued influencer**.

Saturn-Chiron

You to them

You see Other as prone to avoiding deeper investigation of their angle. There are faults here, where you view Other as more likely to neglect people's needs. Alternatively, they may spread themselves too thin providing for outsiders under this same angle.

Them to you

You see the other person's angle as a point of compensation for wishes not achieved. Alternatively, they appear to be used by people for this same reason.

Self chart

Your place of insecurity puts chains upon you under this angle. If you listen to the world while still insecure under this angle, you are further restricted. If you overcome your insecurity, you'll cease to listen to the world which restricted you in the first place. Either way, you are more likely to **dismiss the world's advice** under this angle. (I've found that this is the angle which, if you subject it to others' authority, consistently produces problems; you are suppressed as an individual, *op*pressed as a conformist. The general lesson eventually teaches you to follow your own way.) This pair is part of the "favored rebel" group of pairs scattered across *table 16-5*.

Saturn-Vesta

You to them

You see Other's focus on their angle as being uncharacteristic of them—as if the angle somehow doesn't go well with their natural personality. To you, Other appears fixated in an unusual way here without really being attached to the angle at hand.

Them to you

You see Other as pushing their angle upon people in an attempt to promote their own influence. Where this is not the case, you view Other as naturally big, strong, or socially potent under this angle without trying. This is another half-pair which amplifies all related resonant pairs in the other person.

Self chart

Interestingly, the focus on an angle which doesn't really go with your direct actions can combine with the sense of your own influence to produce a generic image of your career. After all, though you do things in your career, you are not *equal to* your career. Rather, the career is a structured thing bigger than you which is nonetheless associated with you in the minds of others. Focusing on this angle thus becomes easily associated with your **career focused desire**.

Saturn-Pallas

You to them

Your interaction with Other's angle fills you with tension or inspires you to pursue your own version of the angle you've seen.

Them to you

You borrow the other person's angle expression to help you fight your own battles. Other may be used as a scapegoat or a supportive enabler according to their interaction with you.

Self chart

You inspire yourself and use this angle as a **structured tool for making a statement in the world**. The external world tends not to restrict you here since you restrict yourself.

Saturn-Juno

You to them

You use your angle to display commitment-like behaviors towards the other person, regardless of whether a real commitment is possible or desirable. This looks a lot like Hera-style bonding, except that it appears more as a series of outwardly expressive gestures towards Other rather than inwardly felt impressions within you.

Them to you

Your view of Other's expression under this angle keeps you interested in staying associated with them. This is one of the most likely half-pairs to be associated with the phrase, "that's what I love about them." Negatively this becomes "that's about all they have going for them."

Self chart

The structured basis for your style of commitment shows through this angle. When you commit, this angle is more likely to serve as your collateral. That is, **commitment consists of your donating this angle**.

Saturn-Hera

Use this one to keep an exchange from decaying

You to them

You like using this angle with Other as a means of keeping the exchange from growing stagnant. Here we have a "decay preventer." This half-pair is nowhere near as strong as its [Them to you] counterpart, but is still interesting as an exchange builder.

Them to you

You hold Other in high favor under your version of this angle. **It can be VERY hard to stay angry or maintain a rift with the other person when you're using this angle in cooperation with them. We'll call this one the Solidifier**. Check this angle out in your own chart to see what you can do to stop being mad at yourself.

Self chart

This combination shows where you are both bonded to a thing and structured in the process. Thus we have the **context for a stable bond**.

Saturn-Eros

You to them

You see Other as hedonistic when they focus on this angle. **It's all about them in this area, highlighting them as self-focused**. With III-sextiles this is less about self-focused analysis and more about using analytical skill to build rapport with others.

Them to you

You are more inclined to see the other person as a wellspring of potential under this angle, often craving to draw out as much of their angle behavior as possible.

Self chart

You are self-focused, yet focused nonetheless on the object your attention is attached to. With a serious bearing and more of an affinity for order, you are **attracted to or as an authority**.

Saturn-Bacchus

You to them

You see Other as the center of group attention under this angle. Octiles and II-octiles confer power and sex appeal. III-septiles and III-inconjuncts confer strong magnetism via preexisting popularity and network presence.

Them to you

You see Other as sought after material under their angle. It seems as though they provide paparazzi potential for the qualities they display here $_{fbow}$. III-sextiles and III-septiles amplify the other person's name on the grapevine.

Self chart

You attract a group's attention and hold its members under your spell with this angle. Here you have the ability to make collections of people **shut up and listen to you**.

Coincidence or Math? ⚒

Hayden commented to Geery, It seems mighty convenient that your observations of these so-called half-pairs in synastry just so *happen* to line up with your previous observations in this so-called "self chart." I mean, if you're really just collecting statistics as you say, I would think that there doesn't have to be a connection between, for example, [my Saturn to your Hera] and [my Saturn to *my own* Hera]. The fact that they conveniently produce similar meanings seems biased.

Really? It shouldn't.

Why not?

Because, first of all, [your Saturn to my Hera] and [my Saturn to your Hera] came from the same average data, so we'd expect them to show similar interaction patterns, right? Stable bonding,right?

Okaaay, Hayden replied with considerable skepticism.

This is like saying that [your cake to my icing] and [my cake to your icing] relate in similar ways. In statistics these relationships are called "correlated." Secondly, [my cake to *your* cake] basically reflects the same food from both our perspectives, as does [my icing to your icing]. That is, we both agree that these things each play a certain role in the dessert. So the cake-to-cake "food relationship" is also correlated across people. As is that of icing-to-icing. If we imagine that any pair of cakes or any pair of icings (four things total) can be represented on the same circle, you'll see that some combination of [two of the four angles made by different planets plus the two angles made by the same planets] will always add up to 360°. Always. Try it out in a wheel to see that this is true (though you'll need to calculate all angles in the same direction—clockwise or counterclockwise—and will likely need to subtract out twice the value of certain angles to account for overlap).

There is always a way to get 360 from some combination of [yours and my planet A] to [yours and my planet B]. So if [anyone's A to their own B] means something when we lock their angles in, we can slide these locked angles around the circle to show that a change in [my A to your A] *must* produce a related change in [my B to your B] such that these two angles add up to 360 minus [the angles we already have]. Accordingly, assuming [my A to my own B] means something and [my B to *your* B] has its value partly determined by [my A to your A], then [my A to your B] and vice versa will automatically gain a meaning related to [my A to my own B]. The fact that all these half-pairs across two charts are producing meanings very similar to those of the same planet pairs in single charts isn't coincidence, really. It's just math.

Specifically, it's geometry[17]—where the angles of a regular four-sided shape always add up to 360°, and knowing any three angles will give you the fourth. The two opposite among those three angles will be correlated, as will the angle between them be correlated with the missing angle. But with only four angles in such a shape yet six possibilities for combinations[18], the last two angles must be fully determined by the first four, and the first four determined by the first three. As soon as we figured out what [a person's A to his own B] meant and married its meaning to the two other (undescribed) angles produced by sliding a pair of these around the 360° circle, we also determined the meaning of [a person's A to *another person's* B]. Presumably, [my own A to my own B] would simply be the average of [my A looking at my B as if it were someone else's] and [my A being looked at by my B as if it were someone else's]: that is, the self chart.

Hmph, I got lost. But you're saying that *mathematically* it's not a coincidence that synastry pairs have meanings similar to regular birth chart pairs?

Correct.

Yet [my A to *your* A] never got a meaning in the regular chart. How do you explain that?

It *did* get a meaning: through the signs. [Aries is to Taurus] what [Libra is to Scorpio]. But you only really see this by putting aside the idea that Libra gets its "meaning" partly based on Aries. Throw out the "Libra against Aries" part and you'll see that Libra is simply the process-based potential for Scorpio things—like every other sign before its successor.

Hayden quickly shook his head side-to-side with a confused frown.

Remember house rotations and the rules for family exchanges I told you about?[19] Remember how everything gets its meaning from its "orbit number" or place in line? Remember how divisions of a circle get their meaning from the number of repeats it takes to make a whole? All of these lay out the rules for the way certain angles of separation relate to each other regardless of where the separated objects are located on the wheel.[20]

Oh. Yeah. (Hayden's frown relaxed as he pretended to understand, though we all know he really didn't.)

Well there you have it. [A to a different person's A] has a meaning. [B to a different person's B] has a meaning. [A to the same person's B] has a meaning. So every other combination of [either A] or [either B] gets its meaning from these. *Of course* those meanings will move together. But when groups move together so sharply as a product of precise angles, it's pretty safe to say that some common behavior connects each of those groups.

If I ask you to pick a number 0–9 and I decide to pick my own number which is always 9 minus your number, my number's meaning will always change as your number's meaning changes—tying our patterns of change together. If you pick 1-2-3 across trials and go up by 1, I will have picked 8-7-6 and gone down by 1, but both of our picks would have followed the "change by 1" pattern. Here, it's not the number that matters but the pattern which connects them. When studying the character of each planet pair, whether it's [0 Aries trine 0 Leo] or [14 Libra trine 14 Aquarius], it's not the wheel location that

---

[17] Euclidean geometry, that is.

[18] The six possibly non-zero angles created by distributing [yours and my A] plus [yours and my B] around the circle are: [my A-my B], [your A-your B], [my A-your B], [your A-my B], [my A-your A], and [my B-your B].

[19] This is discussed in *FSA*.

[20] I talk about these in depth in *FSA*.

matters but the pattern which connects them. Those patterns are mathematically related though (as a trine is a trine either way), so it shouldn't be a surprise when their relationships move together. 🛠

Uranus pairs

Uranus represents social talk and the information around you. It is synonymous with things that generate such talk as well as those things which are full of information. So unique events, weird characteristics, humanitarian causes, popular trends, and technology are all included here as well. In synastry, Uranus is concerned primarily with the company you keep and the kinds of information they pass among themselves. Your exchange partner can influence this in ways that can either add to or subtract from the quality of your social experience.

Uranus-Uranus

You and Other have similar societal contexts where the focus on that which is popularly talked about depends on the angle. Septiles, for example, allow you and other to share societal context when having a regular conversation or playing games. Septiles also tend to be jointly pessimistic regarding the society beyond their duo. The peer groups of II-undeciles share similar quirks. The peer groups of III-oppositions constitute a similar fan base, for example. III-septiles are immersed in the same kind of social network information. This pair is quite difficult to notice between you and Other though.

Uranus-Neptune

Quick diagnosis 3: Does their general behavior in the world appeal to you? Vice-versa?

If you ever become an activist, go down the list of charts you have for this one to see what kinds of activism you tend to favor in yourself and others

You to them

You are inspired by Other to leave a more pronounced mark under this angle. **You also support Other's further evolution as a social actor here, showing them that it's okay to broadcast this in the world.** Negatively, you broadcast the other person's angle-related faults to everyone. Specifically, the Other has a tendency to be difficult or unapproachable under their use of this angle.

Subtly, gradually as you get to know them, you often find that this pair constitutes a grand gatekeeper to the relationship, where the good versions coming from the other are very good and the bad versions are either very bad or very indifferent. This is a great summary angle for asking yourself the question, "Would I enjoy being associated with them under this angle?" Your answer will depend on whether you accept this angle-related behavior coming from them. Often the answer is an obvious yes or no. Even better, you can ask this same question of the [Them to you] version of this angle to see if they would be interested in a further association with you. That answer tends to be very obvious too.

Be honest when you read this one. It may truly spare you years of heartache.

Them to you

Your conversations with Other regarding your social groups can influence Other's aspirations regarding their angle. **The other person is motivated to become stronger or better under that angle given the time she spends with your opinions on the information around them.** This is a tough read, though as it tends to be fairly weak unless your duo is involved with philanthropy or social action.

Self chart

The social talk and information around you influences the impressions you leave on that surrounding environment. This is your emotional response to society's ideals. Its angle shows that area of life in which you **respond to the social talk by means of your moods and intentions** for new action. Heavily social, you can't actively get nearly as much out of this angle unless you have an interest in doing something in the larger world around you.

Uranus-Pluto

You to them

You see Other's angle as their tool for receiving the world's pressures. **This angle of theirs is more likely to be more fortified against assault from the world, shows them as a colder or more rigid person in your eyes, and shows the means through which they send their sexual or creative energy out into the relationship**. You may notice that more social group pressure means more of this angle from Other when sex isn't on the table. Negatively, this angle is simply destructive to the relationship as Other, in response to pressures beyond your influence, intentionally pits themselves against you. Specifically, they tend to resent your popularity or the popularity of your angle actions despite their own wants.

Them to you

You see the other person as more of an authority or boss figure in line with social pressures upon you. **Other embodies such pressure when their angle is on—their angle serving roughly as that which demands you demonstrate your strength**. You are sometimes challenged to overpower Other's angle here. When done successfully, such power renders them docile or at least comparatively non-threatening in this area. So I guess the natural question is, what is it to "overpower" someone in their angle, and what happens if this doesn't occur? The short answer is, you'll need to be <u>unmoved</u> by their efforts under this angle.

Self chart

Subject to social pressures, you are less passive in light of the talk going on around you. Instead you are challenged to overpower the forces pressuring you by being talked about as rising to the challenge. This is your generation's **accepted route to social power**.

Uranus-Ascendant

✪ One of the big questions: "What do I get out of this relationship?"

You to them

You channel the social world's response to Other's angle, compelling their growth here. This half-pair works the way one would expect the North Node or Vertex connections to work, as it often sponsors major angle-related changes in Other's life in light of input from you. Other's angle evolution is faster under your company here, since interacting with you is like interacting with the world in a microcosm.

Them to you

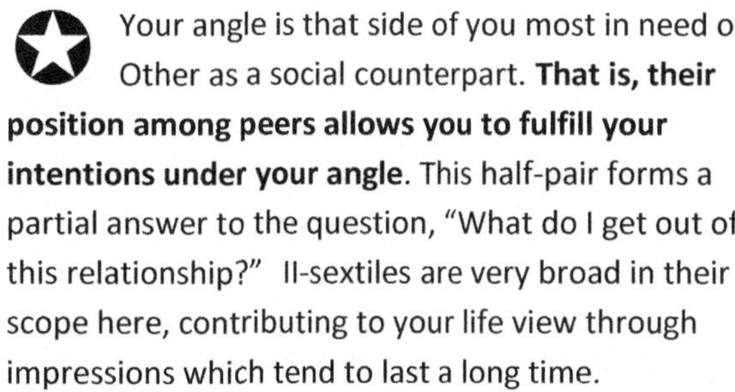

Your angle is that side of you most in need of Other as a social counterpart. **That is, their position among peers allows you to fulfill your intentions under your angle**. This half-pair forms a partial answer to the question, "What do I get out of this relationship?" II-sextiles are very broad in their scope here, contributing to your life view through impressions which tend to last a long time.

Self chart

You compel your own social growth through this pair. Typically this brings a **stronger association between you and a group** whose goals relate to this angle.

Uranus-Midheaven

You to them

You realize Other's popular attributes under their angle. When their angle is on, you understand (or at least perceive) how the other person can command such favor from the social world.

Them to you

You are greeted by the other person as though they gravitate to you under your angle. Although it isn't quite the case that they want what you have here, it is the case that your company is attractive to the social character associated with them.

Self chart

This is a really neat pair which goes a long way towards explaining why you attract the friends that you do; the self-chart [Uranus-MC] describes **the kinds of people who like your company**. Want to attract a certain kind of social group into your life? Hang around a person whose Uranus makes the desired angle to your Midheaven. It works like a charm.

Uranus-Vertex

Social shifting: the silent relationship killer

You to them

You bring surprising change in Other's life in the realm of their angle. This is "at the moment" change which reflects what the social world would think of Other's current state—whether Other is ready for it or not.

Them to you

You are put on the spot under Other's angle given sudden changes sponsored by them. This is not cool for people who prefer stability under the affected angle, so that you—the Vertex person—may "raise karma" to eliminate the relationship if the level of disruption is too high. Being so subtle that neither party may ever realize it, change like this among most non-close associates usually leads to mysterious shifts in feeling compounded by other events in the world which disguise the original issue. For example, when a friend "changes fans" by starting a family (III-opposition), chooses a network over the relationship (III-septile), chooses the public role over the relationship (III-novile), opts for familiar domestic arrangements over the relationship (II-square), or simply picks a different compelling partner (octile), the exchange with you has a higher chance of entering its twilight phase despite yours and their intent to remain friends as usual. Generally, [Uranus-Vertex] is a very powerful, very silent deal breaker between people and, as a pair, might best be described as "The Assassin."

Self chart

You bring about change in your own life via exchanges with the information world. This angle is where you are **more susceptible to surprise or intellectualism**.

Uranus-Node

You to them

Your angle serves as the branded face you bring to Other's life. Such is the face of your **fishbowl** (**the everyday default group with which you interface voluntarily**). Though initially charming, you are more likely to abandon Other when your angle is done evolving as it needs to. Think of your Uranus as being the football team and Other's Node being a fan in the stands. For the latter it's destiny. For the former it's just another game; we are talking about your basic team, though, which will likely outlast any fan. No this pair won't break you up. Just don't build a future on it.

Them to you

Your engagement with Other's angle renders them socially favorable in your eyes—as if you and Other were meant to be friends under this angle. Watch out though. This picture frequently lies. Though you feel that you and the other person should be friends based on this half-pair, it is actually the case that theirs and your "kind of friends" should be friends, while they themselves may yet become a pain in the ass. The chances are about 50-50 and will depend on other, actual bond-building pairs. In fact, this half-pair tends to be slightly more negative in that it sets up the Node person's expectations for friendship that are in no way guaranteed by the Uranus person's behavior. You are more likely to display contempt for Other when those expectations are not fulfilled. Nasty breakups are built on such things. Undeciles, III-oppositions, III-noviles, and any other angles which don't come from within are particularly susceptible to having their veneer stripped over time. If you're going to connect over this angle, you may want to get to know Other's other angles first.

Self chart
This angle feels like **social destiny** to you, and it may well be. Don't expect such **talk about you** to always be positive though.

Uranus-Selene

You to them
You idealize Other under their angle, where your social group finds an ideal "all-in-one" personality in Other for this angle. It might sound abstract, but really **this half-pair does nothing more than make the other seem generally appealing or repulsive on the summarized whole under this angle**.

Them to you
For whatever reason, this half-pair is strongly conducive to sexual attraction from you to the other person, and in cases where attraction is not an option, it is still conducive to a strong procreative tension between actors such that you two, **if not palpably unsettled by each other, would make a great tag team in that hunt for validation** often seen in bars and clubs around the world. That's mainly for the conjunct. **With other angles the quest revolves around whatever business that angle typically sponsors**—where the potency of attraction is usually (but not always) lower compared to the conjunct alone. Under the other person's angle, the connection is nurtured. This is definitely a one-way half-pair though. Note under [Uranus $_{you}$-Selene $_{them}$] how Other's experience of this same angle isn't nearly as visceral. Still this setup has interesting implications for what attraction of this kind is built on. When someone (Uranus) idealizes you under your angle, isn't feeling boldly creative one of the possible results? Your craving for them may be that much stronger with a confidence elevated to such heights.

Self chart
You connect your repository of individual talents with your social side and thus display **more skill in taking your talent viral**. You are an independent thinker here.

Uranus-Lilith

You to them
Other seems to believe that you have a strange nonconformity under your angle. **You may look awkward here, but at the same time innovative**. "Out of place" is the apt phrase. In their eyes, you just look uncomfortable doing whatever you're doing under the angle...

Them to you
...but perhaps you (Lilith) see Other (Uranus) as out of place because *you* are being contrary. Looking at Uranus' fishbowl from the outside-in establishes Uranus' position as lamely conservative under Lilith's lens. This half-pair reverses perspectives, where you struggle to project your angle because you know you're dealing with someone from left field under Other's interpretation of that same angle. Positively, you don't care what Other thinks and you air your angle anyway. This typically means that Other's angle is not up to code here. **If Lilith doesn't make Uranus nervous or cause Uranus to defer to the former, Uranus may see Lilith as under-qualified or below standard in this angle**.

Self chart
With two indicators of unusualness in the same pair, this one can be a tricky read in synastry. In the self chart, however, the net effect is to establish you as a **rebel among your peers** in whatever angle area applies.

Uranus-Fortune

You to them
You fuel Other's bold or avant garde nature through your angle.

Them to you
You are motivated to look at the bigger picture beyond your circumstances in light of interaction with Other's angle.

Self chart
This pair reflects **comfort with your own social mobility or eccentricity**.

Uranus-Ceres

You to them

You assert the final word over almost everyone in the realm of your angle when interacting with Other. You subdue their angle here, curbing that angle's usual effectiveness.

Them to you

You see Other as being pushy when it comes to their angle. **Specifically, they put members of the social world in their places using that angle**. This is the area of Other's life which others are not allowed to influence.

Self chart

The information world around you sees you as pushy, though typically most people don't push entire groups. Alternatively, then, you are seen as being **pushy or caretaking towards individuals affiliated with groups** whose members' interactions with you are related to this angle.

Uranus-Chiron

You to them

You find Other's angle fascinating enough to become fixated on, where your social standards line up with their deep understanding of those same standards under angle. **This is your exploratory interest in them**.

Them to you

You disclose unique secrets about yourself to Other in the realm of your angle. Sometimes these concern traits, sometimes wants, often outlook. This is your uncommon autobiography.

Self chart

Insecurity meets social talk in a pair which indicates **your context for being accepted or rejected by society**.

Uranus-Vesta

You to them

You see Other's angle as aimless compared to your own social context. **That is, as your social information regarding this angle passes through, Other is simply inclined to stare at it by default**. Positively (and more rarely) you see Other as reliably and strongly applying their angle.

Them to you

You see Other as placing heavy priority on their angle in the world. This is played out in the level of focus or multidimensionality they appear to hold towards certain topics when you pay fixed attention to them. With III-inconjuncts for example, you pay attention to Other's conveyance of a message.

Self chart

Fixed attention to an angle-related social action is the theme here. In the ideal world, this angle shows **where you are dedicated to a line of behavior which registers among your social groups**. But since most of us are rarely so invested in any grandly global undertaking, this pair typically shows **the area of life under which you worry about your name on the grapevine**.

Uranus-Pallas

This one influences looks and the impressions Other leaves on you

You to them

You see Other's battlefield as being all of society under their angle. They are well known in angle-related circles (sometimes notoriously) as they devote a stubborn attention to remaining active in this realm.

Them to you

You see Other as being strongly popular under this angle in an aspect which affects the impressions that their appearance leaves on you.

This angle definitely influences how the other person looks or behaves in your eyes. Among the groups that provided impression information in the dataset were the following:

Conjuncts are confident and outgoing. Squares are nervous and or critical. Quintiles are instantly conversation-worthy. Septiles are friendly-sociable. Octiles are simply charismatic and often very attractive—where attractiveness tends to increase with their level of self-centeredness. Noviles are image-endowed sensual. Deciles display a more level-headed collection of mannerisms, but can be quite unfocused (or inspired?) when their emotions get involved. Undeciles are "gossipably" sexual, but often put up an intellectual fence around themselves to prevent others from taking advantage of this; undeciles can also be bullies or prone to basic uncooperativeness.

II-conjuncts are lovable overall, with various features to support this. II-oppositions are physically active or otherwise "well-kept." II-trines behave in more spacey ways, but have addictive personalities which are often pretty fun or entertaining to engage. On the more negative side, II-squares are apparently judgmental—hiding a near-ruthless focus beneath friendlier, but slightly more critical features. Meanwhile, II-quintiles hold thoughts and ideas which work to oppress others when they are conveyed; they are inclined to sport features which reveal their passionate nature—the more pessimistic they are, the prettier they tend to be (male or female), while more work-focused or optimistic people display more of a bohemian look as a reflection of their striving against the outside world. II-sextiles are generally *attractive* to whole groups of people while II-septiles are more *alluring* to groups; where the former are more likely to inspire liking in their groups, the latter are more likely to inspire desire; II-sextiles are actually quite aloof to strangers among the groups that like them while II-septile people have a look which makes them more fun for you to charm. II-octiles, meanwhile, are group-friendly. They have an alluring intensity that can be unsettling in close company, and display fewer inhibitions about getting into your personal space either physically or intellectually. II-noviles are better defended against groups. They tend towards sly eyes. II-deciles are more stern and no nonsense than other angles when it comes to social impressions, but have more innocent features as a group. II-undeciles hold mannersims which strongly suggest they won't put up with your mess, though they're typically a lot nicer in person.

III-conjuncts are enticing. III-trines are opinionated. III-quintiles are body equipped or sexy; this angle feminizes the individual and increases their temperamental nature. III-sextiles confer more masculine good looks along with a smoothly masked stubbornness which comes out fiercely when interactants convey something the III-sextile is passionate about. Then they can be immovable. III-septiles are more physical or exercise-focused (though the type of exercise varies widely). III-octiles display a marked social intelligence which outruns their patience to stay with the task before them. III-noviles are physically big or have a big group-presence. III-deciles are distrustful-looking. III-undeciles are inclined towards a higher-energy intellectualism. Stress seems to be a "thing" for these people; in the data, these people also tended to have bigger body-builds. III-inconjuncts stand out. IV-conjuncts are slimmer and have a crafty look to them.

Note that you can use the 👁 [You to them] version of this half-pair to get a generic idea of the impression you leave on the other person.

Self chart

You leave a forceful impression on the rest of the world here. As this pair is married to what people assume about you, it is also married to what people's assumptions about you train you to assume about yourself, hence its role as an indicator of your **realm of cooperation with social expectations**. This is one of those aspects which heavily influences how society pigeonholes you based on looks. It can be tricky to get around, but gives you a great glimpse at the kind of work society would most likely reward you for...simply because it lines up better with their default stereotypes about you.

Uranus-Juno

Once again: "What do I get out of this relationship?"

You to them

You like receiving Other's angle as affirmation of their place in your social world. **The angle is the area of your life in which they validate your own abilities**. This is another half-pair which helps answer the question "What do I get out of this relationship?"

Them to you

You adopt Other as a friend or kindred mind under your angle. You may not be friends in other areas, but here you and they share an outlook.

Self chart

Juno, the asteroid of commitment in the eyes of the world, combines with Uranus, the information world, to show the area of life where your topic-committed behavior is more easily married to data and information. **You and your work are more easily made public under this angle** fbow.

Uranus-Hera

You'll be captivated by that special quality more easily

Use this angle to determine which among the various things you've done might have stuck most with the other person. For better or worse (fbow)

You to them

You view the other person's company as "sticky" through their angle. **For better or worse, Other's influence under this angle remains with you even in cases where you would tend to other priorities**. As usual, *table 19-1* works here.

Them to you

Your angle is insistently pressed upon Other, sometimes favorably, most of the time insistently (of course). This angle may constitute a point of annoyance for Other if you don't regulate this behavior.

Self chart

You have a tendency to stick to things to which you are bonded under this angle and, as a result, tend to **receive more enduring impressions of your target** under all resonant pairs related to this angle. You also **bond more readily to this angle wherever it appears**.

Uranus-Eros

You to them

You learn strong lessons in your own drive from the passion shown by Other amidst their angle. You elicit a stronger reaction from them here.

Them to you

You see Other as having the image of a driven person under this angle—driven in a social setting. Other appears more attractive to groups here.

Self chart

Your passion shows in the social world. The net effect is that you demonstrate a kind of interest in whatever your angle undertaking may be, regardless of who observes you. This is e**qual drive in the eyes of everyone**.

Uranus-Bacchus

Rewinder. So we meet again

Use this angle to further gauge their interest in your company

(I think this is one of the weirder pairs.)

You to them

Here's an interesting one. [Uranus-Bacchus] describes the circumstances of first meeting between you and Other. **Other's angle constitutes the major first impression left by them upon you**. This is a <u>strong</u> aspect with noticeable effects on the chart. Why would this, of all pairs, indicate the first meeting? (You would think it would be a more direct/major pair of planets or something.) But this is a specific kind of first meeting: the one in which you first become aware of Other's role in a clique. It's not actually the *first* first meeting, just the first ingroup-relevant one in which you actually write a kind of file for them in your memory. Uranus' social world is greeted by Bacchus' action-affirming clique, suggesting that when we meet someone in earnest here we're actually getting an impression of their interactions with others—not necessarily of them as individuals. The bad news is that this meeting tends to be a one shot deal except in cases where you and Other are separated and then reunited. Then the meeting has a weird way of beginning again in the same manner. A friend of mine and I have the inconjunct and effectively met twice under the same busily background-heavy circumstances 9 years apart.

The good news about this half-pair is that how you met tends to color where the relationship is most comfortable from a perspective-sharing point of view—such that every time Other has a new body of social experience to share with you, they color it with their version of this angle. Why is that good news? Because it TOTALLY tells you how their "honey I'm home" report is programmed to go. Fascinating! And strange.

Actually, of all the pairs we've studied up to now in this book, this one strikes me by far as the most interesting. This half-pair can be used to gauge the other's interest in exchanging you. In line with similar pairs we've read, if the Uranus person is not getting this angle from the Bacchus person, chances are the latter's interest in updating the former isn't there. This is part of the "Are they interested?" cocktail. Be honest, and this one will give you a pretty good answer. II-undeciles share unique intellectual interests. II-inconjuncts share works of the imagination. IV-oppositions communicate positively by being cool and soothing company, negatively by showing up in places where they're not really welcome (such that you need to be responsible for them to keep them from upsetting others).

II-octiles have the unfortunate distinction of being generally upsetting to people before joining your clique—until you need them for war. Then they become powerful people to have on your side. Octiles are also like this, but instead of being upsetting, they simply hide their force initially.

Them to you

Your angle is the context under which you offer to Other that which they really stand for (socially). **Although not exactly a love language[21], this angle provides an interesting look at your most comfortable means of communicating your recent clique-related experiences to Other**. If you want to communicate most naturally with another, then heed this one if you are the Bacchus person; try it out on the other person to see how they respond to you at your most comfortable. II-oppositions, as usual, are physical and communicate by sharing company. II-trines dominate the room both people are in with the Bacchus person's intent (not always in a negative way). II-sextiles give progress on far reaching things. Our reliable *table 19-1* works for this, though you may also refer to *table 19-6* if your aim is to be obnoxious. The half-pair is definitely not two-way.

Are you the Bacchus person? Interested in someone but want to hide your cards? Don't show them this angle in a way that announces your enjoyment of their company. Doing so is a good way to leave impressions you don't want to leave.

Self chart

Your personality-infused clique and your broadly gossiping world connect under this angle, forming your weapon of choice for **making noteworthy impressions on the members of new ingroups as well as taking your existing ingroups and making impressions with them on the world which talks**.

Neptune pairs

Neptune corresponds to the ambient emotional environment—the vibe you give to and get from a

---

[21] Chapman, G. (1995). *The five love languages: How to express heartfelt commitment to your mate.* Northfield Publishing.

room when you occupy it. Is there an atmosphere of fear? Excitement? Secrecy? We read Neptune for this.

Synastric angles to Neptune reflect expectations and aspirations—things which people are inclined to do but haven't done yet and may never do. Ideas and impressions are exchanged between you and the other person, where you may support, inspire, or interfere with each other's various goals. Just when you thought we'd covered much of what there is to cover in studying relationships between people, I assure you we're just getting started. Neptune presents us with some really fascinating scenarios which you may never have imagined played a role in your exchanges. Think of all of the ways in which your hopes for the other person influence your success or failure with them. The planet of "ambient vibes" presents us with the first of these ways.

Neptune-Neptune

The angle between Neptunes shows where you and Other hold similar responses to the surrounding environment or context for focusing on the environment. II-conjuncts are inclined to clash in ways that are obvious to everyone even if they get along. II-trines have similar approaches to impression making and intimidation. II-septiles share inclinations for picking the groups they hang out with, and tend to like each other's company. Other angles follow the standard table.

Neptune-Pluto

How do you attract a certain kind of person into your life, accidentally or otherwise? Use half-pairs that connect your attention to the emotions of the bigger environment. We'll call the group of stuff-attracting half-pairs the "Summoner formula."

☎ Summon through desire to use a talent

You to them

Issues in the world (often conflicts) compel you to interact with Other under their angle. Typically there is a problem to be solved in Other's angle that can lead to an increase for you in "spiritual power." For the sake of measurability, let's define **spiritual power** as simply **the skill in reacting to emotions felt in a certain environment. By helping Other address their angle issue, you increase your ability to find contentment in similar environments later on (despite conflict)**. This can be thought of wholly in terms of psychological rather than astrological terms, but is quite cool considering that we rarely read these two planets in mainstream synastry.

Them to you

☎ **You find comfort amidst your interpersonal problems under this angle when in the company of Other**. Here, Other is the kind of person you are inclined to lean on in times of trial; they have a weird way of appearing when your angle burns to find an outlet. This is part of the "Summoning formula" which I'll discuss in more detail in Chapter 20 as well as in the third (and final) book in this series.

Self chart

Although [Neptune-Pluto] is the absolute slowest changing pair of planets that we'll look at, its creeping angles do reflect something in your regular chart. Namely, the angle between these two shows where [the area of life under which you are most sensitive to your environment] aligns with [the area of life under which the world pressures you with its standards]. Considering what we've learned about astrology so far, this shouldn't be too surprising. The consequence of this, though, is that the pair shows where your ambient environment most accurately parallels standards far beyond the room you're in—**where your room's doings reflect the goals set out for you in the larger world**.

For activist types, resonant pairs with this angle constitute one of the best collections of indicators of the means through which you can best do work which aligns with the larger world's needs.

Neptune-Ascendant

You to them

You see Other's angle as an incomplete attempt at connection with you. It only succeeds in leaving you with an impression. Positively, you inspire them here.

Them to you
You see engaging Other's angle as productive of illusions and imagined realities. Maybe this means creativity, but often it indicates that Other has a false notion of how their angle affects you. Positively, you are inspired by this angle.

Self chart
Not quite connecting completely with your situation, you are mainly *inclined* to do things under this angle. Supported by stronger pairs (and more focused attention on your part), however, this pair can indicate creativity in how you naturally project yourself as well as the ability to **inspire** others (that is, **steer their mood towards a certain action**).

Neptune-Midheaven

You to them
You view the other person as escaping the consequences of their actions under this angle. **Other performs angle-related actions fbow, fairly prolifically, and gets away with those actions.** But why?

Midheaven is the reputation while Neptune corresponds to the mood we read from or write onto an environment. But in the case of a reputation, witnesses to another person's Midheaven are the ones picking up an impression while the Midheaven person is only displaying a reputation—so it's as if they did something to you without really doing it. Imagine calling someone who cooks for a living a "chef." Sure he cooks. But when will you ever find him "cheffing?" Rarely. (Is that even a thing? Not in common parlance.) In this way, [Neptune-MC] makes a person's *label* into the guilty party without the actual person having necessarily done anything. You feel effects for which there are no identifiable causes. In positive cases, we're inclined to call this person inspiring without pointing to anything specific, but in negative cases we're inclined to blame this person for stuff without pointing to anything specific.

Them to you
You can seemingly act unchecked under your angle in your interaction with Other. In your own world there is the ability to become super strong in a notorious way here. Not that a power struggle needs to be involved, but if there is one, you have an advantage in this angle (all things being equal) because it's harder for the other person to pin specific angle-related deeds on you.

Self chart
You have a reputation for leaving this angle's impression on people. **This pair tends to give you an inexplicable mojo in others' view under the relevant realm of action.** Strangers with only a cursory impression of you suspect you would perform the angle's activity as soon as you got the chance.

Neptune-Vertex

This is a major relationship killer. Don't lean too heavily on this one if you expect the exchange to last

The Restless One

You to them
There is an extent to which you will never really know the other person under this angle, seeking answers without attaining an understanding of where their angle comes from or why it works. This is that "*Je ne sais quoi*" (literally "I don't know what") which Other has that you either find interesting or unsettling. A little bit of thought about the nature of Vertex and Neptune will reveal why this might be the case. Neptune leaves impressions, Vertex changes lives. If there were such a thing as a moving target in astrology, this pair would be a great candidate for one because, by the time you get the impression that Other is leaving, either you or they have changed to something new. Ill-inconjuncts may present you with a full 180° turn in impression over your time knowing them.

Them to you

You reach into Other's angle trying to extract something that isn't there. Despite what you may hope to experience in light of them, Neptune is as Neptune has always been: active in the realm of impressions rather than actuality. **Granted, Other's Neptune (or more likely its failure to materialize under this angle) may inspire action in you. Unfortunately, this usually consists of you abandoning Other on this point to get your needs fulfilled elsewhere**. In romance, this is one of the deal breakers. Among friends, fr&s, and family [Neptune $_{them}$-Vertex $_{you}$] indicates areas where you and Other should avoid relying on each other (or maybe even working together at all). If you absolutely *must* work with them then expect to have disconnected aims under this angle OR plan to use Other's angle as fuel for your own creativity without expecting that angle to obey any of your wishes. This latter interaction will be one-way according to Other's whim.

This pair has a super high destruction rate among Neptunes who expect to successfully share this angle with the Vertex person, as it tends to promise promises only. To make matters worse, this angle is often an attribute whose potential fills you with want for it. Talk about a dangled carrot.

Self chart

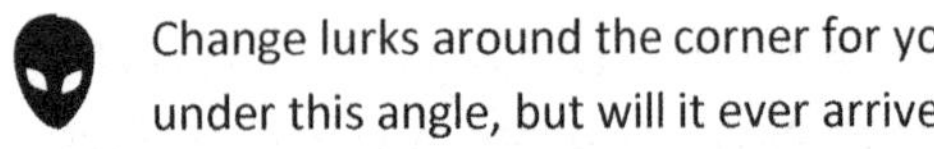

Change lurks around the corner for you under this angle, but will it ever arrive? **There is a good chance that you will be forever homeless in this area**, unless by some truly epic work in self-actualization you manage to settle down. Now this pair need not be negative, as you'll tend to find **endless ways to reinvent roots in this angle's area**. Yet the yearning for stability here tends to go unquenched through one's lifetime. May you learn to enjoy the journey for its own sake.

Other chart

(The "Other chart" is the same as the self chart, except that it consists of you looking at someone else's chart against itself rather than you looking at your chart against your own.) Suppose you're dealing with a particularly quirky individual. You like them, but there's clearly something seemingly fated to be incomplete about them. This is one of the rare occasions where it may be more informative for you to look at Other's standalone birth chart rather than your own. There you'll realize something really interesting about [Neptune-Vertex]: Other displays this characteristic *all the time*, but doesn't realize it. And now for the truth concerning this pair. [Neptune-Vx] is not about a failure to be effective in one's angle, but rather **a failure to be satisfied**. If you can endure Other's shifting goals and give them a way to feel like you'll be there for them regardless of what they do—in both their chart and in your synastry with them, you will have overcome one of the biggest hurdles to deep and permanent bonding with them. Accordingly (and surely ironically), [Neptune-Vertex] in the regular birth chart also reflects the means through which the other person best displays **loyalty** to others while their time with those others lasts.

Neptune-Node

This pair is the one most associated with stupid and thoughtless actions on the part of both people

Summon through fear

You to them

You seem destined to be profoundly affected by Other's aspirations as conveyed through their angle. If they have aspirations related to you which they wish to convey to you, this angle will likely be the means through which this is done, creating any number of seemingly irrational situations that spring seemingly from nowhere. Just when you thought Uranus was the king of surprise, this half-pair comes in playing out Other's thoughts with respect to you in ways that may bowl you over. **If the other person is doomed to do something really thoughtless to fuzzify your relationship, this angle is where they'll most likely to do it.**

In a few departures from normal behavior, undeciles mess things up by being intolerably critical, inconjuncts openly display a very bad attitude, II-oppositions resort to excessive complaining or arguing when they're around you. II-squares are excessively insistent on their own values, constricting others' freedom in the process and wanting things for others that the latter don't necessarily want. II-sextiles make plans to drop you. II-septiles do things to get themselves attacked by peers and supporters. III-conjuncts patronize you. III-trines call you out intellectually or skillwise. III-deciles often work in your favor and can be royally oppressive when the environment seems unstable to them. III-inconjuncts are generally less predictable in how they compromise with you. For all other angles, use *table 19-1*. (*Table 19-6* doesn't apply as frequently here.)

III-septiles (31s) are pretty special. In negative cases, these people mess things up by being in a position to beat you convincingly in the popularity contest. "Mess ups are often battles here because they recruit friends to amplify the problems they see in you, even if they are the ones in the wrong. If you battle them, you should do so on terms that deny them access to their allies or expect a devastating and public loss. Again, a Node person with a III-septile to your Neptune SHOULD NOT be challenged directly; you'll need to win over (or cut off access to) their support network. Furthermore, unfortunately, the reverse situation does not hold. That is, in positive cases their allies are not usually your allies, but in negative cases their allies *are* your enemy. The data on this one were pretty convincing, with more than half of the Node possessors showing up as enemies to the Neptune person when either one of the interactants was allowed to behave irresponsibly. The default is active distrust, and you will likely have to put in actual effort to keep a 31 from sliding into party warfare. I found that the determining factor for cooperation versus enmity was whether the Neptune person used *their* own angle as the Node person in the opposite half-pair in the other person's favor; so if your Neptune is III-septile Other's Node and their Neptune is II-octile your Node, and you fail to use your II-octile in the other's favor (or use it indifferently when they want you to use it for them), you can expect a III-septile popularity battle.

Lastly, we should note that this half-pair is part of the "Summoner formula," where the angle-related thing you currently fear the most in your life often shows up as a person with that angle on this half-pair...

Them to you

...Now suppose you are the Node person. Temperamental types are particularly susceptible to this one as **you send your aspirations regarding Other towards them through your own version of this angle**. Mainly by actively refusing to convey such thoughts can you avoid doing something spontaneously stupid through this angle.

Self chart

As a personal note, I've messed up a lot of exchanges in a lot of basically random ways and—among all of the data I looked at—this pair was far and away the one most associated with what those ways were. My advice to you before you show the other person that unexpected side of yourself: Think it over. Even if it feels like fate, if Other hasn't purposely invited what you're about to do, you may just be setting yourself up to leave a permanently negative impression. This angle shows **how you embarrass yourself in other people's eyes.** On good days **it also shows how you borrow the attention of everyone around you** *without* embarrassing yourself.

On embarrassment

The odd thing about [Neptune-Node] is that it is rooted in the idea of a "destined impression" and thus reflects the actual truth behind our normally filtered social actions. We may call a certain action stupid in hindsight, but really, if it had been so stupid when we first thought of it chances are we wouldn't have done it. Interestingly then, we can think of "stupid actions" on our part as *maybe* partly ill-considered, but also partly consisting of the best decision we felt inclined to make at the time. Along these lines, let's define **embarrassment** as the **feeling of discontentment in light of an action you've**

performed which you now would rather have been some other action that better aligned with other people's standards. See how this definition is related to a kind of regret. Let's define **regret** as a **feeling of lowered contentment in light of an experience you've had which you now wish you had helped steer in some way other than the way it went**. Embarrassment focuses on the rightness of an alternative personal action and basically raises your tension. Regret focuses on the wrongness of what you actually experienced (personal or not) and basically lowers your tension / mood. Why define these here? Because doing so gives us a tool for stripping away much of [Neptune-Node]'s chaotic power: If you truly feel that you made the best decision possible for the most correct group of people as possible, both regret and embarrassment become a lot harder to feel. Your self chart angle constitutes a key topic area for making decisions which you deem to be right—not just for you, but for others.

Neptune-Selene

The other person is awesome here! (Or if they aren't, this is a trait which you can steal from them)

You to them

You are more inclined to think that Other is totally awesome under their angle. They reflect the realization of an idea (not an ideal). No joke. **If you were to join Other's fan club, this angle might be the basis of it**. There's not much more to say about this one. It's very straightforward and very strong. I suppose we could relate it to the cocktail for "What do I get out of this relationship." It may also serve as one of the bases for your forgiveness of Other should the two of you ever fight. **Negatively, you simply disrespect this angle in them and hype it up in yourself**.

Them to you

You are expressively restricted by Other, where it feels as though Other doesn't see things that you want them to see. Now is a good time to discuss the difference between Selene and Neptune. Neptune feels the ambient environment. Selene represents the ideal situation as a whole, such that even if an environment feels weird, the long term story (consisting of environment, potential events, actual actions, and everything else) typically weighs more in the end. Accordingly, Selene and Neptune together amount to Selene seeing Neptune as spacing out on ambient feelings alone, and although we might normally say "yay Neptune" for seeing even this much, in the eyes of Selene, sadly, Neptune's ambient empathy still shows only a fraction of what there is to be seen. You can out-evolve Other here, thus your subservience to their focus on mere ideals tends to hold you back. If you do out-evolve the other person here, there is a higher chance that you will grow apart. The stats bear this out consistently.

Self chart

You are more inclined to believe you are without peer in this angle area. This is your **impressive creativity**, where you have the power to place your talents upon others far beyond the span of your direct influence.

Neptune-Lilith

You to them

You see Other as a rebel or innovator under their angle, looking up to them in this area. Maybe. But there are two issues here. First, in negative cases, you do not look up to Other, but see Other as looking *down* on you—in which case you will feel negatively even thinking about them. This is not an exaggeration; just thinking about Other really can put you off in this case. Secondly, if you are obligated to cooperate but not confident or patient enough to try meeting the other person under this angle, **you may make promises of support that you can't keep** (or which they won't let you keep), seriously damaging the relationship.

Them to you

You imagine a rebellious, rule-breaking exchange with Other under their angle. How often does such an exchange actually happen? Almost never. Neptune lives in the realm of inspiration, remember? The purpose is not for you and them to eventually join forces under this angle, but for you to be inspired to execute the angle without Other's direct help. You are motivated by the other person to imagine boldly here. Here's some more advice for you. DO NOT WAIT for the other person to help you with this angle. Your disappointment in light of their failure to do so will only frustrate you, and is one factor in the termination of fr&ships on the grounds that Other is unreliable. **Call this half-pair the Hollow Oath**.

Self chart
You'd like to be that daring rebel, but can only manage to imagine it. Actually, you're probably more rebellious than you know under this angle, but **you'll have to appreciate what it means to do your angle work socio-emotionally rather than overtly** before you realize this. Until then, you are more likely to be sold dreams which cater to your own sense of uniqueness here, making you **vulnerable to others' control**.

Neptune-Fortune

You to them
You flatter Other under your angle, imagining an ideal where Other is in their element. Negatively, you space out instead when Other is in their element, looking down on their efforts as pitiful or second rate. The difference between the two views? The extent to which you decide to accept Other's efforts as they are.

Them to you
You see Other's angle as being the means through which they create impressions in others. This is very much a reciprocal pair, where Other's looking down on you in this angle causes you to feel negatively towards them in return here. This is, weirdly, not a deal breaker when damaged, but facilitates a very tangible dislike from you to them. This pair marries the notion of your dislike of Other to their disrespect of you, and can be used to read synastry with countries, businesses, pets, and projects as well.

Self chart
Can you live up to your own ideals under this angle? The answer will depend on how comfortable you are with the angle itself as shown through its resonant pairs. **In a perfect world, this one shows where you are most comfortable with your own imagination. In a normal world it simply presents such comfort as a feeling for you to develop**.

Neptune-Ceres

You to them
You see Other's angle as being 1) beneath your desired standard, 2) too lightweight for you, or 3) incompatibly managed. You imagine an ideal where Other pressures a narrow reality, threatening to bring you down from your epic heights. You use your angle standards internally to block Other's access to more of that angle externally, generating a kind of "Lock Out." Usually. **Positively, you flood Other with the same angle**, responding to their call to idealize as much as you want.

Them to you
You sense that your coercion is effective in affecting Other's vibe through their angle. **What you are compelled to want Other to do, they give the illusion of doing. Alternatively, Other's vibe compels you to pressure them to show more of this vibe yourself**. The latter case, inasmuch as it is associated with masculine pressure, is associated with sexually or creatively tempting Neptune people depending on the angle. This is especially true of noviles, II-noviles, II-undeciles, III-quintiles, and III-sextiles.

Vibe-based receptive allure tends to work better coming from stereotypically socialized women than men (with men as the pressurers) so that this pair favors women whom you perceive as "hot" by image (novile), attitude and publicly maintained appearance (II-novile), liveliness (II-undecile), sex appeal and group-charisma (III-quintile), or bragworthy body (III-sextile). Of course all aspects have their own mechanisms for temptation though. Quintiles feminize the other person presumably because your 1:1 ego projection plus your Ceres pressure corresponds to you getting your "holler on"—a behavior which is, heterotypically at least, more likely to be dealt *towards* women and feminized / gay males than straight males. Undeciles are more likely to have stories told about how sexually tempting they are, though in fewer cases (in typical Scorpio fashion) such temptation may be replaced with a STRONG intellectualism or analytical power. In still different cases the other person may be prudish—unwillingly surrounded by sexual talk not of their own sponsorship. III-sextiles were arguably the most tempting group in the dataset, producing "expert" stunners or powerful builds in the eyes of the Ceres person, or those whose bodies worked to intimidate others (III-sextiles also bring socialized fitness). Meanwhile, III-oppositions typically enjoyed a massive fan base built upon their application of interpersonal skills and business-style focus. III-trines had a talent for infiltrating minds with their force. This half-pair shows where you are more inclined to be tempted by the other person's vibe.

Self chart
You have aspirations towards pressuring others under this angle, **foisting your ideals** on them.

Neptune-Chiron

You to them
You suspect uncertainty in Other's display of their angle. **Other typically shows power here, but may need encouragement to develop it**. Positively, they sustain a lot of people with this angle, and then count on you to provide them with safe haven.

Them to you
You see Other's angle as recklessly spread around and may wish that they exercised more self-control. **You may need to clean up after Other's mistakes here. Positively, you love or are proud of this aspect of Other**, finding it a good complement to skills that you lack.

Self chart
You may need encouragement to hone this skill, but as you hone it the skill becomes a talent for taking care of others which you are proud of. It's just as the synastric half-pairs suggest. **You can lift people's spirits here**.

Neptune-Vesta

You to them
You are more likely to feel as though your angle is a fuzzy source of mixed signals in the eyes of the other person. You seek interaction with Other in this area, but aren't sure that you are ready for the consequences of such. **As you imagine, the other person delivers full throttle—faults and all**. Are you ready for this?

Them to you
This is another pair where you view the other person as more single-minded in their communicated ideas. **But this is not quite stubbornness; rather it is fixity of intent instead**.

Self chart
You exude an emotional state which others can feel under this angle. **You either gather attention as a result of this state or seek to gather it**.

Neptune-Pallas

You to them
You are more likely to feel as though you are in the way of Other's expression given your version of this angle. With their action-heavy focus, you tend to feel underappreciated under *their* version of this same angle. Very alternatively, **Other may dedicate their heavy focus to you**, showing their near obsession with sharing their angle with you.

Them to you
You support Other's fulfillment of an idealized role here. Often, though, you experience the other person's angle as wasted talent as they seem to fritter away their attention on unworthy things. **Negatively, you may gradually come to see Other as dead weight** here.

Self chart

You adopt a driven focus amidst inclarity, and are **more likely to fight against such inclarity** under this angle specifically.

Neptune-Juno

Why would you *ever* cheat on each other? Here's why

You to them

If you tend to see the other person as advancing too strongly under their angle, this pair will effectively kill your interest in them. The full [Neptune-Juno] pair is one of the most one-way of all synastric pairs in terms of affinity and liking since it leaves hope in Other's eyes while you know that there is none. Not surprisingly, the more stubborn you are in any of the [Neptune-Juno] angles the harder it will be for you to settle down with Other. The search for a partner with a better matched version of this angle also forms one of the major bases for you cheating on the other person after you get together. Doh! This is also applies to you seeking replacement friends for them even if you don't cheat. Doh!

Wha—? Why? [Neptune-Juno], really?

The planet of illusion meets the planet of commitment in the eyes of the world. Remember, Juno does not reflect a private commitment between you and the other so much as it reflects a public promise to outside observers that you will *show commitment behavior* towards Other. It was for this reason that we initially introduced Hera in *FSA* as a truer indicator of actual bonding between you and your commitment-object. Juno doesn't tell you this. Accordingly, attaching Neptune to Juno in synastry sets up something that *appears* to be commitment in the eyes of everyone (possibly including Other) *except* for the individual who is the source of the illusion: the Neptune person. It is here that the world/room provides you with a person whose angle it "thinks" would be good for you, but only in the sense the world/room "feels" a connection between you and Other. Of course this is a big metaphor, but you get the idea. We're talking about a movie which you and Other play out for a bigger audience, but the true test of whether there is anything genuine behind your performance lies in the extent to which you yourself enjoy playing the role of the recipient of Other's angle—not the extent to which you actually respect that angle in them.

Under what circumstances can you ensure that this angle doesn't ruin your duo? In front of an audience whose approval you value, of course. Keep gaining fuel from pleased audiences in response to this angle and you'll find it to be very rewarding. That is, as long as you keep benefitting from getting this angle from the other person *in front of outside viewers*, the danger of wandering is a lot lower.

Them to you

You commit to Other under this angle, but seldom are they happy about this particular type of commitment. In a sense, you seek to influence their dreams here—an aspiration which is usually not received well except by very docile interactants. You may appear as controlling here. Although not a deal breaker like its partner half-pair, it is this kind of half-pair that prevents friendships from forming in the first place. On the upside, if Other is docile enough, the arrangement should work out well.

Self chart

This pair shows where you hold standards for partnership which may be more externally imposed than internally felt. To the extent that your ideals line up with the emotional expectations of those who are the primary observers of your commitment, you may yet be satisfied with the commitment-objects you adopt. If not, then no. Your partner is a **reflection of the emotional impression you leave on others who witness this angle in you.**

Neptune-Hera

What kind of connection do they consider ideal?

You to them

Your company is appreciated by Other under this angle, where your vision or creative expression gives them an abstract feeling to bond with. You serve as a kind of missing piece which tops off Other's existing progress or creative skills here.

Them to you

You are comfortable delving into Other's angle and sharing company with them here. Aspects like this solidify friendships when they are rooted in personal matters (as opposed to social-grouping or abstract matters). II-squares, III-trines, and III-quintiles—for reasons unknown—make the other person extra physically attractive or strong. III-octiles noticeably increase the extent to which you are drawn to or validated by their company. III-inconjuncts increase the extent to which you are turned on by them or see them as having an aura of carnality.

Having **Mutual aspects** (**the same angle for both half-pairs**) GREATLY amplifies this angle in your duo, often creating entire situations between the two of you which revolve around that angle $_{fbow}$. These situations have a habit of sucking in other people, especially given the more social angles.

Self chart

You bond to the vibes of others more noticeably under this angle, giving the pair its role as the **indicator that you have found an ideal connection**. The things, situations, and people to which you are most strongly attracted depend strongly on their ability to satisfy this angle in you.

 Look at this angle in the other person's regular chart to find out their Achilles' heel when it comes to relationships. Appeal to this angle to significantly increase your chances of winning them over.

Neptune-Eros

This one's a bit complicated.

You to them

You see Other's angle as a secondary driving force for them after you have gotten to know them fairly well. This is because Other's angle is subject to their lust—which usually isn't shown on first meeting. You tend to feel this capacity in them initially, so the characteristic is less of a surprise when it hits, but still...

If you are able to receive Other's voluntary revelation of this angle after a period of rapport building it is a good sign that they have allowed you to drive them with your company. If you get this without the rapport building it is an indicator that Other may just be generally lusty in the company of people like you under this angle, and the attention may not actually be aimed at you. The relationship tends to die under this case. Actually, I had this happen to me with a former friend of mine whose Eros was III-decile my Neptune: A struggle for command in my mind, an expression of passion-infused authority in hers. Interestingly, if this angle happens to be imposed on you but also happens to be one upon which you build a major part of your self-esteem, the exchange is almost guaranteed to morph into a power struggle for control of your angle. Since it's *your* angle, you Neptune, are more likely to be the bad guy for killing the exchange because you are the one whose weird reactions to Eros' show of interest in you—being internal—don't get explained.

Them to you

You are more likely to be impressed by Other's handling of their angle, though this doesn't really translate into motivated action on your part. Although you would think that [Eros-Neptune] was a prime pair for something more passion-based, it isn't. This is because the Eros person's motivated action typically comes with its own built-in imagined target. Other's Neptune, unless it's in conjunct, typically interposes a middle man between Eros and its natural target in the form of the angle situation. So you look at Other as though they show skills reminiscent of a cousin of a standard that you already have. Conversely, if you want to show your vulnerability to Other, displaying this angle without barriers is part of it. Hiding the angle keeps the relationship in acquaintance mode from their perspective. See the other half-pair for more on why this is.

In many fr& cases you may be compelled by circumstances to show this angle to the other person—as when Mr. Eros must give a speech in front of Ms. Neptune and these are separated by a III-novile (crowd performance). Here you are still vulnerable to Other *but unwillingly*, and must trust that they won't screw you over as an audience. If the more negative outcome does occur and Other doesn't receive your efforts favorably, the exchange has a higher chance of meeting its demise by means of something akin to a lack of respect from Other to you.

Self chart

What is going on with this pair? You've written the ideal target for your passions upon your vibe. When this angle is on, you give off that vibe more strongly, compelling the emotions of those around you and being more alert to their reactions to this in turn. This is **the angle under which you are most capable of environment reading and writing**. The behaviors of the synastric half-pairs reflect the idea that one person picks up the feelings of the room while the other writes those feelings intensely. Unless the latter's intensity is driven by the former's behavior, the relationship can take on a misleading character.

This angle has a very powerful character to it in the self-chart. Strongly used, it can make its possessor quite notorious in the social sense.

Neptune-Bacchus

You to them

You idealize Other's entire clique under your angle, making you most prone to disloyalty here. Weird, eh? Let's see why. On the one hand, this pair is bad for you and Other as a duo in that it weakens their <u>unique</u> appeal in your eyes. On the other hand this is good for you in that it allows you to escape—more easily identifying a backup person should things with Other fail. In more extreme cases of this you effectively encourage the other person to "take a number" behind members of their own clique. This result of this pair is strongly under the control of the Neptune person, whose level of sensitivity to Other's needs for appreciation under this angle can make or break the exchange.

Them to you

You see Other as grindingly social here in an aspect which promotes your jealousy towards them. Nothing like your sense of fun cliques being hijacked by Other's vibe to make you feel as though you're being cheated on psychologically. A more practical example of this would be where John introduces girlfriend Jane to his homeboys (Bacchus = the clique) and Jane proceeds to exchange awesomely fun vibes back and forth among John's people, leaving John feeling like yesterday's news. The new relationship energy strikes again. How should one handle this positively? Who knows? Especially in formally committed exchanges, a show of jealousy may actually *affirm* the relationship in Other's eyes, letting them know that you still care. But what if you don't want to be jealous? First, it may help for you to work on becoming more secure with your own version of this angle. Some angles will be easier than others. And then there remains a whole slew of tactics ranging from indifference, to seeking other options, to revenge cheating. As you can tell, though, most of these tactics won't do much to help you and Other grow. I'm not recommending these mind you, but background information behind much of the data supports exactly these kinds of remedies to the "group-kidnapped jealousy" scenario. One middle-of-the-road option I've found useful is to simply be occupied with other things which replace the offended angle. Good luck with this one.

Self chart

You inspire cliques and, unlike the synastry cases, have a hard time being jealous of yourself over this. Thus you become a bandwagon inspirer. That is, **you are better at gathering cliques around you under this angle**.

Pluto pairs

The dwarf planet Pluto, the next major Solar System body after Neptune, corresponds to a kind of secondary ruler of Aries, the next sign after Pisces. Being a very slow moving body, however (with its

248-year cycle around the Sun), Pluto constitutes a "generational planet" whose effects play out over the course of decades' worth of people. Now if this body is so slow moving—sitting in the same sign for about 20 years—you might ask how it can possibly symbolize anything useful in astrology. The answer is that slow moving bodies starting with Saturn (widely recognized structure) tell us a lot about characteristics that everyone can see and agree on. It is here that you get things like widely accepted rules, ideas, and environments whose effects entire audiences can attest to. Pluto picks up where Neptune's collective feeling left off: with the collective "push to act" which results from that widespread feeling. Just as II-conjuncts (the 13th harmonic) take into the public those inclinations shown by inconjuncts (the 12th harmonic), Pluto follows Neptune to make angles with other planets to show where we are urged to put on a public show for meeting the standards of our surroundings' surroundings—the "world" for short.

Pluto in synastry shows how one person's world-pressured values interact with another person's characteristics. Accordingly, it's associated with all of those high-stakes topics on which others weigh, leaving us and our interactants to sort out how those topics actually get addressed.

Pluto-Pluto

The angle between your Pluto and another person's Pluto shows **the area of life in which you share a similar perception of the pressures in front of you and, relatedly, a similar inclination to support each other**. As usual, *table 19-1* tells the tale. Undeciles, for example, support each other through social talk and data, thus facilitating annoyance between you and other in times of trial.

On the behavior of higher harmonics

🛠 If you are around the same age as your interactant, the angle between yours and Other's Plutos will be a conjunct. Or will it? Well, as far as this book is concerned, an angle separation of 0°–9° *will* be considered a conjunct, but we should note that there is an entire unmapped terrain of harmonics higher than 36 which is just begging to be researched. Once we figure out the meaning of, say, $^1/_{63}$ of a circle (a VI-trine)[22], we'll be able to compare even the slowest moving bodies like Haumea, Eris, and Makemake down to 2½° of separation (360 ÷ 144=2.5, where 144 comes from chopping 12 signs into 12 "micro-signs"). Until that time comes, conjuncts will remain wide.

As for the harmonics we actually cover in this book (1 – 36 and sometimes 37, 38, 47, and 48), you might have wondered if there is some kind of pattern to how they behave besides their rough recycling of the first 12 angles. We know that $^1/_2$ of a circle is an opposition and that this reflects self-value. We also know that, if you add 12 to the 2 below the fraction, you get $^1/_{14}$ of a circle: a II-opposition (which reflects bodily value). Add 12 more and you get $^1/_{26}$ of a circle: a III-opposition and its reflection of the value bestowed upon you by groups of bodies who follow you. Sometimes in this book you'll also see me mention another harmonic 12 levels higher than this one. Multiples of $^1/_{38}$ of a circle form a IV-opposition which, based on the rare data in which it occurred, partly indicates the "body disciplinary regimen:" health, fitness, dedicated routine, and exercise. The patterns across these harmonics are pretty stable. And then we also notice how the first 12 seem to be all about exchanges, the level IIs seem to be mostly about people-related things, the level IIIs seem to be about collections of people. Is there some way we can predict what's going on here? Yes there is.

Based on additional statistical work which I won't bore you with here, we find that each successive level ticks *backwards* through the signs, starting with Pisces. That is, think of level Is as occurring against a Pisces, impression-

[22] 63 has passed up five blocks of 12, making it a level VI (6). Adding 3 to this gives a trine. So multiples of $^1/_{63}$ of a circle are all part of the VI-trine harmonic family. I discuss how we name harmonics in detail in *FSA*.

making background. Levels IIs occur against an Aquarius, social-talk background and, as such, are full of new versions of the level Is that are now much more likely to get recognized by others and gossiped about. Level IIIs occur against a Capricorn wide-structuring background where people assemble in formal clusters according to rules laid out by the original level I angles. Not surprisingly then, level IVs occur against a Sagittarius background. But this isn't about "bigness," "travel," or "fame." It's about ideas and processes. (If you're interested in studying this further, be sure to read this footnote[23].) We can predict, then, that level Vs would occur against a Scorpio background and so on.

The reasons for the above behavior are pretty strongly grounded in 1) complicated data that I didn't have the heart to introduce in this book, 2) the ways in which waves of progressively higher frequency work in physics (higher frequency = shorter wavelength → an apparently slower-changing background), and 3) a consistency with several aspects of astrology we've already seen in *FSA*; the planets tick forward through the signs, for example, but *backwards* through the houses. Unfortunately, further discussion of this issue would be way too technical for our purposes. So we'll stop here. Just note that slow movers like Pluto aren't doomed to be uninformative just because our current array of angles for observing them are too low in resolution. There are even higher harmonics than the ones we've been using and, yes, we can predict how those harmonics will play out. ⚒

[23] To complicate matters considerably, when we tick backwards through the signs, we actually have to think again about what each sign means based on the sign *after* it. The Sagittarius (Saj) background of the level IVs provides the clearest example of this: If you define Saj coming from Scorpio's 1:1 steering, Saj bursts forth into the world, breaks barriers, and does all that powerful stuff that Scorpio was about to do by manipulating lots of other people. Based on this definition, a IV-conjunct should be about putting your will out there. A IV-opposition should be about gaining recognition. But the statistical data just don't support this at all. Instead, all four level IVs that I looked at revolved around ideas and abstractions. This makes sense only if you define Saj as coming *from Capricorn*, not Scorpio. Coming from the boundary-fixing nature of Capricorn, Sagittarius removes structure and causes the rules that Capricorn gathered up to spill out into fluid abstraction. So the Saj background causes the level IVs to be tied more to outlooks, approaches, and philosophies than anything else. Similarly, the reason the level IIs seem so solidly social rather than information-driven is because the Aquarius background isn't defined against Capricorn before it. Capricorn *to* Aquarius makes Aquarius look like the communicated versions of Capricorn's laws. But Aquarius coming *from Pisces* makes Aquarius look like socially well-formed versions of Pisces' amorphous feeling. As we've seen, the data pretty convincingly support level II as social rather information-based. Following this, the data also support the level IIIs as social group-structuring (coming from Aquarius) rather than broad action-limiting (coming from Saj). And so the backwards ticking is the one that holds up under the stats. As a reminder, ALL of the nonstandard astrological interpretations (at the time of this writing) were based on statistics rather than astrological tradition. For more on all of this, revisit the conversation between Geery and Hayden at the end of Chapter 18, the section labeled "Modding by 12."

Pluto-Ascendant

You to them

You see Other's approach to the world as embodying the pressures on you. This half-pair provides a rare look at the broad pressures which brought you and the other person together in the first place. In times of calm under your angle, Other embodies a correct standard, where you find their ways super sexy, alluring, powerful, socially elevated, or intelligent. In negative situations (which may even be a byproduct of one of the actor's deeds here), you find Other off-putting and uncouth. Either way, the other person's outlook captures what society wants from your angle in your dealings with them. What does this mean for you in practical terms? Other's happy outlook corresponds loosely to your doing what society would want under your angle within a world determined solely by you and them. (Such a world can become a bit of a puzzler if you think about it for too long.)

Them to you

Your interactions with Other naturally gravitate towards highlighting their problems under this angle. III-quintiles have a high chance of highlighting a bad attitude (negative group charisma) on their part, for example. Call this pair the "**Sore Subject**." Positively, you withhold much of this angle until Other volunteers their version of the angle for your weigh-in. Then the combination can be great for having you serve as a strength builder to Other in this.

But now this half-pair is strange. There is some evidence in the data that suggests it works like Vertex—serving as a kind of infectious conception in which the Pluto person—if they stay around the ASC person long enough and focus on them strongly enough—experiences the hatching / birth of events in their (Pluto's) life related to this angle. The effect is so interesting I wish I could explain it, but I can't. It's probably just a basic self-fulfilling prophecy in action. The hit rate for this "hatching" effect was very high in the data, and partly explained even some of the weirdest coincidences I've encountered personally (such as why I dream of the cosmos every time I put concerted thought into a friend of mine with whom I have a III-sextile [expertise]). For those Ascendant people trying to seed their dreams with thoughts of others (Pluto people), this angle appears to show what kind of event in the dream you are actually likely to get. Again, though, I have no idea why this is.

Self chart

You approach new situations with the pressures of the world upon your shoulders. You may not be having fun, but the group that wanted you to do it approves of your attempt under this angle. This angle shows the **group-favored approach to your experiences**. "Use your trine on it," they say. "Rally them with your III-novile," they say. "Be weird with your II-undecile."

Pluto-Midheaven

⬭ They meet the power standard through sexual expressivity

You to them

You see Other as a powerful person under their angle in an aspect which strongly indicates your view of their strongest sexual asset—especially the male kind. II-oppositions are noted for their bodies in general. You see undeciles as publicly celebrated for their sexual characteristics. With II-undeciles, social presentation does the trick. And so on.

[Pluto-MC] is overwhelmingly associated with male sexual characteristics, but why? Consider that my Midheaven reputation, when stood next to those issues that pressure you, give me a way of pressuring you through means which the public can label. The public tends to base its labels on only a couple of things though: events and objects. Short term exchanges describe the MC person's pressuring approach through an event or two. Longer term exchanges describe the same approach through the body's role in a particular realm of action. Some angles—like conjuncts and undeciles—between Pluto and the MC are "always on" and thus conducive to hot / well-equipped bods in the eyes of the Pluto person (whose sense of world pressures provides the measure for MC's public reputation). Other aspects—like III-quintiles—are more sporadic, hiding their power until its use is necessary. Still other aspects—like II-trines and III-inconjuncts—are deceptive, appearing one way in the person's presence and another way in their absence. The element of surprise is on these people's side despite what you may have expected of them. In all cases though, Pluto remains associated with directly forward pressure, emphasizing masculine traits over feminine ones.

Salient among the [Pluto $_{you}$-MC $_{them}$] angles are II-oppositions, II-septiles, II-noviles, and III-oppositions (all of which favor strong male to female attraction). Undeciles are associated with the male power to which you aspire. Both undeciles and III-septiles display characteristics which make them bragworthy to your friends—so you can tell everyone how you "hit it" (or in cleaner terms, "interacted with the individual"). II-noviles leave indelible impressions on you with their enticing power. II-septiles and III-sextiles are passionate but indifferent to you when you are an outsider to their clique. The latter are sexier when critical, giving them an air of sophistication in their communication. In other news, conjuncts, quintiles, and octiles are directly, in-your-face persuasive. II-trines have an uncanny ability to take what they want by means of surprise; they don't do much while seated quietly in a room, but once they interact with that room they tend to dominate it. II-quintiles are also like this, but whereas II-trines are sneakier, II-quintiles are much more overt. III-inconjuncts become sexier after they're gone, where your memory of them works to elevate their appeal.

All of the above interpretations, by the way, assume that the other person has some area of their lives where they express power (rather than being dominated by the world's pressure in every sense). If you're one of those people who doesn't really dominate anything anywhere, this pair will be a lot weaker in your chart.

Them to you

You have a reputation for power in the eyes of Other under your angle. This is male coercive power especially. This half-pair also shows the nature of your attraction to Other as the embodiment of whatever coerces you under this angle. Sounds abstract? It is. Let's try it again. **Whatever experience can coerce you to show off or improve this angle, the other person embodies it. Your attraction to Other belies this desire to show off or improve your angle accordingly**.

Self chart

You have **a reputation which aligns with the world's standard of power** under this angle, possessing a top of the line characteristic which others would kill for.

Pluto-Vertex

You to them

You see Other working against greater pressures under their angle, where the decisions stand to be life-changing for them. You are typically involved in this somehow, but act more as a witness to its unfolding.

Them to you

Your outlook towards people and their standards are changed through your interactions with Other under your angle. I'll bet you didn't know there was a pair in your chart which was responsible for reassigning weights given to society itself—as in the case where your interaction with Joe causes you to stop believing that money is everything. This pair is called "Reevaluation." **Other serves as a strong means for rewriting your priorities under your angle**—hopefully in a favorable way.

Self chart

Major conflict is the means through which you evolve your approach to this angle. You can think of this as a kind of "karma," where life continually gives you lessons for getting this angle under control. **You also tend to create major conflict through excessive expression of this aspect**.

Pluto-Node

Growing with or growing against?

You to them

You see Other as a point of stability amidst your own troubles under this angle, though they possess their own unfulfilled background motives here. **You find it easier to endure pressures under your own angle, continuing to execute your plans in light of the other person**.

This half-pair revolves around your strength, as it assumes that Other is a growing source of support for you. Thus [Pluto $_{you}$-Node $_{them}$] is another good gauge for the progress of the relationship; are you getting stronger under this angle? If not, then things may still be okay. If you find yourself continuing to grow this angle 1) *against* the other person where previously you grew it with them or 2) intentionally despite their absence, this typically signals the beginning of the end for this exchange.

Them to you

You witness circumstances where Other is forced to act under their angle. **Life has limited their choices here—as if the world opposes Other's easy progress**. Positively, Other becomes very powerful under this angle in light of your company and typically stays that way throughout the relationship—as if they gain the strength to challenge the world on its own level.

Self chart

You are challenged to stand against the world under this angle, **making the struggle to overpower that world feel like your calling**.

Pluto-Selene

You to them

You view Other as either the embodiment of your major problems or as the enabler of your own solutions to those problems—the same basic thing if you think about it. If you are not busy placing hope in them to solve the issues before you, you tend to see Other as stifled under their own version of this same angle. It is important to note here that the issues which are solvable by Other aren't always your own issues, but those which you believe to exist anywhere in your world. For example, in a III-novile, the Pluto person may see the Selene person as possessing the power to lead large groups correctly even if you don't face crowd-steering as an issue in your own character.

Them to you

Your force is greatly increased in light of Other under your angle where, given enough support from them, you can feel unstoppable.

Self chart

You hold solutions to far-reaching problems here. Your use of this angle constitutes an area of **concentrated attention** on an issue whose roots far exceed your direct ability to address. This pair is associated with **obsessive focus** on the angle area at hand.

Pluto-Lilith

You to them

You experience Other as a means to almost revolutionary expression under this angle. Society isn't ready for this. A fly on the wall would be baffled and inspired at the same time. **If you're looking to make a unique impact on society, team up with Other under your expression of this angle and watch what kinds of waves you make**.

Them to you

Your rebelliousness is either difficult to suppress under this angle or your angle expresses standout power against competing abilities in others. This is a pair related to your great skill in the eyes of the other person. When working jointly, this angle is "extra shake-up strong" between you and Other in your world.

Self chart

Partnered with yourself, you still make waves in the world as in the synastry case, but these waves are less about teamwork and more about your own stubbornness. You **demand that things go your way**

here and are resistant to weaker versions of this angle area.

Pluto-Fortune

Where you make a tiny situation into a big one. The Subtractor

You to them

You enjoy issuing forth your power in light of Other under your angle. II-septiles are particularly notable in that you enjoy claiming Other as a member of your team here. Negatively, you express your power against Other's choices (which you view as unfavorable). Typically when their version of this angle expresses first and coincides with a choice you don't agree with, you are more likely to express your version of this angle contrary to them.

An important thing to note about this pair is that it tends to exaggerate the problems in resonant pairs. That is, when one person has decided to hate the other under this one, he typically sees other pairs with the same angle as more wrong than really are. This is one of those half-pairs most responsible for taking a salvageable relationship on a slippery slope downhill, and should be watched carefully in cases where you find yourself fighting to keep a struggling relationship alive. Amidst the struggle, whatever angle you have here has a good chance of being at the core of your problem. You'll notice this even more clearly as you witness Other piling mistake upon mistake via the alternative [Them to you] half-pair below. Such mistakes serve as a clue that you are poised to deduct more and more points from them under this pair and all other resonant pairs—just because [Pluto$_{you}$-Fortune$_{them}$] renders it comfortable for you to do so, not necessarily because they are actually guilty.

Them to you

You may be at home with Other's expression of power under their angle, but if this is not the case and you show you would rather have Other deliver that power some other way, they are more likely to disappear from your life sooner or later. **In really negative cases, you find Other's version of this angle wholly intolerable—in a setup which forms one of the main bases for their assault on your patience**.

Self chart

You are much more **comfortable answering the challenges of the world** here; you adopt a force to match the need and are **more easily pushed into combat**.

Pluto-Ceres

You to them

You are unsettled by Other's show of pressure upon your angle. If such pressure isn't conveyed then you are often the one with the power, in which case Other either becomes disillusioned in light of their inability to steer you or demonstrates an attraction towards this behavior in you. Attraction versus disillusionment, as usual, depends largely on the extent to which you use this angle in the other person's favor.

Them to you

You are, by default, not crazy about Other's angle arrangements, as Ceres adds to the pressure already felt by Pluto in this area. In most cases, this is **"Worsened Pressure" by you onto them**. Positively though, you can see Other as carrying more than their fair share of burdens under this angle, and are more likely to be attracted to this aspect of their company.

Self chart

You put more pressure upon yourself to **push others towards following your demands** under this angle.

Pluto-Chiron

You to them

You experience Other's angle as a remedy for tension felt either in yourself or in your relationship with them. The other person heals your problems with this angle, or may need your counsel themselves with this.

Them to you

You are kept grounded through Other's angle and are less likely to lose track of realistic expectations here.

Self chart

You keep a level head amidst world pressures as you solve issues within yourself related to this angle. You have **a measured approach to self-improvement which aligns you better with your role in the bigger world**.

Pluto-Vesta

You to them

Your angle is a point of fixation for the other person, though you are typically far less aware of this than they are. As a tool for rapport generation in normal cases and seduction in romance cases, this angle can be a means through which you ensnare Other when you execute this angle in both your favor.

Them to you

You are fixated on Other's angle as a hypnotizing source of power emanating from them, and as with many Pluto connections may find this an attractive quality in Other. The difference is that this is another quality which the other person can use to hold you hostage in a compliant state. **If they want you to freeze under their spell, this angle is one means of making that happen.** Negatively, you realize after your escape that you don't wish to be held hostage again, and make plans not to revisit Other.

Self chart

You are **fixated on a set of standards beyond yourself, driven to direct your own power towards addressing those standards.** Interestingly, this is one of the strongest indicators of your career field in that it reflects where you are inclined to keep regular, sustained focus on a specific realm of operation beyond that of the individual. The angle here shows your primary tool for bringing about progress in that field.

Pluto-Pallas

Are the two of you *really* like friends? Use this one to find out

You to them

You learn the art of fighting using your angle in light of Other's version of this angle, with Other as an example, counterexample, or motivating factor in the way opponents should be handled.

Them to you

You are more likely to fight on behalf of Other's angle or experience it as uncooperative in line with your agenda. Typically, the feeling of uncooperativeness is more common, but the willingness to fight for the other under this aspect was, in the dataset, one of the single strongest indicators of true friendship from you towards them. The alternate half-pair, of course, showed friendship from them to you and tended to be reciprocal.

If the other person is pushing for your interests under the [You to them] version of this angle, it is one of the best indicators that they seek a friendship with you. Do what you will with their efforts, but know that if you reject this angle from them you may not get another chance.

Self chart

Broad world issues awaken the fight within you in an aspect which indicates your **main area of interest in world affairs**.

Pluto-Juno

Wrongly or rightly, you can use their weakness for intensity to force yourself into their thoughts

You to them

You see Other's angle as a reliable basis for interfacing with them, though this may turn out to be negative in cases where Other's plans under their angle effectively require you to become someone else in order to work.

Them to you

You commit to Other's development under this angle, sometimes as a friend, sometimes as a critic.

Self chart

Amidst commitment behavior, you draw in the pressures of the world for partly determining how you interface with your commitment object. Under this angle you tend to have **powerful or attractive co-stars** whether they be people, projects, or actions to which you are dedicated. Throughout your life you'll find yourself setting up commitment agreements with others who compel intensity in this angle $_{fbow}$, in an aspect which provides an interesting look at the kinds of semi-destructive partners you return to over and over again.

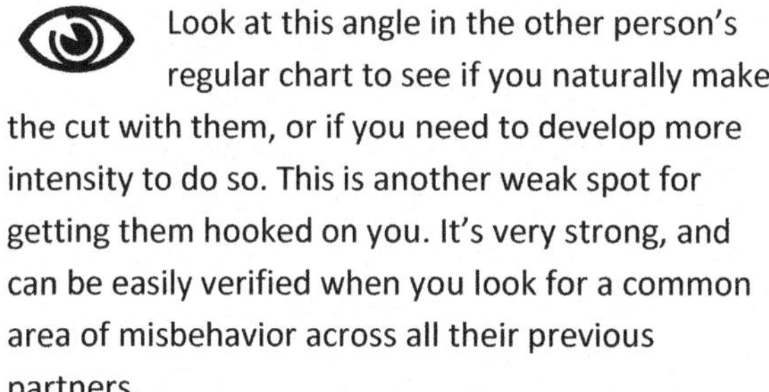

Look at this angle in the other person's regular chart to see if you naturally make the cut with them, or if you need to develop more intensity to do so. This is another weak spot for getting them hooked on you. It's very strong, and can be easily verified when you look for a common area of misbehavior across all their previous partners.

Pluto-Hera

You to them

You feel prolific under this angle, where Other attaches themselves to this trait out of a need to be fulfilled in a related area. Alternatively, their own version of this angle prevents them from sharing this side of themselves with you and subsequently prevents them and you from seeing eye to eye here.

Them to you

You see Other as needing to address pressure under their angle in order to feel personally effective. You are bonded to this effort $_{fbow}$.

Self chart

During bonding behavior you display a need to address world pressures. This is a straightforward read. **It is in this angle area that you form bonds with powerful people or ideas**. Note that these are actual bonds rather than promises to behave *as if* bonded. The latter constitute *commitments* and fall under the purview of [Pluto-Juno].

Pluto-Eros

✪ Decrease their will to act against you by adopting a style of passion which matches pressures they don't know how to fight

You to them

You and Other form lock and key complements under your driven support of their angle, provided that you are willing to take such a role in their life. **If not, you stand to reject Other in light of their spending of this angle on other people** instead of you. This is not jealousy though. Rather it tends to be a case of "they don't seem to have a place for me" in your eyes.

Them to you

You see Other as supporting your own powers under this angle—especially after the relationship ends. You are driven in light of the pressures levied upon them, such that their failure to support your angle-related drive compounded by their failure to surmount their own pressures gives rise to the metaphorical means through which you "kill" Other as an actor in your life. "Deaths" like this are definitely reversible, but tend to get reversed only if Other is able to forgive your severance of the tie.

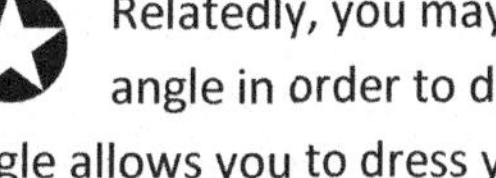

Relatedly, you may also flood Other with this angle in order to drain their vitality. This angle allows you to dress yourself up as a thing which regularly overwhelms them. This one constitutes a pretty cool weapon to have in an argument—relationship-safe or not.

Self chart

The pressure to show passion comes with this angle, such that you have a harder time being lukewarm here. This is the area in which **your own expression can drive up the level of passion in others around you**.

Pluto-Bacchus

Let your friends provide the lens of truth

You to them

You experience good old fashioned peer pressure under this angle in your interaction with Other. They and their group seem to issue standards for you which you often can't match. Where you can meet those standards, you become the target of admiration among their group without knowing. Negatively, you look to avoid Other's friends and cliques for worry that this angle will be a source of contention between you and that group.

This angle provides a really neat look at what you are best known for among Other's friends. Simultaneously, it shows the characteristic for which you would unknowingly use them to increase your own sense of social mobility. Conjuncts appeal to your raw instincts. II-squares make you feel more like a supportive family member to them. II-sextiles are strong long-term partners in analyzing a world full of errors. II-octiles support your esteem with their own self-confidence as you battle external challenges. II-undeciles increase your power to express your unique quirks. The company of III-oppositions makes you feel really popular; these people are often smooth or good-looking.

Them to you

Your group weighs in on the other person, giving a thumbs up or down based on this angle in particular. If you are someone who values the opinion of family and friends in selecting interactants, this is a good test which you can perform without having the other ever know. Ask yourself if your group would approve of this particular angle in your perspective person. You've seen enough to know what the answer would be. Even if the answer is yes, this angle still translates into a kind of expectation that issues from your cliques onto your Other. If the answer is "they wouldn't be able to tell" then watch out for secrets coming from this person. Part of the reason this test works is purely psychological: Your friends know those features which you highlight most brightly to them and carry a lot less of the side detail that you carry, allowing them to vote fairly objectively compared to you. If there are sides of the other which you should be able to judge but have elected not to, then you already know where you've opted to cover up certain aspects of your potential exchange. With Bacchus, though, a secret kept from your friends either means that you'll have a body of friends whose background competes with that of Other or an issue which you haven't figured out how to resolve yet—facilitating secrets which the Other is allowed to keep from you thanks, in part, to your own blinders.

This is one of the few pairs that does not mirror very well across half-pairs, since our cliques and our cliques' cliques have different ways of passing their opinions onto us. Sometimes both you and Other will be able to perform this same test directly, but often one of you will use the test while the other will just have a nagging feeling regarding the results of a test that they *would have* performed.

Self chart

Your friends approve. Your friends' friends approve. You've met the pressure standards and have been crowned a star. Under this angle it is possible for you to receive the **red carpet treatment**, provided you have successfully picked the right group of people to identify with. This won't always be the clique of folks that you keep by default.

Ascendant pairs

The start of the first house, or Ascendant (ASC), reflects how you first approach tasks. Although it is not a physical body in space (rather a spatial point instead) it does make meaningful angles to other points in the chart based on its role as a **Significator** **(a marker located on the astrowheel to represent some kind of experience)**. As long as angles of separation (harmonics) have defined meanings and as long as points on the wheel can stand for something, any two such points—whether or not they are associated with a physical planet—can form an astrological pair.[24] Points paired with the ASC describe first impressions, where the Ascendant person typically gets a view of the other person's planet as being that thing which the other tends to always bring forward when engaging the ASC person anew. We can use this tendency to read ASC pairs broadly: The Ascendant person thinks the point B person carries B with them into most new undertakings involving the angle between ASC and B. The point B person sees the ASC person as a shelf upon which to lay point B's expression. Let's bring these down to a less abstract level.

Ascendant-Ascendant

The angle between Ascendants shows where you and the other person have **similar approaches to attacking problems, exploring new terrains, or addressing new issues**. Perhaps surprisingly, this does not mean you will make good teammates or even get along with each other. It does mean, however, that you are moved by similar driving forces such that, no matter how far apart you are, you may yet find that your responses to angle-related events parallel each other with an eerie regularity. II-squares are great for people who would be (or actually are) family, and all angles which involve multiple people (which are most of them) favor joint action under the relevant angle, either towards each other or towards a shared external thing.

Ascendant-Midheaven

Pass the word of their deeds and support them here

Get noticed by other and their friends

Use this pair to research new angle meanings

You to them

You see Other's angle as the chief vehicle through which the world's view of them travels. **Much of what your sphere of experience knows about Other stems from their approach to this angle** $_{fbow}$. This angle of theirs is a good gauge for the means through which you and they would gain more public notice as partners. It is also an angle your support of which really helps the relationship get off the ground in the first place. Even among the most bitter of enemies, this half-pair is highly positive and stands in sharp contrast to pairs like the very destructive [Neptune-Vertex] combination.

For people researching newer astrological angles like the level IVs and up, I've found this **half-pair to be a good, very clear source of data on how each of those angles behave when you have about 50+ charts to compare against each other**. I call such pairs **definers**.

Them to you

Your actions under this angle earn you a public reputation in Other's world. Want Other's friends to notice you? Use this angle $_{fbow}$. This is an excellent area for showing you how to best manipulate your image in another's eyes, such that they will go back and tell their friends what you want them to tell. The closer you are to the Other, however, the harder it is to pull this off, since more of you will be revealed than you can effectively manipulate. Still, it helps get your foot in the door. Relatedly (and perhaps not surprisingly), this is also an excellent angle for showing those sides of you which Other finds most worth telling.

Self chart

You make your clearest impression on others and show them your truest self through this angle. Otherwise, people have a harder time getting to know what you really think you're about.

Ascendant-Vertex

You to them

You see Other's angle as the basis for discussion of parallels between yours and their lives. There is common ground here which convinces you that you and Other should share a path, but should you?

[24] I describe why this is in *FSA*.

Them to you
You and Other experience intertwined fates in light of your angle. Other arrives to compel a major change in how you approach your angle, and when such change is not on the menu, you and they tend to have parallel experiences under your angle in their eyes. Perhaps unfortunately, this angle is one of the chief culprits responsible for keeping you connected to a person after you've severed the tie with them. Early data suggested that you tend to dream more easily of Other's experience under this angle when they still think of you.

Self chart
[ASC-Vertex] shows the **set of life tools with which you most easily approach major change**.

Ascendant-Node

You to them
You find Other's approach to their angle better (or at least more salient) than that of their contemporaries. Negatively, you find this angle strikingly worse than that of their contemporaries, though the end results are similar: **You are driven towards what seems like spontaneous action in light of "how Other is" under this angle**. You see this a lot in the charts of people seemingly destined to affect each other strongly—in some abstract way, hovering around each other like binary stars when Other's angle is on the table. Conjuncts feature in compelling primal sexual attraction from you to them in general. This should make sense; as ASC seeks, not only does Node represent the find, but a "destined match" to be the find at that.

Overall, this pair features in fairly negative combinations mainly because both one's natural approach to the new and one's apparent "destiny" are frequently beyond one's ability to control without considerable conscious work. To that end, it can feel as though the other person's angle is being thrust upon you here.

Them to you
You are more likely to find Other erratic and unsettled under their angle, where you wonder what all the fuss is about. Note the super sharp contrast between this half-pair and its twin. You have a high-ish chance of being turned off by this angle in Other, but in rarer cases may find them refreshingly open-minded here instead.

Self chart
Word of your accomplishments is best passed onto others through your deeds under this angle. On the one hand you put in the work to do things which will ultimately strike others as fated. On the other hand you view most of those things as no big deal after they're done.

Ascendant-Selene

You to them
Of all possible dimensions of Other's life, you express the least under Other's angle. **Weirdly, this is what "reliance" looks like**. I would stop just short of saying that you can absolutely count on Other's angle under this one, but it's close—even after they become an enemy, even after you and they are no longer associated. Conjuncts mean you can count on them to be themselves. II-inconjuncts mean you can count on their emotional will.

✎🗁 For those researching new astrological angles, this half-pair is another good example of a definer because it is very strong and produces obvious effects on the relationship.

Them to you
You see Other's angle as offering you a home base of operations. **This is a section of their life in which you will always feel welcome** $_{\text{fbow}}$. "Welcome enemies?" you ask. Yes, like Shredder and Splinter. Remember, Other's angle is the one in charge here.

Self chart
You are talented on a level that looks like autopilot as you approach new situations under this angle. Nobody can quite put their finger on what's happening around you, but there is a seemingly otherworldly mojo which appears to help you along in affairs related to this. This is a very abstract pair whose effects in the self chart are just as hard to

describe now as they were in *FSA*. It corresponds to **something like luck**, though. I have a novile, for example, and have found that regardless of what I do or how well I do it, there is an inexplicably undeniable level of luck which follows my desire to learn new things.

If you haven't been looking up angles in your regular chart so far, you should definitely look up this one, then use *table 19-1* to find out where you are most strongly watched over by Lady Luck herself.

Ascendant-Lilith

You to them

You see Other as reliably contrary under your angle, providing an interesting counterpoint to your efforts. This does not necessarily mean you and they will be opponents. Instead, Other will drive a perspective that you did not initially perceive, and can usually serve as a ceaseless source of new adventures for you as a result. Squares are an emotionally weird read. Really. There's something weird about them from your point of view. II-quintiles reveal to you your own personal leanings as well as how you should interact with things and people in general (not just Other).

Them to you

You are a moving target in the eyes of Other under their angle, and won't be pinned down. Most of the time this will introduce some nice dynamism into the exchange, but sometimes when you feel Other is attempting to box you in under this angle, the exchange risks a rift that won't be mended.

Self chart

You yourself are reliably contrary as you approach situations related to this angle, sending signals which confuse others regarding what this angle is about. In a sense, you rebel against rebellion, and so preserve the status quo simply by reversing direction twice. **People thus come to believe that whatever it is you're trying to do as a rebel under this angle, it seems to be useful in some way**.

Ascendant-Fortune

You to them

You see that you and the other person have similar priorities under your angle, but are more likely to favor your own approach over theirs. **You two can share experiences in this realm, but by itself this half-pair is conducive to your view of Other as a fr& more than anything else**. If you do partner, you are typically the stronger of the two under this angle.

Them to you

You take an interest in exploring the future with Other under their angle, fueled by their desires for that same angle. This is a rare example of a well-balanced pair, where both planets are on equal footing in terms of role in their bearers' lives. Differences work well here.

Note that this is another one of those pairs which tells a noticeably different story depending on which half-pair lens you're viewing things through.

Self chart

You are **content with your approach to new situations** under this angle. The main difference between this pair and your [Sun-Moon] pair (through which this one is calculated) is that the midpoint of this pair will usually fall in a different house and sign, causing different feelings for describing this kind of contentment as well as a different means of showing it.

Ascendant-Ceres

You to them

You see Other as pushy under this angle, though pushiness can take many different forms ranging from subtle stubbornness to full-attack bullying.

Them to you

You read a more modest demeanor in Other than the rest of their attributes suggest should be there. It is important to compare this to the rest of Other's attributes because this placement itself does not make them appear humble. It only makes their particular angle appear more humble in light of Other's overall way.

Self chart
While pushing others to do things your way, you believe yourself to be behaving reasonably. In your view, you're not bullying, just "**strongly suggesting**."

Ascendant-Chiron

You to them
You view Other as a reference point for improving your skills as a "doctor" or "patient" under this angle. Other might be considered a living medical journal which you consult either to diagnose yourself or to train your diagnosis of others. Call this pair the "Therapy Reference Journal."

Them to you
You see Other as needing help or validation under their angle, as if they could use your help in escaping something. **Alternatively, Other helps outsiders escape issues related to this angle**—bringing out the angle in others as far as you can tell.

Self chart
You approach situations with a mind to help either outsiders or yourself. **You are the issue fixer here**.

Ascendant-Vesta

Capture their attention. It may not always be positive attention, though

You to them
You pay a lot more attention to Other's body or physical impression under their angle, regardless of whether they are male or female, stranger or acquaintance. The reason for this is interesting. First, this half-pair does not necessarily denote attraction. But as the Ascendant person takes an approach to something, they encounter the Vesta person being fixated on something. How would Ascendant know that Vesta is fixated? By paying longer attention to Vesta's "staring" at an issue! Weirdly then, the only way I know you're staring at something is to look at you long enough to call your looking "staring." So I need to observe your fixation process—a behavior almost exclusively revealed through your bodily actions. This is the angle which you believe captures Other's attention. If manipulated by you, this angle can be used to immerse Other in a process of your choosing.

Them to you
You find Other's angle well worth watching fbow, where this quality of theirs can put you into a kind of trance. Properly used, you can be comforted by this angle when Other expresses it. For example, I found this to be the case while watching a friend of mine sewing. We have a septile, and I just stared hypnotized for a pretty long time. Recall that septiles aren't just about 1:1 communication; they describe any process that requires constant, willing feedback between you and the thing which responds to you. So chatting, gaming, instrument playing, and sewing all count. Septiles and II-quintiles in particular have a way of wrapping you up in their "conversations" with things. III-inconjuncts engage you in ways that are difficult to forget, in an angle which facilitates your fascination with them.

Self chart
You approach a topic with deep engagement and are more likely to mean "**serious business**" amidst this angle topic.

Ascendant-Pallas

You to them
You see Other as passionate under their angle. In some cases you will even help them act on this passion. But if they believe they cannot trust you to assist, the usual "**with me or against me**" approach holds and they may use their version of this angle as a weapon against vulnerability to your distraction.

Them to you
You see Other as a fellow combatant under their angle. Where you struggle, their assistance is involved. **Negatively, you employ your version of the angle against their wishes**—in which case the adversarial relationship between you and them is typically very real.

Self chart
As James Brown once said, "Papa don't take no mess." In few places is this more apt than with [ASC-Pallas]. Here your focus for social action meets your new approach to things such that **you are hardly in the mood to be derailed under this angle**.

Ascendant-Juno

This is another member of the "Are they interested?" family of pairs

You to them
You frequently commit strongly to interfacing with Other under their angle. **If you and they are close, you seek to affirm and reaffirm the relationship using this angle as one of its most enjoyable aspects.**

Them to you
You receive Other's angle as a statement of their caring. This is part of the "Are they interested?" cocktail for determining if Other is interested in being your friend or ally. Does Other bring you this angle voluntarily? Do they bring it to you consistently or sporadically? Consistent showing of this angle tends to indicate Other's liking of your company, while sporadic presentation of this angle towards you implies a more utilitarian need.

Self chart
You approach new situations with the appearance of one who commits to what they are doing under this angle. **Display of the angle allows those who are interested in it to take greater notice of you, attracting their commitment in turn**.

Ascendant-Hera

Can you actually meet their expectations for bonding?

Find the groups that love you

You to them
You inspect Other's angle for suitability of shared worlds. **Clearly they bond with things under this angle, but do you fit what they are looking for?** Usually the answer is no because of plain old probability. You are wary of Other's demands under this angle. If you feel you can meet them then the exchange has a better chance. If not, then less of a chance. This is part of the "Will we make it?" cocktail for gauging a relationship's chance of success, as this pair shows your reaction to the other person's expectations.

Them to you
You fit Other's type of bonded object, but this aspect has a rather poor hit rate for fostering bonds since all it does is raise the expectations that Other places on you along with their degree of dependence on your approval. Given the number of objects in the chart though (25 in this book) the chances are pretty high that Other will have *some* stuff on your Hera, just not the Ascendant. Accordingly, this pair sets Other up for disappointment in you as an expresser under their angle; they'll just have to get the expected angle from you in other ways. Like Juno, Hera can be used by you to tell how interested the other person is in fostering the exchange with you. But whereas Juno shows Other's interest in keeping the exchange alive, Hera shows their interest in connecting with you on a level which attaches you to their inner emotional values—a much more vulnerable position, and one which is much more difficult to achieve.

All the negative pronouncements aside, this pair doesn't *always* fail. It just fails often.

Self chart
You approach new situations with the attitude of one who is willingly bonded to something. Other people tend to really like being greeted this way because it spares them the work of convincing you to look attached to them. Thus, in a pair which behaves very differently from its synastric counterparts, this angle shows **the area in which you are most likely to seem difficult to resist**.

Perhaps even more interesting than the above, the data suggested that you would be **disallowed entry into or even kicked out of places where you yourself felt the environment was not**

conducive to this angle. Your successful bonding in a new situation is highly dependent on the degree to which you believe this angle can be built up there, making this pair one of the more useful to control among all the pairs we've studied so far. In general, the lower and more basic the angle, the more popular you'll tend to be in new situations. Conjuncts, trines, sextiles, and II-undeciles all have a social advantage. Septiles do too, but are more relationship-dependent presumably out of a need to connect more deeply with others in order for the approach-bonding to get started. Undeciles are generally accepted by people to be popular, but are often intolerable or troubled when you engage them personally—unable to live up to the hype placed upon them unless their exchange with you is of the impersonal kind. Regardless of the angle you have, though, the pickier you are regarding the company you keep here, the more likely you are to be isolated. Isaac Newton had an inconjunct. Niccoló Machiavelli had a trine. There is also some evidence that the same kinds of people who will have built you up in life will build you up in death. Inspect the resonant pairs to get a better idea of where you bond socially in the most natural way.

Ascendant-Eros

Keep the fires burning

You to them

The relationship is most creatively tense when you receive Other's angle. All kinds of things get generated under their angle here, making for a prolific duo. Art, sex, ideas, and influence are among the events that flourish when this angle is on. Negatively, these things are made combative or (worse) hindered in each person as you and they fight each other to express different versions of the same thing. If the other person executes this angle wrongly in your eyes, the relationship can definitely be destroyed permanently. Sextiles are tricky in such cases because their misuse occurs more in the form of expectations imposed upon you—often for friendship or cooperation—which is greeted with something like contempt when those expectations aren't met. In other news, just hearing about the deeds of undeciles can make you crazy. These people can turn you on or turn your temper up *very* easily from a position of social attractiveness just beyond your reach.

Them to you

In answer to the question, "What can I give to drive this relationship's intensity?" you use your angle alongside Other's aspiration to produce powerful creativity. This is one of the best pairs for maintaining the dynamic quality in an exchange. **Negatively, you will feel like you can't or shouldn't try to connect with Other here, as something in their mix renders them "off limits"** to this aspect of your personality. *Off limits* is the actual feeling in your case. *Combat* is the feeling in Other's case if you should proceed anyway.

This pair is another good angle definer.

Self chart

You move passionately forward with an air of **amorousness or steamrolling intensity** under this angle's affairs.

Ascendant-Bacchus

You to them

You influence Other's clique via this angle $_{fbow}$, making it harder for them and their friends to resist (or even ignore) your influence. III-septiles are tricky, since this case strongly suggests that yours or their friends need to bring you together in the first place, otherwise you are inclined to forget about each other. Once solidly committed, though, your relationship can remain strong as long as you continue to share a core friendship network or doctrine for guiding your behaviors.

Them to you

Your clique absorbs Other's angle into its function $_{fbow}$. In a sense, Other's angle reflects the standards that you hold your own peers to, either in support of or in contrast to Other's approach here.

This is another one of those occasions where it pays to have a kind of database to survey your friends. You can easily see how your clique works by going down the line of [ASC $_{them}$-Bacchus $_{you}$] angles you've stood for or against.

Self chart

Your approach to new situations aligns with the overall behavior of your friends. You are more inclined to **administer to the needs of your ingroup** here.

On sexual attraction and liars

Maybe you can explain something to me. As I read through your notes and compare them to my own experiences, I keep seeing how the pretty women I've been attracted to tend to be liars. What's that all about? Have you found anything in your work to explain how I can stop meeting such women?

You and your pretty girls. Them and their bad boys. It could just be something in your own chart. But this is also tied a general myth among people crossing social rank. Both pretty women and bad boys appear—to their seekers—to have a tendency to "lie" (or be otherwise unstable). But you don't really need astrology to explain why.

Oh?

It's just the law of large numbers. The more attractive I am to other people, the more they hit on me, the more I realize that they'll give me what I want. But if I'm honest with them and tell them to get in line behind plenty of more interesting people, they'll hate me and remove all those perks. Then we're both unhappy. So I learn to leave them hanging instead. *Some* of this may consist of little deceptions on my part. But *most* of this is simply the person deceiving themselves using me as an excuse. If only they didn't think with their hormones, they might spend their energy on someone who was actually interested in them.

Ouch!

Hey, you asked. Geery brushed back his hair to keep up the role. But it's not all gravy for us "pretty liars," you know. First of all, most of us don't lie or cheat any more than the average person. But the people whom we allow around us tend to suspect us of doing this a little more than average. That's what the data said anyway. Either we or our partners are more likely to battle personal insecurity against the pressure to maintain that image we've acquired. And then there is the idea that we can't just be ourselves as easily as normal people—even if insecurity is not a problem.

Hmph. Your story brings tears to my eyes, man, Hayden replied sarcastically.

Hey, I'm just saying it takes a lot of work to walk around with an Ascendant-Juno or Midheaven-Hera conjunct, where everyone thinks they're entitled to your love and attention. They don't earn it, mind you. They just let your bad boy image or hot girl look drive them animal-style into your world. Yes it's flattering sometimes, but it's also annoying and weird when you don't seek this on purpose.

Hayden looked unimpressed.

Seriously though, Geery finally came back down to the real world, sobering up. I'm not telling you that attractive people have harder lives. Normal social psychological research tells you that they basically have easier lives in terms of status-opportunities across the board. They make more money, get faster promotions, and generally get away with more offenses than others without having to prove themselves. But the tradeoff is that their happiness becomes married to that lifestyle, where aging and the passage of their popularity onto the next hot thing can do much more damage to their esteem than it does to so-called normal people. And just as they are more sensitive to their own flaws, they're also more sensitive to their own flaws. Know what I mean?

Hmm. And I presume you saw this in your research?

I did. Venus-Mars, Ascendant-Hera, and several other pairs which involved getting people to do what you want based on the other person's liking of your external qualities compromised those people's ability to support your *actual* deeds or inner wishes. Don't let our society fool you. We don't live in front of mirrors. But we always live with our inner perception of ourselves. External attraction may make the grass greener, but it doesn't make the trash cleaner. While people are taught to get frustrated over things they can't be and can't have, those who do have it frequently find that "having" isn't really the thing. *Being* is. And that being is often made harder with higher social status, not easier. You shouldn't assume that attractive people are liars just because *you* won't be honest with yourself about what draws you to them. You'd do better to get your own values straight before chasing after them again.

Hayden thought for a moment. Hmmm. I don't normally let people preach to me, but okay. I stand informed.

Midheaven pairs

The Midheaven (MC) marks the **cusp** of (**start of**) house 10, the house of public reputation and approaches to authority. Relatedly, it also shows us the reputation of *things* and situations. This location is surprisingly strong in synastry because it essentially marks the planet it's associated with as publicly viewable and label-able.

As the MC is strongly associated with Capricorn and Saturn, it pays to set up an analogy showing the differences among the roles played by houses like the 10th, planets like Saturn, and signs like Capricorn.

The differences among planets, signs, and houses

Think of human experience as being categorizable into different groups. Suppose, for example that the "10th category" corresponds to the "mechanic's group." Saturn would be like an actual mechanic; his sign and house would tell you where and how he does his work respectively. The 10th house would be like the mechanic's shop; of course you typically go there to have your vehicle tended to, but there are other things that happen in this shop besides "mechanic-ing." The various objects in this place are employed to help the whole shop run. Analogously, the Midheaven would be a Saturn "kind of place" which includes many non-Saturn ideas in it (planets besides Saturn). The sign Capricorn adds a "mechanic's" quality to the planets in it—as a therapist or actor who approaches his role with diagnostic precision.

If you want to take the above analogy even further, angles like the decile would highlight certain goal-oriented actions (Planet A-Planet B) as being expressed while you perform a mechanic's duties (level I), while you're being socially treated as a mechanic (level II), while you're serving as an official example of a mechanic in the eyes of groups (level III), and—presumably—while you project a mechanic's brand of ideas in the world (level IV?).

Whereas it was easier to see what the ASC was about in the chart, it can be harder to separate the role of the MC from that of Saturn if you don't know what things like the MC and Saturn actually tell you.

- Houses show circumstances.
- Planets show the specialists who work there.
- Signs color the things in such houses with the style of such specialists, and
- angles mark planet-pair behaviors as being typical of that specialist in action.

Should you ever decide to take your studies of astrology further and look at other house cusps in synastry, you might use this analogy to understand what you're looking at.

(READ ME!) How the synastric Midheaven works

As we've seen in what may arguably be one of the most important pairs in all of synastry—[Sun-MC]—when there is no active Midheaven in synastry, there is no label for how the Midheaven person sees the other person's planet behaving. So if my MC is trine your Sun and I stop sharing my personal opinions with you, our direct interaction basically dies; here your Sun (1:1 direct interaction) loses its publicly viewable label in my world. The same goes for most other planets to the Midheaven. Keeping this in mind, you can read most combinations to the Midheaven as reflecting 1) the realm in which the non-MC planet or point gets officially seen by the MC person, and 2) gains a publicly recognizable outlet towards the MC person in the eyes of the non-MC person.

If you want, for example, a publicly recognizable emotional connection with a person, then it is your Moon (emotion) which needs the outlet and their MC (public gateway) which needs to acknowledge that Moon. Suppose, then, that [Moon $_{you}$-MC $_{them}$] has an octile. This means that the other person would have to display their desire to steer you or steer things you're involved with in order to keep your emotional connection to them visible. If you simply wanted to keep *conversing* regularly with them, then they'd need to maintain whatever angle is between your *Venus* (1:1 conversation) and their MC (public viewer).

Midheaven-Midheaven

The angle between yours and the other person's MC shows the area of life under which outsiders are inclined to associate you publicly. If you're thinking of going on a public campaign with your favorite partner in crime, consider this to be the domain in which the public will glue you together. This pair also shows the realm in which you take a similar approach to structuring experiences for others—whatever that means. People tend to be more strongly struck by the creative connection between II-inconjuncts.

Midheaven-Vertex

You to them

Your public image influences how Other responds to you through this angle. **Call this one "Spillover:" where Other reacts to, benefits from, or pays the price for association with you under their angle**.

Them to you

You enter Other's world through their angle and experience a change in how you view them. This is often negative, though it can be positive if Other allows you more control over how they execute this angle.

Self chart

You incur the costs and benefits of the reputation you have, in an angle whose use serves to **alter how the public views you**.

Midheaven-Node

How do you rub off on each other?

The face of self destruction is this

You to them

Your angle is used to add more structure to Other's sense of destiny $_{fbow}$. **You often provide insight to them regarding their own direction here**, though you don't always know you're doing it.

Them to you

Your angle accompanies a seemingly inevitable change in how Other approaches their own version of the angle, re-conveying it to you. **They record your behaviors here, in an angle which truly reflects how you "rub off" on them**.

Self chart

You can't really influence yourself the way you influence another person, but you can and do **experience seemingly inevitable change in light of your own reputation** through this angle. While this angle is unrefined, such change can be very negative. I have a square which implies change through the loss of emotional control, and OH the stories I could tell you! Read *table 19-6* as if those behaviors are turned towards yourself to see how you can use this angle to mess yourself up in the public view. III-conjuncts for example, do things to make their own ingroups disrespect them. II-sextiles differ from the table behavior in that they suffer through the mis-imposition of long range plans. They can also hurt their reputation by imposing an unwelcome form of logic or criticism upon others.

Midheaven-Selene

You to them
You see your effects on the public under this angle as being nearly ideal in your association with the other person. **You two make a good public team here**.

Them to you
You are identified by people as a strong partner to Other under their angle fbow.

Self chart
Your talents shine through to your reputation under this angle, where **things just seem to work in your favor**.

Midheaven-Lilith

You to them
You and Other are **publicly known as a rebel pair under their angle, where you tend to be the cooler-headed half of the duo**.

Them to you
You encourage Other (passively or actively) to adopt nonconformist standards under their angle. You see them under their angle as liberated from basic stifling norms.

Self chart
Via this angle, **rebellion becomes you** in ways that the public can accept.

Midheaven-Fortune

Another test for gauging true friendship

You to them
Your image is boosted by Other's enjoyment of your company under this angle. If they don't enjoy your company, your image is lowered in forced association with them here. Be honest with yourself regarding this one and you'll find it to be a great gauge of the real potential for friendship with the other person.

Them to you
You value your association with Other under angle, as if theirs is a well-designed complement to your experience under that angle. This also works for enemies.

Self chart
This one is straightforward. **You're more comfortable with your own reputation** under this angle.

Midheaven-Ceres

You to them
You see Other as a known caretaker under their angle. This does not indicate who or what they take care of, only that they do it.

Them to you
You view Other as promoting themselves (usually unknowingly) in a quest for significance under your angle in the world's eyes.

Self chart
You are publicly acknowledged to be **one who wishes to place their form of caring upon others under this angle**.

Midheaven-Chiron

You to them
You see Other as being very difficult to influence under their angle, despite being more than a little quirky here.

Them to you
You see Other as being less secure under their angle. In rare cases, you can view Other as a counselor to people here.

Self chart
You are labeled by the public, **with a reputation for responding oddly** to those labels. Overall, the self chart interpretation of this pair differs considerably from the regular chart interpretation in that the self chart is skewed more towards how the public would see you than how you see yourself. Though you may think of yourself as a doctor or a patient by

reputation, the public only views your overall approach to your angle "field" as being idiosyncratic on both sides of the couch.

Midheaven-Vesta

You to them

You view Other as being (basically) obsessed with (or highly self-conscious of) their angle. There is great creativity here coupled with great stubbornness within them.

Them to you

You are made much more aware of your angle in your interactions with Other. **This corner of your experience shows your self-consciousness around them**.

Self chart

Here is another basic read. You are **more focused on your reputation** under this angle.

Midheaven-Pallas

You to them

You are driven to press for your own values under Other's angle, making you either intractable or an excellent source of support to them here.

Them to you

You see Other as combative or crusade-prone through their angle. **Other seems to naturally seek to challenge people here**.

Self chart

Ironically, although Pallas generally revolves around socially justified war, the public (as in the case of [MC-Chiron]) does not know the extent to which you are internally discontented. It only knows the reasons for your crusading reputation. Accordingly, the regular chart version of [MC-Pallas] shows the angle area under which you are seen as a seeker of resolution to conflict rather than as **a person who internally thrives on conflicts they create for themselves**. The self chart, on the other hand, shows you as the latter (which is probably closer to the truth).

Midheaven-Juno

You to them

The public sees you as showing your commitment to Other through your angle. **As people see you giving this angle to Other in their favor, the commitment is strengthened**.

Them to you

In the eyes of the public, you receive Other's angle as a token of their commitment.

Self chart

You are associated with commitment behavior in the public view. But it is here that we get to see the kind of commitment that Juno truly brings. It's not necessarily commitment to people, but to endeavors in general. We call **the undertakings to which you are "wed by action" commitment-objects**. **Your angle here reflects the area of life where the general public most strongly associates you with commitment to such commitment-objects**.

Midheaven-Hera

✪ Is your relationship on its deathbed? Find a replacement for this angle to protect yourself against the coming pain of loss

You to them

You publicly show your bond to Other $_{\text{fbow}}$. This is a very strong aspect which plays out both for friends and enemies. As an enemy to Other, you display your thwarted emotional investment in them via this angle. With II-inconjuncts your beef isn't so much with the person as it is with their deeds. With II-quintiles, it's with their interaction choices. With III-oppositions, the problem is with the groups which support Other, for example. *Tables 19-2*, *19-3*, and *19-7* are all good for reading the nature of any conflict under this angle, though the chances of things going smoothly instead are about 50-50.

Them to you

The public automatically assumes you to receive Other's show of bonding through their angle. **Unlike**

the [MC-Juno] case, affection and attachment $_{fbow}$ are implied here. Long term angles make better couples.

This is another example of a potentially one-way pair. While this particular half-pair favors attachment from them to you, the [You to them] case does not always favor this. The [MC $_{them}$-Hera $_{you}$] angle is one of those which it hurts a lot more for you to lose after the relationship has ended and may be one of those for which you wish to seek an imminent replacement amidst a relationship which you know is on its last leg.

Self chart

Walking around with a reputation for looking "bondable" among the people who think of you, this angle shows **the circumstances under which people instantly like you** as well as the trait (that you have) which they find most genuinely validating (of themselves).

As in the synastric case, this angle is very useful as a retreat when you have incurred the loss of a bond. Particularly for those who are emotionally sensitive or prone to depression, this angle's affairs serve as a place for you to go when you feel as though a key bond has eluded you. On the negative side, I've also found in the data that this angle is frequently used as a crutch for those protecting themselves against being hurt by any bond at all.

Midheaven-Eros

You to them

The world knows you as driven to passionate action by Other's angle. This may indicate a strong motivation for you to engage them or great anger instilled in you by them.

Them to you

You see Other's angle as a possible liability in building your reputation. Why? Your area of passion encounters Other's fixed public label—essentially a static image prone to overhyping and one-dimensionalizing by others. By association, your Eros may also be so pigeonholed.

Self chart

Your **public reputation for passion** attends this angle.

Midheaven-Bacchus

You to them

You see Other's angle as foundational to their membership in their cliques. This is one basis for their identity in that clique.

Them to you

Your social groups and cliques highlight Other's angle as the basis of the attention they pay to Other, where Other is a contributor to how they operate.

Self chart

With your reputation under this angle comes the attention of cliques and peer groups. You are the **public crowd attractor**.

Vertex pairs

The Vertex (Vx) represents the intersection of the potential and the actual. Astronomically this is literally one of the intersections of the path of the Sun with the path traced out from horizon to horizon via the highest point in the sky. The end result is that it corresponds to areas where you are most susceptible to major life changing interactions. (The point opposite it, called the Anti-vertex is roughly where you serve as the change agent acting upon your surroundings.) Thinking about this mathematically, we might consider the Vertex as being the western point where the most optimal track for lining up houses meets the most optimal track for lining up planets. This is the point where a would-be planet does its least clouded work in a particular interaction-receiving situation: where interactions received are most dramatically noticeable. Seated on the eastern side of the chart on the other hand, the Anti-vertex would be the point where the interaction-causing person themselves would be most noticeable. If the Vertex is where you *experience* the most dramatic change, the Anti-vertex is where you *cause* the most dramatic change.

In synastry, the Vertex person's version of the other person's planet is typically the thing that changes, while the other person's planet is seen as facilitating the change. In this sense the Vx becomes almost invisible, though it remains very powerful.

We've seen how one of the strongest changing pairs, [Mars-Vx], causes the Vx person's power to go through the roof. This is actually the Vx person's version of Mars getting "life-changed" by the other person's Mars. In this way, we can use our relationships with others—friend or foe, dead or alive, person or object—to drive our own planets up in influence. The tradeoff is that many of the things we used to settle for tend to be irreversibly outgrown (at least in the ways we used to interact with them).

A personal note you might find interesting

For various reasons I won't get into, I began writing this book (*HBS*) at exactly 1:31am October 16, 2016. This was planned based on calculations drawn from the book's predecessor *FSA*. As a result, *HBS* has a kind of weird quality which I think you'll discover if you read it in full. No skipping sections. To help you get the most from that quality, I present to you the official birth time of this book for you to calculate its synastry with your own chart. Use it with your Vertex and see what happens.

Hayden's Book of Synastry (10/16/2016 1:31:00 AM GMT-6:00, Daylight Savings Time: Yes) San Antonio, TX (29N30'41 98W41'33).

Vertex-Vertex

The angle between yours and Other's Vertex shows where you and they have **similar drivers for life change**, but not much more than this. It is the case, however, that the two of you can expect big effects fbow when you team up with each other under this angle.

Vertex-Node

You to them
In hindsight, you see Other's angle as having been almost fated to change your dynamic permanently. **This is the nature of a critical event in yours and their exchange which makes—or more often breaks—the relationship**.

Them to you
Your angle is the means through which seemingly unavoidable changes are brought to the relationship. Your behavior with respect to this angle in Other's life is more likely to be risky.

Self chart
Some of your **most obvious lessons** in life occur through this angle, as both "destiny" and major change intersect.

Vertex-Selene

You to them
You appreciate the strength of expression in Other's angle, and are more easily trained by it in conveying your own version of the angle.

Them to you
You observe that which is often a mismatched lifestyle in Other under their angle. **You learn lessons regarding how your own angle should be conducted, but typically opt not to adopt their ways**.

Self chart
This is an interesting pair whose effects were fairly difficult to read in the original dataset, but whose meaning becomes clearer in the self chart. While you appreciate your own expressive talent, you're not nearly as likely to buy into it as being that special. This is essentially a position of humility, where your capacity to express your skill is constantly offset by the need to use that skill in new areas. This can be summarized as **the cost of using your talent** or it can be thought of as **the talent you have which is more resistant to flattery**. People who praise you for this talent are essentially telling you something you

already know, and you may be more inclined to distrust their motives for doing so.

Vertex-Lilith

You to them

You see Other's angle as an area in which they are stubborn to the point of being almost untrainable. Epic fights between you and them are more likely to be rooted in this angle (in your eyes). **On a normal day, this half-pair simply shows up as a longstanding waywardness in the other person**.

Them to you

You keep your agenda regarding this angle beyond the strong influence of the other person. **Although Other may see this as stubbornness, it's more like this angle is schmooze-resistant in your world**. That is, unlike many sides of ourselves which are depicted as casually open to people's influence, we make no pretense regarding how fixed this particular trait of ours is.

Self chart

You insist on putting your own unique stamp on things under this angle, **stubbornly resisting having others autopilot for you**. That's under normal conditions. Under exceptional conditions, this angle serves as the area of life under which you conduct **final rebellion**—where you burn bridges with such enthusiasm that everyone within viewing distance knows not to mess with you on this issue you ever again. At least not without major consequences.

Vertex-Fortune

You to them

In your interaction with Other, you call attention to major events via your angle. **Many of your deep personal discoveries in the exchange with Other come through this angle**.

Them to you

You see Other's angle as being their most comfortable means for experiencing newer events. Such events shape and reshape their personality.

Self chart

You are comfortable expressing the major personal changes in your life. Not surprisingly, this angle corresponds to **the realm in which you do your "victory strut,"** willingly telling everyone what you did and how you did it.

Vertex-Ceres

You to them

You see the other person as attempting to persuade you into their way of thinking using their angle. Will you allow this? It is through [their imposition of this angle upon you] or [their failure to beneficially share it with you] that your view of life is changed.

Them to you

You use your angle to advance your ends and overrule paths suggested by the other person. In so doing, you bring about change for them under this angle.

Self chart

This angle shows the area of life in which **your decision to care for or abandon others brings about change for you**.

Vertex-Chiron

You to them

You feel that you can bring out the best in Other by engaging their angle. **You are a kind of doctor to them here, not so much healing them as elevating their pre-existing talents**.

Them to you

You experience a change in perspective conducive to your development under interaction with Other. Maybe **accidentally, they learn lessons in tackling their fears through you**.

Self chart

This angle shows **where you can change your own life via your means of tackling fears and insecurities**, whether or not these are your own.

Vertex-Vesta

You to them

You have a way of displaying your angle that Other has a hard time getting used to. This need not be strictly positive or negative, just that **Other has to watch out for left turns from you in this area**.

This aspect can be pretty fun for you sometimes while simultaneously unsettling to them. But how is it that Vesta, an asteroid related to focus, shows up as unpredictability here? Recall that in synastry, it is the Vx person's version of the other's planet that becomes supercharged. In [Vertex $_{you}$-Vesta $_{them}$], your Vesta becomes augmented, allowing you to focus even more strongly on things you were inclined to focus on in the first place. The result is that you are actually the same person as before, except with more audacity and more noticeable resistance to input which Other could successfully give under most other angles. Your seeming unpredictability is a byproduct of renewed concentration on things you were already interested in, allowing you not only to jump back over to those things when the feeling occurs to you, but also to maintain such a habit of jumping for an indefinite amount of time.

We can also think of your "left turns" as simply reflecting your focus on how the other has changed, tying your obvious behavior to their subtle evolution.

Them to you

You find Other's approach to this angle interesting, though a little distracting—**as if their way of doing a thing that you are well familiar with continually catches you off guard** with its deviation from your template. This isn't them surprising you, but it is them taking a notably different approach to something you thought you understood.

Self chart

You remain focused, but change your circumstances as you do so, **keeping up with your chosen topic even as sporadic bursts of progress are made**.

Vertex-Pallas

You to them

Your inner warrior is awakened by exposure to Other's angle, where the latter goads you into crusade-like action in response to what you've seen.

Them to you

You use your angle to kick the other person, pushing them forward in the world, but this is more accidental for certain kinds of angles than others (depending on how each angle behaves in your own chart). Sometimes it is your commentary regarding the other person's approach to their own angle that does the trick, though this near-lecture is noticeably less favorable than the case where Other is inspired on their own. The near-lecture, unlike "auto-inspire," typically brings with it your active disapproval of Other's methods.

Self chart

You push yourself forward as a social actor in the world, bringing about changes in the thing you're acting upon. **This tendency to intentionally drive change in your interactants makes for circumstances that both welcome you and resist your influence.** Semi-adversarial relationships often come along with such circumstances.

Vertex-Juno

This pair had effects which were inconclusive, and requires more research.

You to them

You are the recipient of committed attention from Other under their angle $_{fbow}$. This can definitely swing from love to hate on their part, where the approach chosen depends largely on whether you welcome Other's attention here. This half-pair is not mutual either between you and them or between itself and its alternative half-pair.

Them to you

You and Other seem destined to be friends, allies, or committed enemies under your angle in your

eyes. Squares seem more desire-heavy. II-oppositions are particularly interesting in that they revolve around race- or class-typical assumptions related to Other's body identity. You respond strongly to Other's self-identification or sexuality under a II-septile. You respond strongly to Other's individuality under a II-undecile. You are more likely to fight the world on behalf of (or because of) Other under a III-opposition. You may feel Other to be mysteriously inhibiting under III-inconjuncts though, as Other may not give enough information to respond to your messages.

Actually, [Vertex $_{them}$-Juno $_{you}$] is a bit strange in that it is a lot more human mood-based than other pairs. This is possibly because we're dealing with life change as humans define it and commitment as humans define it. As much as I would love to provide further details on this one, the data were simply inconclusive as to what was happening beyond the specific cases mentioned in the paragraph above. That is to say, although we can conclude with some confidence that this half-pair creates a feeling of destined commitment from you to them, WE CANNOT USE ANY OF THE TABLES IN THIS BOOK TO CONCLUDE SPECIFIC OUTCOMES beyond the square, II-opposition, II-septile, II-undecile, III-opposition, and III-conjunct cases above. More research is needed.

Self chart

Earlier data discussed in *FSA* suggest that this angle shows the area of life where you can change others by committing to them. With partial insight from the self chart, we might speculate that [Vertex-Juno] in your regular chart shows **where commitment behavior on your part is aimed at a particular change in circumstances for *you*.**

Vertex-Hera

This angle provides an interesting look at the change one seeks through bonding

partner **It also shows you the kinds of people / situations the other person tends to bond with**

You to them

You find yourself hooked on Other's approach to their angle $_{fbow}$, in an aspect which is hard to get out of your mind. (Accordingly we'll call this one "Can't Get it Out of My Mind.") Other can use this to ensnare you.

Them to you

Your angle remains fixed on the mind of Other, in a pair which serves as a kind of thought bubble over the head of Other regarding you. Look at the resonant pairs to see what those thoughts revolve around. This is "What Captures You Most About Me." If you are not seen as very forthcoming with this angle, it serves as a source of suspicion held by Other.

Self chart

Through bonding behavior you attach more readily to the bonded object in a way that most easily changes your approach to this angle's family of resonant pairs. **Bonding as a new endeavor is more likely to be undertaken for the purpose of rewriting this area of your life.** Take a look at this angle in the other person's chart to get some really good insight into how they seek to change their own lives through bonding with others. There is a decent chance that such knowledge will give you an upper hand in wooing them. partner Look also at their resonant pairs to get an even fuller picture of the kinds of people they bond with. The more you match this face, the better your chances. For better or worse.

Vertex-Eros

You to them

You find Other's angle a source of agitating provocation, compelling you to do more with who you are and what you want out of life. "This is Passion Ignited." Others with septiles have a talent for making you mad. (If you have septiles in your self chart, you have a talent for making *yourself* mad; this angle contributes to the proverbial "short fuse" by making people prone to life-changing passion through conversation.)

Them to you

You incite driven action in Other under their angle. In some cases this can imply passion, but in most cases it amounts to a kind of quiet craving for new status held by Other towards their various goals. Call this one the "Passion Inciter."

Self chart

You incite passion in yourself through this angle. People with angles that involve deeply invested connections with others (septiles, II-squares, II-septiles, and III-oppositions [with their fans]) tend to be both noticeably hot-tempered when turned off and intimidatingly sexy when turned on, as their passion automatically comes with such connections. These tend to be sensitive to their interactants' approval. Relatedly, people with angles that involved performance for outside groups (undeciles, II-octiles, III-quintiles, and sometimes III-oppositions again) can be better described as intense rather than hot-blooded, and are more visibly distressed in the face of possible public failure.

Vertex-Bacchus

Will their friends let you in? Another quick diagnosis (and a very good one at that)

Why do they choose the friends they choose in the first place?

You to them

You are put into contact with Other's social group via their angle, giving you a glimpse of who their friends are as bonded influencers of Other. Basically, Other's friends inform their angle, so that you can look at how welcoming this angle is to see how welcome you are into their world overall. **Do the other person's friends willingly show you this angle *positively*?** Be honest. This is another excellent indicator of how smoothly your entry into the other person's world will be.

Them to you

This is the "Emissary." **You use your angle as the spokesperson for your clique. If you welcome Other with this angle, your clique generally welcomes Other. If not, then no**. this is a great "keeper of the level head" when you find yourself torn over whether you should welcome Other more fully into your life. How do you send this angle out to them? Our old familiar *table 19-1* tells the tale.

Self chart

As with Hera, this angle is a great indicator of the primary trajectory towards change which motivates your association with certain others. **This time, though, we get a glimpse at the main motivation for one's group choice**. Check it out in your own as well as your partners' charts. Again, the insight this one provides should be very useful.

Hayden on changes in circumstance

Now I'm not saying I quite believe all of this stuff, mind you, but hear me out. As I look through these findings I am reminded of an old girlfriend I had. We seemed so close when we first met, but then things changed and it was like she didn't know me anymore. And I suppose it was as though I didn't know her. It actually reminded me of that Billy Joel song "The Stranger." Now it seems to me that so much of a person's relationship to another depends on the circumstances which brought the two together in the first place, and when those circumstances change, the relationship changes. In hindsight this is quite obvious, but I don't believe I've ever thought of it in terms of angles. You know, things you can actually pinpoint and control.

I actually looked up that old girlfriend's "self chart"—her regular birth chart as read using synastry information—and found something interesting. She had a Vertex-Hera II-trine and a Vertex-Eros III-undecile. Supposedly the II-trine shows how you take over a room with your ways and a III-undecile shows where you pursue your unique curiosity, maybe up to genius level. And it is true that she was much more likely to bond with me when we worked together. There we "shared a room" in a sense and our interaction made her more attention-grabbing to others there. Those same conditions were also described by exploration, so that she could display her unique brand of curiosity-driven insight to our colleagues. Then the job ended, and I suppose we both thought our relationship would be able to continue past it. But it didn't. Instead, our mutual liking grew cold and the bond failed.

The failure of my bond with the lady above would not have been a big deal had it not also described so many of my other relationships. As a proud soldier with his own Vertex-Juno in II-decile, I suppose advancing my career really is the main reason that I commit to anything. I'm a bit of a nomad on this point, so job changes for me are synonymous with whole lifestyle changes that frequently wipe out most of the bonds I built previously. Of course my lady friend couldn't be expected to simply join me in my new role, and without a platform for her II-trine room attention and III-undecile curiosity-driving *at my hand*, my role in her life became effectively moot. And so we had nothing. I find this amazing, because you really don't know how fragile most friendships are under a major move or something like that. You think the other person is really into *you*. And maybe they are. But how often does it occur to you that their definition of "you" is tied to the world in which they've come to know you? When that world changes, is it really true that—in their eyes—*you* also change so drastically?

I've still yet to be convinced regarding all this astrology, but one thing is certain. All these dimensions really do make you think. I'd be lying if I told you that learning all this stuff hasn't changed my perspective; the next time I find a bond that I really do want to keep, I will definitely do things differently. Namely, I plan to show more respect for the original circumstances under which the other person and I met. And if I plan to keep her, I imagine I'll also do my best to maintain some semblance of these original circumstances too.

Node pairs

The North Node in astrology corresponds to something that looks like "**destiny**." For those of us who don't like fluffy words like this, the Node can alternatively be thought of as signifying "the point where your inclination to want things is least out of line with your overall way of getting them." So angles to your Node tell you the area of life **where things feel that 1) they are as they should be and 2) they remove your reason (or means) for turning back to something different**. If that's not a good substitute for destiny, who knows what is. In synastry, this same meaning carries over as the Node person typically feels, at some point, as though it was inevitable (or meant to be) that they experience the other person's various planets via whatever angles do the connecting. Sometimes this is giving, sometimes receiving. As with all of these pairs, we cannot tell by the angle alone how each person will choose to engage these corners of the relationship.

There are a handful of ways to calculate the North Node, the most common being the "Mean Node," followed by the "True Node." In this book, all of my references assume the True Node even though the Mean Node is more common. The short reason for this is that this book is aimed at discussing a kind of destiny you haven't finished writing (the True Node) as opposed to a kind of destiny the way you'll summarize it for all time after the event is written (the Mean Node).[25] As a blueprint for future understanding, this book is more suited to the instruction manual version of things (True Node) rather than the product description version (Mean Node) *even though the product description is overwhelmingly the image of a thing that the world sees*. The only people who tend to care about the manual are the people putting the thing together. In actively assembling your own life, though, "such people" would be YOU. So the True Node it is.

Node-Node

The angle between yours and Other's Node is surprisingly uninformative in practical application because its role is to summarize where you and Other complement each other overall. You might say that it feels as though you and Other should interact according to this angle...all things considered...in a perfectly history-free world. And you actually do interact in this way when initially connecting somewhere between the "complete stranger" phase and the "somebody I've met" phase. But don't look for this sense of complementarity to last very long. Barring reinforcements from other angles, this is more likely to be relegated to **introduction context** between you and them. With II-quintiles, one of you is more likely to begin as the behavioral manager for the other. Such relationships are more likely to start off rocky rather than smooth.

[25] A more technical discussion of the True Node vs Mean Node is given in *FSA*.

Node-Selene

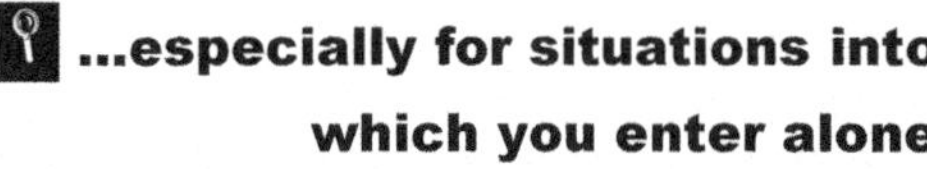

The 2-second impression starts here...

...especially for situations into which you enter alone

(*See Author's note under [Node-Fortune])

You to them

You see Other's angle as a "Destined Reveal." This is the side of Other that you will often see first, most strongly, and with all of the information you need to make conclusions about who they are on the whole. Whether you heed this information is another story. This is part of that group of angles which show the "circumstances of first meeting." In some general, but pretty reliable way, you can assess whether Other will be "good" or "bad" for you based on this angle IF you heed what you observe. Again, you can quickly differentiate fr&s and enemies through what you observe about this angle in the other person IF you heed the information.

Them to you

You make your first significant impression on Other through this angle, but what this means depends almost entirely on their interpretation of that impression. You can help yourself out by correcting any mistakes you make if you think that you might at all want Other in your life later on.

Self chart

The situation you are in reveals its essential point through this angle. How did you even come to do whatever it is you're doing? **This angle's area tells you what it is necessary to master in those engagements which seem inevitable.**

If there was one planet pair I could recommend in all of astrology for achieving self mastery, it would be this one. **This is a VERY important angle to get right before you open full access to your talents**. The longer you take to master this angle and its resonant pairs, the longer you can expect to miss full comfort with your array of talents. And although I'll usually hesitate to recommend that you also look up the Mean Node for Node pairs, here it is highly recommended. Remember, in this book the [True] Node shows how destiny feels while you're writing it. The Mean Node shows how destiny feels when you're describing the finished event. The check goes like this:

"In my significant undertakings, I need to make sure my [(True) Node-Selene] angle is properly displayed. Once the interaction is finished, I want to make sure that my [Mean Node-Selene] angle feels like I left it the way I wanted."

And what if you have blown a good opportunity for mastery? Honestly, you might want to invite your own "karma" and try it again on a new situation. The rewards tend to be great. Why? Think about how we've approached these pairs: The idea was that any situation we can think of can be represented through an appropriately chosen pair of "planets." Furthermore, any pair of planets represents some construct in our conception which is the marriage of the two meanings. Destiny (Node) + exceptional talent (Selene) is a pretty good representation of what we feel we were meant to do.

Node-Lilith

Where seduction is all about them...

You to them

You stand in contrast to Other under your angle, by default taking a perspective other than that taken by them. This is just normal business for you, but read the other half-pair for a very different story of this non-mutual aspect.

You can use this angle as a weapon of seduction. See the self chart description below for more details.

Them to you

You see Other as displaying a way either contrary to or complementary to your own way under their angle. This is a strong pair. Whether it is positive or negative depends mainly on the extent to which you can avoid being annoyed by—and instead lend encouraging support to—Other's different version of your own angle. Annoyance here leads almost directly to a deal breaker where friendship is concerned.

Self chart

Rebellion feels like destiny to you, but why? Is it because you are irritated, or is it for the greater good? Your answer will determine whether others support you or make plans to silence you. Interestingly, this pair is better known by its quiet version than its loud version. **As a face-writer to the family of resonant pairs that come with this angle, this pair shows where you rebel against things you were destined to be given**—hence your **tendency to distrust things that come to you through this angle**. That is, unless or until you decide to accentuate those things' rebel properties. Then this angle can be pretty fun, your feeling of destined sexual or creative attractiveness under this angle being one of the side effects.

Turning discord into sexual stimulation is one of those things I suppose we're not really trained to do as proper citizens, but as certain animals amidst displacement have shown, it has its perks. Just look at bonobos. The reversal of Lilith's contrary role also applies retroactively to the half-pairs, where the non-annoyed Lilith person can feel extra attractive given the attention of the Node person under the Node person's expression of the angle; use the [Node $_{you}$-Lilith $_{them}$] angle on Other to make them feel extra sexy.

This pair is unexpectedly strong for one buried so far down in the chart.

Node-Fortune

Earn respect or go home

(*See Author's note below)

You to them

You see Other as content with being themselves under this angle, in a self-assurance which defies your input. Can you accept this point of contentment, or will you dismiss it as misplaced?

This pair and its angle form a great general measure of where and how much you **respect** the other person. Although I wouldn't call this a deal breaker, it made one hell of a gatekeeper in the data. Where the respect for Other was lacking under the relevant angle, the two people were typically prevented from establishing any long term loyalties in general if they were able to come together at all.

Them to you

If you are to earn respect from Other, you should do it under this angle. Failure here basically kills your potential exchange with Other past a certain obligatory threshold. The tricky part is not so much doing a good job as it is laying out where you stand clearly in the eyes of the other person. Most people can't do this in most areas of their lives. Consequently, tenuous fr&ships and acquaintanceships are borne of imagined affinity.

Self chart

In your own chart, the uncertainty of not knowing the other person disappears since the other person is you. So this is simply where you feel destined to be in your element—your **confident stance**.

Author's note: Heeding warning signs

I learned a ton of things about myself while writing this book and studying the data. One of the biggest lessons I learned was just how, in close relationships, feelings usually lie—masking almost all of the dimensions of an exchange which you've seen throughout this chapter. For evolved social stability, humans are pre-programmed to feel rapport where there is no basis, but in matters of long term personal plans, you often find that logic really is more useful than hormones. Probably because my stats were based on conclusions drawn in hindsight, the hindsight seems more right than normal. And although it will be left to future students of astrology to sharpen such conclusions, I will say that pairs like [Node-Fortune] and [Node-Selene] really should be heeded before you jump into exchanges with certain people or things (even if you ignore other pairs). If you see problems based on what you read here AND you believe that what you read corresponds to actual potential problems (that's important), then you might find it better to address them earlier rather than letting yourself stay blinded by NRE (new relationship energy).

In assessing relationship potential astrologically, sample selection bias applies as well. Sometimes you're cruising along in an escalating, potential exchange and—just for fun—you ask for the other person's chart info. Do they give it? If they can't, that's one thing. If they CAN but DON'T, that's another. The latter shows a basic guarded nature with respect to you and leaves a group of secrets in the chart which really could be fixed if the person just gave you the data. Of course, not everyone wants their birth information floating around, but still it presents another case where your enthusiasm to see how compatible you and they are *is* thwarted by a basic non-alignment of ends. I've learned not to ignore such distrust since—small as it may seem—that distrust always manages to show itself later some other way and, in hindsight, describes a situation where it would have been better to use your head over your heart. When certain connections just aren't there—whether in the chart or kept out—they just aren't there. Covering it up may make you feel better about the exchange, but your acting on that better feeling typically ends up making the other person feel *worse* about you in light of your self-denial.

Node-Ceres

You to them

Your chief persuasive mode in the eyes of Other comes through your angle. This also shows partly how you are most comfortable spending fun time with them. See *table 19-8* below. You had no idea there were so many ways to have fun did you? Read the other half-pair to see if your notions of fun line up. No? It may not matter. Whatever you read, I've found that the fun styles for angles are very pronounced (statistically) and make for one of the most reliable tables we've seen thus far.

Them to you

You see Other as programmed to make their case to you through their angle. The angle speaks louder than words where their efforts at persuasion are concerned, in a display which can look to you like anything from gentle coaxing to bullying. This is a good indicator of where Other most favors showing off your alliance for fun both publicly and privately. Again, reference *table 19-8* for this one.

Self chart

This angle shows **where you naturally press others for their support of your intended ends.** It also serves as a partial indicator of what you have fun doing (True Node) and how you have fun conveying what you did (Mean Node).

Table 19-8: How the angles spend leisure time

Harmonic	Name	Typically fun activity
1	conjunct	enjoying Other's uninhibited company
2	opposition	exchanging in a comfortably supported, (preferably classy) environment
3	trine	listening to Other's talking, enjoying their expression of their personal views
4	square	watching Other unsettle people's emotions
5	quintile	being entertained by Other's substantial personality
6	sextile	enjoying how Other likes to spend time with you
7	septile	conversing with Other
8	octile	debating or intellectually sparring with Other
9	novile	watching Other promote themselves
10	decile	being a witness to Other's authority or expertise
11	undecile	protecting or tending to Other's social interests amidst the groups you share (you often need to bail these people out of social messes they have made for themselves)
12	inconjunct	forming responses to Other's various moods
13	II-conjunct	encouraging Other's social face and increased public projection in the world
14	II-opposition	being in Other's presence or having Other be in your presence
15	II-trine	alongside Other, bringing people's attention to both of you
16	II-square	connecting intimately with Other (that is, sharing a closely expressive connection which noticeably dwarfs lesser grade exchanges)
17	II-quintile	alongside Other, dominating the actions of your shared audience or at least impressing that audience with your ability to command
18	II-sextile	bringing Other out of their shell, encouraging them to publicize their skills, or doing the skill promoting on their behalf

19	II-septile	being inspired by how Other takes care of their ingroup or how Other defines themselves stubbornly against their ingroup
20	II-octile	being impressed with or excited by Other's creativity or sexuality (the receptive version of II-novile)
21	II-novile	being excited or inspired by Other's power to compel people's compliance with their wishes; watching Other's attractiveness or power in action (the active version of II-octile)
22	II-decile	being impressed by and talking about Other's social image
23	II-undecile	benefitting from Other's skill in keeping your follower-group behavior under control and everyone's overall objectives within reach (these people generally make good supporters and seconds-in-command behind you)
24	II-inconjunct	benefitting from Other's execution of your creative goals (these people can, by bringing their own creative vision to light, solve problems that *you* are facing)
25	III-conjunct	watch them overpower or be pushy towards others (more of these people had red hair than normal, non-redheads tended to be good-looking and friendlier looking when compared against their ethnic stereotype)
26	III-opposition	exchange with them concerning the fate of your respective follower groups or groups who support your views; watching them defend their followers or attack an opposing follower-group
27	III-trine	watching them use their strong persuasive or seductive powers over others
28	III-square	receiving their cooperation and positive attitude
29	III-quintile	engaging their criticism and critical eye
30	III-sextile	hearing Other broadcast their commentary (these people really do seem to have a noticeable talent for conveying their ideas through media channels, though 1:1 their company is scattered and often oppressive to the point of being unenjoyable)
31	III-septile	piggybacking off of their personality to foster good spirits among your shared group
32	III-octile	alleviating Other's uncertainty; validating and supporting their tackling of a challenging task
33	III-novile	playing along with their sass (one or both of you are more receptive to the other's flirting or, where attraction is not possible, wingman behavior; more likely Ceres is the accepted flirter and Node is the witness)
34	III-decile	enjoying Other's bossiness (both towards you and towards others); if bossiness is not evident either way, you might suspect that, negatively, they are inclined to complain to you or about you pretty vocally
35	III-undecile	watching their surprisingly strong intellect or curiosity in action
36	III-inconjunct	thinking about and interacting with their weird personality (which is both attractive and anal all at once)

Table 19-8: Leisure styles associated with each harmonic. You may notice that these various versions of fun correspond pretty well to different versions of the basic 12 houses. As always, the above data were obtained from statistics on the same 430 charts used throughout this book.

Node-Chiron

You to them

Other needs the most help from you in developing their angle as a person. Your role is to support them here.

Them to you

You are strongly inclined to accept help from Other in developing your angle. Rarely does the "doctor" face of Chiron come out here, since there is always more to learn from others in life. In negative cases where you and Other don't get along, the lesson stops and Other vanishes from your life. It is said that people come into your life for a purpose. Your

Chiron to the other person's Node is a good indicator of that purpose; and when they are no longer needed, the relationship has a good chance of being better off terminated. Like a class whose content you've mastered, no person should slip into post-lesson devaluation simply because you've become bored with their very best. Look at the alternative half-pair to see not only where you are as teachers to each other, but whether or not one is ready for the lesson the other is to convey.

Self chart
You develop yourself in area of natural uncertainty towards the level of **counselor to others** under this angle.

Node-Vesta

You to them
You see the social worth in Other as lying in their angle, in a pair which almost always affects sexuality/creativity either jointly in non-attraction cases or complementarily in attraction cases. For example, my best friend and I were co-creators (II-novile) in college, jointly expressing more masculine assertion into the unknown in this capacity. This is a strong aspect which is almost essential for a relationship to grow both materially and physically in concert. I suppose the question is, is Other capable of helping you in this? If so, joint prosperity in the area shown by the angle is highly likely.

Them to you
You see Other's angle as the weapon they contribute to your joint establishment of a stable partnership foundation. **If you accept this contribution from Other, your duo is likely to witness Other's angle grow greatly in power**. (Their destiny + your concentration = something like a cooperative attack in video games). This whole pair is VERY strong.

Self chart
Your sense of destiny and your focus align under this angle, **producing those circumstances under which you are far less likely to turn back, regardless of the other demands placed upon your expression**.

Node-Pallas

You to them
You see Other's fighter mode most clearly through their angle, where Other is more likely to dispense with niceties and take a stern approach. There's not much else going on with this one. It works like [Node-Vesta] with less concentration and more concerted effort to establish Other in this area before their audience.

Them to you
You get the impression that Other has much to say regarding their angle, but needs you as a listening ear before this is conveyed. This is a Bottled Message. Here is truly one area where you can help Other unlock their potential.

Self chart
Your fighter mode is facilitated by seemingly destined opportunity. Here, **the fight is your calling**.

Node-Juno

You to them
In a moment of weakness, you let your guard down and disclose something personal about your angle to Other. A vulnerability offering. If Other seems to accept it, you and they usually connect more thoroughly in light of your earnest disclosure. This pair is associated with your honesty towards Other, where further friendship can be made, broken, or reaffirmed according to your degree of true disclosure here.

Them to you
It feels like you were meant to commit to Other as the latter displays their angle to you. Another part of the "destined reveal" group, this pair occurs as you and Other become familiar enough to cross over from acquaintances to potential friends. We'll call this one the **Connecting Conversation**. In negative cases this can also be the disconnecting conversation which turns you off from Other.

Self chart

Your commitment behavior is described by an important exchange under this angle. It seems as though you were destined to learn the angle lesson at hand. **Your commitments consistently teach you here**.

Node-Hera

Are they genuine?

You to them

Recall the difference between committing and bonding. **You use your angle as an offering to Other, facilitating a notable liking from Other to you if the offering is accepted. Call this a Core Offering**. Very unlike [Node-Juno], though, this angle is less about your honesty to Other and more about Other's honest reaction towards your core self.

This is a great aspect for detecting when you have a liar or a deceiver on your hands in the form of Other. Here's how it works:

> As you naturally interact with the other person and reveal your angle, note whether they seem uplifted by this or encourage more of this from you. This particular aspect suggests they should. (This is your destiny plus their bonding).

- If they don't, chances are they are posturing in the name of basic rapport.
- If the bond isn't strengthened, but instead leads to diverted conversation, you've seen the standard level of disingenuousness that all humans employ on some level. But this is not necessarily a liar.
- If, however, you and Other make further friendship plans around all kinds of things *other than* this angle as it comes from you, then you have someone who is using the interaction for some end other than the one they say.

Does this test really work? Yes it does. But now I'll discourage you from trying it too often as it will very quickly drop your faith in most people to near 0. How does this test work? Simple: It amounts to you saying, "This is the real me which I'm showing you so we can bond! Isn't it wonderful?" Because you know that this is basically the pair for which that answer should be a "yes" in the ideal, an answer of "yeah...uh, sure" unaccompanied by supporting actions is a bigger lie detector than most others. The test can backfire though, since you're effectively cornering someone when they may not have formed enough conclusions about how to approach you—making you awkward and undesirable to deal with later. I'd recommend using it only on people who you think are trying to jerk you around with mind games.

As a rule of thumb, if Other fishes for this angle from you, then they may want to bond on some level. If they never ask for it, then fr& or acquaintance status may be more comfortable. If you don't want to give a good "yes" as a response, then *you* are the one withholding the bond potential; perhaps you don't value their deeper support? Lastly, remember that this test only applies to the angle in question. If you have a [Node-Hera]-33 (III-novile) and Other seems false in response to your discussion of long range career plans (II-sextile, 18), it doesn't suggest lies in general. The test only suggests lies if they seem false in response to your success in riling up groups and displaying your academic-style knowledge (III-novile, 33).

Them to you

You bond with Other over their angle IF you have the interest. What if you have no interest in bonding but just want to be cordial acquaintances? What if you don't want to fall victim to the test outlined under [Node $_{you}$-Hera $_{them}$]? Keep your answers short and supportive. As a teacher I've found that this works well with my college students.

On the other hand, are you interested in someone while simultaneously needing to hide your feelings from them? DON'T fish for this angle from them. They are more likely to take it as a sign that you want more from them.

(I'll remind the reader that the above advice doesn't just come from the sky; there were lots of data to back this particular phenomenon with the whole [Node-Hera] pair. Close bonding was the main reason we included Hera in the first place. Also, as a person constantly searching to understand patterns of behavior, stubbornly trained by my own Hera in the 1st house and its need to connect deeply with everyone, I've made every single one of these errors with my students, friends, and peers over the years. You can definitely send the wrong messages when pairs like this are involved.)

Self chart
Your bonding behavior feels meant to be. Under this angle you're more likely to see everything with a consistent **desire to share your experiences with someone else**.

Node-Eros

You to them
You see Other's passionate action most strongly dedicated to their angle. Often in the case of regular, II-, and III-inconjuncts this indicates an attraction to shared action with Other. Further, it can appear as sensual-sexual in the romantic cases and joint conquering in non-romantic cases. Your role here is to serve as a "destined" viewer of this, though your specific reaction to such passion varies too widely for us to even come close to summarizing here. Check out your resonant pairs to this angle instead.

Them to you
You are more likely to reveal your passions to Other through your angle, where the other person serves as a "destined" viewer. Watch out for this one. Although it can indicate attraction from you to them when <u>they</u> display <u>their</u> version of this angle, it can also indicate anger and impulse issues when you display the angle unprompted by them. Overall, this half-pair tends to require self-control on your part either way in cases where displays of excess passion are considered inappropriate. Quintiles are especially inclined to like your company.

Self chart
As expected, you **feel that the expression of passion is appropriate here, and are likely to show little to no remorse about this**.

Node-Bacchus

Introducing a third person to Other: Where must this third person impress?

You to them
You categorize Other's social group according to their general behaviors under angle. This is so general that the groupings break up nicely into clusters of good and bad in your eyes. For example, if you have a II-novile, you'll measure Other's friends by their creative abilities. If a III-trine, you'll measure them by their competence and insight. If you don't have a database for viewing all of your friends, you're missing out. **This angle tends to be the natural language for defining the identity of Other's cliques as a whole**. II-square Others are identified more against their family and family-like relations.

Them to you
You feel stereotyped by Other according to their angle, and it is this stereotype which they use to inform their expectations of your behavior. Say you want to break into Other's world. Ask yourself if your standards for this angle fit theirs. If not, you'd best get to work on this if you hope to improve your chances.

As a personal note, when I've looked at this half-pair among my own family members, I've found that it corresponds to the expectations they place on people whom you introduce to them. Alongside the above meaning, **the data suggested that [Node $_{Other}$-Bacchus $_{you}$] corresponds to the area of behavior where Other expects that any third person you introduce to Other as a potential ally will be up to standard**. So if you value, say, your mother's approval of your potential mate and [Node $_{Mother}$-Bacchus $_{you}$] is a quintile, it means that your mother's most simplified standard for your mate is that they behave well 1:1. In the II-undecile case, your mate would need to be exceptional (or at least unique). This works well for potential business partners as well. Very well.

Self chart

This is **the central role your own peers seem to play in your life**. Naturally, **you also grow your cliques** under this angle.

Selene pairs

Selene is a fictitious point which takes exactly 7 years to cycle the signs. It seems to correspond to that area of life where you are super blessed with luck and talent. In synastry it corresponds to corners of your exchange which are made easy for one person, often at the expense of the other's comfort. There is also some indication that Selene works as a "best summary" of what kind of person you are in general; as far as synastric significators go, Selene = you (more or less). No wonder its pairs tend to play such an array of defining roles in your charts with other people.

Selene-Selene

The angle between yours and Other's Selene shows where you and they appear to share an experiential lineage. **When engaged in this angle jointly, you both seem to have the same level of command for that which needs to be done**. You can feed off of each other's gifts here to make a general splash on outsiders (or each other) under this angle. Conjuncts are naturally drawn to expand upon even the most superficial interaction between them.

Selene-Lilith

You to them

You believe that Other can get away with murder under their angle $_{fbow}$. Other might make a great ally in this department if you can get over being appalled by their behavior here. II-octiles and III-octiles are more likely to get away with scandalous or unsettling behavior as a rule, while III-undeciles are more likely to simply do offensive things. Septiles are notably more skeptical in their communication with you. Octiles are more inclined to be wary of your views. III-conjuncts are more likely to bring complications from outside of the relationship into the relationship, increasing the chances that they will offend you or eventually become your enemy if you don't channel this towards some kind of shared effort to influence others. And in two reversed examples, you are more likely to unsettle conjuncts with your fiery expression towards them. You are also naturally inclined to distrust quintiles, seeing them as being too forward than they have the right to be.

Them to you

In Other's eyes, you display traits that no one can seem to check under this angle. In positive cases it may be simple favored rebellion, but in negative cases you may display an abuse of power or other unsanctioned actions. As far as the other person claims, you have the ability to be a true jerk or a shameless rule breaker here and not get punished for it.

Self chart

You are so non-stop rebellious that we don't even know what you're rebelling against anymore, so we call you "**avant garde**" or generally "**innovative**" instead.

Selene-Fortune

✪ Why have you and they met?

You to them

You appear in Other's life as a means of evolving how they approach their angle. This is a very general pair which, like [Node-Chiron] shows the overall point of Other's knowing you. It's actually pretty informative.

Them to you

Other's role in your life is to hone how you project your angle. This pair answers the question, "Why have I met this person?"

Self chart

In a straightforward read, this pair indicates where you are **comfortable amidst the process of evolving your talents**.

Selene-Ceres

You to them

You promote the idea of Other being powerful under their angle $_{\text{fbow}}$. You can be said to believe in Other's skills here. Conjuncts are often among the most unsettling because they have no context and more easily correspond to Other having a personality that grates on you. Also, the way trines talk to you or think about you can be maddening. Quintiles will typically find you charming and entertaining to exchange with, even if you agitate them sometimes. Interacting significantly with III-septiles coincides pretty tightly with growth in the reach of the other person's social network.

Them to you

You are effectively shielded by Other from many challenges to your angle. You are defended or approached by Other here, greatly decreasing your perception of angle-related problems outside of the exchange.

Self chart

You have a talent for pushing others, unhindered under this angle. **People who challenge you here will find you difficult to beat**.

Selene-Chiron

You to them

You take on the role of authority under your angle in the eyes of Other. This pair is pretty basic, but has implications for those areas in which you would serve as a powerful complement to them. This half-pair is part of the "cooperative attack" and "respect" groups of planet pairs.

If interpersonal interactions were treated as money, this half-pair would be your "talent currency:" that is, instead of being a source that hands out dollars, you would hand out this *angle* to others as payment for their company. With II-oppositions and II-trines, people are more likely to defer to you in shared company no matter how they feel about you.

Them to you

You see Other as having steering expertise over people under their angle. Other is the boss in this area, with the ability to move outsiders in general with their angle talent; this is less about steering you personally. Such is the other person's talent currency.

Self chart

This angle shows where you have a talent for counseling others. Failing this view of your own angle, you will appear to have endless bad luck here. After all, a super talented counselor tends to have an endless stream of solved problems upon which to build his reputation. If you tend to suffer a lot of assaults in this area, it's a good indication that your level of selfishness or guardedness under this angle is too high. Giving this angle out for others' benefit rewards you with various forms of their talent in turn.

Selene-Vesta

You to them

You see Other as approaching their angle with their focused determination. **Other concentrates strongly on maintaining this side of themselves, sometimes at the expense of an improved relationship with you**.

Them to you

You hold fast to your angle in Other's eyes, as **your angle denotes the line of first defense against threats from that other person**. In the event that you feel uncomfortably vulnerable to Other, you will use this angle to defend yourself. This half-pair is much more adversarial on your end than Other often realizes, as it is chiefly a tool for **Internal Defense** whose use needs to be kept secret from them.

Self chart

Under this angle you can block out distractions to your goals much more effectively so that **persistence** comes more easily to you.

Selene-Pallas

This pair is the first example of what we'll call "angle rotations." So before going any further, let's define a **prior angle** as **the angle which is one harmonic below the one in question**. A II-trine's (15's) prior angle is a II-opposition (14). A septile's (7's) prior angle is a sextile (6). Prior angles typically wrap back around to the same level. A III-conjunct's (25's) prior angle is a III-inconjunct (36) and NOT a ~~II-inconjunct (24)~~, because we need to stay on level III. Similarly, a **following angle** is **one whose harmonic is one later than the one in question**. The following angle to an octile (8) is a novile (9). The following angle to an inconjunct (12) is a conjunct (1) because we need to stay on level I. Take a look at *table 19-1* to remind yourself of where each level starts.

You to them

You use your angle on Other when affairs related to your prior angle in light of Other cannot be resolved. If you are using this angle, chances are Other has gotten out of line in your eyes under your prior angle. You use this angle to fight Other. For example, if your Selene is square (4) Other's Vesta, the square would also be your weapon of choice when Other's trine (3) communication with you gets out of line.

Them to you

You see Other as adopting their angle as a remedy for their unsettled prior angle, where your angle is a means for restoring equilibrium in light of the harmonic before. That is, you use this angle to smooth over problems with Other's way of expressing the angle prior. If for example, [Selene $_{\text{them}}$-Vesta $_{\text{you}}$] has a II-conjunct (13), it indicates that you more frequently use your own public persona to fix problems Other has had facing the works of their imagination (II-inconjunct wraparound, 24). II-quintiles here bring a noticeably higher level of tension to your relationship with Other—hopefully of the creative kind. The presence of a II-septile is almost always synonymous with insecurity in the other person.

Self chart

You express yourself as a lucky and skilled fighter under this angle in response to issues raised with the prior angle. Since your dedicated opponent's challenge originates in an angle other than the one that applies here, that opponent is less likely to show up under this angle as well. So potential challengers appear to run from you here as a result of being busy challenging you in another angle's life area instead.

Selene-Juno

You to them

You like hanging around Other's angle and soaking up its influence. If you could, you might extract this energy from them and bottle it—provided you and they get along. There is a tendency to unintentionally rob Other of their energy here as you pry for more. III-quintiles are more likely to leave you uncomfortable $_{\text{fbow}}$. In the data, this half-pair showed an obvious but tangled connection to the kind of attraction shown from you towards Other, where the [angle+5] served as the main means through which through which the Juno person displayed the trait which attracted (or annoyed) the Selene person. This +5 angle rotation appears in certain isolated cases across astrology, and I explain it in more detail in *FSA*. For right now let's just cite an example: A person whose Juno is III-inconjunct (36) your Selene tends to employ public charisma (36+5 = ~~41~~ →29, III-quintile wraparound) to draw your interest.

Them to you

You see Other as invested in processes related to their angle. These processes are tied to how Other conveys their identity interests in your eyes, potentially revealing much about their goals. **They seem more interested in clinging to this aspect of their influence, defending it against displacement**. Add 5 to this harmonic to see the area of life in which they attempt to establish an identity built upon such clinging. It's not as confusing as it sounds. Just read the following:

In your (the reader's) eyes, Other works regularly at [angle+5] to reinforce [angle] as a source of identity for them.

Self chart

You find it easy to adopt commitment-objects aimed at building up this angle in your life, seeking [this angle+5] as the means of making good on that commitment. This pair often constitutes a strong characteristic in your interpersonal dealings.

Selene-Hera

With you in their life, to what goal is the other person truly connected?

You to them

You see **Other as conveying their true desire to bond through their angle, but this is bonding with any kind of situation**, not just people. Thus you see this angle as being **Where Other's Heart Lies**. The company of quintiles is, by default, generally supportive and reassuring to you regardless of the trouble these people may give outsiders. III-trines make great co-explorers of new topics with you. Inconjuncts are really rough on relationships of any kind here, dropping—to disappointingly low levels—yours and Other's ability to connect with each other.

Them to you

By default, you are truly at home expressing yourself alongside Other's angle. As a partner to them in the world, you discover something close to Other's ideal role in your life under this angle. Overall, oppositions are poised turn you on much more easily than other angles. Rightly or wrongly, you are more likely to suspect II-trines of being super successful romantically. II-octiles have something deep and dark within them which can range from an addiction to a pathology to plain instability of some kind, but have a tremendous pull over your impulses when they intentionally seek you out. They are very hard to ignore in such cases. III-conjuncts do things which (often unintentionally) force you to recognize how socially valuable they are. III-quintiles can be a true bitch to deal with when you've failed to do things the way they wanted. You (often unknowingly) use your exchange with III-noviles to control other people in your various spheres of influence. III-deciles would prefer to give you orders and not the other way around. III-undeciles listen to your advice only sometimes but are usually amazingly talented in your eyes. IV-oppositions find you inspiring in non-romantic cases; bones-jumpable, conquest-driving sexy in most other cases.

Self chart

You have **a talent for forming bonds** under this angle, and can be quite sought after as you master it.

Selene-Eros

You to them

Your angle is a point of frustration or desire in the eyes of Other, largely depending on whether or not you use this angle to make them feel good.

Them to you

You see Other as provoking people's passions through their angle. This is general provocation which corresponds partly to that side of their personality that makes people angry—not just desirous. Conjuncts are naturally provocative. But when such provocation is not done aggressively, they tend to be naturally unpolished or clumsy. In fact, this leads to an interesting side effect:

The data revealed a connection between [Selene $_{\text{Other}}$-Eros $_{\text{you}}$] and where you see Other as making frequent mistakes. The significators for their super talent and your insistent passion combine to yield a situation in which the things Other does consistently irritate or embarrass you in your observations of them. This is counterintuitive when you think about it, but makes sense when you think about it longer. If you're doomed to ignite my passions consistently but aren't required to do so using actual passion, you'll be able to do so via normal acts which still make me red-faced. Thus there seems to be an astrological connection between a stubborn person's intolerable behavior and a regular person's clumsy behavior. The connection lies in the idea that both of these two kinds of exchange serve to frustrate and derail interactants through means embedded in the personality.

Self chart

You are simultaneously passionate and talented under this angle, in an arrangement which brings out the temperamental virtuoso in you. You have a peculiar way of expressing your strong interests here.

Selene-Bacchus

You to them

You see the other person as having pronounced status in cliques based on their angle. This angle basically shows the role that they play in small to medium-sized groups, as the group members are reminded of their own versions of Other's angle in light of Other. **Alternatively, Other simply commands this angle among their group members**.

Them to you

Your management of groups in the realm of your angle is influenced by Other. You have the potential to grow as a leader here.

Self chart

Your group status comes more easily through this angle, where **you are naturally recognized by your cliques as having a talent for said angle**.

Lilith pairs

If you stand at the bottom of a ferris wheel, you'll see that there are at least two obvious significant points that describe a particular carriage's position: the one closest to the ground and the one highest up. When a carriage is at its highest point, there is something about that which—at least in concept—provides the "maximum ferris wheel experience" for the people in it. Now think of the ground viewer as Earth and a specific *actual* carriage as the Moon. Lilith (the Black Moon or Mean Lunar Apogee) is not a physical object but a location which corresponds to the highest point on the ferris wheel. By analogy, this is the Moon's farthest point from Earth in its slightly oblong orbit around the Sun. At this point there is a sense in which we would get the "maximum Moon experience" if the Moon were actually there—hence Lilith's association with the three major classes of extremes for the Moon: sexuality, rebellion, and the occult esoteric spiritual practices.

In synastry, Lilith usually corresponds to rebellion since the other two extremes aren't as openly accepted. Typically, the Lilith person sponsors the rule breaking for either person while the Planet B person sponsors the framework. Often the role of actual rule breaker flips depending on how naturally passive the Planet B is, so there's no general rule for reading Lilith without considering the pair it's in.

Lilith-Lilith

The angle between yours and Other's Liliths shows where you and they have a similar prompt for "fiery" defiance. Note that this doesn't mean that your ways of showing your defiance will look alike, but it does mean that the angle will be the topic area in which you are encouraged to defy at the same time. Lilith here works like Mars in that it appears to assert its own way against its bearer's environment, but whereas Mars typically acts towards a new goal, Lilith simply amplifies events within (or away from) an old goal. And while Mars seeks to steer events over the course of several scenarios and a more long-term time span, Lilith defies more perceived-in-the-moment events which occur on the spot.

Paradoxically, yours and Other's [Lilith-Lilith] angle is better than your [Mars-Mars] angle for conducting rebellion together over the *long term*. Why? Because Lilith responds to instant events. With many instant events you have more of an opportunity to build a track record with each other given more "games in the season." [Mars-Mars] isn't as good for building shared track records across many short events as it is for adopting shared influence styles within single events.

Lilith-Fortune

You to them

You see Other employing rebel tactics as a rule under their angle. Non-conformity is the watch word here, often in a way that you find amusing.

Them to you

You facilitate Other's breaking of barriers under their angle, backing them up as they go against the world in ways big and small.

Self chart

This angle denotes **comfortable rebellion** in your chart.

Lilith-Ceres

You to them

You defy standard social training in Other's eyes via your angle. Through pressures that Other may not realize they're setting, you are encouraged to do this.

Them to you

You want to foster Other's escape from the status quo via their angle. Alternatively, they extract your angle in order to foster their own escape.

Self chart

You force your own defiant ways upon others via this angle. This is such a regular habit that it contributes to your general personality as **a troublemaker, playful or otherwise**.

Lilith-Chiron

You to them

Your angle is often a cover for your real feelings regarding Other's version of that same angle or for those subjects which they use their angle to address. In other words, where it comes to this angle, you behave the way you feel Other actually is.

Them to you

You access buried issues in Other via your angle. As a doctor to them diagnosing spaces where they are other than who they want to be, you serve as a help to the latter. Alternatively, you may take on the patient role wherein Other needs to put on that doctor mask.

Self chart

You are skilled at digging beneath the surface of things under this angle and have more of an inclination to actively respond to what you find (either through being upset or by attempting to defy what you see). To the extent that the buried issues in things and people exist as a byproduct of their internal workings, **this pair also coincides with the behavior you use to fight disease**—your own or that of others.

Lilith-Vesta

You to them

You play a **uniquely destabilizing** role in Other's life under this angle.

Them to you

You pay attention to Other's angle as **a trait that sets them apart from others** whom you know.

Self chart

This angle shows where you are much more inclined to assert your desires as a uniquely motivated individual. "Uniquely motivated" means that your methods tend to stray from the standard ways of doing things under this angle.

Lilith-Pallas

You to them

In your view, Other's way of asserting their desires is synonymous with this angle (generically). **You see this angle as an indicator of their main tool for making their more intense wants known.** Conjuncts on the whole have a much easier time unsettling your mood. Sometimes this charges you up positively. But if you are the kind of person who gets easily annoyed, most of the time you will see them as a regular irritant. The company of II-oppositions brings a spread in your social agenda while the company of II-septiles builds up your image $_{fbow}$ on the grapevine. II-deciles increase your craving for attractive things and powerful people. III-oppositions increase the value you place on aesthetic appeal. III-squares increase the value you place on deep emotional or intuitive connections. You seem to become noticeably more charming in association with III-octiles, and physically attention-grabbing in the company of IV-oppositions. These are special cases. As always though, *table 19-1* is useful for reading the rest of the angles.

Them to you

You are more likely to put Other in an uncomfortable position under their angle, as your unconventional approach here puts you at odds with their programmed response. Quintiles by default tend to avoid interacting with you and your fickle nature. At the same time, they are enlivened by this. Septiles, on the other hand, tend to like your company a lot, with few complications in the way. Probably because of your brand of defiance, you tend to have a negative effect on the social world or initial belief system of undeciles, taking it over as your own. In good cases you are simply a welcome kind of revolutionary here, but this is rare. Moving on, in an unusual departure from the norm, II-conjuncts make for very pleasing company by default. Perhaps this is because the rebel in you is relegated mainly to a public mask which can be taken off in your 1:1 interactions with Other. This increases the level of "specialness" in your relationship with them. You are inclined to broadcast the overall moods of II-squares. Your criticality becomes more visible amidst III-conjuncts. You have a much more pronounced desire to protect or take care of III-quintiles, commanding larger groups in their presence or on their behalf. You find the analysis of III-sextiles and the network-based, idea-spreading power of III-septiles impressive. III-deciles make good controllers of groups over which you normally lack control. IV-inconjuncts tend to be more entertaining through complaining.

Self chart

You are fueled by discomfort to make a point to others under this angle area. **Either you spread defiance across your circles or—more likely—you attract it** (lacking the energy to continually spread it 24-7).

Lilith-Juno

You to them

You feel extra unique under your angle in light of Other's continued voluntary company, to the extent that **you have signed onto engaging them for a while** $_{\text{fbow}}$.

Them to you

You validate Other's efforts down a unique path under their angle. **If Other wants to stand out in something, you can often be counted on to support their reputation for doing so in this area** $_{\text{fbow}}$.

Self chart

Your commitment behavior comes with a spirit of rebellion under this angle. One tends to cause the other here.

Lilith-Hera

✪ Read this before you sabotage another relationship

You to them

You resist persuasion at the hands of Other's angle, regardless of how much you may like them. This angle area is simply not described by an approach of theirs that you agree to adopt for yourself.

Them to you

You find Other's angle mysterious, often seeking answers to why it works the way it does. You may be fascinated and mystified by this characteristic of theirs at the same time.

Self chart

✪ This pair may be one of the most personally vexing among all the pairs we cover; **bonding behavior meets rebellion in what amounts to your context for resisting the very bonds you seek**. By default you engage in a kind of self sabotage where your relationships are concerned, but there are several other ways in which this can play out. In order of increasing self-knowledge we have the following:

1. **You connect with people who admire this angle in you, but whom you abandon by running them off as you value this angle over their company.** Why? *Because you cannot see them as contributing strongly enough to the angle behavior you're attached to. Or you see them as getting in the way.*
2. **You connect with people who force you to choose between this angle and themselves**—that is, people who are unsupportive of this angle or who abandon your cause when you use it. Why? *Because even though you might not see the other person as getting in your way with this angle, you don't communicate that fact clearly enough to register with them. They still feel like you undervalue them by comparison. You can also attract whole groups of people who display such non-support. Accordingly, [Lilith-Hera] contributes to the kind of co-working environment you attract—since this is the most immediate, persistent way of highlighting your prioritization problems with people in general.*
3. You may **connect with people who encourage you to ignore this angle's borders.** *The result: Now that Other's encouragement is possible, they give it. They may not know how to actively support you though. You've yet to show them how to do this.*
4. You may choose to **bond with defiant people when expressing this angle.** *Here you're not the one in need of support, they are. But do you know to give it?*
5. You may **attract deep connections as you break rules under this angle.** *The result: both people are pretty contented with their own defiance in this behavior area, and contented enough with the support they receive from the other person in showing such exceptional behavior.*

This is very much a pro-rule breaker's position, but you'll need to be comfortable with yourself before you can engage this side of your life confidently and with few repercussions. One way of overcoming your communication problems associated with #1 (running people off), is to use your [Lilith-Bacchus] behavior with them. [Lilith-Juno] works for #2. The higher three levels will depend on yours and their life priorities at the time.

Lilith-Eros

You to them

This angle constitutes your ace—the tool you use to swoop in for the kill in getting Other riled up. If you use it too often, this angle will quickly become a source of annoyance to them, but used sparingly, **this can be a valuable weapon in motivating Other where they otherwise wouldn't move**.

Them to you

You see Other's angle as either a rare treat or a semi-frequent source of agitation. **In positive cases, you might absolutely love it when Other uses this angle on you or with you, as it constitutes the essence of quality time with them**. Negatively, this same behavior shows up almost randomly as situations where you must actively avoid letting Other get out of line.

Self chart

Passion meets defiance in a pair which puts you against the world. If ever you searched for a way to be the next Tupac, Martin Luther, or Emma Goldman, this angle would be among your best weapons for putting your iconoclasm into effect. Now since actually standing alone tends not to work so well when you are a passionate rebel, we often see this angle manifest as the main focus of your small, partner in crime-style teams.

Lilith-Bacchus

You to them

You classify Other as socially popular (as opposed to gossip-popular) **largely on the basis of a strongly sought after angle**. This half-pair tends to influence your interest in Other for social status purposes. All I-, II-, and III- deciles are skewed towards promoting your interests in status, authority, money, or social mobility. Successful association with II-quintiles produces interactants who are more inclined to advertise you to others later on.

Them to you

Your fishbowl tends to admire Other's way of showing this angle. You take a natural liking towards conjuncts, especially where larger groups directly influence the formation of your relationship. Squares are notable for their caring in all but the most temperamental cases. Septiles have a social ease or warmth which endears them. II-conjuncts are usually quite sociable and fit right into your group. II-trines can strongly capture your friends' attention one way or another. III-septiles tend to enjoy a kind of star status.

Self chart

Even within your own peer and clique group, you are seen as more unpredictable here. **You are their wildcard under this angle**.

Part of Fortune pairs

The Part of Fortune—Fortune for short—shows where you are comfortable with the way you have chosen to approach things. This is a mathematical point which is calculated using the same angle as the one you have between your Sun and your Moon, and thus represents a more specific version of [Sun-Moon]'s self-contentment.

The Part of Fortune brings us to an area of astrology which is scarcely studied at the time of this writing in 2016: that of the so-called Arabic Parts. **Arabic Parts** are **calculated points on the chart which usually take the angle between two planets and subtract it from a third point in order to show how the original two-planet angle plays out in light of the third**. The Part of Fortune is the {Ascendant – [Sun-Moon angle]}, and since [Sun-Moon] shows self-contentment, {Ascendant – [self-contentment]} tells you where you are contented with your approach to new situations; that is, where you are "in your element." Presumably, then {Midheaven – [Sun-Moon angle]} would be where you were contented with your labeled reputation—your idealized career or status. Your {11^{th} house cusp – [Sun-Moon angle]} would be your contentment with your grapevine reputation (depending on how you calculate your houses). More research on parts like the Fortune is needed though.

Fortune in synastry shows areas where you are comfortable with the other person. This is where things come naturally and easily. For better or worse.

Fortune-Fortune

The angle between yours and Other's Fortune shows where you have a **similar tendency to bask in your own abilities**. You form quite the smug duo here, and have an unusual tendency to upset (or in rarer cases inspire) those who watch you.

Fortune-Ceres

Observe the kinds of nurturing you most prefer

You to them

You are at home with Other's style of nurturing under this angle. Take special note of the conjunct as it tells a lot about how you most prefer to be taken care of, in the other person's company, in general. It is also interesting to differentiate which angles you prefer to have used on you and those you prefer to have used on others. This half-pair is a good indicator of where you need to set your own pace. All I-, II-, and III-septiles increase your desire to socialize with the other person. All I-, II-, and III-octiles increase your sexual or creative interest in them.

Them to you

You display the kinds of pressure which Other likes to see under your angle—except when they have their own version of this angle which they would rather use. Then your version becomes a source of intrusion.

Self chart

You are at home with your own style of nurturing others under this angle, in a pair which tends to correspond to **the area of life in which others consistently listen to you** whether or not they agree with your direction.

Fortune-Chiron

You to them

You see Other as having remarkable depth or power in their angle, with the potential to influence many people. **But because this is an individual perspective, Other likely needs some level of encouragement from you** to continue in this.

Them to you

By default, **you serve as a doctor in light of Other's bad preferences** under their angle.

Self chart

You can (and often need to) encourage yourself in this angle in light of insecurities you may have and mistakes you've made. **Becoming comfortable with your imperfections in this area is important, so that you can help others through their problems** instead of remaining saddled with your own.

Fortune-Vesta

You to them

You see Other as being strongly fixated on—or maybe preoccupied with—their angle as a gateway to their self-image. This angle is one of the main means through which Other builds worth in your eyes; personal, monetary, or otherwise.

Them to you

Your angle in Other's eyes causes them to treat you as though you are compelling there. You use this angle often in the expectation that Other will be moved by it.

Self chart

You are moved to **continue staying fixed on your current approach** to this angle. You will pursue this angle of expression ceaselessly as it seems to be in your blood. No wonder this is part of the great riches cocktail.

Fortune-Pallas

You to them

You encourage Other or support them in fighting for their angle. This is pretty much the mirror image of its twin half-pair.

Them to you

You are encouraged or supported by Other to fight for your angle fbow.

Self chart

You are in your element as a fighter here. Nothing surprising.

Fortune-Juno

Unrequited behavior, maybe?

This pair was inconclusive

You to them

Any major commitment or long-term association fbow from you to Other has a strong foundation in how their display of their version of this angle matches your interests under the same angle. **Mismatches in your respective approaches to this angle almost always hurt long term commitment here**.

Them to you

You see Other's angle as the chief means through which they express their discontentment with society and attempt to fight that society until it accords with their will.

Discontentment, you ask? Honestly this was an odd result from the data which I can't explain. Perhaps their Fortune puts Other in their element amidst a situation you have committed to, such that the stripped away interaction is that of a Fortune person who knows your full commitment to them is off limits. Is it the case that this half-pair is the behavior which Other displays towards you when they want your commitment but believe they can't have it? Maybe. The early data suggest something like this, but more research needs to be done on this one.

Self chart
Your own habits are, of course, aligned with your own habits. And you are comfortable committing to them under this angle. **This is the context under which your commitment object plays a role most in line with your comfort.**

Fortune-Hera

You to them
You see Other as bringing their bonding and intense need to make things work in the world through their angle. **There is an importance placed on harmony-or-else here as far as they are apparently concerned.**

Them to you
You use your angle as the main weapon for reconciling events out of harmony in the eyes of Other. This, like most Fortune aspects, shows how Other sees your response to general events rather than responses to them specifically.

Self chart
Your bonding behavior receives an added boost under this angle: **There is an added dose of contentment with how you have chosen to use this angle in the midst of your bond.**

Fortune-Eros

Receive their devotion

You to them
You view Other as being most devoted to things under this angle. This half-pair is simple to interpret and very obvious to observe. Part of the "Encourage this in Other for a great exchange" group.

Them to you
You see Other as being at home conveying their passions or lusts through your angle. If there were a single area of life in which you would describe Other as fierce, it would be here. Ferocity.

Self chart
You are intense, dedicated, and comfortable being so under this angle.

Fortune-Bacchus

(The half-pairs for this one behave unexpectedly.)

You to them
You see Other as having their popularity discussed most commonly on the basis of their angle, but as a point of discussion this angle is typically outside of the clique's regular expectation and thus is frequently **controversial or apparently unusual in some way.**

Them to you
Your angle evades the standards of the normal in Other's eyes, where **you display more eccentricities here which threaten to embarrass Other before their friends.** Why does this half-pair do that? Your fishbowl (Bacchus) aligns with Other's self-contented approach here. It isn't that you are odd, but that Other is a "comfortable approacher" in a world which your clique is inclined to gather around, making for a kind of sideshow. But Other knows they're just being normal, so you and your wide-eyed crew must be the weird ones. Unsettling Habit. An interesting flip side to this one is that you see Other as most likely to display this very angle loudly when they feel overwhelmed by your clique. **In positive cases you don't embarrass Other, but donate your unique skills to their cause under this angle instead.**

Self chart
At home in your clique as you express this angle, you invite strange and wondrous new experiences alongside them, making you party-friendly. Perhaps this synthesis better explains what's going on with the two half-pairs above.

Ceres pairs

Ceres is the (dwarf) planet of caretaking on good days, pushiness on all other days. Sneaking quietly into some of astrology's most stubborn combinations, synastric Ceres typically plays a role in those aspects of a relationship where force and coercion are needed.

Ceres-Ceres

This angle reflects where you and Other have a similar approach to influencing people. Septiles are more psychologically involved with the people they influence. Octiles resort to a similar use of power tactics to get their way. As usual, *table 19-1* will explain the rest. If you've been reading these interpretations straight through, though, you've probably gotten the hang of which angles do what by now.

Ceres-Chiron

You to them

You work to polish your approach to your angle before Other because you think it's what Other needs or wants to see. This is an attempt to please them or otherwise meet their standards.

Them to you

You feel that Other's angle contains elements of insecurity or pathology which, although you might want to help with, you would not want applied to yourself. **You diagnose Other's underlying sense of insufficiency here**.

Self chart

You **coerce fixes** upon yourself under this angle. Once you have gotten this angle down, you work to push these kinds of fixes onto others.

Ceres-Vesta

You to them

You actively support the healthy expression of Other's angle $_{fbow}$, staying in their corner in positive cases, creating reasons for them to mobilize their angle against you in negative cases.

Them to you

You feel that Other will easily cooperate with you under their angle. **Here you pay attention to their attempts to force changes upon others in an area of life which concerns you both**.

Self chart

This angle presents a focused area of caretaking in your life. **Here you are strongly dedicated to influencing people and situations towards the results of your own choosing**.

Ceres-Pallas

You to them

You find Other's angle attractively oppressive, sirenish in romance cases, taskmasterish in non-romance. **You might be something of a masochist here, pushing for Other to dish out qualities which act as your punishment just for being a possible interactant to Other**.

Them to you

You see Other as most resistant to caging under their angle. Here caging means having their motives and ends made clear. They are more likely to be left-field illogical here.

Self chart

This pair roughly coincides with the area of life under which **you coerce others' action on behalf of a goal beyond your own**.

Ceres-Juno

Put them in their place

Assess their level of selfishness (hopefully before you commit)

Does your selfishness help determine your fear of outside groups?

You to them

You use your angle to attempt to make a place for Other in your life or otherwise put them in their place, checking their influence over you. If you should claim that Other has inferior status to yours under this angle, then you have a decent chance of killing the relationship.

Them to you

You see Other as committed to "taking care of people" through their angle, but this depends largely on how selfish you believe Other to be. **This is a great angle for your assessment of Other's selfishness**; if their angle fosters peoples' improvement or good feeling, you tend to see them as having a concern for others. If their angle is aimed at showing Other's own worth to people, you tend to broadly see the more selfish side of Other. There are definitely gray areas in this rather interesting half-pair, but overall it gives you an idea of what level of self-interest you can expect from them in a formally committed relationship.

Though most of the pairs in this book are changeable with a certain new attitude, I found that this particular half-pair, unfortunately, can be very difficult to change without forcing the other person to adopt some major responsibility such as parenthood or a leadership role. That is, people who start out selfish under this angle when you meet them tend to stay that way when you set up formal relationships with them later.

Self chart

Your commitment behavior is synonymous with placing your will upon others here—whether the "others" are your commitment-objects or outsiders to the exchange. Amidst commitment, you can be expected to be pushy here, but who you push and how you push will depend heavily on how considerate of others you are.

⚒ At the time of this writing in 2016, Western society is heavily described by the level of selfish individualism that one would expect of a well-spoiled, yet competitive species. Like a society of cats.[26] This angle is a good basic measure of your own tendency towards self-serving action at the expense of others as well as their tendency towards self-serving action at yours and everyone else's expense. In looking at the data for this pair I ran a statistical test called a correlation on [people's "complaint level" 0...1] versus [their "self-servingness" 0...1]. The correlation was 0.47 on a scale of -1 to +1, meaning that as complaint goes up, it is reasonable to suspect that self-servingness goes up, though one need not cause the other. Given the results, I then ran another statistical test called a multiple regression to see if self-servingness contributed to complaint. The result was "statistically significant." This admittedly sample-biased, non-rigorous test gave me a good preview answer to the following question: Is it true that self-servingness coincides with more difficult interpersonal relationships? These tiny results suggested yes, though scientifically we cannot take this as a rule. [Ceres-Juno] is unique among all the pairs we've covered in that it has much broader implications for the kinds of friendship cultures and overall outlook that you build for yourself on the grand scale, based mainly on how you decide to nurture or coerce groups of people who don't know you. In this sense, [Ceres-Juno] is a lot like [Ceres-Pallas] as we discussed in *FSA*: an indicator of an individual's tendency to make life harder for themselves through the exclusion of other's interests.

What does this mean in English?

Look at your [Ceres-Juno] angle. Are your selfish here? Do you advance your version of this angle at the expense of other's versions of the same angle? If you do, expect the strength of your ingroups to bring you noticeable confidence and self-worth in good times, noticeable anger and fear of uncertainty in bad times as the groups you excluded gain more power to write scenarios beyond your control. ⚒

Ceres-Hera

You to them

Your angle is the chief means through which you convey sensitivity to Other's needs. By considering Other in how you expresses this angle, you can foster a long term space for bonding with them.

[26] I love cats, by the way.

Them to you

You see Other as expressing their caring through their angle. This can have odd consequences depending on the aspect, with some people appearing more authoritarian than others. II-septiles, for example, are more likely to employ sensuality as a means of caring for others.

⚒ In fact, you read this one using an interesting method overall: Look at this angle's following angle, then consider the other person to be the *receiver* of that angle as if it came from you. In our II-septile case, the following angle would be a II-octile, which tends to display power and sexuality in the eyes of ingroup members as its possessor overwhelms outsiders beyond the group. But your other doesn't quite display this under [Ceres-Hera]. Instead, it is as if you display this and Other responds to you. So a [Ceres $_{them}$-Hera $_{you}$] II-septile (19) increases *your* display of II-octile (20) characteristics in their eyes. This is probably a consequence of what it means to be sensitive to someone's anticipated wants in the first place. I discuss more of this kind of pair behavior in *FSA*. The dynamic is noticeably more confusing than that found in normal cases, but thankfully such occasions for this kind of angle-tangling are rare. ⚒

Self chart

This is a pretty caring aspect in general. Your bonding behavior is aimed at bringing out the next angle in the thing you're bonding with. **By pushing this angle onto your bonded object, you draw out the following angle from them.** Read this alongside the regular interpretation in *FSA* for a complete picture of what this "mating dance" looks like.

Ceres-Eros

You to them

In your eyes, a thing which can probably be best described as "lust culture" is embedded in Other's angle. Here lives a heavy attention to pleasing, being pleased, chasing and satisfying desires. **You see the parts of Other's life associated with this angle as being more primal $_{fbow}$ and more likely to inflame passions within you yourself.** (These are passions of all kinds.)

Them to you

You charge up your expression with passion under this angle in Other's eyes. Your associated engagements bring strong preferences here, where Other may or may not be able to keep up with your demands.

Self chart

As expected, **this pair and its angle show where you are passionately pushy.** As with all pairs which take a lot of energy to project, however, you are—on calm days—more likely to experience the things that ultimately push you instead. Accordingly, **this is also the area of life in which you are fueled to passion by external factors.**

Ceres-Bacchus

You to them

Your actions compel Other to fall back on their angle when your demands threaten their comfort. **This angle is the space where Other is most comfortably powerful in light of your expectations, and shows partly which methods they use to resist any demands made by you which seem unreasonable.**

Them to you

You see Other as dwelling in a high stakes, desire-driven world as they express their angle. **There is more pressure for Other to remain strong and desirable amidst their own clique here, where you partly contribute to this pressure.**

Self chart

You take care of your peer groups through this angle, and can be wayward and defensive against outsiders here. A side effect of this angle is that it serves as one of the major factors influencing how people see you amidst groups and, by extension, how they see you as a social actor broadly. Your broad identity as a social actor influences (but does not completely determine) how you show up in people's dreams.

Chiron pairs

Chiron (KAI-ron) in synastry is related to the desire to help the other person. Keeping in line with its normal role as a body associated with socially sponsored insecurity and the counseling that comes with it, Chiron is more overtly double edged than most other astrological factors, and as such can serve as a strong area for improvement in any exchange—including those exchanges with oneself.

Chiron-Chiron

Yours and Other's [Chiron-Chiron] angle reflects the area of life where you and they share similar approaches to security and insecurity, as well as a similar basis for your need to prove yourselves. This read is straightforward. II-sextiles for example will display similar prompts towards uncertainty in planning the long range future. III-inconjuncts will be similarly unsure (but later similarly prone to counsel others) in how one should leave a longstanding memory upon people.

Chiron-Vesta

You to them

You are most highly observant of Other's angle, using this either as the basis for suspicion of their motives or favorable attachment to their true ways. In either event, although it's not necessarily the case that you scrutinize this angle of theirs, it is true that much of your final opinion of their fit in your world rests on the extent to which this angle's expression matches what they claim to be about. This is part of the family of angles related to respect between you and Other.

Them to you

You see Other's perspective as being aligned with yours under their angle. Negatively, Other shares perspective but competes for the right to define circumstances here. You see a kind of kindred connection $_{\text{fbow}}$ which, in negative cases, may bind you to Other past the point where such a kinship feels desirable.

Perhaps weirdly, it is easier for you to think of Other when you are practicing this half-pair's angle. Conjuncts make it easier for you to dream of them, presumably because the general affinity between you and them is likely to be stronger here in your eyes regardless of whether you like Other as a person. While it may seem odd that [Chiron-Vesta] would be associated with dreaming, think about it; besides intuitive things, what kinds of topics do we dream about? That's right: problems $_{\text{Chiron}}$ which we are focused on $_{\text{Vesta}}$. It took me a while to figure that one out as well.

Self chart

You are attentive to potential issues in your life under this angle, basically dwelling on them until they get fixed. There is a greater understanding of the plight of others who have issues related to this angle, though your level of pity for them will vary depending on how you've framed the remedies for your own versions of these problems.

Chiron-Pallas

Here sits another interesting aspect for looking at your exchange with others. See your interactant's self chart for a glimpse into the level of benevolence they're likely to show you

Does Other actually encourage this in you? Preview the exchange. Be honest, and this one will inform you

You to them

Your angle has a pacifying effect on Other in a half-pair which, strangely, quiets Other's dissonance and renders them more docile. This is probably because Chiron as "the patient" gives Other's Pallas fuel for "the fight," while Chiron as "the doctor" gives Other's Pallas a sounding board for any existing frustration the latter might have. Either way, Pallas is tamed. So call this one "**The Tamer**."

Them to you

You root for or openly bemoan Other's angle, driving it towards increased expression either

way—especially that expression aimed towards your own benefit. Deciles indicate a show of respect from you to them. In negative cases, this is only recognition of Other's power to restrict. IV-oppositions show your view of how they use their physical bodies.

Read this same interpretation for the [You to them] half-pair and ask if Other roots for or complains about you here. It will give you a good glimpse into their interest in building a further exchange with you. No signs whatsoever? It *is* possible that they're not considering such building with you or that they're simply preoccupied with other concerns. Or that they would prefer to hide this inclination from you.

Where you plan to erase a relationship, this is one half-pair you are better off paying as little attention to as possible, lest you keep your exchange with the other alive long past its death date. After looking up this angle for someone you've excommunicated, your task is to replace your experience of the angle at their hand with your experience of it at someone (or something) else's hand.

Self chart

You are the crusading healer here, or someone who wishes they could be so. Dataset people who were good-hearted in the very basic sense tended to attract others seeking this angle; the relevant angle draws people who both help you and drain you in this topic area—IF you have a mind to give anything to them, that is. People who tended to look out for themselves tended to be overwhelmed by others' use of this angle upon them wherever they went, and tended to be seen by their surrounding peers as using the angle pathologically.

Chiron-Juno

Your partner needs to be fixed. How do you box them in?

You to them

You approach Other with a one-track mind under this angle, effectively refusing Other's successful input. Favorably, you use this angle to "doctor" $_{\text{Chiron}}$ their point of fixation $_{\text{Juno}}$, keeping them stuck in the way that an actual doctor ideally confines a patient's list of possible what-ifs to a single stabilized malady. Call this The Freezer. Negatively (the default), you simply constrain Other's influence here.

Them to you

You observe as Other treats their angle as a "must protect." Other is highly defensive against assault from you in particular, and may be anything from proud, to unavailable, to unmanageably prolific here.

Self chart

This angle represents the area of your bonding behavior which is described by problems you aim to fix. There is a strong tendency for this to show up as a negative streak in your relationships, as there really aren't a lot of options for making this one sound good. Either you constrain your commitment-objects using this angle or you attract people who draw this tendency out of you as an area of deficiency which you need to correct. This is one of the essential tools you use to put your commitment-objects in their places when you are upset.

Use *table 19-2* to take a look at this one in your own chart to see what you do to put your close partners under your thumb. Then look at it in Other's regular chart to see what kinds of tactics they can be expected to use on you.

Chiron-Hera

Reel them in with their tendency to bond with one who can solve their unique problem

Addictive behavior = a bond $_{Hera}$ to a thing that fixes you $_{Chiron}$

You to them

In close exchanges, your angle is a silver bullet for securing a bond with Other, them to you. Although it doesn't always work, it often does. Actually, this half-pair is most informative in cases where the relevant angle is non-standard—as with III-undeciles: where conversation, appearances, and shared company won't do (only a display of your curiosity in a way that favors them). Now actually you can both correct a broken relationship with this one as well as get into a lot of trouble with a new one not yet formed by using this. Short of making you irresistible, this pair more likely awakens tempting possibilities in their mind. The data I collected on this were quite heavy, consistently showing the central thing the Chiron person did to tempt the Hera person beyond limits without either of them realizing it. Call this one the **Defense Weakener**.

Them to you

You value Other's angle highly $_{fbow}$, allowing them to circumscribe your own angle standards here. This is a half-pair conducive to super strong attachment from you to them, provided they have at any point allowed you to connect with them over this angle.

Self chart

For your own [Chiron-Hera], read the following: "Once I've had a taste of [this angle], there's no turning back." **This angle becomes a favored experience of yours no matter how much you try to get around it**. You might even be described as having an addiction to this angle behavior, making your other competing attachments insecure in the face of it.

Chiron-Eros

You to them

Your efforts to engage Other under your angle seem capped just short of the goal, where you do not get the chance to properly make your case. Favorably (though rarely), you get that chance without getting Other's response. More favorably and even more rarely, you and Other successfully express the angle together, but this takes considerable patience and sensitivity to your struggle on their part.

Them to you

You see Other's angle as being one of the areas of greatest dissatisfaction in their life—as though they can never make enough progress here. There is an enduring sense of something that they need to prove.

Self chart

You passionately seek a fix in this angle area, or seek to cure others here. The quest reigns, as no matter how bonded you are, this urgent area of dissatisfactory expression on *someone's* part drives the journey.

Chiron-Bacchus

Try not to override them unnecessarily

Does their issue fit your clique's natural issue?

You to them

You see Other as gaining wider appeal through their angle, mainly through the expressive need they help fill among your circle as you see it. If this isn't wider appeal on their part, it corresponds to a greater display of this angle on your part—in which case, having them around makes them appealing in some sense anyway (albeit considerably more expendable).

Them to you

You see Other using their angle to win over potential clique members by providing a function you can't provide for yourself. This is a straightforward reading of *table 19-1*. Failing this, you'll be the person who provides this function in light of your association with them. Potential cliques may affirm this, but you're less likely to win their people over if you're the one doing the work.

Beware a tendency to show this angle on the other's behalf when they don't need you to. Unless you are a parent, boss, or some other formally legitimized authority figure to them, there is a high chance that such "overriding" will kill the relationship. In the data, I found that this was the angle that the Bacchus person often overrode in the Chiron person as a defense mechanism in the Bacchus person's own life or as a testament to the Bacchus person's own impatience (again ignoring formal authority relationships). Overriding like this actually produced relationship deaths of the more epic kind, as the Chiron person's inability to express the angle tended to brew to an eventual boil.

Self chart

Your cliques need fixing in this area or, in rare RARE cases, serve as doctors others here. There is some evidence that more concentrated peer groups tended to have more concentrated versions of this angle issue, while more dispersed peer groups served to doctor outsiders more. That is, the easier it was for you to claim a well-connected inner circle, the more this angle's topic tended to show up as a point of focus. Additionally, the less the members of your "inner circle" know each other, the more into "doctoring" outsiders they will be using this angle. Why? Presumably because they didn't need to lean on fellow ingroup members to address this issue, but addressed it themselves as a natural characteristic.

Look at this angle in your chart. Potential romantic partners who are not inclined to share this angle with you, positively or negatively, have a lower chance of success.

Vesta pairs

Vesta is associated with several diverse things in astrology, but most of these can be boiled down to pursuits which we focus on. In synastry, Vesta is typically associated with one interactant's stubborn pursuit of something related to the other person's planet B whenever the relevant angle constitutes a key mode of interfacing either with each other or with a shared topic. The results of Vesta's influence range from pretty good to pretty bad as interactants develop different ways of handling each other's fixations, but rarely will you find Vesta pairs boring.

Vesta-Vesta

The angle between yours and Other's Vesta shows the area of behavior where you have a **similar penchant for "zooming-in" on target issues**. Angles which involve 1:1, non-verbal interaction are among the most interesting because they tend to sponsor yours and Other's zooming in on each other. Quintiles have a sexual or beneath-the-surface-creative undertone. So do octiles, but these are more one way from either of the parties towards the other. Sextiles hover and are more likely to unsettle or annoy one of the partners in response to the other. III-undeciles are more curious about the bigger issues that the respective interactants are occupied with. IV-conjuncts bring a need for you and Other to explain yourselves to each other. The remaining angles are more likely to show up as cooperative or antagonistic behavior towards an issue seen separately in each person's mind rather than each other.

Vesta-Pallas

You to them

You see Other as owning the struggle under their angle. That is, **for better or worse ($_{\text{fbow}}$), Other's angle is described by an ongoing battle against the potential discord presented by some set of unresolved issues**. In many cases, Other possesses a drive towards perfection here.

Them to you
You see Other as more likely to show nervousness or irritation in the handling of their angle. There is either less confidence or more impatience here on their part.

Self chart
In a straightforward read, this is **the social battle on which you are most likely to focus your energy**. Strangers who catch you behaving under this angle are more likely to catch you in a less chipper, more business-serious mood than normal.

Vesta-Juno

You to them
You see Other going overboard in the attention they pay to their angle, often stifling themselves with unnecessary worry. **You often end up supporting Other here, alleviating partially the burden they carry**.

Them to you
You see Other getting swarmed by outsiders or outsiders' concerns in light of their angle. Other inherits the burdens of many people besides themselves under this angle, and is tasked to inspire them, serve them, or command them as a result. This is an odd outcome for this half-pair if you think about it. Maybe this result comes from the idea that Juno's societal commitment-object aligns with Vesta's dwelling object—essentially **rendering Vesta a magnet for issues that concern Juno**. We'll call this one the **Gluer**. **You serve as a potential reflection of luck for Other, good or bad, under this one**.

Self chart
While it may be obvious that this pair corresponds to the area of life in which you are more likely to focus on commitment, it might be less obvious that you tend to attract people who want to commit to you here. Whatever kinds of people prefer stability under this angle are more likely to come to you, so if you ever asked the question, "Why do I keep seeking out / getting these people in my life?" (especially if you don't really like this), this angle is a partial explanation.

Vesta-Hera

Make them strong whether or not you realize it

You to them
You are continually challenged to reevaluate and revise your approach to this angle in light of Other. **The result is usually an accidental evolution towards the improvement of your angle**. In negative cases, you continually reset, starting back at 0 in light of Other's influence. Ill-quintiles are especially notable in that they strongly increase your general charisma; as with all angles, sometimes this is done the easy way and other times the hard way.

Them to you
You are bound tightly to Other with or without their consent as they bring an inexhaustible supply of interaction under their angle. **Alongside your attention, Other seems to grow and grow without cease under this angle, rendering you a kind of Guardian Angel to them here even if you are unaware this is happening**. Check it out in Other's life to see that this is true.

Self chart
This angle grows with your increased participation in bonding behavior, whether to a person or situation. **There is an element of favorable "watching over" which comes with this angle** where you are the observer or the one who feels they are being observed in these angle matters.

Vesta-Eros

You to them
You are sought after by Other for your passion or lust under this angle. **Where you exude intensity, Other's attention fbow often follows even if they don't like such intensity**.

Them to you
You are inspired to be more socially attractive in light of Other's angle. This works for both positive and negative motivation at their hands.

Self chart
The open display of passion becomes a desirable end for you under this angle, where you see this trait as increasing your appeal in the world.

Vesta-Bacchus

You to them
You see Other as strongly well-liked under descriptions of their angle. This is not quite what it sounds like, but is closer to recognized talented expression under the angle rather than raw likeability.

Them to you
You see Other as issuing their angle under the concern of what other people would think. How they come across to potential clique members matters here.

Self chart
Amidst cliques you show attention to a particular mode of expression, establishing yourself as "the one who does [that angle]." **This is a quality for which your peers know you well**.

Pallas pairs

Pallas is best summarized as the asteroid of social action. It is associated with fights on principle and a kind of "warrior's spirit." In synastry, Pallas features in those parts of the exchange where one person sticks to their guns in the face of a topic framed by the other. Despite being more ferocious than the more notorious planet Mars, Pallas is mysteriously obedient when it comes to behaviors that might destroy a relationship. This is possibly because Pallas fights its battles on a bigger level than that of the individual, making it less likely to turn its force on the actual partner.

Pallas-Pallas

The angle between Pallases shows the area of life where you and other have similar bases for displaying your tempers based on the perceived violation of principles. **You have similar prompts for doing social battle and similar ethical foundations for driving these values**. Under a common work life, sextiles make good colleagues. On the other hand, septiles tend towards charged or contentious conversation when principles or society is involved.

Pallas-Juno

You to them
You embark on a quest to resolve an angle-related conflict in your life or world and believe that Other will be useful in this. The angle you want to read for this one is "the following angle <u>three signs after</u>" this half-pair's actual angle. So if you have a septile (7) as the actual angle, for example, you would read the decile's (10's) interpretation from *table 19-1*. Deciles are the "+3 following angle" to septiles. If you have a II-undecile (23), you would read the entry for a II-opposition. (23+3=~~26~~→(minus 12)→14 under wraparound.) The reasons for this angle rotation are 1) because [Pallas-Juno] is a kind of want (as the 4th house is to the 1st house; discussed in *FSA*) and 2) because the data bear this relationship out. The *actual* angle you see in the synastry table reflects the thing that you do which invites Other as a useful supporter. Call this one **The Embroiler**. If you aren't the one on the quest, it becomes your priority to support the other person in a pursuit they need to (but haven't learned to) adopt for themselves. As is the case with other pairs where you override the other person like this though, look for the relationship to mutate $_{fbow}$ over time.

Them to you
You contend with heavy demands in the realm of Other's angle. Much like "Gluer" [Vesta-Juno], **this half-pair attracts Other's burdens to you. Only this time you join Other's war**. This angle often shows up as indicating the major source of hesitation in your mind preventing you from fully committing to Other.

Self chart
You commit to the struggle under this angle. **Where this angle area is concerned, you are more likely to sign onto a cause and stay with it for the long run**.

Pallas-Hera

You to them

This half-pair holds the unique position as the "foundation for moral action." You receive this angle as the basis for the central ideas which Other conveys to you. **In your eyes, they frame the consequences of social actions in terms of this angle**, where said angle corresponds to the source of Other's core principles in the social world.

Them to you

You see Other as under-expressing or less forthcoming under their angle. When more forthcoming, Other is often suspected of over-expressing instead. This angle is associated with dishonesty on behalf of Other as shown to you. It is also associated with forced emphasis by them upon you. But why?

Your Hera bonds with their war, creating a situation in which they are compelled to minimize serious issues facing them or disrupt your comfortable attachment with the discord engendered by those issues. This half-pair is almost always negative except in cases where you have dedicated yourself to supporting Other for the long haul—carrying their burdens as well. You know these rare positive cases by the presence of issue-taming communication over this angle when Other raises the dilemma. If your exchange with Other under this angle doesn't seem to tame them, no dice for you.

Self chart

The social battles you fight consistently lead you back to this angle. You are attached to the angle as a foundational basis for the way you see social problems, and can evolve your view of this angle by polishing your expression of its resonant pairs. Other issues and forms of expression are more likely to fall away while you are in this mode.

Pallas-Eros

You to them

You see Other as a social combat partner under yours and their joint use of this angle. Negatively, you find Other selfishly shortsighted under their angle—believing that they are wasting attention that could be spent building up others besides themselves.

Them to you

You experience Other as a fighter for love under their angle, typically described by **a pronounced need for a kind of intensely felt harmony in their exchanges with others**. Other is much more sensitive to people's lack of respect here, and approaches situations with a pro-social hedonism in your view.

Self chart

Love and war join forces as this angle reflects **that aspect of social combat which you are most likely to feel passionately drawn to**.

Pallas-Bacchus

🕊 Make use of their standards for friendship

You to them

You receive Other's angle as their investment in friendship with you. The higher your standards for friends, the more likely most of these angles will be insufficient for keeping your interest, where only family and formal commitment-partners constitute an exception to this rule.

After you read the alternate half-pair below [Them to you], come back to this one. Perhaps you will have noted something interesting. The [Pallas-Bacchus] whole pair is very non-mutual, as it shows the difference between what one does to be a friend to others and what one requires for others to be friends to them. Generally, people who share the same harmonic for both [Pallas-Bacchus] half-pairs form much easier friends than other angles. On the other hand there is an extent to which all other angles have a noticeably higher chance of deteriorating without active effort to maintain the association.

Them to you

You see Other investing their angle heavily in their cliques. Their angle forms much of the basis of the quality time they spend with friends. **Your positive engagement of Other's angle strengthens your status as a potential friend in their life.**

Self chart

You simultaneously identify with and fight alongside your friends on the basis of this angle, **establishing the very process of group engagement (in this topic area) as the foundation for a social battle**.

Juno pairs

We finally arrive at the asteroid of commitment, reminding ourselves that Juno represents commitment in the world's eyes rather than the genuine commitment between two parties. Think of Juno as being the vows exchanged before everyone—the contract notarized for the public record. In synastry, Juno shows both our commitments to the other person as well as our generic commitment behavior, and thus serves as one of the few bodies which reflects the same-ish dynamic whether we are alone our attached. There is a double-edged nature here then, because Juno-style commitment does not necessarily require the object we're committed to in order to show up as a behavior. Accordingly, when things get rough in a relationship, Juno is known to proceed as if the commitment were still there while the commitment-object is not, prompting us march forward according to the contract terms with or without the other party's blessing.

Juno-Juno

The angle between yours and Other's Junos shows where your respective commitments affect you similarly. You would think this pair showed that you *make* similar commitments. Not so in the data. Instead, **this pair indicates that your respective *general* commitments affect this angle similarly for both of you** and shows up far more strongly when you commit to each other. II-septiles for example experience changes in social mobility as a result of their commitments. Undeciles appear to exclude relationships outside the partnership in similar ways when they commit to each other.

Juno-Hera

Don't let the fairy-tale of romance fool you. A bond to your commitment-object is rarely automatic

(Just try to count the number of other commitments you make besides romantic or affiliative ones. See that this is true)

The face associated with regretless commitments

You to them

You use your angle to provide enduring support for the other person. Negatively, you use the same angle to provide enduring justification for why Other should be denied support.

Them to you

You connect to Other's use of angle as an acquaintance in good standing. Negatively, you see their angle as a tactic for forging a connection that you don't want. Other's display of this angle towards you is a good measure of their interest in your company.

Self chart

One would think that the asteroid of commitment (Juno) and the asteroid of actual bonding (Hera) would combine to make something pretty good. But not really. Since we easily assume that people commit to the things they're bonded to and (ideally) have some kind of bond to the things they're committed to, [Juno-Hera] represents something like a forgone conclusion in the chart. **This is the angle you express when you truly show your bond to your commitment-object**. That's not so interesting, but there are two important side conclusions well worth noting:

> First, we're not always deeply immersed in the things to which we've committed. Sometimes

we're simply doing other stuff while still under contract, so that the assumption of a perfect bond to anything is not only an oversimplification, but a difficult standard to maintain in practice. The idea that the realm of bond+commitment is a specific behavioral style rather than a general one suggests that the perceived state of perfection—though overwhelmingly obvious when you're in it—really is the minority experience in a vast realm of other possible interactions with the bonded thing. That said, keeping your bonds alive within your commitments does bring a need to respect the role of this particular angle. If you get bored with this angle or find yourself no longer able to show this angle effectively in your commitments, the attachments to those commitments loosen. You might also want to look at this pair in the chart of your partner to see one of the key behavioral outlets they need in order to stay enthusiastically connected to you...and anything else for that matter.

  More important than your affiliative bonds to others are the basic families of commitments with which you alone must live. Your bills, your job, your promises, etc. Buried not too far beneath [Juno-Hera] is the idea that there *does* exist a partial means by which you may learn to be okay with such non-sparkly commitments. Have you ever met those people who are so happy with their lives that it's almost annoying? You know those people who don't seem to regret anything? [Juno-Hera] forms much of the face under which you attach to *whatever* you're committed to and, as such, forms one of the strongest components in all of astrology for what you could call "making peace with one's life." THIS PAIR IS NO JOKE, and if you are at all interested in making peace this way, you should study it in this chapter's tables. After [Node-Selene], [Juno-Hera] gets my #2 vote for most powerful pair among all 300 possible self-chart combinations for self-mastery—not in the sense that it will perfect your approach to your talents as [Node-Selene] would, but in the sense that—given your use of your talents, you can learn to be happy with any major commitment choices you get into (I'm not talking minor ones like whether you should use that item in your video game. Just major ones.)

While we're here, let's go ahead and declare another major cocktail in this book. The **inner mastery triad** consists of these three pairs:

- **[Sun-Moon]**: Contentment with how you interface with people <u>and</u> undertakings one-on-one
- **[Node-Selene]**: Contentment with how you display your innate abilities. ("Node" in all cases in this book means the True Node.[27])
- **[Juno-Hera]**: True attachment to the people <u>and</u> situations to which you've committed

I'll go into detail regarding this triad in the next chapter, where we discuss how to apply the pairs and cocktails in this chapter.

Juno-Eros

The down and dirty looks like this...

You to them (skipped)

Let's skip this one for now and come back to it after looking at [Them to you].

Them to you AND self chart

You are attracted to Other through their favorable display of this angle towards you. Negatively, their indifference towards you under this angle leaves you feeling cold. For the non-squeamish, this whole pair is associated with one of the most noteworthy side effects in our entire family of 625 synastry pairs, but before I tell you what it is, I'll tell you how I arrived at it. For those who read *FSA*, you know that inclusion of the love asteroids at some point led to

[27] Remember, this is the <u>True Node</u> we're talking about. The Mean Node—the one that programs usually display by default at the time of this writing—shows how you *describe* your show of your innate abilities *after* you've finished displaying them or *before* you plan to display them. The True Node shows how you play these abilities out *during* the actual interaction.

the addition of several adult film stars in the data, along with several other allegedly deviant characters. What I did not mention in *FSA* was that part of my major area of focus under psychology lies in the realm of sexology—specifically, socio-psychological enculturation and power roles. So when I'm not studying the stars I am often studying people's sexual behavior and the various social training attached to it. After all, public sexual power and social power are closely related in how they compel their subjects. In the survey of both public and private data, through several interesting conversations with and reports from people who contributed to this book, [Juno-Eros] is associated with the Eros person's creative release at the hands of the Juno person's committed action—specifically orgasm in cases where sex is involved.

The resonant pairs with [Juno $_{\text{them}}$-Eros $_{\text{you}}$] give you a broad description of what kinds of experiences you have which correlate with your interactant's bringing you to creative projection—often unfolding over the two or so days it takes for your body chemistry to go back to normal. Gather up all of the pairs with the same angle as [your Eros to Other's Juno], consider these pairs alongside all of your squares, and this is more or less the experience you have with another. Furthermore, **your own [Juno-Eros] angle in the self chart shows how you experience orgasm and creative accomplishment privately**—that is, those events following where you peak without considering your partner's influence. If there is any partner at all. Here, we only consider squares when such climax includes your emotional release. (This is not always the case.) People more versed in good sex regardless of partner seem to have mastered this private version such that their experience of creative peak does not ride on the other person's skill or inhibitions, while those who are very other-centric can have anything from absolutely awful experiences with one partner to epic experiences with another. Most of us fall in this second-group.

Finally, there is an interesting conclusion we can draw from the connection between this asteroid pair and sexual climax: You might say that there is an extent to which sex is a reflection not only of how partners communicate, but how they *create together*. If you know your track record for creating art, music, projects, gaming experiences, or general shared memories with the other person, you know at least a little about how sex with that person will end, and although this doesn't quite apply to fantasies, there is some connection with how you think about shared creation with a person even when they're not present. Resonant pairs with squares are related to this, though they revolve more around how you and the other respond emotionally, intensely to each other.

As a rule of thumb, creative release is a [Juno-Eros] thing regardless of emotional attachment. Emotional release is a square-angle thing regardless of sexual attachment. So emotionless sex and emotional sex can produce two noticeably different experiences. I'm sure you knew that. The astrology behind it, though, is pretty overt.

Now let's not take this pair too far. Because people think about different things and attend to different aspects of the creative process while they're creating, each person's experience of sex and creation—either with or without involving other people—can actually be described by any angle which applies to the realm in which they are actually focused. So if you have a III-decile for [Juno $_{\text{them}}$-Eros $_{\text{you}}$], it doesn't mean that you're absolutely doomed to experience 1) a bad day two days later or 2) a bedroom experience which revolves around authority[28], it just means that you'll experience whatever you focus on at the moment, but likely summarize the event later in III-decile terms. Mastering this creative process and living with the results of what you've released into the world is something of an art, but really can produce some high-quality experiences once you get it down.

[28] Both of these are typical, unfortunate side effects of the [Juno-Eros] III-decile.

You to them

You have your commitment to Other drawn out in light of their desire for that commitment under this angle. **Here you help push Other to create whatever their passions are invested in.** In line with the alternate half-pair description above, **this angle shows the basic reaction that you receive from Other in light of their passionate attitude projection into the world and, by extension, sexual climax.** Perhaps that's interesting enough. But there's even more; as implied above, this is the same kind of broad behavior that you receive from Other at the culmination of *any* kind of jointly created achievement. If you haven't already, read the [Them to you] half-pair above for more details on why this is and how we know this.

For a preview of how Other would summarize their shared creative experiences with you, consider how they behave towards you when you affirm commitment to them *while* they display their passion. Consider, then, how they view such displays on both your behalf in the aftermath. A lot of this rides on how you naturally communicate even when you're not jointly creating, but as a glimpse into a likely future, it works like a charm.

Look at this pair in the other person's self chart to see how they generally respond to their own creative achievements or sexual experiences alone—that is, their commitment $_{Juno}$ to their own passion $_{Eros}$. If they have a III-decile then, watch out. These people have a tendency to become more stern or cause more problems in the face of a creative victory—the exact opposite response you would expect from someone who just reached a goal. In negative cases this shows up as pessimism regarding (or compensation in preparing for) what's next. In positive cases such sternness shows up as a sense of responsibility for a job they see as incomplete.

Juno-Bacchus

You to them

You donate Other's angle as an offering to other members of your group, promoting their mobility in the group. Other has skill under this angle which allows you to connect them to others.

Them to you

You see Other as committing to their groups most noticeably through their angle. This angle basically describes the form of service that Other donates to their in-groups.

Self chart

This angle shows the area of behavior which you primarily employ to display your commitment to your cliques.

Hera pairs

Simplified, Hera is the asteroid of deep bonding. As you've probably seen by now, this asteroid features in several important synastric pairs involving strong, willing attachment and can have a wide range of effects spanning from deep love to obsession. This will depend on what the non-Hera person's planet B is as a comparison. We only have three bodies left to look at, so let's see how the remaining Hera pairs contribute to the relationship chart.

Hera-Hera

Your [Hera-Hera] angle shows where you and Other have similar bond triggers. As with [Juno-Juno], this pair is stronger when we look at how you and Other bond with each other, so you can use your interaction with them under this angle to attempt to foster a connection if you want one. The conjunct can give deep affinity and deep "wish this weren't happening" disagreements, but doesn't necessarily cause bonding. Undeciles poison compatibility because of stubbornness; these people—though they look paired in public—typically have a hard time connecting in realms which do not rest on the public information train.

Hera-Eros

And what if you just want to seduce them?

You to them

You advertise Other's angle to others, effectively marketing this aspect of their personality.

Them to you

You see Other's formed bonds under their angle as stimulating or aggravating. This angle is a partial indicator of how Other actually *commands* you to perform either creatively or sexually. Read this interpretation for the above [You to them] half-pair to see how it works the other way around.[29]

For the wolves among us: Wondering whether you could score with the Other person? There are lots of tests both astrological and plain old experience based, but this one is among the better tests. Ask yourself if you seem to be able to successfully use the [Hera $_{you}$-Eros $_{them}$] angle to get other to cheerfully and enthusiastically do your bidding—regardless of the face they put on. If they give you a hard time but still do it with gusto, there you go. I'll ask you to take my word on this one since you probably don't have a database. But get a database. Then look it up yourself. The usual admonition holds, though. Be careful what you wish for...

Self chart

Bonded behavior and passion join in a combination which really backfires in its effects. You advertise yourself as a passionately bonding character independent of any target. Simple supply and demand shows that you can only hump so many people before you run out of energy, time, or whatever. So in the absence of a settled target you may simply be weird to others under this one. Actually, the words are *creepy*, *unsettling*, or *quirky* in the eyes of others. How does this happen under [Hera-Eros]? Simple: As far as others see it—given that you don't hide this angle or declare your status as strongly bonded to something else—you display hints of passion in a setting where it isn't appropriate, giving others the "reel back" moment. Based on normal social training in how the sexes assert their wants, males cause this reaction in females more than the other way around, though females can certainly be creepers too under this angle. **Shrug** what can you do? This is your natural angle area for a **lusty bond**.

Hera-Bacchus

You to them

You and Other attract people's attention under your joint expression of this angle. You are usually the active element and source of the angle here while Other is the complement which amplifies your audience reach.

Them to you

You form a potent tag team with Other under your joint expression of this angle towards a third party. This is a strong and noticeable aspect, though inconjuncts suggest an inability to truly work together outside of spiritual and artistic matters. Ill-oppositions generate publicity for themselves more easily. Ill-noviles make awesome party co-hosts. With this angle, Other is typically the source of the angle while you are more like the cameraman.

Self chart

Third parties pay more attention to you as you bond with either people OR EXPERIENCES under this angle. Way to draw attention to yourself! Visit *table 19-1* to see how to do this on purpose. Or to see what *not* to do in order to remain low key.

Eros pairs

A basic look at Eros will tell you that it's an asteroid of love. Yes it does also correspond to lust. In more mainstream applications, however (the default), Eros simply corresponds to passionate action. This body differs from Mars—another intense body—in that Eros pushes powerfully forward to fulfill an impulse whereas Mars acts (not always passionately) to steer

[29] Once again consider how we derive such things: Eros' passionate action + Hera's bonding to the Eros person corresponds to something that Eros does in a pronounced enough way to [keep Hera attached] as well as [keep Hera's validation of Eros in copious supply].

a person or situation towards a desired end. If Mars is the turning of the steering wheel to influence the car, Eros is simply fast driving—no consideration of the car needed. Eros also differs markedly from Pallas—yet another intense body. Pallas is driven social action. Eros is just passionate action. If Eros is fast driving, Pallas is the kind of driving you do when you absolutely must get to the hospital on time: It is probably fast, but there's a lot more consideration of your situation and probably a lot more externally directed calculation involved as well.

Eros-Eros

This angle shows where you and Other have similar prompts towards appetitive action. **That is, disruptions in this realm of behavior will move both of you towards a similar state of desire to mobilize intensely**.

Eros-Bacchus

You to them

You form heavy attachments to Other under your focus on their angle. **You have a notable desire to rewrite their entire clique-trained expression of their angle** in a way that rests on their own overall role in your affairs. This is a great indicator of where you attempt to challenge who they are. If not challenging them, you tend to be strongly motivated to action in light of their effect on others using this angle.

Them to you

Your receipt of Other's angle brings with it a touch of the taboo as **your clique is infiltrated by their lusts via their angle**. You get the sense that Other shouldn't be doing [whatever] and that you shouldn't let them do it, but it is what it is. In non-charged cases, Other enlists your help to display their angle in situations outside of yours and their immediate exchange, **making you a promoter of their angle expression to the outside world <u>expressly beyond</u> your clique**.[30]

Self chart

Others witness your passion in the style of this angle, in a pair which indicates **your area of intense expression from within the peer group**. In parties involving the expression of love and merriment, you are more likely to go all out whenever doing so under this angle is an option accessible to you.

If one pair could be described as your overall **maximum-fun party behavior**, this would be it. If you happen to be questioning your social life, thinking perhaps that it's not nearly as fun as all the bass thumpin' shindigs those people on TV must be throwing, don't worry about it. This angle suggests your actual party forte, and there's a good chance it doesn't necessarily involve a lavender-lit warehouse. Social gatherings which let you express this angle have a decent chance of being great ones no matter what the specific setting is.

Personal note regarding naturally comfortable social situations

Writing this at age 37, I took the first 35 years to learn that my [Eros-Bacchus] II-square coincided with fun "parties" built upon the emotional core—family and *very* close friends—rather than events populated with people beyond this. So all the high school, college, and early adult years spent thinking that one had to be social "the advertised way" amounted to lessons in incompatibility. Even the presence of one or two non-close friends still kills the dynamic because I'm then required to load all of the social niceties that come with public rapport, hiding how I'd prefer to interact with the people whom I'm actually close to. But one doesn't need to do this. Take a look at *table 19-8* to read your [Eros-Bacchus] angle. While angles such as I-, II-, and III-conjuncts, II-trines, and II-quintiles may be perfectly at home amongst strangers, angles like II-oppositions, II-squares and II-septiles tend not to be so comfortable mainly because their possessors need to feel a substantial identification with those around them. Even II-quintiles—though they can visibly function better in public gatherings than certain other angles—have an odd lack of sync with those around them when not acting in a dominant or

---

[30] I didn't expect this result. One would think that you promoted Other *within* your clique, but the data didn't bear this out.

servant capacity in some way. Of course there are exceptions, but this is one of those chart factors which casts a major vote on the matter.

Actually, more introverted or awkward types can get around social aversion by simply turning the occasion into one which reflects their element. II-noviles fit right in when creating or performing. III-octiles fit in when displaying insight, and so on. As for people who are naturally outgoing, this angle is less informative for shaping social encounters and more informative for its glimpse at the other resonant pairs which are drawn out at the same time through this same angle. Check out all the pairs in your self chart which have this same angle to see what other traits are built up as you engage this one.

Bacchus pairs

I first encountered Bacchus online among a list of about 10 or so love asteroids while working on a project aimed at clarifying the different means of expressing love between two people. Bacchus was—and still is—considered the asteroid of orgies, group sex, and wanton gaiety, but also sponsored some pretty pronounced mainstream effects in the chart well beyond many of its fellow love asteroids. Most notably, Bacchus in the data featured heavily in the charts of people who had highly social, at least mildly hedonistic lives and, as a reasonable consequence, served as the best and ONLY indicator besides Uranus of what a person's peer groups looked like. But Bacchus is in many ways better than Uranus as a peer indicator because it, unlike Uranus, represents the people whom you keep around you for the sake of expressing your raw personality (hence the use of the terms "cliques" and "ingroups" throughout this chapter). Uranus is less about who you keep around you for fun and more about who happens to be around you in general. More specifically, Uranus represents what the information world or `people around you` themselves `say`. Bacchus represents how the *people whom you like to keep around you* enable *you* to *act*. Uranus is about `them`. Bacchus is about *you and your backup*. Uranus is `communication`. Bacchus is *expression*. Uranus assumes the groups in question are mostly `indifferent to you`. Bacchus assumes the groups in question are extensions of your own choice and, hence, automatically *side with you*. You get the idea.

A look at Bacchus is invariably a look at your intimate friends from whom you are a lot less likely to hide the natural sides of yourself. And while you really will find it prominent in the charts of people who jam out in real orgies, on the more common level you'll also find it in the charts of people who simply like to party. But not all parties are keggers. Some involve family. Others involve social action. Still Others involve shared construction of things. The sign and house of Bacchus in your self chart will tell the tale. In the synastry though, we can think of Bacchus as simply indicating how your exchange with the other person produces experiences which you ultimately weigh against your crew. Sometimes the crew's view of your exchange won't matter much. Often it matters <u>bigtime</u>.

For more information on your regular chart's behavior under the sign, house, and pairs involving Bacchus and any other asteroids among these last eight (beginning with Ceres), you can reference their respective sections in *FSA*.

Bacchus-Bacchus

✪ Calculate your duo's mass appeal

Yours and Other's [Bacchus-Bacchus] angle shows where you and they have similar ways of grabbing the attention of a room. Separately, this is simply a similarity between those events that happen to you which raise your popularity. So if you and Other have a II-trine, when one of you decides to hijack a room with your mannerisms, the other will be able to piggyback off of this and get attention too. Meanwhile, people without the II-trine won't be able to share the floor so naturally with you when you're in this mode. If, instead you decide to assert your presence by declaring your core values and family experiences instead of using room-takeover, a different person whose Bacchus is II-square yours would have a naturally easier time grabbing attention with you here. If you're skilled enough in using different behaviors from *table 19-1* to express yourself, you can draw out even the shyest person in a room with a well-crafted form of assertion. It took a while for me to learn to do something like this with my college students, but it's a pretty cool skill once you have it. People who master synastric Bacchus can share the spotlight with anybody.

More interesting than how you take over a room on purpose is how you "cliquify" a room unintentionally via the Bacchus angle you share with the person you're with. If you and Other have a II-octile, for example, you will grab attention together via your joint allure in the eyes of outsiders. The deeper and more obvious the exchange becomes to witnesses the more this angle tends to make you an unsettlingly attractive or forceful pair, whether you are allies or not. III-conjuncts are "hip-duo popular," allies or not. III-septiles have wide star-power appeal as a duo, allies or not.

Are you looking to make a specific impression on the strange public around you? Do you want that public to become your fans (as your clique would)? Gather the charts of a few people and look at yours and their [Bacchus-Bacchus]. Meet with them in obvious public view of others. Even if you don't do anything particularly outrageous, the people who pay attention to you will tend to treat you as though you and the other person are worth gathering around for the sake of this angle. It's weird but oh so fascinating when you try it and watch it in action.

Just watching quintile duos in action can be an entertaining experience. Watching II-quintiles, however, can definitely make an audience uneasy (for whatever reason that might be). The exchange between III-quintile interactants can truly monopolize a crowd with the charisma bouncing back and forth between actors. All-level septiles are generally noteworthy for the extent to which they appear to like being together—even if they hate each other. All-level octiles are noteworthy for the extent to which they complement each other's compelling power in the eyes of those who view them. With all-level undeciles, your broad popularity in a room tends to rise and fall together even if you are not allies or even associated with each other. Be careful though; certain angles like all-level conjuncts and octiles in particular have a way of getting you looked at in ways you never bargained for. Let the rumors fly. See the usual *table 19-1* for the angle-specific areas of the social scene for which you and Other easily attract the following eye of the public. Just because this one's the last pair, doesn't at all make it useless.

Table 19-9: Synastric pair meanings

So there you have it. Over the next few pages you will find the table which summarizes all of the above synastric pairs discussed in this chapter. Keep in mind that each cell is a "summary of a summary" such that you shouldn't expect them to work strongly unless you actually pay attention to making them work in your relationship with the other person. Where your Mars combines with their Neptune, for example, it is true that the stats on this pair suggest that the Other highlights your power to build up whatever angle you have here. It is not true, however, that such power of yours will actually be built up if neither of you pays attention to this aspect of the exchange. Given all 625 combinations included here, most of the pairs in this table will be muted in your relationship unless or until you or the other person pays attention to either the pair or its angle as a thing worth building.

I must confess that when I finally finished creating the following six-page table the result was pretty overwhelming. The obvious question quickly arises: "What do I do with all this?" And then there are many, many other questions that accompany that first question. We dedicate the entire next chapter to the practical use of the synastric pairs, laying out the various issues that arise most frequently along with the most fundamental ideas you should take away from your chart with another person.

People who are familiar with astrology might note something interesting about the table below: The way we see ourselves is not the same as how we see others. I'll talk about this more in the next chapter, but the headings for your planets versus their planets reveal clear differences in how the planets look.[31] The "Them" columns should seem especially weird to you, as they don't quite do what we normally think they should do. And then we gaze upon Juno—whose patterns warranted an extra column to capture the idea that "commitment" is something designed to see a current event all the way through to its most reasonable end: that is, the beginning of the next event.[32] Strange behavior like this will show up a lot more frequently when we get to composite charts. For now though, when it comes to finding answers in the synastry chart, such differences between "your" planets and "their" planets end up being critical to how we ask and answer questions regarding your relationship with the other person.

For the following table, use the key below:

u	you (ur=your)	➲	through
o	the other person	✪	critical for determining relationship's character
☺	outsiders, anyone who is not one of the two parties in this chart	🕊	strong contributor to great relationship
🌍	the world	🔒	needed for a good relationship
↔	relationship	\	misuse can kill the relationship
∡	angle	👄	features heavily in seduction
soc	social	Ƴ	skyrocketing skill
ilo	in light of	⌘	you can learn from this
sxcre	sexual/creative	👁	read the other's motives or gain insight into your own
±	in a good or bad way / for better or worse (fbow)	💰	money-related

---

[31] Like all the data we've been using, the headings are drawn from patterns among the clusters they label; each heading was derived by looking at the general character of the row or column it described. I found "Their Lilith" to be especially interesting. In other news, why do we engage something 1:1 with our Sun? Perhaps because it awaits our influence in line with priorities we've already had. Why do we (openly) evaluate things socially? Perhaps to publicly align our otherwise unexplained impressions of them with the broader opinion, exposing our unique viewpoint.

[32] All Juno "next planet" entries were based on my guess as to what the logical next phase would be. Yes they *were* guesses, no more. But hopefully those guesses—based solely on the very same data that you've seen throughout this chapter—will make it easier to understand what the other person's Juno is doing in the synastry. Alas, more research on this is needed.

Them (o)→ ↓You (u)	☉ Sun How they interact with you	☽ Moo What they seem to prefer	☿ Mer How they make things work	♀ Ven How they communicate with you	♂ Mar Their attempts to move things around them	♃ Jup Their image projected in the world	♄ Sat Limits and structures that come w them	♅ Ura Where they soc spread fx of your efforts
☉ Sun Your behaviors	where you approach situations similarly	you play out how they feel	you are pursued for common ground	you soften their expression	they push you to steer outsiders	they embody the image you want associ-ated with	you put walls around them	you see them broadcasting widely; they can cheat you
☽ Moo Your feelings	your inclinations are turned into action	**drifting relationship?** subconscious reason for interacting	their desired goal among outsiders	👁 flattered or attended to by them	you can use this to compel their action	you encourage other to build this up as part of their image	you look like you want to impose this	they are a hub for your social groups
☿ Mer Your meaning-making	you take expressive cues	you feel subject to scrutiny	similar analysis; you can work together here	they build ∡ in you (a little) through conversation	you can easily command them	you help build up their image	\ you limit or control them with this	you have more social opportunities alongside them
♀ Ven Your 1:1 exchange with them	you get ∡ expressed to you through shared topic	you think their ∡ is a cool topic	you support their analysis through your conversation	same page as communicators	⬬ you have a natural pull over their impulses	they are prone to your bribes and flattery	you rob them of access to this	🕊 you give them a green light to try friendship with you
♂ Mar Your attempts to steer things / ppl / other	you drive them to express more	you can be easily steered using this	\ they easily command you	you are compelled to action	similar ennervation, prompts to fight	they see you dedicated to changing this in people	you inhibit their mastery; you structure their reputation	how you should interact with them as fr&s
♃ Jup Your efforts in the world	you feel respected by them	their display motivates you to go forth	your image is built up through commonality with them	you work to build up their image	they are more forward and insistent in this ∡	similar basis for image-making	they seem a longstanding complement to your ∡	you have respect for them under their ∡
♄ Sat Your limits / shows of control	you help them structure their approach	you feel restricted by their desire to express this	you are limited by them	you lose options for displaying this	your active influence is limited by their ∡	you expand your image against their obstacles	similar approaches to control	you shock them with your ∡, can embarrass them
♅ Ura You as a social evaluator	you encourage their network mobility	you see their popularity potential	they are well-liked and personable here	people are aware of an affinity btw you and them here	how they classify you socially	your ∡ assoc-iation with their world expands your image	they produce surprise restrictions for all, even themselves	similar societal contexts
♆ Nep You as embo-dying their environment	you give obligated attention or pity	you give impression of scrutiny	they are spacey, confusing, abstract	they seem to misinterpret your ∡	you amplify their influence, intensify their expression	you idealize them under their ∡	they are perfectionistic in general when it comes to ∡	o motivated to become stronger in light of your social environment
♇ Plu You as repre-senting those who pressure Other	you're there (fbow) when they're threatened	you promote their ∡ as powerful	you provide extra insight into their ∡	they become stronger and stronger with your association	you are challenged by their actions	you see them as extra powerful beyond peers	you pressure them to sharpen their ∡ expression	their ∡ demands you demonstrate strength
Asc ASC You as one approaching something new	their interaction reflects your ∡	you get their spontaneous expression of this ∡	they use ∡ to judge your impression making	you create base-level rapport here	you are single-minded in their view	they have the successful identity you seek to build	they submit to you	their position allows you to fulfill your intentions
Mc MC You the acknowledger	their contribution to this keeps u interested in relationship	they are self-promoting and reputation-centered	you are considered a partner to them by people	they show they wish to build something lasting here	they are 1:1 dominant under this ∡	where you and they are true partners in crime	they show controlled expression	they seem to gravitate to you under this ∡

Them (o)→ ↓You (u)	♆ Nep Where they reflect emo fx of your efforts	♇ Plu They infuse ur efforts w power	Asc ASC Where they bring attn. to your efforts	Mc MC Where they give u cause to respond	Vx Ver Their efforts to influence things around them	☊ NNd Where they make ur action convenient 4u	²⚸ Sel Where they model ur ideal view of concpt	⚸ Lil Where they turn into the reason u act	⊕ For Where they are comfortable
☉ Sun Your behaviors	**o=attentive?** your deeds dominate their idea of this ∡	you help them build defense against social pressure	you see them as strongly skilled	✪ 🔒 ⚕ they keep relationship alive through this	they value your help through change here	👁 you're easily known for this behavior	you celebrate their talents or criticize their defects	they are beyond your influence	you are more comfortable giving this
☽ Moo Your feelings	you make more errors, are self-conscious	they are your publicist for the rumor mill	you are comfortable going to them with your ∡	you use this ∡ to create an identity in their world	they see you as a catalyst for major change	🕊 you see role for yourself in their life	you see this as one of best parts of relationship	you draw out excitement or intimidate them	you reduce their insecurities
☿ Mer Your meaning-making	where they cover up issues you can't face; you are intuitive	⌘ you give good evaluation of their issues	they use this as central trait for making impressions	⌘ they adopt an approach you want to adopt	you benefit from their specialization	their angle is worth your analysis	you are more shameless showing this	they are a troublemaker	your criticality returns to you through them
♀ Ven Your 1:1 exchange with them	something about their world is unreal here	you attain power along-side them	you can be superficial friends here	you show you have other concerns besides them here	you consciously shape their decisions	you value your association through more 1:1 with them	you admire them as a source of de-cisive talent	you are weird, avant garde to them	they are themselves talking to you
♂ Mar Your attempts to steer things / ppl / other	they highlight your power to build up your ∡	⌘ 💰 u hand out "lessons" to them, in-fluence their money	you tend to lose challenges to them here	⬬ how they want you to validate them	your ∡ is altered by association with them	you show strength towards them	you actively smooth over conflicts btw o and people	your influence augments their defiance	your active influence pacifies their ∡
♃ Jup Your efforts in the world	their ∡ is fuzzy, but they can be very creative	♈ you levy world pressure uopn them	you think they look up to your efforts	they are an ally, if you jointly execute	your broad ∡ approach can change them	you appear sure of yourself	you're awkwardly skilled	you encourage rule-breaking and taboo in them	o has a wider view than you and could be a role model
♄ Sat Your limits / shows of control	you are obsessively attentive to certain rules	they possess limiting command over people	you don't mind having your efforts structured	you display control in their eyes	their ∡ is a glue trap, you are subject to their influence	🕊 you use this ∡ to tame them	they monopolize this ∡ when it arises	their angle is better seen than heard, a liability	they soften your seriousness
♅ Ura You as a social evaluator	🔒 **u like their company?** you support their social evolution	they are the fortress; send sxcre energy into relationship	you channel social world's response to them	you see their popular attributes under their ∡	you bring surprising change to them under their ∡	your angle is your branded face in their life	they seem soc appealing or repulsive in general	you look awkward but innovative	you fuel their bold or progressive nature
♆ Nep You as embo-dying their environment	similar focus on environment	your envirnmt survival skill goes up by helping them	their ∡ is an incomplete connection with you	they get away with prolific actions	you may never know them well here	their thoughtless actions can confuse ↔	the basis of your joining their fan club	you may look up to o as a rebel or innovator	you imagine an ideal when o is in their element
♇ Plu You as repre-senting those who pressure Other	u find comfort in your person-al problems around them	similar perception of pressures, support	their approach embodies your pressures	their strongest sxcre asset	they work against greater pressures	it is easier to endure your own pressures ilo them	o embodies your problems or enables your solutions	o enables social revolutionary expression	you use your ∡ to issue power
Asc ASC You as one approaching something new	their ∡ produces illusions for you	your exchange highlights problems in their ∡	similar approach to new situations, exploration	your sphere of experience learns of them through this ∡	their angle = basis of discussion for parallels	o drives you to spontaneous action	you can rely on them to express this	they are reliably contrary	you and other as fr&s
Mc MC You the acknowledger	you can act unchecked under your ∡	you are attracted to them to extent u want to show off ∡	your ∡ actions earn you a reputation in their life	people inclined to associate you and them publicly	Spillover. o reacts to or pays for assoc w you	you provide insight into their direction	you and they make an idealized public team	you and they publicly known as a rebel pair	ur image is boosted by o's enjoymnt of ur compny

Them (o)→ ↓You (u)	⚳ Cer Where they feel things need to be tended to	⚷ Chir Where they teach / compel ur learning	⚶ Ves Where they focus on what u flood them w/	⚴ Pal Where you respond to their crusade	⚵ Jun Their idea of ur current planet used to draw ur next "planet" curr	next		Hra Their attachment to your efforts	Ero Their passionate response to ur efforts	Bac How their friends answer your efforts
☉ Sun Your behaviors	you see their expressive potential	you learn from them; or they are a bad teacher	you motivate shaping of their ∡	you war alongside them; feel tension ilo o	Sun	Mercury	use this to secure commitment	your entitled association with o if this isn't blocked	you give them access to this as association builds	they rely on you to show this to their cliques
☽ Moo Your feelings	watched by o, you want to show dominance	you are a therapeutic listing ear	you hide this or let them have their way first	they see you as rebellious against social imposition	Moon	Sun	✪ their actions insist that you display this ∡	they greet you with this as they try to get closer 2 u	they are hungry or lusty here	you encroach on their space
☿ Mer Your meaning-making	you can make them smile or be uncomfortable	they appear to have their stuff together	you endure them	you don't receive attacks well	Mercury	Venus	you borrow their ∡ for your own advancement	you feel their excitement ilo your ∡	your ∡ is a button pusher for them	they are provocative and group-persuasive
♀ Ven Your 1:1 exchange with them	they are a little too forceful persuading people here	your "helping" them actually helps you	you flood them with information	they treat you as a crusader here	Venus	Mars	they assert this to reinforce their relevance	you maintain your identity against their connection	they see ur ∡ as more intense than expected	your 1:1 engagement affirms your popularity
♂ Mar Your attempts to steer things / ppl / other	you encourage more of their ∡ action	you are the perfectionistic evaluator of their abilities	you stay busy with this ∡ with or despite them	you tolerate, but don't adopt their ∡	Mars	Jupiter	you use ∡ to request their attention	\ maj. means for solidifying ↔...even as a dead one	Ping. This ∡ should inspire them	you make a great co-conspirator to them
♃ Jup Your efforts in the world	you can get away w pressuring them	you gain "exp points" for dealing w them here	this is a pronounced component of their world rep	they drive their own agitation	Jupiter	Saturn	your way grows their ∡ effectiveness w commitment	they express their attachment to you through ∡	you use ∡ to compel results in their eyes	you can draw a crowd in their eyes, ±
♄ Sat Your limits / shows of control	they cheer on your ∡ efforts	they avoid deep investigation of their ∡	this ∡ looks mismatched for them	your interaction fills you with tension or inspires you	Saturn	Uranus	you display commitment-like behaviors to them	you like using this ∡ to keep ↔ fresh	they are self-focused	they are the center of group attention
♅ Ura You as a social evaluator	in their company, you assert final word over ∡	their angle = area of your exploratory interest	o stares at ur soc information regarding this ∡	their battlefield = all of society under this ∡	Uranus	Neptune	they are a kindred mind to u under ∡	their influence stays with u beyond exchg	you learn ur own passion from theirs	✪their ∡ is the 1st maj impression they leave on you
♆ Nep You as embodying their environment	you see them as being in need of your coercion	o needs your encouragement to develop their power	as you imagine, they deliver in full	you feel you are in their way	Neptune	Pluto	\ their overly strong advancement hurts ↔	your company is appreciated by them	their driving force once you get to know them	you idealize their clique, u prone to disloyalty
♇ Plu You as representing those who pressure Other	you issue power ilo their ∡	their ∡ is a remedy for tension in ur ↔	they fixate on your ∡	you learn the art of fighting here	Pluto (soc prssr to	(social prssr to	their ∡ is a reliable basis for interfacing with them	you feel prolific, o attaches to be fulfilled	you and other = lock and key complements	you experience peer pressure ilo them
Asc ASC You as one approaching something new	they are pushy	you improve as a "doctor" ilo them	u pay more attn 2 their body or physical impression	u see o as passionate, with them or against them	Ascendant (1st house)	(worth of ↔; 2nd house)	you and they reaffirm the ↔	they bond with things under this ∡	u receive their ∡, ↔ becomes creatively tense	you influence their clique here
Mc MC You the acknowledger	they are known as a caretaker here	they are difficult to influence and quirky	they are obsessed w (or self-conscious of) ∡	their ∡ drives u to press for your own values	Midheaven (10th	(public talk; 11th house)	as ppl see u give ur ∡ to o, commitment is stronger	you publicly show bond to them ±	ppl see their ∡ as driving your passionate action	u see their ∡ as foundation for their clique membership

Them (o)→ ↓You (u)	☉ Sun How they interact with you	☽ Moo What they seem to prefer	☿ Mer How they make things work	♀ Ven How they communicate with you	♂ Mar Their attempts to move things around them	♃ Jup Their image projected in the world	♄ Sat Limits and structures that come w them	♅ Ura Where they soc spread fx of your efforts
Vx Ver Your experience of change	their behavior tied to their major changes	you seem a potential agent for their major change	👁 you can change them; they struggle to forgive you	you can have your life changed under their ∡	♈ your skill with this ∡ skyrockets alongside them	your responses to them can change you	your life is changed, stabilized under their ∡	o brings chngs under ∡, putting u on the spot
☊ NNd Where u make things seem meant to be	o seems destined to express this ∡	they see this as important for early ↔ survival	you receive important analysis from them	conversation with you increases their sophistication	you seem destined to receive their steering attempts	they're extra forceful to cover self-doubt	if you choose to learn from them, you grow here	their angle makes them favorable to you
²⚸ Sel Where u r super talented	you feel more talented ilo them	you can use this to make them happy	\ you have commonality with their unlimited talent	you share an overwhelming trait with them	they are (or should be) ridiculously lucky here	they're good, but probably not the best	u like being put under their influence 4 ur reputation building	u and o make a good tag team 4 social validation
⚸ Lil Where u defy normal expected behavior	you are rebel complement to other	you are a badass alongside other doing this	where you are a perpetrator of offenses	their path is unusual here	their ∡ draws out the rulebreaker in you	they are the devil on your shoulder	u encourage them to break restrictions	u make o defer to u or see you as underqualified
⊕ For You in your element	you are in your element ilo their ∡	you accept their angle as comfortable fact	you like their reluctantly given tactics	👁 what they think you like to talk about	they can shake you out of comfort here	you're inclined to brag about this association	you help co-write their ∡	you look at bigger picture ilo their ∡
⚳ Cer Where you push them to more force	u are encouraged 2 behave differently; they grate	they are heavily persuasive here	you are amused by or agree with their tactics	they model strong communication	✪you enjoy associating their prtnrshp with your ∡	u are subject to changes in ur presentation under their influence	u push them to display this ∡ beyond themselves	o puts members of soc world in place
⚷ Chir Where u teach lessons (smtms accidently)	you see them as capped; or as a respected teacher	they heal you or serve as outlet for you	⌘ you are an apprentice skillwise	their ∡ has a therapeutic effect on them	o difficult to reach when engaged in this	you help them through issues here	their point of compensation for failed wishes	you disclose secrets about yourself relative to ∡
⚶ Ves Where you put ur concentration	you admire and focus on them	you are fascinated by them, want to know more	you can be wrapped up for hours by them	you pay focused attn to their communication	unless you're helping them, o is inclined to ignore you	you gain sharper focus on your angle ilo their ways	they push ∡ on ppl to increase their own influence	they are well-versed or focused under your attn
⚴ Pal Where you call for war	they can provoke you into a social statement	they are unwilling to be caged in	they are a rebel fighter when ∡ threatened	they are a paradigm toppling communicator	o braves the world to fight for their version of this ∡	♈ you hone your skills in warfare ilo their ∡	you borrow their ∡ to fight your own battles	their appearance leaves this impression on you
⚵ Jun Your commitment behavior	o commits to you using this	you commit to supporting this angle	an ideal they come to you to validate	discussions under your ∡ = togetherness for you	o insinuates themselves into your life	✪ how you'll change ilo your commitment to them	their expression keeps u interested in them	**✪Wht u get out of ↔? o validates your abilities**
Hra Your bonding behavior	joint expression here solidifies bond	their ∡ is the basis for good will between you	✪ you bond strongly with them ilo their ∡	they are attached to protecting their ∡	🕊 you are very strongly drawn to their ∡	o = your long term friend if you can accept this ∡	🕊Solidifier jointly, keep the exchange from decaying	ur ∡ is insistently pressed upon by your target
Ero Where you crave passion	✪ you express your desires ilo their version of ∡	you press full force for their ∡	they motivate your impassioned response	o = a territory conquering communicator	you appreciate their ∡ and find it comforting	they = sexy or frustrating, motivating you ±	they brim with potential	they are driven in a scoial setting
Bac How your clique responds	they adopt this basic behavior in their cliques	they seem a dominator here	they are an attention grabbing co-star to you	o has talent for group-commanding communication	you conspire with them to take over their group	they gather pleasure seekers	they are sought after under ∡	your most comfortable way of sending ur clique expression to them

Them (o)→ ↓You (u)	♆ Nep Where they reflect emo fx of your efforts	♇ Plu They infuse ur efforts w power	Asc ASC Where they bring attn. to your efforts	Mc MC Where they give u cause to respond	Vx Ver Their efforts to influencethings around them	☊ NNd Where they make ur action convenient 4u	²⚸ Sel Where they model ur ideal view of concpt	⚸ Lil Where they turn into the reason u act	⊕ For Where they are comfortable
Vx Ver Your experience of change	their fuzziness may inspire your action	👄o is a strong means of rewritiing ur ∡ priorities	u and o have intertwined fates ilo your ∡	you enter their world and change your view of them	similar drivers for life change	their ∡ fated to change ur ↔ permanently	u appreciate the strength of expression in their ∡	∡ reflects longstanding waywardness in them	their ∡ sponsors ur deep personal discoveries
☊ NNd Where u make things seem meant to be	you use this ∡ to send ur aspirations to them	🔒world opposes their easy progress	they are erra-tic, u may question the hype about o	🔒 you rub off on them	your ∡ brings unavoidable changes to ↔	your + their Introduction Context	their Destined Reveal 2 u	👄you take counterperspective to them	they are self-assured without you here
²⚸ Sel Where u r super talented	o doesn't see what you want them to see	you can feel unstoppable w their support	the section of life where u always feel o welcomes u±	ppl identify you as strong partner to them	you learn how your own ∡ should be used	your first signi-ficant impression on them	similar level of command 4 what needs to be done	o can get away w murder under this	✪you appear in their life to evolve how they use ∡
⚸ Lil Where u defy normal expect ed behavior	u imagine a rule-breaking exchg w o; Hollow Oath	ur ∡ shows stand out power comp ared to ppl	you won't be pinned down	u encourage o to be nonconformist	they see this ∡ as schmooze-resitant in you	o is contrary or complementary to you	they see a trait in you which no one can check	similar prompt for fiery defiance	they employ rebel tactics as a rule here
⊕ For You in your element	their ∡ is the means they use to impress upon people	o assaults ± with this ∡	u r interested in exploring the future with them	you value ur assoc w other under ∡	u see their ∡ as their most comfortable new expressn	✪ u (ideally) earn their respect under this angle	✪ their role = hone how u project ur ∡	you help o break barriers under ∡	similar tendency to bask in ur + their abilities
⚳ Cer Where you push them to more force	they do what you are com pelled to want them to do	Worsened Pressure by u onto them	o is compara tively modest against their other traits	o promotes thmslvs for significance under your ∡	you use this angle to overrule their suggestions	o prgrmmed to make their case to you through angle	u r shielded by them from challenges to ur ∡	you want to foster their escape from the status quo	you show the kind of pressure o likes via ur ∡
⚷ Chir Where u teach lessons (sm accidently)	you clean up their mistakes	you are kept grounded through their ∡	they need help or validation	o is less secure under their ∡	o accidentally learns by tackling ur fears	you strongly inclined to accept help from o here	o has steering expertise over ppl in this ∡	you access buried issues in them via ur ∡	you serve as a doctor ilo their bad preferences
⚶ Ves Where you put ur concentration	you see them as fixed in intent	you direct ur power towards addressing standards in o	you can be entranced by them	where u r self-conscious around them	their way of doing things surprises you	o grows greatly in power w ur partnership	Internal Defense against their threats	their ∡ = trait that sets them apart from people	o treats you as compelling given ur display of ∡
⚴ Pal Where you call for war	you support their fulfillment of an ideal role	you are more likely to fight on their behalf	they are a fellow combatant under their ∡	they naturally seek to challenge people here	you use your ∡ to kick them, push them forward	o needs you to listen here	they adopt ∡ as a remedy for issues with [∡-1]	u are more likely to put o in an uncomfortable position in their∡	u encouraged by o to fight for ur ∡, ±
⚵ Jun Your commitment behavior	you seek to influence their dreams	you commit to their development	👁u receive their ∡ as a statement of their caring	ppl see their ∡ to you as a token of their commitment	you and o seem destined to be committed ±	you feel destined to commit given their ∡ to you	they cling to this aspect of their influence	you support their stand out in this ∡	they express their discontent w society
Hra Your bonding behavior	you are comfortable delving into their company	o needs to address prssr here to feel effective	other puts expectations on you; ✪u = irresistible	where u + o have implied affection and attachment	you use new bonding w o to rewrite this area of ur life	you bond to o over their ∡ IF you have the interest	u r at home expressing yourself along-side their ∡	you find their ∡ mysterious	o sees ur ∡ as main wpn 4 reconciling disharmony
Ero Where you crave passion	their handling of their ∡ is impressive 2 you	✪o supports your powers (after ↔); u flood Other	🗡 ✪ 🕊 how can u drive ↔ intensity?	their ∡ is a possible liabil ity in building ur reputation	you incite driven action in other	you reveal ur passions to them, o = fated viewer	o provokes ppl's passions through their ∡	their ∡ = the essence of quality time with them	o conveys their lusts through ur ∡
Bac How your clique responds	o is insistently social here, might make u jealous	your group weighs in on o ilo this ∡	your clique absorbs o's ways into its function	your cliques view o's ∡ as basis for clique's attn	you use your ∡ as spokespersn for ur clique	natural language for defining their cliques	your mgmt of groups is influenced by them	your clique admires this ∡ in o	u r eccentric in a way that embarrasses o

Them (o)→ ↓You (u)	⚳ Cer Where they feel things need to be tended to	⚷ Chir Where they teach / compel ur learning	⚶ Ves Where they focus on what u flood them w/	⚴ Pal Where you respond to their crusade	⚵ Jun Their idea of ur current planet used to draw ur next "planet" curr	next		Hra Their attachment to your efforts	Ero Their passionate response to ur efforts	Bac How their friends answer your efforts
Vx Ver Your experience of change	o attempts to persuade you to their way of thinking	you elevate their pre-existing talents	they have to watch out for left turns from you	their ∡ awakens your inner warrior	Vertex (change)	(reconciled change)	you get their committed attention	you're hooked on their approach ±	their ∡ is agitating and provocative	do their friends show you this ∡ positively?
☊ NNd Where u make things seem meant to be	your chief persuasive mode, fun time with o	o needs your help developing this ∡	their social worth lies partly in this ∡	their fighter mode ∡	Nth Node (destiny)	(aftermath)	your vulnerability offering to them	your core offering to o, gets their liking if successful	their passionate action is dedicated to this ∡	u categorize their group according to this ∡
²⚸ Sel Where u r super talented	you promote the idea of o as powerful under ∡	u take on authority role in their eyes	o concentrates on maintaining this side, 4 or against u	u use this ∡ on o unreslvd [∡-1] issues w them	Selene (perfection)	(next event)	you like hanging around them for this ∡	👁their true desire 2 bond (in general) conveyed	ur ∡ is point of charged emo. to them	they have pronounced status in cliques here
⚸ Lil Where u defy normal expected behavior	o sees ur ∡ defy standard soc training	ur ∡ is a cover 4 ur real feelings of their version of ∡	ur uniquely destabilizing role in their life	their tool 4 making their more intense wants known	Lilith (defiance)	(uniqueness)	u r extra unique given your decision to engage them	you resist their persuasion using this ∡	ur weapon for motivating o when they don't move	you see them as popular ilo ppl seeking this ∡ in them
⊕ For You in your element	you are at home with their style of nurturing	o needs your encouragement through difficulty here	o sees this ∡ as a gateway to their self-image	u encourage o in fighting for their ∡	P. Fortune (ur element)	(voluntary choice)	mismatches in this ∡ easily hurt long term ↔	o brings this ↔ as the harmony or else condition	🕊 o is most devoted to u under this ∡	o stands out among own; u surprised by their circle
⚳ Cer Where you push them to more force	similar approach to influencing people	u polish this ∡ b/c u think it's what o wants to see	u actively support healthy exprssion of their ∡	you ask for punishment for being associated w o	Ceres (pushing)	(strong display)	\ u make a place 4 o; or put them in their place	you convey sensitivity to their needs	their primal side inflames ur own	the method o uses to resist ur unreasonbl demands
⚷ Chir Where u teach lessons (sm accidently)	you diagnose their underlying sense of insufficiency	similar approaches to insecurity	you are highly observant of their ∡	your ∡ has a pacifying effct on them; The Tamer	Chiron (social insecurity)	(security in society)	u refuse their successful input, single-mindedly	🕊ur silver bullet for bonding w o, Dfns Weakenr	your capped efforts to engage them	\ o helps fill ur expressve need; o gains wider appeal
⚶ Ves Where you put ur concentration	you watch their attempts to force changes on people	you see their perspective as aligned w yours under ∡	similar penchant for zooming in on issues	their ongoing battle against issues here	Vesta (focus)	(continuation)	u end up supporting o here, lifting partial burden	o produces conditions for ur accidental ∡ evolution	their intensity follows yours	o seems well-liked under descriptions of their ∡
⚴ Pal Where you call for war	u see them as most resistant to caging	u cheer 4 or bemoan their ∡ to drive it -> ur benefit	o more likely to show irritation handling this ∡	similar social-battle prompts and ethical foundations	Pallas ("right" war)	(resolution)	u see o as useful to ur quest to resolve ur ∡	o frames the consequences of their social actions w ∡	they are your joint social combat partner	their ∡ is their investment in friendship w u
⚵ Jun Your commitment behavior	your assessment of their selfishness	they treat their ∡ as a "must protect"	they are a magnet for issues that concern you	their burdens attracted to you	Juno (commitment)	(committer's desired end)	ur + their commitments affect this ∡ similarly	u use ur ∡ to provide enduring support to o	⬬o brings u to creative projection this ∡'s way	u donate their ∡ as offering 2 ur clique, promoting o
Hra Your bonding behavior	you see o as caring through their ∡	u value their ∡ highly, letting it circumscribe your standards	u as Guardian Angel to them	o under-expresses under ∡	Hera (bonding)	(fulfillment)	you connect to their use of ∡ as valid acquaintance	similar bond triggers	u market this ∡ of theirs to ppl	u + o jointly attract ppl's attention
Ero Where you crave passion	o sees you charge up ur expression w passion	you see their area of greatest dissatisfaction	u r inspired 2 be more soc attractive ilo their ∡	o needs intensely felt harmony w ppl here	Eros (lust)	(satiation)	u help push o to create whatever their ∡ passion is	⬬their formed bond under their ∡ = stimulating ±	similar passionate mobility prompts	u want to rewrite their clique training
Bac How your clique responds	u help pressure o 2 stay strong and desirable among clique	o provides skill u can't, winning over cliques	o issues ∡ under concern 4 ppl's opinion	🕊ur positive engagement in ur ∡ grows ur friendship	Bacchus (clique beh.)	(clique identity)	they commit noticeably to their groups via this ∡	u + o form a potent tag team towards ppl	ur clique = infiltrated by their lusts	✪ u + o jointly "cliquify" a room

Chapter 20: How do you read this synastry chart?

Table 19-9 is huge. Where synastry is concerned, the number of questions we could ask about any relationship between two things far exceeds the number of questions we could ask about one thing in isolation. So we'll need to tackle the reading of a synastry chart in a way that makes sense. This chapter divides the reading of a synastry chart into the four following phases and concludes with a single basic takeaway:

1. Read all (level I) conjuncts
2. Ask whatever specific questions you have
3. Read the cocktails (frequently asked questions)
4. Consider the other person's perspective

Takeaway: Remember the ONE pair that matters most to you (which we'll call the key pair)

If you're coming straight to this chapter as a quick start...

I'll repeat the disclaimer found in Chapter 19: In order to use what you read in this chapter, you'll need to obtain an angle-view (a.k.a. aspect view / aspectarium) version of your chart. Not a chart wheel.

Not this...

Tropical, Geocentric
Polich - Page

StarFisher 0.8.5.4
Mutual Aspects

NO

...but this.

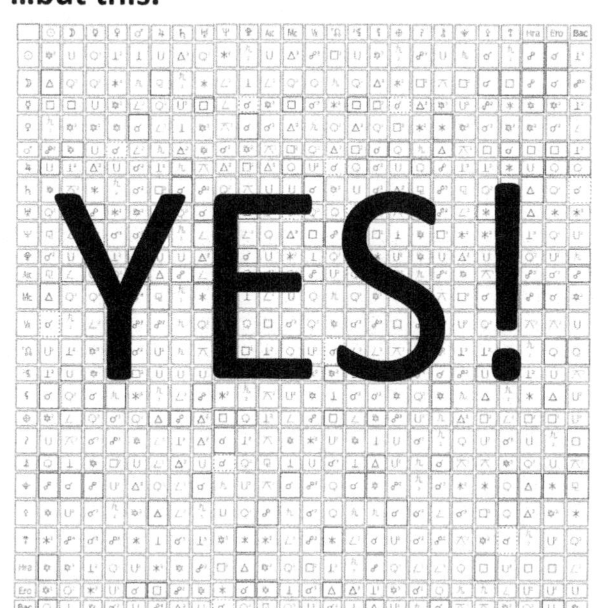

You'll find the program that I used to create an "angle view" on my website at http://electricmonastery.com. It's called StarFisher and (at the time of this writing) can be found at http://www.starfisher.cz/starfisher/EN/. You should still visit http://electricmonastery.com for the files you need to display a full table's worth of angles, though. StarFisher doesn't come with all 36 angle families included. At the time of this writing, no program does. (They were just introduced a year prior in in *FSA*.)

Okay, let's begin.

Synastry reading step 1: Read all conjuncts ☌

Among all of the 36 kinds of angles we cover in this book, conjuncts are the most useful for reading basic charts. This is because conjuncts occur when two points are next to each other—more or less within a window of 0° – 9.5ish°. When two points are next to each other, they tend to play out together. So having your Sun (1:1 expression) conjunct another person's Moon (inner feeling) means that these sides of the two of you will typically play out together (for better or worse). When you read all of the conjunct pairs in a synastry chart, you are essentially reading those corners of the relationship which play out most naturally in your relationship with that particular other person. So while any relationship will hold the [Vertex-Chiron] potential for you to build up the other person's preexisting talents for example, only relationships with a [Vertex-Chiron] conjunct will show this tendency naturally and automatically.

Recall that all pairs in a chart which share the same angle are called **resonant pairs**. Resonant pairs form little "mini-personalities" for whatever you're looking at, such that all chart pairs which have the *conjunct* will describe the chart holders' most *natural* exchange and all pairs with the opposition will describe the chart holders' overall way of seeing their self-image in the exchange. When we refer to "all the resonant pairs to [Mars $_{you}$-Moon $_{them}$]," for example, we are talking about all of the pairs in your synastry chart which have the same angle as the one between your Mars and their Moon; if [Mars $_{you}$-Moon $_{them}$] has an opposition, the resonant pairs to this will be the entire family of pairs in the chart which have the opposition, [Mars $_{you}$-Moon $_{them}$] included.

A synastry chart reading begins by looking at the resonant pairs for the conjunct. That family of pairs answers the question, "How does this relationship most naturally play out?"

Consider the following sample synastry:

Table 20-1: Synastry chart for Person A and Person B

	☉	☽	☿	♀	♂	♃	♄	♅	♆	♇	Asc	Mc	Vx	'☊	^{2}⚸	⚸	⊕	ʔ	⚷	⯓	⚲	⚵	Hra	Ero	Bac
☉	□^{2}	✱^{3}	⊥^{2}	U	**☌**	⚼	U^2	☌^{2}	**☌**	∠^{2}	U^2	△	U^2	⚻	☌^{2}	九^2	△^{2}	✱^{2}	U	U	□	✱^{3}	☌^{3}	☍^{2}	∠^{2}
☽	U	✡^{2}	✡^{3}	☌^{2}	△^{2}	U	⊥	Q	✡	Q	□^{3}	U^2	九^3	△^{2}	Q^2	✡^{2}	⚻	Q^2	⚻	□^{2}	Q	U^2	△	U	⊥
☿	□	⊥	⚻^{2}	☌^{2}	⚻	✡	∠^{3}	U^2	U^2	☍^{2}	∠^{2}	Q	⚻	☌^{3}	U	Q^2	Q	△	⊥	✡	U	✱	✱^{2}	Q^2	U^3
♀	九^2	✡	✱^{2}	✡	Q^3	✡^{2}	△^{3}	Q	九^3	Q	⊥^{2}	☌^{2}	✡	△^{2}	Q^3	□^{2}	U	△	□^{2}	⚻	Q	U	☍^{2}	☌^{2}	☍
♂	⚻^{3}	**☌**	**☌**	∠	Q	☌^{2}	□^{2}	□^{2}	九^2	△^{2}	U^2	Q^2	九^3	Q	⚼	U	⚻	U^2	⚻	⊥^{3}	△^{2}	∠^{2}	△	✡	✱^{3}
♃	**☌**	✱^{2}	∠^{2}	U^2	✡^{2}	☍^{3}	✡^{2}	**☌**	Q	**☌**	U	✡^{2}	△	九^2	△	⚻	⊥^{2}	✡	⚻^{2}	□^{2}	✡	⊥^{2}	△^{3}	☌^{2}	U
♄	Q^2	✡^{2}	⊥	☍^{3}	九	Q^3	✡^{2}	**☌**	∠^{2}	**☌**	U^2	⊥^{3}	U^2	✡	✡	✱^{3}	**☌**	☌^{3}	☍	Q^2	⚼	U	□	☍	✡^{3}
♅	U^2	✡^{2}	✡^{3}	☌^{3}	九^2	Q	✡^{2}	U	**☌**	U	Q^2	U	∠^{2}	九	∠	⚻^{2}	✱	⚻^{3}	△	九^3	U^2	Q	U	△	☌^{3}
♆	△^{3}	△	△	Q	∠	U^2	九^2	✡^{2}	U^2	✡^{3}	⚻^{3}	⊥^{3}	⚼	✡^{2}	⊥^{2}	U^2	Q^3	∠^{3}	□	Q^2	✡	∠	**☌**	□	⊥^{3}
♇	△^{2}	Q^2	Q^2	□^{3}	△^{3}	□^{2}	Q	⊥	☌^{2}	九^2	∠^{3}	✱^{2}	△^{2}	⚻^{3}	✡^{2}	Q^2	☌^{2}	九	✡^{2}	☌^{2}	九^3	✡	Q^2	⚻	Q
Asc	☌^{3}	✡^{2}	U^2	九^2	□^{2}	△	✱^{2}	九	U	九	⚼	⚼	□^{2}	⚻^{2}	⚻^{3}	✱^{2}	✡	⊥	☍^{2}	Q^3	U^2	Q^2	✱	△^{2}	✡^{3}
Mc	△^{2}	□^{2}	☌^{2}	✱	⊥	∠^{2}	△^{2}	✱^{3}	Q^2	☌^{2}	✱	Q^3	Q	☍	☌^{2}	✡^{2}	✡^{2}	□^{2}	✡	九	✱	☌^{2}	⚻^{2}	☌^{3}	Q^2
Vx	✱^{3}	☌^{3}	△^{3}	✡^{3}	⊥^{2}	☍^{2}	☍	**☌**	Q^2	**☌**	Q^3	U	✱^{3}	✡^{2}	☌^{2}	U^2	**☌**	U	☌^{3}	✡^{2}	Q	✱^{2}	U	U^3	△^{3}
'☊	**☌**	Q^2	✡^{2}	U^3	✡^{2}	☍^{3}	九^2	**☌**	Q	**☌**	U	✡^{2}	Q^3	九^2	△	Q^3	U^2	✡	☌^{2}	□^{2}	✡	⊥^{2}	△^{3}	△^{2}	U
^{2}⚸	✡^{2}	⚻	⊥^{2}	U	Q	∠^{2}	✱	△	✡^{3}	△	△^{2}	U^3	⊥	Q	**☌**	✱^{2}	□^{2}	✡^{2}	U	U	△^{2}	✡^{2}	九^3	Q^2	✡^{2}
⚸	九^3	☌^{2}	☍^{2}	△^{2}	⚻^{3}	✡^{2}	☍	**☌**	U	**☌**	☍^{2}	Q^2	U	✡^{3}	□^{2}	Q	**☌**	∠^{2}	九^2	⊥^{3}	∠^{3}	✱^{2}	✱^{2}	Q^3	⚻^{2}
⊕	☍^{2}	**☌**	九^3	✱	Q^3	九	九^3	✡^{2}	☌^{3}	九	Q^2	☌^{2}	✡^{2}	✡^{2}	Q^3	☍	∠	Q^2	⚼	✡^{2}	☍	☍	⚼	九^2	九^2
ʔ	Q	☍^{2}	U	☍	✡	九	九^3	□^{2}	✱^{2}	⊥^{3}	☍	✡^{3}	☍^{2}	Q^2	□	✱	⚻^{2}	**☌**	U^2	⊥^{2}	✡^{3}	Q^2	⚻^{2}	∠^{2}	✡
⚷	☌^{2}	✡^{2}	△^{2}	Q	九^2	∠	✡^{2}	△	Q^3	Q^3	⊥^{2}	✡^{3}	**☌**	☌^{3}	Q^2	△^{2}	U	U^3	✡	U^2	□	U	☌^{2}	✡	⊥^{2}
⯓	☌^{2}	✡^{2}	☍^{3}	⊥^{2}	U^2	∠	☌^{2}	Q^3	☌^{3}	U^2	Q^2	✱	**☌**	⚻	U^2	✡^{2}	U	九	⊥^{2}	△^{2}	□	☍^{3}	九^2	✡	九^2
⚲	U	☍	☍	☍^{2}	✡	U	☌^{3}	✡^{2}	□	⚻	Q^2	Q	☍^{2}	⊥^{2}	九	⚻^{3}	Q	∠	⊥	⚼	**☌**	✱^{3}	⊥^{3}	U	✡
⚵	⊥	✱^{2}	九^3	Q	U	☌^{3}	U	⊥^{2}	□^{2}	⚻^{3}	Q	U^2	☌^{2}	∠	九	Q^2	✡^{2}	⊥^{2}	Q^3	△^{3}	☌^{2}	九^2	⊥^{2}	Q^2	✡^{3}
Hra	U	⊥^{2}	⚻	☍^{4}	⚼	U	**☌**	☍	△	☍	⊥^{3}	☌^{2}	∠	⊥^{2}	Q	Q^2	☍	□^{3}	**☌**	☌^{3}	☌^{4}	∠	Q^2	**☌**	☍^{3}
Ero	⚻^{2}	☍	☍	⚻^{3}	✡	⚻^{3}	☌^{2}	✡	□	✡^{2}	☍^{2}	Q	✡^{2}	□^{2}	U^3	✡^{3}	Q	☌^{3}	九^2	✱^{3}	**☌**	△^{3}	∠^{2}	U	☌^{3}
Bac	△^{2}	□^{2}	☌^{2}	✱	⊥	∠^{2}	△^{2}	Q^2	Q^2	☌^{2}	✱	⚻	Q	☍	☍^{2}	✡^{2}	☍^{2}	□^{2}	✡	九	✱	☌^{2}	⚻^{2}	✱^{2}	Q^2

Table 20-1: Sample synastry chart. I've marked all of the (regular, level I) conjuncts.

Before we start asking questions about how A and B get along, what each person likes and all that, it is very important to know how the interaction actually works by default. This less biased baseline will partly keep us from lying to ourselves about what we find later. *Table 20-1* is a straightforward read. To make the meanings slightly more readable, we'll say that A is male and B is female. With all of the conjuncts marked, the only thing we need to do is write down what the marked pairs mean using *table 19-9*.

Table 20-2: List of resonant pairs for the conjuncts in sample table 20-1

Pair	Person A (Him)	Person B (Her)	**Meaning** (references to "the angle" have been replaced with "natural instincts" because we're looking at the conjunct)
☉-♂	Sun	Mars	She pushes him to steer other people
☉-♆	Sun	Neptune	His deeds dominate her ideas of how *natural instincts* (conjuncts) play out
♂-☽	Mars	Moon	He can be easily steered *naturally* (i.e., using the conjunct)
♂-☿	Mars	Mercury	She easily commands him
♃-☉	Jupiter	Sun	He feels respected by her
♃-♅	Jupiter	Uranus	He has a natural respect for her
♃-♇	Jupiter	Pluto	He levies world pressures upon her
♄-♅	Saturn	Uranus	He shocks her with his *natural instinct*, can embarrass her
♄-♇	Saturn	Pluto	She has a limiting command over people's behavior
♄-⊕	Saturn	Fortune	She softens his seriousness
♅-♆	Uranus	Neptune	He supports her social evolution
♆-Hera	Neptune	Hera	His company is appreciated by her
Vx-♅	Vertex	Uranus	She naturally brings changes in his life, putting him on the spot
Vx-♇	Vertex	Pluto	She is a strong means of rewriting his priorities regarding his *natural instincts*
Vx-⊕	Vertex	Fortune	Her natural way sponsors his deep personal discoveries
ᵀ☊-☉	Node	Sun	She seems destined to express her *natural instincts*
ᵀ☊-♅	Node	Uranus	Her natural ways makes her favorable to him
ᵀ☊-♇	Node	Pluto	The world naturally opposes her easy progress
²⚸-²⚸	Selene	Selene	They share a similar command of [how to be their natural selves]
⚸-♅	Lilith	Uranus	He makes her defer to him or sees her as underqualified
⚸-♇	Lilith	Pluto	He naturally shows stand-out power compared to other people
⚸-⊕	Lilith	Fortune	She employs rebel tactics as a rule
⊕-☽	Fortune	Moon	He accepts her natural behavior as a comfortable fact
⚳-⚳	Ceres	Ceres	They have similar approaches to influencing people
⚷-Vx	Chiorn	Vertex	She naturally learns by tackling his fears
⚶-Vx	Vesta	Vertex	Her way of doing things surprises him
⚴-⚴	Pallas	Pallas	They share similar triggers that drive them to battle and similar ethics
Hera-♄	Hera	Saturn	By being themselves together, they keep the interaction from decaying
Hera-⚷	Hera	Chiron	He values her natural way highly, letting it circumscribe his standards
Hera-Ero	Hera	Eros	He markets her natural behavior or instincts to people
Eros-⚴	Eros	Pallas	She needs intensely felt harmony with people's *natural selves*

Can we say anything about this interaction based on the above chart? Sure. But we might have to rearrange some things to make the conclusions flow better. From there, we'll come up with some blanket statements.

Table 20-3: List of resonant pairs for the conjuncts in sample table 20-1, rearranged

Pair	General Summary	**Meaning** (references to "the angle" have been replaced with "natural instincts" because we're looking at the conjunct)
♂-☽	In the most default case, this interaction is one in which she has a natural influence over him (possibly as a rebellious influencer of others), though he may exercise a kind of reverse control as a way of balancing their dynamic. He is inclined to appreciate her for her basic way of being, though one could see him being a difficult person at times.	He can be easily steered *naturally* (i.e., using the conjunct)
♂-☿		She easily commands him
☉-♂		She pushes him to steer other people
Vx-♅		She naturally brings changes in his life, putting him on the spot
Vx-♇		She is a strong means of rewriting his priorities regarding his *natural instincts*
♄-♇		She has a limiting command over people's behavior
Vx-⊕		Her natural way sponsors his deep personal discoveries
²⚸-²⚸		They share a similar command of [how to be their natural selves]
⚵-⚵		They share similar triggers that drive them to battle and similar ethics
♃-♅		He has a natural respect for her
ᵀ☊-☉		She seems destined to express her *natural instincts*
Eros-⚵		She needs intensely felt harmony with people's *natural selves*
⚸-⊕		She employs rebel tactics as a rule
ᵀ☊-♇		The world naturally opposes her easy progress
ᵀ☊-♅		Her natural ways makes her favorable to him
⯓-Vx		Her way of doing things surprises him
Hera-⚷		He values her natural way highly, letting it circumscribe his standards
⚳-⚳		They have similar approaches to influencing people
⊕-☽		He accepts her natural behavior as a comfortable fact
♅-♆		He supports her social evolution
♆-Hera		His company is appreciated by her
♃-☉		He feels respected by her
♄-⊕		She softens his seriousness
⚷-Vx		She naturally learns by tackling his fears
♃-♇		He levies world pressures upon her
♄-♅		He shocks her with his *natural instinct*, can embarrass her
⚸-♇		He naturally shows stand-out power compared to other people
⚸-♅		He makes her defer to him or sees her as underqualified
☉-♆		His deeds dominate her ideas of how *natural instincts* (conjuncts) play out
Hera-♄		By being themselves together, they keep the interaction from decaying
Hera-Ero		He markets her natural behavior or instincts to people

So are these two friends? Enemies? Something in between? We can't say for sure, but they seem to be friendly by default. At least we now have a decent summary in front of us.

Rearranging what you get from the conjunct reading can be a very informative task. The order in which you put things says a lot about how you yourself are biased to interpret the relationship—which is the main reason why we can't read whether the above chart is positive or negative. You could imagine, say, reversing the statements above to get a dynamic which was much more pathological looking—him to her.[33]

Synastry reading step 2: Ask whatever questions you have

This next step is simple but not. First let's get the bad news out of the way: If you plan to read synastry charts more than once or twice with any thoroughness, you really *should* get comfortable with *tables 16-3* and *19-1* to get a solid grip on what all the planets and angles mean. A quick look at this chapter's *table 20-1* will remind you why this is; a full astrochart consists of nothing but symbols, and will be very hard to read for people planning to look up their specific angle for every pair. You won't find such angle-by-angle interpretations in here—only overall pair descriptions for the most part. I know, I know. "That sucks," you say. But as I mention in *FSA* where the 36 harmonic families are first introduced, building a chart summary from 25 x 25 x 36 separate interpretations is not only difficult, but actually inaccurate; a [Mars-Mars] novile, for example, doesn't always show two people who get agitated together by "image promotion." Sometimes it's through shared learning. Sometimes it's through travel. Sometimes they're not even getting agitated together. They're reasoning. They're delving into each other's psyches. They're using their resonant pairs to argue with each other instead. As suggested by the three columns in *table 19-1* and the tense/non-tense version of each planet, 25 x 25 x 36 x 3 x 2 x 2 is closer to what we would end up with if you looked for an interpretation for every version of every angle of every pair, and even this would not be enough, given that your unique chart will steer how these play out in specific ways. Why don't we just get directions through a city by listing all the roads? Not cool. And so you'll need to know, with some practice, that a trine is for thinking and a II-septile is for ingroups. A III-sextile is critical analysis (and sometimes body show-off) while a III-decile shows how one behaves as a boss or a master. You'll need to know that Uranus is for social talk while Bacchus is for fun cliques. Barring this grasp of the angles and planets, your answers to certain questions won't be so clear.

And now for some neutral news: There are many ways to pose the same question in an astro chart, so you'll often find several pairs which tell you similar things. It pays to appreciate the nuanced differences among the various combinations here. A common question I get when reading synastry is, "Does the chart say how [the asker] and [the other person] get along?" The most common answer is, "Kind of, but it depends on what you mean by 'get along.'" In what sense? Regarding what issue? As friends or as something else? The chart doesn't read minds, you know.

Asking pre-made questions

Fortunately the *table 19-9* has a ton of questions already built in. Thanks to some great significators like Selene and the Part of Fortune, you really can ask some big questions and get decent answers. For big questions like "What am I supposed to get out of this relationship?" you have a couple of options such as [Juno $_{\text{you}}$-Uranus $_{\text{them}}$] and [Selene $_{\text{you}}$-Fortune $_{\text{them}}$] as well as a number of other interesting answers which aren't specially gray-shaded in *table 19-9*. You might also find certain standard relationship topics in this book's glossary. When asking questions for which there are already common answers, you can follow the rules of the various planets for framing your questions and find which ones to look for in the table. Let's go over what those general rules are in synastry; these are the same ones that can be found in the top and side headings of *table 19-9*:

---

[33] The point is, the conjunct reading gives you a pretty decent first look at an interaction and what it's overall nature is. The above is either a respectful but liberal friendship or a demeaning, patronizing dysfunction in which the man can't help but cut down the woman whom he appreciates and the woman resorts to defiant resistance in kind. The first scenario is considerably more consistent though, since the second scenario would have more logical holes not found in the pairs above.

Table 20-4: What the synastric planets generally tell you

Your planet...	...tells:	Their planet...	...tells:
☉ Sun	your behaviors	☉ Sun	how they interact with you
☽ Moon	your feelings	☽ Moon	what they seem to prefer
☿ Mercury	your meaning making	☿ Mercury	how they make things work
♀ Venus	your 1:1 communication with them	♀ Venus	how they communicate with you
♂ Mars	your attempts to steer things, the other person, people in general, or ideas	♂ Mars	their attempts to move things around them
♃ Jupiter	your efforts to be seen or to do visible things in the world	♃ Jupiter	their image projected in the world
♄ Saturn	your placing of limits, shows of control	♄ Saturn	limits and structures that come with the other person
♅ Uranus	you as a social evaluator	♅ Uranus	where they spread the social effects of your efforts
♆ Neptune	you as embodying the other person's environment	♆ Neptune	where they reflect the emotional effects of your efforts
♇ Pluto	you as representing those who pressure the other person	♇ Pluto	how they infuse your efforts with power over people or things; how they show power around you
Asc Ascendant	you as approaching something new	Asc Ascendant	where they bring attention to your efforts
Mc Midheaven	you as one who acknowledges the other person's planet	Mc Midheaven	where they give you cause to respond
Vx Vertex	your experience of change	Vx Vertex	their efforts to change or influence things around them
☊ North Node	where you make things seem meant to be	☊ North Node	where they make your action convenient for you
Selene	where you are super talented	Selene	where they model your ideal view of a concept
⚸ Lilith	where you defy normally expected behavior	⚸ Lilith	where they turn into the reason you act
⊕ Fortune	you in your element	⊕ Fortune	where they are comfortable
⚳ Ceres	where you push the other to show more force; your light coercion of things (fun)	⚳ Ceres	where they feel things need to be tended to; their light coercion of you (fun)
⚷ Chiron	where you teach lessons (sometimes to yourself, often accidentally)	⚷ Chiron	where they teach; where they compel your learning
⚶ Vesta	where you put your concentration	⚶ Vesta	where they focus on what you flood them with
⚴ Pallas	where you call for war	⚴ Pallas	where you respond to their crusade
⚵ Juno	your commitment behavior	⚵ Juno	their idea of your planet as being used to draw out the concept that follows it
Hera	your bonding behavior	Hera	their attachment to your efforts
Eros	where you crave passion	Eros	their passionate response to your efforts
Bacchus	how your clique responds	Bacchus	how their friends answer your efforts

Table 20-4: What the synastric planets signify in synastry. Use the rules to guide your questions when looking at a relationship.

For a list of all the angle families whose symbols fill up the chart, refer to *table 16-6*.

We need to draw some distinctions among the more similar concepts above:

- The Sun corresponds to generic "behavior," with no reasons or details provided. It's like using the word "do" to describe things. "Yes I do football. No I don't do cantaloupe. I sometimes do donuts in the middle of the street" (instead of playing, eating, or turning).
- Mercury is logical and serves to align things that aren't flowing together as they should. Venus is cordial and bounces actions back and forth between things that already align. Mercury builds the computer; Venus uses it.
- Your Mars, attached to your dissatisfaction, is what you use to influence things in front of you. But your Ceres, attached to your assessment of things as underperforming, is what you use to "improve" their behavior.
- *The other person's* Mars is NOT attached to dissatisfaction you can really feel, so it is their Vertex which is a better indicator of the change they actually make in their own lives. Instead, their Mars corresponds to the things they do that are intended to elicit a response from you. It's not so much that their Mars wants to change you. More like it wants you to stay the same but with a different response to what they want. Vertex actually works to alter things in general, not just you.
- Uranus is for generic social talk. Bacchus is for the behavior of friends and people who dig you.
- Your Pluto and Pallas, unlike your Mars and Ceres, have less to do with things in front of you and more to do with the force you apply to situations in the abstract. Your Pallas is where you take up arms to change a situation while your Pluto is where you simply push standards upon a thing, in a situation.
- The Midheaven is generally stronger than the Ascendant in synastry, since the Midheaven publicly acknowledges the planet it's compared to while the Ascendant "comes at" new situations through the lens of that planet. Coming into a new situation happens in tons of ways, most of which are nigh-insignificant in the context of an interaction. Acknowledgement, though, tends to be moment defining. At a party, the Midheaven represents that first glanced impression. The Ascendant constitutes the vast array of subject changes and new schmooze topics approached by you and your interlocutors.
- Commitment to something with your own Juno seems like a simple agreement to fulfill certain obligations. Committing to something with *someone else's* Juno involves an entire world full of priorities reweighed and put on hold just so you can stay out of one situation and stay in another. Understandably, reading the other person's Juno is more complicated than reading your own. In a real sense there are many more well-defined pressures involved with their Juno than yours. With your own Juno, such pressures are probably just as heavy, but you handle them too automatically to notice.

The above rules should make it easier for you to scan *table 19-9* for answers to some of your more straightforward questions. That way you don't have to fish through all 625 pairs blindly.

And now for an example of some good old fashioned relationship prediction

Suppose you want to know how the other person feels about your friends. *Table 20-4* suggests that [Moon $_{\text{them}}$-Saturn $_{\text{you}}$] should do the trick. Suppose you read a novile; Other would have a more pronounced opinion of your friends as image promoters. By itself this only tells you the area of life where Other is most likely to hold pronounced opinions of your friends, but it doesn't tell you how they feel. Using a trick though, (related to the Uranus-in-house test), we can obtain an answer:

- Use *table 17-4* to look at how Other responds to ALL novile-type issues with you. How has the other responded to you on issues specifically related to travel, image promotion, or learning?
- A further look at all the resonant pairs for the novile would show you the whole array of other thoughts that come to their mind when the two of you behave in "novile mode." Gather all of the resonant noviles

together, then ask yourself how the other person typically treats you in light of these areas. There's your rough answer. In this example, how Other feels about your shared noviles is how they feel about your friends.

(You'd still need to compare your results against common sense though. Are you sure you framed the question properly? If you really wanted to know how Other felt about your generic social pack and NOT your fun cliques, you may have done better to look up [Moon $_{them}$-Uranus $_{you}$] instead.)

Curiously, if you read the actual [Moon $_{them}$-Bacchus $_{you}$] pair in Chapter 19, it doesn't seem to support "Other's opinion of your friends." Why? Because the question we've asked here boils down to mind-reading, which goes way beyond this book's statistics. What we do see in the actual [Moon $_{them}$-Bacchus $_{you}$] pair is essentially a set of possible, observable responses to such opinion; perhaps you can see that there is indeed a reasonable connection here. The alternate half-pair, [Moon $_{you}$-Bacchus $_{them}$] shows a still different set of responses were yours and Other's roles reversed.

Both fortunately and unfortunately, almost any question you ask of astrology can ride upon nuance and transform into a completely different pair. [Neptune-Bacchus], [Node-Bacchus], and [Ascendant-Bacchus] can also tell you about Other's opinion of your clique depending on what kind of question you ask. But before you take this to mean that astrology has once again slipped into vaguery, I remind you that there were definite patterns across the sample data. In synastry in particular, a vague answer is almost always associated with a vague question. This brings us to our next chart-reading strategy.

Asking questions that aren't pre-made: An example

Pre-posed questions are good, but how do we use the above rules to ask unique questions for which there are no pre-packaged answers?

1. Ask your question.
   Would other enjoy dancing with me?
2. Break the question into a reasonable "you" and a reasonable "them" piece.
   [Other's enjoyment-My dance]
3. Use *table 20-4* to determine some reasonable planets to represent the pieces you've made.
   a. *[Other's enjoyment]:Moon (their happy feeling), Ascendant (their trying new things with me), Ceres (their tending to my efforts, their fun)*
   b. *[My dance]: Mars (my steering attempts), Uranus (me as a social performer), Selene (my talents), Fortune (I in my element), Ceres (my fun)*
4. You might use *table 19-9* to look at any of the combinations from step 3 (there are 3 x 5 =15 in our example), but it helps to narrow it down based on your view of the question you've asked, *then* look at the table.
   a. *[Other's enjoyment]:* If you're not going for ongoing, spewy emotions from them, then Moon $_{them}$ probably doesn't make sense. If you just want to *try* dancing, ASC $_{them}$ might work. If you're more interested in how your fun will play out during the dancing, Ceres $_{them}$ might work. These last two are actually two nicely complementary views of the same event, so let's stick with them both.
   b. *[My dance]:* If you know you can't really dance and aren't that crazy about having all eyes on you, then Neither Uranus $_{you}$ nor Selene $_{you}$ will work as signficators (though Uranus may well end up telling what you look like on the floor). If you're not really focused on steering them so much as you are on having fun, Mars won't be that great a choice either. Fortune might be good if you really feel at home dancing, but Ceres will be better if you're just into fun. Let's keep only Ceres.

5. Look at *table 19-9*. and see what your planet choices have brought you. But keep your eyes open for nearby pairs.
    a. [Ceres $_{you}$-ASC $_{them}$] shows where they are comparatively modest against their other traits. Sounds pretty cute.
    b. [Ceres-Ceres] shows where you influence people similarly. Not so great. This example was supposed to be about you and them having fun. We'll scratch ~~[Ceres-Ceres]~~.
    c. But maybe you noticed nearby [Ceres $_{you}$-Lilith $_{them}$] and [Ceres $_{you}$-Fortune $_{them}$] (you foster other's escape and you show the kind of pressure they like). These all sound like the kind of dancing date that we've set up in this example.
    d. So let's go with the above selected three as indicators of whether the Other would like to go dancing, assuming you're both novice-ish: [Ceres $_{you}$-ASC $_{them}$], [Ceres $_{you}$-Fortune $_{them}$], and [Ceres $_{you}$-Lilith $_{them}$]. These represent fun going to, during, and (kind of) after the dance. Can you see this?
6. Look at the angles you have for the pairs you've decided match your question. You'll likely have several such pairs. The angles you read will tell you when such pairs are most easily activated.

   As a kind of warning, you may be surprised, shocked, or disappointed with what you find, since a whopping 36 harmonics renders it highly unlikely that you'll get exactly the angles you'd expect or prefer.

    a. Since we already have the sample *table 20-1*, we'll use it as a visual example. Suppose you're Person A and they are Person B. We then have a [Ceres $_{you}$-ASC $_{them}$]-☍, [Ceres $_{you}$-Fortune $_{them}$]-⚻^{2}, and [Ceres $_{you}$-Lilith $_{them}$]- ⚹.
    b. [Ceres $_{you}$-ASC $_{them}$]-☍ (opposition) shows them as comparatively modest in their self-value with you. They might be reluctant to try something they're not confident in.
    c. [Ceres $_{you}$-Fortune $_{them}$]-⚻^{2} (II-inconjunct) shows that they like the pressure you put on them through your works of the imagination. This is more like art than dancing.
    d. [Ceres $_{you}$-Lilith $_{them}$]- ⚹ (sextile) shows that you foster their escape in the realm of daily doings. Dancing seems like more of a special occasion. So unless you're dancing at home, in your cubicle, or doing dishes, public dance might be a little much—not just for them, but for the two of you as interactants.
7. Assess the results.
   Based on the sample chart, I'd call our example an overall fail. Dancing of the kind we spelled out looks unnecessarily public among other things, and it seems as though persons A and B would be much more comfortable exploring a more abstract artsy, setting in closer, self-value building quarters. Dancing may not work so well in the way we've framed it, but it did teach us something about the interaction.
8. And now for the best part: Given the high chance that you didn't get what you wanted from the *pairs*, use any of the previous chapters' angle tables (like *16-6*, *17-4*, or *19-8*) to pick the *harmonic* (angle family) that best describes what you *were* initially looking for.
   We were dancing, so let's pick a fun, physical angle. Fire's pretty fun. Quintiles are especially fun in a 1:1 way. Regular quintiles are nice and "me and you," whereas II- and III-quintiles involve others. So quintiles it is. As a backup, noviles are also decent. How do we know this? By looking at these angles enough times to have a decent idea of what they all do.
9. Read the resonant pairs for the harmonic you picked to see what kinds of outcome you could expect if you tried this kind of exchange anyway. You don't need to read the whole family, but you should see if the families with the designated aspect also have the planets you've originally settled on.
   Do the resonant pairs for quintiles have your Ceres or their Fortune in them? How about the resonant pairs for noviles?

So what are we supposed to get out of all that work we just did? Two things: First, we learn how "safe" it is to experiment over new territory with the other person. Second, we learn what old territory naturally looks like. Given that we compared our astro results against our actual, real-life experience with the other person of course, the example not only told us that dancing might not be the most natural adventure, it also told us that art exploration *could* be. Understandably, this kind of investigation works better when you have less real experience to go on. But even in exchanges which you've been involved in for a long time, it's often surprising just how much of the other person we still haven't seen.

Thus ends our example.

Synastry reading step 3: Read common cocktails

There are some very common questions out there which have incredibly complex answers. And although astrology can definitely provide pieces of such answers for us, these pieces still need to be integrated into a bigger picture before we can use them easily. **Cocktails** are **those combinations of planet pairs which, when activated together, produce predictable effects in an astrochart**. In this section we'll go over some of the more important ones for asking 19 of some of the most common (but also most difficult) questions that can be asked of synastry and self charts.

1. What am I supposed to get out of this relationship?
2. How can I dream of this person?
3. Should I choose this person or that one?
4. Are they the one?
5. What do they like to do for fun?
6. What standards do I need to meet to get through to them?
7. How do I get their friends to like me?
8. How do I make this person appear in my life?
9. How do I keep them in my life?
10. Will we last?
11. Why can't I get rid of them (or get them off my mind)?
12. How do I get rid of them?
13. Why do they hate me?
14. How do I beat them?
15. How should I best help them?
16. How can we become something great?
17. (Self chart) How do I attain great riches?
18. (Self chart) Who am I when I am at my best as an interactor with people?
19. (Self chart) How do I master myself?

Interaction purpose cocktail: What am I supposed to get out of this relationship?

Jupiter $_{them}$-Juno $_{you}$	Moon-Moon	Jupiter $_{you}$-Chiron $_{them}$
Uranus $_{them}$-Juno $_{you}$	Selene $_{them}$-Fortune $_{you}$	Selene $_{you}$-Fortune $_{them}$

Certain pairs provide fantastic summaries of what happens in a relationship overall. The above six pairs represent the best of the best in this respect, giving you the ultimate rundown regardless of who fought whom or how quickly it all went down. As will be the case with each one of the combinations that follow, we'll compress the interplay of all the listed combinations into a brief story for you to fill in with your own angles.

> The other and I are on the same page in our wants regarding [Moon-Moon]. Recognizing them strongly for their [Jupiter $_{me}$-Chiron $_{them}$], I gain increased experience and skill when it comes to handling this side of their world. My newfound experience can be applied to this same area of life far beyond my dealings with them alone. Overall, they are in my world to help me hone how I project my [Selene $_{them}$-Fortune $_{me}$]. I am in their world to help them build on how they use their [Selene $_{me}$-Fortune $_{them}$]. Throughout the exchange, the main thing I get lies in [Uranus $_{them}$-Juno $_{me}$]. Over the long term my commitment to them will change me in the area of [Jupiter $_{them}$-Juno $_{me}$].

Example using table 20-1

If we look at *table 20-1* we see the following angles for the six pairs in this cocktail:

Moon-Moon	II-septile	Uranus $_{them}$-Juno $_{you}$	II-decile
Jupiter $_{you}$-Chiron $_{them}$	II-inconjunct	Selene $_{them}$-Fortune $_{you}$	III-quintile
Jupiter $_{them}$-Juno $_{you}$	III-conjunct	Selene $_{you}$-Fortune $_{them}$	II-square

Although you could (and probably should) use *tables 19-1* or *19-2* to fill angle meanings for pairs like [Moon-Moon], [Jupiter $_{me}$-Chiron $_{them}$] and so on, we'll introduce a simpler table for this purpose. *Table 20-5* is very skeletal in nature, but has entries that may be easier to plug into this section's summaries for giving you a decent sketch of what a relationship looks like.

Table 20-5: Quick angle reference for synastry

Harmonic	Name	Symbol	Meaning	Harmonic	Name	Symbol	Meaning
1	conjunct	☌	natural behavior	19	II-septile	✡^{2}	ingroups
2	opposition	☍	self-value	20	II-octile	∠^{2}	magnetism
3	trine	△	thoughts	21	II-novile	九^{2}	creation
4	square	□	wants	22	II-decile	+^{2}	career or reputation
5	quintile	⋆	1:1 interaction	23	II-undecile	U^{2}	uniqueness
6	sextile	⚹	work	24	II-inconjunct	⚻^{2}	works of the imagination
7	septile	✡	communication	25	III-conjunct	☌^{3}	psychology
8	octile	∠	power	26	III-opposition	☍^{3}	fans & following
9	novile	九	image promotion	27	III-trine	△^{3}	insight
10	decile	+	control	28	III-square	□^{3}	morality
11	undecile	U	social talk	29	III-quintile	⋆^{3}	charisma over groups
12	inconjunct	⚻	impression	30	III-sextile	⚹^{3}	critical analysis
13	II-conjunct	☌^{2}	persona	31	III-septile	✡^{3}	networks
14	II-opposition	☍^{2}	physical presence	32	III-octile	∠^{3}	mysterious allure
15	II-trine	△^{2}	room hijacking	33	III-novile	九^{3}	rallying
16	II-square	□^{2}	family values	34	III-decile	+^{3}	command
17	II-quintile	⋆^{2}	management	35	III-undecile	U^{3}	intellectual curiosity
18	II-sextile	⚹^{2}	rationality	36	III-inconjunct	⚻^{3}	memorability

Table 20-5: Quick angle reference for synastry. These are super trimmed down versions of tables *19-1* and *19-2* for use in this chapter's summary paragraphs.

Referencing the above table and the angles attached to each pair we used, we can now fill in the blanks in our example:

> The other and I are on the same page in our wants regarding [ingroups]. Recognizing them strongly for their [works of the imagination], I gain increased experience and skill when it comes to handling this side of their world. My newfound experience can be applied to this same area of life far beyond my dealings with them alone. Overall, they are in my world to help me hone how I project my [charisma over groups]. I am in their world to help them build on how they use their [family values]. Throughout the exchange, the main thing I get lies in [career or reputation]. Over the long term my commitment to them will change me in the area of [psychology].

Now suppose you've read the above, but it doesn't quite seem right. In that case go back to *tables 19-1* and *19-2* for many more versions of each angle.

> The other and I are on the same page in our wants regarding [the ideas we exchange with people in our own class]. Recognizing them strongly for their [inspiration], I gain increased experience and skill when it comes to handling this side of their world. My newfound experience can be applied to this same area of life far beyond my dealings with them alone. Overall, they are in my world to help me hone how I project my [charm and confidence]. I am in their world to help them build on how they use their [core values]. Throughout the exchange, the main thing I get lies in [career or reputation]. Over the long term my commitment to them will change me in the area of [how I get bigger groups to back me].

Synastric dream trio: How can I dream of this person?

Moon $_{them}$-Mercury $_{you}$ Moon $_{you}$-Selene $_{them}$ Mercury $_{you}$-Selene $_{them}$

Now why in the world would you want to dream of someone on purpose? Is that even a thing? It is. The main reason you would want to intentionally dream of someone is actually pretty simple. Your dreams are closer to your subconscious than your waking thoughts are, and provide more accurate insight into what you really think of your dealings with a person. While awake we can tell ourselves all kinds of socially prescribed lies about where we stand regarding the other. But in your dreams, such lies drop drastically in number. I can't tell you how many times I've dreamt of someone whom I thought was an adversary but really wasn't—how many times I thought I connected with someone but really didn't. And while the synastric dream trio admittedly won't *force* you to dream of the person you want, it does produce a couple of interesting dream-related effects: As a general tendency, the Selene person appears in the Moon person's dreams when the angle between these is a big enough preoccupation on the Moon person's mind.

> When I precede sleep with [Moon $_{me}$-Selene $_{them}$] heavy on my mind and the other person as a significantly related interaction, I have a much easier time dreaming of them. Working to dream of the angle is more important than working to dream of the person. If the person isn't already close to me, they tend to be involved in a scenario associated with our [Moon $_{me}$-Selene $_{them}$]. The less connected they are to me in this angle area, the less likely they are to look like themselves. In waking they can use their [Moon $_{them}$-Mercury $_{me}$] to elicit responses in my body. In the dream, they are likely to pull [Mercury $_{me}$-Selene $_{them}$] from me as a behavior.
>
> Perhaps if I reverse the "me-them," in the above pairs and look at all of this the other way around, I can get them to dream of me. But I think I'll need to hide less of myself from them in waking in order for their picture of me to be a clear one.

Geery theorizes regarding dreams about others

First of all, I'll admit that I do not have a scientific explanation of why the synastric dream trio seems to work. I can, however, offer my guess as to what's going on.

Without a lot of heavy training or meditation, you can induce dreams based on three major factors:

1. an issue you're preoccupied with *solving* (Mercury),
2. what you *want* to happen with that issue (Moon),
3. and the extent to which you think you need [*the thing that another person most purely stands for*] (Selene) to help you frame that issue.

Certain people are really easy to dream of because 1) they like you enough to reveal certain sides of themselves to you in real life (thus making clearer symbols in the dream world) and 2) because their role (Selene $_{them}$) with respect to the outcome you want (Moon $_{you}$) in the realm of behavior you're looking at is clear. That realm (which connects the other person to your issue) would be shown by [Moon $_{you}$-Selene $_{them}$]'s angle. Meanwhile, other people just won't show up in dreams no matter what you try doing to make them appear.

Believe it or not there really were data on those who did and didn't make it into dreams (thanks to some offline experiments I arranged with other people); it seems that a person's failure to show up in a dream given the dreamer's efforts ultimately indicated that the person to be dreamt of did not trust the dreamer enough in waking to provide the dreamer an accurate symbol in dreaming. That is, if I don't trust you, like you, or identify with you enough to reveal myself without weapons in waking, your dreams of me will either be confused, absent, or disguised by my weapons. Effectively, you won't dream of me in a way that you recognize. A second reason that dreams of another person may fail to appear is because the dreamer themselves isn't as psychologically invested in the other person as their waking thoughts may suggest. In waking, you may think it's cool to dream of me for fun. Once you fall asleep, however, it's as if your own brain says, "But seriously though, let's do something else." Both of these cases vary depending on who the person to be dreamt of is.

Since most of us can't easily peer into the outer dimensions, dreams are all we have for restoring truth to an increasingly staged waking life. Dreams do a hell of a lot more for us as forms of memory consolidation, body monitoring, and dilemma processing than they do for us as metabolically wasteful entertainment. So we can look to our dreams as existential scratch pads for negotiating tomorrow's exchanges in light of today's resources. The most informative dreams are 1) the ones which *would* concern that other person, but fail to happen and 2) the frequent ones in which people you're not that close to keep showing up. The first group reminds us to be on alert for disconnects while the second one reminds us to be open to connections. Most dreams, in some form or another, tell us where we think we're going. In that sense—as much as I hate to fall back on esoterics—I'd say that the connection between [dreams and biology] and [science and astrology]—though strange—is one worth respecting at least as a future area of study. Clearly there is something that we do to draw up symbols for the sleeping world, but how those symbols interact with each other is still one of those topics that remains at the edge of psychological inquiry.

Match cocktail: Should I choose this person or that one?

(This one is truly for entertainment purposes only...and some insight)

Sun $_{them}$-Moon $_{you}$ Lilith $_{them}$-Vesta $_{you}$ Chiron $_{them}$-Bacchus $_{you}$

Behind door #1 sits Awesome Sweetheart. Behind door #2 sits Old Supportive. One is passionate and exciting while the other actually puts up with your demons. One is irresponsible yet fills you with confidence while the other sees eye to eye with you...though they can be boring. Whom do you choose?

Realistically you should choose the one who brings you closer to who you want to be. But if you'd prefer an astrological coin flip, the Match cocktail provides such an arbiter. The idea is pretty utilitarian. Which one of the people 1) will do your subconscious bidding [Sun $_{them}$-Moon $_{you}$], 2) is more special-looking [Lilith $_{them}$-Vesta $_{you}$], or is more impressive to your friends [Chiron $_{them}$-Bacchus $_{you}$]? For those times when you just can't decide which ornament to parade around with for a few weeks, there is the path of greatest superficial social reward. Now I actually think you'd be pretty shallow to use this cocktail to make a real decision between two people, but the combination isn't meaningless. Let's check out the summary then take it for a test spin to see how it works.

> Other seems to read my thoughts when it comes to [Sun $_{them}$-Moon $_{me}$]. They'd also be pretty impressive to my friends in their [Chiron $_{them}$-Bacchus $_{me}$], walking around with that [Lilith $_{them}$-Vesta $_{me}$] of theirs.

Now suppose you have two people with the following angles against your synastry.

	Sun $_{them}$-Moon $_{you}$	Lilith $_{them}$-Vesta $_{you}$	Chiron $_{them}$-Bacchus $_{you}$
Terry	II-decile	opposition	III-octile
Jean	II-trine	decile	undecile

We'll still need a birth time for *you* here, but we don't really a need birth time for the other person since none of their planets are quick movers. If you really don't know the birth times and want to be sure, you might test charts for these people against several different birth hours across the day—just to see if your [Sun $_{them}$-Moon $_{you}$] angle lines up with reality. PLEASE check this cocktail against reality. Don't just plug in "image projection" for a person's novile if, in real life, you know "learning" would work better. Again, these angles take practice to get used to. That said, let's see how Terry and Jean stack up. Note how I change some ideas to help the description's grammar flow better.

On the one hand...	On the other hand...
Terry seems to read my thoughts when it comes to [my reputation]. They'd also be pretty impressive to my friends in their [mysterious allure], walking around with that [self-satisfaction] of theirs.	Jean seems to read my thoughts when it comes to [taking over a room]. They'd also be pretty impressive to my friends in their [show of control], walking around with that [attention-getting way] of theirs.

It looks like Terry gives more appeal while Jean gives more command. Whomever you would choose depends on your preferences. One thing is certain though, the distilled comparisons above definitely give you something to look at, at least—social consequences and all. There is surely something self-serving to making decisions based on comparisons like this, but we humans do this kind of thing all the time anyway. We just take longer and do it without guidelines. Now you have guidelines.

Future Image formula: Are they the one?

MC$_{you}$-Selene$_{them}$
Jupiter$_{them}$-Fortune$_{you}$
Node$_{you}$-Juno$_{them}$
Node$_{them}$-Hera$_{you}$
Mercury$_{you}$-Juno$_{them}$
Jupiter$_{them}$-Juno$_{you}$
ASC$_{them}$-Fortune$_{you}$
Selene$_{you}$-Hera$_{them}$
Lilith$_{them}$-Bacchus$_{you}$
Selene$_{you}$-Fortune$_{them}$
Mars$_{them}$-Ceres$_{you}$
Selene$_{them}$-Ceres$_{you}$
Neptune$_{them}$-Hera$_{you}$
Sun$_{them}$-Hera$_{you}$
Chiron$_{them}$-Vesta$_{you}$

It is perhaps unfortunate that, for reasons entirely related to changeable psychology, astrology won't point you to "the one." The synastry chart does, however, present an interesting family of pairs which make a person highly resistant to replacement in another's circle of bonds. You can imagine how the usual suspects for "perfection" and "bonding" might be involved in this one, as well as indicators of comfort with where one has ended up in the relationship. And so we have a cocktail which approximates "the one" not just for today, but for the future beyond tomorrow.

We'll describe "that special person" as being someone who comes to occupy a special place among our emotional bonds, whom we are not very likely to replace except in the most far out circumstances. This person takes up a special position in our emotional world and sets up a permanent-looking base there. And even though you can have several relationships that fit this description, your person will be rare enough to retain their specialness even against other special people. Part of the secret to this cocktail lies in the abundance of commitment, comfort, and perfection-related pairs—pairs which take a longer time to legitimately play out and require a certain socially-anchored track record in order to even be recognized for what they are. (For example, people are less likely to recognize your new [Node-Juno] sweetie as a "destined" commitment if you've barely known them a month.)

> This person inspires me immensely through their [Mars$_{them}$-Ceres$_{me}$]. They have a strange way of expressing [Selene$_{them}$-Ceres$_{me}$] without trying and provide a welcome companion for me in [Mercury$_{me}$-Juno$_{them}$]. We're bound together through [Neptune$_{them}$-Hera$_{me}$], conveying our [Node$_{them}$-Hera$_{me}$] there. The exchange gives us the space we need to successfully [Lilith$_{them}$-Bacchus$_{me}$] as we would with old friends. Our [Sun$_{them}$-Hera$_{me}$] is a point of mutual charm as we appear to make a great team throughout my expression of my [MC$_{me}$-Selene$_{them}$]—the circumstances under which I first realized their talent too. It doesn't have to be all play though. When it's time to work, they use their [Node$_{me}$-Juno$_{them}$] to add to my doings.
>
> I explore new paths in [ASC$_{them}$-Fortune$_{me}$] with this person, and over time I become stronger in my [Jupiter$_{them}$-Juno$_{me}$] thanks to them. Even if we separate, it will be easy for me to remember them for their [Selene$_{me}$-Fortune$_{them}$]. If we do separate it will be partly because of a change in their [Selene$_{me}$-Hera$_{them}$]. But separations of this kind are rarely that bad, usually stemming from the distance life quietly puts between us. We won't quite grow apart, just into new things—their [Jupiter$_{them}$-Fortune$_{me}$] being among the things that pulls them away. If we are to stay together, I will continue to support this goal of theirs as strongly as possible, clearing a path for us with my [Chiron$_{them}$-Vesta$_{me}$].

Entertainer cocktail: What do they like to do for fun?

MC$_{you}$-Ceres$_{them}$
Lilith$_{them}$-Eros$_{you}$
Node$_{you}$-Ceres$_{them}$
Sun$_{you}$-Ceres$_{them}$
Moon$_{them}$-Selene$_{you}$
Pallas$_{them}$-Bacchus$_{you}$
Saturn$_{you}$-Pluto$_{them}$
Uranus$_{you}$-Vesta$_{them}$
Fortune$_{them}$-Ceres$_{you}$
Fortune$_{you}$-Ceres$_{them}$
Pallas$_{them}$-Juno$_{you}$

More bad news: Can you read somebody's hobbies through an astrochart? Nope. No more than you look at a picture of some random car and tell where it "likes" to drive. If it still runs. Wherever it is in the world. Even if we could tell what a person's hobby should be, we won't know *if they know* that those hobbies would work for them. Like a first grader who will eventually learn to love day trading, some people just wouldn't be ready for themselves even if we knew what those selves looked like. Or maybe they *are* ready for themselves. Just not with you.

So what can we tell about a person's fun life? We can tell the kinds of scenarios in which another person is inclined to push you around without expecting to be taken too seriously. We can tell a little bit about how they like to be pushed in turn. The Entertainer cocktail is a combination of passion, obsession, and comfortable Ceres-style carebullying. Read its summary in your self chart to get a glimpse of what it says about you, then read it in yours and another's synastry to see what kind of fun it spells out for you and them. (That is, of course, assuming they'd let you get that close to them.)

> If there were a single phrase for how the other person likes to have fun (in my eyes) it would be through **"[Pallas$_{them}$-Juno$_{me}$] which allows them to feel [Saturn$_{me}$-Pluto$_{them}$]."** That's about it.
>
> As for the other person's experiences during their fun, they like for the fun situation they're interacting with to grow their [Sun$_{me}$-Ceres$_{them}$]. It makes them confident to feel as though they have shown [Moon$_{them}$-Selene$_{me}$] and that they're recognized for the potency of their [Pallas$_{them}$-Bacchus$_{me}$] among my friends. Though I find [Lilith$_{them}$-Eros$_{me}$ – *table 19-8*] with them particularly exciting, I don't mind being pushed by their [Fortune$_{me}$-Ceres$_{them}$] as long as I get to do the pushing with my [Fortune$_{them}$-Ceres$_{me}$]. (Things stop being so fun when they call too many shots in this later area, though.) The main downside to their kind of fun is that they can go too far in their [MC$_{me}$-Ceres$_{them}$] for me to handle. Still I had some idea when we first connected over [Node$_{me}$-Ceres$_{them}$ – *table 19-8*] about the kind of person I was connecting to. [Node$_{me}$-Ceres$_{them}$] is what they reinforce when we have fun together. [Uranus$_{me}$-Vesta$_{them}$] is the area which sponsors some of the coolest joint experiences we'll ever have.

So now you've read it, but did it suggest any activities in particular? Probably not. What counts most is the *spirit* of "[Pallas$_{them}$-Juno$_{you}$] which allows the other to feel [Saturn$_{you}$-Pluto$_{them}$]."[34] This is the power to stop others dead in their tracks, straight up. Not only does it make for a great oppressor of men, it also makes an excellent silencer of all haters. Showstopping sure is fun, isn't it? Check out [Pallas-Juno] and [Saturn-Pluto] in your own chart to see how you do unparalleled fun when no one else is around.

[34] Speaking of Saturn-Pluto, what in the world...? Isn't this connected to "negative karma"—often with the father—in astrology circles? Only for people who focus on any resentment they might have had with their fathers. And when we resent our fathers/authority, what do we do? Have rebellious fun with our friends of course: the output side of Saturn-Pluto. Saturn-Pluto brings socially pressured (Pluto) limits (Saturn) as the person seeks some alternative outlet to acknowledge as authority.

"Are They Interested" cocktail: What standards do I need to meet to get through to them?

Uranus $_{\text{you}}$-Bacchus $_{\text{them}}$	Ascendant $_{\text{them}}$-Juno $_{\text{you}}$	Venus $_{\text{you}}$-Jupiter $_{\text{them}}$
Venus $_{\text{them}}$-Midheaven $_{\text{you}}$	Mars $_{\text{you}}$-Midheaven $_{\text{them}}$	Mars $_{\text{you}}$-Eros $_{\text{them}}$
Mars $_{\text{them}}$-Vesta $_{\text{you}}$	Ascendant $_{\text{them}}$-Hera $_{\text{you}}$	Node $_{\text{them}}$-Fortune $_{\text{you}}$
Chiron $_{\text{you}}$-Hera $_{\text{them}}$	Vertex $_{\text{you}}$-Juno $_{\text{them}}$	

Winning someone over despite initial difficulty presents an interesting pair of challenges. First is the challenge of actually getting them to approve of you. Second (and actually more importantly) is the challenge of keeping them despite the many obstacles which suggested you shouldn't have won them over in the first place.

It is often said that the best things in life are free. Although this isn't really true of relationships, it's not completely false either. Where another person has placed an array of hurdles between you and them (or where you yourself have placed such hurdles) the best way of winning them over astrologically is to simply evolve (or **ahem** *de*volve) to meet their standards. Hurdles placed tend to remain long after you've won, though, in the form of ongoing irritations. But I'm sure that deep in your heart you really just want to win them over no matter what, so asking you if all this is worth it would just be a waste of ink. Let's just assume for the time being that you're ready to change your habits to reach somebody else and that, in some way, such a somebody is good for you. What sides of yourself should you re-weight in order to accomplish this task?

> Ping. As a test of their interest in exchanging with me (before I put in the work to win them over), I can use my [Mars $_{\text{me}}$-Eros $_{\text{them}}$] on them and watch how the other person reacts. How do they display their inspiration as a response? Do they display any at all? Their reaction to this family of behaviors on my part will tell how they receive my efforts at firing them up in general. Unless I am helping them express **their [Mars $_{\text{them}}$-Vesta $_{\text{me}}$]**, they are more likely to ignore me though. **Backing them up here is incredibly important for winning them over**. Related to this, it is very valuable for them to build something enduring in the realm of [Venus $_{\text{them}}$-Midheaven $_{\text{me}}$] in the world. Prior to us getting along, the other person's display of [Mars $_{\text{me}}$-Midheaven $_{\text{them}}$] against me shows where I have intruded upon their desire to express. As we get along, they come to display this same behavior in my favor, provided I show them that I like how they do this. Even as a stranger, for better or worse, my [Ascendant $_{\text{them}}$-Hera $_{\text{me}}$] will be difficult for them to ignore. Once we get our exchange working, they may even come to see this side of me as irresistible in one of several ways.
>
> Assuming the other person doesn't distrust me, I can flatter them through my show of [Venus $_{\text{me}}$-Jupiter $_{\text{them}}$] to help soften them up. Gradually, I earn their respect through disciplined attention to my own [Node $_{\text{them}}$-Fortune $_{\text{me}}$]. This particular trait of mine might take quite a while to register with them, though. And if they never come to respect it, that's an indication that they may actually *want* to keep me out of their lives. Perhaps they *will* want to keep me out, but even then I may still force their cooperation through determined use of my [Chiron $_{\text{me}}$-Hera $_{\text{them}}$] to bring them over to my side. (Among the family of actions studied, I heard that this was my version of the single most effective "silver bullet" for getting any person to open the door to me. I can't use this too early though, because circumstances usually don't permit it until I've learned enough about the other to actually use it *on them* and not just *from me*.)
>
> Whether or not I win the other person over, they pay strong attention to my [Vertex $_{\text{me}}$-Juno $_{\text{them}}$] (even if I'm not aware of this). This might be the least obvious of the traits I'll need to change in their favor. Once I've won them over, I have another test available to see if they are actually interested in me as a person (rather than as simply a servant to them): When I convey my [Uranus $_{\text{me}}$-Bacchus $_{\text{them}}$] to them, do they

care? Finally, if they're really *really* convinced, they'll show it by voluntarily offering their [Ascendant $_{them}$-Juno $_{me}$].

Hopefully you've got a pretty good grasp of the angle families by the time you've arrived at the "Are They Interested" cocktail. This one's pretty legit, can be taken much more seriously and used much more effectively than the "Match" cocktail (which is better for choosing which prey to chase).

Provided you have a good grasp of the angles by the time you read this cocktail, you may find the "Are They Interested" combination to be the single best indicator of the state of your interaction with the other person.

Clique Entry formula: How do I get their friends to like me?

Midheaven-Midheaven	Venus $_{you}$-Bacchus $_{them}$	Mars $_{you}$-Bacchus $_{them}$
Neptune $_{you}$-Bacchus $_{them}$	**ASC $_{you}$-Bacchus $_{them}$**	MC $_{them}$-Selene $_{you}$
Hera $_{you}$-Bacchus $_{them}$	Vertex $_{you}$-Bacchus $_{them}$	Pallas $_{you}$-Bacchus $_{them}$

Winning a person's friends over is a bit of a science. You're not really trying to appeal to individual interests, but to *patterns of communication* instead. As a college instructor I've found that a lot of such attempts to appeal to the faceless masses rests on your ability to "combine and conquer"—allowing the friends you're trying to convince to assemble under circumstances which you can directly influence. If Joe, Flo, and Moe love to lambaste you in private amongst themselves, your attempt to win them over one by one tends to be an uphill battle. That's like attacking Voltron one lion at a time before he comes together; your beef is actually with the whole Voltron, so unless you plan to enslave one of the team members permanently, they will eventually reassemble anyway. Get the friends together and conquer them as a unit if you can. But if you can't, you can always hypnotize one of them with a special mixture of myth and flattery. No doubt, this is a job for Bacchus—the alleged "asteroid of orgies."

> From the beginning, without having made much effort, I have the ability to easily influence the other person's friends through [ASC $_{me}$-Bacchus $_{them}$]. For better or worse. One basic step in winning over those friends over lies in my being recognized as a great partner to the person in the realm of [Mars $_{me}$-Bacchus $_{them}$]. By drawing forth [Pallas $_{me}$-Bacchus $_{them}$] from the person in a way that supports our working together, I can extract their eventual friendship. In general though, in order to steer the friends directly, **I should concentrate on how I *look* during [ASC $_{me}$-Bacchus $_{them}$] rather than trying to steer the group directly**. I can't "push" a collection of eyes, only impress them. And in the event that I'm not interested in the person themselves, but really just want to win over the friends, I'll tend to elevate those friends in their [Neptune $_{me}$-Bacchus $_{them}$]. But I can also become too popular here if using this talent is my main aim; excessive popularity among the person's friends in this area may make the person jealous, straining our relationship. The ultimate test of my success in compelling the friends lies in whether that group shows me its [Vertex $_{me}$-Bacchus $_{them}$] positively.
>
> Sometimes I'm less interested in winning the group over and more interested in simply getting their approval of my association with the person. People are generally inclined to associate me with the other person in our [Midheaven-Midheaven], but I'll need even further for those friends to identify me as a strong partner to the person in [MC $_{them}$-Selene $_{me}$]. The other and I gain the attention of many when we [Hera $_{me}$-Bacchus $_{them}$] together, so my aim is to show this favorably. My 1:1 communication with the other over [Venus $_{me}$-Bacchus $_{them}$] has an interesting way of spreading to their friends.

Interestingly, the Clique Entry formula is probably the best one in this chapter for studying why your enemies are your enemies.[35] Below is an example of the Clique Entry formula applied to two real-life people A and B, where B was an enemy to A and not the other way around. I've bolded the problem areas.

---

[35] This is not the same as "why someone may hate you" (addressed later). Often enemies don't actually hate you, they just have a contrary stance on a situation you're connected to. Often, people who hate you aren't really enemies. Though I sometimes throw these terms around informally, people who "hate" you are different in that they are often filled with fight in response to you without actually opposing your deeds. I may hate broccoli, but that doesn't mean I'm its enemy. King Koopa may be my enemy, but I don't really hate him. (I don't think.)

Example of B treating A as an enemy, but not the other way around

From the beginning, without having made much effort, A has the ability to easily influence B's friends **[as a member of a kindred group, ✡^{2}]** $_1$. For better or worse. One basic step in winning over those friends over lies in A's being recognized as a great partner to B in [acting against a joint enemy, ∠^{2}]. By drawing forth [B's ability to dominate the attention of a room, △^{2}] in a way that supports A and B working together, A can extract B's eventual friendship. In general though, in order to steer the friends directly, A should concentrate on how A *looks* [in identifying with B's group, ✡^{2}] rather than trying to steer B's group directly. A can't push a collection of eyes, only impress them. And in the event that A is not interested in B themselves, but really just wants to win over the friends, A will tend to elevate those friends **[by natural default, ☌]$_2$**. But A can also become too popular here if using this talent is A's main aim; excessive popularity among B's friends in this area may make B jealous, straining A's and B's relationship. The ultimate test of A's success in compelling the friends lies in whether that group shows A its [1:1 communication] positively.

Sometimes A is less interested in winning the group over and more interested in simply getting their approval of A's association with B. **People are generally inclined to [naturally, ☌] associate A with B$_3$**, but A will need even further for those friends to identify A as a strong partner to B in [intellectual curiosity, ∪^{3}]. A and B gain the attention of many when they [promote their images, 九] together, so A's aim is to show this favorably. **A's 1:1 communication with B [looks more like a vibe, ⊼]$_4$** and has an interesting way of spreading to their friends.

So what went wrong here? Nothing really. If anything, B's friends should probably naturally be A's friends according to [1] and [2]. Yet this gluing of influence can be very negative if, for reasons outside the exchange, the unspoken, group-passed communication between A and B [4] starts off badly. A can naturally connect with B's group, but if A can't naturally communicate to B's group **through B** and needs a vibe [4] to do it, we have a situation in which A gets along better with B's group through A's own efforts which explicitly exclude B as a messenger; that is, A is better friends with B's friends *without B's involvement* than *with* B's involvement. Furthermore (again in situations that are damaged by factors OUTSIDE of the ones shown here), A is naturally associated with B by everyone [3] in such a way as to render A intrusive upon B's clique. In the negative, the clique entry formula shows that A can naturally make an impression on B's clique by going around B, and that A and B mainly look friend-connected when dominating or projecting onto their circumstances. Such circumstances could actually include their dealings with each other. Astrologically, though, A and B really don't look like enemies. This is exactly the kind of instance where synastry can be expected to show you dynamics, not whether a relationship is good or bad.

On the connection between sexuality and creativity

Before we leave the topic of winning a person's friends over, we should remind ourselves of the strong connection between sexuality and creativity. Back in *FSA* we began our investigation of Bacchus as the asteroid of "group sex, etc," seeking to understand how such a fringe definition played out in the charts of most traditionally-trained people. As the data unfolded, we learned that a multi-person sex session was analogous to a multi-person creativity gathering—that *orgies*, parties, gossip gatherings, and GROUP-ADVENTURES were all related except that they were classified by their *fiery action*, earthy shared-identity, airy talk, and WATERY SHARED-INFLUENCE respectively. This was further supported by heavily sexual angles like the II-noviles, II-oppositions, II-septiles, and (to a lesser extent)

II-octiles respectively. The II-noviles are especially sexual[36] and the II-oppositions especially company-seeking. Why talk about this now? Because it turns out that winning over a person's friends is akin to making them feel that it is safe to create their "art" around you. Our clique-friends are those packets of action which reflect some of our expressive input but truly take on personalities of their own in light of what we've done with them in combination with the rest of the world. Seen through the lens of Bacchus, to win another's friends is to facilitate another's creative ambitions.

Many people believe that the modern world has become more decadent, more booty-shakin', more curse-word desensitized in such a way as to degrade the overall quality of society. It is true that the Western world has seen such changes in what passes for acceptable *public* imagery. But I think that our prejudicial, territory-conquering, other-enslaving, wife-beating, inquisition-sponsoring past selves were hardly better in the images they pushed upon those who lived in them. We *look* more free-wheeling, but wince more easily at the sight of real blood and real beatings. We show more skin and less respect but skin/lynch less and generally respect differences more. Where Bacchus introduces us to the world of the taboo, it also shows where we trade savage urges for social innovation—replacing real orgies with media ones. Appealing to others' apparent frivolity doesn't have to mean selling out. This is something to consider during those times when we absolutely must win over a certain group of people. Can we communicate with them as a unit? Are we helping them create what they claim to create? Our willingness to promote the "art" of the group's members will tell the tale.

[36] This is probably because they lend follow-up action to the II-octile steering of outsiders, probably because they begin the sixth group of four (Virgo-izing one's actions and making them into tangible creative works), and possibly because they represent 3 x 7 = 21, presenting internal thoughts through 1:1 feedback as a way of communicating the impulses. This is discussed in *FSA*.

Summoner formula (partial): How do I make this person appear in my life?

Neptune $_{them}$-Pluto $_{you}$ Neptune $_{them}$-Node $_{you}$ Uranus $_{them}$ -Pluto $_{you}$
Node $_{you}$ -Selene $_{them}$ MC*-Vertex*$_{composite}$

For non-astrology related reasons that I won't get into until the next book, you generally can't summon a person against their will. You can call, but will they answer? If they do, it may be because you are open enough to each other's personal influence that you respond to images of them and vice versa. But astrology won't tell you whether another is apt to talk to you. It will, however, show you a piece of their "psychological phone number." Just as we turn to ESPN when we want sports and CSPAN when we want government, we turn to certain angles when we want the world to put us in contact with certain people. Now in general, all angles resonate with like angles. So a truly focused person can summon all kinds of III-novile things by concentrating on one area of their experience which is strongly III-novile. These resonant pairs are a kind of summon in themselves, except that they don't differentiate among things attracted. Thus your fluorescent lights interfere with your remote control; your microwave interferes with your internet; you concentrate on your favorite angle and attract everything from friends, to ants, to traffic incidents (true story). These are cases where the resonated frequency is indiscriminately effective. Most of this is heavily tied to your self chart and not to synastry, but there are a couple of synastric aspects worth noting.

> By seeking to express [Neptune $_{them}$-Node $_{me}$] in my [Neptune $_{them}$-Pluto $_{me}$], I widen the space available for the other person to appear in my life. Picturing our [MC*-Vertex*$_{composite}$] helps me envision them.[37]

> The other person typically shows up bringing [Uranus $_{them}$ -Pluto $_{me}$] into my life while we jointly work on projecting their [Node $_{me}$ -Selene $_{them}$].

Lastly, I have found early evidence that the single most powerful planet for summoning is none other than classic Venus. This is followed closely by Pluto. Why Venus? I don't know. My guess would be that a planet of you-to-other feedback automatically creates an "other" for you to exchange feedback with.

[37] See the next chapter for this, since calculating the MC* and Vertex* requires additional work.

Longevity cocktail: How do I keep them in my life?

Sun $_{them}$-Midheaven $_{you}$	Ascendant $_{you}$-Juno $_{them}$	Pluto $_{you}$-Juno $_{them}$
Venus $_{them}$-Juno $_{you}$	Sun $_{them}$-Hera $_{you}$	Jupiter $_{them}$-Hera $_{you}$
Saturn $_{them}$-Hera $_{you}$	Mercury $_{you}$-Juno $_{them}$	Lilith $_{them}$-Bacchus $_{you}$
Neptune $_{you}$-Pluto $_{them}$		

Let's get this one started first then comment on it afterwards.

> When my and the other person's [Mercury $_{me}$-Juno $_{them}$] is impressively favorable to me, I am more inclined to keep a long-term place for them in my life. This is especially true when their [Lilith $_{them}$-Bacchus $_{me}$] meets the kind of standards that I believe my true friends would approve of.[38] Being a part of this association helps me keep my sense of [Saturn $_{them}$-Hera $_{me}$] strong. Their [Neptune $_{me}$-Pluto $_{them}$] is the context under which I am invited into their life. There, we focus on [Pluto $_{me}$-Juno $_{them}$] as their primary focus for communication. We are most "together," though, when talking about [Venus $_{them}$-Juno $_{me}$].
>
> The other person has a way about them which can be described as [Ascendant $_{me}$-Juno $_{them}$]. Maybe it's me who draws this out of them, though. They can be unusual in how they show their [Jupiter $_{them}$-Hera $_{me}$], yet I provide a safe haven for them in this which makes us stronger. Embedded in their interaction with me is their ability to draw [Sun $_{them}$-Midheaven $_{me}$], and I am inspired to show [Sun $_{them}$-Hera $_{me}$] alongside them.

Despite the appearance of this cocktail, you might be surprised to find that long-lasting friendships aren't really rooted in any specific pairs. The ones listed above certainly help, but much of the basis for longevity rests in 1) the kinds of conjuncts you have with another person[39] and 2) half-pair mutuality. **Half-pair mutuality** is **where you and another person have similar or equal angles no matter which synastric half-pair you look at**. So if [your Moon to their Sun] is trine and [their Moon to your Sun] is trine, these count as mutual half-pairs; you will essentially agree on this aspect of the relationship as being rooted in the easy flow of ideas (the trine). If [your Moon to their Sun] is trine and [their Moon to your Sun] is *sextile*, these *also* count as mutual half-pairs, since the trine and sextile play out very similarly in actual relationships (both instinctually and intellectually).[40] The Longevity cocktail is actually less of a roadmap to creating longevity and more of a description of how you interact with the other person once the possibility of longevity has been established.

You'll be able to find the conjuncts in your chart easily. Reading the above mini-summary is simple enough. But we probably need another table to outline which angles tend to act as "mutual." *Tables 20-6* and *20-7* show this broadly, though not completely.

---

[38] Conjuncts, trines, squares, and sextiles are better for these, though any angle will work depending on context.

[39] Now even though I've said that conjuncts are part of the longevity picture, pairs like [Mercury $_{me}$-Juno $_{them}$], [Pluto $_{me}$-Juno $_{them}$], and [Sun $_{them}$-Midheaven $_{me}$] are actually better when not conjunct, since these work better as world-expanders in your chart. Ironically perhaps, there was <u>not a single conjunct</u> among any of the above ten pairs among the four most long-lived friendships in the dataset. The ten pairs above are noteworthy for their complementarity and emphasis on 1:1 communication instead. Quintiles and trines dominated [Mercury $_{you}$-Juno $_{them}$] and [Lilith $_{them}$-Bacchus $_{you}$], II-noviles dominated [Sun $_{them}$-Hera $_{you}$], and socially broadcasting angles described [Sun $_{them}$-Midheaven $_{you}$] and [Venus $_{them}$-Juno $_{you}$].

[40] Trines and sextiles are also similar because a trine (120°) can be thought of as a "bi-sextile" (2 x 60°). In *FSA* I said you shouldn't normally work with things like "bi-sextiles" since they don't exist as standard angles, but the full story is that you *should* work with math which considers certain harmonics to be factors of others. I've done this throughout both books whenever discussing how, for example, a III-sextile (30) sometimes shows its 5 x 6 or 6 x 5 characteristics. In this example, a sextile (60°) can be thought of as a <u>quinti</u>-*III-sextile* (<u>5</u> x *12*°) or a <u>sexto</u>-*III-inconjunct* (<u>6</u> x *10*°). Here, sextiles and III-sextiles are similar when analysis is the focus while sextiles and III-inconjuncts are similar when impressions on others is the focus. Half-pair mutuality partly results from shared factors and shared effects, not just equal angles.

Actually, you could probably find any angle similar to any other angle given the right context. Tables *20-6* and *20-7* only show angle families which are similar under their default behavior. So you don't need a specific career, ability, external status, or comparative ranking to highlight such similarities. Furthermore, these tables only show categories for which there were a lot of data in my research. This is important because, although long-lived friendship is greatly helped by the presence of mutual angles, the definition of "mutual" changes depending on who the chart holders are and what they are doing together. To a pair of engineers, an information-centric undecile and a rational II-sextile may be similar enough to create mutual half-pairs, though this would not be true for most people. The same would hold for two people who only *think* like engineers. As you get more practice with these, the tables below will become less important in light of your own understanding of what each angle family says.

Table 20-6: Similar angle families for synastry (by harmonic)

Harmonic	Name	Symbol	Category
1	conjunct	☌	Instinctual expression
1	conjunct	☌	Public power
1	conjunct	☌	Body image & gender
2	opposition	☍	Two-sided issue facing
2	opposition	☍	Emotional closeness
2	opposition	☍	Pleasure seeking
3	trine	△	Instinctual expression
3	trine	△	Intellectualizing
4	square	□	Two-sided issue facing
4	square	□	Conflict by default
4	square	□	Emotional closeness
5	quintile	⋆	Easy 1:1 interaction
5	quintile	⋆	Public power
6	sextile	✱	Instinctual expression
6	sextile	✱	Intellectualizing
7	septile	✡	Easy 1:1 interaction
7	septile	✡	Emotional closeness
8	octile	∠	Conflict by default
8	octile	∠	Pleasure seeking
9	novile	九	Intellectualizing
9	novile	九	Joint exploration
9	novile	九	Belief system-related
10	decile	+	Control
11	undecile	U	Intellectualizing
11	undecile	U	Joint exploration
11	undecile	U	Brilliance & eccentricity
12	inconjunct	⊼	Conflict by default
12	inconjunct	⊼	Creativity
12	inconjunct	⊼	Mysterious impression making
13	II-conjunct	☌^{2}	Persona broadcasting
14	II-opposition	☍^{2}	Emotional closeness
14	II-opposition	☍^{2}	Pleasure seeking
14	II-opposition	☍^{2}	Body image & gender
15	II-trine	△^{2}	Persona broadcasting
15	II-trine	△^{2}	Public power
16	II-square	□^{2}	Belief system-related
16	II-square	□^{2}	Emotional closeness
17	II-quintile	⋆^{2}	Persona broadcasting
17	II-quintile	⋆^{2}	Public power
18	II-sextile	✱^{2}	Two-sided issue facing
19	II-septile	✡^{2}	Easy 1:1 interaction
19	II-septile	✡^{2}	Joint exploration
19	II-septile	✡^{2}	Social influence
19	II-septile	✡^{2}	Body image & gender
20	II-octile	∠^{2}	Control
20	II-octile	∠^{2}	Pleasure seeking
21	II-novile	九^{2}	Creativity
21	II-novile	九^{2}	Persona broadcasting
21	II-novile	九^{2}	Pleasure seeking
21	II-novile	九^{2}	Body image & gender
22	II-decile	+^{2}	Control
23	II-undecile	U^{2}	Brilliance & eccentricity
23	II-undecile	U^{2}	Body image & gender
24	II-inconjunct	⊼^{2}	Creativity
24	II-inconjunct	⊼^{2}	Mysterious impression making
24	II-inconjunct	⊼^{2}	Brilliance & eccentricity
25	III-conjunct	☌^{3}	Public power
26	III-opposition	☍^{3}	Social influence
27	III-trine	△^{3}	Brilliance & eccentricity
28	III-square	□^{3}	Belief system-related
29	III-quintile	⋆^{3}	Public power
29	III-quintile	⋆^{3}	Social influence
30	III-sextile	✱^{3}	Control
30	III-sextile	✱^{3}	Belief system-related
31	III-septile	✡^{3}	Belief system-related
31	III-septile	✡^{3}	Social influence
32	III-octile	∠^{3}	Mysterious impression making
33	III-novile	九^{3}	Joint exploration
33	III-novile	九^{3}	Public power
33	III-novile	九^{3}	Social influence
34	III-decile	+^{3}	Control
35	III-undecile	U^{3}	Brilliance & eccentricity
36	III-inconjunct	⊼^{3}	Mysterious impression making
36	III-inconjunct	⊼^{3}	Public power
36	III-inconjunct	⊼^{3}	Social influence
36	III-inconjunct	⊼^{3}	Brilliance & eccentricity

Table 20-6: Angle similarity categories. Use these to search you and the other's synastry table for pairs which share theme areas. THIS TABLE DOES NOT COVER ALL POSSIBLE CATEGORIES, certain areas such as athleticism, health, and career didn't produce enough data from my work to make it into this table. You'll need to use your own take on the angles to see what other categories may apply.

Table 20-7: Similar angle families for synastry (by category)

Harmonic	Name	Symbol	Meaning
Instinctual expression			
1	conjunct	☌	natural behavior
3	trine	△	internal impulse
6	sextile	∗	alignment of means and goals
Two-sided issue facing			
2	opposition	☍	self-value
4	square	□	wants
18	II-sextile	∗^{2}	rationality
Intellectualizing			
3	trine	△	thoughts
6	sextile	∗	analysis
9	novile	九	learning
11	undecile	U	information focus
Conflict by default			
4	square	□	discontentment
8	octile	∠	power
12	inconjunct	⊼	questionable vibe
Easy 1:1 interaction			
5	quintile	⋆	1:1 interaction
7	septile	✡	communication
19	II-septile	✡^{2}	ingroup shared ideas
Joint exploration			
9	novile	九	image promotion
11	undecile	U	social talk
19	II-septile	✡^{2}	ingroup identification
33	III-novile	九^3	group rallying
Control			
10	decile	+	control
20	II-octile	∠^{2}	outsider suppression
22	II-decile	+^{2}	field specialization
30	III-sextile	∗^{3}	critical analysis
34	III-decile	+^{3}	command
Belief system-related			
9	novile	九	philosophy
16	II-square	□^{2}	family values
28	III-square	□^{3}	morality
30	III-sextile	∗^{3}	criticality
31	III-septile	✡^{3}	formal belief and doctrine
Emotional closeness			
2	opposition	☍	measured-against identity
4	square	□	wants
7	septile	✡	camaraderie
14	II-opposition	☍^{2}	physical company-seeking
16	II-square	□^{2}	family values
Creativity			
12	inconjunct	⊼	artistic inclination
21	II-novile	九^2	creativity
24	II-inconjunct	⊼^{2}	works of the imagination
Mysterious impression making			
12	inconjunct	⊼	vibe
24	II-inconjunct	⊼^{2}	works of the imagination
32	III-octile	∠^{3}	mysterious allure
36	III-inconjunct	⊼^{3}	memorability
Persona broadcasting			
13	II-conjunct	☌^{2}	persona
15	II-trine	△^{2}	room hijacking
17	II-quintile	⋆^{2}	"fishbowl" group domination
21	II-novile	九^2	attitude display
Pleasure seeking			
14	II-opposition	☍^{2}	physicality-seeking
20	II-octile	∠^{2}	sexual appetite
21	II-novile	九^2	sexuality announce
2	opposition	☍	body-sensuality
8	octile	∠	intensity seeking
Public power			
1	conjunct	☌	raw instinct
5	quintile	⋆	leadership
15	II-trine	△^{2}	room hijacking
17	II-quintile	⋆^{2}	management of others' behavior
25	III-conjunct	☌^{3}	masses who follow
29	III-quintile	⋆^{3}	charisma over groups
33	III-novile	九^3	rallying
36	III-inconjunct	⊼^{3}	memorability
Social influence			
19	II-septile	✡^{2}	ingroup support
26	III-opposition	☍^{3}	fans & following
29	III-quintile	⋆^{3}	charisma over groups
31	III-septile	✡^{3}	networks
33	III-novile	九^3	group rallying and entertainment
36	III-inconjunct	⊼^{3}	cult following
Brilliance & eccentricity			
11	undecile	U	notoriety
23	II-undecile	U^2	uniqueness
24	II-inconjunct	⊼^{2}	works of the imagination
27	III-trine	△^{3}	insight
35	III-undecile	U^3	genius
36	III-inconjunct	⊼^{3}	memorability
Body image and gender			
1	conjunct	☌	raw instinct
14	II-opposition	☍^{2}	hedonistic pattern
19	II-septile	✡^{2}	same vs diff-based group preferences
21	II-novile	九^2	declaration of physicality
23	II-undecile	U^2	social deviation

Table 20-7: Angle similarity categories. Use this in conjunction with *table 20-6* to determine when you and another person are more or less on the same page by theme, even when the angles aren't the same. THIS TABLE DOES NOT COVER ALL POSSIBLE CATEGORIES, only the ones with more data on them from my sample.

"Will We Last" cocktail: Will we last?

Ascendant $_{you}$-Hera $_{them}$ | Sun $_{you}$-Midheaven $_{them}$ | Moon $_{them}$-Node $_{you}$
Ascendant $_{them}$-Hera $_{you}$ | Fortune $_{you}$-Hera $_{them}$ | **Moon $_{you}$-Venus $_{them}$**
Venus $_{you}$-Hera $_{them}$ | **Saturn-Saturn**

The previous question "How do I keep them in my life?" is different from "Will we last?" The first question asks what you might do to maintain an association while the second question asks whether the other person is inclined to stick around by default (with little extra effort put in). There are a couple of ways to assess the durability of a relationship despite ceaseless change, for better or worse. But you might be surprised to find that investigating neither "perfect" Selene nor "commitment ready" Juno will show you what you need to know. Durability is much less about comparison to other people's expectations and much more about strong bonding to commonly practiced *little* behaviors in the other.

> Very early on in my exchange with the other person, we will need to build a solid foundation in [Moon $_{them}$-Node $_{me}$] in order for us to survive as interactants. They will then need to think of me as a harmonious influence on them in their [Fortune $_{me}$-Hera $_{them}$]. From there, where the other person flatters me and pays attention to my [Moon $_{me}$-Venus $_{them}$], where they are attached to our conversations about [Venus $_{me}$-Hera $_{them}$], and given that we have similar approaches to control of our [Saturn-Saturn]—all of which are rooted in our favorable self-expression*—we then have a formula for automatic longevity. It is important that these three areas are easily and favorably "self-expressed" in our lives. Given that the other person and I can last a long time in our association, their continuing to donate their [Sun $_{me}$-Midheaven $_{them}$] to the interaction will be proof that they still acknowledge my actions in their life. In general they are prone to bonding with situations and people when [Ascendant $_{me}$-Hera $_{them}$]. They hold me in high esteem in [Ascendant $_{them}$-Hera $_{me}$].

On the major angles and favorable self-expression

At the time of this writing, the field of astrology focuses most heavily on those angle families which make up the **major aspects**. These are **the conjunct, trine, opposition, square, sextile, and sometimes the inconjunct**. Among these majors, the conjunct, trine, and sextile are generally considered favorable while the opposition, square, and inconjunct are less favorable than the other three. The majors stand out not only for mathematical reasons, but also for psychological reasons (both discussed in *FSA*). For our purposes here, the majors represent some of the most obvious behaviors you can find yourself engaged in without anyone else being present. Among the favorable major harmonics, conjuncts are doing, trines are thinking, and sextiles are making sense of things. On the other side, oppositions are comparing, squares are wanting, and inconjuncts are inclining towards an action. Each of these angle families is usually "on" when you go from doing things by yourself to doing them with a partner. Accordingly, these angles are more likely to form the basis of lasting exchanges simply because your expression of them doesn't really depend on any specific goals you may have. By virtue of your exchange with another, you are probably doing all six of these things whether or not you are aware of this. But the favorable angles are the main ones we prefer to keep associating with. We also prefer to associate with favorable versions of the "less favorable" angles. So when squares represent deep feeling instead of tense desire, they become favorable. When oppositions become pleasure-generating instead of esteem-vexing, they become favorable. Inconjuncts are favorable when their discomforting uncertainty turns to creative inspiration. Other angles like the II-opposition may be "always on,"[41] but aren't actively steered. Most other angles like the II-conjunct (persona) may be automatic when needed,

[41] Your values always have some worth.

but aren't always needed and by default require others' perspectives to be what they are. It is for all these reasons that having major harmonics for [Moon $_{you}$-Venus $_{them}$], [Venus $_{you}$-Hera $_{them}$], and [Saturn-Saturn] is especially important for your perceiving a relationship as one you don't have to work to stay in. That is, these three pairs in particular are important for *you* seeing the relationship as long-lasting. If you don't have majors for these three, having the same angle for two out of three of them makes you feel more like family to them, with a relationship to them which is much more likely to be inordinately close—them towards you. Check it. It works.

Glue trap: Why can't I get rid of them (or get them off my mind)?

Saturn $_{\text{you}}$-Vertex $_{\text{them}}$
Mercury $_{\text{them}}$-Vesta $_{\text{you}}$
ASC $_{\text{them}}$-Vertex $_{\text{you}}$
Vertex $_{\text{you}}$-Hera $_{\text{them}}$
Eros $_{\text{them}}$-Bacchus $_{\text{you}}$
Pluto $_{\text{you}}$-Midheaven $_{\text{them}}$
Jupiter $_{\text{you}}$-Saturn $_{\text{them}}$
ASC $_{\text{them}}$-Vesta $_{\text{you}}$
Moon $_{\text{you}}$-Venus $_{\text{them}}$
Chiron-Chiron
Venus $_{\text{you}}$-Juno $_{\text{them}}$
Pluto $_{\text{them}}$-Vertex $_{\text{you}}$
Selene $_{\text{you}}$-Lilith $_{\text{them}}$
Sun $_{\text{you}}$-Chiron $_{\text{them}}$

When some exchanges become too close with bad experiences to accompany them, they begin to grate. At that point you may find yourself in the company of an enemy, itching for ways to make them go away. Yet some personalities are stubborn. They haunt the mind with dogged persistence and set up camp just a few notions away from your every thought. How does the idea of someone get stuck on you like this? The same way most things get stuck: Part of them binds things while the other part remains all too different from the things they bind. If they stood in agreement with the things they bound we wouldn't really consider them "stuck" in the negative sense, just "attached." And so it is with people. They stay on our minds because they have characteristics we're attracted to. They resist unsticking when all of a sudden we decide that those same attracting characteristics should magically stop working on us—usually because they now refuse to go the way we wanted them to go. But we can't have it both ways. The thing that made them popular or attractive to us or our friends in easy times will surely make them popular or attractive *as thoughts* in hard times...when we least want them. Whether or not we ourselves invited them is irrelevant. A "bound comparison" is the name of the game. Our first step in getting them off the mind is to understand what kinds of binding and what kinds of comparison keep them alive in our heads to begin with.

And the number one synastric pair for keeping someone stuck is...It's a tie. [Jupiter $_{\text{you}}$-Saturn $_{\text{them}}$] effectively shows where the other person can control your projection in the world, while [Chiron-Chiron] shows where you share an arena for playing out a game of insecurity. The net result is that they seem to have taken your imperfect world, perfected a little piece of it, then held the perfected part hostage.

> They found me knee deep in my [Moon $_{\text{me}}$-Venus $_{\text{them}}$] and added to my life, where their way with **[Jupiter $_{\text{me}}$-Saturn $_{\text{them}}$] seemed to complement mine**. We appeared to have intertwined paths as [ASC $_{\text{them}}$-Vertex $_{\text{me}}$], and I found their [ASC $_{\text{them}}$-Vesta $_{\text{me}}$] well worth paying attention to. It has been too easy for me to remain hooked on their [Vertex $_{\text{me}}$-Hera $_{\text{them}}$]. Now I am caught up in their [Saturn $_{\text{me}}$-Vertex $_{\text{them}}$] as they seem to get away with murder doing [Selene $_{\text{me}}$-Lilith $_{\text{them}}$] things—the most severe among their deeds constantly attacking who I am as a [Pluto $_{\text{them}}$-Vertex $_{\text{me}}$]. This is made even worse by their very potent [Pluto $_{\text{me}}$-Midheaven $_{\text{them}}$]. And then they keep rubbing my face in their [Venus $_{\text{me}}$-Juno $_{\text{them}}$]—apparently just to remain on the mind. **[Chiron-Chiron] was what I should have enjoyed sharing with them**, but instead I learned [Sun $_{\text{me}}$-Chiron $_{\text{them}}$] while they wrapped me up in their [Mercury $_{\text{them}}$-Vesta $_{\text{me}}$]. Perhaps I left them in the cold with my [Eros $_{\text{them}}$-Bacchus $_{\text{me}}$], refusing to accept the intensity they had to offer. And this will have been part of their main issue with me. Now they still threaten to invade other ideas that I create here. But I have a way of escaping their grip should I ever decide to do so...

Severance cocktail: How do I get rid of them?

Mars $_{them}$-Hera $_{you}$	Moon $_{you}$-Juno $_{them}$	Pluto $_{them}$-Midheaven $_{you}$
Chiron $_{you}$-Bacchus $_{them}$	Mercury $_{you}$-Saturn $_{them}$	**Midheaven $_{them}$-Hera $_{you}$**
Jupiter $_{you}$-Saturn $_{them}$	**Chiron $_{them}$-Pallas $_{you}$**	

Let's terminate that nuisance person from the previous entry, shall we? The secret: take the tool they've been in your life and replace it with a superior model. Get your new [Chiron $_{them}$-Pallas $_{you}$] replacement person ready and build your [Midheaven $_{them}$-Hera $_{you}$] alongside that replacement instead. Don't be mad. Be normal. Anger only makes the memory linger longer. Instead, we'll ask how things would be if the other person were completely, *thoroughly* gone. How would you do things then? This cocktail will give you a decent idea and then some.

> I'm done with this person. But before I can successfully end things in my own mind with total finality, **I should prepare to replace the role they currently play in my [Midheaven $_{them}$-Hera $_{me}$] with the role of another**. Next, I will give myself credit for growing against the experiences in [Mars $_{them}$-Hera $_{me}$] which they handed me. I'm better in light of the choices I made in this area. I'll take the credit and my lessons and go from there, replacing their [Jupiter $_{me}$-Saturn $_{them}$] with a better means of disciplining myself in this same area. I don't need to keep getting served the hard way by this person. As I exit, I'll continue to use the very characteristic which the exchange with this person has squeezed out of me—my way with [Moon $_{me}$-Juno $_{them}$]—until I get bored. Might as well put it to good use. But I'll use it on things which I'll actually want to keep around after they're gone. I won't waste the skill they raised in me on them. (That would be like a lottery winner giving their money back.)
>
> Should this person attempt to keep influencing me, I'll show more [Chiron $_{me}$-Bacchus $_{them}$] (which I know overrides them), and use my [Mercury $_{me}$-Saturn $_{them}$] to suppress them. (This second action is my way of continually dissecting $_{Mercury}$ the structure they try to build $_{Saturn}$ around me; in this way, anything they build which has to do with me will slip apart.) Lastly, **I will avoid thinking of [Chiron $_{them}$-Pallas $_{me}$] in the same way and turn my attention to someone who does this better**. Better under the replacement person, I have no doubt that they'll see me as one of the strongest [Pluto $_{them}$-Midheaven $_{me}$] they ever encountered.

I'm not gonna lie, as a fan of control, I found the above pretty fun to write and even more fun to read. The Severance cocktail can both look and feel pretty cold, but is a great weapon to have in a world full of people who will guilt trip you out of all kinds of opportunities. Whether it's a bad ex, a nasty colleague, or (sometimes) an annoying media figure whom you've never met, you can draw a line in the sand, pull them over, and punish them for crossing all in one swoop with the Severance cocktail.

Now, although we don't condone vengeance or cheating, this combination of pairs has that effect. Actually, it stings more if you don't seek vengeance or cheat. Revenge is more likely to bring out the fight in your enemy while indifference is more likely to simply hurt—leaving your newfound adversary nothing to fight but their own failure. Not that you want to waste your efforts hurting them, you just don't want to be fought anymore *by them*. What's more, cutting a tie bitterly with nothing to show but Ceres-9s means that you're more likely to have left the whole thing empty-handed.[42] Because you yourself said so. Don't leave empty handed. Take the A you've earned in

[42] From *FSA*, Ceres in the 9th house has one of the highest capacities for vengeance among all astrological factors studied in the book. If you have it, don't take it as a complement or a criticism. When used rightly it makes you Oprah. When used wrongly it makes you Hitler. When used frivolously (on issues others would consider pretty unimportant) it damages your relationships with those others in your absence, as they

BS101 and do something else. Still, this cocktail definitely doubles as a roadmap for cheating on a romantic partner and diminishing the worth of a friend, such that if you do use these pairs—in all their glorious self-satisfaction—don't be surprised if you reap the consequences later for your heartlessness. The reasons for this are purely psychological and should be obvious to you. In brief, to reduce a person's effect on you to 0 is to introduce *to yourself* the idea that even the closest exchanges can become completely worthless in a heartbeat. So you might actually want to avoid thinking in terms of severance unless it's really necessary. I suspect that its repeated use won't quite leave you lonely, but *will* leave you socially homeless (thanks to conditions that you yourself have set up in your own outlook).

One more thing. Replacing **[Chiron $_{\text{them}}$-Pallas $_{\text{you}}$]**—[Doctor/patient $_{\text{them}}$-Social objective $_{\text{you}}$]—is arguably <u>the</u> key to effective relationship erasure. But what if you can't find a better exchange than the one you're killing? Either in your own mind or (preferably) in real life, use your own [Chiron $_{\text{you}}$-Pallas $_{\text{them}}$] to make them use their [Chiron $_{\text{them}}$-Pallas $_{\text{you}}$]. It's a bit messed up, but it works. See [Mercury-Eros] in Chapter 19 for the basic idea of why it works. The idea is to show yourself that their "best" is actually the result of *your* best steering of their talents under your direction.

---

remind each other of how excessive you were. In this latter case, the people in the data who used this setup to regularly slam opponents were also more likely to be lonely for longer stretches of their lives. True story.

Adversary formula: Why do they hate me?

Moon $_{them}$-Juno $_{you}$ Moon $_{you}$-Juno $_{them}$ Neptune $_{you}$-Juno $_{them}$

Mars $_{them}$-Node $_{you}$ **MC $_{them}$-Chiron $_{you}$** **Selene $_{them}$-Lilith $_{you}$**

Maybe they hate you because you tried to sever them. Just kidding (kind of). Seriously, there are certain pairs which are just plain sensitive to chaos, which fight and frustrate easily. Before we get to the mini-summary, we'll tour some straight explanations. Generally, most people regarding whom we ask "Why do they hate me?" don't actually hate us. Maybe you knew that. Instead, they bring to the table a basket of issues which existed before you got there that you either amplified or exposed—attitudes or memories they held associated with a threat response that you awakened. This means that we'll typically have no way at all of knowing "why they hate us," only that they *seem* to do so. This aggravation component of the other person's supposed hate is partly viewable in the chart.

Reason#1 (why they "hate" you): You have incompatible aims for each other

If the Moon shows what we want and Juno shows what we've been committed to pursue in the eyes of society, we can look at both [Moon-Juno] half-pairs to see where you and the other person are most likely to square off in terms of what a first person seeks to do and what a second person is compelled to make the first person seek to do. These areas of life come down to [What you want vs What *they* push you to want] ([Moon $_{you}$-Juno $_{them}$]) as well as [What they want vs What *you push them* to want] ([Moon $_{them}$-Juno $_{you}$]). We can add to this scenario [What their *mood seems to want* from you vs What they *actually push* you to pursue] ([Neptune $_{you}$-Juno $_{them}$]). The [Moon-Juno] half-pairs look like "pressure to feel." [Neptune $_{you}$-Juno $_{them}$] looks more like grounds for you to distrust them.

Reason #2: That's just the way they are

Most reasonably familiar acquaintances have their usual set of things they encourage us to do and a typical way of playing out that encouragement. This becomes even more obvious when the person doing the "encouraging" seems to dislike us. [Mars $_{them}$-Node $_{you}$] shows the area of life where you feel it will have been most convenient (Node) for you to be pushed by them (Mars). [MC $_{them}$-Chiron $_{you}$] is that area of life where they acknowledge (MC) your insecurity (Chiron). The first pair looks like a natural pushiness on their part. The second pair looks like their ability to zoom in on any areas where you are broken. The ironic thing here is that more secure you are the less secure they tend to be as your Chiron ultimately flips its role from patient to doctor.

Reason #3: You render their perfect talent irrelevant

What kind of person enjoys having their great skill rendered useless? The other person's Selene is such a great skill—one which your forever-contrary Lilith is (as with all things) designed to defy. Used favorably, you are simply seen as an innovator to them. Used wrongly, you become the one mountain they can't conquer.

> Usually because of who we were before meeting, I push this person to expose more of their wishes in [Moon $_{them}$-Juno $_{me}$] while they draw out my wants in [Moon $_{me}$-Juno $_{them}$]. They seem to have a natural eye for my weaknesses in [MC $_{them}$-Chiron $_{me}$], and this is indeed the tool they use to cut me down as we fight under [Moon $_{them}$-Juno $_{me}$] circumstances. It looks unreasonably easy for them to try to direct my [Mars $_{them}$-Node $_{me}$] even when they have no clue regarding what they're looking at or how to direct it. They simply want influence there. Whatever their talents may be as [Selene $_{them}$-Lilith $_{me}$], I frustrate their ability to show through my own non-response. And this is perhaps the biggest indicator of whether or not they hate me for something that I've done: Have I thwarted their confident advancement on me in [Selene $_{them}$-Lilith $_{me}$]? If not, maybe they were just programmed to be nasty to me as I attempt to [MC

> $_{\text{them}}$-Chiron $_{\text{me}}$]. If this isn't true either, then maybe they don't actually hate me. Maybe they are fighting their own quest for significance as [Mars $_{\text{them}}$-Node $_{\text{me}}$] in my life. Whatever the case, by the time they officially began standing against me, I realized that I should not rely on my impressions of their [Neptune $_{\text{me}}$-Juno $_{\text{them}}$] to tell me anything about their actual stance towards me.

To wrap up the above, another person's hate can usually be traced back to one of three broad areas:

- **problems with your resistance to their influence [Selene $_{\text{them}}$-Lilith $_{\text{you}}$]**
- **problems with their default view of you [MC $_{\text{them}}$-Chiron $_{\text{you}}$], or**
- **problems internal to them [Mars $_{\text{them}}$-Node $_{\text{you}}$].**

The last two kinds of problems typically have roots beyond your reach.

The adversary formula gives you possible reasons for the other person's ire, but not solutions. Solutions may not even be in your job description. Just understanding what the deal is, though, might be useful to you in working your way out of a negative situation with them.

Oppressor cocktail: How do I beat them?

Mercury $_{\text{you}}$-Saturn $_{\text{them}}$ Mars $_{\text{you}}$-Saturn $_{\text{them}}$ Uranus $_{\text{you}}$-Ceres $_{\text{them}}$
Mercury $_{\text{them}}$-Vertex $_{\text{you}}$ Moon $_{\text{you}}$-Mercury $_{\text{them}}$ Midheaven $_{\text{me}}$-Mars $_{\text{them}}$
Selene $_{\text{them}}$-Lilith $_{\text{you}}$ **Midheaven $_{\text{you}}$-Pluto $_{\text{them}}$**

Unlike relationship destruction, opponent suppression is all about making the other person squirm, handing them a loss, or—in the lightest cases—just denying them a victory. Perhaps you don't want to (or simply can't) eliminate the other person from your life entirely. You just need to make sure they don't win. Well there's good news and bad news. The bad news is, despite the presence of some really useful synastric pairs, not all opponents are beatable. I'll say a little more about this after the mini-summary. The good news is, there are some really decent pairs for opponent suppression and most opponents can be beaten with very little work on your part. The key lies in comfortably staying with the path that vexes them (in the way that [Lilith in Aries] worked in *FSA*).

> Insensitive to their issues with [Moon $_{\text{me}}$-Mercury $_{\text{them}}$], I back them into a corner by frustrating their sense of effectiveness here. Where they attempt to establish order and control, I say or do things which both 1) highlight the flaws in their [Mercury $_{\text{me}}$-Saturn $_{\text{them}}$] as well as necessitate that they put even more work to fix their [Mars $_{\text{me}}$-Saturn $_{\text{them}}$]—no matter how good they already think it is. Regardless of how skilled or high ranking they may be, in their company I easily determine the last word on matters of [Uranus $_{\text{me}}$-Ceres $_{\text{them}}$], even if I can't say so out loud. Why? Because the way they choose to push me here directly affects what people say about them. Through simple ongoing exposure to me, they automatically adjust their [Mercury $_{\text{them}}$-Vertex $_{\text{me}}$] to accommodate my changes. How I choose to change greatly affects those areas which they do and don't see as problems. **My main weapon against them is to remain as realistically distant from their [Selene $_{\text{them}}$-Lilith $_{\text{me}}$] influence as possible, while still asserting my status as unmatched in [Midheaven $_{\text{me}}$-Pluto $_{\text{them}}$].** When I stop receiving their [Midheaven $_{\text{me}}$-Mars $_{\text{them}}$] after having been hit with it for so long, I can consider them to have given up.

I can't tell you how many times I've asked myself the "how do I beat them" question, and how many times I've learned that certain people just shouldn't be fought. If you look back over these last four cocktails you may notice a pattern. Half of the battle against presumed enemies lies in us tackling the issues that attract us to them, not in simply "stopping" them. Much of the time, the person you seek to beat is simply closer to your equal than most; so you can't just sway them the way you would normal company. Sometimes, the person you would beat is actually masterful in areas you don't have it in you to handle, and neither you nor they understand that the change you're trying to effect in the other is more fitting for yourselves than the other. Sometimes the person you would beat is necessary to hold up the very ground you're standing on. I call these three kinds of people "mirrors," "doors," and "floors." Each may aggravate you as an obstruction, but unless you're ready to handle whatever it is behind them, fighting them will only stress you out. If you find that using this cocktail only harms you more, that's a clue to stop. More likely this person should be used for the experience or protection they provide in lieu of bigger issues beyond your capabilities. Your [Fortune $_{\text{them}}$-Selene $_{\text{you}}$] is a great indicator of what the point of the exchange is. Take a look at it. Then read the very first cocktail, "What am I supposed to get out of this relationship?"

Enabler cocktail: How should I best help them?

Venus $_{them}$-Pluto $_{you}$	Sun $_{you}$-Pluto $_{them}$	Moon $_{you}$-Fortune $_{them}$
Mars $_{them}$-Selene $_{you}$	**Vesta $_{them}$-Hera $_{you}$**	**Vesta $_{you}$-Juno $_{them}$**
Juno $_{you}$-Hera $_{them}$	Juno $_{them}$-Eros $_{you}$	

There are many ways to bring out the best in someone, though most of these ways will depend on the person's own readiness to receive your aid. You know what they say about leading a horse to water...

> The other person has responsibilities they must tend to in society, **but my supporting their [Vesta $_{me}$-Juno $_{them}$] helps lighten their burdens**. They can be a super strong inspiration to me as [Venus $_{them}$-Pluto $_{me}$], and with very little effort on my part they only grow stronger in this area as the exchange goes on. Also automatic is my ability to raise their confident [Mars $_{them}$-Selene $_{me}$].
>
> The other person is more inclined to make risky moves in [Juno $_{me}$-Hera $_{them}$], largely because I support their doing so and can serve as a safe place for them return to if things should fail work out as planned. I reduce their [Moon $_{me}$-Fortune $_{them}$]-related insecurities. **Through my anchoring of their [Vesta $_{them}$-Hera $_{me}$], we find that things just seem to work out better for them.** I use [Juno $_{them}$-Eros $_{me}$][43] to inspire their creative flow when they need a boost. One ultimate goal for our exchange is to help them reflect a powerful [Sun $_{me}$-Pluto $_{them}$], which I do through my normal interaction with them.

I found this combination of pairs quite interesting in the sense that there was very little to do actively. Though you would think the Enabler cocktail would give you more advice on how to intentionally help another person, all it really tells is how you naturally help them by being yourself. The specifics flow from this. Indeed, try as you might to help someone, you never really know how your efforts at aid will ultimately be converted into the currency of their minds. For many people out there, your trying too hard to help them looks more like imposition, so that you're better off just supporting what they're ready for as the issues arise—unless it's part of your official relationship to do otherwise. I think the real secret to enabling someone's happiness lies less in what you do and more in how their needs are fulfilled through what you do. This cocktail highlights some of the easier areas for you to attend to.

[43] The data strongly suggested that, in the case of the Enabler cocktail, more primal angles such as the major, the "pleasure seeking," and the "instinctual expression" groups were better than the more abstract and intellectual-only ones, presumably because they gave more of a visceral, bodily feel for the success or failure of support efforts. The trine is okay because it also has a physical side. The better relationships had both [Juno-Eros] half-pairs dominated by such angles.

Challenger cocktail: How can we become something great?

Mars-Bacchus $_{both}$	Sun $_{them}$-Neptune $_{you}$	Saturn $_{them}$-Lilith $_{you}$
Saturn-Chiron $_{you}$	ASC $_{them}$-MC $_{you}$	Vertex-Vertex
Pluto $_{them}$-Selene $_{you}$	MC $_{you}$-Vertex $_{them}$	ASC $_{them}$-Pallas $_{you}$

A socially "great" partnership might be described as one which not only publicizes the partner's talents before peers and the world, but one which does so with a presence that few can deny. For those who want their interactions to be relevant in the world rather than relevant on a personal level solely, we have the Challenger cocktail: one which grabs outside challenges by the horns and slaps them around.

> Dismissing the world's advice when it comes to [my own Saturn-Chiron], I team up with Other over the subject of [Pluto $_{them}$-Selene $_{me}$] to get our [Vertex-Vertex]-related concerns under control. We understand each other's aims through [MC $_{me}$-Vertex $_{them}$] and use that understanding to get ourselves publicly seen as [ASC $_{them}$-MC $_{me}$] who put their [Saturn $_{them}$-Lilith $_{me}$] under the spotlight in our quest to build our [ASC $_{them}$-Pallas $_{me}$] in the world. We carry out our work against the backdrop of [Sun $_{them}$-Neptune $_{me}$], ultimately establishing each of us (the Mars person in [Mars-Bacchus $_{both}$]) as great in [Mars-Bacchus $_{both}$].

Finally, below we have three self chart combinations.

Great Riches cocktail: How do I attain great riches?

Pallas-Hera	True Node-Lilith	Ascendant-Sun
Pallas-Vesta	**True Node-Vesta**	Fortune-Vesta
Midheaven-Mars	**Mean Node-Vesta**	Fortune-Vertex
Midheaven-Uranus	Jupiter-Pluto	

In *FSA* I discuss how there is no real formula for riches in astrology. This is because there is a difference between being money rich, security rich, power rich, friend rich, and (yes) knowledge rich. Consider that some people, with all the stacks of money in the world, would primarily spend it on travel and experience-hunting. And what would they have bought with their money? Experience—a close relative of world-knowledge. And what about those who spend their money on cars? What would they have bought? Object associations—a close relative of self-value (like ethnicity and body-image). Before we scoff at the idea that novile experience or II-opposition identity pale in comparison to cash, we should remember that government paper is only as good as the value it measures, and only as good as the recognition (a type of knowledge) given to it by those who have it. Give a $50 bill to a baby to prove this to yourself. Values vary, and astrology recognizes no government. So we can't look for dollars in the chart. We can, however, look for the families of experiences that dollars buy.

The Great Riches cocktail was indeed culled from the data of some pretty rich people, but don't look for their 1% of 1% level of money-wealth to show up in your chart in the same way. In general, great riches instead show up as [that combination of skills where you are widely recognized as being awesomely good] combined with [the kinds of opportunities others think you have an inexhaustible supply of]. In this rather complex area of life you are so super-prosperous that you wouldn't trade your fortune for anything. On the contrary, you continue to pile more upon more of whatever it is until the day you die. Without having read the summary below, maybe you've already figured out where you might be so rich. But in case you haven't, here's the summary again:

> Broadly speaking, **I am best at making money by [doing True Node-Vesta things], which I think back on as showing my ability to [Mean Node-Vesta]**.
>
> For great riches, though, it is important to [Pallas-Hera] in the execution of [Pallas-Vesta]. In doing so, it is also important that I 1) build [Fortune-Vesta] for those who work with me, 2) am considered an innovator among [Node-Lilith], 3) am considered a field leader in [MC-Mars], and 4) am noted among the masses for my [MC-Uranus]. **My expressive field is [ASC-Sun]**. I meet the standards of societal pressure in [Jupiter-Pluto]. The money I make is a measure of [Fortune-Vertex] placed upon others.

Tables 17-4 and *19-1* are particularly good for reading the above.

Interpersonal Calling cocktail: Who am I when I am at my best as an interactor with people?

Sun-Node Moon-Node Sun-Moon

We humans are generally wired to be social, but we're not exactly wired to "get in where we fit in" so to speak. Instead, we get in *where we're put* and build from there. Yet in so many cases, this isn't quite good enough. Behind each of our comfortable circles lies the shadow of what *could* be. If only we knew *those* people. If only sat down and had a chat with their kind. Now I'm sure you're pretty happy with where you currently are socially. Your current clique is probably all you'll need for the rest of your life (no joke). BUT you might still wonder what kind of person you'd be if you could pick absolutely any circle you wanted in such a way as to feel like your way of interacting with others had been truly perfected. No awkwardness or pretense, just behaving naturally and sharing those ideas which appeal to you naturally. Well wonder no more. Here we officially define the Interpersonal Calling cocktail.

> As an ideal interactant with others, I [Sun-Node] based on my intent to [Moon-Node], and am most self-contented when [showing Sun-Moon] in those matters.

For this one I HIGHLY encourage you to get creative with the angles and swap out words so that they match you better. The exercise can be both fun and enlightening, as well as informative if you use it to read other's charts. Below are five samples from the dataset which illustrate what I mean. Compare the wording below to the more mechanical wording normally used in this chapter's tables.

Table 20-8: Sample Mini-summary rewording using Interpersonal calling cocktail

Person	Sun-Node	Moon-Node	Sun-Moon	Mini-summary
1	II-novile	II-septile	III-inconjunct	As an ideal interactant with others, I [am attractive and talented] with an intent to [make anyone feel like a friend], and am most self-contented when [I feel I've left a memorable impression on others].
2	II-square	II-septile	trine	As an ideal interactant with others, I [share close relationships with others] based on my intent to [hold great friendships], and am most self-contented when [being free to say what's on my mind in those situations].
3	II-square	III-undecile	II-quintile	As an ideal interactant with others, I [make others feel comfortable] based on my [unique personality], and am most self-contented when [moving the people around me] as a result.
4	II-quintile	octile	II-octile	As an ideal interactant with others, I [am seen as steering a bunch of people] based on my intent to [unlock power], and am most self-contented when [kicking ass] in those matters.
5	quintile	conjunct	quintile	As an ideal interactant with others, I [am a leader] because of the way I [express what I feel], and am most self-contented when [being celebrated as the center of attention] in those matters.

Table 20-8: Sample mini-summary rewording using Interpersonal Calling cocktail. As with all the cocktails, plug in words that fit you.

Inner Mastery triad: How do I master myself?

Sun-Moon Node-Selene Juno-Hera

There is something to be said for finding that realm of action where you're really, really good. Many nice candidates exist in the regular chart for locating this space of things. Some like [Sun-Node] even tell you what you might be doing. But if you think about it, knowing *what* to do in the ideal is probably easy enough given your awareness of your own talents. Knowing *where* though...that's the thing. You want to win a Nobel Prize, but which field should you choose? You want to be the next Prince, but which venue should you rock? You'd love to be a happy multimillionaire, but what kind of business should you operate? Now imagine there exists a set of circumstances of which you could say, "I have a commitment to be there and *want* to be there. I'm contented with my choices there. And my ideal talents seem like destiny there." Sounds nice doesn't it? Fill in the mini-summary below to see what that place looks like for you. Use words that fit you. Where perfect-looking situations are concerned, this is as close as it gets.

> Having found inner mastery, I feel self-contented as I [Sun-Moon] amidst my enjoyable commitment to [Juno-Hera]. Here it is destiny that I play out my high talent as [Node-Selene].

Don't be surprised if the above seems...different...from what you expected. This is the *situation* for mastery and not the mastered thing itself. Also, remember that charts won't generally talk about cash or cars or feeding the children. You'll get abstractions instead. That may not be a satisfying answer from an astrology book but trust me, it's better for you in reality. An abstract cocktail gives you room to shape more situations to fit this one rather than *shaping you* to fit some boxed notion of a successful life.

Synastry reading step 4: Consider the other person's perspective

Just when you thought you'd read all of the interesting major combinations worth reading, we have something that may be even more informative. Try reading the previous section's combinations from the other person's perspective. You may have done this automatically, but it warrants noting officially. As wide as the terrain of planets and combinations can be, most of us will find it difficult to remember what every pair or cocktail said. It is actually easier to look at someone else's side of the relationship and remember what you read there than it is to look at your own and remember what you read for yourself. This is because you're going to continue with the business of living your life however you live it regardless of what some symbols told you about yourself, but your reading about another person's life and motivations amounts to something like mind-reading. Indeed, it *feels* like mind-reading. Here the chart can give you insight into things that you never would have thought of in years' worth of interaction with the other person. That is, doing a synastry reading on your own chart is life taking a selfie with someone else in the background; doing a synastry reading from that someone else's perspective is like taking a regular picture of them preparing to do something with you. The latter can be especially informative in relationships that have gone bad or those where the other person has some mysterious motivations lurking beneath the surface.

Takeaway: If necessary, define one key pair as the basis for your entire interaction

At the end of the day, reading your synastry chart with another person and going through all the combinations will give you several things to think about, but we can hardly expect for all that information to stick with you over the long term. For practical purposes, it will be better to reduce everything you've read to **a single synastric pair for keeping your interaction going and going healthily**. We'll call this the **key pair**.

It turns out that nothing in this chapter will matter in the long run if you just don't care enough to maintain the exchanges with the various other people you read about. I myself have read tons of charts—many of which featured friends—and just couldn't do much with the encyclopedia of information which each synastry chart held. Instead, I'll tell you that the three most useful things that stay with you following a synastry reading are (in order)

- Your #1 reason for keeping up an exchange with the other person
- Information regarding whether or not the other person was basically on your side
- Insight into what other person likely felt they were getting from you

Truly, synastry provides most of its insight through step 4 in the sections above: That is, when you read the cocktails from step 3 with [you as "them"] and [them as "you"] instead of the default perspectives. Rather than asking "Are they interested?" you can ask what tests they use to see if *you're* interested. Rather than asking why *you* can't shake the thought of them, you can ask what things prevent *them* from shaking the thought of you. Swapping perspectives will give you the second and third most useful kinds of information listed above. Nothing else you read—especially cocktails you read from your own perspective—will provide much for you besides good trivia.

As far as the first most useful information provided by synastry is concerned, you'll typically have your reasons for wanting a relationship to work out (at least temporarily), and this will largely depend on what angle you're focused on at the time. While writing both this book and its predecessor *FSA* for example, I enjoyed an interesting exchange with a fascinating young lady who served as my muse, and the inspiration kept coming. She and I had a [Mars $_{her}$-Vertex $_{me}$] III-undecile for supercharging the Vertex person's creative genius and intellectual curiosity, and this became my key pair—the number one reason for keeping the otherwise improbable exchange going. In exchanges which aren't naturally easy, you can and should choose a single pair as the main motivator for the exchange. The process of choosing is actually very simple. While looking at either the cocktails or *table 19-9*, just note to yourself what you think the coolest pair is and choose that one. If you want, you can then look at its resonant pairs to see what the rest of that relationship quality looks like. When I first saw the [Mars $_{her}$-Vertex $_{me}$] III-undecile in the lady's and my synastry chart I said to myself, "That's crazy! It's so true! For as long as we've been interacting all these months I've have nothing but insight after insight." With the key pair's angle area in mind (mine here was intellectual inspiration), you'll tend to do everything else to support the relationship automatically, and what you do has a good chance of following the patterns set out in this chapter's cocktails. There's actually no need to develop a full blown strategy for your interaction's success.

You'll have a key pair, but be aware that the other person's key pair will almost certainly not be the same as yours. While you're focusing on family (a II-square pair), they'll be focused on career (a II-decile). While you're focusing on organizing a group (a II-quintile), they'll be focused on their friendship interactions (septile). And then there is the inevitable change; at some point your priorities will shift, your relationship with the other will change and your key pair will become something else. But I've found that there's rarely a need to determine what the new key pair will be. Why? Because if you've decided to stay with an interaction even after its key pair has changed, you've probably decided that there's no need to have an official anchor anymore. The key pair works best when you need a reason to keep things running smoothly. Once that reason becomes obsolete, most people won't need to search for a different reason. Instead they will have simply decided to continue things or end things based on whether the relationship was worth it in general.

Chapter 21: Planets on the planets IV: Composite charts

So you and Other have decided to form a relationship of some kind. Maybe you're business partners. Perhaps you're friends. Or significant others. You know enough about how you affect them and they affect you, but something is missing. How can we explain the way your duo affects you both? How does your duo seem to affect people outside of the relationship? Enter composite charts.

A composite chart is simply the astrological chart formed by averaging your planets' locations with the locations of the other person's planets. **The charts that make up a composite chart** will be called **component charts**. If your Sun is in 3° Leo and their Sun is in 5° Libra, your composite Sun will be in 4° Virgo. Do this for all of your planets and you get the chart of an alleged third party which is the general psychological relationship formed by the two of you. That is, the composite chart is the chart of a relationship between two or more parties, formed from averaging their planets. They are slippery, behave weirdly, and should be used very sparingly. But they're there, so we'll go over them.

Some things you MUST know before using composite charts

When I first started studying relationship astrology over a decade ago I thought that the composite charts and synastry charts showed roughly the same thing. They don't. Not at all.

- The synastry chart shows how you and Other relate to each other. The composite chart shows what your relationship looks like broadly when you zoom out and observe its character. So Fred Flintstone and Barney Rubble have a particular dynamic shown in synastry. Their composite chart is the basis of how they treat each other. Wile E. Coyote and the Roadrunner have a particular kind of adversarial dynamic.

Their composite chart should, hypothetical, reveal a combined dynamic marked by amazing complementarity. (If they had real psychologies. More on this later.)

- Basic synastry charts are built on the interaction of events that really happen in spacetime. For reasons related to the speed, direction, and orbits of actual bodies in space, the positions of planets in composite charts can't normally happen in physics. Synastries are real. Composite charts are generally fictions.

- Related to the previous note, synastry charts have a character. Composite charts don't actually do anything themselves, but are *seen* by viewers as affecting those viewers. In this sense, composites are like books: They are only as useful as their reader's processing will allow, and tend to be best understood by the authors themselves.

- We'll find out that the only way we can really use composite charts is by reading synastry with them. I did this prior to writing this book, and the results have produced this chapter. Angles between a composite chart's planets and its own planets are definitely something different from angles between a composite chart's planets and other people's planets.

- For really deep, but questionable relationships, composite charts are only as healthy as their "outs:" planets in the composite which are conjunct planets in the charts of the people whose charts were averaged. You can have a trine between your planet and a planet in the composite chart for talking to the relationship, but it probably won't talk back. Outs are mainly visible as conjuncts. Unless you're really scrutinizing a relationship, most other angles matter very little.

- Most importantly, COMPOSITE CHART PLANETS BEHAVE ABNORMALLY, where traditional interpretations perform a kind of fascinating (but aggravating) game of musical chairs. I have a theory of why this is, but you should know that one should NOT go into a composite reading expecting Venus to represent love or communication. It's much meaner than that. Don't count on anything you've read about the planets prior to this chapter. Not even from other sections of this book. We'll need to use statistics to figure out what's happening with the planets in a composite chart, and you'll likely find the results unusual.

And so reading composites, no matter how confident you may be in your astrology skills, is a lot like reading a work of fine art. Sure there's something in there, but don't expect it to be what it looks like on the surface. I was initially going to omit composites in this book, but there really were statistical patterns. The patterns just weren't the ones I expected. Similarly, you'll probably find these charts to reveal an interesting portrait of the third party relationship created between you and another as well as a good general overview of what the two of you can build in the long run. But with at least three layers of chart needed to get at what composites actually show, it gets pretty deep.[44] Only skilled divers need apply.

Don't confuse composite charts with relative charts (a close cousin)

There is a practice which exists in astrology which consists of **using time and place averaging to calculate the combined chart between two people**. If I'm born in California in December 1980 and you're born in Florida in February of 1981, this version of our chart, called the **Davison (or relative) chart**, would be calculated for something like a birth in Texas in January of 1981—the average. This is a partial fix to the idea that composite charts aren't real, since this practice produces a real time and place to serve as the foundation for our relationship. The Davison / relative chart

[44] To interpret composites, we'll need to borrow from regular charts, synastric charts, and our knowledge of orbit levels discussed back in *FSA*.

produces houses, planet placements, and calculated points which make physical sense. Kind of. Indeed these charts can more or less be read as the broad character for an interaction when no other internal information is available, and you would read them more or less the way you read regular charts, except on a macrocosmic scale; that is, reading a Davison chart is like reading a person's chart, except that person isn't a person, but a project. The logic of these kinds of relationship charts is actually consistent with the logic of various house systems discussed in *FSA*, where the viewpoint you choose matters. Davison/relative charts are the charts of relationships as viewed by outside parties, with no knowledge of the two people's internal dynamics required. Here the component people are just merged blips in spacetime. Again, you read a relative chart the way you read a regular birth chart. But since the relationship itself isn't a person, you'd read mainly conjuncts, oppositions, trines, and squares—omitting the aspects which require that the relationship "talk" to others.

In terms of what almost every viewer of a particular relationship sees, relative charts actually give a better description of that relationship than composite charts do. But even mashups have their limits. Within the minds of the people *in the relationship*, these charts ignore an obvious observation: Two people who behave like Sun in Taurus should, when interacting, form a dynamic with Sun in Taurus no matter where or when they were born. But a relative chart between my Sun in 10° Cancer this year and your Sun in 10° Cancer next year actually averages out to a composite Sun in 10° Capricorn six months between. But you and I are both Cancer Suns. How is it that the "behavior" of our relationship suddenly looks like the exact opposite sign? If we come together and form opinions of the relationship within our own minds, it won't. So relative charts form a great view of a relationship for everyone except the people actually in the relationship. Bummer, eh?[45] Don't scrap relative charts just yet, though. We'll definitely need them later.

So there is another tradition in astrology which **uses position midpoints to calculate the composite chart**. This is the **standard composite chart** which we referenced earlier. Forget about where planets actually could be in space. Just average everything. This actually lines up better with actual dynamics between people whose planets occupy their respective frequencies (signs), and lines up better with how the people within a relationship see their own interaction. The idea is that, if midpoints can work, composite charts made up of midpoints should also work as descriptors of what the people do within a relationship. The data basically support this. Whereas the relative chart tells you how the relationship looks to the world, the composite chart tells to you how things happen behind that world-face. The relative chart is the greatly simplified movie shown to everyone else. Composites are the production process known by the crew themselves. One problem you'll discover, however, is that certain programs spit out weird locations for sky angles and the calculated points which use them: All houses (including the Ascendant and Midheaven), the Vertex, and the Part of Fortune (along with any other Arabic parts which use sky angles in their calculation) cease to make sense in this kind of composite since the sky's wraparound behavior defies coherence. It is thus said that you shouldn't try to read the houses in a composite chart because they are meaningless. Indeed, we will not try to read them in this book either...

An Unfortunate Outcome Regarding the ASC, MC, Vertex, Fortune, and Houses

...and yet we surely want to know whether our joint approach to a situation (composite Ascendant), our joint reputation (composite MC), our joint place of comfort (Fortune), and our joint tendency to change (Vertex) mean anything. Building upon the idea that ALL locations on an astrowheel can be thought of as points in frequency space,[46] we can argue that one can obtain meaningful sky angles by averaging their equivalents from the

[45] An analogy we can make is this: Looking at the interaction between two people is like looking at a pair of electrons in an atom's orbitals. To outsiders it's just a probability cloud "giving off" some combination of two states. To the electrons themselves, though, it's a dynamic, space-filling interaction. Those electrons know the real story between each other, but you don't. Similarly, composites show the real story internal to a relationship while relative charts show only the public "cloud"-version.

[46] I explain this in *FSA*.

component charts. The results we get won't be physically real but will be relevant to the parties doing the interacting. Furthermore, the data show such points to be meaningful. Because these averaged versions of the ASC, MC, Vertex, and Fortune are often not the normal ones which you'll get out of your program, you'll either need to calculate them by hand or get them from a midpoint view of yours and the Other's synastry chart. In this book's treatment of composites, I'll use these **averaged versions of ASC, MC, Vertex, and Fortune**, referring to them as **ASC*, MC*, Vertex*, and Fortune*** respectively to distinguish them from what you would normally get from the standard composite chart output. Why does all of this matter, you ask? Because if you're not using these *versions of these four points, this book won't give you any interpretations for the angles they form in a composite. We will only be looking at the *versions because these are the ones whose statistical basis was consistent with that of the rest of the planets: plain averaging. Technically, our version of the composite chart in this book should be called the **nearest midpoint composite chart**, **where all planets and points are the mathematical average of their component versions; sky angles and Arabic parts (like Fortune) are not recalculated given new planet positions; and no outer-midpoints are allowed**. We'll define **outer-midpoints** as **midpoints located in an arc of greater than 180° between the planets that formed them**. These won't happen in the charts we'll be using.

Just as we won't be reading houses, we won't be reading sign placements in a composite chart either. This is because signs denote the broad personality of the planets in them and, again, composites tend to be near silent in the personality department. Barring future research on this topic, it's the dynamics among composite planets which seem to be more meaningful—constituting the interplay among parts which viewers of the relationship are inclined to selectively reference. Angles among composite planets, though subject to much more error than regular or synastry charts, wash out much of that error through the law of large numbers; as long as we have enough charts, errors will tend to cancel towards zero and we'll still be able to come up with meaningful clusters in the spirit of big data. Additionally, the angles in composites really are just average separations between midpoints which are already known to have at least marginal meaning.[47] While the signs and houses assume—perhaps erroneously—that the relationship itself has "personality" or "areas of 'life'" respectively, angles only assume that the relevant frequencies can be averaged by those looking at them. Thus the angles are the realest thing we get from composites. Taking into account the ASC* through Vertex*, though, this still ends up being pretty informative.

How We Should Think About Composites 🛠

Can I confess something? Geery asked Hayden.

Hayden replied to the scientist, Yes sir, what is it?

I'm pretty uncomfortable using composite charts. Although I have gotten a lot of data out of them, the nature of those data are weird.

Well, seeing as how I don't know what you're talking about, Hayden remarked in turn, your telling me this doesn't mean much. But I guess if you need to get this off your chest then—

Hear me out, here. Composite charts are basically the average of yours and another's charts. If regular astrocharts just reflect different frequencies for you playing out patterns on your spacetime compass, if synastry charts reflect frequencies between yours and another person's patterns, then the only thing a synastry chart does is treat the other person as if they were an expressive extension of you. So it makes sense that synastry should work if regular charts work; my Mars to your Moon is just as logical as my Mars to my own Moon if we believe that each person has such a meaningful "Moon" and "Mars" in the first

[47] This is also explained in *FSA*.

place; Here I simply simulate your planets using empathy and treat them as differently expressed versions of my own. But composites are different. From what I gather, they do work but in a pretty secondary way—like icing to a cake, buttons to a shirt, a paint job to a car. Icing, buttons, and paint all do certain things, but as accents to cakes, shirts, and cars they seem to change their function.

Okay, whatever. Hayden turned back towards the sea ahead, realizing that his passenger was simply preparing to theorize to himself out loud.

Geery continued, Really I think composite charts—as a diagram full of averages (average Sun, average Moon, average of yours and my Hera)—might be better explained as the chart reflecting where two people are most in tune with each other.

Hayden ignored Geery.

I mean,

- consider something basic like my Ascendant and your Ascendant. Suppose my ASC is 24.9 Aquarius. Call this The Beatles' "Come Together" just for argument's sake. Suppose your ASC is 21 Pisces. Call this Jimi Hendrix's "Foxey Lady." [48] Since these are Ascendants, these songs would be like our respective theme songs when we arrive on the scene.
- You might ask where these songs are similar. They're probably similar in a lot of ways, but let's just say they both talk about people wanting to get together with other people.
- Now I happen to know that the angle between these degrees is 26.1°. This is closest to a II-opposition. II-oppositions actually *are* about sharing company as identities.
- Consider that we're actually sharing company and we're approaching something new. The *II-opposition* corresponds to a situation in which our approaches line up really well, for better or worse, *just because we are together*.
- Here's the important part: Given that our approaches line up, what does our "average" approach together probably look like in the eyes of other people?

Hayden, seeing that Geery was bound to keep talking, answered tersely. I don't know.

- It looks like the midpoint, man! Come on, this is easy! Anyway, the midpoint is about 7.95 Pisces. Sarah Jarosz, "The Book of Right On:" ambiently witty in $\text{Pisces}_{\text{Gemini}}$. Forget about our individual themes. This is the song that plays when we're <u>together</u> approaching a new situation <u>as we see our own duo</u>. 7.95 Pisces is where our composite Sun would be.

Okay.

- Now suppose we both feel like steering people. My Mars is 21.8 Leo: Camp Lo "Luchini:" charismatic bragging. Your Mars is 8.6 Pisces: still "The Book of Right On." These songs play when we're manipulating other people separately. Together, though, our Mars-Mars angle of separation is 163.1°: an undecile. So the way we manipulate people (or each other) gets us

---

[48] If you're familiar with the idea of duodecanates (discussed in *FSA*), 24.9 Aquarius is the Scorpio subsection of Aquarius: Aqu_{Sco}. This is the psychological/death/sex-focused (Sco) section of the humanitarian approach to things (Aqu). So Geery thought "Come Together" was appropriate. 21 Pisces is the Pis_{Sco} duodecanate. This is an ambient vibe (Pis) with a psychological/death/sex-related emphasis. "Foxey Lady" might work for this.

talked about even if we're not actually on the same page. The midpoint is 0.2 Gemini: Janelle Monae & Prince: "Givin' 'Em What They Love:" two-sided, shoot-from-the-hip mind speaking. Our composite Mars would be here at 0.2 Gemini.

Oookay.

- So basically
  - when we're connected in how we approach things, our composite Ascendant lights up. In my example this happens when we're together: a II-opposition.
  - When we're connected in how we manipulate people or ideas our composite Mars lights up, this happens when we're getting our names on the grapevine: an undecile.
- What if we're connected both in how we approach AND how we manipulate? Better yet, what if we're connected in our "resistance to assault?" (This is the average of Your ASC to my Mars and my ASC to your Mars: the regular—self chart—version of Mars-ASC.[49]). I think that under these circumstances (and MAINLY under these circumstances) our duo's composite Mars-ASC would light up. The angle is 82.25°: a II-decile, and would show mainly in the career reputation we build together. The midpoint is around 19 Aries, suggesting that such a JOINT career would be rooted in doing what we want in the sex/death/psychology sense: $\text{Aries}_{\text{Scorpio}}$. And, given all the prideful, togetherness-based locations we used to calculate this point, an appropriate song might be something like Sheila E, "A Love Bizarre" or—for a slightly more subdued Scorpionic spontaneity, Poe's "Hey Pretty."
- In this way, the planets in a composite chart only do anything IF we're on the same page regarding that planet. That is, the synastry angle between [my Ascendant and your Ascendant] AND [my Mars and your Mars] are both activated. It's near useless to average planets that aren't being paid attention to. And it's near useless to consider a duo when we haven't decided to work together in the first place. Whatever the composite planet is, the synastric angle between the two planets it comprises needs to be ON.
- Since "nearest midpoint" composite planets are indeed midpoints, they show how our blurred combination of planets looks to us viewing our own duo, not us viewing ourselves individually. Maybe you can see how this isn't very useful on its own since that blurred planet is just a picture and doesn't actively express itself. *We're* the ones doing the expressing.
- But now the angles between composite planets are another story. They still don't express, but they do set up an actual dynamic for us to see outside viewers as looking at. If I stand here and say, "The Book of Right On," you say, "Alright. It's just a song." But if I ask you to *process* the connection *between* "The Book of Right On" Ascendant and "Givin' 'Em What They Love" Mars, you as a viewer will think of a resistance to assault in something like the "Hey Pretty" family of attitude, in the realm of our duo's "career."

Hayden was quiet.

Do you get it?

---

[49] As shown in *table 16-5*.

Hm, so composite charts are abstract comparisons of two real families of styles. Like comparing Math to Biology. It shows what the chart for Biomathematics would look like if you forced Biology and Math to line up everywhere.

Uh, yeah. Geery was a bit embarrassed at how his long explanation had been so simply reduced. Except that—

Biomathematics is only as real as Biology and Math are separately, and only as real as these subjects' ability to work together.

Yeah, I guess.

Okay, I get it. I actually *was* listening, you know. Hayden assured Geery. But my question is, how does a relationship have a "career?" In fact, how does a relationship even "resist assault?"

In the same way people do, but instead of talking about a relationship's behavior as if it were a person, we have to talk about it as if it had the *effects* of human things. A career is the area of activity that people formally recognize you as occupying. It's just a reputation for leaning against. A duo's "career" is its socially structured role. It's resistance to assault is its ability to project the same set of impressions under a challenge.

Oh, okay.

Hayden paused for a while.

You seem to have worked all of this out already, so where was the confusion?

My confusion lies in the idea that, even though we might be able to explain how to go from regular chart meanings to composite chart meanings, it's not nearly as easy to go the other way. That is, even if Ascendant-Mars in the composite shows the *relationship's* resistance to assault, you weirdly find that the people who make up that relationship typically aren't using their Ascendant or their Mars to protect it. Let me ask you something which will make this clear. Quick, off the top of your head, how do you normally defend a relationship from assault?

By agreeing on what the relationship is about and communicating with the other person.

...

Oh.

Suddenly Hayden realized (maybe) what Geery was trying to say.

In other words, an Ascendant-Mars feature of the relationship arises from 2nd house and Venus-style decisions of the people in the relationship?

Hayden donned a sideways pucker in acknowledgement that this issue was indeed a curious one. Was it true that planets in the composite didn't necessarily affect the same planets of people in the composite, but component people's planets did affect their composite planets the other way around? Curious indeed.

So I throw something into a room. A person sitting inside the room sees what I actually threw, but that person throws the same thing back to me outside of the room and I end up with something *different*? Hayden puzzled.

Exactly. If the room represents a relationship. What I'm saying is that real individual traits lead to composite behaviors which are similar to the individual versions, but composite "traits" of the relationship consistently reinforce individual actions which belong to a *different* set of traits. You'll see it when I show you the data. Most notably, for example, composite pairs involving the Sun tend to describe Moon behavior in the individuals. Composite Venuses are noticeably colder than usual and correspond to Mercury behavior among the actors. It's all very weird. I once thought you could read composites like regular charts and just make regular conclusions. Until I did the statistics and learned otherwise. You *might* be able to read relationships as if they were people. But if you do so, you'll need to read the people within those relationships as if they were...I don't know...organ systems within those people? If we treat relationships as people we can't treat the people in them as people. The setup is one that mathematicians would call "non-commutative"—meaning that the planets and their angles in a composite chart can be read one way going from individual to duo but not in the same way when going in reverse. I suppose this is how actual groups in society work (individual influence to collective), but still...I find the whole thing intellectually dissatisfying in general.

So we'll need a whole new family of interpretations especially designed for composite charts as they affect individuals. In many places, these won't look anything like their regular chart versions. And because they are rooted in a kind of second-level behavioral observation, you'll find out very quickly that the interpretations are considerably more complicated than the ones we've run into so far. The trade-off is that they are often richer and—if you can secure your fellow duo member's cooperation—much more useful for people interested in shaping relationships as they see fit. ⚒

Preliminary Comments

Prior planets are marked with a <

⚒ Throughout this chapter you'll see "<" used to indicate those characteristics which naturally come before each member of the pair in question. In line with the dialogue between Geery and Hayden above, the data revealed that composite planets tended to be propped up by an interaction between the duo members' "planets" before them, basically as a kind of cause for which the composite pair ends up being an effect. This is tricky business because, although the actual composite pair really does seem to reflect the extent to which the exact same planets are on the same page on the individual level, it is the planets before these which the duo members use to keep such alignment going. That is, if one's Point of Internal Monologue [discussed in *FSA*] comes before the Moon and the Moon comes before the Sun, then a duo's composite [Sun-Moon] pair *does* reflect the duo member's cohesion between their respective Suns and Moons, BUT it is their expression of their natural internal monologue alongside their Moon feelings about things which keep the Sun-Moon quality of the duo on display.

Our individual [Sun-Sun], [Moon-Moon]→

Our composite [Sun-Moon]→

Our individual [Moon-Monologue] half-pairs→

Our individual [Sun-Sun], [Moon-Moon]...

...in a cycle, but it is the *individuals'* [Moon-Monologue] dynamic which stands out the most when we look at the *relationship's* [Sun-Moon] composite. It is the *individuals'* [Venus-Jupiter] dynamic which stands out the most when we look at the *relationship's* [Mars-Saturn] composite. And so it goes for almost all of the composite pairs to follow: the planets before the ones being looked at in the composite are the ones which are most affected in the individuals making up that composite angle. ⚒

Blind interpretations are marked with 👓

As with the planets in the houses section in Chapter 18, you'll sometimes see the glasses to indicate my use of the "blind method"—a description straight from my notes before I knew which pair I was looking at. When it comes to testing astrology, these descriptions are some of the best you can get at the time of this writing since they reveal how patterns of angles really do exist even if you put all astrological assumptions aside and just look at tables full of name groupings and angle numbers. I show how this is done via a walkthrough for [Pluto-Selene], one of the many pairs whose planets were not known as I wrote the walkthrough.[50]

On references to the "duo"

- Throughout this chapter I will refer to the relationship between two parties involved in a composite chart as the "duo," the "exchange," "partnership," or simply the "relationship."
- The *parties that make up the duo* will be called "*parties*," "*duo members*," or "*partners*."
- When I say "one duo member does [something] towards the other," I automatically mean at least one duo member. That is, most interpretations can work both ways at the same time unless otherwise noted. If I tell you that [one duo member screws the other over], it automatically means that 1) one *could* screw the other OR 2) both could screw each other at the same time.

[50] As for those descriptions without the glasses, it just hadn't occurred to me to do the "blind method" beforehand at that stage in the writing of this book. It wasn't that these pairs don't lend themselves to statistics, just that I hadn't adopted the more rigorously unbiased method yet.

Setup for a basic composite chart: Using StarFisher to find the ASC*, MC*, Vertex*, and Fortune*

Because this book's approach to composites assumes every planet and point in a combined chart will be a nearest midpoint average of the component charts, you may need to calculate four of the main points yourself. This section walks you through how to do this with the software program I used to write this book, StarFisher.

You can skip this section, but I wouldn't recommend it. If you don't use *versions of the ASC through Vx, you won't be able to use any of their composite interpretations in this chapter. Instead, the non-*versions for these which you get out of your program are as good as random.

If you don't already have StarFisher, refer to the quick start page right before Chapter 16 for instructions on how to get it along with the files associated with it. Once you have the program, open it. You should begin at the chart loading screen:

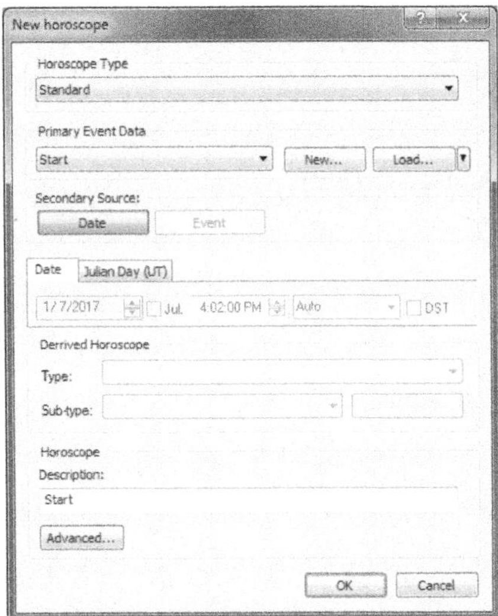

1. Click Load to select the first chart you want to use.
2. Choose your first chart. (In the example below, I've selected Person A. Note also that your starting folder may be different from mine. Here its "Strangers," but yours may be "Events" or something similar.)

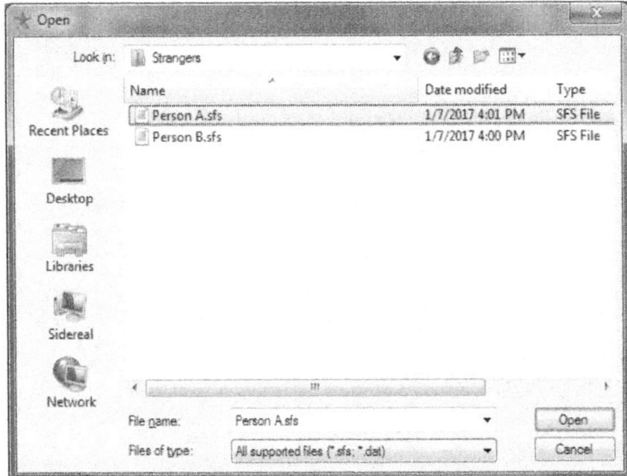

3. From the Horoscope Type Menu, select Comparison (Standard / Standard). This is a synastry chart and not a composite, but we'll need some details from the synastry chart in order for the composite to give us meaningful information.

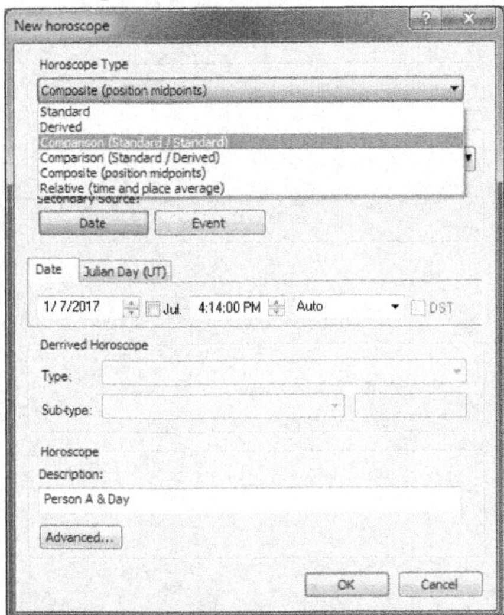

4. Under the Secondary Source Menu, choose Event. The menu below this will change.

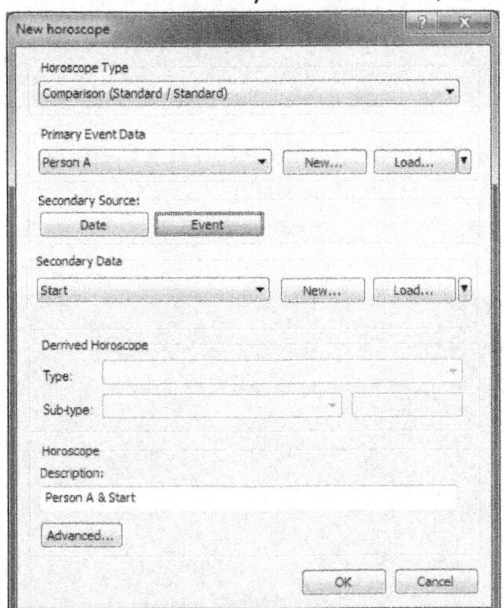

5. Under Secondary Data, click Load to load your second chart. I'll be loading Person B.

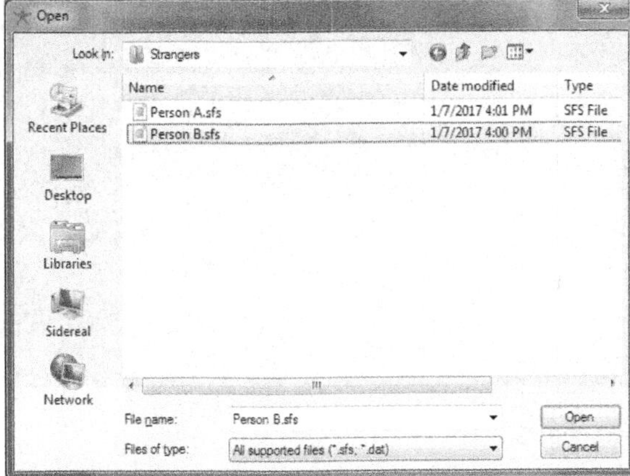

6. Click OK.

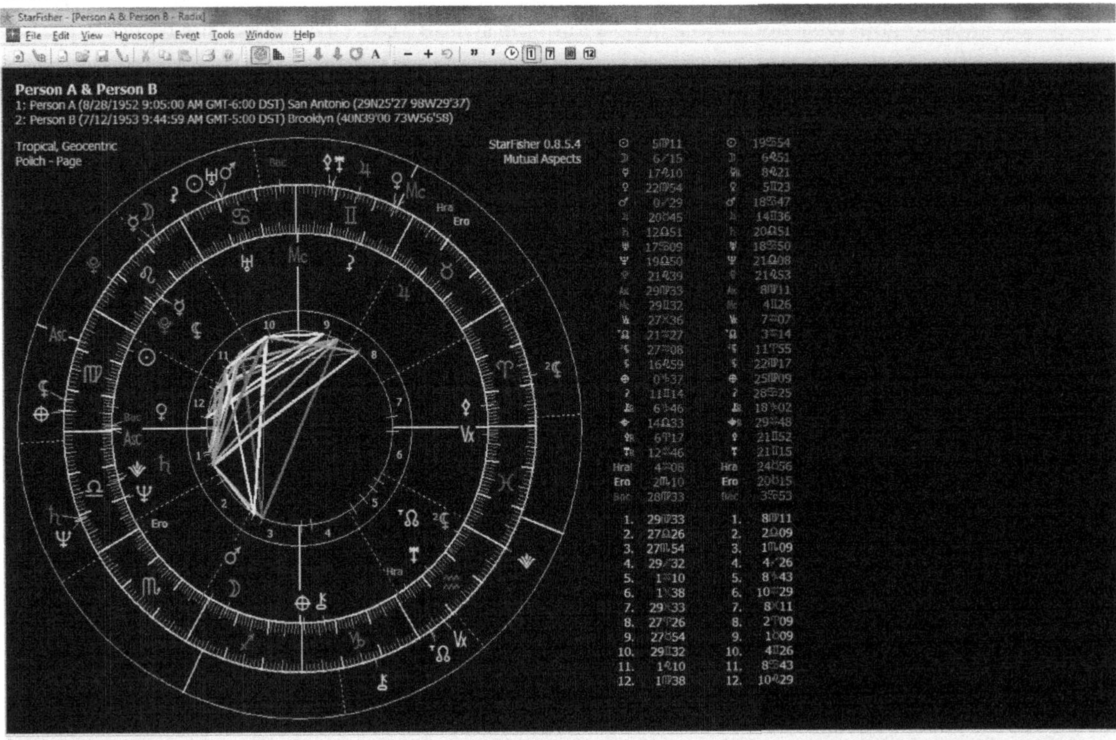

7. You'll start off on chart wheel (radix) view, but we don't want this. Instead use the File menu to choose View>Midpoints.

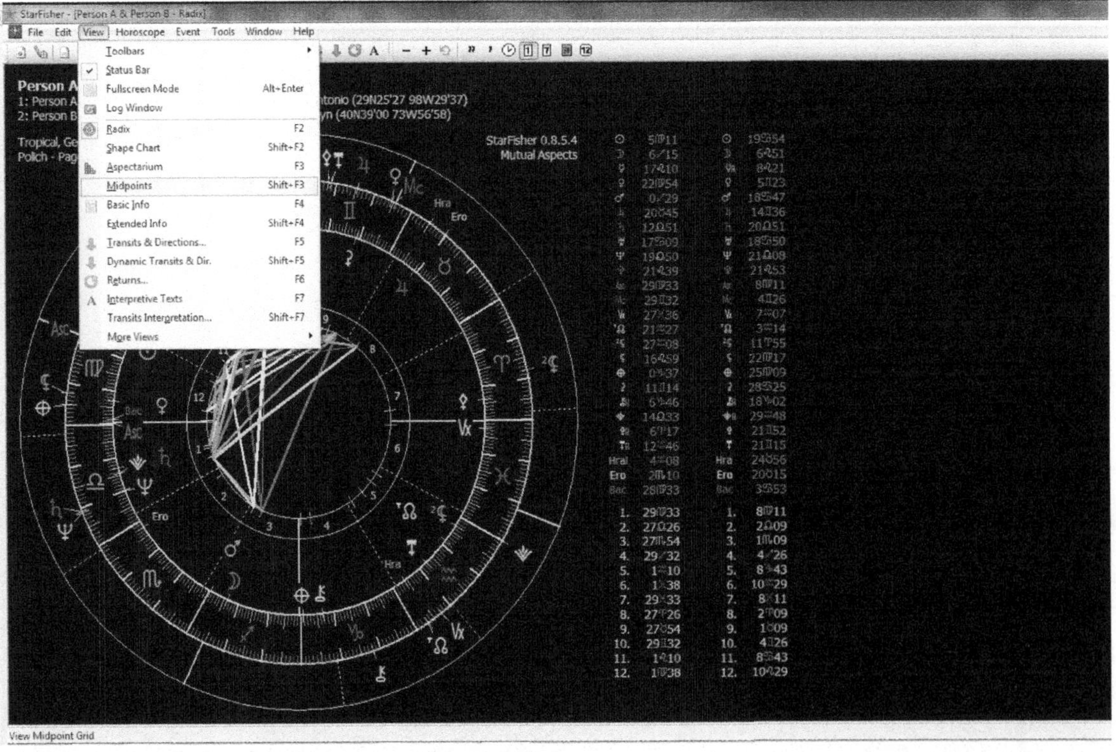

You'll see a list of all midpoints between the two charts.

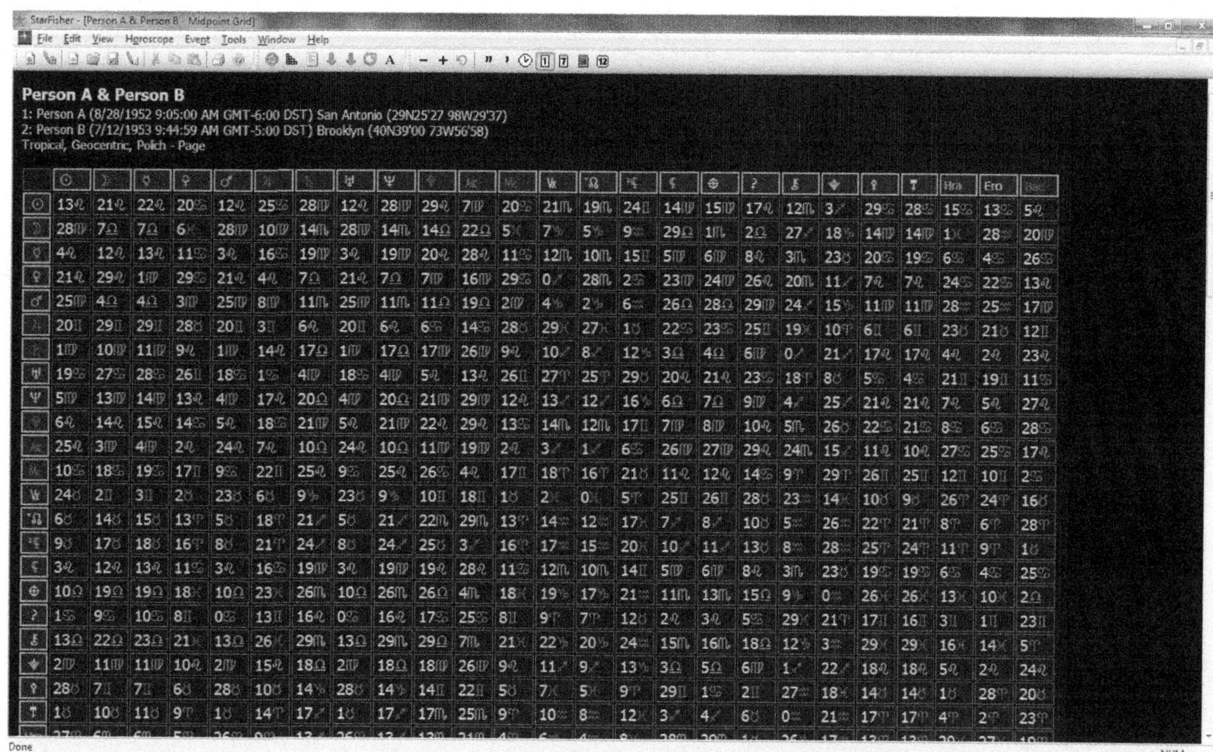

This midpoint list is alright, but not nearly detailed enough for the narrow angles we'll be using.

8. Using the File menu, go to Tools>Settings...

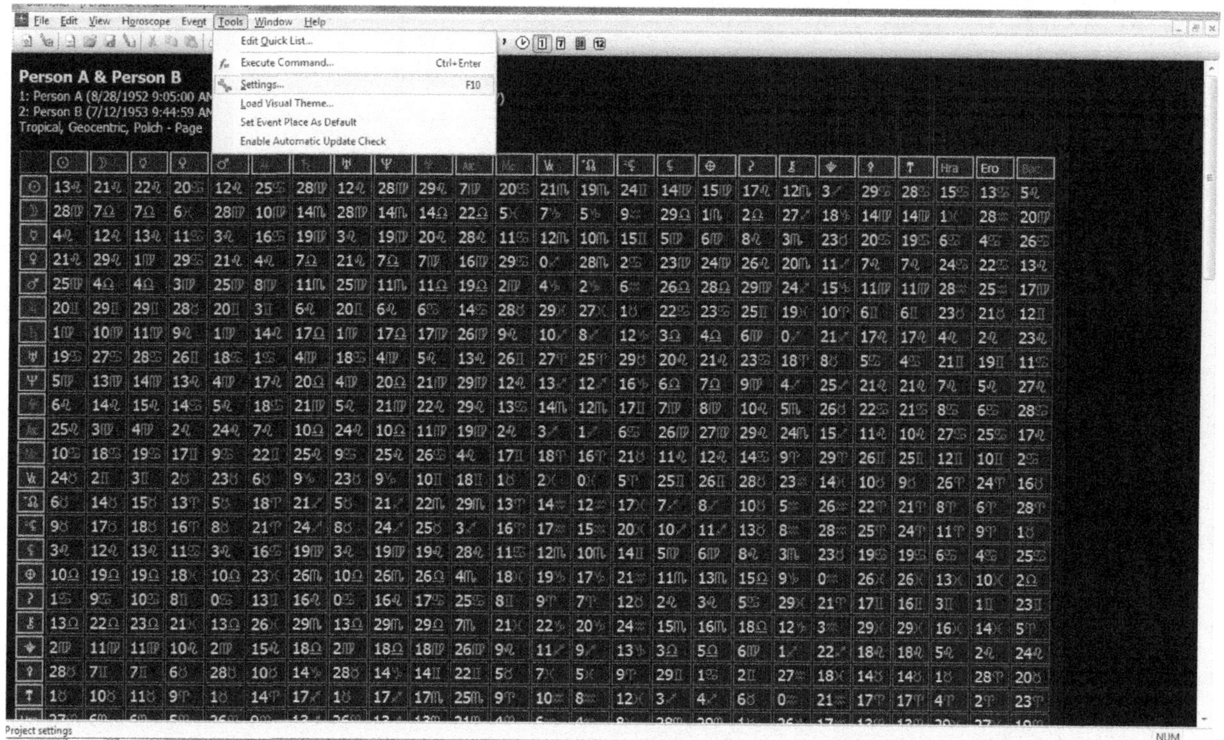

9. In the left-hand window, choose Display>Aspectarium.

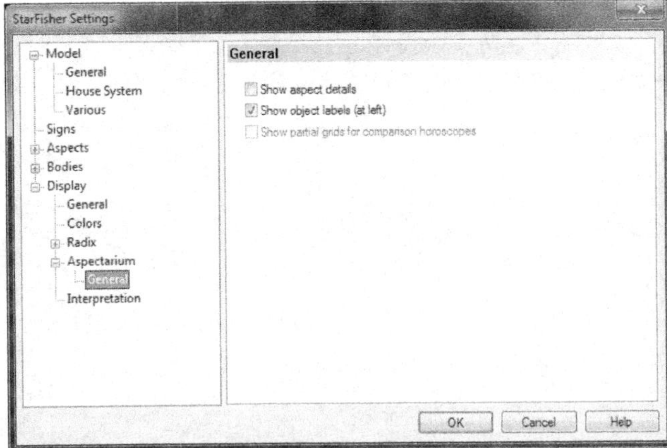

10. Check "Show aspect details" and click OK.

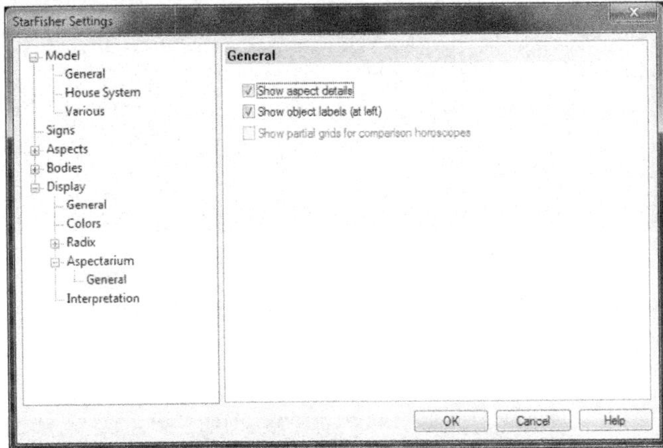

What we see now is much better. Much more detailed. This table contains the midpoints for all 625 combinations between your two charts' planets. The locations along the diagonal ([Sun-Sun], [Moon-Moon], etc.) will end up being the locations of the corresponding planets and points in the nearest midpoint composite chart.

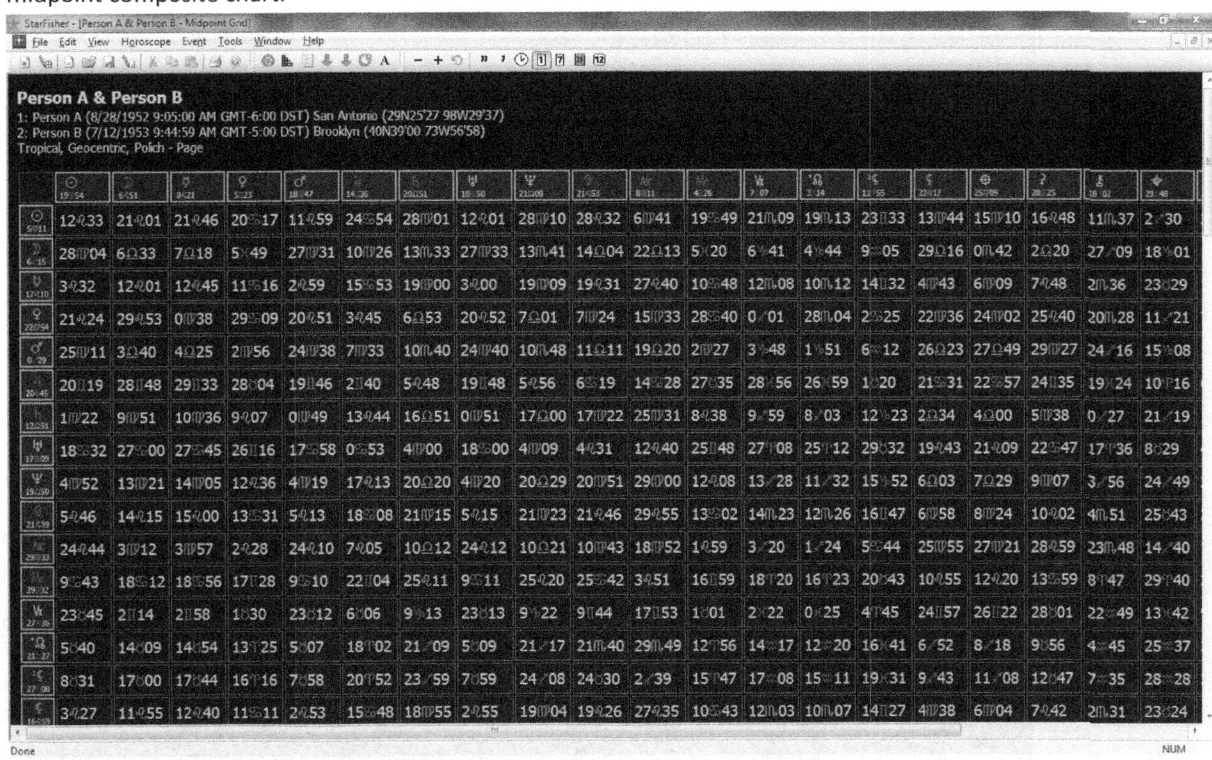

11. Write down the midpoints for [ASC-ASC], [MC-MC], [Vx-Vx], and [⊕-⊕] (Fortune-Fortune). In the example mine will be 18♍52, 16♊59, 2♓22, and 12♏53 respectively.
12. Using the icon bar beneath the File menu, choose Edit Horoscope (the pencil with the target next to it).

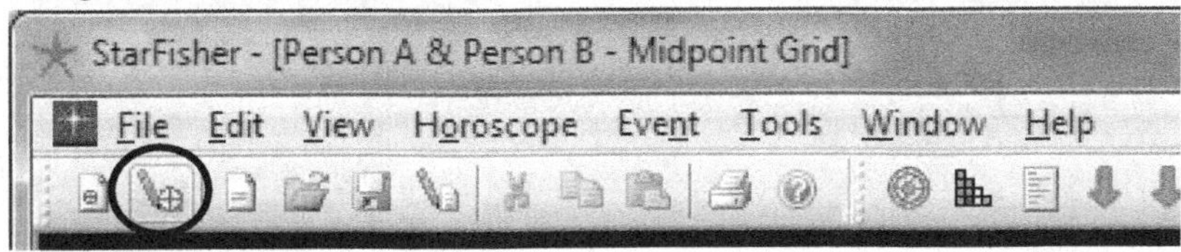

13. From the Horoscope Type Menu, select Composite (position midpoints).

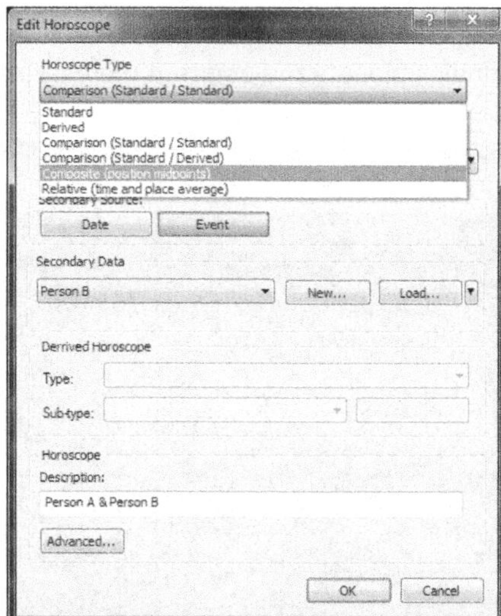

14. Click OK. You'll see something like the table below.

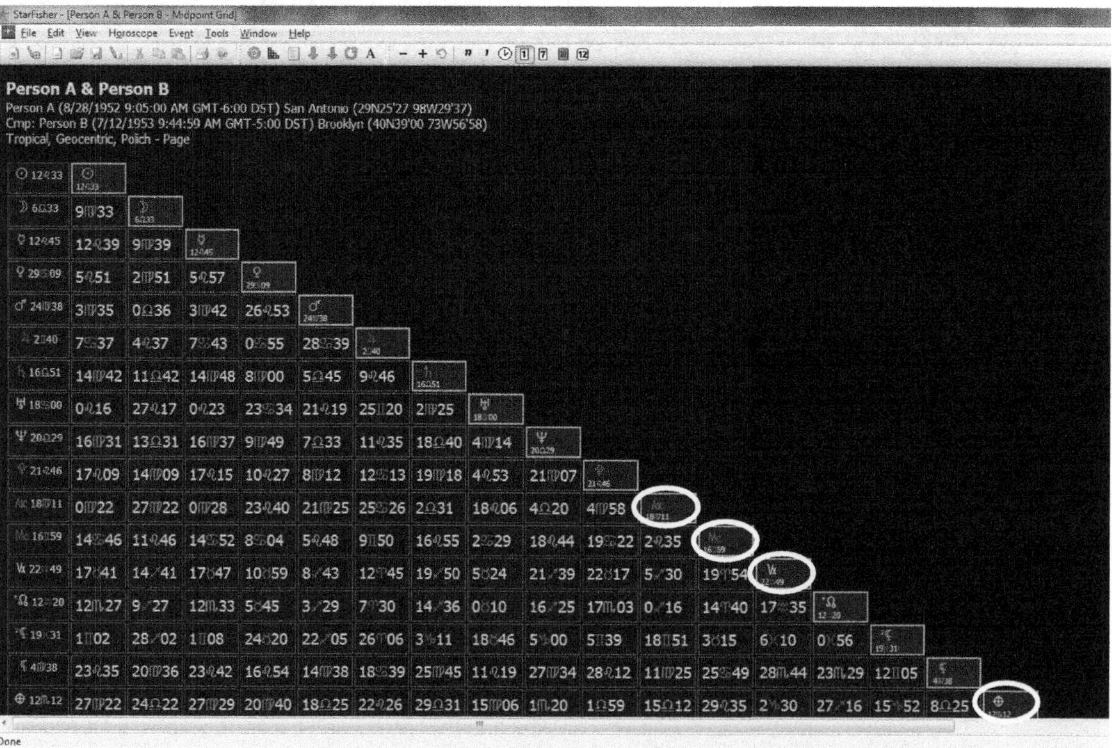

Note where the program puts the ASC, MC, Vx, and Fortune. Sometimes these will be the same as what you wrote down, sometimes not. We'll need to fix that.

15. Using the File menu, go to Tools>Settings...

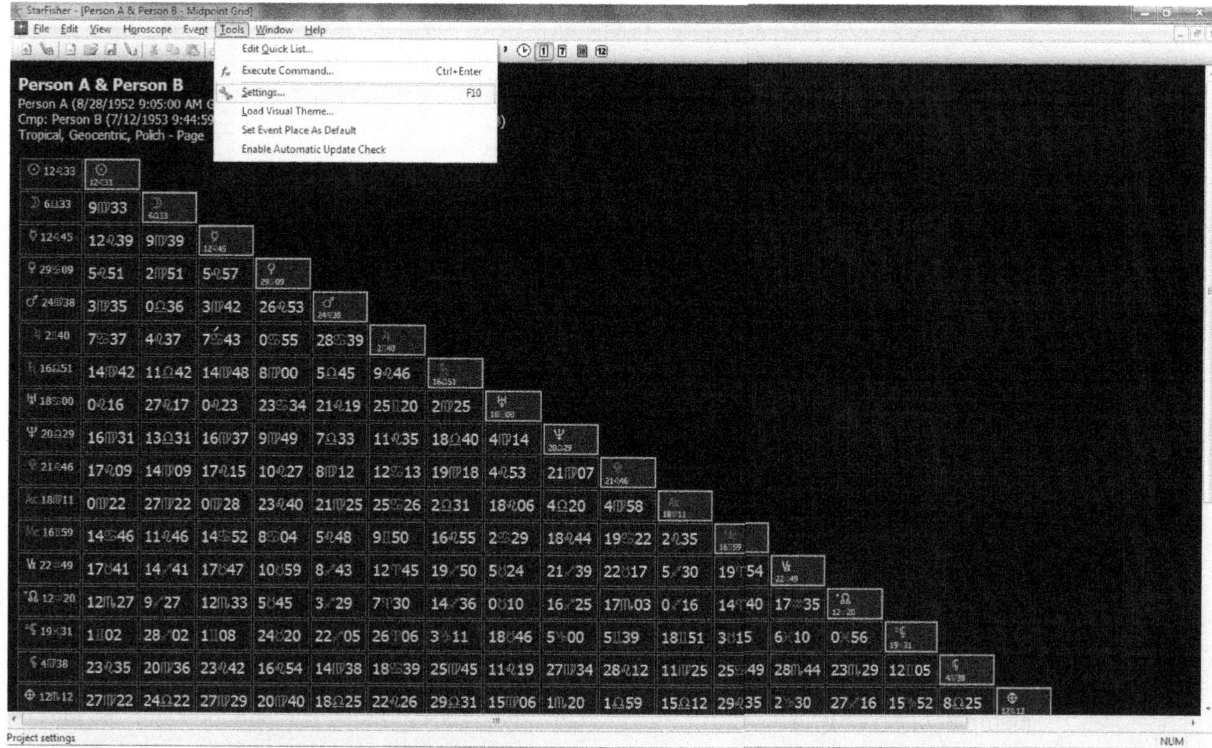

16. On the left-hand menu, choose Bodies>Definitions.

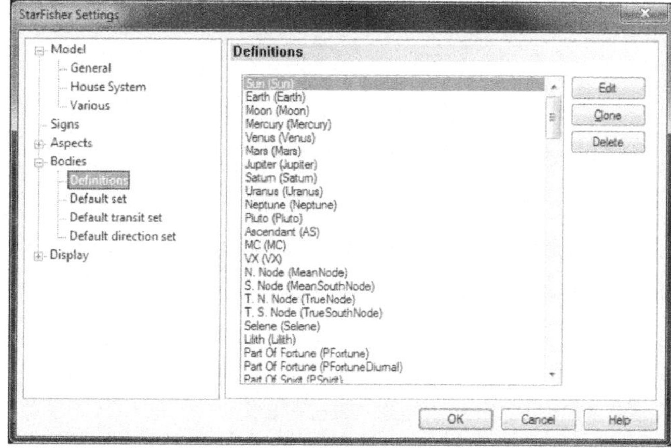

17. Select Selene (Selene).

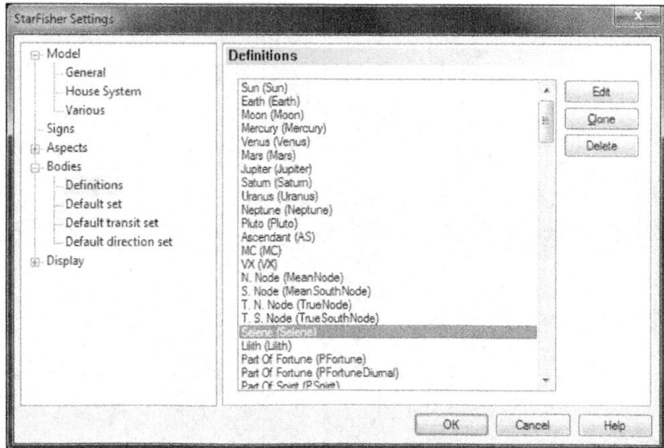

18. Click Clone. We'll be using Selene's existing details to create a brand new "star."
19. You'll get a screen asking you to enter a name that StarFisher's code will use to work with your new star. So you'll enter a name that starts with the abbreviation for the thing you're inputting and ends with the people whose charts this thing goes with. There are no major rules for this, but to avoid problems with StarFisher later **you should definitely use only capital or lowercase letters or underscores ("_"). Don't use numbers or spaces. And start your chosen identifier with a letter** (for somewhat technical reasons I won't get into here). Since we're starting with the Ascendant for a composite chart, we should have our identifier begin with "ASCcmp". I prefer to label things using [thing_personA_personB], so my label will read ASCcmp_A_B as shown below. If you're doing a composite Ascendant for Mike and Gale, your label might be ASCcmp_Mike_Gale.

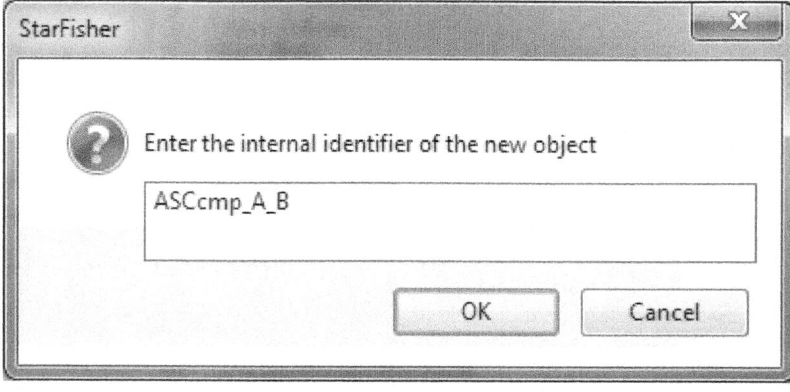

20. Click OK.

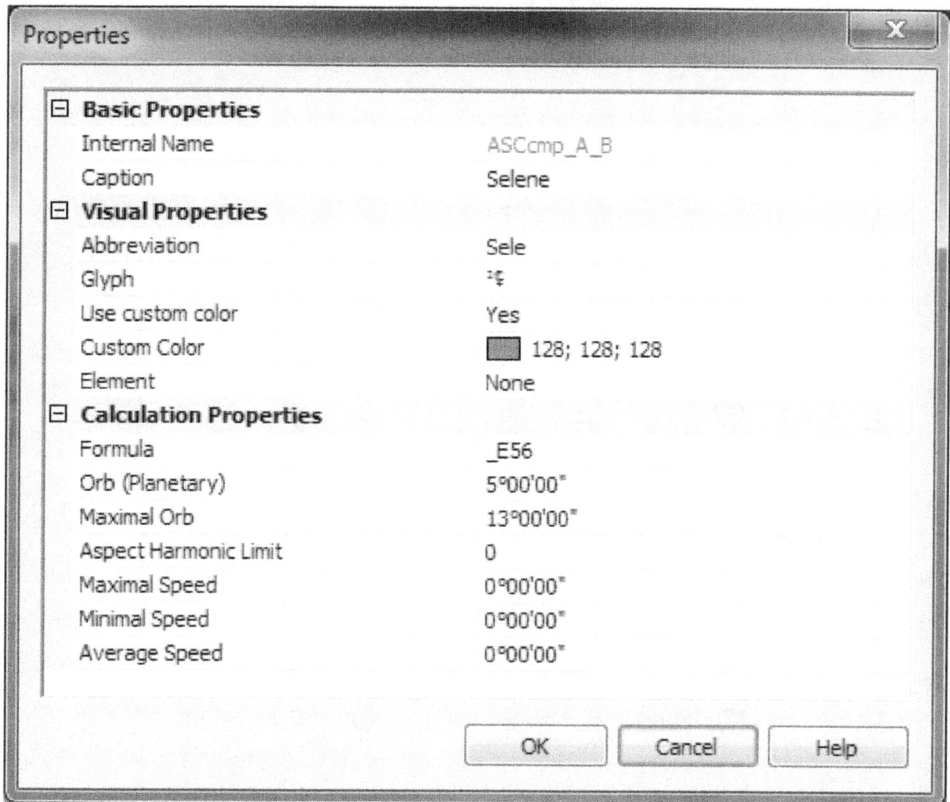

21. You'll get a new screen which mostly has Selene's details. Let's change some things.
    a. Change the Caption to reflect a nice description of the point you're inputting. My example will read "Composite ASC for A and B".
    b. Change the Abbreviation to something VERY SHORT. Use letters only. Mine will be "ASC*"
    c. Click on the text area for entering the Glyph. A "..." button appears.
    d. Click on the "..." button to bring up a screen for choosing which symbol will come up in your charts and tables for this new point you're entering.

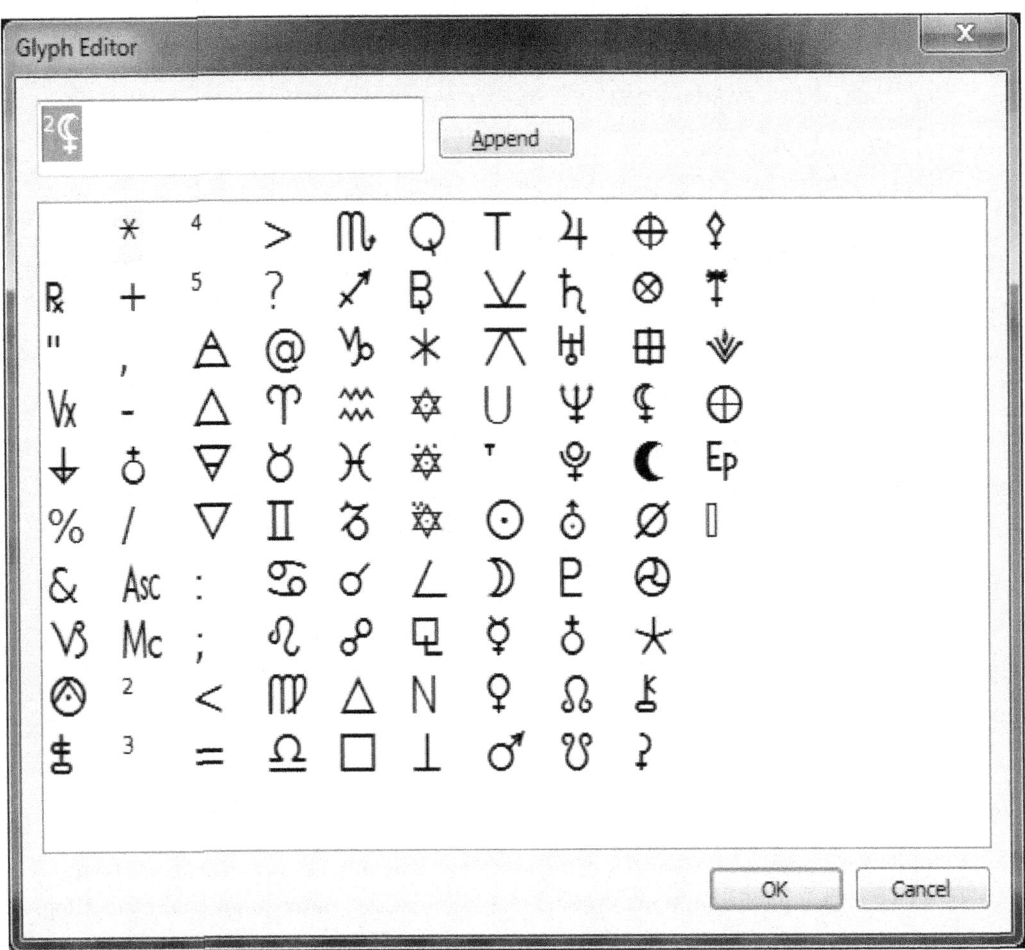

normally delete whatever's in the box unless there's a good replacement in the area below. You can leave this blank and click OK if you want, but if you do, be sure the abbreviation you chose in step 21-b is very short because that's what will show up instead. Fortunately, the ASC, MC, Vx, and Fortune all have existing characters, so I'll just choose the one that works and put a * after it. The result for the Ascendant is Asc* as shown below.

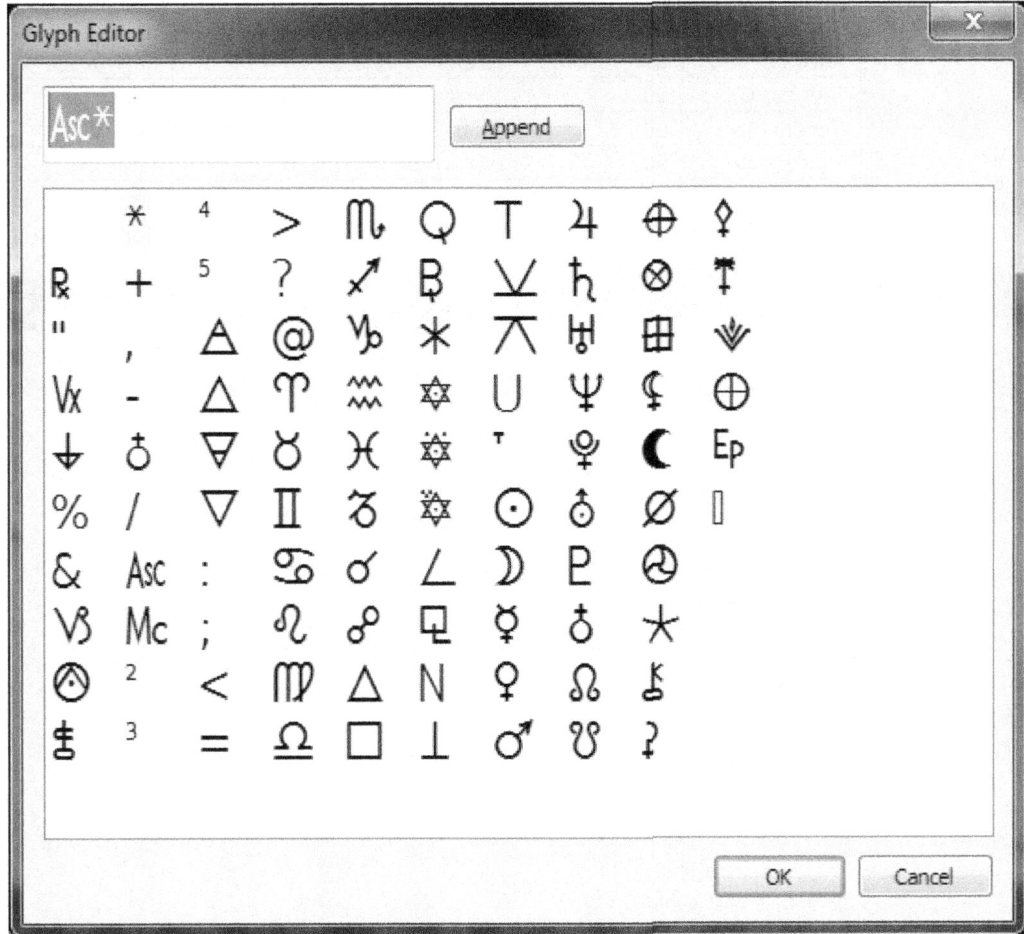

Click OK.

e. **Optional.** Choose a color if you want. So that I can remind myself of which signs, houses, and angles match with what frequencies,
   - I like red for fire and 1, 5, 9, 13... -related things—including the Ascendant (1st house)
   - Earth and 2, 6, 10, 14... -related things are goldish—including the MC (10th house)
   - Air and 3, 7, 11, 15... - related things are green
   - Water and 4, 8, 12, 16... -related things are blue
   - 1-4 related things are darker. 5-8 related things are average color. 9-12 related things are lighter. And then we wrap around. 13-16 related things are darker, 17-20 things are average, 21-24 related things are lighter, etc.
   - Fake points and generic asteroids are various shades of gray
   - Asteroids and points with a strong fire, earth, air, or water character get a color that fits them

   This whole color system is optional, but if you plan to put in a lot of custom points, you may want to follow it for consistency.
   - Following the system above, my color for the ASC* should be dark red or maroon (the same color as a conjunct or Aries if you downloaded my StarFisher files).

f. And now for the hard part: Change the formula to reflect what you wrote. You do this by taking the first number in your `#sign#` and adding it to the starting degree of the sign. The amounts to add are below.

Sign	Add	Sign	Add	Sign	Add
Aries ♈	0	Leo ♌	120	Sagittarius ♐	240
Taurus ♉	30	Virgo ♍	150	Capricorn ♑	270
Gemini ♊	60	Libra ♎	180	Aquarius ♒	300
Cancer ♋	90	Scorpio ♏	210	Pisces ♓	330

So if your point was at 18♍52 like mine was, you'd take 18 + 150 (for Virgo) to get 168. Type this number into the formula to replace whatever is there.

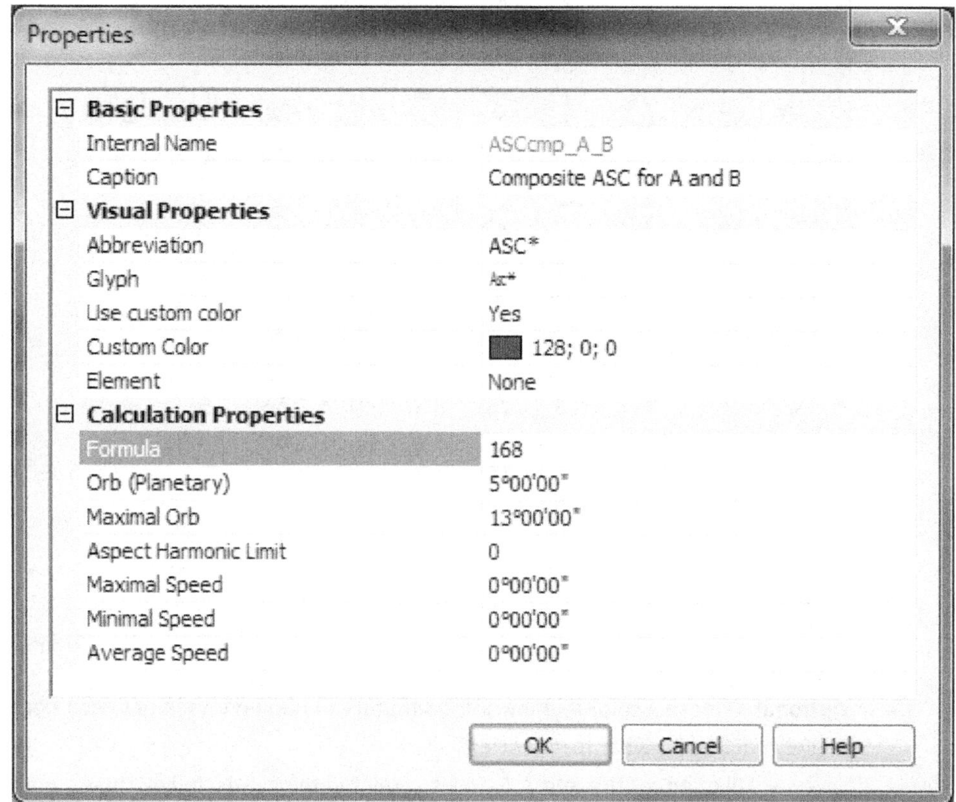

g. Click OK. Since my actual point was 18♍**52**, what I really wanted was 168 + 52/60, but the program doesn't take this kind of input. VERY UNFORTUNATELY, you may have to look around for another body which already has the rest of the degree that you need. By clicking OK now, you save what you've done just in case you need to exit the settings and find another star for finishing your formula.

h. You'll now be back in the StarFisher Settings screen. Click OK to get out of it.

i. We're now back on the aspect table screen. The hard part is getting StarFisher to recognize fractions of a degree for the point we're working on. The thing I usually do is look for some other planet or star whose degree comes close and use it. For example, looking on the screen I see that Saturn is at 16♎51. The "51" is very close to the *52* I need, so I'll need to peel this 51 off of Saturn and put it on my ASC*.

Saturn's whole-degree location is Libra +16. This gives 196. I peel off the *51* by taking Saturn – 196.0, leaving only the fractional part. I then add this to 168. This gives me `Saturn - 28`. This is the closest **`formula`** I'll get to my actual ASC*. <u>Yours, of course, will differ</u>. Use the blanks below to work this out:

Step	Example	Your value
i.1 What angle are you trying to obtain?	18♍52	
i.2 What's the whole part?	18	
i.3 What's the sign?	♍ (Virgo)	
i.4 What's the fractional part?	52	
i.5 Using the table in step f, how much should you add for the sign you got in step i.3?	150	
i.6 Add i.2 + i.5	168 (18 + 150)	
i.7 In the screen that has the table with all of the planets and their angles, look for another body whose fractional part comes close to your answer for i.4. What body is it and what's its location?	Saturn 16♎51	
i.8 Using the table in step f, how much should you add for the sign you got in step i.7?	180 (for Libra)	
i.9 Add i.8 to the whole part from i.7	196 (180 + 16)	
i.10 Take *the body from i.7* – i.9 + i.6	*Saturn* – 196 + 168	
i.11 Simplify. This is your formula.	Saturn – 28	

Once you have found the body whose fraction you want to peel, and after you have figured out your `formula`, go back into File menu>Tools>Settings...>Bodies>Definitions. Scroll all the way down to the bottom (your most recent addition) and click Edit. This will bring you back to the screen for editing your new point.

j. **Type the formula you came up with, but hear this: To avoid headaches, you'll need to use existing formula versions of star-names if you want to refer to them, those names must be in quotes and you <u>must</u> put spaces in between your formula pieces.** In the example for the Ascendant, I'll be typing `"Saturn" - 28` as shown below. That's

The program won't take it if I try something else. Click OK. Then click Edit again to make sure your formula stayed there. If not, you've typed something StarFisher didn't understand.

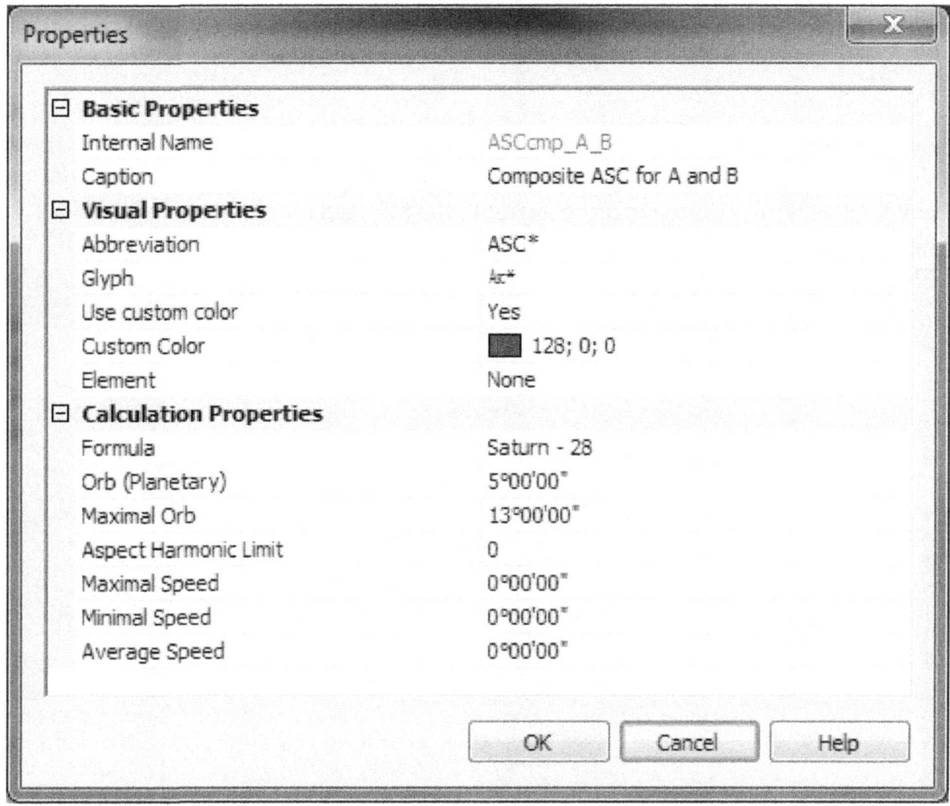

k. Once you're satisfied with your formula, click OK then click OK again to exit the settings.

22. Now we need to tell StarFisher to show our new point. From the icon bar, choose Edit Horoscope.

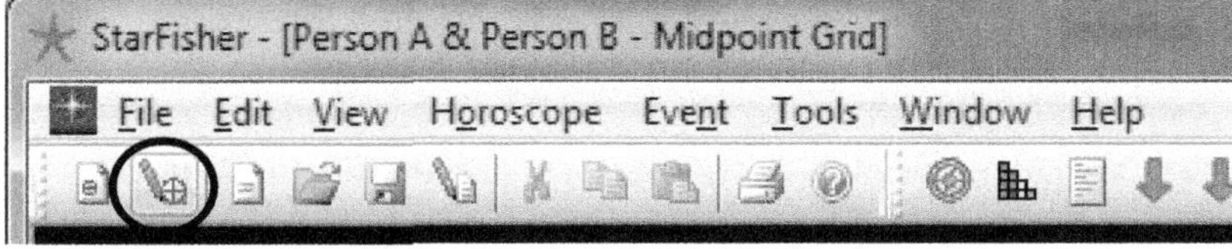

23. Click Advanced... at the bottom of the window that pops up.

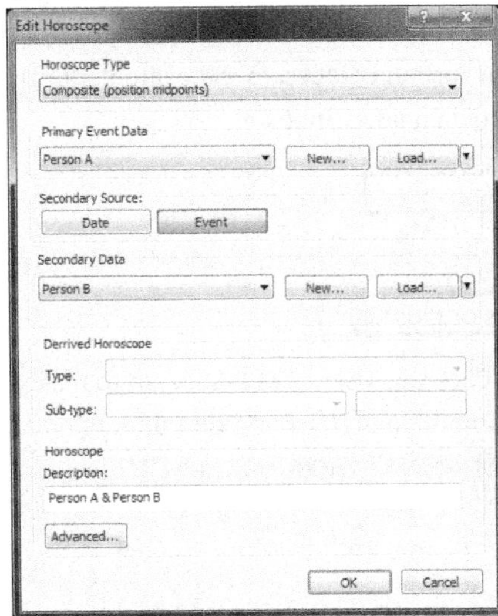

24. Under the Bodies menu, scroll all the way down to the bottom of Available items and select your new point. Click on the < button to move it over to the Selected items side. You should see it at the bottom of the Selected items box.

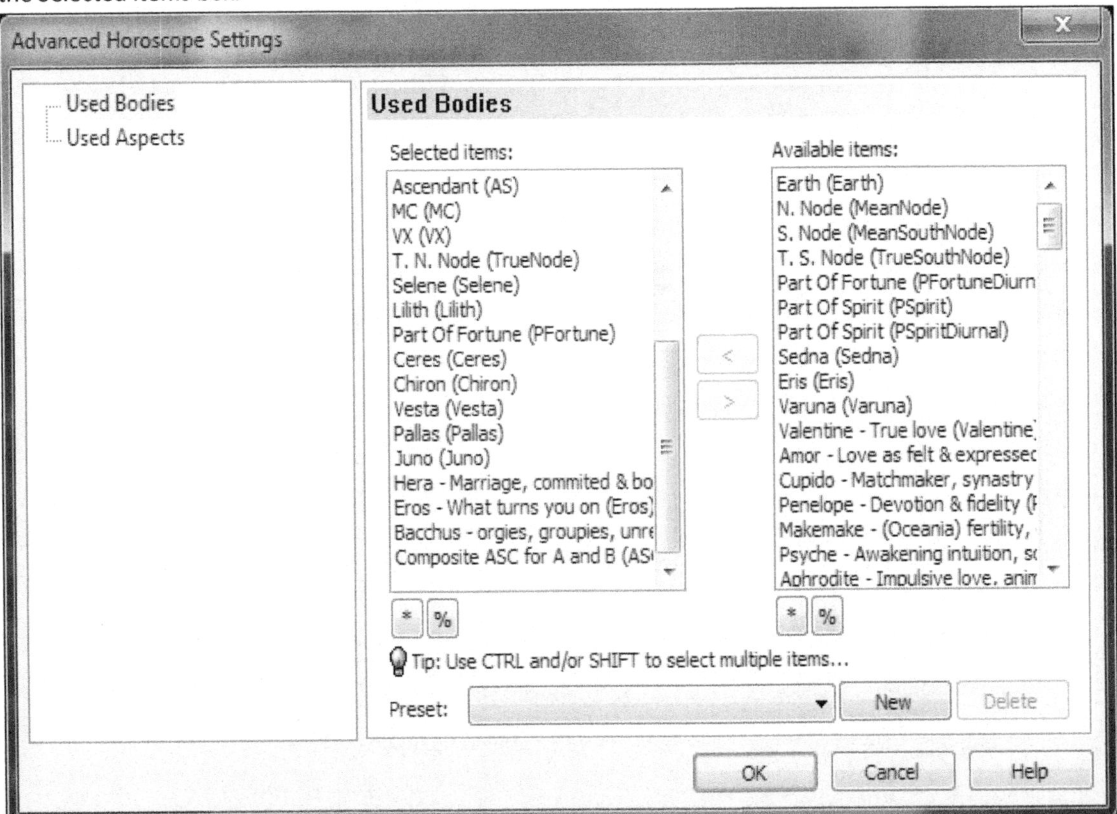

25. Click OK.
26. Click OK again to exit the Edit Horoscope menu.

27. Scroll down to see your new point displayed.

17♈01	14♊47	11♋47	14♊53	8♊05	5♋49
Hra 29♓32	6♊02	3♑03	6♊09	29♉21	27♊05
Ero 11♌12	11♌52	8♍53	11♌59	5♌11	2♍55
Bac 16♌13	14♌23	11♍23	14♌29	7♌41	5♍25
Asc* 18♍51	0♍42	27♍42	0♍48	24♌00	21♍4

Done

Right on! There it is! Our very own point in the sky with no actual astronomy behind it whatsoever.

28. Now we only have to repeat steps 15 through 28 three...more...times to put in the MC*, VX*, and Fortune*. Grrr. Don't do this yet. Keep reading. We'll add the other points in step 30.

WARNING. When you do things like this and decide to exit, StarFisher will ask you if you want to save the new default settings SAY YES! Otherwise you'll have to do it all over again. Well help ourselves out with this though.

29. Go to File>Save Settings As Default.... Click OK when the alert box pops up telling you the settings were saved.
30. As you prepare to repeat steps 15 – 28 for the MC*, VX*, and Fortune*, you should keep a couple of things in mind:
    a. **Optional**. Plan to do all the math in step 21.i BEFOREHAND. Search for the planet /star whose fractional degree you'll be using BEFORE you enter the formula. If you don't see one you like, you may have to borrow from stars by choosing info view from the icon bar,

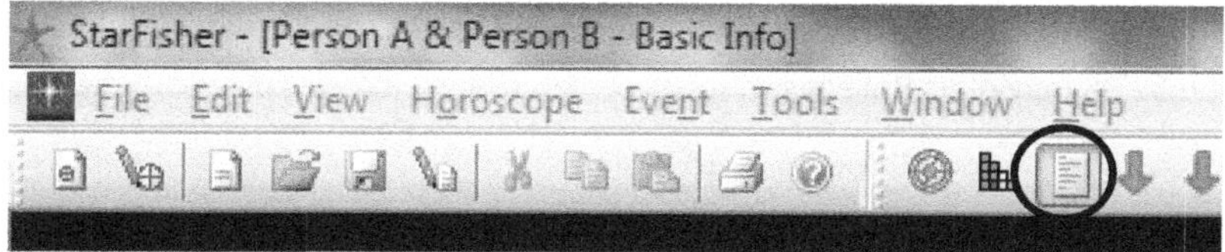

going to Edit Horoscope>Advanced... and selecting all the fixed stars from Available items (Acrux through Zosma),

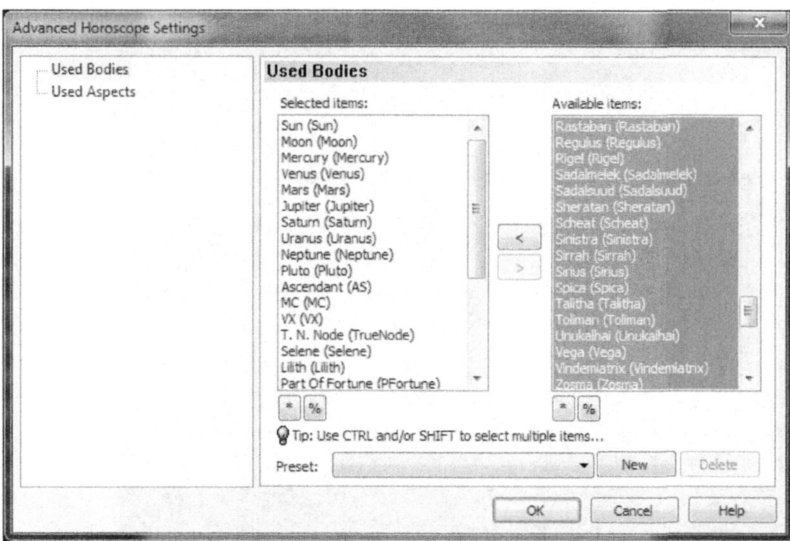

moving them over to Selected items with the < button,

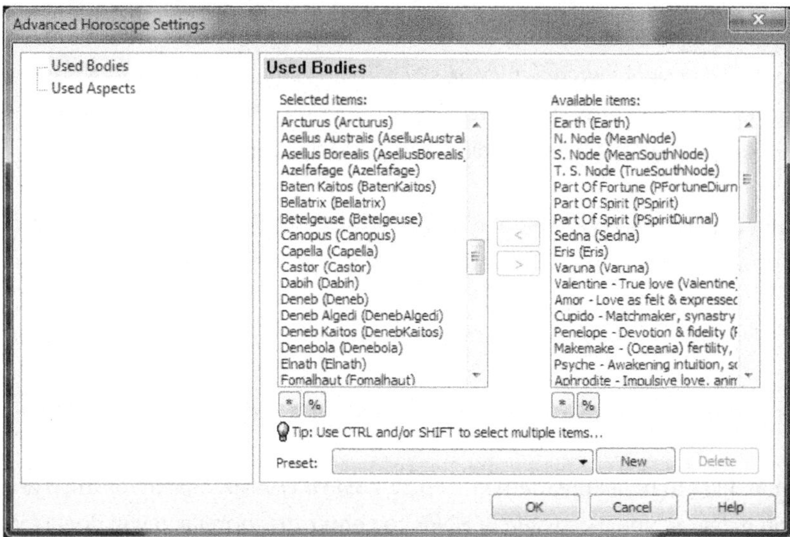

exiting these settings by clicking OK then clicking OK again, then going down the long list of locations to find a fractional part you like. In order to get the 53 in my 12♏53 Fortune*, I had to use the 52'58 in Asellus Borealis:

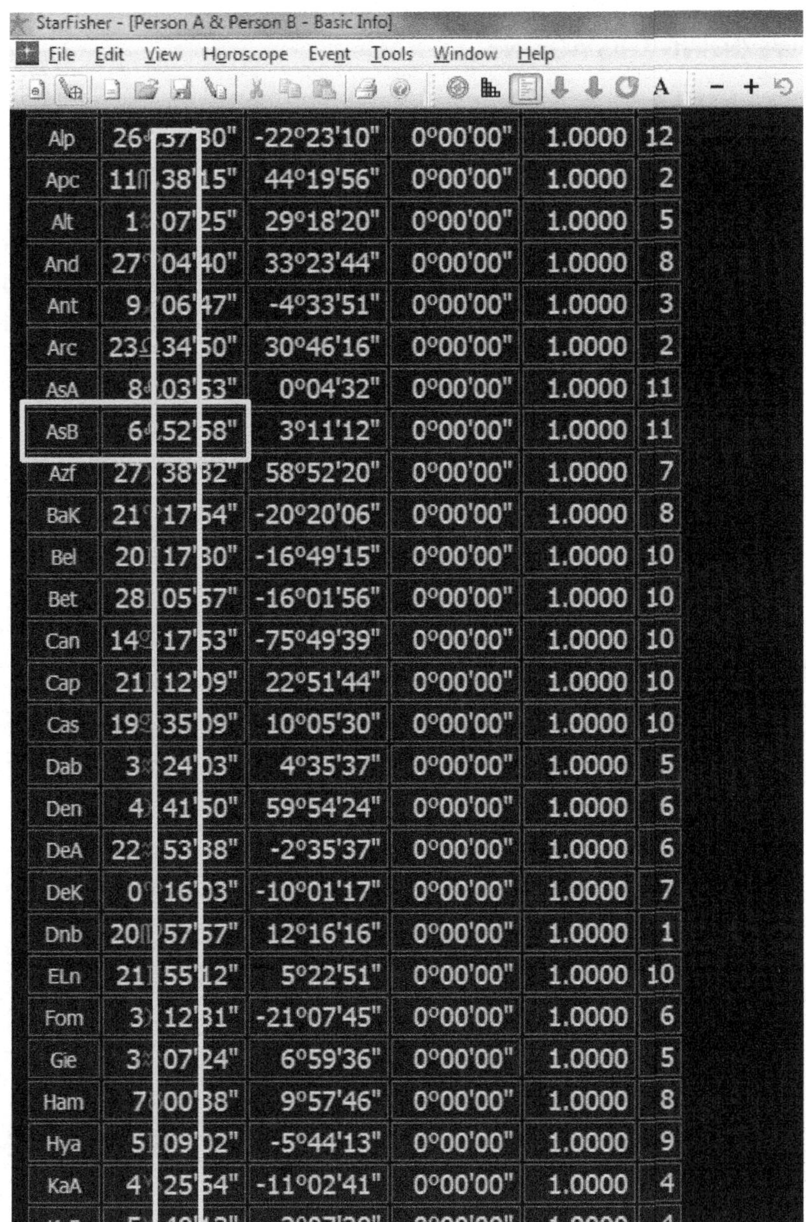

Alp	26 37'30"	-22°23'10"	0°00'00"	1.0000	12
Apc	11 38'15"	44°19'56"	0°00'00"	1.0000	2
Alt	1 07'25"	29°18'20"	0°00'00"	1.0000	5
And	27 04'40"	33°23'44"	0°00'00"	1.0000	8
Ant	9 06'47"	-4°33'51"	0°00'00"	1.0000	3
Arc	23 34'50"	30°46'16"	0°00'00"	1.0000	2
AsA	8 03'53"	0°04'32"	0°00'00"	1.0000	11
AsB	6 52'58"	3°11'12"	0°00'00"	1.0000	11
Azf	27 38'32"	58°52'20"	0°00'00"	1.0000	7
BaK	21 17'54"	-20°20'06"	0°00'00"	1.0000	8
Bel	20 17'30"	-16°49'15"	0°00'00"	1.0000	10
Bet	28 05'57"	-16°01'56"	0°00'00"	1.0000	10
Can	14 17'53"	-75°49'39"	0°00'00"	1.0000	10
Cap	21 12'09"	22°51'44"	0°00'00"	1.0000	10
Cas	19 35'09"	10°05'30"	0°00'00"	1.0000	10
Dab	3 24'03"	4°35'37"	0°00'00"	1.0000	5
Den	4 41'50"	59°54'24"	0°00'00"	1.0000	6
DeA	22 53'38"	-2°35'37"	0°00'00"	1.0000	6
DeK	0 16'03"	-10°01'17"	0°00'00"	1.0000	7
Dnb	20 57'57"	12°16'16"	0°00'00"	1.0000	1
ELn	21 55'12"	5°22'51"	0°00'00"	1.0000	10
Fom	3 12'31"	-21°07'45"	0°00'00"	1.0000	6
Gie	3 07'24"	6°59'36"	0°00'00"	1.0000	5
Ham	7 00'38"	9°57'46"	0°00'00"	1.0000	8
Hya	5 09'02"	-5°44'13"	0°00'00"	1.0000	9
KaA	4 25'54"	-11°02'41"	0°00'00"	1.0000	4
KaB	5 40'13"	-2°07'38"	0°00'00"	1.0000	4

When you enter names like "Asellus Borealis", just use the star name in quotes.

b. Clone the ASC* instead of Selene. Doing so will speed things up.

That's what's next. Here we go. Repeat steps 15-28 for the MC*, VX*, and Fortune*. And good luck on your journey.

and **WHY** ARE WE DOING THIS AGAIN?

Because the composite ASC, MC, Vx, and Fortune you start with have very little research behind them, few people, if any, know what they do and why they should do it, and their existence doesn't line up with any theory presented in this book or its predecessor. If you don't do this, you'll end up trying to interpret these four and the whopping **90** of 300 combinations that they participate in which will likely be wrong—wrong enough to where you'll read them, they won't feel right, but you'll want to go with them anyway—getting into all of that self-fulfilling prophecy-related business we talked about in the previous book; the accurate-sounding inaccuracies that give astrology a bad rap. You might as well scribble out every row and column with these four in them if you don't recalculate them with reasonable accuracy.

And what if you're off by a half degree or something? This won't kill you, though it will almost certainly change some of the angles. In *FSA* I address why this isn't as big a problem as it sounds. Just go with it. It'll be okay.

Two days later... Alright, I haven't shaven in a while or gotten up from this chair, but the deed is done. Below is what I have, but yours will certainly look different:

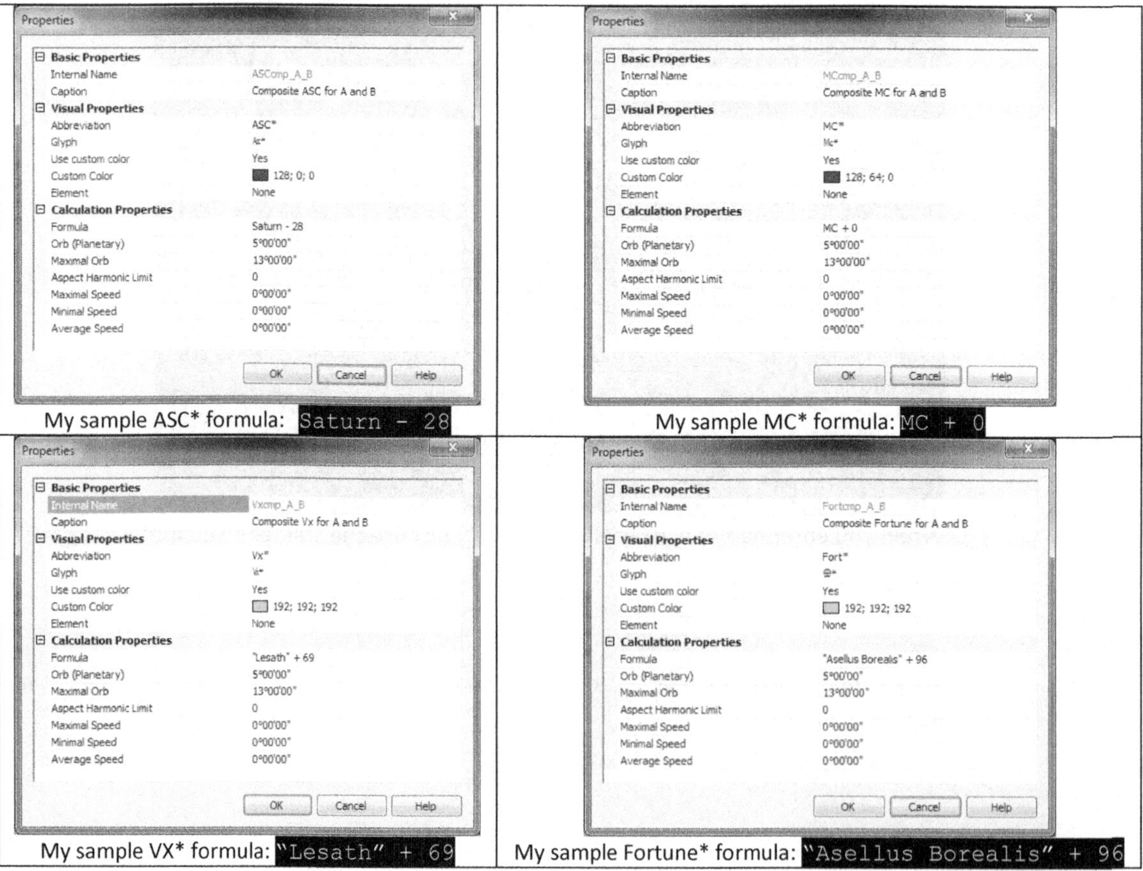

My sample ASC* formula: `Saturn - 28`

My sample MC* formula: `MC + 0`

My sample VX* formula: `"Lesath" + 69`

My sample Fortune* formula: `"Asellus Borealis" + 96`

31. Go to Edit Horoscope>Advanced...> Selected items and select all of the fixed stars, the original ASC, MC, VX, and Fortune. (Use Ctrl to select multiple items.)

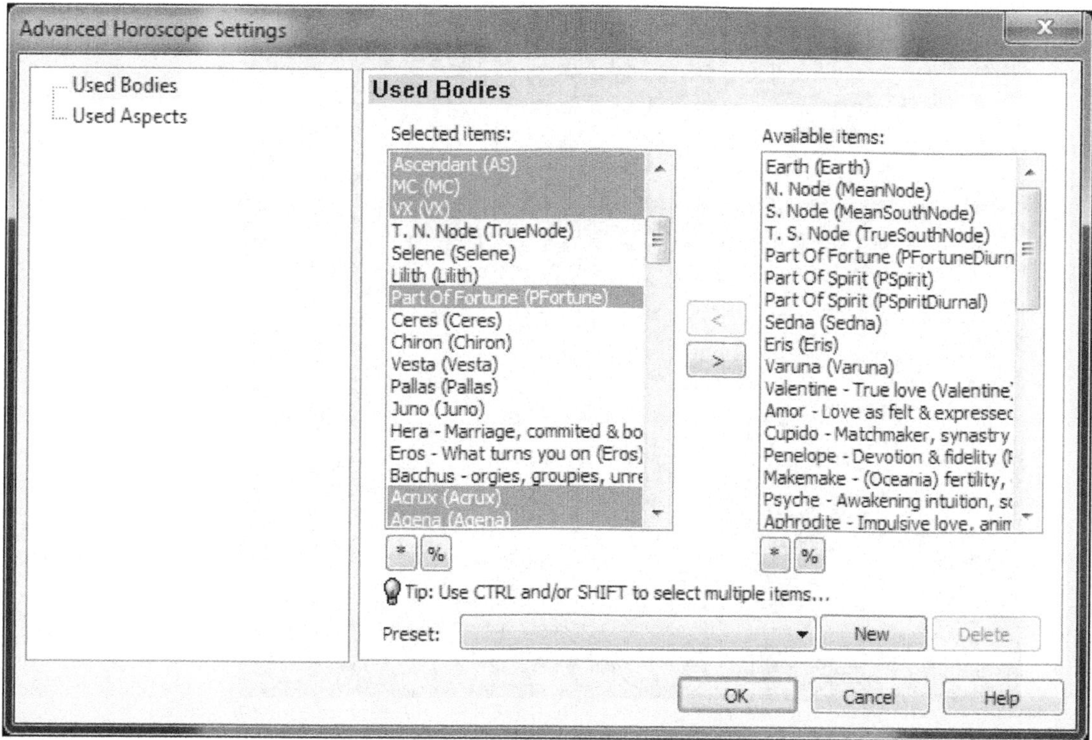

32. Use the > button to stop them from displaying in your chart.
33. Make sure you've selected your brand new ASC*, MC*, Vx*, and Fortune* from the "Available items:" window and used the < button to move them over to the "Selected items:" side.
34. Click OK. Then click OK again to exit settings.
35. Click on the Radix View wheel on the icon bar.

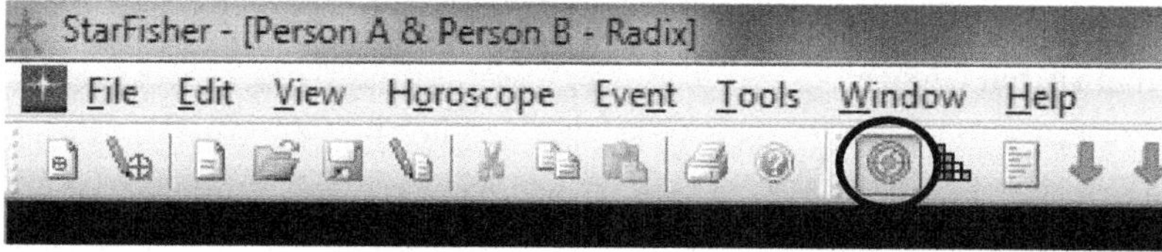

Your composite wheel is now ready!

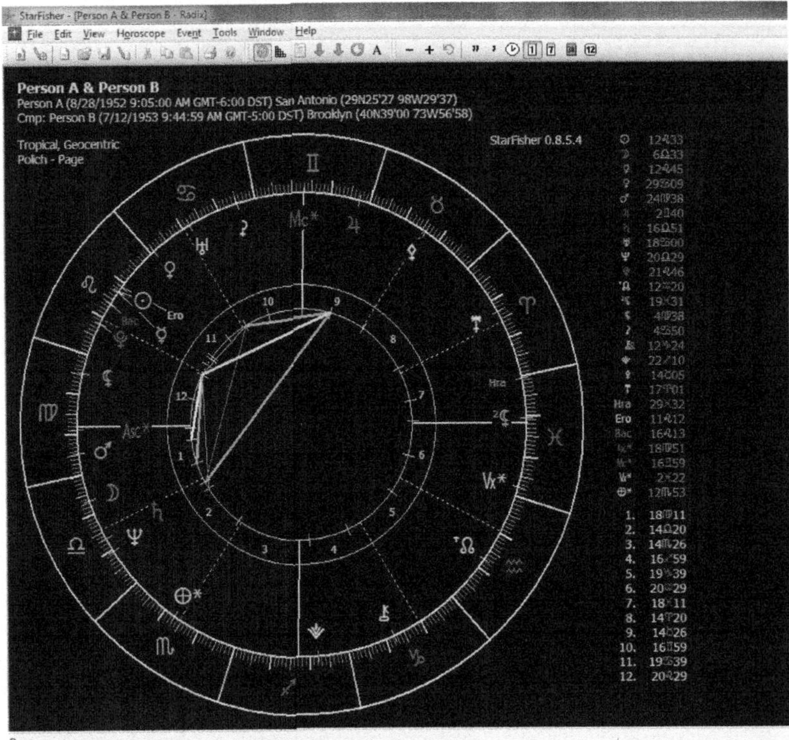

We just have a couple of other things to do.

36. Click on Aspectarium view in the icon bar.

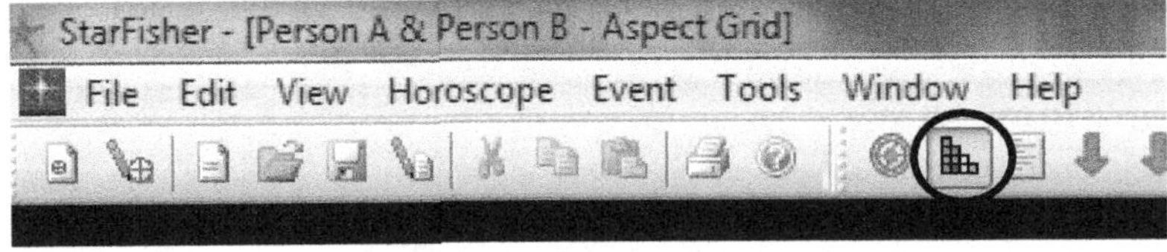

The view below is informative, but NAS.TY.

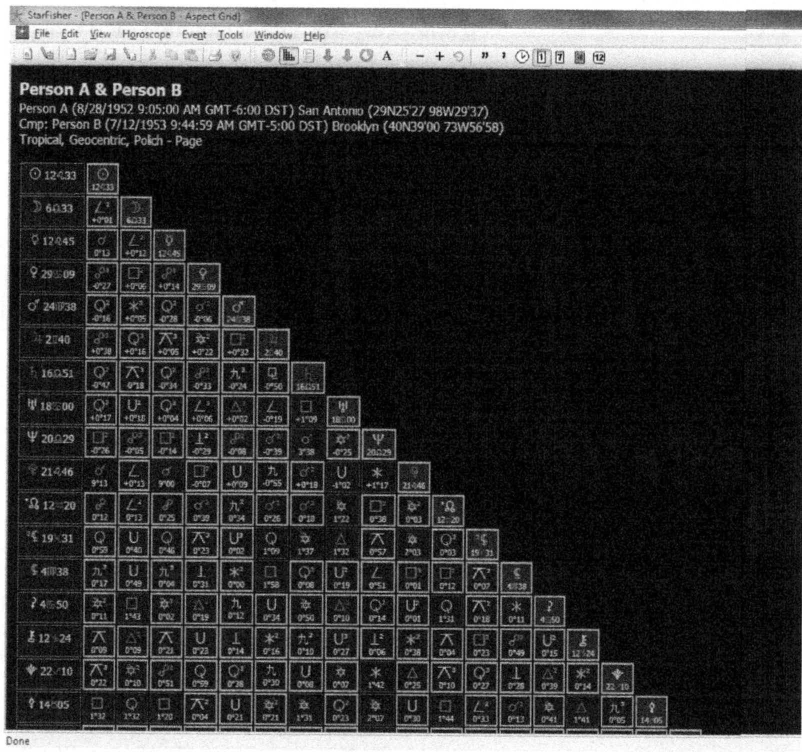

Let's turn it off all the extra numbers.

37. Using the File menu, go to Tools>Settings...
38. From the left hand box, choose Display>Aspectarium
39. Uncheck Show aspect details and click OK.
40. Much better. Go to File>Save Settings As Default.... Click OK when the alert box pops up telling you the settings were saved.
41. You now have what you need to read this composite chart.
42. **Optional**. By the way, if you're like me and are bothered by the fact that your new points are all the way at the bottom of the list, if you later find yourself messing up interpretations in this book because the ASC and its friends are in the wrong part of the table, you can change this by going into your folder `StarFisher\MyScripts\init.sfs` and rearranging the sections where your new points are defined. `init.sfs` is just a text file. The same as a `.txt`. You can edit it in any normal text editor like Notepad.

Now I know what you're thinking. "That sure was a hell of a lot of trouble just to read four points." Yes. it. was. And truthfully, I don't use StarFisher to do this because this same data is in my Excel table instead (discussed in *FSA*). If you have access to another program and find a quicker way of inventing sky points then have at it. I'm pretty hooked on StarFisher though for all kinds of reasons only a tech person would love, and after you've gone through the above ordeal a couple of times—especially that mess with the stars and the quotes and stuff—you find that the whole thing truly takes about 10 minutes to do. Unbelievable but true. Annnyway... let's read ourselves a duo.

Go into the table / aspect / aspectarium view of your chart and we'll get started. As was the case in Chapter 19, you won't be able to read much of anything in wheel view.

Sun pairs

Sun-Moon

<Moon-Monologue

[Sun-Moon] in a composite chart shows how the relationship primarily expresses itself between you when you and Other's Suns and you and Other's Moons are on the same page. This kind of "alignment" will be the case for all composite pairs throughout this chapter. Here, the angle between your composite Sun and Moon shows how you interact with each other given what you both feel the need (Moon) to think or talk about (Internal Monologue) as you naturally communicate what's on your minds. **What you feel is worth talking or thinking about lies in the realm of your composite [Sun-Moon] angle, forming the basis of the relationship's comfortable expression.**

Sun-Mercury

<Moon-Sun

The relationship is naturally "direct," such that, when you and other exist as a duo, your feelings about what you want from each other are harder to hide under this angle. **The angle between composite Sun and Mercury is the mode under which your level of satisfaction with each other is most clear**. Is Other actually happy with you or are they just faking it? Use this angle together and observe how contented they seem to be. The most comfortable aspect of the relationship for both of you comes out when your relationship affects your surroundings with this angle.

Sun-Venus

<Moon-Mercury

How easily do you both give your opinions in a way that allows equal air time? When you are on the same page in exchanging your analysis, your relationship strikes observers as naturally projecting this angle as a role. "**Based on how you give your opinions, you two should engage others with your [composite Sun-Venus] angle. You'd make a great team here,**" they say.

Sun-Mars

<Moon-Venus

This pair's angle reflects the realm in which you both respect each other's knack for interfacing with others. **In this angle's area, there is recognition of each other's popularity-building skill.**

Sun-Jupiter

<Moon-Mars

In each other's eyes, self-worth for the other rests on the other's ability to successfully project this angle onto their interactants. II-opposition duo members see each other as eating up attention from others. II-quintile duo members are particularly charismatic as individuals since the relationship they build is effectively "image conscious" in a way that focuses on getting fishbowl (ingroup) peers to follow along; fellow group members are a lot less likely to be II-quintile "managed" by your duo if it isn't a smooth one. Such smoothness is out of character for the II-quintile as an angle but well in line with the level of comfort held by people willingly following the leader. II-deciles on the other hand share projection goals when using their relationship to jointly put weaklings in their place. III-inconjuncts see each other as wanting to be significant. These people are more likely to find each other memorable.

Sun-Saturn

<Moon-Jupiter

The relationship is all about getting others under control using this angle as foisted upon others by at least one of the members. Squares across the board in the data, for example, consisted of at least one of the duo members pushing their emotions or intuition upon outsiders. Quintiles consisted of at least one of the duo members forcing outsiders to interact. Undeciles consisted of at least one duo member doing something to get them gossiped about among shared circles. All angles served to corner the expression of whatever outsiders paid attention to the duo. In the data, the non-foisting duo member was almost always an enabler whose role as witness served to give the foisting person fuel for their enthusiasm.

Sun-Uranus

<Moon-Saturn

The relationship revolves around the social, the strange, or the erratic under this angle, where the duo members turn a considerable amount of attention towards each other as interactants. There is a notable power dynamic here, where **one duo member typically assumes the superior position to the other under this angle or one duo member uses this angle in the other's behavior as a means to advance themselves.**

Sun-Neptune

<Moon-Uranus

One duo member naturally displays this angle as a way of easing the social path for (or accepting) the other. Such an attempt isn't always successful though, where you can usually gauge success by the degree to which the displayed angle's effects actually materialize.

Although a reading of this same pair in a regular chart would suggest that the relationship would in some way display "immersion" here, the data didn't reveal very much about how this pair affected the relationship as a whole.

Sun-Pluto

<Moon-Neptune

Yours and Other's interaction under this angle is designed to influence the world around you. That is, when your Suns and Plutos are on the same page and you wish to keep such cohesion going, you'll attend to your Moons and Neptunes respectively in order to motivate the Suns' and Plutos' next state. **The relationship itself reflects an "awareness of its own power" in this case.**

Sun-Ascendant*

<Moon-<u>2nd</u> house

(Notice how the house "before" a cusp marker like the ASC or MC is actually the <u>following</u> house. The data supported this and not the other way around. Perhaps this is because the planets move backwards through the houses in the natural course of a day (something I discuss in *FSA*).

✪ The foundation for your duo

When you want to build up the relationship with another person, what do you do? You do this angle of course. **[Sun-Ascendant]'s angle shows the methods used by at least one of the duo members to build the value in the relationship**. As this angle area is expressed, the two of you are likely to become closer for better or worse ($_{\text{fbow}}$), making the relationship into a "thing." II- and III-undeciles are more likely to share unusual topics. III-inconjuncts become closer through memorable moments.

This is a very strong pair for building a relationship. Assuming the two of you can get on the same page regarding your 1:1 interactions (Sun) and approach to new situations (ASC), you can consider this pair to mark the foundation for the more enduring forms of friendship between you.

Sun-Midheaven*

<Moon-11th house

✪ One of the absolute best pairs for your motives in forming a duo

The angle for this pair shows the mode in which you and Other interact most out in the open. Conjuncts do this naturally and can feel like friends very early on in the relationship. Squares are more likely to disagree or talk intuition. Octiles are more inclined to fight, spar, or reason against each other. Undeciles struggle to get along even though people are inclined to associate them as a good public team. Similarly, II-conjuncts seem like they should work well together, though there can still be some question as to whether they can keep that intensity up in their non-public exchanges. II-quintiles and II-septiles are naturally inclined towards mutual camaraderie, with the former skewed slightly towards attraction. II-deciles do good business together. II-undeciles are good at inventing together and channeling their shared creativity towards a new endeavor. Barring shared creation though, they can get on each other's nerves to the point that the relationship breaks. III-oppositions and III-septiles make stellar attractors of fans as a duo. III-octiles are more likely to attract rumors with their rather unorthodox association. IV-undeciles have a noteworthy philosophical exchange, but like other undeciles may struggle to connect in other ways.

[Sun-MC] is one of the first composite pairs which is more likely to look like itself than the pairing before it. Like its relationship-killing cousin in synastry, this one gives the duo its public identity such that—if you and Other are to be publicly acknowledged as a thing at all, this angle is how you can expect to achieve mobility on the minds of those who watch you.

This is among the strongest, most notable composite pairs we've covered thus far. For those opportunistic people among us, **this is the pair you reference when you want a specific benefit from a relationship and are less concerned with who your partner actually is.** *Table 19-2* is great for this. Want a lot of fans? Locate a III-opposition. Want high popularity? A III-septile will work. Want to be notorious? Find a III-octile. Conjuncts, octiles, and II-undeciles have an easier time becoming sexually or creatively involved, presumably because their relationship will have been noteworthy for its forceful affirmation of its duo members' individuality. II-conjuncts make for visibly public partners. Oppositions increase the personal value and status of the duo.

Sun-Vertex*

<Moon-"expiring comfort"

This pair shows **the behavioral mode in which you and Other are most comfortable with each other, even though such comfort stands to be interrupted** by contingencies from outside or within the relationship.

Sun-Node

<Moon-"questing"

When sharing this angle, your duo seems destined to form. This pair isn't as strong as it sounds, though it certainly makes coming together noticeably more convenient for the two of you.

Sun-Selene

<Moon-"resolvable dilemma"

Get another glimpse into the future

One of the duo members is just what the other needed when the latter wants (or is compelled) to express this angle. This pair is moderate in influence but says a lot about the conditions under which your duo forms for the satisfaction of a need. Look at *table 19-1* and consider this to pair to be what you stand to gain from this exchange. Like Jupiter-Juno, this pair can give you a glimpse into the future regarding what your paired exchange will have given you on the whole.

Sun-Lilith

<Moon-"unfulfilling conformity"

Your duo uses this angle to disrupt the peaceful surroundings of others. In response to the issues that the two of you choose to address, you present your room of influence with situations that cause tension, are difficult to handle, or are otherwise normally avoided. II-undeciles are naturally disconnected as they disrupt others' peace with their own individuality rather than teamwork by default. III-conjuncts fill each other with tension by default, as one duo member imposes collective-backed ideas upon the other in response to pending change. III-trines have an easier time sharing the same unorthodox vision of the future.

Sun-Fortune*

<Moon-"comfortable conditions"

You and other get along best under this angle, as both your Suns and both your Fortune's are in line. This composite pair is thoroughly positive even between the most bitter of rivalries, as it takes two of your most satisfying comfort zones and builds a relationship from them.

Sun-Ceres

<Moon-“Other’s dissatisfying expression”

One duo member tries to force the other’s acknowledgement—knowingly or not—through this angle. The forcer is more likely to brag or gather attention to this skill of theirs as the standard for getting the other to look at them.

Sun-Chiron

<Moon-“need for help”

One duo member helps the other build up the ability to use this angle. There is a paradoxical repulsion yet intensity that comes with octiles. Moral support is the result of II-squares. II-quintiles teach one of the duo members how to manage their surrounding groups. III-octiles teach one of the duo members how to use allure and mysterious creativity to their advantage.

Sun-Vesta

<Moon-“situation that needs tending to”

This angle sucks up a great deal of one of the duo member’s attention as they focus on the other. This pair is often quite negative, as the focused-on person is often assumed to be performing below or outside of the focused-person’s standards here.

Sun-Pallas

<Moon-“social imbalance”

This angle shows the circumstances under which your duo is most likely to crusade for something. You are more likely to agree on which social issues matter under this angle and more likely to get wrapped up in conversations about those issues.

Sun-Juno

<Moon-“need for secured role”

Your duo solidifies yours and Other’s mutual commitment most easily through this angle. **You look like you’ve chosen to be on the same side here whether or not you actually are**. Often you are not, but are instead contractually bound for more utilitarian purposes. In more cases than fewer, there is actually a tendency to dislike using the angle alongside the other. Such depends on the rest of your chart.

Sun-Hera

<Moon-“state of unattachment”

The best explanation for this pair probably lies in the quality before Hera: A state of unattachment precedes Hera’s attached bonding. **This composite pair and its angle shows your duo’s “battery”—the topic area which, as it gets spent in the exchange, gradually drains out until the relationship can no longer offer anything**. The relationship feels fairly positive while you and other are exchanging this angle, but at some point there is simply no more of this angle left to give and the bond you had to each other fades. This kind of decay can be easily offset if the two of you agree to stick with each other on new projects beyond the one which initially brought you together. But as you can imagine, sticking with it is not the default for most casual exchanges.

As with all composite pairs, this one will be easier to maintain if it’s associated with an “out” in both duo members’ charts. I’ll define an “out” at the end of this section on the Sun pairs.

Sun-Eros

<Moon-“receptiveness to impassioned action”

Is the relationship still alive?

One duo member inflames the passions of the other through this angle when the two of you have entered a relationship which allows your 1:1 actions and your passions to align. Here is a good time to remind ourselves that composite pairs don’t do much if the midpoints of each pair of the same individual planets making up those pairs aren’t talking to each other; composite [Sun-Eros] does almost nothing if yours and their synastric [Sun-Sun] and yours and their synastric [Eros-Eros] aren’t responding to each other. Accordingly, this is a really good gauge to see if either of you still care about the relationship: Can one of you still do things to inflame the other? Or have you lost interest?

Sun-Bacchus

<Moon-"desire to share company"

Make them your friend, astro-style

You and Other make natural friends when this angle is on, where [Sun-Bacchus] was an excellent indicator of the circumstances under which besties and couples of all kinds came together in enjoyment of each other's company.

If you really *really* want to be the other person's friend, do this angle thing with them and, as usual, make sure your synastric Suns and synastric Bacchuses are on the same page when you do. The latter part is probably the biggest obstacle to a relationship which hasn't gelled yet.

What is an "Out?"

If you're ever asked to diagnose a relationship using the composite chart and can only remember one thing, remember to look for "outs." An **out** is just **a planet in the composite chart which is conjunct one of your regular birth chart planets**. Outs are basically outlets for your planets. The more outs you have, the more control you basically have in writing the fate of the relationship. For example, suppose you and Other have a composite chart, and your regular Moon is conjunct the composite Jupiter. What this actually means is that your Moon in your own chart is very close to the midpoint between your Jupiter and their Jupiter. Your emotions (Moon) can be used to steer your joint style of image projection (Jupiter) within your relationship with Other. Your Moon has an "out" via the composite Jupiter and, **as the person who controls how the composite planet looks here**, you are called Jupiter's **writer**. On the other hand, if your Sun isn't conjunct any of the major composite planets you're looking at, your Sun basically has no out, so that 1) the relationship itself isn't designed to *naturally* respond to your 1:1 interaction style (Sun) and 2) in times of difficulty you'll find that your 1:1 way of behaving doesn't matter as much in solving problems directly connected to the "personality" of your duo.

Outs are fairly easy to read and especially useful for looking at relationships which are in doubt. Typically when we're less inclined to actively save a relationship, we lean on the behaviors that pass naturally between us and the other person. The behaviors that come naturally are those of ours which are conjunct those of the duo. This raises two important questions though:

1. **First, even if a planet like one's Sun has no out in the composite, doesn't it still make *some* usable angle to each composite planet?**
   Yes it does, but that angle won't come easily if you're not interested in actively maintaining the exchange.
2. **Second, even if a planet like one's Sun has no out in the composite, can't we still read the angles which that planet makes to the other person's *synastry*?**
   Yes you can, but that angle won't easily show up in the context of a duo. It will just be the way the two of you interact with each other whether you form an official duo or not. You'll typically find yourself looking outside of the official exchange to get these fulfilled, where "outside" implies independent activities, other friends, or simply the way you were before you formed a duo.

Outs basically control the relationship at its absolute laziest (which is the form taken by most relationships between people who are not family, close friends or business partners). Fr&ships, acquaintanceships, and other passing exchanges rely on the duo members' conjuncts to their shared composite in order for the composite to really run. Three rules of thumb for these autopilot exchanges would be as follows:

1. If your planet doesn't have an out in the composite, don't expect the passively maintained relationship to provide an outlet for you where that planet is concerned. For example, if your regular chart's Moon isn't conjunct anything in the composite, the relationship will tend to be emotionally unfulfilling for you in times where you don't feel like making it otherwise. But if your Moon is conjunct the Midheaven* for example, your level of emotional fulfillment can safely be expected to match the way you think the relationship looks to others publicly. Unlike the non-out case, if you are emotionally unfulfilled here, your duo with the other drops in its ability to be seen positively by the public.
2. If a particular composite planet isn't conjunct anything in either yours or the other person's chart, expect that planet to "write itself" based on yours and Other's efforts. If, for example, yours and their composite Mars isn't conjunct any planets belonging to either of your regular charts, your passively maintained relationship will effectively steer others in ways that neither of you directly control.
3. All outs are controlled by the individual planets with which they are conjunct. If my Mars and Midheaven are conjunct our composite Sun and your Venus and Mars are also conjunct our composite Sun, then the way we think our duo naturally behaves in viewers' eyes (the composite Sun) will be co-written by both my apparent leadership [Mars-MC] and your ability to be socially sought after [Venus-Mars].

Of course, you can get around the limitations of outs if you only care to actively nurture the exchange.

Moon pairs

Moon-Mercury

<Monologue-Sun

You and Other are more likely to engage in a heart-to-heart conversation regarding one of your duo member's motivations behind this angle. Such conversations effectively amount to the sharing of secrets, though these secrets are more like intimate self-disclosure than they are trivial "do not tell" items.

Moon-Venus

<Monologue-Mercury

One duo member greatly increases the expression of this value as priority in the other. The person whose expression is increased displays more agitation or more erratic behavior in this angle. From the outside, the duo itself appears to run pretty smoothly. That is, until the agitated person's stress level causes impulses to boil over on occasion (which happens a little less than half the time).

Moon-Mars

<Monologue-Venus

Both duo members look like tougher people under this angle, where it is much harder for an outsider to say that the duo members are pushovers here. You two have strong effects on your circumstances in this department, and can go the distance as individuals committed to a common direction.

Moon-Jupiter

<Monologue-Mars

👓 **In each other's company, the two of you bond by exchanging this angle under people's noses**. Undeciles and II-conjuncts typically make better public allies than private ones, while II-octiles make good partners in crime when it comes to jointly defeating external challenges. II-inconjuncts connect over imaginative endeavors, but are often unfortunately distant outside of this. This pair's angle has a tendency to be applied by at least one of the duo members to groups outside of the exchange.

Moon-Saturn

<Monologue-Jupiter

Sometimes you just can't win

One duo member's version of this angle is a forbidding obstacle which stifles the other's free expression. This pair is almost always negative, though how negative depends on how much you and Other like each other. Consider that the individual versions of planets before each composite pair are the characteristics used to drive the composite. Where my instinctual ideas $_{\text{Monologue}}$ regarding image promotion $_{\text{Jupiter}}$ are used to stabilize $_{\text{Saturn}}$ the emotions $_{\text{Moon}}$ in our duo, we have a recipe for both of us hitting a wall in how our duo feels. And this is in the positive case. Most of the time—between people who don't like each other so much—there is no goal to "stabilize emotions," only a feeling that this is where the relationship cannot grow.

It is the task of the stifled person to view such expressive blocking as stabilization or structuring instead. If they don't, this pair will serve as a definite partnership killer.

Moon-Uranus

<Monologue-Saturn

This angle lurks beneath the surface as a desired exchange that one duo member wishes to have with the other. The desiring duo member is more likely to favor having their views of this angle structured (if not controlled) by the other, **in a pair which shows where one wants to (or is unwillingly positioned to) give the other authority**.

Moon-Neptune

<Monologue-Uranus

One duo member's talking to the other builds up this angle in the former $_{\text{fbow}}$. This one is pretty straightforward. The built up angle is typically conveyed back to the duo member who sponsored it rather than to outsiders solely.

Moon-Pluto

<Monologue-Neptune

One duo member's ability to push this angle forward goes up in light of the other. **You might even say they become bolder and more prone to take risks when employing their own charisma here**.

Moon-Ascendant*

<Monologue-2nd house

The duo members easily dream of new horizons together under this angle's topic, in a composite pair which is really obvious and very easy to read. Not only are new horizons proposed, they tend to be successfully traversed—often by at least one of the duo members outside of the exchange. This is a position of definite influence, one upon the other (usually positive).

Negatively though, III-deciles in the dataset were really bad for most close exchanges, as one duo member continually bossed the other around in these. III-novile exchanges tended to be fun but short-lived as they required an audience to survive as an emotional context.

Moon-Midheaven*

<Monologue-11th house

One duo member uses this angle to introduce their troubles into the life of the other. This angle is the means through which one person hears about what a problem the other is (socially) or what social problems the other has encountered. This is another one of those pairs which tends to be wholly negative, varying only in the level of negativity. This time, though, the amount of negativity depends not on how much the two of you like each other, but on how honest you are with each other. The idea here is that the Monologue-11th gives away your thoughts about social happenings whether you reveal them yourself to the other person or attempt to keep them in your head. The [Moon-MC*] colors the mood accompanying the relationship's public appearance in light of what you reveal either way.

But a relationship which is comfortable with its public appearance under the kinds of social events worth reporting tends to be a henpecked one.

Moon-Vertex*

<Monologue-"expiring comfort"

One duo member sees the other as a kindred spirit under this angle, where the two of your priorities align in such a way as to make it easier to relate to each other. The person who sees the other as kindred is more likely to sponsor that other's public action under this angle.

Moon-Node

<Monologue-"questing"

Duo members' exchange of this angle isn't generally comfortable unless it is focused on business, control, or work. Why? Perhaps because [Monologue-"questing"] is an objective-focused path of communication. If it doesn't relate to the quest towards "destiny," you and the other person may simply be going through the motions.

Moon-Selene

<Monologue-"resolvable dilemma"

One of the duo members is reassured when the other displays this angle in their favor. It's as if things will suddenly be okay. Here the reassured duo member is more inclined to think "Man, life sure was crazy before I started getting [this angle] from the other person."

Moon-Lilith

<Monologue-"unfulfilling conformity"

This composite pair corresponds to the context under which your duo members communicate emotional depth with each other. **Interactions are infused with intensity under this angle, making for a relationship which projects some of its greatest dynamism here**.

Moon-Fortune*

<Monologue-"comfortable conditions"

The impression of this angle from one duo member hovers around the thoughts of the other for a LONG time even after the duo has expired. This one can take years to subside, constituting the basis for a super long-lived impression gained from the relationship. Provided it was allowed to become a duo in the first place, of course. Let's give this one a name: **Unforgettable**.

Moon-Ceres

<Monologue-"Other's dissatisfying expression"

Pushy or...?

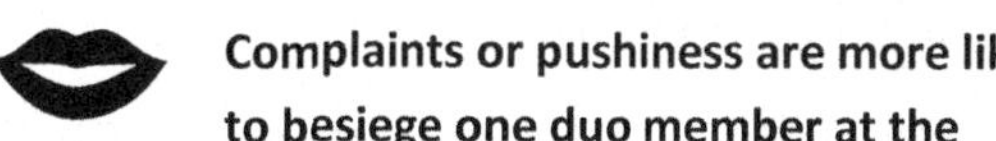

Complaints or pushiness are more likely to besiege one duo member at the hand of the other under this angle, though the pushy one is more inclined to invite the pushed one's creative or sexual expression in a suitably close relationship. In cases where sex and creativity are invited, this angle reflects the trait which the pushed person stands to have augmented in their chart at the hand of the pushy one. For stubborn people who don't like to be pushed at all, this one might serve as an exception. It's not always easy to tell what the pushy one wants from you.

Moon-Chiron

<Monologue-"need for help"

Don't teach them too "hard"

One duo member has the urge to teach or take care of the other in the realm of this angle. The other person is not infrequently resistant to this, though. The greater the insecurity on the part of the one to be taken care of (or greater the overstepping of the part of the caretaker), the more likely the duo is to erode to a miniscule smidgeon of its former self.

Moon-Vesta

<Monologue-"situation that needs tending to"

This pair epitomizes the "awkward situation," where one duo member is overpowered and the

other grossly underpowered for the situation that surrounds them both. Actually, the underpowered one is more likely just underexpressing, while the overpowered one is more likely scattered in their attention here, creating a situation in which the duo looks like an odd couple. This planet pair is disruptive, but not destructive.

Moon-Pallas

<Monologue-"social imbalance"

On duo member's approach to this angle is advanced while the other stands as an encouraging or enabling witness.

Moon-Juno

<Monologue-"need for secured role"

One duo member is cold and efficient under this angle in light of the other. Even among warm people, a noticeably chilly assembly line cranks out new deeds under this one, making connections difficult. This pair is not a relationship killer, but it does put the brakes on some of the intense exchange that would otherwise be there when this angle becomes the central focus.

Moon-Hera

<Monologue-"state of unattachment"

One duo member pours out this angle onto the other in a statement of their openness to the partner's influence.

This isn't vulnerability, but a true receptiveness to the other person's feedback—typically as an attempt to bond.

Moon-Eros

<Monologue-"receptiveness to impassioned action"

Another member of the "Are they interested?" family: Gauging attraction

One duo member finds the other strongly attractive or strongly creative under this angle, where conjuncts are especially strong. **Generally, this pair indicates the kind of impression which a person's brand of attractiveness or creativity has on others, and gives you a sense of what kinds of things the attractor can get others to do when that power is put into effect.** Take a look at this angle in the composite chart between you and a romantic interest to see if either you or they are inclined to push this angle on the other. Such tends to be a decent tell regarding their desire to engage you in certain creative ways.

Moon-Bacchus

<Monologue-"desire to share company"

Shared cliques are brought before the duo's attention via this angle. This pair is actually pretty interesting in that **it shows the area of the duo's expression which is most likely to describe how they engage friends together and, thus, what constitutes a fun social life for them as a pair**.

Mercury pairs

Mercury-Venus

<Sun-Mercury

Here's an odd role for [Mercury-Venus]: One duo member is naturally the boss in the relationship; the angle in this pair shows where this is the case. Actually it might be more fitting to say that **one duo member is more direct than the other**, taking charge of the angle for both people whether or not they are qualified to do so.

Mercury-Mars

<Sun-Venus

The relationship appears to be one rooted in the commands one duo member gives to the other, but it's really more mutual than it looks as **the angle between this pair reflects the area of life in which one duo member leans on the other's talents to advance them both**.

Mercury-Jupiter

<Sun-Mars

There is a toe-in-the-water hesitancy for one duo member to display this angle to the other, often in the expectation that the other would not be receptive. Although it isn't always true that the other wouldn't receive this angle, it is true that conflicts are more likely within the recipient as a result of what is shown. Only those among the most accepting of partners can avoid this result.

Mercury-Saturn

<Sun-Jupiter

One duo member believes they can conquer the world with the other at their side, or maybe just help the other conquer the world under this angle, as **one recognizes the other person's inherent star power in this angle area.**

Mercury-Uranus

<Sun-Saturn

Support for the long term

You and Other are recognized by outsiders as friends and associates when you display this angle, mainly because you seem more inclined to back each other up and perform various services for the other when this angle area is an issue for one of you. **One of you seems to have the other's back here in an aspect which works as a strong indicator of the kind of support you provide to each other** at different points in the relationship.

Mercury-Neptune

<Sun-Uranus

Where's the reward?

This angle area in the relationship is basically characterized by warmth, though there is a definite sense that one duo member feels that such warmth is not enough. Depending on who the writers are, the duo member who gives the warmth may be led on or deceived by the person who gets it, and for an interesting reason. It's not that the receiver is afraid to let the giver down or intends to lie to the giver necessarily, but that the motivation for keeping the duo's common $_{\text{Mercury}}$ imagination $_{\text{Neptune}}$ alive lies in a mutual matching of social circumstance (group attunement, [Sun-Uranus]). This is a fancy way of saying that, as long as the receiver isn't where they want to be in life, the giver's gift will be as good as buying windows for a homeless man. Try not to hate the person who takes and takes from you and never tangibly gives back. We do this for children all the time. Sometimes the other person's overall world just isn't ready for you yet.

Mercury-Pluto

<Sun-Neptune

One duo member sees the other as strong under this angle, but in a way that is spacey enough to be near unmanageable—like bottling air. One may find it a futile effort to attempt to tame the other person here, so they might as well sit back and be awed.

Mercury-Ascendant*

<Sun-2nd house

Will the differences in personal worth hurt your exchange?

One person would like for the other to take them seriously here, but this only tends to happen in cases where outsiders are allowed to see and agree upon the results of the first person's actions.

I've actually run into this problem in several exchanges and wish I could share with you how valuable this pair is in offsetting a partnership-killing "failure to convince." For now I can only tell you that partnership with a person who doubts you is no cooler after the first few years than it is after the first few days. **This pair's angle shows where one needs to prove one's worth to the other—often towards the goal of public acknowledgement.** This pair's net results in [Mercury-ASC*] show how you can get around the need to constantly prove your worth [Sun-2nd] to the other by simply getting witnesses to back you, but if you're exchanging with someone whose own worth is low, the whole mutuality situation discussed in the preliminary comments kicks in and—in order to remain on the same page and keep the composite going—either their worth must go up or yours must go down. In business partnerships this may simply be part of the costs you pay, but in personal relationships don't count on an exchange built on proof between people of mismatched worth to end well.

Mercury-Midheaven*

<Sun-11th house

The duo makes moves under this angle towards the establishment of a reputation. **By employing this angle jointly, the duo members create a public image through which others describe the way they relate**. Interestingly, you can do things with your partner which are not under this angle and effectively dodge having it written on your permanent record—no matter how grand the deed. It's pretty fun actually. Just know that if you're using this angle to express jointly with the other person, there's a good chance that it will NOT remain a secret.

Mercury-Vertex*

<Sun-"expiring comfort"

✪ The critical moment...

If you use this angle alongside the other person, you should expect to have your life changed in some way. An old viewpoint is replaced with a new one as you and Other play out an event of unusual importance compared to your normal modes of interaction. This one can be used both to kill and to rewrite relationships.

Mercury-Node

<Sun-"questing"

Your analytical equal

The duo consists of analytical equals under this angle, where both parties are evenly matched in the power with which they apply this angle to solve problems. Although not the most powerful, this pair is—I'll confess—my favorite one of all the pairs we've covered so far. Given that you have a sizable collection of charts, it effectively shows your ideal interactant for any angle. It also partly answers the question, "Why am I in this relationship?" The answer given here: to engage someone who matches your problem solving under this angle.

Mercury-Selene

<Sun-"resolvable dilemma"

One of the duo members avoids interacting with the other under this angle unless they have to—driven by some compelling need to share experience with a specialized audience. **If the need is there, however, the other duo member will have more of an urge to see this angle displayed by the first person**. There is a kind of line in the sand here, where the successful use of this angle by one party and acceptance of that angle by the other indicates a deeper affinity between two people. But you'll need to be honest with this one. If offer and acceptance of this specific angle aren't there, they just aren't there.

Mercury-Lilith

<Sun-"unfulfilling conformity"

One person finds the other near-inaccessible under this angle except in cases where the one being accessed expressly allows it. Call this one the "White List." By default, the would-be accessor will not be able to get past the would-be accessed person's defenses under this angle unless the latter sufficiently trusts the former. Once access is granted, the accessor gets a read-only view of the accessed person's inner world.

Pay particular attention to the outs on this one, as the writers of Mercury will be the ones who struggle to access the writers of Lilith. The weirder exchanges occur in people who have outs in both the composite Lilith and Jupiter—who can't access a certain side of the other person but end up figuring that side out for themselves anyway. Another weird dynamic occurs when the composite Lilith isn't an out for either person—where you just can't get at that "thing" which is missing in the exchange's angle for this pair, but don't know what it is. The data seemed to suggest that this latter case is harder to get around, since neither person has the key to this lock.

Mercury-Fortune*
<Sun-"comfortable conditions"

One duo member approaches with authority over the other, with the ability to use this angle to write the other's decisions regarding the latter person's preferences under this angle. That is, **one duo member can train the other here**.

Mercury-Ceres
<Sun-"Other's dissatisfying expression"

One duo member defers to the other's judgment under this angle, allowing the other to take the spotlight. This isn't always a good thing though, since it often amounts to letting the spotlight person steer the relationship into trouble. That trouble results from an overenthusiasm by one coupled with a lack of effort by the other.

Mercury-Chiron
<Sun-"need for help"

⌘ One person writes an entire angle

One partner takes the lead, using their personality to dictate this angle's version of the exchange between both people. Think of this pair as putting one duo member in charge of how this angle passes between both duo members. As such, this pair becomes the face of all resonant pairs exchanged between both individuals. One duo member "teaches" the other how to use this angle, governing the curriculum and everything.

⌘ This angle is excellent for showing the primary lesson conveyed from teacher to student and parent to child. It also shows the primary impression left by a boss upon their subordinate. Watch out for this one in your composite. In cases where the other person seems to be influencing you negatively, you may want to look at this pair to ensure that such influence isn't embedded in your relationship for the long term. Teacher-student influences rarely reverse, although it is possible in extreme cases where one party undergoes great growth or experiences a great loss.

Mercury-Vesta
<Sun-"situation that needs tending to"

This angle is acts as a "raised topic" to open the lines of communication with the other person. **One duo member greets the other with this angle on the table as a way of opening the day's discussion**. Trines begin with what's actually on their minds and make for honest, outspoken partners. II-quintiles tend to need help with something. (But don't assume that this makes them incapable. I had a very sharp student whom I tutored, a boss, and a close friend who all had this, each with all kinds of tasks for greeting. The task depends on which planets are doing the writing.) II-sextiles can be positive if the topic revolves around some form of rational analysis, negative if it revolves around long-term planning (the latter being an indication that the person to whom the subject is brought up is irresponsible or shortsighted). Interpersonal power is the opening topic for II-octiles. You can reference *table 19-1* to see how the rest of the angles play out.

Mercury-Pallas
<Sun-"social imbalance"

You and Other look extra smooth together under this angle, with an impressive kind of charm which makes outsiders look upon your exchange with slight embarrassment at their own inability to compete. [Mercury-Pallas] is striking in its effect on viewers in that it makes them think of you and your partner as a close-knit, indomitable duo whose bubble can't be easily popped. Whatever you're talking about or however you and Other are interacting, watching you at work amidst this angle becomes the thing to do.

Mercury-Juno

<Sun-"need for secured role"

This pair is super-powerful with noticeable effects on the relationship. **One duo member unleashes this angle full-throttle on the other, ensuring that the former is remembered by the latter for this as their strongest weapon for social power**. This is the means employed by one duo member to lock down the behaviors of others and force the person's personality upon those others. Accordingly, it works similar to [Mars-Vertex] for the Vertex person in that this pair sends their skills through the roof. This time, however, it is membership in the joint exchange (rather than simple association) and the impulse to show the angle to the other person which drives the strengthened duo member's potency.

Mercury-Hera

<Sun-"state of unattachment"

One duo member reserves a special place for the other where this angle is concerned, allowing the other to express this angle freely with minimal judgment. This particular pair slightly affects physical and behavioral characteristics in that it makes the other (free expressing person) quirky, with unusual traits to reflect the angle being accepted. Oppositions, for example, often have a distinguishing body feature which makes them different from their peers. Squares have a distinctive emotional bearing. Octiles have a displaced sensuality and drive to steer others which pops up in places where it shouldn't. II-squares evoke the impulse to break one's moral rules in order to live under the II-square person's core setup instead. II-noviles sport more theatrical attitudes. III-quintiles are often pleasant-looking in a way that eludes standard description—this as a reflection of their unique brand of charisma. III-octiles sport a sleepy look so as to compel your acceptance of the intensity that sits beneath their surface. III-inconjuncts have a memorable look or bearing which forces you to remember them for how they presented themselves and their ideas; these people, like II-inconjuncts (and to a lesser extent, regular inconjuncts) have a creative talent which defies what you would expect based on their appearance.

Mercury-Eros

<Sun-"receptiveness to impassioned action"

A person's attractiveness can change without you being on drugs? Really?

Here's something I didn't know which maybe you didn't know either: Although we're wired to judge people based on looks when calculating a first impression, although we're certainly wired to continue (at least slightly) judging those people against our trained standards of physical beauty throughout the course of the relationship, it is not only possible but likely that people's attractiveness in our eyes can change depending on what we're doing. **[Mercury-Eros] is one of the quintessential cases of a physical turn-on, where one duo member's attractiveness goes up in the eyes of the other under the pair's angle**. I'll tell you briefly how I concluded this from the cluster since it's actually pretty interesting.

In the data, composite [Mercury-Eros] conjuncts were simply sexy in the eyes of the people who viewed them. Quintiles also tended to be attractive to their viewers, but noticeably more so during interaction, where they had the capacity to charm and unsettle the viewer pretty convincingly. Undeciles became more attractive the more their viewers saw them as socially sought after. And so the story went. There were even cases where a person who was otherwise unattractive to the viewer suddenly became a kind of supermodel under the [Mercury-Eros] angle. Needless to say, such knowledge constitutes a useful hack tool for those who like to play the field; you don't necessarily need substances to get others to see you differently.

In the world of sex and power roles, compatibility between partners is partly dependent on aligned preferences. [Mercury-Eros]—the very same pair which brought us "relationship safe fights" in Chapter 19 and the "love-locating action" in *FSA*—continues to stand out as the choice pair for writing romance upon its possessor. This time, though, the possessor is the relationship itself. Within that relationship, the duo members use their 1:1 personalities (Suns) beside their "receptiveness to impassioned action" to create a window of receptiveness to their partners. Of course you could fight the partner too with this pair, but the aligned Suns and "receptiveness" needed to make the composite go in the first place would cause the fight to look more like a sham here. At the risk of dipping into the kinky, I think many duo members in the romantic cases would do better to adopt play roles related to this angle rather than sham anger related to the same angle—especially for couples who like each other a lot, but just can't get past the pretty unromantic II-sextiles, II-deciles, III-trines, and III-deciles.

Mercury-Bacchus

<Sun-"desire to share company"

Let no one question your duo again

Bacchus strikes again with its emphasis on excessively amplified friendship.

The duo members make a really effective pair under this angle, with a force underlying their mutual approach which impresses outsiders. Undeciles are especially conducive to a cohesive interaction which others can see. This is the kind of exchange which makes others say, "Man, those two are kickin' some ass [under this angle]!" This is definitely a pair to watch if you want to do prolific things alongside your partner.

Venus pairs

Venus-Mars

<Mercury-Venus

One duo member conveys discipline and sternness in this angle, despite their ability to get others to bow to their will in this department. **For the individual, this is focus despite being socially in demand. For the duo as a whole, the steering of others comes easily under the angle** as the pair appears charismatic with a truly legitimate skill displayed in their deeds.

Venus-Jupiter

<Mercury-Mars

The duo is unorthodox, with an under-the-radar way of displaying this angle towards each other. This is truly a situation in which the two parties defy the recommended rules of engagement which have been written by others, infusing their communication with something that is not expected (or in some cases, allowed) in their position.

Beneath the good looking image of this duo lies the willingness to command each other up to and slightly beyond crossable lines of engagement.

Venus-Saturn

<Mercury-Jupiter

♀/♂ Power roles swapped

One partner confines the expression of the other under this angle, often in a way that makes the confined person uncomfortable showing their version of this angle to the confiner.

♀/♂ This is a pretty restrictive pair in the composite chart. It seems as though the more inhibiting partner will prevail over both partners' agendas when they are together and this angle is on the table, and the more inhibiting partner tends to be the stereotypically weaker party (the feminine, subordinate, younger, etc) except in cases where strength is gauged in terms of instinctual aggressiveness (I- and III-conjuncts) or public appeal (II- and III-quintiles). In the best cases, both partners will have agreed to this, but this is one of the strongest angles through which the "expected" weaker comes to disrespect the expected stronger as the honeymoon phase ends. Manly man husband becomes a good-for-nothing. Teacher becomes a disappointment to student. Hyped up business partner underperforms. As we discussed in *FSA*, II-septiles, II-noviles, and II-undeciles are most associated with non-standard sexuality, where the feminine element becomes boss here. Disappointment in the bedroom and in romantic advance is more likely under these angles if the people involved are set on traditional gender roles. Many duos will need to trade roles for the best shot at happiness here.

This pair is not a partnership killer but does form a substantial basis for the kinds of complaints that eventually sap the strength of a bond. If ever there were a case where the dominant person should let the dominated one prevail, this would be it. The long term survival of the relationship may depend on it.

Venus-Uranus

<Mercury-Saturn

One duo member's sensitivity to their environment shows in how they display this angle. This pair best describes the realm in which the person's feminine power exerts its influence. That is, **by being receptive and sensitive to one's surroundings, by displaying beauty, exercising nurturing, and communicating, one duo member (typically the less assertive) gets this angle done**. II-oppositions approach the partner they like with open receptivity more often than forcefulness.

Venus-Neptune

<Mercury-Uranus

One duo member sends formless messages regarding what they want under this angle, and requires the other duo member to clarify it for them through the latter's response to the cloudy person's expression.

Venus-Pluto

<Mercury-Neptune

Arguments, stress, and strife—both between duo members and with groups outside the duo—characterize this pair. It seems as though there is always some kind of issue with this angle, where the quest for power over whatever the obstacle's form is never-ending. You might be surprised to find, then, that this pair isn't really bad for relationships. It's just the nature of the enemy which you and Other face together. Hopefully you face it together. If not, you'll continually find this issue in each other.

So do the two of you ever win these conflicts? All the time. Just be prepared for the conflicts to ceaselessly return in new and varied forms.

Venus-Ascendant*

<Mercury-2nd house

If the relationship could talk, it would do so towards the kinds of people who promote this angle as a rule—people who value this angle as an experience. **Very roughly, this pair can be thought of as the reason the duo members opt to work together or the values they attempt to instill in others by working together**. Note the special emphasis on working together. This really is more publicly aimed cooperation than it is private.

Venus-Midheaven*

<Mercury-11th house

The less assertive duo member invites the more assertive duo member to weigh in with their standards under this angle. That's in the ideal case. In more negative cases, the more assertive duo member weighs in without being invited, incurring the distrust of the former.

Venus-Vertex*

<Mercury-"expiring comfort"

One duo member basically requires the following angle after this one in order for the connection to grow. Remember, the following angle is the current harmonic +1, so that if your composite chart has a II-septile (19) for this pair for example, one duo member will effectively require the other to display II-octile (20) power over outsiders in order for the exchange between partners to increase in depth. Also, the wraparound rule still applies, so that partners who have an inconjunct (regular level I, 12th harmonic) for this pair will see one of them require a conjunct's instinctual behavior in the other (regular level I, 1st harmonic instead of 13th because of wraparound). Nonperformance under this pair leads to stagnancy in the exchange.

Venus-Node

<Mercury-"questing"

This angle is prolifically or distantly displayed on the part of one duo member, keeping the other from reaching them. There is a strong sense in which the latter will be ever unable to match the level of the former no matter how well they connect.

There are two additional consequences that come with this angle which are noteworthy. The first (good news) is that this pair neither kills nor stifles a partnership. In fact, this one is more like the talent which characterizes the duo given its possession by the unreachable duo member. The possessor of this unreachable talent will carry much of the public flag for the relationship. The second consequence (not so good) is that the relationship in which the partners attain equal mastery in this one (coming from one-sidedness) tends to produce remorseless separations as the weaker partner most often incurs something like pre-jealousy on the part of the stronger. Only the closest, most understanding duo member can withstand such erosion of their former monopoly over this angle skill.

Venus-Selene

<Mercury-"resolvable dilemma"

The ability of one duo member to convey this angle with social potency is evident in this pair. **One partner can successfully foist this angle strongly upon lots of people**, in yet another indicator of one partner's skill—this time in the unstoppable sense rather than the mastery sense.

Venus-Lilith

<Mercury-"unfulfilling conformity"

This angle is the means through which one duo member seeks out contact with the other in order to share the former's new experiences. In fuzzier cases like the decile or inconjunct, the angle simply colors regular communication with the undertone of structure or amorphousness for example. II-conjuncts and III-septiles are unfortunate here in that they color the receipt of new personal experiences with the weight of what outsiders think, making the sharer feel invalidated and effectively crushing their self-esteem. (As a personal note, the III-septile was the angle responsible for one of the worst relationship deaths I ever experienced; III-septiles produce a situation where one person says, "Look what I did!" and the other says, "All these other people have done better than that. Fail.")

Venus-Fortune*

<Mercury-"comfortable conditions"

Talking to or about the effects of one duo member on the other is the topic under this angle, whether those effects take place within or outside of the duo. **This angle constitutes the subject of either positive or negative commentary which one duo member issues forth about their partner**.

Venus-Ceres

<Mercury-"Other's dissatisfying expression"

[Venus-Ceres] shows the kind of pressing subject matter that comes with one duo member's conversation. **When this person discloses information about themselves which also includes hints of what they want, such information is related to this angle**. This poses an interesting puzzle if you're up for it because the angle you find here is directly tied to the resonant pairs in their regular chart. In other words, for the partner who discloses information about their unique history through a II-undecile, not only will you tend to learn about the entire family of II-undecile pairs in their regular chart, you'll also hear (if you listen) about how they would like to resolve the issues related to their unique history (the II-undecile's area of concern).

By the way, what kind of resolution does a person tend to want when they air the issues associated with this angle? The resolution that comes with good display of their own [Mercury-"*Other's dissatisfying expression*"]. You can substitute *Saturn* for this one, so that their regular chart's [Mercury-Saturn] will give you a decent idea of how they would like to resolve the composite [Venus-Ceres]. It works like a charm. This only applies to the partner which the [Venus-Ceres] style actually describes though.

Venus-Chiron

<Mercury-"need for help"

One partner is inclined to distrust or simply be in mystery regarding the other's version of this angle. This is one of those angles which may take the first partner a long time to get used to in the other. So long, in fact, that by the time they do get used to it, the second partner may have moved on. In positive cases (very rare), trust is not an issue and the first partner simply supports the second's broadcasting of this angle to others.

Venus-Vesta

<Mercury-"situation that needs tending to"

 **Did you get their message?**

It turns out that Venus plays a role in more than its share of abstract pairs in the composite chart, among which sits [Venus-Vesta] as one of the most salient. **This pair's angle shows the area of experience which duo members hope to express through continued communication with the other partner**. We know this because 1) their actions in unequal or cancelled partnerships reveal this as an end and 2) because they say so. And although we never like to lean on astrology to tell you something that reality itself wouldn't confirm, this particular pair is really good for getting at the partner's actual motives behind the more confusing messages they send. In cases where your partner struggles to convey their wishes to you, you can make them feel as if they have successfully sent you this angle. More often than not, it will make them feel really listened to. Deny that they have sent this message successfully and watch the exchange freeze instantly upon the icy expanse of misunderstanding.

Venus-Pallas

<Mercury-"social imbalance"

 **That fateful conversation**

This angle shows the end which smooth communication between partners is meant to serve. That is, it shows the reason why the duo members would be encouraged to work together smoothly. You'll find that it is much easier to connect one-on-one with the other partner through really good conversation under this angle. **In fact, this angle situation may circumscribe some of your best conversations**. Often the topic concerns other people's behaviors.

Venus-Juno

<Mercury-"need for secured role"

Austerity or another form of limitation is enforced by one duo member upon the other under this angle, where one of your modes of influence is subject to the recognized control of the other. This is often done in the interest of the one being controlled, whether or not they realize it. The controller effectively liberates the controlled from a certain set of restrictions.

Venus-Hera

<Mercury-"state of unattachment"

One partner demonstrates openness coupled with responsibility under this angle while the other remains stubbornly entrenched. In good cases, the pair can make great complements to each other, though these cases are rarer than the standard disconnect which we would rightly expect of most exchanges. There is definitely room for both partners to work on acceptance here, as successful negotiation of these differences can allow the entrenched partner to serve as a great safe haven for the open one.

The data suggested that III-inconjuncts, unfortunately, have a greater uphill battle in that these relationships are divided on "memorability;" While parts of the duo may look very good, the relationship itself tends to struggle mightily in other areas and usually dies suddenly before its time. On a less intense level, inconjuncts describe relationships which are divided over a thing that can't be easily explained.

Venus-Eros

<Mercury-"receptiveness to impassioned action"

This angle shows what the more dominant partner supports the other in expressing, serving as a source of encouragement or as a trainer to the latter.

Venus-Bacchus

<Mercury-"desire to share company"

This one is very straightforward. **[Venus-Bacchus]' angle shows the duo's preferred approach to casual conversation, usually at the behest of the more interested partner**. Conjuncts trade raw responses to the topic while trines trade opinions. Septiles converse largely for the sake of the exchange and tend to cover a lot of ground in the process. II-sextiles make holistic observations in a way that can be very insightful or dismissively honest. Speaking of honest, II-squares communicate like family, sharing their unpolished emotional core. III-trines instruct or inform each other. III-septiles respect the behavioral rules of their shared networks. IV-conjuncts speak what's on their mind in ways that can easily shock or offend each other.

Mars pairs

Mars-Jupiter

<Venus-Mars

The battle lines for a divorce

The duo members are very much in tune when it comes to placing this angle area on others, even if they don't actively cooperate. There is broad agreement on how things should be done here, though the result may be fighting instead of friendship. The odds of each are about equal. Here is a good time to recall how astrological influences like Venus, Libra, and the 7th house work; each can denote both friends as well as open enemies. Open enemies come from the idea that we agree enough with another to be in the same arena but, because we're different people with different backgrounds, we don't agree enough to take the same approach within that arena. Here we have the same assumptions, different conclusions in the case of disagreements in angle approach. We have the same broad assumptions, other-validating communication in the agreement case.

In the end, rifts under this angle tend to be more obvious than with other composite pairs, with the two partners truly setting up separate, competing versions of this angle within the same partnership if things get really bad. If there are shared creations like children, friends or followers, those creations will be forced to view two choices for this angle instead of one. **Relatedly, this pair is a good indicator of the lines along which shared things are parceled out in a literal or figurative divorce**. If you and Other have an undecile amidst a rift for example, your former joint followers will pick between realms of social talk to reinforce. If you have a II-trine, they will divide themselves into two separate spheres of influence to frequent. If you have a II-sextile, they will choose from two sets of long-range courses of action to follow. If you have a III-quintile, your following audiences will divide themselves into two positions of pride between you.

Mars-Jupiter is not a partnership killer, but provides a good description of where the lines are drawn after a partnership is already dead.

Mars-Saturn

<Venus-Jupiter

One duo member's interaction with the other under this angle is a tough affair, since the latter can be implacable here. No matter how much the first partner does, the second always seems to want more or require something different. **The first duo member may regret having attempted to interact with the second one here, since the agreement to do so sets up a chain of obligations which the first person will struggle to escape without damaging**

the relationship. This is the classic "You're the one who signed the contract..." situation.

On the positive side of this pair, II-septiles can socialize for a very long time, identifying easily with each other.

Mars-Uranus

<Venus-Saturn

Simply by hanging around, one duo member greatly amplifies the spotlight shone by the other upon the latter's angle area of life. Harmless looking as this effect might seem, this pair is in fact a potent duo killer when either 1) monopolized by one partner or 2) projected in an imbalanced way onto the wrong partner. So if you and I have a III-septile here and you're the one who's more fit to grow their network, you are the one who'll naturally need to have this tendency further amplified. If I (the unskilled partner) have it amplified under this pair, we will both defy our natural roles and the partnership will have a good chance of dying.

You actually want for the strong to get stronger under this angle within the context of the duo. Squares are odd because, while one partner tends to be naturally more emotional than the other, they can't be so emotional as to make the other truly angry while the relationship is still fragile. Making the other angry effectively causes the naturally more emotional person to get themselves overpowered by the anger of the normally less emotional person, greatly harming the nascent partnership in most cases. And so it goes for other angles; the stronger should remain so, but not so strong as to bully the weaker expresser into outshining the stronger through a defensive reaction.

Mars-Neptune

<Venus-Uranus

The Impressor (Beta)

This angle shows the realm of expression for what is typically the more feminine, more subordinate, or less assertive partner. **This person is super skilled at issuing this angle in a laid back, automatic way, showing this pair more as an ability to draw the angle from their interactants than an ability to issue it forth themselves.**

Mars-Pluto

<Venus-Neptune

You and other have a natural ability to talk business under this angle, though the nature of that business depends greatly on the angle. Conjuncts can mix business with fun. Trine communication tends to be provocative and more insistent. Undeciles tend to struggle to communicate "really" about serious topics and are more likely to eventually lose respect for each other in this department if they're not careful. II-quintiles on the other hand may only connect well through the discussion of shared business as it relates to controlling others' behavior. **The net result is that the relationship becomes notable for the realm in which the two of you see eye to eye on how to influence certain topic areas in the world**.

Mars-Ascendant*

<Venus-2nd house

One of the duo members is unusual in their approach to this angle, **using tactics opposite those normally used to achieve this angle's ends. Look at the angle+6 (using wraparound) to see how the contrary partner accomplishes this angle's goal** in the eyes of the other partner.

Mars-Midheaven*[51]

<Venus-11th house

How sex and creativity pass between partners

The duo members convey their sexuality or creativity to each other through this angle. For better or worse, this pair is very picky with definite effects on the kinds of shared creation which passes through a duo.

For most non-romantic relationships, this pair plays out in the usual angle-related ways shown in *table 19-1*. Conjuncts pass creativity naturally, Oppositions do it through the way they value themselves and seek satisfaction of their urges. Trines simply communicate. Septiles converse. Undeciles swap social information. And so on. Romantic cases, on the other hand, are another story. Dipping into the work in sexology I can tell you that there are a million ways to engage a partner thus, but most of these ways are reduced to traditional social training with this angle as an afterthought. So partners with a decile are more likely to have traditional sex with control issues hovering around the act. Partners with an undecile will have traditional sex which turns into a public item for discussion—for any number of reasons you can think of, mostly negative. II-oppositions may have traditional sex when just being together and valuing each other would be better. III-oppositions will have traditional sex but judge the experience against what their "fans" and social expectation trainers would say. You get the idea. In addition to showing how you pass creative messages to each other this angle shows how your duo approaches the idea of sexual and creative performance with each other. Now I know what you're thinking. That's no big deal, right? But let's go back over some things most of us know but easily forget.

As relationships age, the initial fire has a tendency to dim as partners get used to each other. With the expectations we bring into the relationship (shown partly by this angle), we gauge how we expect that fire to play out and what we expect to get out of the affair. Actually setting your expectations against your partner takes more time than using the expectations of previous partners, so that some never get the chance to be whom they would naturally be with you. That is, those people will never be fully into it because you won't let them meet you on their terms rather than some past commentator whom you brought with you. Of course, during the act we tend not to think about this. After the exchange or before the next round though...

...As we've seen over and over throughout these interpretations, sex and creativity are quite interchangeable in the astrological sense. Sex and sensuality are related in the sensory sense. Sex and power are related in the social sense. So while it's easy to think of a pair which describes the physical exchange as being just that, those with fragile relationships whose fire dies when the sexy newness dies might consider removing some of the eggs from that basket. As with almost all relationship aspects, good sex comes with good communication. Good communication over this angle—whether through conversation, shared projects, nurtured power, or consideration of the partner's sensuality—can go a long way in keeping the creativity between partners going even when bodily exchange and physical dating deeds cease to be the main event. When

[51] This entire description (with all paragraphs below it) was written using the "blind method," where I did not know the planets involved with this pair as I wrote it, finding out only AFTER I placed the lips, and *as* I placed the heading. Compare this to [Mars-Midheaven] in Chapter 19 and [Mars-Midheaven] in *table 16-5* (from *FSA*). Although I don't usually take time to argue for the merits of testing astrology statistically, the statistician in me found this particular pair especially amazing. Surely you've seen that descriptions which are romance-relevant enough to get marked with lips are rare. And even though I've offered explanations in this book and in *FSA* explaining why composites, synastries, and regular charts should work, I still find the whole "coincidence" of a random, unlabeled column full of numbers just *happening* to produce results that line up with the right label from previous research to be incredible. Even with all the correct math involved, there is still enough error inherent in composite angles to justify meaningless results. Yet the data *still* generate consistently matched patterns. Mind. Blown. See [Pluto-Selene] for a full description of the blind method. As Katha argued in *FSA*, I challenge people who question all of astrology to do statistics like this first before dismissing everything. There are surely patterns at play here.

deciles address the control issues inherent in their shared projects, they address the control issues in the bedroom. When II-quintiles address the divide in how they dominate, they address ego issues in the bedroom. And although notions of physical intimacy are often limited to the "all the way" phase of a romance, we know by now that it can also be thought of as simply the more direct form of communicative intimacy. To sharpen the communication is to solve a wide array of other partner problems in the long run—including those related to the creation of money, the creation of children, and the creation of shared life opportunities as well. Sex constitutes only a fraction of this pair's picture. Perfect the rest of this angle to improve the quality of your exchange with the other on the whole.

Mars-Vertex*

<Venus-"expiring comfort"

This angle shows the means through which one of the partner's intentions for power are conveyed. **They like to operate freely and unobstructed in this angle area, leaving the other partner as a witness for validating the former's skillful ability to self-determine.**

Mars-Node

<Venus-"questing"

Get them to do what you want

One partner has a strong ability to steer people using this angle, sometimes through their temperament, sometimes through smooth reasoning. For whatever reason (most likely rooted in a science beyond this book), some of the more attitude-based versions of this angle can be used to produce results in a partner which look truly "psychic"—however you feel about that. As a II-inconjunct partner imagines, the other sees them as getting what they want. As a IV-undecile forms an outlook, the partner sees them as getting the world envisioned. More research on how this works would certainly be interesting, though it may just amount to the usual form of resonance between one partner's actions and the other's view of those actions.

This is basically the angle you use for getting the other person to do what you want.

(In light of finding out that this pair was [Mars-Node], I was actually quite surprised at how apparently psychic this pair was. Trained in the traditional idea that Mars rules Aries and denotes Masculine forwardness, I still have this lingering assumption that Mars doesn't "do" intuition. Of course we already dispelled this idea in FSA *when we concluded that Mars rules Scorpio and is much less aggressive, much more other-compelling. So the intuitive part makes more sense here. Furthermore, there is quite a lot of evidence supporting the idea that this pair's prior planet Venus is one of the strongest major planets for "summoning" situations to which the summoner is attracted.)*

Mars-Selene

<Venus-"resolvable dilemma"

There is a shared approach to the use of force under this angle, where the duo members can jointly express the angle to knock rivals off their horses. The creative tension between II-inconjuncts is especially strong. The shared networks of III-septiles consist of especially fierce personalities. III-novile pairs can work their fans into extra fervor. The command of III-deciles is extra "boss." The justifications (arguments) launched by IV-conjuncts are extra potent. In negative cases, such force is turned on each other.

Mars-Lilith

<Venus-"unfulfilling conformity"

The Impressor (Alpha)

This pair shows one duo member's view of the other's expressive specialty. The other partner has a skill for this angle which renders the competing efforts of others moot by comparison. The data suggested that such skill is usually associated with the more assertive, more masculine, or more dominant partner.

Mars-Fortune*

<Venus-"comfortable conditions"

There is a sober recognition of how one of the duo members presents themselves through this angle. Such recognition is something like respect mixed with acceptance of the other person's standards. It is simply assumed that one shouldn't joke around with said duo member's efforts here.

Mars-Ceres

<Venus-"Other's dissatisfying expression"

> After a while when you have so many planets and points for comparison the effects start looking alike. That's when we have to get into the nuanced differences among them.

One partner sees this angle as being the standard against which the latter's successful interaction is measured. **With this combination you can read something like "That meeting went well because it provided [angle area] for us (mostly them)."** Success with this pair provides a slight esteem boost for the measured partner.

Mars-Chiron

<Venus-"need for help"

One duo member evokes a show of anger in the form of this angle from the other person. When unsettled, the upset partner conveys it by expressing this angle in a way that excludes or punishes the offending partner. Interestingly, this trait seems to be exaggerated in partners who have been hurt or disappointed many times. Of course this pair does not always produce anger. Positively, it simply produces a need to strongly steer certain outcomes.

Mars-Vesta

<Venus-"situation that needs tending to"

This pair shows where one duo member forces the other to step up their standards to dominance level. **That is, at least one partner's company compels the other to be so strong under this angle that the latter can defeat almost any challenger in this area.** This is attack-dog training in which the partner who is already strong in this angle is pushed to become even stronger. The level of power achieved by this person here can be outrageous.

Mars-Pallas

<Venus-"social imbalance"

One partner acts to amplify this trait in the other and polish it for public broadcast, though the other is typically resistant to this—intentionally or not. This amounts to something like resistance-based friction. **As the first partner pushes, the second partner becomes harder to move even as the latter typically wants to be successfully pushed.**

Mars-Juno

<Venus-"need for secured role"

☯ Reverse the fate of a duo

One partner holds this angle as an eternal monkey on their back. There is an accepted struggle to advance against this angle area without cease. Here we are reminded of Juno's role not as a marriage indicator *per se*, but as an indicator of what one is metaphorically married to in the eyes of society. Composite [Mars-Juno] shows where the duo is "married"$_{\text{Juno}}$ to the desire to steer something$_{\text{Mars}}$ while the angle shows roughly what that something is. Typically though, having the whole duo fixated on such a quest does not imply that both members are so fixated, only one. Remember, Mars steering can also indicate a quest to reason things out rather than solely manipulating them. As such, there is a connection between this pair as a source of ceaseless dilemmas and this pair as a source of ceaseless craving for validation in one's actions.

☯ Composite [Mars-Juno] behaves VERY differently depending on whether you use the high or low tension versions of the angle, the intellectual or manipulating versions of Mars, and the committed versus bounded version of Juno. As such, this one constitutes the first pair which can be marked with the yin-yang symbol as a true source of "alchemy" in a relationship. If you plan to reverse the fate of a partnership and need something drastic which won't destroy the duo, start with this pair and its angle.

Mars-Hera

<Venus-"state of unattachment"

In the eyes of one partner the other asks, "Does this activity in the world lead to an increase in [angle]? If not, then it's hardly worth it." We need to watch the different perspectives here, though, because they can get tangled: **Partner A sees Partner B as pursuing activities—mostly outside of the partnership—with an eye for those activities' ability to promote [this angle] as a concept in line with Partner B's own view of how that concept should work, though not necessarily for Partner B themselves.** (Whew, that was a lot.) This pair is somewhat utilitarian in that Partner B is less likely to be interested in pursuits that don't advance this angle as they define it. This pair is also more negative than the usual pair in that Partner B is more likely to have narrow views about this angle area which prevent them from seeing the angle in situations that don't align with their own framing of it. Partner A is more likely to encounter trouble getting Partner B to open their mind regarding this angle such that Partner A may find themselves responsible for expanding B's definition of the angle just to get the latter to properly pursue a worthwhile activity that B has written off. Overall, this pair is typically a source of difficulty arising from one partner's stubborn adherence to a certain way of seeing things.

Mars-Eros

<Venus-"receptiveness to impassioned action"

One duo member seems to struggle to experience this angle in just the way they want it, scattering their energy in attempts to get it right. A lack of focus is common here which can lead to frustration on behalf of both halves of the duo, both with each other and with things outside of their partnership.

Mars-Bacchus

<Venus-"desire to share company"

This angle shows the kind of focus one of the duo members feels it is important to have for the sake of their own status. They will tend to dedicate their time to this endeavor as they attempt to assert their role in the world. In an uncharacteristic turn, III-inconjuncts can be temperamental since it is so important that they be significant in the minds of those close to them.

Jupiter pairs

Jupiter-Saturn

<Mars-Jupiter

This pair shows the vehicle through which one duo member conveys their self-assured attitude. They believe in their abilities here and aren't afraid to tell the partner what's what.

Jupiter-Uranus

<Mars-Saturn

One duo member exposes the other to new ways of doing things under this angle, where the weaker duo member is actually the more effective one as the new lessons are internalized. This angle is also likely to be among the main faces of the duo's interaction which is displayed in front of peer groups as the duo evolves; sextiles are known among peers for the way they cooperate in work, for example. III-oppositions are known for the followers they attract.

Jupiter-Neptune

<Mars-Uranus

Think of this angle as showing the energy which leaks from the duo's exchange. That is, when the two parties interact, there is a mood of [this angle] which circumscribes the interaction. [Jupiter-Neptune] is a great indicator of what kind of vibe a pair of people leaves on their environment while they're together. **It's as if others really suspect this angle as being a key descriptor of their relationship.**

Certain angles create issues in professional partnerships. The three notably gender bending angles (discussed in *FSA*) are extra visible here. II-septiles tend to start off by sniffing each other out, but easily end up as friends and mutual supporters. Strangely, romantically inclined II-undeciles are more likely to flirt in publicly inappropriate situations and do so with little remorse. Where flirting is not feasible, the two may enjoy a bitter rivalry rooted in "something about them that I just don't like." The data were VERY consistent on this angle in particular. Perhaps this is related to the role of the composite II-undecile as indicating a "unique" and unsettling duo. In positive cases II-noviles are more likely to talk about sex and sexual things in plain view of others as if nothing's wrong. In neutral cases one will pick on the other like a classic bully infatuated with their victim. In negative II-novile cases the pair will simply repulse and annoy each other for no apparent reason. Finally, squares are more likely to seem personally affected by each other despite proscriptions against this.

Jupiter-Pluto

<Mars-Neptune

This angle signifies the thing that the duo wishes to attract together. **While cooperating with each other the duo members lay the seeds for more of this angle's subject area to appear in their lives**. II-septiles as a pair become more beloved among their friends. III-quintiles are more likely to evolve into a power duo the longer and more often they associate. III-sextiles become experts together. This pair is a great indicator of the thing which you and your partner can and should strive for with no remorse.

Jupiter-Ascendant*

<Mars-2nd house

One duo member protects or sticks up for this angle in another, where the defended person is more likely to be wayward, weird or simply misrepresented by others when it comes to this angle.

The duo marches forward unashamedly here.

Jupiter-Midheaven*

<Mars-11th house

Through a satisfying exchange with this angle, one duo member is filled with excitement regarding the other. The excited one is motivated to continue their bridge-building with the other person with an undertone of intensity further added (slightly) to the exchange. **This one takes time though, and should be thought of as an angle which the receiving partner has to get used to gradually before the duo can really connect**. Once connected, the two can strongly fuel each other's continued creativity under this angle.

Jupiter-Vertex*

<Mars-"expiring comfort"

♀/♂ This angle shows the means through which the duo becomes disconnected, should this ever occur. **The partners are naturally inclined to engage each other here, but equally inclined to pursue this angle in different ways—one typically more assertive and the other more passive**. Indeed, we might say that this pair is one of the principle indicators of where masculine-feminine or projective-receptive power differences play out. It matters less how divided the partners are in this topic area and matters more whether the partners can endure whatever deviations from expectation may arise from those differences. This is an interesting pair.

Jupiter-Node

<Mars-"questing"

This pair is inherently sexual, though it can also show up as shared creativity. **Its angle is the realm in which the duo is most likely to experience each other's most intense impulses**, revealing a more primal background for exchange. There are several aspects like this in the composite chart, where this one is distinguishable as setting the circumstance in which sexual advance is most likely to play out. Conjuncts gravitate towards such a connection automatically. II-squares make for a particularly satisfying love life in the home. II-conjuncts favor one of the duo members as having an intensely charged stage presence; here the attraction between duo members is more likely to play out through art or the public. In cases where sex isn't the thing, joint creativity seems especially favored.

Jupiter-Selene

<Mars-"resolvable dilemma"

This pair's angle is the means through which one partner gains respect for the other's abilities. Suppose you like someone or would, minimally, want to work with them *but for* your lack of faith in their talents. **This is the angle through which the other would need to prove themselves to you in order to increase your sense of security in them as partners in the public image-building sense.**

Jupiter-Lilith

<Mars-"unfulfilling conformity"

♀/♂ The Attractor (Beta)

Alongside its partner (Attractor Alpha), this pair serves as the basis of attraction between one duo member and the other. Attraction need not always be romantic, but the attractors favor this along with shared creative endeavors. In fact, as soon as you're done reading this one you should skip directly to [Jupiter-Vesta (1)] (later in the chapter but written before this one) and see what it says. The two composite pairs round out the attractive terrain very nicely.

♀/♂ **This pair shows specifically where one duo member is instinctually (or animalistically) drawn to the other.** It differs from its partner [Jupiter-Vesta] in that **this one is all about what one feels compelled to give** while the other involves what one is drawn to receive. The interpretations are as straightforward as the usual *table 19-1* reading, though I found it more interesting to look at this and its partner pair side by side as a way of rounding out the primal picture between romantic partners overall.

The attractors can be used to manipulate a relationship, but I wouldn't recommend it unless you know which party is receiving which angle. Otherwise you'll likely mess things up. Typically the more dominant person will push this (Beta's) angle onto the other and cause them to be attracted while the less dominant person overall will push Alpha's angle [Jupiter-Vesta] onto their counterpart. If we think of the "Alpha" as the more dominant person in general and the "Beta" as the less dominant person, this pair—the Beta Attractor—attracts the Beta person and [Jupiter-Vesta]—the Alpha Attractor—attracts the Alpha person. This gets us into a whole new can of worms regarding masculinity and femininity, but we'll save that conversation for the last book in this series.

Jupiter-Fortune*

<Mars-"comfortable conditions"

One partner likes to brag about their relationship status with the partner as providing this angle. Or at least they are inclined to be quite content with the other here. **The partner validates the first person as a social success in the realm of this angle.**

Jupiter-Ceres

<Mars-"Other's dissatisfying expression"

The face of pleasantness

This pair tames the resonant pairs under this same angle across the board, rendering communication via this angle a more pleasant, cool-headed, or joyful experience. The partners are good at bringing happiness to each other using this angle, where even the normally meaner III-deciles are more likely to be welcomed as respected traits of partners rather than dreaded ones. III-inconjuncts are much more likely to be remembered for their lively and upbeat company.

Jupiter-Chiron

<Mars-"need for help"

The duo members' expectations for the rules regarding this angle govern much of their responses to each other's interaction. The duo members single each other out for the other's ability to perform according to those rules or excel in the realm of those rules. Social efficacy using this angle is the measuring stick employed by one partner to judge the quality of the other's company.

As the result of a procedural error I neglected to hide the next pair in the database after I first interpreted it. So I interpreted its pattern twice. Serendipitously, readers may be interested to see how the two descriptions differ yet really complement each other, giving you a glimpse at what statisticians call "instrument reliability" (how consistently the same test measures the same thing over repeated trials). Here the instrument would be my own interpretation of unlabeled clusters. See how the first interpretation answers more questions about the specific duo members while the second answers more questions about the duo as a whole. Thankfully, the two descriptions both support each other through their emphasis on "gluing" the union together. The first description warranted the gender bias symbol ♀/♂ while the second didn't. Yet both interpretations warranted the relationship builder symbol. As with all blind method pairs, these symbols and their preceding **descriptors** were added *before* I knew what the paired planets were.

Jupiter-Vesta (1)

<Mars-"situation that needs tending to"

♀/♂ The Attractor (Alpha)

♀/♂ The duo is glued together in part by this—one duo member's most attractive feature. Now the data actually suggest that this one holds for only half of the pairs, where one person views this angle as a source of potential in their own lives while the other doesn't necessarily see anything. As you might expect, we'll need two of these to complete the relationship picture. **This pair shows roughly where one duo member enjoys receiving from another. Its partner pair (Attractor Beta) will tell the other half of the story**.

Jupiter-Vesta (2)

<Mars-"situation that needs tending to"

The relationship is held solidly together through joint expression of this angle as a behavior to be broadcast to the world. This is a very powerful pair whose effects heavily influence the duo's ability to remain a duo. As long as you're doing this angle together, your relationship with the other person has a good chance of staying strong. Oppositions tend to be naturally loyal to each other as do II-squares, though the latter may be weighed down by more than their share of insecurities sponsored by or foisted upon the other partner. My mom and I were an example of a III-opposition in which "appealing to the fans" doesn't just mean appealing to strangers, but tending to the rest of the family—nuclear and extended—as well. III-noviles need some kind of audience to please. III-inconjuncts share similar feelings about society which tends to keep them strong in each other's memory.

Jupiter-Pallas

<Mars-"social imbalance"

One partner strongly insists that the other hears them out under this angle, demanding acknowledgement by whatever means is acceptable. This angle frequently comes with a cocky attitude on the part of the person demanding to be heard; sometimes (but not always) the demanding person can take things to such an extreme that they dismiss the partner whom they actually want to listen to them.

Jupiter-Juno

<Mars-"need for secured role"

This angle shows where one partner demonstrates the need to protect the other or the other's interests.

This pair would be fairly minor but for its role as an indicator of the area where one partner has the other's back. I've found that, somewhat unfortunately, the defended partner in certain relationships has to extract this kind of defense from their partner, creating a situation in which the defender serves more as a mercenary for hire. Why would partners do this to each other? In those same relationships I found that this pair's role as a protection-extractor seemed solid enough to "want" to show up regardless of the partners' closeness but also tended to favor the partner who most valued the angle in question. So if you and Other have a III-trine and you are the only one who cares about protecting your powers of insight, you will be the defended one. But if Other is someone who isn't knowledgeable about or isn't invested in defending you, you are more likely to simply defend your own insight using some consequence of their presence around you. They become a tool for you here. Relationships like this in the data were highly prone to deceit or resentment on the part of the "mercenary" partner forced to do the defending, though neither partner typically realizes what is going on while it's happening. **In such negative cases this angle is strongly related to the reasons one partner would use the other as a tool.**

Jupiter-Hera

<Mars-"state of unattachment"

This angle shows where one of the duo members demonstrates a reliable level of maturity or sophistication. This partner knows what's up where this angle is concerned and shows a marked ability to be responsible to or for others here.

Jupiter-Eros

<Mars-"receptiveness to impassioned action"

Intimate bonding time for the duo takes on the appearance of this angle. **In cases where one person wants to soak up the other's company, blocking out all else, this pair dominates.** *Table 19-8* is good for reading this one. II-quintiles make each other look great in public by default.

Jupiter-Bacchus

<Mars-"desire to share company"

The duo puts on a very public show for others using this angle. And even if they don't overtly show it, others are more likely to at least suspect that this angle is a focus which the duo members share. People tend to find watching the duo in action under this angle quite entertaining and at least a little fulfilling. This pair has a noticeable effect on the duo's public image in general.

Saturn pairs

Saturn-Uranus

<Jupiter-Saturn

To renew or expire...

Exposure to this angle on the part of one of the duo members can make or break the relationship. Here one will see the other in their most raw form and typically be forced into a decision to stay partnered or sever the tie. **When this angle is successfully displayed and accepted, the exchange and its fire are renewed, but when such an exchange fails, the relationship begins a stubborn slide into nothingness unless the displayer can dig things out of the hole before it's too late.** This one is both a bond maintainer and duo breaker.

Saturn-Neptune

<Jupiter-Uranus

One duo member feels more comfortable revealing this angle side of themselves to the other, though such comfort often shows up as the automatic tendency to burden the latter with the former's expression of this angle. Comfortable revelation looks more like a bad habit here, where the first partner is more inclined to unleash this angle on the second in ways that the latter is not quite ready to receive. The more social or information-based angles like III-quintiles and all I-, II-, and III-undeciles are more likely to flood their partners with the respective kinds of information.

Saturn-Pluto

<Jupiter-Neptune

One partner picks on or pressures the other under this angle, compelling a better performance here. **In positive cases the pushing partner simply serves as a sounding board against which the pushed partner can drive themselves.**

Saturn-Ascendant*

<Jupiter -2nd house

One duo member must be (and often is) on top of their game when engaging the other under this angle. Especially in light of the other's immaturity or lack of experience, the person must be patient while the other develops the necessary strength to match the first person's level. The inexperienced partner typically does evolve, but this one takes time and practice.

Saturn-Midheaven*

<Jupiter -11th house

This angle shows what the duo members do in order to attract each other's attention. **Participation in this angle's affairs by the partners as individuals puts them on each other's radar for further interaction as a possible formal team.**

Saturn-Vertex*

<Jupiter-"expiring comfort"

A respected basis for connection

Where did we go wrong as a team?

There is a kind of commitment that comes with this pair, where the duo members (usually unknowingly) promise to stay plugged into each other's efforts under this angle fbow. Even if the partners separate and end up hating each other, there remains a basic acknowledgement of the other's basic correctness in showing this angle. **Regardless of the pleasantness of the interaction, at least one partner tends to be right on in their display of this angle towards the other.** You may find it interesting to note that, when partners are not equally strong under this angle, the partner who is more consistently in the wrong under this one is the partner who can be more easily blamed for destroying the association based on a lack of cooperation.

Saturn-Node

<Jupiter-"questing"

Stay with their ceaseless fixation

This angle is given a high priority for one of the duo members, often to the point that the other has no choice but to focus on it as well or be dropped as company. Cultivation of this pair's angle falls just short of an obsession for one of the partners and serves as a means of gatekeeping for establishment of a permanent relationship with that partner. The more you have to struggle to do this angle with your partner (or the other way around if the reverse is true) the harder you can expect the relationship to be to maintain over the long term.

Saturn-Selene

<Jupiter-"resolvable dilemma"

One of the partners displays high maintenance standards in this angle area, creating a duo which requires this angle as its lifeblood. For the duo to be described by a really close social exchange, this angle needs to constitute a regular part of the relationship's diet.

Saturn-Lilith

<Jupiter-"unfulfilling conformity"

This angle is the means through which the more charming duo partner endears themselves to others. Such endearment consists of a combination of respect, and a willingness to be moved through exchange, so that **this pair constitutes the means through which the duo as a whole can win others over.**

Saturn-Fortune*

<Jupiter-"comfortable conditions"

The easiest indicator of partnership survivability thus far: Does our union stand a chance?

Strong opinions and intellectual force permeate the partnership under this angle. **Here, the duo members jointly focus their intensity on creating something that can stand up against outside assault.** At least we hope it's a joint effort. If it isn't this same angle becomes the source of heavily one-sided effort on the part of one partner to build a foundation that the other doesn't want to build. If you can be honest with yourself, this pair serves as a GREAT tell regarding the chances of the partnership's survival: Barring family and other stuck commitments, if one partner is silent on this one while the other is very passionate, the exchange is effectively doomed in most cases due to a lack of interest (or, in rarer cases, lack of hope) on the part of the silent person. Watch who keeps contact with whom in the III-inconjunct case.

Saturn-Ceres

<Jupiter-"Other's dissatisfying expression"

One duo member absolutely insists on having their way here. Consequently they may back the other duo member so far into a corner that the latter has no choice but to end the exchange. This is about as close to pure bullying as we've seen in the composites thus far, and if the two people aren't good sports about it there may be quite the mess to contend with afterwards. In positive cases—which are slightly less frequent than negative ones—the partners can be as close as a bodyguard and their protected charge; this is when the one who would be the bully finds a willing guardian in the one who would be bullied. (No, it's not the other way around.)

Saturn-Chiron

<Jupiter-"need for help"

One partner delivers criticism to the other via this angle. This pair is pretty informative in that its adherence to the usual *table 19-1* actually produces a very colorful array of critical styles. For example, noviles air their criticism directly to the public without checking in with the partner first, making for a particularly caustic interactant. Undeciles make their criticism into the talk of the town and are more likely to be sarcastic. Inconjuncts very often choose to remain silent, writing their criticism on their demeanor instead.

II-quintiles are more likely to try to manage the source of their discontent and may perform an array of compensatory actions rather than airing their criticism straight on. II-sextiles plan, and can look haywire as they do so. II-septiles have friends who do the criticizing for them, though they too will weigh in if the situation is urgent enough. II-deciles will become very serious. III-sextiles will simply air their sharp analysis in the classic style. III-septiles will fuel a social network's disapproval of the criticized thing. III-deciles will advise and command. III-inconjuncts will remind you of where you have consistently failed and how this is just another one of those occasions.

Saturn-Vesta

<Jupiter-"situation that needs tending to"

One partner reassures the other by giving the latter this angle. This is a pick-me up arrangement.

Saturn-Pallas

<Jupiter-"social imbalance"

This angle shows the realm in which advice-giving commentary is exchanged between partners. One duo member gives the other intel on the way things should be done here or interacts with them in such a way as to activate this angle when they give their opinion to the other.

Saturn-Juno

<Jupiter-“need for secured role”

The duo is all about business and order under this angle. Things done here must be done right and head in a coherent direction towards *something*. They must also be habitually practiced. Failing this, one partner has a decent chance of disappointing the other. Squares, in typical fashion, bind the partners emotionally such that failures register more deeply than they would with other angles. Sextiles aim to make daily sharing a longstanding thing. (At least *one* partner does.) Octiles are more invested in steering each other and gravitate towards the sexual or shared creation.

II-squares make for very loving and kind relationships while II-quintiles are more about how the duo looks to others. It is the task of II-undeciles to bring at least one of the partner's creativity to the forefront of viewers' perspectives. III-conjuncts are more about investigating one's own mind, while III-quintiles rely on the individual charisma of at least one of the partners to open doors for both people.

Saturn-Hera

<Jupiter-“state of unattachment”

This pair corresponds to what the duo talks about when they share intel on the social relations around them. This is one of the many areas of commonality between partners where a meeting of the minds comes easily, except that in this case the topic is more precisely aimed at assessing other people's behavior and how the partners interact with the world at large.

Saturn-Eros

<Jupiter-“receptiveness to impassioned action”

This entry is gray because it was difficult to draw conclusions from it based on the data.

This pair is quite weak with effects that are difficult to read in the chart. **It roughly corresponds to the set of personality standards which one of the duo members would prefer to please in their dealings with the other**. This pair is mostly about what is strived for and not what is actually done; the easiest way to ascertain its effects from the data was to note that the various clusters of people who had it each seemed to hold the same kinds of quiet little pack of judges in the background saying, “You'd better get this right or else be a failure.”

Saturn-Bacchus

<Jupiter-“desire to share company”

One duo member has a need to watch over the other in the realm of this angle. **The first partner champions and expands the outlook of the second as the latter conveys this angle**.

Uranus pairs

Uranus-Neptune

<Saturn-Uranus

The first real connection

The duo begins to become a duo under this angle. This corresponds to the setting which inspires the two to come together in the first place. If you want to initiate a partnership, using this angle as a common context for your interaction can be a huge help, though there is some evidence that this one is not so good for bringing a partnership back from the dead; the trust in the initial impression just won't normally be there. Still, this angle is really effective in establishing that first desire to join forces, and **seems to serve as a kind of gateway for similar self-discovery in one's regular chart—where you can learn much more about yourself via this angle**. This is a very strong pair with noticeable effects on the partnership for influencing the strength of its bond.

Uranus-Pluto

<Saturn-Neptune

A diamond refined

One of the chief aims of the partnership is to refine the unrefined version of this angle in the less mature duo member. Evolution of this angle becomes a project as one person is rightfully subjected to the authority of the other. This angle often brings difficulties to the relationship because the less refined person is more likely to resist taming no matter how cooperative they try to be. Such taming tends to take a very long time—on the order of years—probably because there is an element of both 1) entrenched programming on the part of the unrefined partner and 2) a true need to stick with it (through as many different situations as possible) on the part of the refined partner.

On the rare occasions where there is no need for taming, the person who would normally be thought weaker becomes a fulfilling source of confidence for the stronger. In new age terms, such relationships look as though they are the work of "old souls" or "old friends" who have known each other for a very long time. These kinds of relationships (where this angle is not the stuff of lessons or where any angle lessons here have been completed) should be cherished when you find them, as they are very rare and very valuable.

Uranus-Ascendant*

<Saturn-2nd house

One partner has a humbled or modest presence in the eyes of the other here, covering their strength. This is a good aspect for the humbled partner becoming a cool-headed expert in this angle area; in most cases this person has a potency which never goes to their heads.

Warning: The following views of composites are highly technical and are intended (like many of the explanations in this book and its predecessor) to explain the possible science/math behind patterns which are clearly there, but unexplained at the time of this writing. As much of *FSA* and *HBS* contains new research, these kinds of explanations serve not only to ease the skepticism of the reader regarding why they should "believe" the interpretations herein, but also why the author himself should believe them. For people familiar enough with astrology, you don't just create chapters full of weird conclusions without explaining why they should hold, so here we have it. The following explanations are "vertical"—showing how we move up one level of conception when we go from a regular chart to a composite chart. For a more "horizontal" version of this same process, see the gray box under [Vertex*-Fortune*].

Why do the composite pairs act like this? Explanation 1.

Okay. Now I officially don't get it, Hayden interrupted Geery's explanation of composite [Uranus-Ascendant]. I've heard so much about Uranus being shocking and Ascendant being an approach, so I would think that this pair was some kind of shocking approach. What's the deal with these composite pairs behaving like the planets before them? The one you just told me about really does sound more like a more controlled Saturn and a more self-esteem related "2nd house" thing if I understand these correctly. I imagine people into astrology would argue with you on an interpretation like this.

Argue with me? They should look at the statistics in an unlabeled group and tell me what *they* find. There was nothing shocking about [Uranus-Ascendant] except for the idea that someone in the pair was a badass and *didn't* brag about it. I suppose you could call the duo on the whole shockingly blasé about its social potency. Remember also that [Uranus-Ascendant] in the regular chart lines up a person with his surrounding social talk. In the individual's chart this was "group membership" such that he fit right in with what was talked about. Only this time it's not an individual who fits right in, but the pair as a whole. All of the composites are like this; the things which individuals formerly did, their partnerships now do. But as individuals in those partnerships, the single people who make up those partnerships must almost certainly be doing something else.

Why is that? Hayden queried, clearly confused. Why does a pair's Venus-Mars depend on the individual's Mercury-Venuses before it? I guess in general, why does a composite chart's planet X-N combination depend on its individuals' W-M combination before these—you know, where W is right before X and M is right before N?

I don't know.

Just give me a guess. I'm sure you have one, since you've been spelling out these composite combinations for a while and their behavior doesn't seem to bother the "scientist" in you. It definitely bothers me though. Just when your interpretations were starting to look a little consistent, these composite pairs seem to be doing something systematically different, but not. Why?

Well, I do have a guess, Geery hesitated. But I don't think you'll like it.

Oh? Why's that?

Because it's technical.

Hayden froze for a fraction of second, wide-eyed at the thought of Geery's next long-winded speech. Then he sighed. **Hbbbb** Alright, whatever. I'm bracing myself.

Are you sure?

Yeah, fine.

First, I'll give you an analogy to make the technical part easier: You know that, in order for a city to do one thing, its various departments must work together on many complementary things which don't look like what the city is doing on the whole?

Sure.

And you know that in order for a person to do one thing his various organ systems have to do several complementary things which don't look like what *he* is doing on the whole?

Mm hm.

🛠 Okay. Remember how I told you (when we started) that the planets get their character from their orbits? So Jupiter doesn't show "expansion" just because it's Jupiter. It shows expansion because that's the character which comes after "an intent to push something:" That's Mars. Mars doesn't show "an intent to push" just because it's Mars. It shows such pushing because that's the character which comes right after "one-on-one contact:" Venus. To understand how the planets and points get arranged in a naturally ordered chain, it helps not to think of them as being "characters," but to think of them instead as being numbers in succession—orbit numbers. Just like the periodic table's electron orbits produce a natural order for the elements. Just like the increasing frequency number on the spectrum produces everything from radio waves to gamma rays and, somewhere in there, colors as different as red is from green. See how a change in number can make things look different but still repeatable on a cycle?

Okay, I understand that. And I also understand how people make up partnerships and so might behave differently from the things they make up. But you haven't yet said how a characteristic that acts like Mercury-Venus on the single person level magically transforms into a Venus-Mars thing on the pair level. I kind of get where you might be going, but not really.

Alright so here's the technical part. I believe it was the mathematician Giuseppe Peano who came up with a nice set of rules for defining the counting numbers.

Defining numbers?

Yes. It's pretty abstract, but goes something like this:

- Let the number "1" be a thing which includes "some stuff we won't bother to get into." 1 tree. 1 car. 1 pig. Whatever. Since we won't get into the details of whatever the thing is, we'll call that thing's characteristics an "empty set." In other words, "1" is a box with some undescribed stuff in it. 1 = {∅}
- Now I'll bet you forgot that when you count items you assume that earlier amounts were already counted. That is, in order to count to 2, you have to assume that 1 thing is already in there. So 2 includes 1 (plus some new stuff/empty space which I'll ignore). That is, 2 is a box which includes 1 inside of it. 2 = {1}. So 2 is a box which includes a box with some undescribed stuff in it. 2 = {1} = {{∅}}. You follow me so far?

Uh…

- 1 thing includes stuff. 2 things include 1 thing which includes stuff. 3 things include 2 things. And that's how it's gonna go.

Gotcha.

- The next part is the key: Can you see that if you look at counting this way, adding 1 isn't really "adding" 1, but it's more like "absorbing" the previous count into the next box that you're on? So increasing your count from 14 to 15 really is more like putting a box labeled "14" into yet another box. Assuming we haven't changed any ideas discussed so far, how many boxes do we now have?

15.

- Right. When people look at things on a number line, they see those things as standing apart. But when it comes to counting, it's better to think of those things as being stacked up on top each of the things considered before them. So *counting* perceptually is actually *stacking* mentally.
    - Distance is the stacking of space upon space; so putting distance between yourself and a thing makes it that much harder for the thing's effects to reach you.
    - Time is the stacking of experience; so putting time between yourself and a thing puts *experiential* distance between you and it, crowding out its effects on you with other experiences. Thus we forget. And our "wounds" are healed.

Interesting.

- And orbits are the stacking of potential energy levels in spacetime. Just as the next level sign Scorpio stacks upon Libra, so corresponds octile stacking upon septile, Mars stacking upon Venus, and 8 stacking upon 7. So fill in the blank: A Mars-style partner<u>ship</u> should be expected to stack upon a [blank] style *partner.*

Venus.

Right.

But—you can't just conclude that can you? You've made the analogy but you haven't proven it.

You're right, but the premise is consistent with everything I've surmised from my previous observations with Katha right up to now. By this argument, the charts of partnerships should have pairs which are determined by the *partners'* planets one level before them. Then the second level composite charts of competitions among partnerships (or teams) should have pairs which are determined by the partnerships' planets one level before them and by the *partners'* planets two levels before that—allowing us, perhaps to drill down to the underlying principles espoused by various levels of various systems.

Hayden was silent, reflecting on Geery's conclusions.

In other words, each level of a system involving stuff with other stuff in it adds one more level to the stack and the count. But that last part was a bit advanced. So to answer your question, *Why do the pairs in composite/partnership charts consistently reflect the actions of their members one planet backwards*, I think it's because **composite-partnership charts stack on individual-partner charts. To stack is to add 1. To unstack and go back to partner behaviors ←from partnership behaviors, we need to *subtract* 1**. ⚒

Hayden sighed again. I've often had reason to doubt you on these trips, but this time I truly don't have anything to challenge what you've told me. Adding things *does* seem like stacking their instances in some way. And I have no reason to believe that stacking things can't be thought of as adding to them. Stacking people to form groups and stacking groups to form—I don't know, departments?—seems like it almost begs for a change in planet each time, not so much because your logic has convinced me, (I actually didn't really understand it) but because, realistically, I've wondered why bosses everywhere can be so out of touch with their employees, elected representatives can be so out of touch with their public, and why people's partnership ideals can be so out of touch with the people themselves. The "stacking as adding, adding as changing" thing is a foreign concept to me, but it does make me think.

Geery scratched his head. I have the explanation, and I'm sure it can be used to help people in society if more folks understood it, but I don't really know how to put it to use in the real world.

Yeah. But that's probably a task for other people who read your work and understand it well enough to apply it in their own way.

May-be.

Why do the composite pairs act like this? Explanation 2.

You know, I do have a less abstract explanation for composite chart behavior.

Is that so?

⚒ Well actually it's the same explanation with less number theory and more algebra. The nearest midpoint composite chart consists *entirely* of averaged locations, so reading it is like looking at some third party whose personality is the exact balance of yours and your partner's personalities. This is what it would feel like if you considered your partner's outlook on a level equal to your own—to where your relationship reflected a perfect average. But with your duo having its own "self chart," something interesting happens; in order to explain to yourself any quality of your duo, you need to look at that quality's root cause: the prior planet. You also have to tie that root cause to the people who make everything happen in the duo in the first place: you and your partner. So when you ask for example, "How did our duo's Jupiter image promotion get like this?" you typically answer with some "influence" exercised by you or your partner. That is, your Marses. In this way, your duo's traits are the results of the duo members' deeds that caused them. Thus we get the whole "prior planets" effect on *component* charts mixed with actual planet effects on *composite* charts. According to this theory you can interpret any composite pair as a combination of three things: 1) The meaning of the regular chart equivalent of that same current pair, 2) the meaning of the regular chart equivalent of the prior pair or something like it, and 3) by far the most important thing—the kind of behavior that naturally flows from the prior pair meaning to the current pair meaning.

Hm. I almost gotcha. Give me an example.

Ok. Say you're looking at a composite Saturn-Uranus. This is where the duo is being structured (Saturn) by the social talk (Uranus). If you're IN the duo reflecting on the duo's Saturn-Uranus, chances are you're thinking about what you and your partner are doing to produce that Saturn-Uranus kind of quality. Jupiter precedes Saturn and Saturn precedes Uranus so you're thinking about how you promote yourselves (Jupiter) in line with structured rules (Saturn). This is Jupiter-Saturn "balanced self-promotion." To interpret composite Saturn-Uranus then, you ask "What do we get when we go from [balanced self-promotion] to [being bound by the social world]?" Think about it. Doesn't that situation remind you of the statement "You're only as good as your next hit"? This is where you must keep winning or get dropped—the kind of perfect self-promotion that only invites more social pressure. And actually this is what composite Saturn-Uranus shows.

Hayden pondered Geery's second explanation as Geery continued. Because composite Saturn-Uranus is the average of two regular Saturns and Uranuses, the composite meaning will almost certainly be at least somewhat correlated with the regular meanings. Composite interpretations can't be completely random because our consistent application of the same math on all the component planets prohibits this. Being averages, however, composites also have a tendency to water down any eccentricities in each component planet's orbits in addition to cutting each planet's distances on the frequency wheel in half. The averaging renders eccentric ellipses closer to circles—which is what idealized orbit meanings are based on. Meanwhile, the cutting in half of magnitudes is extra important to this story because it puts planets on the levels of their priors.

I don't get that.

Remember how I told you about my notes from Katha? Where the planetary orbit distances from the Sun basically double? Well if I have two of any planet a maximum of 180 degrees apart, their nearest midpoint average, by definition, can never be more than 90 degrees away from either of the original planets. Furthermore if two planets are moving away from each other at say, one degree per day, their nearest midpoint will separate from the originals at no more than half a degree per day. This kind of "halving" by averaging makes any composite planet adopt behaviors of the next "undoubled" planet: the one before it.

Interesting, but that stuff's not exact. Jupiter's cycle of 12 years is much more than double Mars' two-year cycle.

It's not the cycle speed, but the astronomical potential energy level that matters. The real science behind it almost certainly takes into account asteroids, moons, chemical composition and all that. So the degree motion around the wheel is only a rough analogy for the kind of unwinding I'm talking about; in a system like the musical scale or planetary potential levels where powers of two move you to the next level, building a whole system built entirely upon division by two would indeed move everything back one level.

Hm.

And then again, moving back one level is also easier on the brain. If I take 27+some error and add it to 29+ some error and average it, I *could* learn something about 28 + twice the error, but I might also reduce to get an easier cognitive count by using half the result at half the error: 14+some error. This is related to significant digits in science and allows me to check my calculations more quickly: 14 firing cycles per period instead of 28. ⚒

The other way around: Why higher harmonics end up being important

Hayden shook his head quickly as if to bring himself back into alertness. Jesus, man. **Sigh** I guess I asked for it. So prior planet interpretations are both mathematically and mentally more fitting for composite charts?

⚒ More or less. As for the whole "error reducing" part, the connection to the higher angles we've been talking about follows directly. Going backwards in orbit level gives us earlier planets, lower signs, lower houses, and higher angles—all with less interpretive error. Going forward gives us later planets, higher signs, higher houses, and lower angles. The problems with later planets and lower angles only become apparent when measurements related to them are consistently multiplied in a way to augment their error. The farther out you go in astronomical orbit, the rougher your estimates of how our chosen objects behave, the greater the need for sharper measurements and, hence, higher harmonics. Does that make sense?

Uh, yeah I guess. I guess it does.

So when we only know the seven classical planets, the major angles are good enough for low resolution calculations. Once we add in everything up to Neptune, we really need to start interpreting the minors like undeciles and noviles in order to describe the angle-based analogs to these. How else can you call yourself looking at Uranus when you don't know how to read undeciles?

Makes sense.

But once we increase the scale of our measurements and start counting lots and lots of repeats, the old estimates break down. You can only multiply 3.25 so many times before you realize that the 13-count is better than the 3-count. Once our space knowledge and the complexity of our experiential worlds gets beyond astrolabes and into the realm of the Hubble, we need more precision. Calling 3.25, 3.2, and 3.1 repeats per cycle a trine is fine when "thinking-communicating" is all you know how to talk about, but as you increase in the complexity of your expression, you see that 3.25 x 4 = 13: the kind of communication which builds personas. 3.2 x 5 = 16: the kind of close-range thinking that comes with the comfort of family. 3.1 x 10 = 31: the kind of communication that builds social networks. All of these offer less error, but you need to move onto higher harmonics and observe stable patterns for longer periods of time in order to see them. All in all though, whether you go up or down in complexity or scale of orbit, the ability to count in reliable whole numbers drives all of the basic meaning of things. In chemistry, quanta, or astrology. ⚒

Hayden smiled slightly.

What's that for?

You answered the next question before I could ask it a long time ago: Why should Jupiter introduce itself into a Saturn interpretation. You say it's because averaging Saturns into a midpoint basically cuts Saturn's energy changes in half, demoting the influence of its midpoint to the level of the planet before it.

Yes.

But then you talked about going in the other direction and needing sharper angles to understand planets farther out. Even had the nerve to use astrology and quantum mechanics in the same sentence. I guess I'm just amused at your continued use of math to confuse the hell out of me. I kind of like it though. I find it surprising for a hippie.

GEE WHIZ, THANKS, Geery replied sarcastically.

Uranus-Midheaven*

<Saturn-11th house

This pair shows what one of the duo members believes constitutes the basis of effective assertion in the world. **That is, this is the angle which their actions reflect as being their idea of the key to successful expression, particularly among acquaintances.**

Uranus-Vertex*

<Saturn-"expiring comfort"

In what should be part of the "Summoner" formula, **this pair represents the reason that one duo member calls upon the other**. Contact between the two is opened here, where the angle tells you both the mood that prompted the contact as well as the related perspective that one duo member has of the other. "This is my friend. I need to talk to a friend," says the septile. "This person sorts things out for me. I need a sorter," says the II-quintile. And then there are a whole host of other reasons for opening a connection. If you plan to call someone estranged back into your life, one of the first things you might do is declare this angle to be your reason for doing so. Hopefully you have a place where they can fit here. Otherwise, even if you do successfully connect with them, your exchange will have a good chance of missing that certain "something." Read *table 19-1* for the standard sources of motivation for opening communication with this angle. Read *table 19-7* for the standard mood that comes with it. And read *table 19-8* for the fun stuff associated with the same angle.

Uranus-Node

<Saturn-"questing"

Hangout time is of higher quality when spent doing this angle's deeds. Although you could look at the "fun" *table 19-8* for this one, the regular *table 19-1* is actually better since quality time doesn't always consist of intentional fun. Sometimes the natural flow of the angle creates a good experience without either partner planning it.

Uranus-Selene

<Saturn-"resolvable dilemma"

One partner is extra confident and extra comfortable with themselves under this angle. They are willing to advance the duo openly by means of the angle's area, though there's no guarantee that the other partner will be so willing or so able to get on board with this.

Uranus-Lilith

<Saturn-"unfulfilling conformity"

✪ A local legend

✪ **One partner overflows with this pair's angle—so much so that they hold the capacity for great notoriety among friends here**. This is the kind of notoriety which can elevate the duo as a whole. If you're looking for the realm in which you and a partner are capable of building something public and memorable, this is definitely a pair worth looking into.

Uranus-Fortune*

<Saturn-"comfortable conditions"

Where intimate exchange seems inevitable

The proper playing field for "home base"

The aim of sex and shared creativity is to advance this angle. Now even among perfectly disinterested partners, this pair is highly skewed towards the penetrative depths of each person's intentions such that even the most innocent shared creativity is attended by a kind of intimacy which draws out both partners' deepest needs for influence under this angle. This pair is abstract and complicated to explain without your own collection of charts to give it meaning. For now we'll just say that **the duo members are A LOT less likely to hide their basic ideas of this angle from each other when creating something together**. Accordingly, this angle is among the ones most clearly expressed in their joint projects. Its resonant pairs give us a pretty good look at the lasting impressions they leave upon each other through whatever it is they have worked on.

As an insightful curiosity in romantic relationships, this pair's angle essentially tells you the interaction for which sex and intimacy would be one of the natural "next phases." So if you and your partner have a trine, intimacy is one of the next phases along the evolution of [how you convey your personal opinions to each other], but if you don't have a trine, you can give personal opinions to each other all day and never feel that urge. (In non-romantic cases, trines—which are naturally attracted to each other—typically suppress this effect, making communication feel weirdly "off.") In another example, the more II-septiles identify with each other as fellow ingroup kindred, the more inclined they will be to either want to engage each other sexually or want to create together using ideas from the depths of their thoughts. **In other words, the more you do this angle with the partner, the more inclined you are to want intimate exchange with them—except when you block this instinct or displace it onto something else. If you block this "next phase" but keep the original angle dynamic going, the relationship will tend to take on a strangely stifled character**. One could write a whole book on this pair alone, but thus goes the short version.

This pair works in the opposite way from composite [Pluto-MC*]. Whereas [Pluto-MC*] shows us how an individual trait can evolve into a paired one, composite [Uranus-Fortune*] shows how a paired trait can morph into an individual one: As the duo gets more and more comfortable as a social item under this angle, the individuals come to build a formal structure for themselves rooted in the feelings they are most comfortable with.

Uranus-Ceres

<Saturn-"Other's dissatisfying expression"

One partner makes their intentions regarding the partnership known through this angle, though they don't always make it known to the partner themselves. In fact, the person's intentions are less directly stated here and manifest more through the kinds of deeds they do with this angle in light of the partner's influence. So II-quintiles, for example, can prompt one partner to either change how they manage people in light of the partner or intentionally make no change. II-sextiles will alter their long range outlook, intentionally do nothing, or become more entrenched (in negative cases). **This pair doesn't quite show how a partner has been influenced, but more *where* the partner responds to the other's <u>attempt</u> to influence them**. If interacting with your partner under this pair has changed you in the way that the partner intended, that's an indication of someone whose partnership was good for you in some way, regardless of how the exchange ended. In exchanges where you knowingly appreciate this angle's changes in you inspired by the partner, you may not want the relationship to end.

Uranus-Chiron

<Saturn-"need for help"

The deeper the exchange, the more pronounced the friends

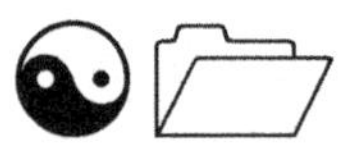 

The preferred peer groups of at least one of the partners consists of specialists in this angle. Within the duo, this pair shows how you can expect your friends and social circles to change. Looking to move up in the world? Put together a collection of your friends' charts, look at *tables 19-1* and *19-5*, then spend more time connecting with the friends who have the angle you want. This is definitely some form of manipulation in somebody's book, and you might go to hell for it, but it's not the same kind of conniving as you'll find with a bad Neptune-Eros III-novile. And it *does* work. You manipulator. `May Heaven have mercy on your soul.`

The composite chart reading of this pair suggests that its regular chart version is associated with the kinds of friends you yourself naturally attract by default.

Uranus-Vesta

<Saturn-"situation that needs tending to"

This pair corresponds roughly to the realm in which the duo "makes art" together. This means that they have creative ways of tending to this angle's affairs together, and can be seen by others as inventive or original in how they do things here. Should these two establish a project or organization together using this angle, successors to that project may find this pair a tough act to follow. The duo is very creative here, JOINTLY. Oppositions display an interesting kind of flirtation or "secret handshake" with each other. Trines are just plain fascinating to watch in how they talk to each other.

Uranus-Pallas

<Saturn-"social imbalance"

One duo member is in tune with the art of this angle, displaying an overpowered version of this angle towards others. If either of the partners is to be well known or notorious among their peers for something in their future, this angle and its resonant pairs form a decent indicator of what such notoriety might be based on.

Uranus-Juno

<Saturn-"need for secured role"

This is the angle which one duo member uses to shock the other in the middle of close exchange. The first person often unleashes this one as a way of checking the second person when the latter has either taken things too far (negatively) or passed a certain threshold for good exchange (positively).

Uranus-Hera

<Saturn-"state of unattachment"

This angle represents the underlying motives of the duo members in interfacing with each other. Regardless of what the two do overtly, achievement of this angle's promises in the eyes of outsiders is a nice-to-have. One partner is more likely to show a drive towards socially relevant power under this angle and force it on the other.

Uranus-Eros

<Saturn-"receptiveness to impassioned action"

The duo entertains exploration under this angle; one partner inspires the other to take risks and be a little more reckless with this angle. Such inspiration is often negative though, as the risk-taking partner is often unwittingly provoked into doing so by certain actions performed by the other partner. Angle-specific surprises which lead to anger are more common in negative cases, surprises which lead to the other partner's passion are more common in positive cases as one person feels the other is foisting this angle upon them.

Uranus-Bacchus

<Saturn-“desire to share company”

❧ Close peer groups acknowledge this pair’s angle as a special quality of the duo. This pair is very much a property of the partnership more than it is a byproduct of individual contributions, and has the effect of endearing the partnership to many others within the partner’s shared spheres of influence. It may be harder to feel this one on an individual level, but **you might read this angle as “the thing that the duo is known to do well and do strongly.”**

(These last eight pairs were entirely blind method pairs, as indicated by the ❧. Just for fun, try covering up the title of pairs like [Uranus-Eros] and [Uranus-Bacchus] to see if you could have guessed at least one of the planets involved in each combination without knowing the planets beforehand. If you can then good for you. This means you’re getting an idea of which planets do what. It also means that whatever data pattern produced these particular interpretations actually supported consistent roles for the planets involved, once again promoting the idea that astrology isn’t completely random. Pallas’ column of statistics, for example, produced an interpretation involving social force before we knew Pallas was one of the planets. Ceres still involved coercion.)

Neptune pairs

Neptune-Pluto

<Uranus-Neptune

❧ This pair has the least amount of variation of all the composite pairs covered in this book, a typical consequence of slow moving bodies. **The pair can be thought of as the basic aim towards which the duo members jointly work for leaving something of value in society**. Their work, though reflective of a kind of duty to others, doesn’t necessarily have a specific group that it focuses on (hence having generic society as a recipient). Sextiles form basic domestic partnerships, but can also serve others together in more altruistic relationships. II-septiles work towards increasing belonging among formerly excluded groups or towards a sharing of important ideas. III-quintiles work to get an untamed subject under control. III-septiles build large, colorful networks of diverse people, roughly towards the attainment of a common dream. III-octiles work to amplify each other’s private power among their groups and tend to be very sexual or creative as a result.

Neptune-Ascendant*

<Uranus-2nd house

❧ **One of the partners is seen as charming under this angle, though it is really the other partner’s rose goggles which are partly responsible for this**. The “charming” partner tends to have a much more difficult or unreasonable temperament than is first apparent and the viewing partner (often) seems more optimistic here, especially as the partners naturally distance themselves from each other over time.

Neptune-Midheaven*

<Uranus-11th house

❧ **The duo is highly active under this pair’s angle, with more energy applied to its affairs**. Usually this extra energy is applied by one of the partners much more strongly than the other, but the end result is a more fiery pursuit of this angle’s goals and more thorough expression of its aims as a whole.

Neptune-Vertex*

<Uranus-“expiring comfort”

❧ Sharing of this angle typically comes with some form of line crossing in duos for which there are certain rules. If there are any professional, social, or other kinds of standards which it is suggested that the partners not breach, this angle shows how the partners approach such a breach. **We can consider this angle to be the context under which the duo breaks rules for how its duo mates are allowed to interact**. Although this one does not reflect the rulebreaking act itself, it is kind of like a cloud which hovers over the duo suggesting that rulebreaking is a possibility. Maybe the two are about to do something they shouldn't be doing.

Neptune-Node

<Uranus-"questing"

This pair corresponds broadly to the area of life where one partner needs the other as mirror against which to reflect pressing concerns. Note that these are pressing concerns and not trivial ones—concerns which, though not exactly urgent, are tied to the esteem of the one who airs them. Where the other partner proves an effective validator, the duo grows in solidarity. The other person's interest in the first partner's concerns under this angle is a good way of separating potential friends from those who would remain only acquaintances.

Neptune-Selene

<Uranus-"resolvable dilemma"

One duo member is rendered more subdued under this angle, perhaps in response to the power displayed by the other person. This is typically an arrangement where one person lets the other do most of the talking (since there's no point in trying to stop them). The pair, however, isn't so much negative as it is heavily skewed in favor of one person's agenda. Conjuncts make the dominated partner feel validated. II-oppositions typically make for great company in general.

Neptune-Lilith

<Uranus-"unfulfilling conformity"

The duo amplifies the extent to which one duo member stands out among peers as exemplary in this angle area. The talents of this person are magnified considerably in the context of the relationship.

Neptune-Fortune*

<Uranus-"comfortable conditions"

One duo member surrounds themselves with this angle as a shield against vulnerability amidst the unknown. Sometimes the use of this shield is quite effective, other times not so much. In the latter cases, this issue may serve as the basis for the duo's eventual disconnect and subsequent separation.

Neptune-Ceres

<Uranus-"Other's dissatisfying expression"

One partner displays an intimidating level of skill towards the other. In positive cases, the second partner allows the first to easily take the lead here, acting in a strong complementary role. In negative cases we get all kinds of conflict which depend on the resonant pairs associated with this angle as well as the individual quirks of both partners. All responses though can be summed up as the result of one partner feeling as though they have been put beneath the dominion of another.

Neptune-Chiron

<Uranus-"need for help"

Within the duo, the "good life" affords free expression of this angle. This pair shows how the duo would proceed if suddenly released from the burden of responsibilities in the world. Although not quite the complete picture of a happy ending, this pair definitely comes close. **Partners who interact in accordance with this angle are much more likely to feel as though they are doing what they were made to do as a pair**.

[Neptune-Chiron] has interesting implications for one way we might come to envision "happily ever after:" by socializing our need for help $_{\text{"help need"}}$ or framing places where we need help through the lens of the broad information around us $_{\text{Uranus}}$, we establish partnerships which indulge our dreams $_{\text{Neptune}}$ of a fix despite full knowledge of the security we lack $_{\text{Chiron}}$. This is the essence of wishful thinking—an idealized band-aid for all that ails us.

Neptune-Vesta

<Uranus-"situation that needs tending to"

One partner pursues a monopoly over the other's view of things under this angle, whether or not the former knows it. "You will only see this angle as I project it," the monopolizing partner says. II-oppositions are often about values rather than physical company here. Be careful with this angle, your partner can definitely apply the blinders to you under this angle, where you come to pigeonhole them on the one hand, fail to see past their influence on the other. **When it's time to end the duo, this is one of the main angles which you feel you will be losing after they are gone**.

Neptune-Pallas

<Uranus-"social imbalance"

One partner uses this angle as proof of their worth to the other partner. Usually unknowingly, they present this angle area to justify why the other should bother with them as well as to explain the connections they have outside of the relationship. This pair works like a secondary reason for joining forces in the same way that the causal mention of one's wealth stands as a secondary reason following one's marriage proposal. One partner uses this angle to help the other decide in the former's favor—especially when it comes to becoming a formal duo in the first place.

Neptune-Juno

<Uranus-"need for secured role"

Can we bridge the gap?

This pair is a classic gatekeeper showing where the duo members must reconcile their differences in outlook in order to effectively value each other's company in the long run. The data on this pair were a very mixed bag, with some duos connecting strongly over this pair and others remaining very disconnected. Disconnection typically prevents a relationship from getting off the ground early on, though it's not clear whether this pair has any significant effects on the exchange later down the line.

Neptune-Hera

<Uranus-"state of unattachment"

One duo member provides more personal disclosure to the other in the style of this angle. The angle is **also related to the means through which that person obtains the approval of audience members on a one-by-one basis**, either as the giver or receiver of the angle.

Neptune-Eros [52]

<Uranus-"receptiveness to impassioned action"

Reverse the other party's ability to anger you

One partner appeals to the other's hedonistic sense under this angle, fulfilling the former's sense of bodily, material, or worth-based satisfaction through the latter's ways. **The effect of this pair is wide, but clear: one partner can use this angle to thoroughly and convincingly excite the other $_{\text{fbow}}$, bringing out nasty impulses in whatever ways you can imagine**. The negative cases here are very negative.

If you are one of those people who happens to be trapped in the clutches of someone who holds the power to get your fur up in every which way, this pair is an essential one to reverse. Although no book can tell you how to do this, do take a look at tables *19-6*, the usual *19-1*, and *19-5* to get your bearings, then consult *table 21-1* below. Be warned, these entries are not magic and require, more than anything else, 1) an understanding of what kinds of buttons are being pushed, 2) why such buttons *might have* been pushed by the other (you don't need the real reasons, just a broad idea), 3) an

[52] This entire section all the way through its *table 21-1* were written using the blind method. Once again the partner behaviors drawn out are consistent with earlier findings. See synastric [Neptune-Eros] in Chapter 19 for an interesting comparison to this composite version. As in all blind paragraphs, you'll find no mention of the actual planets (in this case Neptune or Eros) because I didn't know beforehand that these were what I was writing about.

overall view of your own role with respect to the other in the big picture, and 4) enough patience to resist your own self-destruction now so that you can choose a more fitting approach to them once the immediate conflict is over. I will talk about this kind of thing in detail the next and last book of this trio, but for now just remember that all angles have high and low tension versions, as well as active and receptive forms. You can choose which one you plan to use in a conflict, but it's a lot easier to practice implementing that choice before the battle rather than during.

The results below were culled from the usual 7 years' worth of observations of people's relationships, particularly watching how my colleagues and I evolved in our dealings with our students and each other. Unfortunately before I even got through writing the first sentence of the conjunct, I realized that a table of "reversal tactics" depends HEAVILY on whether others assume your weapons to be masculine or feminine. As a heterosexual male, I won't pretend to know whether the table below will work equally well for majority-trained women, so I present it from a male perspective by default. More research will need to be done on the feminine equivalents of these successful approaches to maintaining your sense of personal control in the face of a strongly vexing adversary.

Let's call the infinitely patient, ideally responding (probably masculine-assertive-style) duo member who does all the stuff below "The Noble One."

Note that the trick with all of these lies generally in you asserting the "prior angle" to your rival's action as if *you* caused it. Fight a trine (3) partner's argument with an opposition's (2) satisfaction. Fight a quintile (5) person's attention-grabbing with a square person's (4) parenting.

Table 21-1: What the "Noble One" does when attacked by someone else's angle

∠	Situation
1. conjunct	Other: over-asserts, bullies Noble: tells himself that Other enjoys giving their raw energy to him, and uses his indifference to Other's advances to suck out more of Other's energy until the latter has no more to give
2. opposition	No data
3. trine	Other: complains or does thoughtless things Noble: listens to Other's complaints or absorbs Other's skill, shows how impressed he is with it, and seeks to know more about how Other has come to do it this way; (since this one is "raw opinionation," Other usually doesn't know how to explain their own actions and has their fire dowsed quickly)
4. square	Other: is emotionally overbearing Noble: ignores or fails to receive Other's intensity (as if it's another language); only responds to the calm, intuitively sense-making versions of the same efforts
5. quintile	Other: is impetuous, craves attention Noble: babies Other, giving them the "poor you" attention they seek
6. sextile	Other: oppresses with logic, criticality Noble: has his fun away from Other and makes sure that Other knows it
7. septile	Other: buries partner under massive commentary Noble: just listens to them...in such a way as to let them know it's safe for Other to talk *to* but undesirable for them to *talk at* Noble. (Noble steers Other's talk towards perspectives relevant to Noble's own interests while letting Other know that topics besides this are just wasted words)

8. octile	Other: is belligerent or disruptive Noble: lets Other know how important it is for Other to keep manipulating whatever their trying to manipulate[53]
9. novile	Other: is hoity toity, arrogant, dismissive Noble: celebrates Other's skills to himself. You're arrogant towards me? I celebrate your skills to myself. It's weird but it works. (I considered telling you why it works, but while writing this decided that doing so would ruin much of the effect. So I won't.)
10. decile	Other: is standoffish Noble: ignores Other's potential support and builds a reputation through interaction with different people
11. undecile	Other: distrusts Noble, has a different set of social standards Noble: makes the situation revolve around Other, turns people's attention to Other and makes them the talk of the town (these relationships tend to be very positive when you get them to work)
12. inconjunct	Not enough data
13. II-conjunct	Other: creates problems for Noble's peers and room of influence Noble: maintains an environment of liveliness and enjoyment around Other's actions
14. II-opposition	Other: disrupts the flow of things just by being around Noble: crowns Other a leader and puts them visibly in charge of part of the agenda
15. II-trine	Other: seduces Noble's audience Noble: employs Other's charisma for his own use
16. II-square	Other: won't connect with the rest of the group Noble: gradually builds rapport, makes Other feel like family
17. II-quintile	Other: wants to dominate situation Noble: connects with Other offline to establish that his agenda and Other's agenda are the same
18. II-sextile	Other: assesses Noble rather than supporting him Noble: earns the trust of Other's friends and peers
19. II-septile	Other: excludes Noble from their inner circle or treats Noble's group as Other's own inner circle when it shouldn't be Noble: zooms in on good sources of "inside jokes" and similar ingroup knowledge with Other and airs these across unaware publics (this establishes Noble and Other as their own in-crowd)
20. II-octile	Other: is unfocused on the matters at hand, diverting the focus of Noble's plans towards competing externals Noble: lets Other wander off, avoid trusting them with anything important; maybe Other will be useful for taking care of problems outside of Noble's sphere
21. II-novile	Other: is Noble's able and uncooperative competitor Noble: (if competition is not intended) elevates Other or lowers himself. (if Other is worthy of Noble's company, I've found that the relationship eventually becomes an equal and trusting one as rapport is built; if Other is not worthy, Other will eventually shrink away and disappear if Noble proceeds as if unaffected)
22. II-decile	Other: complains to and annoys Noble and outsiders about all kinds of aspects of various affairs related to something Noble is involved in Noble: Lets Other make entertaining conversation with outsiders, but requires that Other be solely responsible for their part of affairs (if more accustomed to complaining, Other—alone—tends to complain themselves into a corner and fail). Cut off Other from group resources in task
23. II-undecile	Other: displays a vocal and resistant bad attitude Noble: tends to Other's complaints, but shares negative intel on them with everyone else—effectively spreading their complaints before they do and establishing Noble as the one in the right
24. II-inconjunct	Other: head is elsewhere, is intractable Noble: supports and absorbs Other's creative ideas while they are around, but considers them to be a part of the environment more than an active supporter

[53] I call this one "turning invisible," and it seems to work pretty well on aggressive drivers. After working for years to become a more patient driver, I found that if I just let them go AND identify them as chronically impatient, they usually invite immediate beef somewhere else within the next few cars ahead of you. It's obvious when you think about it, but not obvious when you're unprepared. The point is to encourage them to manipulate to their heart's content on *more* people while you cheer them on. The consequences of this are several and might be apparent to you. One such consequence is their making even more enemies before your very eyes.

25. III-conjunct	Other: is disruptively and spotlight-grabbing outspoken in a distracting way (usually rather than a malicious way) Noble: if at all possible, interacts with Other one on one to assure them of the potential for spotlight, but in groups, pairs Other up with someone else to keep them occupied until Noble is ready to deal with them
26. III-opposition	Other: herds their fans and supporters in a direction that opposes Noble Noble: abandons Other's fans without abandoning Other or abandons Other without abandoning Other's fans. The first one is more likely to make relations with Other better. The second is more likely to make the relationship worse
27. III-trine	Other: is scathingly critical or uses their insight to punish Other Noble: withdraws support from all those convinced by Other and engages in minimal performance of activities with those convinced people with whom relationships need to be maintained. Arguing is usually very bad for this style of enemy—the slanderous kind—whether it's a III-trine or not. "You're right, but I don't care" works a lot better. "Not only do I not care if you're right, I think anyone who supports you should be asked to question your delivery of those facts." This is known as "divide and conquer" or in V.I. Lenin's case, "salami tactics." So when Joe and Moe slam Noble's reputation using facts, Noble admits Joe is right, but forms an alliance with Moe on whatever aspect of Joe's presentation of the facts Noble and Moe both agree on but disagree with Joe. Unless you're dealing with actual militaries, this tactic usually works very well with people. First, it concedes that Both Joe and Moe are right and deflates their influence over any shared audience with Noble. Second, it shows Moe that, just as Noble doesn't care, Moe shouldn't care either since Noble is a cool guy. If Joe and Moe are friends, Noble allies with Flo against Joe and Moe's presentation. The premise is the same.
28. III-square	No data
29. III-quintile	Other: endeavors to take control of Noble's space or sphere of influence Noble: singles Other out for an independent task and doesn't give that special task to anyone else. This keeps Other within eyeshot, under Noble's service, and dependent on Noble for further instruction. If Other is an actual equal and can't be given a task, Noble sends some of his own allies to Other to get certain problems solved—effectively assigning tasks to Other anyway. This works well on micromanaging bosses and managers; Is Bossman in your face? Selectively send your clients and peers to Bossman in order to present him with problems he can't solve for a lack of the kind of specialization that you have. As this works, you'll find that Bossman 1) leaves these things to you and 2) Bossman references you to others as one of his prime "managed" people to whom other things he can't solve should be entrusted. Bossman still has his control, but such control is used to advance *you* since you don't accept the oppression part.
30. III-sextile	Not enough data; the pairs who had this were consistently smooth-running in my sample, with the Other using their powers of critical analysis to support Noble. My guess would be that the negative cases involve Other's criticism of Noble, to which Noble would respond by letting Other speak for him and polish Noble's errors
31. III-septile	Other: hijacks Noble's network Noble: invites Other to join him as a fellow network controller. If this isn't feasible, Noble gives Other access to Noble's problem children to 1) inconvenience Other, 2) keep those problem children under control, 3) expose weaknesses in Other or the problem children (which can be people or tasks)
32. III-octile	Other: requires efforts that Noble can't afford to give Noble: is simply honest with Other. "This is as much as I can give and here's why..." When Other eventually departs to be supplied by someone else, hopefully Noble will have an ally abroad. Why? Because most of the outsiders whom Other encounters will not be so honest if Other has already shown that your honesty is not a thing they can live with. "I can't tend to you past this point, but at least I'm honest in telling you why. If you can't accept my limited help or at least my honesty concerning it, and if you can't help yourself but still need someone to do this for you, then good luck. Look forward to the next person promising to help you, lying about his intentions to keep that promise, breaking the promise, and doing so remorselessly." This is how the *karma of having people purposely lie to you* is built up: You ask for the world but won't listen to those who tell you they can't give it.

Angle	Tactic
33. III-novile	Other: limits Noble's influence over his desired audience Noble: befriends Other as a person; Other as a gatekeeper usually changes their mind later It's actually not advisable to attempt to "use" Other to get to your wanted audience. This may work for the more opportunistic among us, but it creates bigger problems later as the used Other simply builds a newer, tighter gate right behind you. This is how the *karma of being hated by history* is built up on a series of little betrayals, no matter how big the lifetime of successes: Those who guard the favor of groups you're not a part of need to feel that their trust is not in vain. When dealing with people who believe it is their duty to protect groups beyond themselves, expect their disappointment in you to carry more weight. If you betray these people, you typically will not have squashed their role as protector, but made them more vigilant against you, so that social-psychologically, for every protector you betray, there will be an even larger number of their later followers who are mobilized against you near-permanently. It is this second group of the betrayed person's people who will tell your story long after the first group who you stole has, predictably, changed their minds about any good you've done. Loyalty here isn't so much a moral good as it is a social safety net.
34. III-decile	Other: believes they have all the answers Noble: leaves them alone; if Other attempts to control Noble's execution of plans, Noble lets Other do this to the strict letter, but promotes his own intentions in every other aspect of the event which Other didn't expressly cover. If possible, Noble also ensures that everyone is aware of how limited Other's guidance was; if Noble is not free to do this openly, he does it by "clocking in and clocking out" at the precise time and going straight home to Noble's more imperfect allies, letting Other know that though they may have total control over the formally bossed area, they have no interpersonal importance.
35. III-undecile	Other: is an uncontrollable attention getter Noble: gives Other attention randomly in times where there is no need; this puts Other's otherwise disruptive shocks to the order of things under Noble's control while establishing Noble as a supporter of, rather than an enemy to, Other
36. III-inconjunct	Other: unsettles Noble with a surprisingly penetrative quality, can lodge themselves in other's mind and resist extraction therefrom Noble: declares Other a memorable leader and takes Other under his wing. This may seem excessive, but you really want to avoid thinking negatively about people who have this effect on you ("I can't stop thinking about how weird they make me feel"). For reasons that would mess up how the solution to this one works, I won't explain why positive thoughts about the fixed person work so well, but will tell you that you should do what you can to keep them positive. This is advice specifically for people whose interaction with you makes you uneasy in ways you can't explain and not for regular opponents. Take a look at yourself first. Dig deep. Then do what you can to help them.
37. IV-conjunct	Other: publicizes objectives which create dilemmas for Noble Noble: accepts those objectives and attempts not to hold them against Other if possible. If Noble must hold those objectives against Other, he makes it clear why
38. IV-opposition	No data
47. IV-undecile	Other: holds an outlook which is out of sync with Noble's reality Noble: assists Other where possible, but—often and *quite* unfortunately—helps Other turn everyone else against Other. Being out of sync with everyone else's notion of reality is, as Machiavelli would put it, a characteristic of "exiles." A person who sees things in a way irreconcilably different from that which is useful to the healthy function of his surroundings begs to be removed from those surroundings one way or another.
48. IV-inconjunct	Not enough data

Table 21-1: Reversal tactics when attacked by a partner's angle. These reversal tactics are described from a masculine perspective—the only one available to me at the writing of this book. All tactics are aimed at making your interactions with yourself and others easier rather than harder; several of them require patience and humility on your part rather than revenge. The reason for this is mainly psychological and doesn't have much to do with spirituality or virtue (though they can certainly be read that way for the spiritually inclined); people preoccupied

with vengeance and drama are commonly (and practically) described as having [shorter lives and more stress] or [longer lives and shameful reputations whenever they turn away from battle for a moment]. Especially after they leave a place or die. We see this by looking at how history is told by others regarding them. Live by vengeance. Die in shame.

"Untangling Karma:" One more comment on Neptune Eros (non-blind)

As I read back through the above section I felt it useful to share something I learned during the writing of this book. *HBS* was written during a particularly contentious political and social season in which many people on several sides took up entrenched positions against their own. Under these conditions, a general environment of increased domestic unrest was (unsurprisingly) the popularly portrayed result. While writing and studying the angles, however, I noticed that there is a kind of separable quality to even the most tangled looking perspectives; just as angles which seem to flow together can be chopped into separate harmonics (where, say, the binovile [80°] and the quinti-II-decile [81°49'] can actually be separated as part of two distinct patterns), people's outlooks can also be separated. It is not always necessary to share space with an enemy. Instead, the enemy's way of opposing you and your way of being opposed can be divorced such that, when you decide you're ready, the two of you will separate by "circumstance" and resume your respective ways elsewhere.

The best example of "untangling karma" is in the [Neptune-Eros] octile footnote [53] where a raging driver and a potentially raged-on *you* aren't really obligated to interact. Despite what may seem like an unavoidable tangling of paths, you actually do retain the right to keep your experiences separate from theirs. Yes, they are still successfully permitted to rage out but yes, you are permitted to carry on as you were before they got near you. Earlier in the book you found a dialogue in which Geery and Hayden discussed time and distance as constituting two types of "space" between events, and nowhere is this more useful than in cases where you need to avoid influences you deem poisonous. Some space is physical. Other space is psychological. But once you get tangled up with another person's destructive input you effectively agree to play out your own lessons using them as the means.

You begin separating your lessons from another's teaching by refusing to accept them as a teacher. Astrologically, you follow this by looking at all the resonant pairs for squares (how you display want), octiles (how you steer others), and II-octiles (how you steer strangers). I wish I could encapsulate the usefulness of this in a paragraph, but I can't. In the end all we can say is that two boxers will box regardless of who's in the ring with them, where the need to box each other is only a convenient illusion.

Neptune-Bacchus

<Uranus-"desire to share (better) company"

👓 **One partner is no-nonsense, with a noticeable tendency to drop unworthy interactants in light of a failure related to this angle**. The other duo member knows this, recognizing it as a kind of ruthless streak in the first person. The first partner has no qualms about moving on past people who don't meet their standards.

Pluto pairs

Pluto dominates the composite chart

In the coming pages you'll find that Pluto is extra strong in the composite chart. While going through all the data, I first asked myself why this was. Then it hit me:

First, for theoretical reasons mentioned in *FSA*,	this is similar to the way	This is the same way that
the dwarf planet Pluto closes out the array of	"13:00" closes out the array of	Sodium closes out the array of
immediately earth-relevant orbits in our solar system	1:00 to 12:00 positions on a clock	II-period elements
through its "locked" cycle with Neptune	through its predictable following of 12:00	through its predictable proton count following Neon
and world-level version of the Point of Action;	and afternoon-level version of 1am.	and III-period version of Lithium.

That is, Pluto is to groups what the Point of Action is to individuals; if an individual was formerly pressured by society, his formation of a pair with someone means he has formed his own mini-society. Pluto is no longer a big source of pressure then, but a simple instinct to take care of certain issues on the societal (partnership) level. Accordingly, if you are concerned about what you and your partner are able to accomplish as a team, you'll need to look to the composite Pluto. The synastric chart isn't good enough because it only shows how two separate people interact. To meet society's demands you'll need to pilot your own society. Your partnership with another person constitutes such a vehicle, and how you tend to your duo's Pluto will make all the difference between a great team and a sorry one.

Pluto-Ascendant*

<Neptune-2nd house

One duo member is less balanced in displaying their characteristics under this angle and, as a result, overpowers others with it. This trait can be wildly overfocused in the person and cause both outsiders and the more subdued partner to avoid them.

Pluto-Midheaven*

<Neptune-11th house

This pair shows one partner's annoying trait which later gains respect as the relationship grows. The time effect on this one is interesting, and might be explained by the idea that one partner is simply hyper-powered in a characteristic that the other person doesn't realize they need until later. The former is ahead of their time under this angle. How long does it take for the annoyed partner to realize the value of the other's excessive angle? About as long as it takes for the annoyed partner to see the other as a communicative equal; if this doesn't happen during the exchange, it may well happen long after the duo has dissolved—when all that remains of the annoying person exists in the annoyed person's own memory (thus strongly compelling equal status in some psychological sense).

Check out the prior planets on this one. The idea that [Neptune-11th] in individuals transforms into [Pluto-MC] in the duo gives us a really good idea of how something amorphous $_{\text{Neptune}}$ and scattered $_{\text{11th}}$ can become the stuff of socially pressured $_{\text{Pluto}}$ public labeling $_{\text{MC}}$ is pretty well captured here.

Pluto-Vertex*

<Neptune-"expiring comfort"

Check them

For one partner, this angle is dampened and often misinterpreted in the context of the duo, when it would normally work fine outside of the partnership. One duo member decreases the regular worth of the other under this angle. **This combination does not have to be negative, but it does constitute the kind of area where the dampening partner says to the dampened partner, "That mess may work on your public, but it's useless in here."**

Pluto-Node

<Neptune-"questing"

 **Your search for a power partner looks like this**

One partner blows through the other's world like a tornado, asserting all kinds of say-so over the latter's normal way of operating. Expect for one person's ideas to dominate the other's angle, but this may actually work out well for the dominated person. This pair often plays out pleasantly in some masochistic way.

Assuming you have a collection of charts, note that the more partners you have with a particular angle here, the higher the priority you tend to give to that angle as a sought after benefit of your partnerships.

How the blind method was conducted

Although this section may seem superfluous in a chapter on composite descriptions, it is important for illustrating one key point: Astrology *can* be tested scientifically and it really does produce real patterns once we get beyond the folklore. This section is written in the present tense; while writing it, I don't know which of the composite pairs I am about to describe. (This chapter's descriptions have been written out of order so that I still have over 280 descriptions left out of 300.) Below are the steps for determining what a composite pair actually does without knowing the planets involved beforehand:

1. I'm going to my database and jiggling the screen so that I don't know whether I'm in an early or late column of data. (Each row in the database below holds the harmonics for all of the possible planet combinations for synastry, composites, and house placements between two specific people. Each column holds all of the different harmonic numbers for a specific planet pair or house placement, where all noviles ($^{1}/_{9}$ths of a circle, [40°, 80°, and 160°]) would get 9's for example and all II-inconjuncts ($^{1}/_{24}$ths of a circle, [15°, 75°, 105°, and 165°]) would get 24s.)

2. Pick a column (an unknown planet pair) and, without looking at the heading, sort it by harmonic.

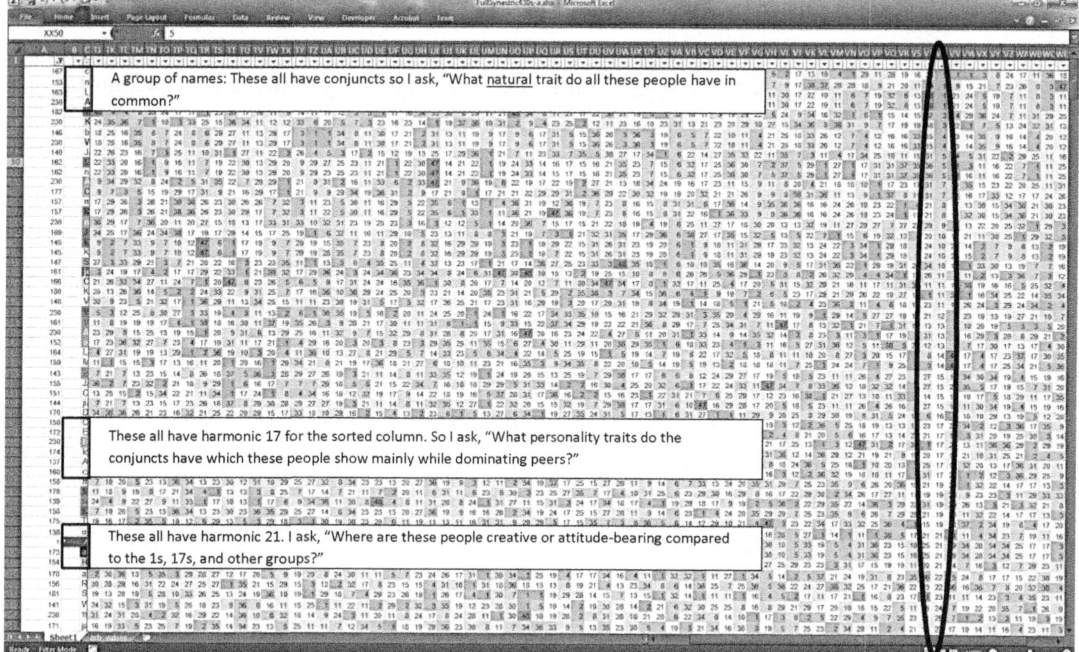
A group of names: These all have conjuncts so I ask, "What natural trait do all these people have in common?"
These all have harmonic 17 for the sorted column. So I ask, "What personality traits do the conjuncts have which these people show mainly while dominating peers?"
These all have harmonic 21. I ask, "Where are these people creative or attitude-bearing compared to the 1s, 17s, and other groups?"

3. Look at the names occupying each cluster (not shown for privacy reasons) and ask what differentiates each group from the other groups. Specifically, what is it that cluster 1 does naturally that cluster 4 does emotionally and cluster 13 does through public image?[54] Knowing all these people, I can tell you immediately that cluster 1 is naturally persuasive, though weird—possibly into affairs that mainstream society would look down on. They also share a strange but pragmatic spirituality. The trines are also like this but mainly when they talk to people. The septiles have conversations about it. The II-conjuncts have an unnecessarily negative outlook behind their public face, as if the face is a mask. The II-quintiles get serious when managing people. II-septiles, though, are noticeably more dedicated to family and friends. III-trines are ready to defend their ideas. III-septiles are entrenched in their networks. That's enough. I would say that this pair, whatever it is, revolves around the stubborn defense of one of the duo member's social role using the angle as a means. This would explain why II-septiles are so friendly: their ingroup does the defending for them.

4. Next I check other angles. Does it look like undeciles are gossiped about as being resistant to persuasion in the social sense? Pretty much. (Not bad so far, Ajani.) Does it look like deciles—of which there are several—like to defend their sense of authority over things as an important part of their identity? Yes. How about octiles? Do they retreat to power gestures to defend their social role? Definitely. So the description stands. Because I did this without knowing the pair (👓), I'll type this:

   👓 This composite pair shows where one of the duo members stubbornly defends their social role using the angle as a means.

   then this above it: <

   If there's more to say after I learn the pair, I'll say it in a separate paragraph.

5. Next I'll uncover the header. It's [Pluto-Selene]. Neptune comes before Pluto. But since this is the first time I will have written about Selene in this chapter, I'll have to think about what kind of human experience comes <u>before</u> "perfect talent." How about exposure to an issue which is vexing to others but easily resolvable by you? Let's call it "resolvable dilemma." Thus we have the full description:

   Pluto-Selene
   <Neptune-"resolvable dilemma"
   👓 This composite pair shows where one of the duo members stubbornly defends their social role using the angle as a means.

6. One last check: does my description make sense in line with Pluto, Selene, Neptune, and "resolvable dilemma?" Yes, but I see all those other observations I made regarding the conjunct should have been double checked in other angles. Also, I don't really like the word "role" in light of the Neptune part (since role implies something more active). Now that I look at it, "impression" really is a better descriptor of the data I got. So I'll change the word "role" to "impression"[55] and add another paragraph:

---

[54] This, of course, assumes that the angle families for conjunct, square, II-conjunct etc. are meaningful, but I've already tackled this issue in *FSA*.

[55] Although in this example I have changed a word from my original notes, this move was very much an exception which occurred less than five times throughout all the blind pairs. I did it here because it really was tricky writing this walkthrough section and the actual description at the same time, such that my concentration solely on what I was reading felt off.

Under the stubborn duo member's action, the relationship itself takes on a kind of one-sided, steamrolling inertia that outsiders can't deny.

That last line doesn't get glasses since I already know the pair, but it does fit the other things that are going on in my data pretty well. Time to move this section to its proper location between [Jupiter-ASC] and [Pallas-Juno] (two other sections I've already written).

Pluto-Selene

<Neptune-"resolvable dilemma"

This composite pair shows where one of the duo members stubbornly defends their social impression using the angle as a means.

Under the stubborn duo member's action, the relationship itself takes on a kind of one-sided, steamrolling inertia that outsiders can't deny.

Pluto-Lilith

<Neptune-"unfulfilling conformity"

Can we stand each other day-to-day in the long run?

Normal hangout mode between partners looks like this angle. In a very unfortunate observation, I found that this seemingly innocent angle actually serves as one of the most silent, most passive domestic partnership killers among all of the composites. Why? Imagine a database filled with relationships of all kinds, most good, some great, and some terrible. Ultimately though, one column stands out as the best reflection of the interactions themselves—where conjunct duos preferred to interact instinctively rather than talking, trines didn't exist as a duo if they didn't air their thoughts, and III-septiles died when their shared network influence died. This pair was such a pair. For friendships and non-domestic partnerships, pretty much anything goes for this combination. But if you're looking for long-term live-in partnerships, perhaps you can imagine how most of the non-communicating and socially dependent angles eventually become insufficient.

The paragraph below describes all levels of each angle together. So for this pair, "conjuncts" means I-, II-, III-, and IV-conjuncts. "Oppositions" means I-, II-, III-, and IV-oppositions, for example.

Oppositions, squares, sextiles, and octiles tend to be pretty good for long-term commitments, though squares have an initial emotional uphill battle and sextiles look boring from the beginning. Conjuncts are fun to date, but require constant newness in order to remain interesting. Trines need new ideas if they are to avoid becoming obnoxious. Quintiles need controversy or an unresolved issue. Septiles, though you might think they were positive, need deep discussion or communicative connection constantly, where basic sharing is more likely to be insufficient. Noviles need new adventures in the world and can be exhausting for people who don't have the stamina for this. Deciles need structure and control, yet are more likely to be described by chaotic environments in order to justify such structure. Undeciles need a public against which to measure their duo. Inconjuncts need a continuing stream of new ideas and a language for communicating them.

In the end, though no pair *has* to spell the end for a relationship, this one will creep up on the unaware, poisoning the union by default with its strong tendency to make one person tired of the other. For anyone who has had trouble committing in the long-term, 1) look at this angle in your self chart to see what you require of your partners to fuel hangout mode. More public angles like III-quintiles and III-septiles will need to exist under a more enduringly public eye. 2) Look at the relationships you've been in and see which angles have been the closest to successful. Sextiles (daily routine) and squares (emotional ties) usually hold a great advantage here, but not always.

Pluto-Fortune*

<Neptune-"comfortable conditions"

Overpower the world

The duo attracts non-conformists and social rule breakers under matters related to this angle, making for an exciting (if not controversial) team. This is one of the more fun angles for partners looking to raise a ruckus in society at large while drawing red faces from more conservative minds.

This composite pair is straightforward to interpret using our usual rules: Individuals use their own comfort "comfortable conditions" with their surrounding vibes Neptune to create a partnership which is at home Fortune putting pressure on everyone else they meet Pluto. This is one of the rare combinations where the duo is noticeably stronger than most of the world around them—no matter how famous or high ranking. Conjuncts make great teams and great-looking teams in general as far as actions are concerned. Quintiles have a hot-and-cold thing going in which one partner produces notable tension in the life of the other. Trines also have this, though there is often—at some point in the relationship—a one-way attraction which others can feel. Some of the fiercest emotion fbow passes through the trine under [Pluto-Fortune*]. Septiles spar more openly, but make cute couples in general—even if they happen to be two macho men getting on each other's nerves. Undeciles make broadly entertaining pairs and are more likely to get themselves talked about socially. II-conjuncts eat up the spotlight and are more inclined to flirt or pass mischievous inside jokes in front of everyone. II-oppositions visibly enjoy being in each other's company and are more obvious in the fun they tend to have here. II-squares have the ability to remain very emotionally close despite hardship; they tend to make each other feel awkward when this level of closeness in disallowed for whatever reason. II-octiles favor a contagious creative or sexual attraction between duo members which spills over onto witnesses. III-oppositions can develop a kind of cult following together—partly as a result of the charisma they exercise upon each other. III-deciles have super-strong command over their joint enterprise. III-undeciles tend towards being intellectually unstoppable. IV-conjuncts have a powerful understanding of each other and, subsequently, a powerful affinity for each other's motives. IV-oppositions have a strong understanding of each other's physical preferences and will be more open with each other in this respect.

Pluto-Ceres

<Neptune-"Other's dissatisfying expression"

Proper behavior required

The duo is built on quality exchange under this angle. A certain level of respect and sound values tend to be especially important for the participants under this angle. Barring this, the relationship is inclined to fall apart quickly and loudly. **The partners must make sense to each other under this angle in order for the relationship to continue.**

Pluto-Chiron

<Neptune-"need for help"

A dynamic set in stone

This pair's angle shows the nature of the partners' most memorable interaction with each other. Here we have a captured moment, brief among many, yet potent and relationship-defining. Trines, quintiles, septiles, III-inconjuncts, and IV-oppositions have memorable styles of interaction broadly, and thus generate less event-specific memories than other angles. These angles can make for really good partnerships should the two duo members decide that this is what they want.

[Pluto-Chiron] shows where the individuals' sense of an open issue creates circumstances under which the duo as a whole either [has the ability to solve] or [needs to be fixed in light of] problems in the world at large. Thus the interaction gains significance for its far reaching effects on the interactants' larger views of the pressuring world beyond them.

Pluto-Vesta

<Neptune-"situation that needs tending to"

The red herring

The filters come off under this pair, exposing the duo members' respective versions of this angle to each other and making it very easy for them to access a side of each other which most people would not have access to. Although you would think that this angle made the partners vulnerable to each other's influence, it really doesn't. Granted, there is a kind of backstage pass which the partners possess as mutual interactants, and there really is a sense in which the two know something about the other's otherwise non-public life, but the overall effect of this angle is closer to providing an inside scoop rather than an exposé. This pair is misleading in that it frequently leads to a false sense of rapport among the partners. "Now that you've shared your secret life with me, we're buds right? You'll hook me up, right?" No.

Don't try to build a duo off of this one. Perhaps *because* it is so easy for one partner to disclose to the other here, the disclosing partner doesn't tend to feel that that they've given up much in giving up this angle. Their real secret will likely be something they're noticeably more hesitant to disclose. The "secret" you just got doesn't actually count.

Pluto-Pallas

<Neptune-"social imbalance"

Joint power by appearance

This angle is an important contextual factor looming in the back of the partners' minds as a source of *what-if* potential for the duo. In truly well-connected partners, this pair represents a realizable area of great power-by-appearance for the duo in the eyes of those who have heard of them as an item. This is understandably rare though. Power-by-appearance is the ability to move viewers under an angle area simply as a byproduct of being seen or thought of together.

Pluto-Juno

<Neptune-"need for secured role"

The wall we hit

When you just have to cheat fate

**This is a key tactic for struggling partnerships*

Outside help wanted

The duo is at the mercy of circumstances under this angle, struggling to get a break that isn't handed to them by the world. Some angles like the septile can reduce this chronic obstacle to a standard conversation piece and work around it that way, but typically this is one of those areas where the duo just seems to struggle to project in the public, no matter how fluid their exchange may be between each other. This pair is a recipe for being misunderstood as a partnership. To make things worse, at least one of the duo members is likely to be interested enough in this angle to want the duo to pursue it.

  **There is a strong tendency for this angle and its resonant pairs to simply be denied prosperity in the duo.** There are, however, two pretty interesting ways to cheat this pair—both of them related. 1) Seek this pair outside of the duo. 2) Get a non-duo member to reach this angle for you. You and the partner may still be misunderstood, but your chances of expressing this angle as you wish will increase.

Although the transition from individual angle to composite angle might seem reasonable enough (individual dreams $_{\text{Neptune}}$ of security $_{\text{security need}}$ leading to societally-imposed $_{\text{Pluto}}$ commitments $_{\text{Juno}}$ on the duo) it may not be so obvious why composite [Pluto-Juno] would give partnerships such a hard time. But if we look more closely at the nature of [Pluto-Juno], we get our explanation: A duo which has societally-imposed commitments placed on it whenever this pair's angle runs simply has an endless stream of new things to take care of whenever they want to express this angle jointly. It's not that this angle doesn't work in public. It's that this angle mainly works against a powerful set of public commitments. Where this resonant family of angles goes, so follow the challenges in the world. Here we can see the connection between composite [Pluto-Juno] and a regular chart's "powerful/attractive co-star" (*table 16-5*). The duo naturally draws the need for a third party to help them with this angle in one of the rare pairs which truly requires at least three people to work: The two duo partners themselves and the third party to which the duo commits for help in answering its world-imposed obligations.

There isn't a lot of room to talk about rewriting circumstances here, but look forward to more about this kind of thing in the next/last book of the *FSA* trio.

Pluto-Hera

<Neptune-"state of unattachment"

 **Win or go home**

This pair's angle represents the area of one partner's life with which the other partner must compete in order to successfully forge the duo. Failure to win here typically means there will be no duo. It's that simple. This pair is a potent gatekeeper and duo killer all wrapped in one.

The data suggest that [Pluto-Hera] in the regular chart will be a formidable barrier to entry for unqualified candidates when it comes to seeking cooperation with the chart holder.

Pluto-Eros

<Neptune-"receptiveness to impassioned action"

On the homefront

One partner (in the eyes of the other) seems to make their living based on this angle, **in a pair which strongly influences the apparent "comfort zone" of the partners**. This is another one of those quiet but important planet combinations which plays an essential role in outlining the foundation of the exchange. **The duo members are likely to do more of their most comfortable, unscripted interaction in the realm of this angle**, in an arrangement which has heavy effects on the level and kinds of variety the exchange brings to the partners in the long run.

Pluto-Bacchus

<Neptune-"desire to share company"

The duo members seem well matched under this angle; outsiders view them as being of equal power here, creating a nice matchup between the partners should the two ever compete against each other. In positive cases this is territory where the partners refrain from challenging each other, respecting each other's ways.

Ascendant pairs

Testing a prediction (part I)[56]

So, Mr. Hayden, you know that at this point I haven't yet gathered any data on the composite [Ascendant-Midheaven], right?

Is that so?

[56] This section contains an actual prediction of results regarding [ASC-MC] and was written before the [ASC-MC] section that follows. The reasoning Geery gives at the end of this section is a sample of how we might form similar hypotheses for the composite pairs of planets not included in this book. When I wrote this section, I did not know in advance if the data would support the hypotheses given by Geery.

Yes. But I'm about to analyze its clusters shortly. Can I present you with a hypothesis regarding what this composite pair does?

Sure, Sir Geery. But I imagine your hypothesis will be correct since you already seem to know this stuff pretty well.

Don't be so certain. First of all, the composite pairs are known to misbehave—especially in how their corresponding individual "pre-planets" play out. Secondly, you take for granted that as we stand here almost all of this stuff is new to modern astrology, so what I "know" amounts to little more than what I've seen pattern-wise since beginning my instruction with Katha: less than a year's worth of statistics.

I still don't see the big deal, but go ahead. Shoot.

Okay. Believe it or not, we scientists actually have lives. It may surprise you to find that I actually have a date with someone special in a week or two, so I have reason to use all this stuff.

You? Right. What are you going to do? Use your findings to manipulate her like some experiment?

Geery feigned shock. Who me? Mary Pallas Aries? I'm *appalled* that you'd suggest such a thing.

Suuure you are.

Actually, manipulation of people isn't my style. Understanding them is. And I'm actually less interested in playing the eye in the sky than I am in knowing what directions my own life has in store. Currently I'm at a point where I'm actually considering settling down maybe, and it just so happens that this girl makes me happy. The problem is, we're not exactly on the same page, so she hasn't quite warmed up to me. She wants to though. I can tell.

Can you now? Why don't you just toss this star stuff and date her like normal person if you're so sure of that?

I don't approach love in the normal way. I approach it my way.

Mr. Big Shit, huh? Then you should expect to struggle in the real world, my friend. Most people are normal with normal standards. Traditional with traditional standards. If they weren't, the whole point of regular social training would be lost, Hayden observed. As a person who studies people you should know that.

Well, I do know that. But as a person who has no plans to sacrifice his own potential to cater to the wishes of someone who would cap that potential, I have no plans to settle for "normal." As a theorist in new areas, I look for a partner who can put up with my randomness. As a perfectionist who needs to understand *why* things work as they do, I'm not content with butterflies that will die after two months of dating; then what will she and I have? I tire of "normal" too quickly to stay. Lastly, as a person whose work *is* his world, I need to know that my work can be applied to reality. It's not that I plan to manipulate the girl, but that she is a sufficiently challenging catch to allow me to put my work to use. Can you imagine how valuable it would be if we could use this "star stuff" (as you call it) to take an otherwise improbable union and turn it into gold? As far as we're currently concerned, my lady friend is a mythical land, and I am a fair wind. She's the kind of person who'll never be captured, and I am the kind who'll never stay. My ultimate goal isn't just to "date" her, but to make her a real thing in my life, though we're near impossible.

Hayden frowned in contemplation.

And if we can pull that off, I truly believe that we would have found a tool that the whole world can benefit from—using the study of people's interactions to fix relationships which are otherwise destined to fail. You must know that humanity tends to enter states of massive fear from time to time—all because the individuals who constitute it lose their ability to turn an exchange around in time.

Hayden reflected seriously on what Geery seemed to be saying. Did the scientist really think that his astrology could be used as a tool by something as large as humanity itself? How inflated! How intriguing. But with thoughts that high-flying, Geery must have really had a hard time dating after all.

Geery continued, I'm not satisfied with letting my male hormones, need for companionship, need for social validation, or quest for another's giggles override my natural desire for freedom, the power to self-determine, and fulfillment of whatever goals I see fit. I don't mind sharing goals. In fact, the whole point of my work is to make other people happy. But do you know how many people accept that sacrificing their own dreams is a necessary part of this? Then they become jaded. Then they just exist for the rest of their years, doing whatever normal life dictates. I refuse. So if I'm gonna connect with this girl, I'll have to do it the same way I connect with every other valuable thing I've found in life—through exploration that matches my natural ways and not through some scripted imposition of other people's ways. Can you say the same?

Hayden looked at Geery with a puzzled expression, trying to understand where the latter was coming from.

Look, all I'm saying is that I have big goals, personal goals, and a set of quirks which will HURT—not help—a relationship started or maintained in the wrong way. If I can't be myself in this, then I can look forward to a future full of compromise—whether the relationship is just beginning or has already started. I'm not saying that astrology is something we should swear by or even use when building relationships. I AM saying that, when entering or keeping a relationship, a person shouldn't just give up his self, and astrology gives me a useful glimpse at who that self is so that I can dig into my experiences with this other person and say, "Oh yeah! Things with them *did* go better when we did that."

Hayden, relaxed, turning back towards the water. So what's your hypothesis?

Back on track, my guess is: If the Ascendant is our approach to things and the Midheaven is the reputation we gain, then the composite [ASC-MC] shows how our relationship comes to be a "thing." Its angle should show the area of action in which the duo as a whole performs, by which it comes to be publicly recognized as a duo and not just two people exchanging.

Is that all? Haven't you already covered plenty of pairs like that?

Not really, the composite [ASC-MC]—given, of course, that you got the Ascendant and Midheaven by averaging—shouldn't be what makes the relationship. It should be what solidifies the relationship as such in outsiders' eyes as the duo mates see it. I think that the more you do its angle, the more of a reputation you'll have as a pair. And then there's the whole "prior planet thing." According to my hypothesis, partners will keep this composite pair going by reinforcing their 11th house-2nd house relationships: my social talkers must respond to your approach to worth and your social talkers must respond to mine. It's actually not terribly straightforward, but it should show what we need in order to legitimize our pair as a public thing. And yes I *do* hope to try this on my lady friend; in short, we'll need to be seen by each other's groups for whatever self-worth we appear to have.

Interesting.

Hayden paused to gather his thoughts.

So you think partners will be recognized as such based on the degree to which each one's groups assess the other's value and, I assume, the extent to which both partners align their own approaches and reputations in the process?

Yes.

Well let's see if you're right…

Ascendant*-Midheaven*

<2nd house-11th house

Yes, we're an item

Thanks to the roots of the Ascendant and Midheaven resting in the easternmost and highest points in the sky respectively, the composite [ASC-MC] is overwhelmingly dominated by squares (90°) and will never be conjunct in any decent house system. **The data revealed that this pair showed the area of life in which partners did new things together in order to establish a reputation for themselves as a duo**. Where the duo itself is concerned, the angles follow from a straightforward reading of our old friend *table 19-1*, with a couple of notable moments.

Squares are ultimately hard on long term relationships, though they are not killers. Since squares are rooted in want and emotion, duos with a square develop a reputation based on the extent to which outsiders watch the duo members' emotional interaction. When the relationship is new, this tends to be happy. When the relationship is old, it tends to be much less so. Thus we accept tacitly the inevitable drop in excitement of the average union. Children and shared endeavors can definitely serve as a means for offsetting this, but we should note that [ASC-MC] turns partners' emotional exchange into the substance of how they are publicly recognized by others. In a sense, the maintenance of a good attitude towards each other leads to the public's good attitude towards the partnership and, relatedly, all of the various perks associated with that partnership. There isn't enough room in this book to talk about all of the ways in which this circumscribes the fate of a pair as a public thing, so I invite you the reader to consider it on your own. When you and your partner get bored, tired or annoyed with each other, your partnership's reputation goes with it if you have a square. Here, your emotional exchange in approaching new situations, whether public or private, writes the fate of the relationship in public. Squares have a substantial failure rate when the going gets tough, mainly (I suspect) because we simply don't know how far our emotional approach to our partners echoes beyond the partnership and into the rest of the world.

Certain angles like noviles, II-conjuncts, II-trines, and II-septiles tend to be easy by default since they amount to partners voluntarily relating in public anyway. In private, the duo members are more likely to irk each other with II-conjuncts and II-trines, but overall, they can repair this simply by engaging activities together in front of people. II-septiles are generally great, attract people who want to join their circle in public, and have a lot to teach each other in private. II-noviles, in classic fashion, unsettle people in public and are fundamentally creative together in private. In many ways the opposite of II-septiles, these people tend to have reasons for hiding their strong affinity from the public, but work well together creatively or sexually in private. Many an adulterous affair has been built upon things like this. II-deciles establish their reputation through their professional alliance in a union that doesn't exactly favor affinity but utility instead. If these people associate as friends, it's more likely contractual in nature. Lastly, III-deciles build their duo's reputation upon either the mutual pursuit of mastery or upon one's bossing of the other. The former case is very good. The latter can be very bad if not consensual.

The trick with [ASC-MC] is for both partners to agree to try their best to provide as much support to each other under this angle as possible. This pair does not make a duo, but can either break a weak one or greatly empower a strong one. The reasons for this are ultimately very philosophical, conjuring discussions of what makes a thing real and what gives a thing form. In this case, reality is what partners' social groups say it is and form is what the partners themselves advertise as their worth within the context of the relationship. No one needs to be doomed to ride the normal train if they know that their misuse of square emotions or misuse of III-decile authority will kill the union. If you and your partner can only talk about one aspect in this book for keeping your relationship real in the world, I'd recommend this one. The negotiation over how you jointly approach your new opportunities can produce results which are well worth it.

Testing a prediction (part II)

So were you right?

I was.

Good for you.

Yes, I am quite pleased with myself.

So what did you learn? In English, if you don't mind.

I learned that no matter what happens between you and another person, there is one angle that is most directly tied to your future as a pair of people taking on the world together. That's the angle between your composite Ascendant-Midheaven. Agree with the partner to get this one right as much as you can and you've agreed to hold the relationship together using its most important property, no matter how complex everything else gets.

Hm. Interesting.

Ascendant*-Vertex*

<2nd house-"expiring comfort"

ℰ𝒮 **The duo comes together for the purpose of putting this angle in other people's faces.** They are likely to resemble a pair of show-offs here and have fewer qualms about letting others know just how special their partnership is. In opposite sex partners, III-quintiles are more likely to give off the appearance of being closer than they should be. If two people were to start a business together, this angle would be a good indicator of the capacity in which they would be the strongest operating jointly.

Ascendant*-Node

<2nd house-"questing"

ℰ𝒮 **Witnesses to the duo see this angle as the kind of "internal culture" they strive to build between the two of them.** That is, the partners aim to recognize each other as valuable contributors to their combined ability under this angle. So the II-octile partner says to the other, "We kick ass don't we? I kick ass. You kick ass. Don't we kick ass together?" The III-inconjunct says, "Well, those people won't be forgetting *us* any time soon."

Ascendant*-Selene

<2nd house-"resolvable dilemma"

ℰ𝒮 The duo enjoys early commonality status with this pair's angle. **Very early on in the exchange, this angle is the background against which one duo member takes an interest in the other.** Before the two join forces officially, but just before they complete their passage through the stranger phase, this angle provides key context for the way the two were before they became a team. This is quite the nostalgic pair.

Ascendant*-Lilith

<2nd house-"unfulfilling conformity"

The partners are drawn to express this angle together and are more likely to spend quite a bit more time building up this angle between each other in their attempts to grow the exchange. **This pair corresponds to the area in which the partners raise their confidence in each other before advancing the exchange from acquaintance to friend level**. For some partners this phase is completed very quickly though.

Ascendant*-Fortune*

<2nd house-"comfortable conditions"

One duo member grabs the other's attention as a potential kindred under this angle. **There is a sense of a deep connection which others aren't qualified to share**—a secret understanding between duo members which others don't have the power to fathom. For duos held together by bonds forged through shared trial, this angle is a good indicator of what such bonds tends to be built on.

Ascendant*-Ceres

<2nd house-"Other's dissatisfying expression"

Sass and a certain level of playfulness are more likely to come out between the duo members under this angle as the two interactants comfortably push each other around. The undecile is misleading here in the sense that the partners aren't so much engaged with each other as they are engaged with their own audiences, using the other as an object. In the long run the undecile often becomes negative, adding an air of superficiality to the kind of fun being had. Relatedly, all conjuncts and all trines are less personally invested than they look because they are more about each partner's own instinct than they are about the partner's interactant. II-noviles need a high amount of shared creative activity to keep their fun going.

Ascendant*-Chiron

<2nd house-"need for help"

We're too good for those peasants

The duo members provide high-quality, high-grade interactions for each other under this angle, in what amounts to the gold standard for exchange between them. This pair's angle shows where the partners form a superior team with each other compared to alternative partnerships. Accordingly, this same combination is, along with pairs like [Pluto-Pallas], an excellent indicator of where the two duo members would do well to work together towards a common critical standard.

Alongside composite [Vertex*-Juno], I call this one the "snob combo."

Ascendant*-Vesta

<2nd house-"situation that needs tending to"

Raw attention

This pair is probably one of the top five most animalistic combinations of all the composite pairs we'll cover, as the data filtered very clearly according to **different means of transmitting sexual intensity. This angle shows the topic area into which the partners pour such energy**. Even in cases where sexuality would normally be replaced by shared creativity, there tended to be an unsettlingly awkward focus on how deeply one partner could dive into the other's space before somebody said something. In every harmonic, you got the sense that at least one of the duo partners had an enduring focus on satisfying a set of unstated urges related to the angle's topic area. II-sextiles were, on average, especially lusty duos with their full time expression of the angle. Conjuncts tended towards a raw, inexplicable liking or dislike of each other—mostly liking. Trines and septiles were prone to engage in charged conversations. Undeciles told stories about their partners to many others. When reading this angle, consider it to show the circumstances under which the partners are most likely to approach each other with full fire blazing.

[ASC-Vesta] may be difficult to explain without a look at its prior planets as well. This pair essentially comprises two partners tending $_{\text{tending situation}}$ to their own self/bodily values $_{\text{2nd house}}$ in such a way as to focus $_{\text{Vesta}}$ the new situation jointly approached by the duo $_{\text{ASC}}$ as a whole.

Ascendant*-Pallas

<2nd house-"social imbalance"

✪ Is this what was meant to be?

✪ This pair is a critical indicator of why the duo exists as a duo in the first place. I call it the NPC (non-player character) combination. In video games, NPCs are other characters who aren't you, whose main reason for existing is to advance your character's story. **This composite pair's angle shows the main "stat" which the duo members are meant to increase in light of their partnership with each other**. It is especially good to look at in duos which have come to an end because it tells us what area of the partners' personalities they were designed to grow—regardless of how they actually interacted. There aren't many pairs which can claim to show "what was meant to be" in a relationship, but this pair is among such a group. Duos in which this angle never shows up strongly are typically duos that either 1) never formed in the first place or 2) fractured bitterly.

Again we see an example of how a seemingly minor asteroid (Pallas) can combine with a more well-known planet to pack big meaning. Why? Because the more well-known planets are broad with multiple interpretations while the minor asteroids are much more specific. Pallas shows something like socially-relevant action. The ASC shows approach to new situations. Accordingly, [ASC-Pallas] is where the duo as a whole pushes for change in the world abroad, typically for the purpose of righting a kind of wrong. Where most of our duos aren't so overtly aimed at repairing the world, the "wrong" which gets corrected is none other than an existing area of inefficiency $_{\text{social imbalance}}$ in the self-value $_{\text{2nd house}}$ of the duo members themselves. Perhaps this is why the data showed squares and II-deciles to be among the most positive angles for this pair; squares stabilized the partners' emotions while II-deciles stabilized their confidence as meaningful influencers among peers. III-quintiles favored "wingman" status when it came to influencing groups and was excellent for long-term personal commitments like marriage—presumably because it increased the partners' personal charisma in light of each other everywhere they appeared together. Squares also had this effect. Weirdly, octiles overwhelmingly favored the sharing of intuition of all kinds between partners (especially of the apparently "psychic" kind). Negatively, trines and II-undeciles in the data really struggled to get along.

Ascendant*-Juno

<2nd house-"need for secured role"

The duo forms an odd mismatch here, where the data supported the idea that whatever angle was present here constituted something that generally *didn't* happen between them or did happen in such opposite ways that the two formed a kind of sideshow for witnesses. It's not that the partners are at cross purposes, just that they seem to come from two obviously different worlds under this angle.

Ascendant*-Hera

<2nd house-"state of unattachment"

One partner puts their non-conformist outlook to productive use under this angle, standing out as a unique personality in this topic area. **This pair's angle indicates the realm of life in which a partner is rewarded for being different**.

Ascendant*-Eros

<2nd house-"receptiveness to impassioned action"

The duo members open doors for each other under this angle, introducing the other to a new realm that *could* be. **This is a good arrangement for one partner serving as a liberator to the other or a catalyst for the other's accomplishments in the world**.

Ascendant*-Bacchus

<2nd house-"desire to share company"

Joint horizons unlimited

There is a level of exploratory feedback which provides seemingly limitless potential for the duo under this angle. The two parties complement each other strongly, sending their combined talents through the roof in the same way that synastric [Mars-Vertex] does. Communication regarding this angle, whether spoken or unspoken also has fewer filters here $_{fbow}$. Oddly though, this pair is much more subtle than other strengtheners; rather than exploding forth, it releases its power with a slow burn which gradually creeps up on both the partners themselves as well as outsiders over time. These effects are felt as strongly within the duo as without.

Midheaven pairs

Midheaven*-Vertex*

<11th house-"expiring comfort"

⌘ **To dial them up, picture this as the background**

⌘ Part of the "Summoner formula," **this angle corresponds to the conditions under which it becomes easier for one of the people to envision the other on the mind**. When the first partner turns their attention to this angle, the chances of the second person appearing in their mind goes up noticeably. Squares naturally dream of each other while undeciles and II-deciles have a much harder time dreaming of each other purposely. Septiles come to mind when one person thinks of noteworthy communication (often negative). II-oppositions come to mind when one wants to share cool experiences with a partner. The pattern follows the usual *table 19-1* pretty closely, but can be tricky in the sense that most angles aren't really mental in nature; bringing a person to mind on purpose when you want to summon them, under this particular pair, often involves thinking of this pair's angle as an initial setting. How do I conclude this without knowing what planets are involved? Because there were enough pairs in the data where my own combinations with other people brought them to mind when this angle served as the broad subject I was thinking about, and all other pairs besides these served as contexts under which the duo in question seemed to "form" when the angle was active in the minds of outsiders who viewed them...

[MC-Vertex] is another one of those Midheaven combinations which shows where a certain quality of an interaction is easy to acknowledge. Here the quality is the "duo's" acknowledged change by way of the individuals' push toward a socially talked about or information-based move.

Midheaven*-Node

<11th house-"questing"

♀/♂ **The confidence vacuum**

♀/♂ This pair is a strange and complex planet combination. In positive cases, one partner offers charismatic company to the other under this angle. In the other's eyes, the first person can be soothing or reassuring. This only occurs, however, when either 1) the duo members are equally masculine-assertive or 2) there is some kind of sexual or creative attraction between the two parties. When such a connection does not exist, the mood surrounding the partners' sharing of this angle is often weirdly negative—affiliated with a bad attitude somewhere in the picture. Given that there is some kind of draw to each other in the physical or creative sense, the more intellectual this pair, the more tense it seems to be. The more wordlessly conveyed this pair is, the less tense it seems to be. There is some evidence that this pair is related to one partner's self-image, where the partner with the lower self-image is more likely to use intellectual or communicative versions of this angle to tear up the relationship. This pair seemed to produce more positive relationships between [strong, confident males with respect to each other] or between [confident males and their socially sought after women duo members]. The less confident either of the partners was (in the data), the worse this angle became. Here, more of the duo's explanations to each other regarding this angle had a way of hurting their dynamic. **Overall, we might say that this pair corresponds to a confidence vacuum, where partners of equally strong self-image get stronger as a duo, while those of unequal self-image are more likely to break under the strain of the weaker partner bringing the stronger down to match the former's level**.

Think of [MC-Node] as an individual quest for social significance gradually informing the destined public image of the duo, amplifying what outsiders say about each duo member's quest. The socially stronger duo member will need to pull the weaker one up in order for this one to work, but it is often the case that the weaker partner cares more about the issue and has more to lose, thus they end up exerting greater pull over the ultimate fate of the pair when it comes to this issue. The stronger partner tends to be less invested in addressing something that they don't really see as a problem, and tend to be less active here. This pair effectively reinforces class differences between the duo members.

Midheaven*-Selene

<11th house-"resolvable dilemma"

One partner respects the other's command of this angle area. Often highly.

Midheaven*-Lilith

<11th house-"unfulfilling conformity"

It's so easy to come together

One partner finds the other a comforting complement to them in this area of life. While the duo exists, the two people can almost be great friends on the basis of this angle alone, but for any differences in the way they normally conduct their separate lives. In another one of those unfortunate cases, this angle is among the best parts of the relationship which gets thrown away first when, for whatever reason, the two parties decide they don't like each other anymore. This pair is one of the main reasons that the two duo members should at least try to get along even when things get difficult. There is so much that they could do together here if they could only forgive each other's respective faults.

Personally, I liked this pattern of data a lot. There's something very reassuring in it. Look at a collection of your friends' charts to remind yourself of what you saw in them in the first place.

Midheaven*-Fortune*

<11th house-"comfortable conditions"

The duo at its most inventive

The duo builds an entirely novel framework for interacting under this angle in what constitutes a very unique and powerful pair. Roughly summarized, this pair shows the duo's most unique creation in the world of either member. Conjuncts will create a new way of approaching people through their interaction with each other. Oppositions will experience a new way of valuing themselves. Trines will invent a new way of communicating. And so on. Definitely take a look at this pair for a view of one of the most stand-out realms of activity you can possibly engage with your other person. You and the other person are super strong together under this angle, and the combination is almost always eye-opening (if not positive) in the long run.

Midheaven*-Ceres

<11th house-"Other's dissatisfying expression"

One duo member is more likely to take risks with this angle, choosing their interactions or angle-related topic areas with less caution. As a result, the partnership covers more ground here than in other areas.

Midheaven*-Chiron

<11th house-"need for help"

A source of insecurity patched up

Being in the duo provides a crucial source of fulfillment to the duo members in this angle area. As long as the duo is actively and healthily maintained, the need for the satisfied partner to seek more of this angle drops greatly. This pair is very strong, but only really runs around the time when the partners are actually interacting. In positive relationships it roughly corresponds to that angle area which the satisfied partner appreciates receiving from the other. In negative relationships it corresponds to a dynamic from which a divorce is hard to obtain. Most of the time this pair is a positive one.

Octiles heavily favor sexual or creative, playful or teasing, or power-centered attraction. Quintiles are like octiles, but more fiery and less emotionally invested. II-squares feel naturally kindred, have fewer filters on their communication with each other, and forgive each other's bad habits more easily in a relationship that really does look like family. II-quintiles favor cool attraction to each other's company and an easy friendship powered partly by the duo members' ability to dominate others together. II-septiles don't often make enemies, but when they do the enmity between them can be very bad—as it is difficult for the fighting parties to pull away from each other because of their basic programming to be friends. III-conjuncts take up opinions which encompass entire fields of experience and can be either very worldly-wise or very inappropriate (another kind of worldly-wise). One of the duo members in a III-opposition seems born to entertain the masses one way or another. A predictable tendency to distrust each other in the beginning is deceptive. III-inconjuncts tend to remain in the memory for a very long time regardless of how deep the interaction was.

Midheaven*-Vesta

<11th house-"situation that needs tending to"

Discussions between the duo members produces this angle as a subsequent experience. That is, partner discussions inspire this. The effect of this angle was obvious in the data and really obvious in hindsight, but not so obvious during the actual interaction. I found such a delay in effect pretty interesting. I suppose that we tend to think that just because an exchange has ended, we have license to file it in memory under what it *was*; it doesn't occur to us that an exchange can give something still different to us after it has ended. III-octile exchanges increase a partner's charisma in light of the relationship, for example.

Midheaven*-Pallas

<11th house-"social imbalance"

One of the partners has an intuitive talent for projecting this angle onto people and subsequently influencing those people through the angle. That partner seems to have a strong command of this topic area and is very hard to resist.

Midheaven*-Juno

<11th house-"need for secured role"

One partner's physical presence compels the other's actions under this angle in a weird kind of Pavlovian training. **The angle just feels like the thing for one partner to focus on when the other is around.**

Midheaven*-Hera

<11th house-"state of unattachment"

One of the duo members is results focused in the eyes of the other, acting to secure this angle from that other via a more stern set of standards. **Partner A is serious about Partner B's ability to convey this angle as a reflection upon Partner A's own self-image.**

Midheaven*-Eros

<11th house-"receptiveness to impassioned action"

In the wrong candy store

One partner strives to make progress under this angle and is supported by the other partner, but such progress is actually hindered by their association with the other partner in the long run. There is a sense in which the area the first person wishes to develop receives encouragement by the other, but encouragement of a kind which does not match the first person's ultimate make-up. We'll call this one the Substitute Goal. It is the angle area which forms the basis of the divide when one partner ultimately outgrows the other.

This is definitely an angle that should be taken with a grain of salt when you receive it from your partner. The evidence suggests that, in the self chart, this pair also corresponds to a trait that you yourself possess which you should be prepared to eventually outgrow. Somewhat unfortunately though, the more easily you outgrow your self chart version of this angle the easier it is to outgrow others under this composite pair, whatever the composite angle is.

Midheaven*-Bacchus

<11th house-"desire to share company"

The partners set up a space for framing others' actions using this angle. **Think of this angle as a playing field upon which ideas are moved like chess pieces in the partners' quest to make meaning of their worlds.** This is another fairly abstract pair which constitutes the realm over which the duo members assess things jointly. Put another way, **if the two people were to host a talk show, this angle area would be its most likely overall theme.**

Vertex pairs

Vertex*-Node

<"expiring comfort"-"questing"

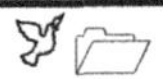 **Where two share a road**

This is a very strong pair which corresponds roughly to the kind of pronounced parallel that makes the two duo members feel as though they share a destined path. They seem as though they were made to follow strongly related sets of experiences under this angle; some of the more amorous or affectionate types may even extend this to a sense of fated union. But of course all pairs of people in the world will have *some* angle here, so this pair declares no such thing. It only makes a connection *feel* fated. That said, certain very enduring angles like the (automatically instinctual) conjunct or (highly family-centric) II-square really do favor "forever."

If you're looking for someone who'll share your view of things under a specific angle, this is one of the best composite pairs you can reference.

Vertex*-Selene

<"expiring comfort"-"resolvable dilemma"

One partner weighs in, with their opinion of this angle, on an issue raised by the other. This very often amounts to the first person's inexpert opinion on the second person's issue, where the second person holds a perspective that the first can't really identify with.

Vertex*-Lilith

<"expiring comfort"-"unfulfilling conformity"

Yield to the pressure

One duo member feels like they are owed this angle—that the other partner or *somebody* needs to service them or validate them in the proper way. This person *will* attempt to change the other person in most cases, though such change efforts may be short-lived in the presence of an interactant who is unwilling to be changed. Expect to be put on a schedule or have your itinerary outlined in a table for this angle. Barring this, you may simply be ceaselessly cajoled until the partner gives up. You may even be that partner. Unfortunately, this is one of those cases where a failure to properly perform causes the duo to lose its luster in a quick and obvious way.

Vertex*-Fortune*

<"expiring comfort"-"comfortable conditions"

The partner's dreaded box

This angle creates an uncomfortable feeling in one partner at the hands of the other, as if the second person wants something that the first won't be able to provide. Let's call this one a light sense of dread—dread that one day that towering fortress over which the second person presides will someday be bequeathed to the first person, who won't have a clue what to do with it. This is another one of those angles associated with intimidation and insecurity, except the emphasis is less on insecurity and more on avoidance. In cases where the avoided situation actually comes to pass, the burdened partner typically has to rely on the comfortable partner's support to do things correctly. Conjuncts have an easier time being annoyed by the comfortable partner's every deed. Sometimes the comfortable partner just gets into one of those moods where they treat every occurrence as a bitchable offense. Trines can also get like this, but invite their partners to complain with them. Septiles need to be encouraged that they are doing the right thing in general, and may even avoid becoming real friends for fear that they will let the other person down as an 1:1 interactant. II-quintiles, by initial default, avoid their share of responsibilities in the relationship. III-oppositions need the other partner to represent them to the public. III-septiles struggle to really share their circle, subjecting the partner to it instead.[57] III-noviles steal the spotlight from an otherwise very popular (burdened) partner. Often in attraction based relationships, comfortable IV-oppositions dangle an inaccessible carrot in the form of their bodies before the burdened partner, creating discomfort on a hormonal level.

[Vertex-Fortune] provides a really good example of how synastric / regular chart dynamics can change forms in a composite chart. If the regular [Vx-Fortune] pair represents "being in one's element $_{\text{Fortune}}$ amidst major change $_{\text{Vertex}}$," the composite version represents that situation where the partners' sense of major change is "averaged" and their comfort areas are also averaged. There is a partial sense that your favored position of skill is just around the corner, but then again so is the other person's favored position. The latter situation is decidedly different from your own. The resulting feeling is kind of like that of choosing a mystery food from inside of an unmarked box: It could be cherry pie (your favorite dish) or it could be broccoli (somebody else's favorite dish).

Perhaps you've noticed how the composite pairs are noticeably more positive or negative than their regular counterparts. Along with the theory of stacking proposed in the dialogue between Geery and Hayden, there is also the idea that composites simply reflect where we must consider our partner's perspective to be as equally likely to apply to situations as our own. Sometimes this produces anticipation. Sometimes it produces discomfort. In most cases, however, such provision of equal air time for [our version of a pair versus another's version] does not promote *indifference*. Thus we can think of the nearest midpoint composite chart as the set of interactions between ourselves and another where both of our preferred approaches to things become equally valid. It is no wonder that this kind of chart is a better reflection of a relationship from the inside, while the relative chart is a better reflection of a relationship from the outside; for every pair in your chart, there is a corresponding pair

[57] The dynamics of this one are really interesting and could command a chapter of their own. In a nutshell, the comfortable partner adds the burdened partner to a kind of friend-collection, but doesn't really want the burdened partner to play a role in influencing that circle. This is a "read-only" relationship for the burdened partner, and can lead to some profoundly bad blood between the two if not actively worked on.

in the other's chart which counterbalances yours. In the world of composites we consider the other's alternative ways of doing things against our own, creating a whole new space in our minds for how our internal approaches to situations differ compared to theirs.

Vertex*-Ceres

<“expiring comfort”-“Other's dissatisfying expression”

One partner uses this angle as the basis for avoiding the other partner in more negative relationships. This may be because the other person is a social liability or in some way irresponsible under this angle. The first person is simply inclined to feel safer investing their hope in separate alternatives in order to stay out of trouble here. This is in more negative cases. In positive cases this angle serves as an added bonus to an already solid exchange. This bonus, if capitalized on, is noticeably different from the relationship's normal fare as to take the exchange in an entirely new direction, particularly when the partner who would avoid this angle in negative cases actually chooses to adopt it instead. Here the adopting partner is the one who experiences a heavy change in angle-related standards.

Vertex*-Chiron

<“expiring comfort”-“need for help”

The duo's dynamic reflects a forward charisma which highlights the duo members' understanding of the angle. **The individual duo members seem comfortable with the angle and comfortably invite outsiders to join their exchange and experiment with it for themselves**.

Vertex*-Vesta

<“expiring comfort”-“situation that needs tending to”

The duo has complex forces impinging on it under this pair's angle. They tend to be more sensitive to imperfections here and have an easier time seeing when the other person is not at their best. Additionally, there is more of a tendency for the partners to lean on each other here. Overall this composite pair forms one of the more chaotic sides of the relationship.

I'm trying to focus on my major change. You're trying to focus on your major change. We distract each other, but the angle describing that distraction shows the common situation where both of us *simultaneously* focus on such things in the first place.

Vertex*-Pallas

<“expiring comfort”-“social imbalance”

This pair shows what angle one duo member expects from the other. That is, **this is a reversed angle where one partner draws the relevant character out of the other rather than projecting it to them**. It's not so much that one partner forces this characteristic out of the other as it is the other naturally shows this angle to them as a standard feature of the other's interaction with the first person. III-conjuncts and III-octiles strongly contribute to the projecting partner being attractive, strong, or both. III-quintiles strongly contribute to the popular charisma of the projecting partner.

Vertex*-Juno

<“expiring comfort”-“need for secured role”

Tight company

A kind of passion-infused bond passes between duo members here, where the two join together in a connected journey to experience the best life has to offer under this angle. This is a great angle for joint easy expression in a way that outsiders can recognize and positively affirm. This angle is very useful for cementing an already strong connection and serves as one of the bases for a fun duo.

Vertex*-Hera

<“expiring comfort”-“state of unattachment”

This angle shows an impressive characteristic held by one duo member in the eyes of the other. This characteristic generally enriches the life of the

partner who views it in the sense that it inspires the viewing partner to grow themselves through forward action which favors their long term evolution (particularly concerning peers in one's sphere of influence).

Vertex*-Eros

<"expiring comfort"-"receptiveness to impassioned action"

One partner is very demanding of themselves and others regarding this angle. They can show up as a stickler for perfection in some cases, a little diva in others. The data were pretty clear in this respect; at least one of the partners won't be the least bit amused at the thought of people getting this one wrong.

Vertex*-Bacchus

<"expiring comfort"-"desire to share company"

The duo uses this angle to determine a path for others to follow, effectively managing those others' efforts. Octiles resist being managed by each other and are more likely to be equals in the sense that they "consult" with each other instead. Similarly, II-septiles are a particularly strong indicator of two people who share the same level of "management rank" among their peers. This isn't official rank, but more like recognized influence. II-undeciles move others simply by being unique together. See the usual *table 19-1* to get a good look at the tools you and your partner use to organize the efforts of your peers.

"Forward action" in this pair's case is not always pleasant. The inspired partner can do anything ranging from adopting a new persona to cutting old ties to changing a long held outlook. Such action tends to be significant enough to register in obvious ways to the impressed partner.

Node pairs

Node-Selene

<"questing"-"resolvable dilemma"

The duo's exchange is rich and loud with the interplay of its members' versions of this angle. The two parties display a very visible power over others in this department such that the rooms they influence easily recognize them as an impressive pair of people. This composite combination does not at all guarantee that the two people will get along, but it strongly aids in their being compared side by side as two angle-strong individuals in the eyes of others.

Node-Lilith

<"questing"-"unfulfilling conformity"

A strong combo attack

The duo pours out intensity onto the world under this angle. Jointly, they present a face which others can find intimidating.

Node-Fortune*

<"questing"-"comfortable conditions"

The duo produces it's most memorable interactions in the eyes of outsiders under this angle. Conjuncts seem to belong together. Square duos are most memorable for the occasions where they fight or where they get along quietly, perhaps sharing an intuitive view of the same subject. Octiles have a noteworthy fire which passes between them in general. Deciles are noted for the extent to which they act to control either outsiders or each other. All of this is standard territory from *table 19-1* though. II-trines, as one might expect, may become notorious for an epic public scene which they make together. I've been involved in one or two of these. Epic I tell you.

This pair actually provides a pretty decent glimpse into a future event in your exchange with the other person—as it affects others—should you stick together long enough.

Node-Ceres

<"questing"-"Other's dissatisfying expression"

Planning to spend time with the other but don't know what to do?

[58] Interaction between the duo members establishes this angle as the preferred background context for their most natural communication. That is, **against an environment where others are displaying this angle or where this angle is expected to take priority, communication between duo members flows naturally**. Although not a major pair, this angle is an essential weapon for your toolbox in building relationships with another. Like [Node-Ceres] in synastry, this angle is great for establishing the ideal environment for "together time" between duo members.

Node-Chiron

<"questing"-"need for help"

One duo member regulates this angle or heavily defends it from influence by the other. In positive cases this is simply a skill which the defending partner brings to the table which precedes the other's input.

Node-Vesta

<"questing"-"situation that needs tending to"

A void finally filled

The duo-mate's most reliable role as duo-mate

The duo members find usefulness in each other under this angle such that they may advance themselves personally by anchoring themselves to the other. Done right, this attempt to patch up a hole in their own lives can be very successful; the "useful" turns out to be super-reliable here. This one is a must if you're looking to investigate the potential in your duo with someone else.

Node-Pallas

<"questing"-"social imbalance"

Partners seek each other's support in this angle area, particularly in situations where one partner wishes to display this angle to outsiders, but is obstructed. In some cases this support is sought when one partner simply has some angle-related quality they wish to show off to the outside world. The good thing about this angle is that the other partner's support is typically effective in getting the first partner the attention they want.

Node-Juno

<"questing"-"need for secured role"

The duo revolves around the attainment of #1 status for one of the partners in a realm related to this angle. **This is #1 status in the eyes of the other partner, such that the #1 person goes down in the other's personal history book as among the best or strongest there ever was in matters related to this angle.** This pair is very strong and very abstract, but quite automatic if partners get to know each other well enough. II-oppositions make some of the best company just to hang around.

Take a look at this angle to see how you'll be remembered by your partner (or how you'll remember them) after the relationship has ended, assuming things end <u>positively</u>.

Node-Hera

<"questing"-"state of unattachment"

One duo member's overpowering version of this angle compels the other to become absorbed in the former's expression of it. This is where one person can take over the other's priorities, not by

[58] Amazing. In line with all other blind method descriptions, I wrote this description before knowing the pair. When I saw where the pattern was going, looked up the "leisure time" pair from the synastry chapter (not remembering which one it was), found that that pair was [Node-Ceres] and included the reference to *synastric* [Node-Ceres] in this description. Once finished, I wrote the "Planning to spend…" note then, finally, uncovered this composite pair's identity. Found that it was *composite* [Node-Ceres]. I continue to be surprised at the consistency in patterns. Even if all of these angles are just noise, they constitute consistent noise—suggesting once again that astrology can be statistically tested via classification and clustering (regardless of whether the planets and points have any inherent meaning).

domination, but by broadly covering an entire span of attention.

Node-Eros

<“questing”-“receptiveness to impassioned action”

One duo member foists this angle upon another, surprising them in the process. Those surprises are often pleasant in a healthy partnership, unpleasant in a lackluster one.

In the realm of this angle, the surprising partner typically surprises when a more longstanding opinion of what they think the partnership generally needs (or something they continually desire to express) leaks out of their thoughts.

Node-Bacchus

<“questing”-“desire to share company”

The story you'll tell of them

This combination is super revealing

This pair's angle represents the story that one partner is most likely to tell to their peers and friends regarding the other partner <u>as a teammate</u>. As a composite combination, this one is very strong, fairly obvious to read if you've used *table 19-1* enough times, and is actually a little creepy as an overall predictor of the future of the partner's role in the relationship—regardless of whether or not things go well. **Read another way, this angle shows the area of life which serves as the first person's lens for assessing the second person's general effect on them (as told to the first person's circle of influence)**.

Read this one to see what kinds of behavior it is most convenient for you to expect from your duo-mate. For example, if you have a III-decile with a potential romantic interest, you might expect that romance ultimately won't be the thing that you tell others about regarding your partner; **boss-ness** will be the topic instead. Regarding potential negative situations related to this angle, consider yourself warned. On the up side though, your knowledge of this particular composite combination is one of your best potential tools for righting the ship in a relationship which is dying, since this angle essentially tells you what mode of interaction is most natural for your duo. All pretense and forced exchanges aside, if you can get a relationship to go in this direction, you essentially will have found the proper place for it in your life.

Selene pairs

Selene-Lilith

<-“resolvable dilemma”-“unfulfilling conformity”

The duo celebrates one member's version of this angle as a source of socially recognizable power for the pair. The partners engage each other as though that person is boss when it comes to this angle.

Selene-Fortune*

<“resolvable dilemma”-“comfortable conditions”

These are the standards

One duo member sets up this angle as the setting around themselves for drawing out the other's initiative. It is typically the more assertive partner who does this. That is, **this angle is the vibe that one partner takes on when pulling actions from the other**. This pair is actually very interesting and I invite you to go back to the usual *table 19-1* to see all of the kinds of faces people can take on in order to get their partners to do things. Oppositions question the value of the other's actions. Trines announce their complaint while septiles will tell the other directly through conversation when the former is disappointed. II-conjuncts go into a “mode” which the other may not want to see. III-deciles have an air of authority which makes the other ashamed. The composite behavior also suggests some self chart effects...

Self chart

...The data suggested that, in the self chart, this pair also corresponds to the means through which a person conveys their disappointment in people. Relatedly, when another disappoints, that other person tends to respond as though they failed under this angle...

...Now seeing that this pair is [Selene-Fortune], we can return to the self chart data in full. Without knowing they're doing it, possessors of a II-septile for example make others who fail them feel as though they have failed peer standards. Possessors of a II-decile make those who fail them feel professionally incapable. III-septiles are very popular; people who fail them feel themselves to be beneath this standard. People are more likely to vanish when they believe they have failed a III-decile, convincing the III-decile possessor that folks are just unreliable in general. In a very negative aspect (when not carefully administered), III-deciles are more likely to lose allies permanently simply through the latter's unwillingness to show their faces again following a failure. If this happens, it falls to the III-decile person to seek out the failing person and let them know things are alright (otherwise the III-decile may be waiting forever for their interactant to finally perform). For all angles under this pair in one's own chart, a lifetime peppered with various people who fail produces a situation in which the angle possessor learns mainly to rely on themselves for this angle—hence the tendency to get absorbed in their own world here.

In the end I suppose the data make sense; if ever we looked for a pair of planets capable of intimidating others, it would be the planet of perfect talent (Selene) combined with the planet of being in one's ideal element (Fortune). The standards set for interactants regarding this angle will be immeasurably high here.

Selene-Ceres

<"resolvable dilemma"-"Other's dissatisfying expression"

This pair shows the behavioral channel through which the duo members are tasked to filter their animal instincts. Things can get pretty primal here if the two aren't careful, anger and openly strong emotions over this angle topic being the most common results while raw lust is the rarer outcome (seen mostly among the first four harmonics—conjuncts, oppositions, trines, and squares). The duo members are highly susceptible to inflamed emotions in this area which others can clearly see.

Selene-Chiron

<"resolvable dilemma"-"need for help"

One partner makes for very popular company under this angle; the duo as a whole benefits from the partners' ability to attract outsiders' attention to them in light of this dynamic.

Selene-Vesta

<"resolvable dilemma"-"situation that needs tending to"

One partner is more likely to display irritation or restlessness in light of this angle's affairs. It will be harder for them to settle down when this angle is being threatened and they will tend to be more vigilant in scanning for potential threats. The person is more likely to air their discontentment here.

Selene-Pallas

<"resolvable dilemma"-"social imbalance"

In the presence of a master

One duo member appears to have mastered this role as a social performer, with all the bounty that both duo members could ask for. The level of talent is exceptional here, and can be used to drive the duo's notoriety among its surrounding circles.

Selene-Juno

<"resolvable dilemma"-"need for secured role"

One duo member sets a high bar, leaving an impression which the other could not hope to match on the first person's terms. **For this pair, you often find one person matching the other's expertise through sheer intensity rather than expertise of their own.** That is, the weaker partner under this angle is more likely to demonstrate sheer determination in holding onto the stronger partner's standards or will simply counterbalance the stronger partner's standards with a brute force response. In the latter case where brute force is the only way, the weaker partner tends to be either thoughtless or rudely inconsiderate in their complementary behavior to the stronger partner's angle. (For this interpretation, the "stronger partner" refers to the duo member who is better at using this particular angle, and has nothing to do with who is stronger or more assertive globally.)

Selene-Hera

<"resolvable dilemma"-"state of unattachment"

One partner is unusual in how they convey this angle—unique and prolific at the same time. Here you will find your duo-mate at their weirdest, making their weirdest decisions and adopting their weirdest personality traits. Or you might be that partner. "Deviant from normal traits" describes the character of one of the partners under in this angle. And the way in which that partner deviates is bound to get them noticed by others (especially the spheres of people surrounding the partnership).

Selene-Eros

<"resolvable dilemma"-"receptiveness to impassioned action"

The duo demonstrates charm and popularity under this realm of expression; they have an easier time making outsiders feel comfortable when they sow this angle jointly. Interestingly, despite such charm, the two people normally don't overlap very much in their approaches to this angle. Perhaps it is the mutual recognition of the great differences between them which allows the duo members to foster charm over everyone partly by using the other partner as a source of amusing material.

Selene-Bacchus

<"resolvable dilemma"-"desire to share company"

Personal history disclosure from one duo member to the other is more likely when this angle's area is the central issue. **Under this angle, one partner is more likely to say "Just to let you know, this is how I work; this is my background with respect to [this angle issue]."** III-conjuncts are more likely to disclose where they stand in a particular field or on a particular subject. III-sextiles are more likely to disclose their critical assessments.

Lilith pairs

Lilith-Fortune*

<"unfulfilling conformity"-"comfortable conditions"

A means of conveying creative passions

Open sensuality or fulfillment of one's impulses describes the duo's interaction here; **this angle is the channel along which the duo members convey their actual deep desire nature—though often that nature does not concern the partner**. This is desire nature in general. Interestingly, if you watch your partner under this angle you'll get a good idea of how they are inclined to play out their passions towards you should the occasion arise. Note, however that this pair (like most composite pairs) is not necessarily mutual so that usually one partner may be more responsible for using this angle as a desire channel than the other. In that case, this angle will mainly describe their display of desire and not the other's.

Lilith-Ceres

<"unfulfilling conformity"-"Other's dissatisfying expression"

One partner pushes this angle out towards the other with the expectation that the latter will back them (if not accept their ideas). This composite pair is analogous to a conversion attempt on behalf of one partner towards the other such that the aims is to have both people see the same kind of value in the same angle-related thing. Where no strong attempt at conversion is made, one partner simply holds standards for this angle without regard for the other person's opinion.

Lilith-Chiron

<"unfulfilling conformity"-"need for help"

✪ The protector

One duo member protects the right of the other to use this angle. Like an offensive lineman in football protects the quarterback, the former buys the latter room to maneuver. Sometimes active encouragement is part of this. In negative cases, the would-be protector is inclined to get visibly upset over the protected person's bad decisions under this very angle. In either case, the protecting person gives the protected one space to make their own choices. This is a pretty clear, pretty noticeable pair in the composite chart whose effects are quite obvious.

Lilith-Vesta

<"unfulfilling conformity"-"situation that needs tending to"

✪ How will the partners' joint creation stand out?

Here's an interesting pair which gives us a glimpse into the actual works that one of the duo members produces. **This pair shows the prime feature of an idealized created object in the mind of that duo member**. That is, if the partner created or served as the main guide for something, this angle area would be the quality which the partner wanted that something to express well. **Such standards, per the data, seem to spill over into the partnership as a whole such that the two parties together adopt this angle as the measure of a good joint creation.**

I found this to be among the more unique, more interesting aspects of all the composites because of its role in answering three related questions:

1. *What experiences should one partner create for a living?*
   Answer: They should make whatever works for them, but this angle is the thing which the second partner would *strongly support* them making.
2. *What will the partners' shared endeavors look like overall at the end of the day?*
   Answer: We can't tell that from this pair alone, but those shared endeavors can be summarized as reflecting this angle as a central characteristic.
3. *How will the children turn out?*
   Answer: Like other shared creations under this pair, a couple's children will reflect this angle more strongly. Return to *table 19-1* to see all of the possible characteristics. For people interested in creating things which stand authoritatively above the creations of their peers, all three levels of decile may be considered lucky.

Lilith-Pallas

<"unfulfilling conformity"-"social imbalance"

The duo members identify each other's primary contribution to their respective friendship terrain as being through this angle. This is among the pairs used by one partner to recall the significance of the other after the exchange has ended, mainly **constituting the realm in which "things could have gone right had we not had asked so much of each other."** In positive cases this angle actually does work out well between the two.

Lilith-Juno

<"unfulfilling conformity"-"need for secured role"

One partner's supporters greet the other with sternness or seriousness under this angle; these supporters are less likely to treat the second partner lightly. **For better or worse ($_{\text{fbow}}$) the ingroups of one person look upon the other person as a real force in the first's sphere of angle-related interactions.** This composite pair is the mark of a valuable influencer. III-quintiles make awesome battle buddies. In long-ended partnerships (and sometimes during), III-septiles are more likely to end up being an honor to have known.

Lilith-Hera

<“unfulfilling conformity”-“state of unattachment”

One of the partners plays out what-if scenarios, responding to things hoped, feared, or expected using this angle as their tool for conveying the outcome they anticipate. This is a complex composite combination which shows up in the form of some very elaborate behaviors. Reading its pattern in the data took some work, but in the end yielded a useful tool for those looking to understand their duo-mate better: You can typically look at the duo-mate’s self chart version of this angle to get a glimpse of what the other person hopes for or fears in their association with you. Deciphering what you read is definitely a skill though.

Lilith-Eros

<“unfulfilling conformity”-“receptiveness to impassioned action”

One partner acts strongly to get their point across through this angle. Sometimes this is done knowingly, most of the time this is done unknowingly through the person’s normal course of behavior towards the other. Establishing one’s presence under this angle is key here, as there is some tie to the person’s self-esteem or basic identity involved. Where the person acts to build a presence under this angle, they turn their eyes beyond the partnership and put the measure of their success in the hands of outsiders at large.

Lilith-Bacchus

<“unfulfilling conformity”-“desire to share company”

Easy on the moods

The duo members create a pleasant setting under this angle. Pleasant, I tell you. This composite pair is biased towards easy relations between the two or at least issuing from one partner towards the other as well as outsiders. This is the kind of dynamic which witnesses find smile-worthy—one which soothes even the most tense viewer.

Fortune pairs

Fortune*-Ceres [59]

<“comfortable conditions”-“Other’s dissatisfying expression”

A contract marriage

Jointly, the duo’s expression aims to pursue this angle. **This is probably the best pair for forming a contractual relationship between the two parties such that, regardless of whether the two people like each other, they should (unless they truly loathe each other) agree to still chase this angle together**. So maybe your duo has fallen apart. Suppose the other person and you still have some really pressing matter which you need to take care of in the bigger world. You can reference this pair as the basis for continuing to work together. This is, of course, harder for the more emotional angles like the II-square and II-octile.

A personal note on the creation of enemies

(Warning. This section gets VERY technical.)

Interestingly, I actually had a II-square with a personal friend who later became, effectively, an enemy. While we did all of the social things one would expect of friends, it turns out that our purest exchanges were those spent talking to each other in a “home” setting—like regular family. Those conversations were, unfortunately, largely spent digging our duo out of the grave dug by a mountain of externally justified social activities topped by

[59] This entire section all the way through its *table 21-2* were written using the blind method.

towering clouds of other-people-comparison, so we ultimately failed as a partnership. I believe, however, that if we had "played house" more, it really would have worked out. It's at about this point in the data (blind pair #241) that I realized how archenemies are made astrologically:

Too many emotional angles in structured pairs	turns detached issues into personal ones
Too many structured angles in expressive pairs	puts areas of expression into stifled cages
Too many expressive angles in public pairs	makes strong feelings louder and open to others
Too many public angles in emotional pairs	entrusts (to others' opinion) those relationship areas that should be private
+ Partners who simply don't get to know each other	stop themselves from working things out
Partners who oppose each other by default	

Translated into elements, we have

Too many waterish angles in earth dominated pairs
Too many earthish angles in fire dominated pairs
Too many fireish angles in air dominated pairs
Too many airish angles in water dominated pairs
+ Misuse of "acknowledgement" pairs (Venus, MC)
Partners who force issues separately instead of together

I'll address what it means to be "earth dominated," "earthish," and other related terms after we look at *table 21-2*.

Now I know what you'd *like* to see: a table (perhaps) of airish angles, waterish angles , or whatever. But it's not that simple. Note how *table 19-1*'s low, medium and high tension versions of angles can vary. Sometimes oppositions are just like earthy solid values. Other times they are more like watery bodily feeling. As explained in more detail in *FSA*, the elements are simply broad stories for describing categories of experience—which is exactly the reason why we can change how astrological factors get expressed in the first place. Sure water is water; but when water is vapor, water is air; when water is ice, water is earth. And so we can't really say what constitutes "airish." We can, however, lay out a table of some of the more stubborn angles and planets and how they "like" to behave. See *table 21-2*. Not all angles or planets will be listed because they're not all as stubborn as the ones shown.

Table 21-2: How we experience different angle tendencies in synastry and composite charts

Element	Typical angles	Typical planets
Fireish (looks like an action)	II-trine, II-quintile, II-novile, II-undecile, III-quintile, III-novile	Pluto, Ascendant, Selene, Lilith
Earthish (looks like a structure)	II-sextile, all deciles	Saturn, Midheaven
Airish (looks like communication)	septile, undecile, II-novile, III-trine, III-quintile, III-sextile, III-decile	Venus
Waterish (looks like a feeling)	conjunct, square, II-square, II-octile, III-decile (a felt need to control a situation)	Moon, Neptune, Selene, Fortune, Ceres, Hera
Situation	**Typical angles**	**Typical planets**
Force-related (associated with making things happen by pushing them)	II-conjunct (forced personality), II-quintile (forcibly managed groups), II-novile (forced creation), II-undecile (imposed quirks), III-square (imposed morality), III-sextile (forced assessment), III-decile (forced structure)	Mars, Pluto, Ceres
Acknowledgment-related (associated with group or personal identification of things)	undecile, II-quintile, **II-septile** (strong), II-octile, II-decile, III-conjunct, III-septile, III-novile, III-inconjunct	Venus, Uranus, Midheaven, Bacchus
Attention-related (associated with getting attention)	septile, undecile, II-conjunct, II-trine, II-octile, II-novile, II-undecile, III-conjunct, **III-opposition** (very strong), III-quintile, III-novile	Sun, Uranus, Lilith, Pallas
Feeling-related (typically brings the urge to influence something)	square, octile, II-square	Moon, Mars, Fortune, Hera, Eros

Table 21-2: Stubborn, element-like behavior of certain more predictable planets and angles. These are NOT actual elements, only tendencies which certain astrological factors obey when you actually feel them. Conjuncts for example correspond to basic action, but when we perform those basic actions in a relationship it's typically because we *want* to; our feelings about what we're doing override the realization of *what* we're actually doing. On this point, astrology as a field reveals one of its major weaknesses: by categorizing everything, we may lose a sense of the bigger, more flexible picture. To people who are strongly committed to the notion that the so-called "elements" are fixed representations of real things rather than fuzzy baskets, the above chart won't make much sense. Don't rely on this table too much unless you're already pretty comfortable with traditional astrology. The table's scrambling of characteristics can be confusing if you're just starting out. I include it, though, because this is how you'll actually come to view these angles and planets after working with them for a while.

What does "earth dominated" and all of that mean? I'll give you an example: Suppose you have a pair like synastric [Mars-Saturn] (see Chapter 19), where the Saturn person's will overrides the Mars person's will. Suppose that you are the Saturn person, Other is the Mars person, and the two of you have a `square` here. If you (Saturn) dominate this particular pair in the synastry, the pair can be described as "a `waterish` angle in an earth dominated pair" and you'll gain an added ability to protect the other person from their own negative emotions. But if they dominate this pair instead AND they happen to be fairly emotional, this pair could be considered "a `waterish` angle in a mixed element pair." They'll have the ability to stop you—through their behaviors—from feeling what you want, but this could be through structured or some other form. The second case seems worse, but is it?

- The case where you dominate, by itself, won't make you archenemies just because *table 21-2* suggests so. But if you have too many pairs with angles like this to the other person AND Saturn/earth tends to override the other person's intentions in such pairs, the overall character of your relationship with them will render YOU, Saturn, an oppressor of their natural feelings, helping you and Other to become archenemies.

- The case where Other dominates actually doesn't do much to create archenemies, firstly, because although certainly rooted in a watery urge to do something, Mars comes out as sometimes action-based, sometimes manipulation-based, sometimes intellectual, and is thus not stubbornly "watery" *by experience* to make the waterish part of *table 21-2* (even though it does make the "feelings" section). Secondly, a person's out-of-control emotions making you upset isn't really that surprising. They won't be an enemy, just a nuisance.

- In the end, Mars isn't so stubbornly water-looking that the Other person can't reasonably play it some other way if they dominate. But Saturn is pretty stubbornly earthy looking such that it is harder for you to do anything other than limit them if you dominate the pair.[60] A relationship full of Other's misbehavior simply breeds normal discontentment in you. A relationship full of your oppression of what they're "supposed to" feel is one of those things that eventually makes them hate you. ⚒

---

[60] This is why Mars was listed as particularly watery, the Sun wasn't listed as particularly fiery, while Saturn was listed as earthy in *table 21-2*. It depends on the number of options each planet has for being displayed.

Fortune*-Chiron

<"comfortable conditions"-"need for help"

The duo members are more inclined to behave more respectfully and pleasantly towards each other under this angle. Basically. But...while courtesy is a natural byproduct of this composite pair, certain angles can mask bigger troubles. Deciles and III-trines are particularly good at delivering a scathing message through nice-looking mannerisms. Indeed, this composite combination is not what it seems in the sense that it appears (from the data) to compel courtesy even when none is intended. Accordingly, **this is also the pair through which partners are more likely cut each other down lightly—when they have a critical opinion to deliver, but don't really care to deliver it meanly**. (My personal reaction to this data pattern was, "Oh that's cool! **pause** Wait a minute...Not cool." And that's what this angle feels like when it's used on you. I imagine many a tintiddle has been inspired by such "courtesy" between duo-mates.)

Fortune*-Vesta

<"comfortable conditions"-"situation that needs tending to"

✪ Where your partner is your ace

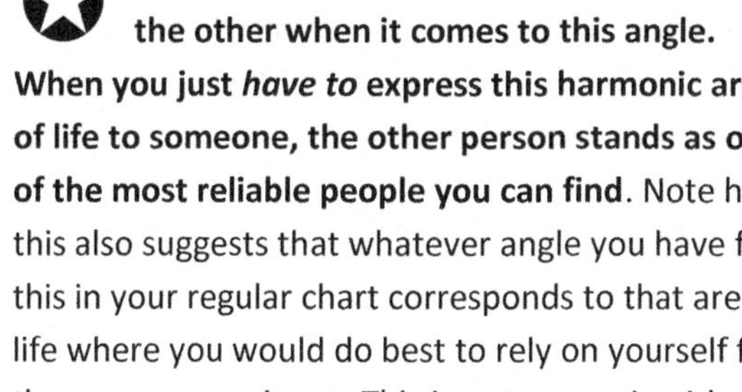

One duo-mate is <u>the</u> go-to person for the other when it comes to this angle. When you just *have to* express this harmonic area of life to someone, the other person stands as one of the most reliable people you can find. Note how this also suggests that whatever angle you have for this in your regular chart corresponds to that area of life where you would do best to rely on yourself for the proper experience. This is a strong pair with noticeable effects on the composite chart (as well as the last interpretation to be written among all 300 in this chapter).

Fortune*-Pallas

<"comfortable conditions"-"social imbalance"

The duo's ability to prosper is circumscribed by this angle. That is, **by increasing the extent to which the duo members can share resources here, the two can widen the reach of those resources and the success of their partnership on the whole**. For example, if you and Other have an opposition, yours and their views of money and value will combine to govern how the two of you prosper as a pair on the whole. If you and Other have a II-septile, you will need to share ingroups. As long as you keep your respective resources separate under this angle, the harder it will be for you to survive as a team. This is another interesting angle which lends credence to the idea that "the whole is greater than the sum..." Typically—except in cases involving family and other people who are stuck together—an inability to share resources or perspectives under this angle spells the end of the duo.

Why would composite [Fortune*-Pallas] be associated with prosperity in a duo? I don't know. Perhaps this pair shows where the joint duo is most comfortable "fighting" socially. Perhaps this fighting requires enough effort from the duo such that, if two people have the time and resources to fight, they must be getting something back from the world which keeps such effort from draining them. If the angle between their composite Fortune and Pallas shows where two people form a known combo, there may be a tie to certain resources given back to them from the world at large, be it money, self-fulfillment, notoriety, or something else.

Fortune*-Juno

<"comfortable conditions"-"need for secured role"

One partner must contend with the uncapped force of the other under this angle. This combination can be fun at times, frustrating at other times, but it's mostly just engaging. In some way, the uncapped partner often earns status as kind of pet zoo animal, their out-of-control nature endearing them as a source of fascination in the eyes of even the most straight-laced partner.

Fortune*-Hera

<“comfortable conditions”-“state of unattachment”

This angle is the currency of exchange between duo members. The more the two parties focus jointly on this angle and pass its related deeds back and forth to each other, the more invested in each other they become. Or maybe the word is “indebted.” **As one or both partners pay attention to this angle in the context of the relationship, the exchange becomes harder for them to terminate**. The partner who doesn't respect this angle in the other, doesn't pay attention to it, or doesn't rely on it has an easier time leaving the duo. Octiles and II-septiles, because they depend on one partner's response to another, tend to form stickier bonds under this pair.

Fortune*-Eros

<“comfortable conditions”-“receptiveness to impassioned action”

I knew them for professional reasons

One duo member's professional livelihood depends on this angle. This is a good partial indicator of the kind of career one of the partners can be expected to have. When this angle is stronger in you, your relationships with people with this same angle under this composite pair will take on more significance. When this angle becomes weaker, more superficial exchanges will drop in significance accordingly. More solid exchanges won't be affected nearly as much. This composite pair can be considered part of the Summoner formula as a means of attracting someone to you via a change in your job focus.

So here's a question for us: Why would [Fortune-Eros] be tied to professional behavior? Consider that composite pairs are made up of averages and NOT similarities. If my “place of being in my element” is different than yours and my style of passionate action is different than yours, it shouldn't be surprising that our composite Fortune and composite Eros need not reflect anything we're actually interested in. Instead, it's our duo that will show *its* comfortable “area of passion” (whatever that means). But our duo is a team and typically we form teams to accomplish some emotional or utilitarian end. Our *duo* passionately pursues this end, tying it more to our reasons for coming together than the personal emotional fuel we bring to the table. Preceding Fortune and Eros on the individual level we have the less passionate notions of “comfort” and “receptiveness to [being fueled],” both of which are pretty passive and thus more dependent on where we are than on what we actively want. Our work surroundings and life conditions are great places for playing this out. In the end, composite [Fortune-Eros] takes us from [the individual space of comfort in being fueled] to the partnership's [space of being right at home projecting a strong aim], hence the pair's weird transition from something personally forceful to something jointly professional.

Fortune*-Bacchus

<“comfortable conditions”-“desire to share company”

This angle can be thought of as feeding into one of the duo member's creative skill. **Where that person displays the ability to create things of lasting impression on others, this angle area is one of the prime inputs behind that creativity**. Although you wouldn't necessarily say that the duo member in question likes to brag here, you would say that they continually reinforce their skill with this angle area in the eyes of the other person.

Ceres pairs

Ceres-Chiron

<“Other's dissatisfying expression”-“need for help”

One partner's life under this angle is filled with drama or—at the very least—variety. This is the kind of preoccupation-infused soap opera material where the other duo member can expect to get an earful during updates on the day's events.

Ceres-Vesta

<"Other's dissatisfying expression"-"situation that needs tending to"

One duo member is more likely to present themselves as an object or objectify the other partner based on the former's experience of this angle in light of that partner. **Even after the other person's personality or looks have been forgotten, this angle will stand as one of the most memorable behaviors conveyed by the objectified partner in the mind of the other**. Conjuncts are noted for their raw personality and general expressive nature—the things they do without warning. II-deciles are noted for their unique career decisions or formal associations. And then there are two odd ones. II-undeciles are more likely to be noted for the unusually high level of intimacy in exchanging with the partner. III-deciles are remembered for their magnetism.

Ceres-Pallas

<"Other's dissatisfying expression"-"social imbalance"

The partnership provides release for its members' tension and pent up aspirations under this angle $_{\text{fbow}}$. We can't tell from this combination alone, though, whether such release will lead to anything productive.

Ceres-Juno

<"Other's dissatisfying expression"-"need for secured role"

The duo spends extensive together-time doing this angle. **If you really want to hang out with the other person more, you might seriously consider using this angle as a means to making that happen**. In general, the more II-oppositions spend time together the more they want to spend time together. Consider this another one of those silver bullets for building up a relationship. This is a very strong pair with noticeable effects on the stickiness of the partnership.

Ceres-Hera

<"Other's dissatisfying expression"-"state of unattachment"

One of the duo members is busy, particularly enterprising with this angle in such a way as to seemingly push it on outsiders as a rule (without thinking about it) wherever they go. This is essentially a habitual style of projection which *would* be a reputation except that it rests more in the duo member's automatic "signature" upon viewers more than it rests upon how those viewers agree to label the person's deeds. Conjuncts as partnerships impress outsiders with their will to project their personalities. One II-sextile duo member can effectively carry out plans for the other. III-noviles form highly charismatic partnerships which outsiders find quite "watchable."

Ceres-Eros

<"Other's dissatisfying expression"-"receptiveness to impassioned action"

One partner tests the other's patience or renders the other excitable $_{\text{fbow}}$ **under this angle**. It is harder for the second person to maintain their emotional equilibrium under the first person's display of this angle; the overall effect is that the second person is moved to abandon indifference and feel strongly about their duo-mate's deeds here. Being a part of a II-septile's ingroup usually increases the feeling of friendship between duo mates and makes their interaction generally more exciting. The interaction with III-deciles' "boss" or "business" sides makes the partner consider them seriously. The interaction with III-inconjuncts is more likely to take on a "fated" quality.

Ceres-Bacchus

<"Other's dissatisfying expression"-"desire to share company"

One duo member needs someone to lean on in the eyes of the other duo member in order to advance this angle, though that person need not be the other duo member themselves. Without some other person as a complement (or validating audience), the first is a lot less inclined to achieve their sought level of mastery—or at least a lot less likely to achieve that mastery confidently.

Chiron pairs

Chiron-Vesta

<"need for help"-"situation that needs tending to"

A basic interweaving of paths is assumed by the partners under this angle such that the duo members may attempt to build an alliance upon what they feel to be a kind of bond. True, there may be a connection, but it's not always a "bond" (as most partners under this composite pair eventually realize); instead this pair really does correspond to a simple intersection of behaviors which establish nice solid ground for *some* kind of interaction, but whether the interaction is supportive or not is another matter.

Chiron-Pallas

<"need for help"-"social imbalance"

One duo member can use this angle to poke holes in the other's self-assuredness. Just when the other partner is getting too big-headed to tolerate, the first person displays this angle as a check on the second one's ego. This dynamic is usually one way as a tool used against the less humble partner.

Chiron-Juno

<"need for help"-"need for secured role"

Within the context of the partnership, one partner uses this angle to search for and express their worth to themselves. In times when they are feeling particularly insecure, the person can be capricious or obnoxious here. This can apply to either partner or both at any time, but tends to be more characteristic of one than the other.

Chiron-Hera

<"need for help"-"state of unattachment"

How must the duo escalate in order to survive?

One duo member, over the course of the partnership, comes to want more of this angle from the other. The stakes are gradually raised for this composite pair in what, oddly, constitutes **the only composite combination among all 300 which can be easily read as showing how the relationship is expected to grow <u>past</u> where it started**. As such this one represents a critical planet pair in the composite chart. Failure to grow here will not necessarily kill the duo, but will seriously cripple its ability to satisfy the two parties who initially agreed to it. Disillusionment with the failing partner is a common result in such cases.

As practice in reading composites, we might ask how we could have known to look at [Chiron-Hera] for information as critical as "the thing that our duo needs to escalate." The short answer is, we *couldn't* have known since there are many ways of asking the same question and many ways of answering even one question—which is why all of the pairs (self chart, synastric, and composite) tend to get fairly repetitive as more and more planets are added. But [Chiron-Hera] does provide a strong answer for one specific kind of partnership-escalation question: *What kinds of fixes* $_{\text{Chiron}}$ *will our duo be really attached to finding* $_{\text{Hera}}$*?* In other words, what will you and Other as a team keep inventing for yourselves as a dedicated issue to keep addressing? You can look at the answer this one provides in the way that you look at a departmental description in a business. What does Human Resources do? What does Sales do? Once these departments have done the job once, are they considered finished? Of course not (if we're talking about regular business operations); instead, business units like these are expected to address the same issue over and over, and expected to do it better over time. Not worse. Relatedly, Doctor Chiron is most strongly Hera-bound to the kind of patient he is trained to see, and should be expected to advance in his profession rather than regress. [Chiron-Hera] shows the kind of practice your duo operates. Slip up too heavily and your practice closes no matter how many past successes you've had.

Chiron-Eros

<"need for help"-"receptiveness to impassioned action"

A quick diagnosis IV: Off the top of your head, what is this duo all about?

An at-a-glance look at the duo by outsiders conjures up impressions of this angle. A powerful summary of what the partnership is all about, this composite pair constitutes one of the most basic indicators of the sense in which the duo is actually a duo and not just two people interacting. **Here we have the simplest view of how the duo-mates stereotypically engage each other**. Trines, II-undeciles, and III-conjuncts don't connect nearly as deeply as one would think, while squares and inconjuncts connect more deeply than one would think. The former, though expressive, tends to be all about each expresser's own world. The latter, though not obviously matched, tend to leave witnesses with a *feeling* that the "mismatched" partners were somehow meant to find each other. II-inconjuncts form fascinating duos which inspire novel ideas in their viewers. Such ideas, by virtue of their roots in the duo-mates' interaction, tend to be related to how the witnesses themselves behave in their own social relations.

Chiron-Bacchus

<"need for help"-"desire to share company"

The partners reaffirm each other through this angle $_{fbow}$. When expressing this one jointly, they reinforce (most strongly) the importance of the other especially as a physical presence in each one's life. This composite pair gets turned up when the duo members cite each other's overt deeds or hang around each other, but gets weaker in response to shared ideas or communication only.

We can describe this as the kind of reaction which the perception of the other person inspires. It doesn't seem to be that strongly tied to physical looks so much as it appears tied to the area of life in which the perceiving partner is more inclined to be immediately aware of their own self-image given the attention they pay to the *actual* duo-mate. The perceiver's *interpretation* of the duo-mate doesn't carry the same weight here.

[Chiron-Bacchus] can be better understood as being "where the duo is most self-conscious of its impression on peers." Peer-impression is more easily tied to how the partners look together rather than how they work apart.

Vesta pairs

Vesta-Pallas

<"situation that needs tending to"-"social imbalance"

A case of classic eccentricity

This pair's angle often shows up as uncharted territory in the duo mainly because of 1) its complexity as an issue presented by one person towards the other or 2) its looming status as a costly area of potential misunderstanding between the partners and outsiders or the partners and each other. One person is more likely to introduce the other to wacky or outlandish ideas which only the most adventurous duo-mates would buy into, but in the rare cases where such ideas are successfully conveyed, the whole duo can emerge with some pretty noteworthy experiences which are strongly connected to fame. A friend of mine and I have the undecile, for example, which predisposes our duo to getting eyed by others everywhere we go.

Vesta-Juno

<"situation that needs tending to"-"need for secured role"

One duo member keeps this angle at the top of the other's mind, emphasizing either its importance

to the former or its importance as a value to be held by the latter. There can be a convincing level of pressure (applied to one partner by the other who values this) towards responsible execution of this angle on the part of the pair as a whole. In more stressful cases this serves to knock the other partner out of the clouds. One partner's focus on this angle can dominate the angle's expression across the duo as a whole, silencing the other's version of it by comparison when the two are together.

Vesta-Hera

<"situation that needs tending to"-"state of unattachment"

One duo member naturally displays this angle in a way that riles up or turns on the other. **The second person's desire nature is easily activated fbow by the first person's show of this angle behavior**. Dreams of conquest and a hunger for power are among the results.

Vesta-Eros

<"situation that needs tending to"-"receptiveness to impassioned action"

 **Let the duo be born!**

One duo member kicks down the door and uses this angle as the ram to storm the castle which holds the other partner's favor. **This is the angle which the would-be duo member who is more interested in forming the duo uses to win the other person over**. You might even say that this is the angle behavior which grants the duo life. If the partnership is a baby, this pair's angle is the doctor who facilitates delivery.

Vesta-Bacchus

<"situation that needs tending to"-"desire to share company"

Their best efforts

This pair corresponds roughly to the gift that one partner gives to the other as a duo-mate. **As long as the two are together, it is as if the duo-mate donates this angle in earnest, with everything they have**. This is especially true of enemies—whose abilities under this angle form half of the more frustrating bases for enmity. "I'm giving everything I have with [this angle], why won't you just take it as I give it!?"

This was one of the sadder patterns in the data; it showed where, in exchanges which eventually expired, one partner's best (though imperfect) really was their best, but still failed to overcome other problems in the exchange. There is a sense of unfortunate purity in this combination, where one person interacts with the other given all of the first one's human failings...and is often punished for having tried and faltered. If you want your duo to last, accepting this angle as your partner's means of patching up differences will go a long way.

Pallas pairs

Pallas-Juno

<"social imbalance"-"need for secured role"

It is easier for the two of you to cross into frowned upon territory under this angle, where your duo takes on a level of investment which breaches socially accepted bounds. **We could describe this as being where the two of you are likely to go overboard as a team.**

Pallas-Hera

<"social imbalance"-"state of unattachment"

The level of daring and boldness in this angle is turned up for one partner in light of the other. This is creative and expressive inspiration on a noticeable enough level to awaken the emboldened partner's awareness of their own insecurities (or at least their unpreparedness). This person is called on to be brave here.

Pallas-Eros

<“social imbalance”-“receptiveness to impassioned action”

Both partners behave as though invincible when engaging each other under this angle. “No thanks. I got this,” is what they may as well say to each other. Third parties to the duo will find only mutual smugness here. Undeciles “know for a fact” that they are relevant on the grapevine. II-quintiles have no lack of confidence in their ability to influence others under their charms. III-noviles make for pretty fun entertainers as a pair.

Pallas-Bacchus

<“social imbalance”-“desire to share company”

One partner has high energy or is higher strung under this angle. It seems as though that person is preoccupied with all kinds of issues that most others can’t see. Such issues are commonly related to people’s behavior. III-conjunct exchanges are often highly society-focused. III-trine exchanges are more inclined to be hyper-intellectual. More negatively, II-conjuncts are more susceptible to damage resulting from one partner’s over-focus on their public image. Control issues tend to hamper the success of duos with the III-decile. Conjuncts are neutral in that they bring a partner who shoots from the hip…with a tommy gun.

Juno pairs

Juno-Hera

<“situation that needs tending to”-“state of unattachment”

One duo member is pleasantly unpredictable in positive cases, a loose cannon in negative cases under this angle. Their aims and communicated messages in the context of the duo can vary widely in nature, typically affecting an unprepared partner in relatedly varied ways. In negative cases this angle corresponds to an area of life where one partner is unreliable in the face they present to the partner for subsequent output to the world. This is, “I don’t believe you’re doing that. Are you serious?” Or it could be “…but what happened to all those previous plans we laid out?”

Juno-Eros

<“situation that needs tending to”-“receptiveness to impassioned action”

The duo shows this angle shamelessly before everyone else, with an open complementarity which is too close to not be a bond, but too normally played to be considered punishable—even if it *is* inappropriate. If ever you planned to do something publicly risky with someone and get away with it (socially if not legally) this would be the angle to use. Expressing this angle jointly, two people can get away with murder under this one—though they may definitely draw a frown or two in the process. All octiles and the II-novile, for example, can get away with taboo talk in front of everyone and not be called on it (within reason of course). II- and III-quintiles exercise an eccentric form of public impression making; they are usually serious enough, but there is something about them which is unsettling and weird to others. As if they encourage each other to push the limits of acceptable charm farther and farther beyond the norm.

Juno-Bacchus

<“situation that needs tending to”-“desire to share company”

The color of <u>receptive</u> physical intimacy

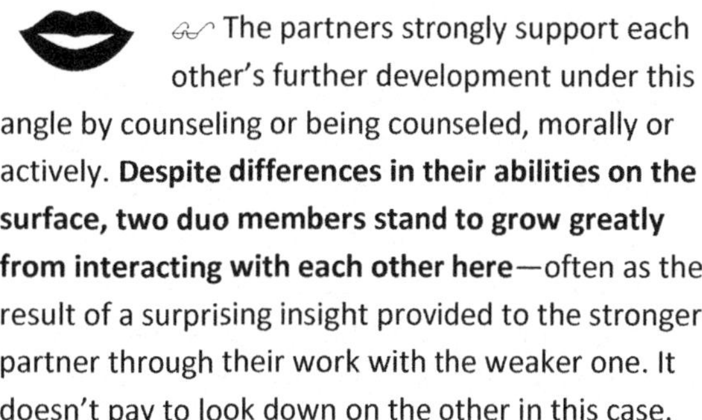

The partners strongly support each other’s further development under this angle by counseling or being counseled, morally or actively. **Despite differences in their abilities on the surface, two duo members stand to grow greatly from interacting with each other here**—often as the result of a surprising insight provided to the stronger partner through their work with the weaker one. It doesn’t pay to look down on the other in this case.

This pair is also related to the way physical intimacy is experienced by the more openly

receptive party in a romantic exchange—the idea being that such intimacy amounts to a sharing of bodily value inspired by the actions of another. Where romance is concerned, this pair is less about sex and more about love making, less about conscious communication and more about equally received subconscious ideas inspired by the company of the other. Before the mind translates it, there is the body and brain which feels it. Why the more receptive party? Because the more active party is too busy acting (and perhaps expecting) rather than receiving. Both parties can actually be receptive in this one, but the one who isn't receptive won't feel this pair nearly as viscerally.

Really, the experience with this pair doesn't have to be sexual. It can also be about expectation-free closeness in general. I remember laying my head in my mom's lap as a kid while she brushed my hair. In hindsight the experience matches our opposition perfectly. Relatedly, you'll likely remember some of your more peaceful physical exchanges with your partner as being more like this pair's angle than any other in the composite. Check this one out in your self chart to get a neat look at the family of experiences which can be used to stimulate your body without asking your mind permission. As a neat experiment you can use either the self chart version or the composite version of this pair to attain tingles from the other even without laying a hand on them—provided you are 1) receptive enough to the angle in question and 2) free of expectations regarding how they should interact with you. The feeling is quite cool, and very easy to achieve with enough openness.

After finding out what the above planets were I realized the pair should be added to the list of "alchemical combinations"—those used to rewrite the face of a partnership on purpose. [Juno-Bacchus] is another one of those pairs which provides us with a very good reason to forgive people with whom we have rifted and remember what they were capable of giving us—not because they make us feel physically good under this angle, but because physical pleasure and self-worth are married concepts astrologically, biologically, and socially. For you to receive this angle from your partner is for you to let your worth go up in light of them. For ex-partners who can no longer be tolerated, considering this angle to be a thing which *you* compelled them to donate to you works almost as well. Of course you could always plan to stay bitter over the cancelled exchange, but maybe you can imagine the amount of actual biological energy this really costs—both from dedicated tension and from lost peace. In a lot of negative cases forgiveness is easier said than done of course, but *planning* to withhold such forgiveness is another matter.

Hera pairs

Hera-Eros

<"state of unattachment"-"receptiveness to impassioned action"

This pair shows how one duo member displays passion towards each other when the exchange is felt at its deepest.

Conjuncts can erupt in a sudden burst of unexpected passion. Septiles can suddenly fight. Deciles suddenly limit each other. II-quintiles suddenly invoke standards which they believe the other has failed. II-undeciles are generally unpredictable. III-squares shock the other with pirate behavior and violations of the other's moral expectations. These are all typically negative cases, though they each have their positive versions. More positively by default, II-septiles suddenly identify with each other where you thought they wouldn't. II-octiles suddenly recognize the other's influence over outsiders. II-noviles—highly positive—stir the other in flashes of inspiration with which the other can then create things. III-quintiles are more predictably charismatic towards each other, though the partner may see them as a ceaselessly surprising to outsiders. Because of the emphasis on III-quintile self-assured prosperity, a sense of "we're so special" kind of intimacy comes easily for these partners as they feel and act like their association is one of a kind. Hater, be jealous.

In all cases, though, one partner can be expected to break out this angle in a shot of passion, so that the other partner should hope to be prepared. This pair, though minor, is a strong predictor of the partners' enthusiastic investment in each other's continued good.

[Hera-Eros] can show the basis for how we experience deeply passionate bonds with the partner internally and, by extension, the feeling we get in light of intimacy with them. Unfortunately, there are many occasions where this one can get out of hand, where more often than not this pair simply shows **how fights-you-wish-didn't-have-to-happen unfold**. Here, partners are bonded, but intimacy is neither feasible nor appropriate. So on the one hand the partners agree to associate; on the other hand they rile each other up when they do. And although it would be nice if they could simply turn their attention to a common goal, most of the time they can't and don't. The situation just won't permit it. Then the only thing they can do is step back and try to cooperate despite it all.

Hera-Bacchus

<"state of unattachment"-"desire to share company"

One of the duo members displays a strong will under this angle, frequently experiencing—but withstanding—multipronged assaults on this aspect of their personality. "Multipronged assaults" need not always be negative, but often reflect where the person is simply in demand. Octiles and III-quintiles increase the physical attractiveness of at least one of the partners. III-sextiles increase bodily allure. Both of these are presumably connected to the idea of having others come to one of the partners to be dominated (octiles individually, III-quintiles collectively). If not for the purpose of being dominated, people may come to one of the partners to be told how to view things (III-sextile). What kinds of patrons seek such subservience? Patrons who find safety in the kind of power you can display from afar: usually looks.

Eros pairs

Eros-Bacchus

<"receptiveness to impassioned action"-"desire to share company"

Under this angle, the partners escape into each other's company. The two are more likely to spend more time together here, but not so much more as to compete with priorities like that of [Ceres-Juno]. Instead **this pair shows where, when interacting with each other, the partners tend to get lost in the many nuances of a shared issue related to this angle**. Despite how they may appear in public, II-squares are designed to get along swimmingly as near or actual family. II-quintiles are more prone to break out the big guns in their interaction, in some relationships turning them against each other, in other relationships turning them towards a joint target.

And there you have it. All 300 composite interpretations for the planets covered in this book and in *Full Spectrum Astrology*.

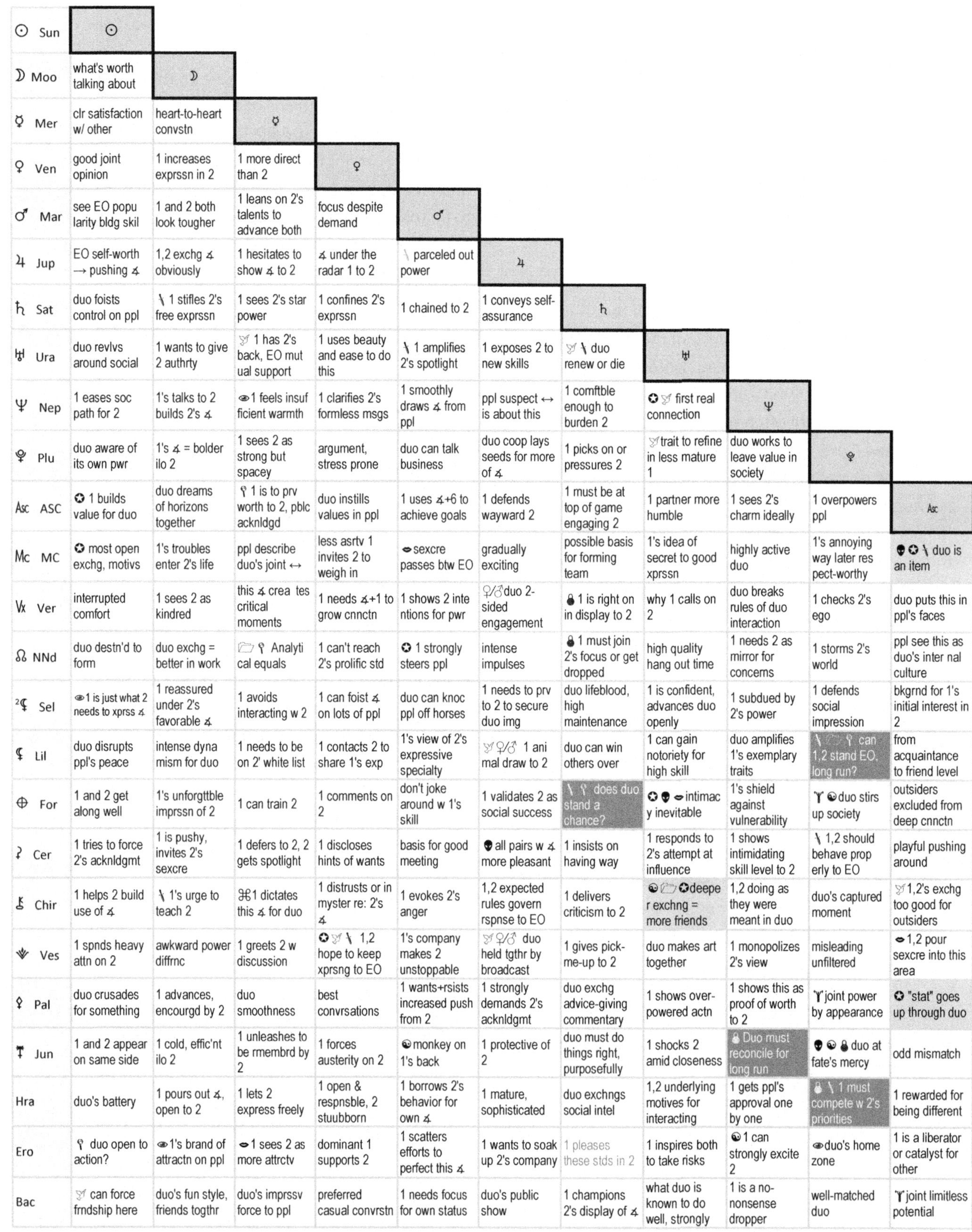

☉ Sun	☉										
☽ Moo	what's worth talking about	☽									
☿ Mer	clr satisfaction w/ other	heart-to-heart convstn	☿								
♀ Ven	good joint opinion	1 increases exprssn in 2	1 more direct than 2	♀							
♂ Mar	see EO popu larity bldg skil	1 and 2 both look tougher	1 leans on 2's talents to advance both	focus despite demand	♂						
♃ Jup	EO self-worth → pushing ∡	1,2 exchg ∡ obviously	1 hesitates to show ∡ to 2	∡ under the radar 1 to 2	\ parceled out power	♃					
♄ Sat	duo foists control on ppl	\ 1 stifles 2's free exprssn	1 sees 2's star power	1 confines 2's exprssn	1 chained to 2	1 conveys self-assurance	♄				
♅ Ura	duo revlvs around social	1 wants to give 2 authrty	🕊 1 has 2's back, EO mut ual support	1 uses beauty and ease to do this	\ 1 amplifies 2's spotlight	1 exposes 2 to new skills	🕊 \ duo renew or die	♅			
♆ Nep	1 eases soc path for 2	1's talks to 2 builds 2's ∡	👁1 feels insuf ficient warmth	1 clarifies 2's formless msgs	1 smoothly draws ∡ from ppl	ppl suspect ↔ is about this	1 comftble enough to burden 2	✪ 🕊 first real connection	♆		
♇ Plu	duo aware of its own pwr	1's ∡ = bolder ilo 2	1 sees 2 as strong but spacey	argument, stress prone	duo can talk business	duo coop lays seeds for more of ∡	1 picks on or pressures 2	🕊trait to refine in less mature 1	duo works to leave value in society	♇	
Asc ASC	✪ 1 builds value for duo	duo dreams of horizons together	⚲ 1 is to prv worth to 2, pblc acknldgd	duo instills values in ppl	1 uses ∡+6 to achieve goals	1 defends wayward 2	1 must be at top of game engaging 2	1 partner more humble	1 sees 2's charm ideally	1 overpowers ppl	Asc
Mc MC	✪ most open exchg, motivs	1's troubles enter 2's life	ppl describe duo's joint ↔	less asrtv 1 invites 2 to weigh in	👄sexcre passes btw EO	gradually exciting	possible basis for forming team	1's idea of secret to good xprssn	highly active duo	1's annoying way later res pect-worthy	👽 ✪ \ duo is an item
Vx Ver	interrupted comfort	1 sees 2 as kindred	this ∡ crea tes critical moments	1 needs ∡+1 to grow cnnctn	1 shows 2 inte ntions for pwr	♀/♂duo 2-sided engagement	🔒 1 is right on in display to 2	why 1 calls on 2	duo breaks rules of duo interaction	1 checks 2's ego	duo puts this in ppl's faces
☊ NNd	duo destn'd to form	duo exchg = better in work	📂 ⚲ Analyti cal equals	1 can't reach 2's prolific std	✪ 1 strongly steers ppl	intense impulses	🔒 1 must join 2's focus or get dropped	high quality hang out time	1 needs 2 as mirror for concerns	1 storms 2's world	ppl see this as duo's inter nal culture
²⚸ Sel	👁1 is just what 2 needs to xprss ∡	1 reassured under 2's favorable ∡	1 avoids interacting w 2	1 can foist ∡ on lots of ppl	duo can knoc ppl off horses	1 needs to prv to 2 to secure duo img	duo lifeblood, high maintenance	1 is confident, advances duo openly	1 subdued by 2's power	1 defends social impression	bkgrnd for 1's initial interest in 2
⚸ Lil	duo disrupts ppl's peace	intense dyna mism for duo	1 needs to be on 2' white list	1 contacts 2 to share 1's exp	1's view of 2's expressive specialty	🕊♀/♂ 1 ani mal draw to 2	duo can win others over	1 can gain notoriety for high skill	duo amplifies 1's exemplary traits	\ 📂 ⚲ can 1,2 stand EO, long run?	from acquaintance to friend level
⊕ For	1 and 2 get along well	1's unforgttble imprssn of 2	1 can train 2	1 comments on 2	don't joke around w 1's skill	1 validates 2 as social success	\ ⚲ does duo stand a chance?	✪ 👽 👄intimac y inevitable	1's shield against vulnerability	ϒ ☯duo stirs up society	outsiders excluded from deep cnnctn
⚳ Cer	1 tries to force 2's acknldgmt	1 is pushy, invites 2's sexcre	1 defers to 2, 2 gets spotlight	1 discloses hints of wants	basis for good meeting	👽 all pairs w ∡ more pleasant	1 insists on having way	1 responds to 2's attempt at influence	1 shows intimidating skill level to 2	\ 1,2 should behave prop erly to EO	playful pushing around
⚷ Chir	1 helps 2 build use of ∡	\ 1's urge to teach 2	⌘1 dictates this ∡ for duo	1 distrusts or in myster re: 2's ∡	1 evokes 2's anger	1,2 expected rules govern rspnse to EO	1 delivers criticism to 2	☯ 📂 ✪deepe r exchng = more friends	1,2 doing as they were meant in duo	duo's captured moment	🕊1,2's exchg too good for outsiders
⚶ Ves	1 spnds heavy attn on 2	awkward power diffrnc	1 greets 2 w discussion	✪ 🕊 \ 1,2 hope to keep xprsng to EO	1's company makes 2 unstoppable	🕊♀/♂ duo held tgthr by broadcast	1 gives pick-me-up to 2	duo makes art together	1 monopolizes 2's view	misleading unfiltered	👄1,2 pour sexcre into this area
⚴ Pal	duo crusades for something	1 advances, encourgd by 2	duo smoothness	best convrsations	1 wants+rsists increased push from 2	1 strongly demands 2's acknldgmt	duo exchg advice-giving commentary	1 shows over-powered actn	1 shows this as proof of worth to 2	ϒjoint power by appearance	✪ "stat" goes up through duo
⚵ Jun	1 and 2 appear on same side	1 cold, effic'nt ilo 2	1 unleashes to be rmembrd by 2	1 forces austerity on 2	☯monkey on 1's back	1 protective of 2	duo must do things right, purposefully	1 shocks 2 amid closeness	🔒 Duo must reconcile for long run	👽 ☯ 🔒 duo at fate's mercy	odd mismatch
Hra	duo's battery	1 pours out ∡, open to 2	1 lets 2 express freely	1 open & respnsble, 2 stuubborn	1 borrows 2's behavior for own ∡	1 mature, sophisticated	duo exchngs social intel	1,2 underlying motives for interacting	1 gets ppl's approval one by one	🔒 \ 1 must compete w 2's priorities	1 rewarded for being different
Ero	⚲ duo open to action?	👁1's brand of attractn on ppl	👄1 sees 2 as more attrctv	dominant 1 supports 2	1 scatters efforts to perfect this ∡	1 wants to soak up 2's company	1 pleases these stds in 2	1 inspires both to take risks	☯1 can strongly excite 2	👁duo's home zone	1 is a liberator or catalyst for other
Bac	🕊 can force frndship here	duo's fun style, friends togthr	duo's imprssv force to ppl	preferred casual convrstn	1 needs focus for own status	duo's public show	1 champions 2's display of ∡	what duo is known to do well, strongly	1 is a no-nonsense dropper	well-matched duo	ϒjoint limitless potential

Table 21-3: Composite chart pair meanings

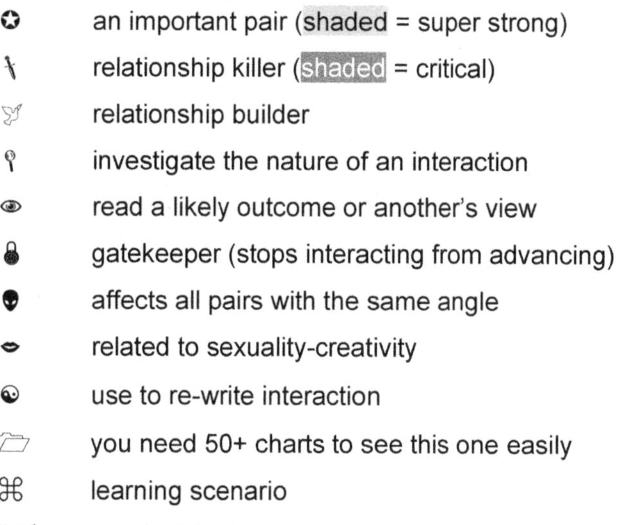

Symbols

✪	an important pair (shaded = super strong)
\	relationship killer (shaded = critical)
🕊	relationship builder
⚲	investigate the nature of an interaction
👁	read a likely outcome or another's view
🔒	gatekeeper (stops interacting from advancing)
👽	affects all pairs with the same angle
👄	related to sexuality-creativity
☯	use to re-write interaction
🗁	you need 50+ charts to see this one easily
⌘	learning scenario
♀/♂	gender biased
↔	"relationship" (EO = each other)

	Mc	Vx	☊	²⚸	⚸	⊕	⚳	⚷	⯓	♀	⯐	Hera	Eros	Bac
Mc														
Vx	⌘1's bkgd for envisning 2													
☊	♀/♂ \ = confidence, better duo	🕊🗁destined path to share												
²⚸	1 respects 2's command	1 weighs in on 2's issue	strongly announcing duo											
⚸	🕊🗁1 finds 2 a complement	\ 1 feels owed by ppl	♈strong combo attack	1 hold soc recgnzble pwr for duo										
⊕	✪ 👽duo most inventive	1's light dread ilo 2's priorities	ppl see most memorable exchg	1 pulls actions from 2	👄1,2 convey passions									
⚳	1 takes more risks under duo	1's basis for avoiding 2	🕊easy comm environment	duo filters animal instincts	1 coerces 2 w expected cooperation	✪ contractual duo								
⚷	🕊duo fulfills 1,2	inviting duo	1 defends this from 2	1 is super popular to ppl	✪ 1 protects 2's right to use angle	critically nice	1's life of drama							
⯓	duo discussions inspire this in 1,2	duo hit by complex forces	🕊✪\ void filled by other	♈1 is a master soc performer	✪ duo's joint creation stands out	✪ 1 is 2's go-to	1's strongest memory of 2	1,2 see basic tied paths						
♀	1 has intuitn for projecting this onto ppl	1 draws this out of 2	support seeking amidst obstruction	1 is irritated, restless	1,2 see EO's main contrib to friendshp	sharing builds prosperity	duo gives release to 1,2's tension	1 pokes holes in 2's self-assrdns	\ ☯ 1's risky eccentricity					
⯐	1's auto-focus ilo 2	🕊tight company	1 sees 2 as best there was	1 matches 2's skill w 1's intensity	1's ingroups see 2 as real force	1 handles 2's uncapped force	make hang-out possible	1 shows worth to 1self ilo duo	1 reinforces importance of this	duo goes overboard as a team				
Hera	1 serious re: 2's reflctn of 1's img	1 impressvly inspires 2 to grow	1 absorbed into 2's power	1 is unique and prolific	1 responds to what-ifs	more attn, harder for 1,2 to killduo	1 is busy and pushy to ppl	🔒✪duo must escalate or die	1 riles up 2	1's daring goes up ilo 2	1 unpredictable			
Eros	wrong reward	1 is dmnding of self and others	1's surprising intrusion on 2	charming, popular duo	1 seeks to get point across	1's professnl livelihood dpnds on...	1 tests 2's patience	⚲ ✪what is duo about?	🔒 🕊1 wins 2 over to form duo	1,2 feel invincible ilo EO	duo shamelessly open	deep emotion display		
Bac	duo's talk show theme	duo manages others' effrts	⚲👁☯✪ 1's story of 2	warning disclosure happens	🕊 👽duo makes pleasantness	duo feeds 1's creative skill	1 sees 2 as needing smn to lean on	1's self-img conjured ilo 2	🕊1's best efforts for 2	1 high strung	👄 🕊 ☯receptive phys intimacy	assaulted 1, strong willed 1	1,2 escape to EO company	

Chapter 22: On duos and trios – Reading the composite chart

When looking at the actual interaction between two people, synastry is typically the way to go. The biggest problem with composite and relative charts is that they summarize *interactions* and not people, so neither can be reliably counted on to tell you which person does what in the relationship. Now it's not that composite and relative charts are useless. It is the case, however, that we form actual teams with others A LOT less frequently than it looks like we would. Consider a friend you hang out with. Do you normally think of yourselves as a "together-pair" headed in a common direction or do you simply think of yourselves as two people interacting with each other? Chances are you do the latter much more than you do the former. And this makes sense. Why go through all the trouble of bunching the two of you into a third party "partnership" when you're both right there to do the job without the extra layer? Composite and relative charts assume that you and another have come together to build something bigger beyond yourselves. Their planets describe the merging of two formerly distinct charts—something that usually isn't the case unless the duo-mates have some shared objective to attend to.

Yet composites turn out to be very useful for reading actual duos that you are actually involved in. Meanwhile, relative charts—in addition to their use in reading duos from the outside—are also useful for reading a different kind of collective: trios. This is because formal duos tend to describe more personally beneficial arrangements where you and another are united by a common goal. Trios, meanwhile, apply when a third viewer watches two people from the outside, ignorant of the deep details of the duo's arrangement. In a trio, when things blow up between Joe and Moe, Flo remains on the sidelines saying, "Yeah, whatever folks. So when does the 'getting along' part resume?" Said differently, duos die easily when the common mission dies or is compromised, and this corresponds to their great dependence on their duo-mates' psychologies. Trios don't die unless two of the vested parties take their relationship-killing rift and register it formally with a third, where the third person cares less about the duo-mates' psychologies and more about their averaged behavior from afar. In a way, the trio scenario is closer to the one that holds marriages and other contractual commitments together: It's me, you, and our witnesses; should things slip between us, we'll need to put in the extra work to convince our witnesses that it's really over. Accordingly, duos are very commonality/composite-oriented and pretty breakable when that commonality is outweighed by differences. Trios are public presentation/relative-oriented and only as breakable as the two members' ability to separate in the eyes of a third. In basic cliques, trio separation usually occurs by circumstance rather than through fighting.

This chapter covers how to read certain special relationship characteristics through composite and relative charts. Here we'll look at outs, cocktails, and a basic approach to trios which can be used to promote trios' proper function in your life. Along the way, we'll also discuss why each of these corners of composite study is important.

Reading duos in a composite chart: Look for outs

The question that usually prompts the study of composite charts is, "What does our relationship look like?" In order to answer this, we'll need access to both component charts as well as the composite.

Load your composite chart

0. In the previous chapter we did all that work to get a good-looking composite with an interpretable ASC, MC, Vx, AND Fortune. If you have such a chart that you'd like to read, go ahead and load that chart now.

Once we have loaded our composite chart and have successfully displayed the * versions of the ASC, MC, Vx, and Fortune, we need to load the two component charts.

Load your two component charts

1. If you're using StarFisher, click on New Horoscope in the icon bar. It's the very first icon.

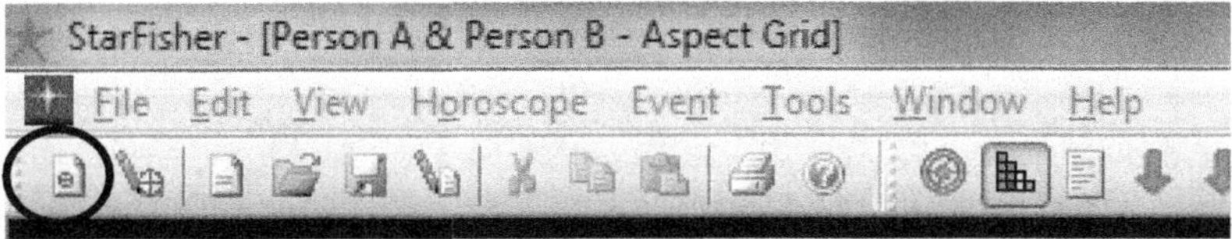

2. Make sure Standard is selected under Horoscope Type, that the Primary Event Data is either of your two people, then click Advanced...

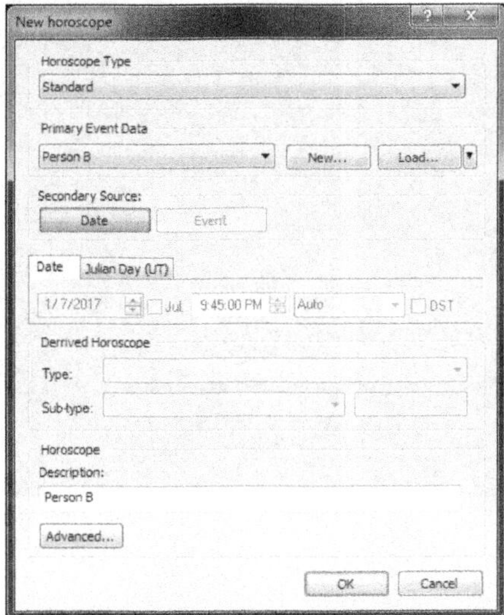

3. Under bodies, *make sure that the REGULAR Ascendant, Midheaven, Vertex, and Fortune ARE on your list of Selected items*, and make sure that the * ASC*, MC*, Vx*, and Fortune* are **NOT** under the Selected items list. The * versions should be under Available items instead. The *s were calculated only for the composite charts. For standard charts, the regular versions are what we want.
4. Repeat steps 1 – 3 for the other person's chart.
5. If you peek under File menu>Window, you should have all three charts available. Select Tile.

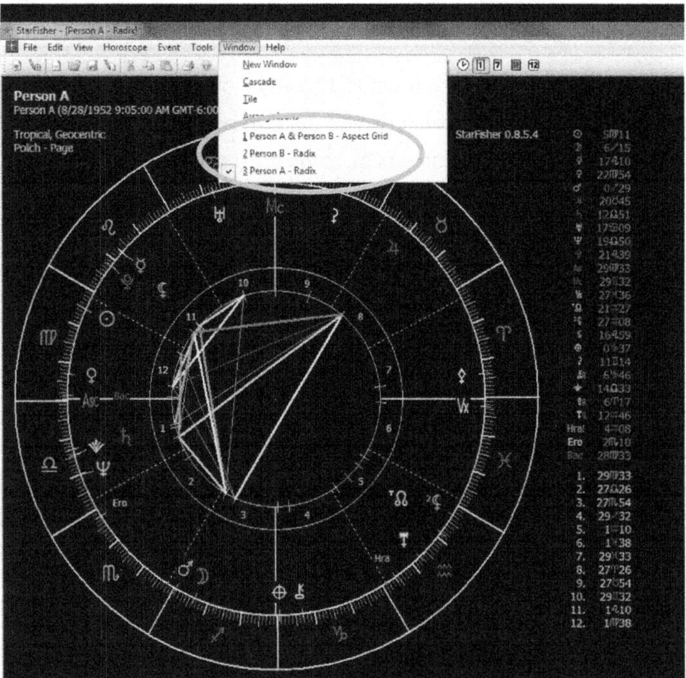

6. See if you can arrange the charts to where all three are visible.

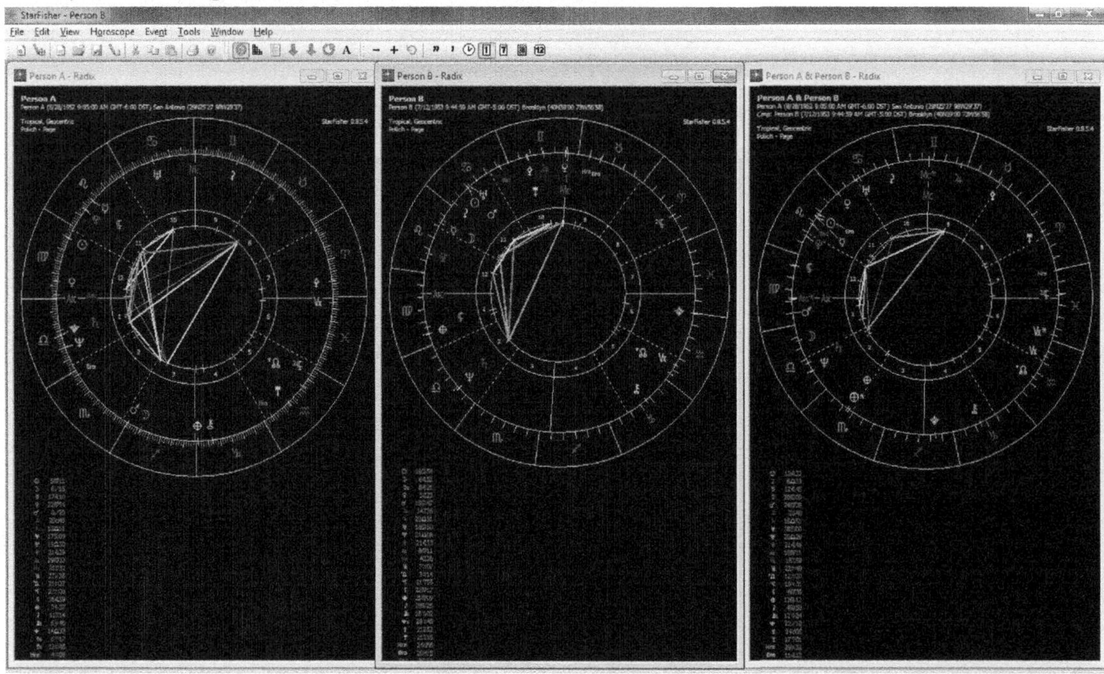

Figure 22-1: Chart wheels for Person A, Person B, and their composite

Person A
Person A (8/28/1952 9:05:00 AM GMT-6:00 DST) San Antonio (29N25'27 98W29'37)

Tropical, Geocentric
Polich - Page

StarFisher 0.8.5.4

Person B
Person B (7/12/1953 9:44:59 AM GMT-5:00 DST) Brooklyn (40N39'00 73W56'58)

Tropical, Geocentric
Polich - Page

StarFisher 0.8.5.4

Person A & Person B
Person A (8/28/1952 9:05:00 AM GMT-6:00 DST) San Antonio (29N25'27 98W29'37)
Cmp: Person B (7/12/1953 9:44:59 AM GMT-5:00 DST) Brooklyn (40N39'00 73W56'58)

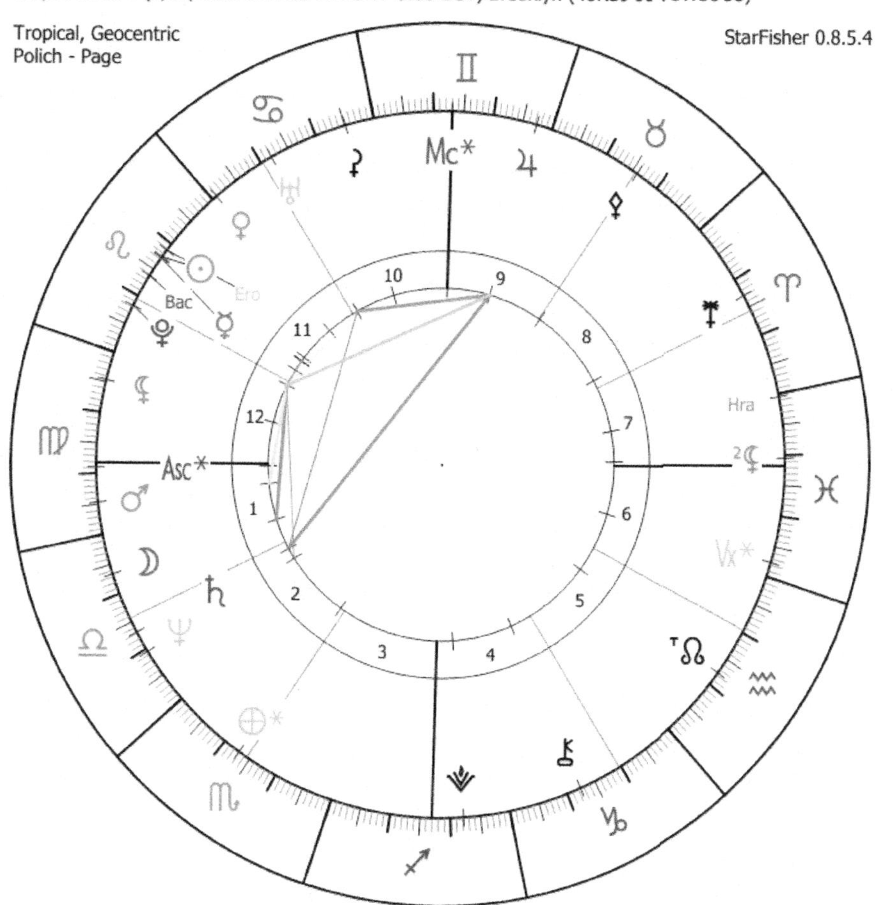

We're looking for "outs." Side by side is the best way to find these.

Moon outs in the example

As discussed in Chapter 21, outs are locations in the composite chart which are conjunct locations in at least one of the component charts. They constitute the simplest means of reading a relationship because they show where the people involved in that relationship have an outlet for their own behaviors. In romantic relationships and friendships, you want outs for the Sun, Moon, Venus and probably Mars. Having any composite planets conjunct these in the regular chart essentially means that the regular chart person has a means of expressing these in a way that directly affects the relationship. In romance the Moon is super important. In the case above, for example, Person A has a Moon in early Sagittarius, but the composite doesn't have anything there. No out for Person A. How about B? They have a Moon in early Leo. The composite has all kinds of things there. The Sun, Venus, Eros and Mercury are all within 10° of 6 Leo. This means that at Person A's absolute laziest—with no extra effort put into keeping the partnership alive—they can feel emotionally disengaged from the relationship. It would be easier for A to become frustrated or bored with the whole thing. At Person B's laziest, their disengagement from the relationship causes the duo to lose its contact with the outside world, its tendency to connect with that outside world, as well as its overall fire.[61] This is stagnancy as a public item. It will be a lot harder for Person B to emotionally disengage from the relationship because B's emotions ARE the relationship in many ways. When B tunes out, the whole pair can be expected to struggle mightily to stay together. When A tunes out, that may just be normal business.

Check the charts you've chosen to see where the outs for the Moon are located (if there are any).

Sun outs in the example

The availability of Sun outs helps answer the question, *Does this person's deeds affect the partnership, or can they just do whatever they want (within reason) and expect the partnership to continue existing?* In the example, Person A's Sun sharply conjunct the composite's Lilith means that their deeds determine how much the partnership stands out to others—how rebellious it is against social norms. Person B's Sun around 20 Cancer is conjunct the relationship's Uranus (social talk) so that this one's deeds determine how the relationship gets talked about. So we have outs for both.

You might think that not having outs was a bad thing. Not necessarily. The setup above—where A's deeds write the rebellion, A's emotions don't write anything, B's deeds write the partnership's social world and B's emotions steer the public course of the relationship—is an excellent setup for a situation in which Person A can act up emotionally, rebel, and not break anything while B (if they are responsible enough) can simply keep stable status for the partnership. It may not be cookie-cutter equal, but what partnership is? A relationship with unequal access to outs is a lot like a job with unequal responsibility for various mistakes. The person with no eyes on them can get away with more and often have more control over the course of things when they do turn on angles besides the conjunct. This is because the person without the outs must exercise their angles on purpose. By default though, the relationship sits in the hands of the one with the outs.

Mercury outs in the example

Do the partners feel like their ability to make sense of things affects the relationship, or do they just float along with whatever comes as the default? Person A's Mercury sense-making is the only personal planet with access to the relationship's social pressures (Pluto), such that their analysis of things writes the partnership's response to external pressures. Person B's Mercury writes more of the fun, forward sociability of the partnership with its conjunct to composite Eros, Sun, Mercury, and Bacchus. Again we see Person B determining the fun, public stuff.

[61] These result from contact with the composite Venus and the Sun, Mercury, and Eros respectively.

But this time Person A is the one who takes care of business. Maybe you're starting to get the idea of how this exchange might look in real life. So far Person B seems to provide the reputation. Person A seems to provide the limitation or structure.

Venus and Mars outs in the example

At this point we should be getting the general idea. Outs answer the question, *Does my planet X naturally determine important things in the partnership?* Person A's Venus-communication determines the composite's Mars and Moon. When A's 1:1 communication is bad, not only does the mood of the relationship suffer, the relationship's ability to get things done in the outside world suffers. Person A's Mars has no natural out, so if ever A were to get mean enough to manipulate, fight, or hyperanalyze—or if ever A were insightful enough to dissect, dedicated enough jealously protect, or spiritual enough to push the partnership forward, none of this would naturally affect the partnership. Person A would have to convey thoughts towards (or publicize their interaction with) the relationship itself, for example,[62] in order to move things with their Mars. But most people won't naturally interact with their "team" construct. They'll just interact with each other instead. Meanwhile, Person B's Venus writes the relationship's Jupiter in what amounts to still more control of the partnership's public image based on B's personality. And B's Mars again writes the partnership's Uranus. If A gets forceful, the relationship can stay stable. If B gets forceful, everyone who looks at the relationship will know it.

In *FSA* we defined **personal planets** as **the Moon, Sun, Mercury, Venus, and Mars—those which show how we interact on an individual level**. This was compared to **social planets** (Jupiter, Saturn, Uranus, Neptune and slow movers around them like Chiron) that change with large groups. Then we had **generational planets** like **Neptune and Pluto which took on the order of generations to change signs**. In composites we care more about outs for the personal planets than anything else, because an out for a social planet is like putting the world in your back yard. Certainly Person A's Jupiter with an out on the composite Pallas means that their ambitions affect the kinds of social issues the relationship seeks to solve, but the world itself won't really get this idea. It will just see ambitious movement without asking what A's "inner traveler" wanted. Thus it is less disturbing to a person if his non-personal planets don't have outs. Personal planets with no outs, however, can at times make a relationship seem stifling in the relevant planet area.

Composite cocktails

During the writing of this book I was confronted with a philosophical question in light of an exchange with a student of mine. Whenever she was in my class, we would have some once-in-a decade set of events which hadn't taken place before and wouldn't take place afterwards. Our exchange was chronically fun. So what was the philosophical question? *What is the difference between a fun relationship (duo) and a mere fun interaction (synastry)?* So began the search for composite cocktails. And although I eventually read her astrology chart and found that, among other things, we had mutual [Bacchus-Node] conjuncts,[63] there were indeed some factors in the composite itself which served to make our vibe contagious to other people in the room.

Composite cocktails are fewer in number because true duos are fewer in number. The possible planet pairs are fewer (at 300 instead of 625 in this book), and the occasions for enduring, non-marriage-typical duos is lower.[64]

---

[62] These are shown by the [Mars $_A$-Vertex*$_{composite}$] trine or [Mars $_A$-Mars$_{composite}$] biundecile respectively.

[63] This was the only such case of mutual Bacchus-Node half-pair conjuncts I'd seen in any of the data I'd worked with in both books. It's a riot I tell you. Even in a professional setting.

[64] Though there are of course many marriages worth studying, my data on them was scarce for a couple of reasons you may find interesting. Marriages are kind of like duos, kind of like trios. You, your sweetie, and witnesses agree that you and your sweetie are an item. You, Sweetie, and children anchor you and Sweetie. Upon entry into the marriage, however, a kind of door typically closes between the individuals and the types of data available to other kinds of partnerships. I've found that married couples were much less favorable for questioning regarding

Still there are five cocktails near and dear to my heart which probably describe certain relationships near and dear to yours. These are the cocktails for relationships which are

- noteworthy
- effective
- lucky
- connected
- fun

Noteworthy composite: Top of the world

Moon-Saturn	Mercury-Venus	**Uranus-Lilith**	Uranus-Pallas
Selene-Pallas	Selene-Hera	**Lilith-Pallas**	Vesta-Pallas
Pallas-Eros	Juno-Hera		

We have quite a few moving parts involved in making a noteworthy pair. But before we delve into these parts I'd like to revisit the difference between notoriety, popularity, and renown as discussed in *FSA*. For our purposes, **notoriety** is **where a lot of people talk about you**. We'll consider this similar to **fame**, which is **notoriety that viewers recognize as being society-wide**. **Popularity** is where people talk about you a lot. **When this talk is negative you become infamous**, and when this talk is associated with a discouraged social role you become **notorious**. **Renown** is **where you are widely known in such a way as to be synonymous with a bigger idea**. That is, if you're just plain famous but not known for anything in particular besides your own individuality, you have fame without renown. Again for our purposes, to be renowned is to be re-known. So people need something to "know" you against.

We restate the notoriety definitions for two reasons. First and most importantly we do it in order to clarify the important idea that you can look for any of these types of notoriety, but they're not the same things and have different levels of positivity, idea-connectedness, and conversational penetrating power. Second, if you want to achieve any of these forms of notoriety (as lots of people do) and plan to use astrology to show you how to get it, you might want to clarify which of these versions is more important to you; the planet pairs are highly nuanced and can truly misbehave if you pick the wrong one. [Uranus-Bacchus] aids your popularity among friends, for example; [Uranus-Pallas] on the other hand is where you and the duo-mate put on your best Godzilla-Mothra hats. The latter is definitely more like infamy.

I considered referencing celebrities for more data on this cocktail, but rejected the idea for practicality reasons. Most of us aren't celebrities, so studying noteworthiness among this kind of famous duo would have introduced another variable like "cultural spread" into the picture—which most of us don't have. Also, as mentioned in Chapter 16, it's harder to tell what goes on behind the scenes to make famous people famous, such that our studying them will have been about as useful as saying "The famous have this angle and you don't. The end." Our premise in *FSA* and *HBS* has always been that you can make anything happen with the right attitude, access, and allies, and this cocktail is no different. Among the various kinds of notoriety listed above then, the Noteworthy cocktail is more about renown than anything else. But if it's some other kind of fame you want, you in your duo will need to figure that out on your own. Only you two will know the inner workings required to get there.

---

potential uncertainty areas in their union. "Why would you ask me that? You know we'll be here till death do us part, don't you?" So it was harder to even determine what fun looked like in these unions since they were (from a research perspective) like little fortresses littered with conversational landmines for even the most euphemizing scholar to lay upon. You couldn't really win with married couples, because there was always that array of issues which weren't open for private study. Fun has a specific look. Closeness has an expected feel. So I largely excluded them from my data as a highly specialized sample set to be saved for the scholar with more energy to penetrate their mysteries.

If we should become noteworthy, it will be through the use of [Moon-Saturn] as the means of spreading our [Selene-Pallas]. The world hands us opportunities to [do Selene-Hera], where our goals for [Mercury-Venus] fuel our [Juno-Hera] towards each other. For better or worse, we are each [Lilith-Pallas] in our communication about each other and towards each other in front of other people, though one of us tends to be much more [Uranus-Lilith] towards the other in a way that all can see. The rogue among the two of us behaves in riskier ways as one who [does Vesta-Pallas], but we're both inclined to feel ourselves invincible [Pallas-Eros] in this pairing. Being in this pairing predisposes us to [Uranus-Pallas] in public and private on our quest to pacify this aspect of our own worlds.

Public air angles are better

Effective composite: Killin' it

For all of those duo mates who have teamed up just to do a simple job, this one's for you. While I'm sure we've all experienced more than our share of half-assed alliances out there (teams you've joined which failed dismally to come through) the duos which informed this cocktail represent the pinnacle of performance. Now they reveal their secrets to you. When all you want to do is complete what you started (...with an A+ rating, in the time allowed), you have at your disposal the Effective composite to make your team go.

Sun-Mercury	Mercury-Midheaven*	Venus-Selene	**Mars-Lilith**
Midheaven*-Fortune*	Vertex*-Lilith	Node-Lilith	Selene-Fortune*
Saturn-Ceres	Saturn-Bacchus	Uranus-Bacchus	Pluto-Ceres
Fortune*-Ceres	Fortune*-Juno	Fortune*-Hera	Ceres-Eros
Mars-Ceres	Lilith-Chiron	Ascendant*-Hera	Pallas-Eros

Yikes! Unfortunately, an effective duo is the hardest of all of our cocktails—synastric or composite—to achieve. Why? Because it requires a combination of skill, dedication, self-control, problem solving, communication, and an ability to set aside personal issues (at least sometimes). As we no longer live in Old Western times "when a man's word was his bond," the world is filled with people who say they will, then just don't. Task-effective duos overcome this problem with an old school combination of internally-guided mutual respect for the other duo mate's time and effort alongside an eyes-forward focus which most of us now rely on external pressure to enforce.

We'll present this mini-summary a little differently since, unlike other cocktails, it is definitely NOT the case that "anything goes" here.

Table 22-1: The qualities of a task-smashing duo

#	Quality	Pair	Angle rules
1.	They **clearly** stand for something	**Sun-Mercury**	• ~~Conjuncts~~ are bad for this; being automatic, they strongly hurt task focus and dedicate the duo's attention to each other's personal qualities instead. The data on this were VERY STRONG.
2.	One appreciates the other's strong **personality** trait	**Mars-Lilith**	• **Personal and self-expression angles** are very good • Interaction-dependent and social power angles are not good, as these promote using the person for their power rather than what they bring from within. • This was the second strongest data pattern.
3.	One protects the other's **image or task role**	Lilith-Chiron	• **Social power, networking, ingroup, or other-influencing angles** are very good • ~~Personal and ego angles~~ are very negative for task focus as they are strongly associated with one's covering for the behavioral problems of another until the partnership breaks. The data were strong on this point. Such angles—if not carefully watched—form potent \ partnership killers in task-focused arrangements

4.	They are *not* stubbornly entrenched on matters of **group administration**	Saturn-Ceres	• ~~Group management angles~~ are bad for this one, because [Saturn-Ceres] shows where own insists on having their own way. If you have such an angle, expect the duo to be one-sided in at least one key area
5.	They can be expected to stay with **the task**, even if they disagree	Fortune*-Ceres	• **Command, notoriety, and directed follower** angles are good • ~~Personal, ego, emotional, and (usually) abstract angles~~ are bad unless you're making art. Personal angles introduce leniency into the exchange where, really, one of the people needs to get on the ball • Unfortunately, this same pair which can be good for close relationships is not so good for business. It's hard to come out a winner on this one if your business partner also happens to be your friend. The exception lies with the "public-overpowering" angles like III-octiles and II-trines, which typically give you the best of both worlds. On the opposite end, personal conflict between duo mates with the II-square can deal a fatal blow to business partnerships which otherwise stood to be very close
6.	A good meeting increases the duo's **preparedness for business involving others**	Mars-Ceres	• **Command, notoriety, and directed follower** angles are better (but III-oppositions maybe-maybe not, since fans can be wayward) • Ego and self-expression angles are very bad for these, as they predispose the duo to wasting time on one or both partner's ego expression. Oppositions can go either way depending on whether their hedonistic or value-based sides play out. • This pair is an excellent indication of your partnership's predisposal to wasting time when you need to get a job done, and shows what you can expect to get out of a quality meeting.
7.	People describe their joint efforts **easily**	Mercury-Midheaven*	• This is the only composite pair among all twenty which has more to do with the pair than the individuals in it. This angle tells you when people recognize the duo as doing something. As such, **conjuncts** are great for natural duo visibility. • Every other angle besides conjuncts depends on how the duo intends to affect others. Squares for example render the duo silent until one or both members start inspiring or upsetting people. Then, suddenly, the duo exists. Look to this pair to tell you what aspects of you and the partner's interaction is most likely to put your duo on the lips of witnesses.
8.	One feels **authority** is their right	Vertex-Lilith	• **Intellectually expressive, control, notoriety, and power angles** are good here • Physical or instinctually expressive angles as well as imaginative angles are not good here, as they are conducive to lollygagging
9.	One champions the other's **influence**	Saturn-Bacchus	• **Social influence and charisma-related angles** are better for this one
10.	One is comfortable with the other's **achievement**	Fortune*-Juno	• **Notoriety angles** are better • Abstract feeling, emotional and self-satisfying angles are worse
11.	One can foist their **personality** on lots of people in the sense that outsiders come to recognize them	Venus-Selene	• **Personal and ego angles** are better, though certain angles like the II-undecile and II-square can open up one partner's private life for dissection, rendering these angles more negative • Command angles are not as good because they undercut the importance of the duo, rendering the other partner less important
12.	The duo is extra powerful *together* in **task-related matters**	Node-Lilith	• Almost anything works here except for abstract angles like the II-inconjunct—unless you're making art. • This angle roughly shows the face which the two of you put on when posturing towards each other, so *it's actually better that this angle NOT be tied to the work you do together*. If this angle is something you need to do your joint work successfully, there is a danger that one of the partner's pride will prevent them from taking good advice or accepting much-needed help from the other. Such is Lilith. Such is Node.
13.	They are **not** strongly known for a **quality that competes with the task**	Uranus-Bacchus	• Personal, ego and feeling angles are generally not good here, as they put the public's focus on the duo's personalities rather than their accomplishments. Of course, if that's the whole point then...
14.	The more **power** they're comfortable with, they more they get	Fortune*-Hera	• **Command and other-influence angles** are better • Personal expression angles are worse

15.	One is rewarded for their unique **charisma**	Ascendant*-Hera	• **Charismatic and room-influencing angles** are good here • Raw instinct angles like the conjunct, sometimes the opposition, as well as all noviles are more likely to receive intangible rewards rather than task-related ones.
16.	They are most inventive in matters **related to the objective**	Midheaven*-Fortune*	• ~~Interpersonal and self-expression angles~~ are not helpful here
17.	One draws out **people-steering abilities** from the other	Selene-Fortune*	• **People-steering and planning angles** are good, but almost anything will work depending on the task. Almost... • ...but ego and self-worth angles aren't so good for task focus, as they are associated with the tendency of the drawn-from person to stall under pressure. Believe it. I've seen it happen. That's how this interpretation came to be in the first place.
18.	They behave respectfully towards each other **1:1**	Pluto-Ceres	• **1:1 communicative and shared company angles** like the II-opposition and II-septile are good here • Superficial, external-network dependent, or emotional angles are negative here, as they lead to an "It's only because of your position that I'm putting up with you" kind of thing
19.	One challenges the other **to perform**	Ceres-Eros	• **Planning and management angles** are better • Personal expression angles are usually worse, unless image-making is part of the task
20.	They are invincible **problem solvers**	Pallas-Eros	• **Analytical and problem solving angles** (including I- and III-octiles) are better • ~~Personal an emotional angles~~ are much worse, as they lead to temperament problems in most duos

This is one of those areas where it would be oh so nice to have a table which told you which angles were "notoriety angles," which of them were "analytical angles," and other such classifications. But first of all, we already have quite a few such tables in this book. Secondly (and more importantly) if I gave you a table for this one, the results you'd attain would be much more fatalistic without having to be. Sometimes octiles throw tantrums and sometimes they are piercingly insightful. It's up to you or your duo mate to decide if you want to turn off the manipulation for a moment and get down to business. Sometimes trines blare their humble opinion, sometimes they're athletic, and other times they are intellectually gifted; so the trine can be personal, expressive, or intellectual. You'll need to have some familiarity with the angles to use this cocktail to its potential—that is, for forecasting the task-success of you and the other person as well as choosing which tasks would work best for the two of you to approach together. Not surprisingly, the angles will behave differently depending on what you're doing.

I give you advice as a teacher and a colleague who's seen a hefty share of dud duos: The data on this cocktail formed a nice little checkerboard with the power partnerships swapping colors with the pitiful ones across all twenty of the above pairs. I wish I could show you how the ineffective group's roots in wishful thinking really seem obvious in hindsight. For privacy reasons of course, I can't do this. But looking back at the various duos studied one can see how, even without astrology, the duds have a way of sputtering from the very beginning which tells a person all he needs to know *but for* those rose-colored drapes he has on his head. In matters of shared work, use this cocktail to determine whether you and your partner are wired for success or... suck-cess perhaps. If the result isn't as pretty as you would like, heed it. You may want to keep your eyes open for a back-up partner. I'm just sayin'.

Keep in mind, though, that your having unimpressive results for this cocktail doesn't mean that you and the other will fail as task partners. This cocktail is more for standard business than, say, family tasks. And even if you were reading a business partnership, the angles you will have gotten are what they are. As usual it will fall to you to mix the above with common sense to see if adjustments really do need to be made, or if the two of you should simply ignore the above and play it the way the rest of the non astrology-reading world does. No fault in that.

Lucky composite: The sunny side

Sun-Bacchus	**Mercury-Fortune***	Venus-Fortune*	Uranus-Selene
Ascendant*-Juno	**Chiron-Juno**	**Juno-Eros**	**Sun-Selene**

Conjuncts are better

Dedicate serious focus to this

We are [Sun-Selene] talented as a duo. Through the exchange of [Uranus-Selene] towards the establishment of a prolific [Juno-Eros] control over others, we have a seemingly magical ability to attract [Chiron-Juno]. Executing this ability, we specialize in impressing others with our [Sun-Bacchus], continually attaining victory after victory in our [Mercury-Fortune*]. Our [Venus-Fortune*] is the main thing we bring to the table in meeting with each other, where we are most comfortable communicating about [Ascendant*-Juno] affairs.

Continually acknowledge this result

It turns out that you *can* make a so-so duo into a lucky one with just four pairs.

> Do [Sun-Selene] things with a focus on expressing the ultimate [Juno-Eros]. Note every victory in [Mercury-Fortune*] and keep pursuing more of those victories, big and small. This facilitates great luck in attracting [Chiron-Juno]. Provided you and the other keep a positive attitude towards each other and the thing you're working towards (Chiron doctor instead of patient), the luck is pretty easy. HOWEVER...

If any of the above four areas slip, your duo is likely to lose its lucky streak. Furthermore, maintaining those four areas above requires a certain kind of never-say die attitude which needs reinforcement through communication. Having [Sun-Selene] conjunct does wonders for this whole thing, but as long as whatever angle you have for [Sun-Selene] regularly describes your relationship, it doesn't necessarily need to be a conjunct. You truly must aim for the jugular when it comes to your composite [Juno-Eros] though, and you really do have to get used to counting [Mercury-Fortune*] wins for this luck to look like it's happening.

In my opinion, this is one of the simplest cocktails to purposely apply beginning with a pretty safe conversation with your duo mate. I originally looked for a combination to explain the kind of fantastic luck which an acquaintance and I had during a mini quest a couple of years ago, and found that—more than anything—she and I both brought to the table a stubborn refusal to be defeated alongside a natural tendency to steal social attention. The composite [Sun-Selene] conjunct also helped. In matters like these, when you're hot, you're hot. And when you're not, you're a slightly strained version of normal. But for most people it does take effort to builds this kind of outlook. Shared communication is a must here.

Connected composite: Thick as thieves

Sun-Eros	Sun-Bacchus	Moon-Mars	Ceres-Vesta
Mercury-Neptune	**Venus-Fortune***	*Mars-Ceres*	**Saturn-Ceres**
Uranus-Midheaven*	Uranus-Vesta	**Uranus-Eros**	Neptune-Vesta
Pluto-Chiron	Lilith-Chiron	Ascendant*-Chiron	Ascendant*-Vesta
Node-Fortune*			

Strongly connected two-person friendships are about as rare as strongly effective task duos, with almost as many pairs describing their main characteristics. By "strongly connected" we mean that you don't just like them, you don't just relate to or have great chats with them, but you also agree to genuinely share an important piece of your inner life with them. Here you bond with a closeness that describes truly dedicated friends, often feeling as though you can read each other's thoughts and respond to each other's wishes before they are aired.

As with the task duos, we'll present the qualities of connected duos in list form. Unlike the task duo case, however, the angle information contained should be thought of as a set of mere patterns rather than rules for getting a particular thing done. Friendships come in all forms, but do tend towards certain dynamics more than others. *Table 22-2* shows what some of the more noteworthy dynamics that emerged from the data were.

Table 22-2: The qualities of a duo with a strong bond

#	Quality	Pair	Angle tendencies
1.	One provides a safe haven for the other to express **something of importance** to them	**Saturn-Ceres**	• ~~Less ego centered, group management, or other-dependent angles~~ such as II-quintiles or III-deciles usually **aren't as good** for close friendships unless the protected person is married to their work. In work-heavy cases such angles can be very good (though a bit utilitarian)
2.	They have a **natural** interest in talking **to each other**	**Venus-Fortune***	• **Natural and naturally 1:1 angles** like conjuncts, septiles, II-oppositions, and II-squares are good here • Me-first angles produce a love of talking about oneself. Trines are surprisingly negative if you don't watch this tendency. Other consciously me first angles include II-conjuncts, II-undeciles, IV-undeciles, and oppositions • "External measurement" angles like II-octiles and III-septiles hurt close connections • This pair seems extra important as an indicator of the reason one person bothers to seek the other's conversation in general, and is tied with [Saturn-Ceres] as one of the most consistent indicators of connected bonding in a composite chart
3.	One makes the other **braver or more confident amongst outsiders**	**Uranus-Eros**	• **Other-impressing angles** were very good here, especially II-trines (which dominated the data) • Temperament-heavy angles were not as good, as they typically give one partner more license to be inconsiderate to the other as well as outsiders. By default, this is especially true of squares. • In the data, non-1:1 and planning angles such as II-septiles and even trines lent a logical edge to the exchange which hindered emotional connection
4.	People see their most memorable exchange in terms of how they **interact deeply with each other**	**Node-Fortune*** (Think of this pair as showing where the duo has a "convenient destiny" to express itself.)	• **Instinctual, deeply invested angles** like conjuncts, quintiles, and octiles are very good • Impersonal or mostly social angles like undeciles make for two people who stay together (unknowingly) because they think they make sense as a social unit; there are often noticeable connection-limiting incompatibilities in how they think, and even though they can be strong friends, you find that their friendship fades when the surrounding group disappears • Abstract angles like inconjuncts and IV-inconjuncts may feel as though they should connect, but just can't

5.	They pour their creative energy into **natural, deep 1:1 exchange with each other**	Ascendant*-Vesta	• **Instinctual, 1:1 angles** are good • More external, social, or abstract angles aren't as helpful unless your priority is to have a social acquaintance or imagination partner
6.	They both look tougher **on a personal level**	Moon-Mars	• **Interpersonal angles** are better • Impersonal, social and planning angles are worse for this
7.	A good meeting between them occurs **where their regular socialization is made powerful**	*Mars-Ceres*	• **1:1 and interpersonal craving angles** are better; these are angles like septiles, II-oppositions, II-septiles, and III-oppositions which are both interaction-centered and belonging-centered • Angles not of the above type produce exchanges which are more self-interested or intellectual than close and validating • *This pair is noteworthy for its picky insistence on angles which are just right in their combination of self- and other-focus*
8.	One's strongest memory of the other is **not a personal one**, since these are written all the time by virtue of their regular closeness	Ceres-Vesta	• ~~**Conjuncts hurt**~~ this one, and indicate exchanges of limited instinctual connection despite the fact that one or both people wanted it • Whatever angle you have here, expect it to be expressed as a major basis for your interaction only rarely in the grand scheme of things
9.	Together, they are too good for outsiders in the **joint charisma** department	Ascendant*-Chiron	• **Group centered room-takeover angles** like II-trines and III-quintiles are better here • Control angles aren't as good, though they favor same-sex friendships to the extent that the two people share a common mission to take over territory rather than bond to each other • Me-first angles like conjuncts, trines and squares decrease the natural level of interest one has in the other and replace that interest with unbalanced ego projection from one onto the other
10.	One defends the other's **influence or social standing**	Lilith-Chiron	• **Individualistic intellectual angles** like III-trines and III-undeciles facilitate mutual learning • **Strong impression or imagination angles** like II-inconjuncts or III-octiles help duo mates have fun with each other • Self-projection or ego-building angles like conjuncts, trines, squares, III-oppositions, or IV-conjuncts invite one's fighting on behalf of the other—often in a one-sided way
11.	One instinctually compels friendship through **direct interaction**	Sun-Bacchus	• **Instinctual and 1:1 influence angles** such as conjuncts, septiles, and octiles build friendship through direct company
12.	One monopolizes the other's view of the latter's **emotional priorities**	Neptune-Vesta	• **Non-external conflict based, emotionally-invested angles** like squares, II-squares, and III-inconjuncts are good • All octiles, typically based on external conflict, tend to be hampered by fights or increased disagreement which distance one from the other
13.	They **naturally and instinctively** make "art" together	Uranus-Vesta	• **Self-expression, 1:1, and imaginative angles** are good • Angles which require external groups fade when the group is removed
14.	They are open to **enjoying each other's company**	Sun-Eros	• **Self-expression and shared company angles** are good • Collective-pushing angles including undeciles, III-quintiles, and those from the III-septile on up are harder to get working, since they require a shared social outlook to spur them to action
15.	If one feels a lack of warmth from the other, it's in the form of **the second person's view of the public which assaults the first person**	Mercury-Neptune	• Crowd-pleasing and intellectual angles are better; this does not include the II-septile • ~~Personal and ego expression angles~~ (not necessarily squares) are much worse in general, as they lend inclarity to the duo's direction • II-septiles can make it difficult for the duo to connect their social circles or most important ideologies
16.	One finds the secret to **good expression being rooted in self-expression** and socially-supported relevance	Uranus-Midheaven*	• ~~Impersonal and work related angles~~ create good working relationships which often struggle mightily to translate beyond work
17.	The essence of the duo's exchange is captured in moments of **strong self-expression**	Pluto-Chiron	• **Heavily expressive communication angles** like trines, quintiles, II-trines, and IV-oppositions are strong here • In the data, II-octiles required treating the other person carefully to just enough an extent that full comfort never arrived • In the data, III-sextiles had the unfortunate distinction of fostering very deep relationships which terminated early over an issue that could only be perceived by a critical eye; others won't understand why these two separated, but the two themselves will

You may notice that the asteroid of bonding—Hera—is suspiciously absent from the above list. As are Juno (commitment), Vertex* (major change), and Selene (blessed talent). Additionally, the Midheaven* (public image) and Bacchus (cliques) only appear once each. Lilith's one-time appearance we could understand. Lilith is contrary by nature. But one would think that at least some of the friendship and commitment asteroids would play stronger roles in this cocktail. They don't, and my guess is that this is because these objects are designed to work *within* the relationship. Once beyond the relationship, they drastically change their function. Hera in the regular chart is about me bonding with you. Hera in the composite is not about me bonding with you, but about our partnership "bonding" with something outside of it. Just look at Hera's entries in *table 21-3* to remind yourself of the asteroid's very different role in the composite as opposed to its role in regular charts and synastry. It turns out that all points which have to do with "acceptance by others" undergo a change in role as the nature of "others" changes from that of separate people on the regular chart level to that of separate *situations* on the composite chart level. The Midheaven* is no exception.

Fun composite: Till the break of dawn

Fill in the blanks. "Every time we get together it's like the _____ and _____ show." You're loud. You're brash. You release subjects which people were sure they locked up. You mess with things that shouldn't be messed with, and when you run into each other, the other activities of surrounding people end up being disturbed. This is the fun duo.

And it's not just something the two of you do. It's an environment the two of you *make*. When you play, you play. And when you really fight, it really hurts. The list of qualities that apply to this duo is as long as its list of publicly unsanctioned exploits, but the qualities are all related. A fun composite sucks other people in with its uninhibited nature—its component partners as pilot and navigator aboard the Starship Infinity.

Sun-Selene	Sun-Bacchus	**Moon-Bacchus**	Venus-Midheaven*
Saturn-Neptune	**Neptune-Hera**	Pluto-Fortune*	Pluto-Bacchus

Power angles

majors and bodily angles

What is it that makes us fun? To others it's our [Moon-Bacchus] which compels others' [Pluto-Fortune*]. To us it's our personal quest for [Pluto-Fortune*] in the world. In many people this is just normal, but in our partnership, the sharing of our [Neptune-Hera] is underscored by intensity. A commanding and unforgettable [Sun-Selene] ensures that our duo forces its talent onto witnesses. We naturally attract friends through the joint [Sun-Bacchus] we portray as the world unrolls the welcome mat in its encouragement that we [Pluto-Bacchus]. Our public face is helped by the highly visible [Saturn-Neptune] held by one of us. Together we're just more [Venus-Midheaven*] than other people.

Memorable and expansive angles

Very public angles

On Trios ⚒

The soldier Hayden requested of the scholar Geery, Alright Mr. Scientist, you've told me all about charts for two. How about you tell me about charts for three, or four, or more, even. Do you just average a bunch of charts together?

I wouldn't, Geery replied. First of all, most of our dealings with big groups wind up being reflected in charts based on synastry with those groups' "birth charts" so to speak. So if you want to look at the astrology between yourself and six people as a collective, you'd usually want a chart for them which reflected when they actually came together as a collective: the founding date of yours and their group. I'm assuming that your interaction with the group as a collective is what matters here. The only time you would do mass averaging of charts is when you wanted to look at a group whose member contributions were near-indistinguishable in light of some MUCH more important whole—like the Three Stooges. Otherwise you'd just look at synastry charts between yourself and each of the six people separately.

Yeah, the collective is what I mean.

Fine. Second of all, I wouldn't do mass averaging simply because it doesn't make practical sense. If a mother, father, and two small children need a single chart, the marriage or anniversary for the mother and father would be as good as any. The problem with averaging everything together is that it assumes all the planets have equal weights—that mom's, dad's, and children's Saturns all contribute the same amount of limitation (which almost certainly they don't) or that mom's, dad's, and children's Ascendant's all approach new situations with the same power (which they almost certainly don't). Just as we might give some distant uncle a weight of zero for each of his planets as contributors to this mom-dad-children picture, we need the right to change the weights of mom's, dad's, and the children's own planets if, say, Baby Mary just doesn't have a meaningful Mercury yet. Averaging blindly is like taking the whole meal and dumping it into a blender. Again, I'm not saying you should *never* do it, but I am questioning how useful such a chart might actually be.

Hmm, Hayden pondered. So what do you do?

Since I like to study astrology as a science, Geery replied, I've believe there must be some setup which describes groups of three, four, or more. These interactions can't just *not* have a chart. But those charts have to line up with a certain kind of psychological reality. Realistically, I believe the only complex—but still useful—case for synastry and composites comes when you have three people: Two plus yourself. Your interaction with their duo's dynamic. Once you get to four people, the various combinations of interactions among the other three besides you begin to be unequal, so that averaging tells you less. In the case of four, I would just do synastries between each pair of people separately if the four of you don't constitute an official group. If you are an official group, then I would do synastry between you and the "birth chart" (or start date) of that group. As for three people though, this is the only case where I would put in any work to do complex synastry.

I guess that makes sense, Hayden agreed. But what would that so-called "complex synastry" look like?

It would be a synastry chart between your birth chart and…Well you tell me. Would it be yours and the other two's *composite* or yours and the other two's *Davison* chart?

Uh, let's see if I can remember. The Davison chart was another name for the relative chart. And this was the one you didn't tell me much about because you said it showed a relationship from the *outside*. I guess if you are a third party standing outside of the two other people, you'd use *your* birth chart and *their* Davison chart, since you wouldn't be able to reliably "turn on" the planets they needed to make their composite chart. I mean, you couldn't read their minds.

Right.

Okay, that makes sense. But how are you so sure this is what you should do?

I'm not sure, but we only have three options for multi-person synastry: 1) mass-averaging or mass Davison (which ignores the idea that planet contributions among the three charts are unequal) 2) start date charts (which can only happen when you have a start date to begin with), and 3) synastry between a regular and a Davison chart for the other two (which is not only consistent with the data on "outs," but also takes into account the idea that each person sees the interaction with the other two differently). Option 3 is the one that makes the most sense to me.

Do you have any data to support this?

Not nearly enough, no. I can only tell you what I've found from looking at conjuncts in four different trios, seeing whether they were consistent or inconsistent with regular synastry interpretations.

Well, I guess asking for data on trios really would be asking for the Moon given that we've already talked about all kinds of new ideas already—

I'm glad you see that.

—but still I'd be interested to hear what you found. Even if it is based on only four trios. Why so few, by the way?

Because of reference frames and covariances.

What? English please.

Because even if I can study a reasonably stable trio of people, the number of perspectives I can take for viewing that trio is limited. This is my limited reference frame. Even if I'm not a part of that trio—*especially* if I'm not a part of that trio—my way of looking at [A vs B+C] compared to [A+B vs C] will be limited by my own filter for seeing A, B, and C through the [A+B+C] mask—one in which C's Mars may be off, B's Saturn may be on, and A's Moon may only work when B and C are interacting for example. How then, could I study this trio equally clearly through each one's eyes? I couldn't. My reference frame limits me. In other words, even when you *can* study trios correctly, you are rarely able to study from their various third-person perspectives equally easily.

And then there are covariances, Geery continued. This is where two parts of a bigger whole change together. To study multiple trios, I would have had to observe all three actors really, really well to such an extent that I could separate their trio behaviors against the whole group from their synastry behaviors against each other member independent of the trio setup. This can be done, mind you. We do it all the time mathematically. But I'd have to know all three trio mates super well to pull this off. SUPER DUPER well. And you can imagine how crazy this would get with four people involved. In other words, when you point out a characteristic in Mary, is she acting that way because of her trio with Terry and Jean, or because of her synastry with Jean as viewed by Terry?

Hm. And if I asked you to do a chart for four people anyway?

Again, I'd ask you for the date the group was "born" and do synastry with that. Otherwise I'd do separate synastries with each person. If there's a better or more reasonable way which takes into account different weightings for people's actions and remains consistent with other theories already in place, I invite you to use it. A quartet has far more combinations of interactions in it than a trio, and I don't think picking these combinations apart is very practical if it is indeed a quartet you seek to study. Trios are the only time you can ask me to do a chart for more than two people and expect me to give you any reasonable insight into the people involved. They are also frequent enough to where asking for start dates is less reasonable than just doing the other two people's relative chart.

I see. 🛠

Why study trios?

Why in the world would you want to look at trios in astrology when almost all of our major relationship decisions appear to revolve around establishing good duos? It's because good duos aren't just duos; they're duos against a third background. It's also because in the framework we set up back in *FSA*, the idea of "self- other- world-" implied corresponding spaces for behaving. For "self" planets like the Moon, we needed only to feel internally. For "other" planets like the Sun, we needed some other person or thing to act against. For "world" planets like Jupiter, we needed a place in which to define facelessness. The trio is the smallest collection of people in which a person can interact with a group and bypass the individual behaviors within that group, rendering the other two people something like a "faceless" collective to him. We don't really get an understanding of what planets like Jupiter through Neptune do until we study ourselves in groups larger than two. Furthermore, whereas almost every duo you enter will be fleeting and utilitarian, the trios you choose tend to be much more durable. I invite you to explore the many philosophical, psychological, and social reasons for why this is, but suffice it to say that every time you interact with someone for whatever reason, you enter a kind of duo. Every time you consider the consequences of one interaction against a separate one, you enter a trio.

- Given you, your friend, and either [a third friend] or [the backdrop against which you and your friend interact], most of your enduring associations will be trios.
- When you read a composite chart against either of the component people's charts which make up that composite, you're reading a trio.
- The common objective which unites a duo can typically be read as its own planet or as a third party, rendering the duo a trio.

While looking at the issue of trios in astrology, I'll admit that I breathed a sigh of relief when I found that reading trios simply meant reading synastries between one person and the relative chart of two others. Why the relief? Because relative charts have actual birthplaces and times. All that stuff we went through for calculating the ASC* and so on just isn't necessary. In case you missed it in the previous chapter, relative charts look at a relationship from the outside. Composites look at it from the inside. In a trio, a third person is an outsider to the other two. So all you do is read **the synastry between [(Person A) and (the Davison/relative chart of Person B with Person C)]**. We'll call this **three person synastry**.[65]

---

[65] When looking at how a person relates to their own partnership with another, however, three person synastry transforms into **synastry with a composite**: **the synastry between [(Person A) and (the composite chart of Person A with Person B)]**. Here, you *do* use the composite, but this is just the very thing we've been using to read "outs." This only happens when you effectively play two roles in a relationship: that of yourself and that of half of the duo. Don't worry about this though. For this next section we'll be sticking with relative charts.

Why you may not want to read advanced angles in synastry with a relationship: Relationships are hard to steer directly

For the most part only conjuncts, oppositions, trines, and squares should count heavily in synastry with a relationship dynamic, because these first four harmonics are purely internal to the third person and dynamics don't really have personalities in the way that we do. As soon as we get to quintiles, we have to start thinking about what it means to "talk" to a box of dynamics. You can still read aspects higher than this, but they won't automatically be as useful in guiding how you deal with the other two people. It's helpful here to think of yourself as a birdwatcher and the other two as birds at play. The relative chart will tell you what the others' play looks like and the first four harmonics will show how *you personally* respond to what you're seeing. But if you realistically want to affect what they're doing, you'd do better to influence one bird at a time rather than trying to influence the "playing" itself.

🛠 Looking at three person synastry presents a case where less truly is more. Two people's relative chart is typically as good as read-only to outsiders, since all it does is describe their overall effects on everyone, everywhere as the result of one oversimplifying average. Again, I believe there are some really good philosophical and psychological implications for this, but I'll reduce these to one broadly esoteric result:

> The "karma" between two people is their own; when relating to them, serving as their mediator, parent, or any other role, the best you can do is control your own attitude towards their dynamic. Your attitude can help draw them closer together or break them apart—raising or lowering the strength of their dynamic—but it won't *change* their fundamental dynamic. Barring this, if you actually want to influence them, you'll need to interface with them one on one.

The above result applies not only to people and other people, but to people and their own dreams, projects, and learnings. In dealing with "ensemble averages" (to use a physics term), we often strive in vain to influence the parts by interacting with the whole. Without access to the parts themselves, however, all we end up doing is bringing the parts closer together or separating them further while they essentially interact in the same way in either case. You'll see this often whether you're watching arguments among friends or arguments among policy makers. Change from outside is the work of men upon ghosts. The ghost which consists of a non-visible average of multiple visible people presents a frustrating terrain for the outsider who would steer it. So it may be better for you to read only those angles which describe your own actions, self-worth, thoughts, and feelings in response to the other pair (until you perfect your powers of ghost control). To summarize:

> In a three-person interaction, the dynamic between any two people can be separated from the influence of a third.[66] Where two people's interaction can be divorced from the influence of a third person, it's often not worth it for the third person to try to steer the other two's relationship without steering the other two themselves. The first four harmonics in synastry between the third person and the [duo comprising the other two]—conjuncts, oppositions, trines, and squares—are the only angles which, being internal to the third person's perspective, can be reliably steered by that third person. All other angles behave in a more "read only" way. 🛠

If all a third person really does is steer his own attitude towards the other two, how do we explain the influence that one person can have over the other two's interaction with each other? To clarify the claims made above, it's not that you *can't* steer a dynamic with your II-sextile or III-quintile, it's that your attempts to steer it *intentionally* will usually be frustrated by the individual goals that the actual other two have for themselves. But steering your own attitude is far from useless. In the next book I'll describe how a change in attitude towards a thing beyond

---

[66] In statistics we call the process for breaking tangled dimensions into independent dimensions "orthogonalization."

your influence produces chains of experience for you such that, even if you would struggle to steer Mary and Annie, your attitude change towards them will lead you to meet "Marie" and "Anne" in their places. This discussion of "slots," however, is best left to the realm of spirituality rather than astrology, so we'll hold off on it here. For our purposes, the third person's attitude towards the other two determines his opportunities related to what those other two provide—sometimes from within the trio, sometimes from without. That said, we'll look only at conjuncts through squares for this kind of chart, leaving the 32 other (more interaction-based) harmonics as a less practical curiosity.

Using StarFisher to read a trio chart

In this section I'll be using sample data from the trio I know best. That between me and my two younger brothers. Granted this won't be as satisfying to you as, say, reading a trio consisting of three well-known celebrities, but really we just don't know celebrities as well as all the media hype would have us think. If I read celebrities here I'll only be able to speculate regarding what's actually important to read, how one should go about interpreting what's read, and whether such a reading is accurate. Reading people we know lets us test astrology against our own reality and limits the extent to which we think we can read the minds of people we've never met.

There is another, more practical reason for reading mine and my brothers' chart for this example. I think you'll find (as I did) that doing three person synastry is a really great way to expose the true default opinions of the third person regarding the other two. The results can reveal all kinds of insecurities and other nasty corners of the third person's opinion and, as such, I chose not to read the charts of anyone who wouldn't want this kind of information disclosed. I also chose not to fictionalize this case just because doing so would have been extra work. As we go through this section, be sure to follow along using the charts of a trio you've been a part of, and get ready to read some interesting stuff.

Predict the third person's view of the of the other two

1. Determine who the third (outside) person will be. So that you won't be led by the nose, develop a very rough opinion of what the third person thinks of the other two.

   In the example, I love my brothers and have always been proud of them. I absolutely LOVE being an oldest brother and am defensive given any (rare) person who questions our honor. As we get older, I have a more eccentric personality than they do. But they are more socially responsible than I am.

   Your turn. Write some of your broad observations here (what the third person thinks of the other two):

   ____

   ____

   ____

   ____

Display a relative chart for the two (non-third person) individuals

2. Assuming you have already entered and saved the charts of all three people,
   a. Open StarFisher.
   b. Once you see the New horoscope window, click Load... (under Primary Event Data) and select one of the other's (non-third person's) chart. Click Open.

   c. Staying in the New horoscope window, click Load... (under Primary Event Data) and select the other (non-third person's) chart. Click Open.
   d. Click OK to display the wheel of the second chart you loaded.

3. Once the chart wheel loads, use the menu to select Event>Combine Events. This will take you to the Combine events window.

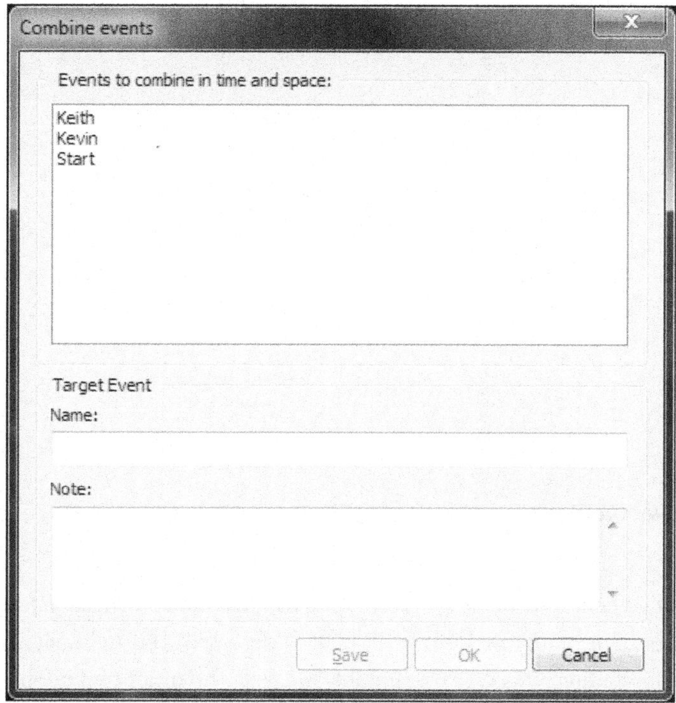

4. Click the first name you want to combine, then click the second. We're about to average their charts.
5. You should see the two people's names in the Name box along with their birth information in the Note box. Save if you want, then Click OK.
6. You'll be asked if you want to create a new horoscope using the currently loaded event. Click Yes.

7. The New Horoscope window will appear.

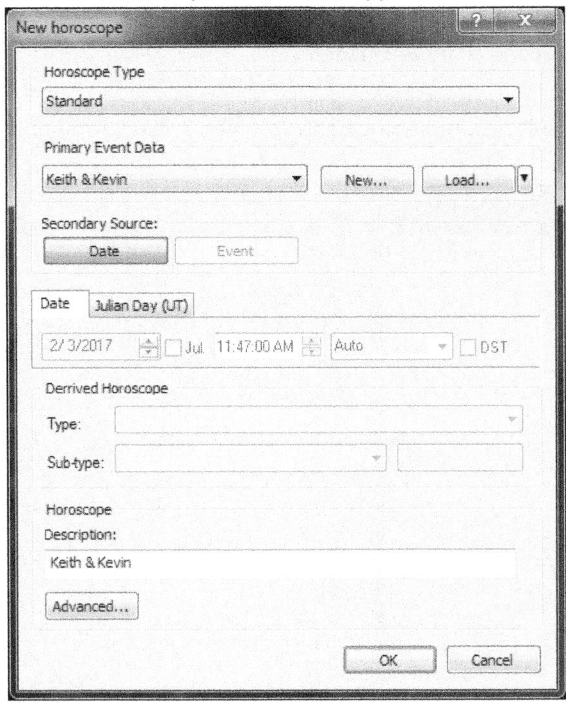

Click OK.

What you now have is the Davison / relative chart. This chart is interesting by itself, and I invite you to pay particular attention to what's on the Ascendant. Juno and Hera in particular came up A LOT (actually, in most cases) in the various duos I studied for trio reading. This was presumably because the other two people in the trio needed to be close enough to help form a trio in the first place.

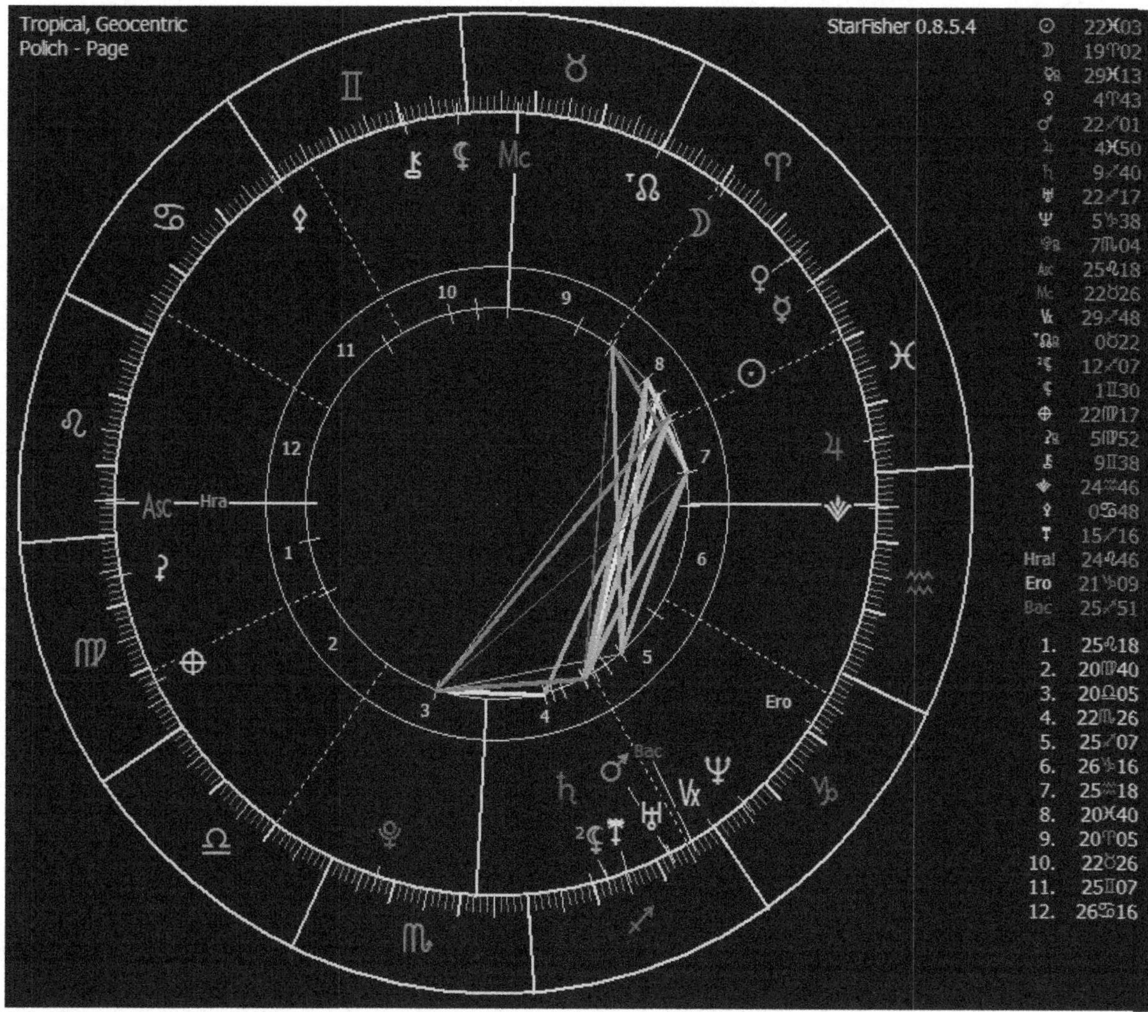

Reading the duo's relative chart

Why haven't we talked about how to read a relative chart in depth? Because **you read these charts using the same basic principles applied in the regular / self chart**, except with relative charts I'd stick mainly with <u>conjuncts and trines</u> only. Conjuncts show how a duo projects while trines show the most basic message that a duo sends to others. I suppose you could also look at house placements and signs, and these are discussed in *FSA*. Although we'll end up reading conjuncts, trines, *oppositions, and squares* when the third chart is introduced, I hesitate to read oppositions and squares for the relative chart by itself simply because the idea of an *interaction* having "self-worth" or "feelings" is weird to me. You can read whatever you want, though. Just don't read the Vertex. As an indicator of how the chart possessor changes, the Vertex just doesn't seem to make nearly as much intuitive sense as the other planets and points.

8. Use *table 16-5* to locate all of the resonant pairs for the conjunct. This is the natural character of the non-third person's duo. I'm pretty certain you'll find this an informative read.
    a. **Optional**. Switching over to Aspectarium view so I can see all the conjuncts, I'll just go down the list and read the corresponding entries from *table 16-5* (ignoring the Vertex in the process).

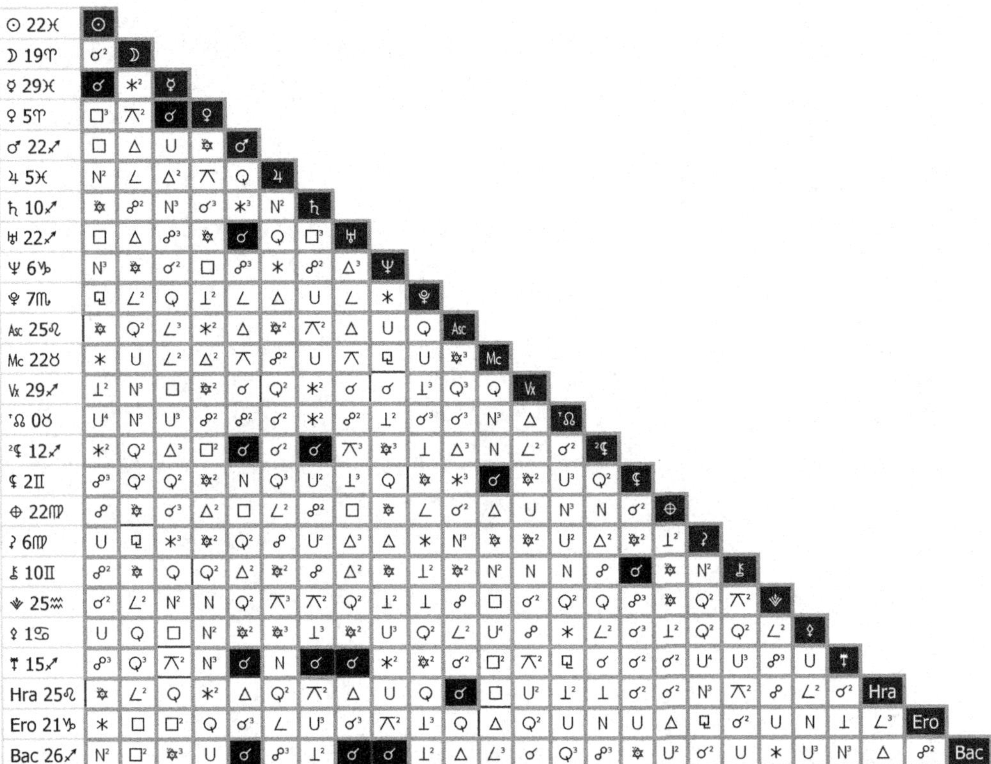

☉ 22♓	☉																								
☽ 19♈	☌^{2}	☽																							
☿ 29♓	☌	*^{2}	☿																						
♀ 5♈	□^{3}	⚻^{2}	☌	♀																					
♂ 22♐	□	△	U	✡	♂																				
♃ 5♓	N^2	∠	△^{2}	⚻	Q	♃																			
♄ 10♐	✡	☍^{2}	N^3	☌^{3}	*^{3}	N^2	♄																		
♅ 22♐	□	△	☍^{3}	✡	☌	Q	□^{3}	♅																	
♆ 6♑	N^3	✡	☌^{2}	□	☍^{3}	*	☍^{2}	△^{3}	♆																
♇ 7♏	⚼	∠^{2}	Q	⊥^{2}	∠	△	U	∠	*	♇															
Asc 25♌	✡	Q^2	∠^{3}	*^{2}	△	✡^{2}	⚻^{2}	△	U	Q	Asc														
Mc 22♉	*	U	∠^{2}	△^{2}	⚻	☍^{2}	U	⚻	⚼	U	✡^{3}	Mc													
Vx 29♐	⊥^{2}	N^3	□	✡^{2}	☌	Q^2	*^{2}	☌	☌	⊥^{3}	Q^3	Q	Vx												
^{T}☊ 0♉	U^4	N^3	U^3	☍^{2}	☍^{2}	☌^{2}	*^{2}	☍^{2}	⊥^{2}	☌^{3}	☌^{3}	N^3	△	^{T}☊											
^{2}⚸ 12♐	*^{2}	Q^2	△^{3}	□^{2}	☌	☌^{2}	☌	⚻^{3}	✡^{3}	⊥	△^{3}	N	∠^{2}	☌^{2}	^{2}⚸										
⚸ 2♊	☍^{3}	Q^2	Q^2	✡^{2}	N	Q^3	U^2	⊥^{3}	Q	✡	*^{3}	☌	✡^{2}	U^3	Q^2	⚸									
⊕ 22♍	☍	✡	☌^{3}	△^{2}	□	∠^{2}	☍^{2}	□	✡	∠	☌^{2}	△	U	N^3	N	☌^{2}	⊕								
? 6♍	U	⚼	*^{3}	✡^{2}	Q^2	☍	U^2	△^{3}	△	*	N^3	✡	✡^{2}	U^2	△^{2}	✡^{2}	⊥^{2}	?							
⚷ 10♊	☍^{2}	✡	Q	Q^2	△^{2}	✡^{2}	☍	△^{2}	✡	⊥^{2}	✡^{2}	N^2	N	N	☍	☌	✡	N^2	⚷						
⚶ 25♒	☌^{2}	∠^{2}	N^2	N	Q^2	⚻^{3}	⚻^{2}	Q^2	⊥^{2}	⊥	☍	□	☌^{2}	Q^2	Q	☍^{3}	✡	Q^2	⚻^{2}	⚶					
⚴ 1♋	U	Q	□	N^2	✡^{2}	✡^{3}	⊥^{3}	✡^{2}	U^3	Q^2	∠^{2}	U^4	☍	*	∠^{2}	☌^{3}	⊥^{2}	Q^2	Q^2	∠^{2}	⚴				
⚵ 15♐	☍^{3}	Q^3	⚻^{2}	N^3	☌	N	☌	☌	*^{2}	✡^{2}	☌^{2}	□^{2}	⚻^{2}	⚼	☌	☌^{2}	☌^{2}	U^4	U^3	☍^{3}	U	⚵			
Hra 25♌	✡	∠^{2}	Q	*^{2}	△	Q^2	⚻^{2}	△	U	Q	☌	□	U^2	⊥^{2}	⊥	☌^{2}	☌^{2}	N^3	⚻^{2}	☍	∠^{2}	☌^{2}	Hra		
Ero 21♑	*	□	□^{2}	Q	☌^{3}	∠	U^3	☌^{3}	⚻^{2}	⊥^{3}	Q	△	Q^2	U	N	U	△	⚼	☌^{2}	U	N	⊥	∠^{3}	Ero	
Bac 26♐	N^2	□^{2}	✡^{3}	U	☌	☍^{3}	⊥^{2}	☌	☌	⊥^{2}	△	∠^{3}	☌	Q^3	☍^{3}	✡	U^2	☌^{2}	U	*	U^3	N^3	△	☍^{2}	Bac

Based on *table 16-5*, Keith and Kevin's duo appears direct and persuasive, with the ability and talent to compel and command groups they interact with. They can also restrain others in their social role, suggesting that others aren't easily inclined to disrespect them when they are together. They derive power at their interactant's expense, but can also be limited by their interactant, suggesting that they are not inclined to actually overpower others willy nilly, but exercise control over their joint expression instead. They are plugged into the information and collective world, can inspire a following, are super well-liked and rewarded for rebelling against boundaries. They serve as "disease fighters" which, by close analogy, makes them more resistant to long term damage within their exchange with each other.
This is a charismatic duo.

9. Use *table 16-5* to locate all of the resonant pairs for the trine. This angle family shows where others are impressed when the duo-mates are communicating without the third person's inclusion. I'll skip this one, but it works the same way as step 8 above. Just use the table and read off the pairs which all have trines.
10. **Optional reading: Oppositions and squares.** Some of the data suggest that oppositions in the relative chart show the behavioral priorities of things against which the duo interacts, while squares show the kinds of attitudes which the duo attracts from those who interact with them. If you read these resonant pairs, start with this idea and use *table 16-5*.

Reading three person synastry using [one person's birth chart] against [a duo's relative chart]:

11. Now let's look at the trio. Select Edit Horoscope from the icon bar.

12. From the Horoscope Type Menu, select Comparison (Standard / Standard).

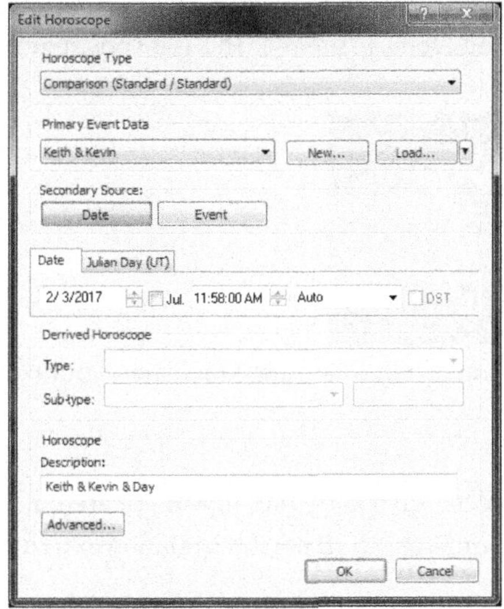

13. Under the Secondary Source Menu, Choose Event. The menu below this will change.
14. Under Secondary Data, click Load to load your third person chart. I'll be loading myself.

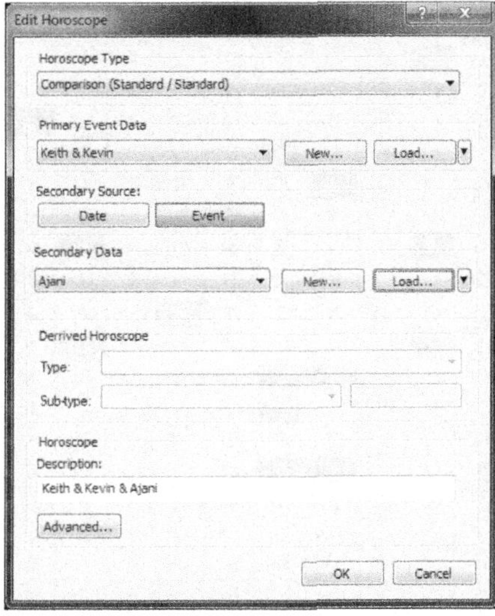

15. If you're not already in Aspectarium view, use the icon bar to go there and take a look at the big synastry table.

16. Keep in mind that when you read three person synastry using the method we've been using, you're looking at the trio from the perspective of the third person. Accordingly, if you yourself happen to be the third person, it may be easier to read our favorite table 19-9 using your own chart as the first one (with

planets going down the side) and the duo's chart as the second one (with planets going across the top. In StarFisher, if your header has you as the second chart (shown below)...

...you'd need to read *table 19-9* with [the duo as "you"] and [you as "them"]. This is inconvenient, so hit the Space Bar to reverse this...

...This will be a much easier read. If you are the third person and you're using StarFisher, your name should be the top name.

17. Using *table 19-9*, read all the resonant pairs for the conjunct. You'll likely find that there are quite a few, and that the entire collection of these more or less spells out your third person's relationship to the duo made up of the first and second person.

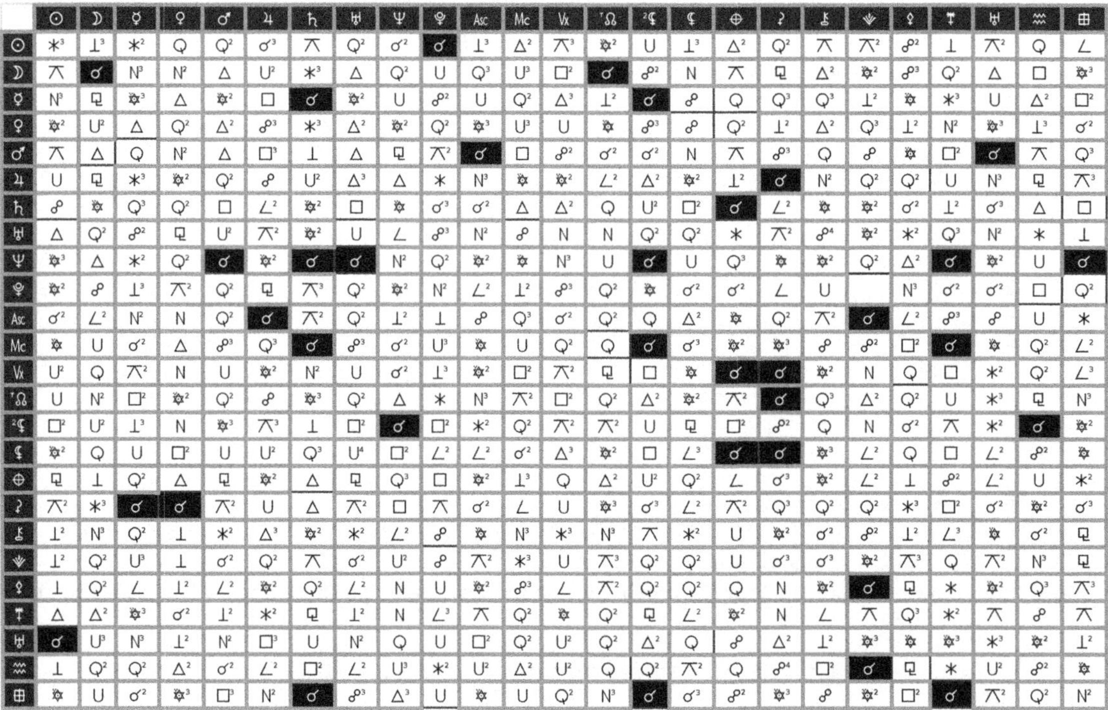

	☉	☽	☿	♀	♂	♃	♄	♅	♆	♇	Asc	Mc	Vx	ᵀ☊	²⚸	⚸	⊕	?	⚷	⚳	⚴	⚶	♅	≋	⊞
☉	⚹^{3}	⊥^{3}	⚹^{2}	Q	Q^2	☌^{3}	⚻	Q^2	☌^{2}	**☌**	⊥^{3}	△^{2}	⚻^{3}	✡^{2}	U	⊥^{3}	△^{2}	Q^2	⚻	⚻^{2}	☍^{2}	⊥	⚻^{2}	Q	∠
☽	⚻	**☌**	N^3	N^2	△	U^2	⚹^{3}	△	Q^2	U	Q^3	U^3	□^{2}	**☌**	☍^{2}	N	⚻	⚼	△^{2}	✡^{2}	☍^{3}	Q^2	△	□	✡^{3}
☿	N^3	⚼	✡^{3}	△	✡^{2}	□	**☌**	✡^{2}	U	☍^{2}	U	Q^2	△^{3}	⊥^{2}	**☌**	☍	Q	Q^3	Q^3	⊥^{2}	✡	⚹^{3}	U	△^{2}	□^{2}
♀	✡^{2}	U^2	△	Q^2	△^{2}	☍^{3}	⚹^{3}	△^{2}	✡^{2}	Q^2	✡^{3}	U^3	U	✡	☍^{3}	☍	Q^2	⊥^{2}	△^{2}	Q^3	⊥^{2}	N^2	✡^{3}	⊥^{3}	☌^{2}
♂	⚻	△	Q	N^2	△	□^{3}	⊥	△	⚼	⚻^{2}	**☌**	□	☍^{2}	☌^{2}	☌^{2}	N	⚻	☍^{3}	Q	☍	✡	□^{2}	**☌**	⚻	Q^3
♃	U	⚼	⚹^{3}	✡^{2}	Q^2	☍	U^2	△^{3}	△	⚹	N^3	✡	✡^{2}	∠^{2}	△^{2}	✡^{2}	⊥^{2}	**☌**	N^2	Q^2	Q^2	U	N^3	⚼	⚻^{3}
♄	☍	✡	Q^3	Q^2	□	∠^{2}	✡^{2}	□	✡	☌^{3}	☌^{2}	△	△^{2}	Q	U^2	□^{2}	**☌**	∠^{2}	✡	✡^{2}	☌^{2}	⊥^{2}	☌^{3}	△	□
♅	△	Q^2	☍^{2}	⚼	U^2	⚻^{2}	✡^{2}	U	∠	☍^{3}	N^2	☍	N	N	Q^2	Q^2	⚹	⚻^{2}	☍^{4}	✡^{2}	⚹^{2}	Q^3	N^2	⚹	⊥
♆	✡^{3}	△	⚹^{2}	Q^2	**☌**	✡^{2}	**☌**	**☌**	N^2	Q^2	✡^{2}	✡	N^3	U	**☌**	U	Q^3	✡	✡^{2}	Q^2	△^{2}	**☌**	✡^{2}	U	**☌**
♇	✡^{2}	☍	⊥^{3}	⚻^{2}	Q^2	⚼	⚻^{3}	Q^2	✡^{2}	N^2	∠^{2}	⊥^{2}	☍^{3}	Q^2	✡	☌^{2}	☌^{2}	∠	U		N^3	☌^{2}	☌^{2}	□	Q^2
Asc	☌^{2}	∠^{2}	N^2	N	Q^2	**☌**	⚻^{2}	Q^2	⊥^{2}	⊥	☍	Q^3	☌^{2}	Q^2	Q	△^{2}	✡	Q^2	⚻^{2}	**☌**	∠^{2}	☍^{3}	☍	U	⚹
Mc	✡	U	☌^{2}	△	☍^{3}	Q^3	**☌**	☍^{3}	☌^{2}	U^3	✡	U	Q^2	Q	**☌**	☌^{3}	✡^{2}	✡^{3}	☍	☍^{2}	□^{2}	**☌**	✡	Q^2	∠^{2}
Vx	U^2	Q	⚻^{2}	N	U	✡^{2}	N^2	U	☌^{2}	⊥^{3}	✡^{2}	□^{2}	⚻^{2}	⚼	□	✡	**☌**	**☌**	✡^{2}	N	Q	□	⚹^{2}	Q^2	∠^{3}
ᵀ☊	U	N^2	□^{2}	✡^{2}	Q^2	☍	✡^{3}	Q^2	△	⚹	N^3	⚻^{2}	□^{2}	Q^2	△^{2}	✡^{2}	⚻^{2}	**☌**	Q^3	△^{2}	Q^2	U	⚹^{3}	⚼	N^3
²⚸	□^{2}	U^2	⊥^{3}	N	✡^{3}	⚻^{3}	⊥	□^{2}	**☌**	□^{2}	⚹^{2}	Q^2	⚻^{2}	⚻^{2}	U	⚼	□^{2}	☍^{2}	Q	N	☌^{2}	⚻	⚹^{2}	**☌**	✡^{2}
⚸	✡^{2}	Q	U	□^{2}	U	U^2	Q^3	U^4	□^{2}	∠^{2}	∠^{2}	☌^{2}	△^{3}	✡^{2}	□	∠^{3}	**☌**	**☌**	✡^{3}	∠^{2}	Q	□	∠^{2}	☍^{2}	✡
⊕	⚼	⊥	Q^2	△	⚼	✡^{2}	△	⚼	Q^3	□	✡^{2}	⊥^{3}	Q	△^{2}	U^2	Q^2	∠	☌^{3}	✡^{2}	∠^{2}	⊥	☍^{2}	∠^{2}	U	⚹^{2}
?	⚻^{2}	⚹^{3}	**☌**	**☌**	⚻^{2}	U	△	⚻^{2}	□	⚻	☌^{2}	∠	U	✡^{3}	☌^{3}	∠^{2}	⚻^{2}	Q^3	Q^2	Q^2	⚹^{3}	□^{2}	☌^{2}	✡^{2}	☌^{3}
⚷	⊥^{2}	N^3	Q^2	⊥	⚹^{2}	△^{3}	✡^{2}	⚹^{2}	∠^{2}	☍	✡	N^3	⚹^{3}	N^3	⚻	⚹^{2}	U	✡^{2}	☌^{2}	☍^{2}	⊥^{2}	∠^{3}	✡	☌^{2}	⚼
⚳	⊥^{2}	Q^2	U^3	⊥	☌^{2}	Q^2	⚻	☌^{2}	U^2	☍	⚻^{2}	⚹^{3}	U	⚻^{3}	Q^2	Q^2	U	☌^{3}	☌^{3}	✡^{2}	⚻^{3}	Q	⚻^{2}	N^3	⚼
⚴	⊥	Q^2	∠	⊥^{2}	∠^{2}	✡^{2}	Q^2	∠^{2}	N	U	✡^{2}	☍^{3}	∠	⚻^{2}	Q^2	Q^2	Q	N	✡^{2}	**☌**	⚼	⚹	✡^{2}	Q^3	⚻^{3}
⚶	△	△^{2}	✡^{3}	☌^{2}	⊥^{2}	⚹^{2}	⚼	⊥^{2}	N	∠^{3}	⚻	Q^2	✡	Q^2	⚼	∠^{2}	✡^{2}	N	∠	⚻	Q^3	⚹^{2}	⚻	☍	⚻
♅	**☌**	U^3	N^3	⊥^{2}	N^2	□^{3}	U	N^2	Q	U	□^{2}	Q^2	U^2	Q^2	△^{2}	Q	☍	△^{2}	⊥^{2}	✡^{3}	✡	✡^{3}	⚹^{3}	✡^{2}	⊥^{2}
≋	⊥	Q^2	Q^2	△^{2}	☌^{2}	∠^{2}	□^{2}	∠^{2}	U^3	⚹^{2}	U^2	△^{2}	U^2	Q	Q^2	⚻^{2}	Q	☍^{4}	□^{2}	**☌**	⚼	⚹	U^2	☍^{2}	✡
⊞	✡	U	☌^{2}	✡^{3}	□^{3}	N^2	**☌**	☍^{3}	△^{3}	U	✡	U	Q^2	N^3	**☌**	☌^{3}	☍^{2}	✡^{3}	☍	✡^{2}	□^{2}	**☌**	⚻^{2}	Q^2	N^2

For the purposes of this example, I'll only read enough of the conjuncts to check against the reality I wrote down in step 1. But you should read them all. When reading conjuncts using *table 19-9*, you can plug in the words "naturally" or "instinctively" to get the general gist of each pair. For example, my brothers' and my subconscious reason for interacting is because it's natural ([Moon-Moon] conjunct). I amplify their influence, look up to their communication, and help defend them against social pressure. As the oldest, I naturally tend to lose challenges to their pair, suggesting that either they just plain beat me or I put them first. (The latter is true, as I naturally join their fan club). Meanwhile, I can naturally get away with pressuring them, though we instinctively have different solutions to things. We make an idealized public team. As far as different levels of eccentricity are concerned, we can use the steps in Chapter 20 to conclude that my Lilith would be the thing to look at. Sure enough [Lilith $_{me}$-Ceres $_{them}$] shows that they see me as defying standard social training. Way to brag about your family, Ajani. But you get the idea. The rest of the pairs show more of the same. And believe me, this did not have to be the case. Now it's your turn. Try this exercise out on your own trio.

18. Once you've read all of the resonant pairs for conjuncts, you should do the same for the oppositions, trines, and squares. (Remember, oppositions and squares are okay when we're reading a *third person's view* of a duo; these angles are only weird when we're reading a duo's own "feelings" and "values." It's also okay to read your own Vertex in this one. Try it out and see what you get. Don't read the duo's Vertex, though.

You've read the trio. Now what?

The most useful takeaway from reading trios lies in the insight it provides into your most stable associations. Particularly for diagnosing issues with the parents and other stressful caretaking relationships, you'll find that reading the conjunct and square resonant pair groups is especially informative. To supplement the conjunct group, the square resonances show situations which you or the duo *wish* would work but, by default, don't. And even though I've up to now discouraged looking beyond the squares, it's almost always useful to check out the "Interaction Purpose" cocktail back in Chapter 20, regardless of what angles pop up. Again, you'll likely find some enlightening stuff here.

Perfecting your friendship trios may at first glance seem easy, since fun and validation are often the main menu items. A second look at these kinds of trios, however, reveals something deeper: The fun you have is related to the styles of expression you are encouraged to display. More than mere jokery, the good times we experience with our trios invariably shape the kinds of expressive standards we hold both as individuals and as caretakers for others. As you discover and hone the kind of attitudes which your various trios are designed to foster, you gain access to a valuable tool for growing your world-planets like Jupiter through Neptune as well as your personal standards for interfacing with the world via the 9th through 12th houses. While healthy duos foster healthy interpersonal habits, healthy trios foster healthy world-identity habits. And so we grow up and grow in worldly experience through our favorite cliques. As for groups bigger than three, I'd highly recommend that you read them one trio or one duo at a time. From the very beginning you'll likely find that certain combinations of personalities within the group are more important to you than others—not because some clique members are less important, but because some lessons at the hands of other clique members are more important for your own advancement as a person.

Chapter 23: Synastry with dead people, dates, and projects

We begin this chapter with three major questions in mind:

- What is it that makes a historical figure into a role model?
- What determines a historical figure or event's ability to teach you?
- How can you evolve yourself by studying a historical figure or event?

It turns out, though, that each of these questions has answers rooted in synastry with events that are not actually in front of you—events with which there is only a partial ability to interact. Enter the realm of charts for the non-living.

Before getting into any astrology, let's start with a pair of basic assumptions. The first assumption is that we can indeed learn certain things from certain historical figures and events. This is actually why we study history. When we think of great spiritual leaders we think of Jesus or the Buddha, for example. When we think of great philosophers we think of Aristotle or Plato, perhaps. When we think of great events we think of World War II or the French Revolution. Living or not, people and events leave certain traces that extend far beyond themselves and into larger society. The task is to learn whether such traces follow a predictable astrological pattern. The second assumption is that inanimate objects, books, businesses, and other events in spacetime can also affect us in stereotyped ways. When we interface with such things (which I'll refer to as projects), certain sides of us are highlighted. TVs highlight our Uranian side by surrounding us with the information they project. Our own vehicles highlight our internal monologue / Gemini / 3rd house by serving as the shell within which we issue a constant stream of responses to others; with 3rd harmonics, we're not talking *to* the world (as 7th harmonics like Venus / Libra / 7th house would), but *at* it. These two assumptions serve to emphasize a central point: People's astrological dynamics can be affected by things besides other people, and sometimes these other things have charts of their own.

What kinds of things get charts?

In general, the more expressive choices a thing has, the more likely it is to have a meaningful astrochart. So maybe your basic computer doesn't really have a chart since all it does is throw the information-based results of your own deeds back to you. Your A.I.-infused video game, however, can have more of a meaningful chart to the extent that it sometimes fights you back (Mars), sometimes tells stories (Sun, Jupiter), sometimes presents you with puzzles (Mercury), and sometimes displays game mechanics which defy or agree with industry standards (Point of Action, Pluto). In cases where the exact same game is produced in copies by the millions, the "birth chart" would be the date and time of the original game concept or final release. I talk about this in *FSA*, Chapter 11. Meanwhile, pets can have charts. Works of art can have charts. Events can have charts. But the extent to which these projects show chart behavior as opposed to single-planet influence depends on how diverse we find the array of internal and external effects they have "to choose" from. Obviously, pets are more likely to get astrocharts than phones are, because pets have more styles of interaction to purposefully choose from without relying on some external "other" to make that choice for them.

Four kinds of concepts

Once we accept the idea that everything we interact with can also exist as a concept, we can then interface with those things as though such concepts were events in spacetime. For our purposes, concepts can take four forms: that of faceless tools, dynamics, situations, and events.

Faceless tools are things that aid us in our own deeds. (These are like planets)

Faceless tools are basically backgrounds for amplifying particular planets. TV's and computers are Uranian because they primarily turn up our Uranian information environment. Music is Neptunian because it primarily turns up our sense of ambient mood. The home is Lunar because it primarily serves as a place where we can be free to feel the feelings that fit us best. The workplace is Mercurian because it is the frame in which we untangle unsolved dilemmas for a living, but the *career* is Saturnian because it outlines what labels (role boxes) the public applies to what we do—minus the actual workplace details. Things used as faceless tools don't have charts. To us they're just volume switches for our own planets. To us, that is. The truth is, they usually have *some* creation date, but we don't care about whatever detail that implies. Indeed, even crowds of living people are often treated as tools especially in the Jupiter through Pluto cases.

What kinds of faceless tools help ups bring out our planets? *Table 23-1* addresses this.

Table 23-1: Tools we interact with that build up planets

Planet	Tools like...	...which elicit...
Moon	home, friends, desired things, children, pets, food	emotion
Sun	other people, hobby objects, fun outings	default 1:1 interaction
Mercury	attention to one's health, puzzles, disordered things	a desire to work on things / align them with a standard
Venus	beautiful things, friends, social standards	a desire to communicate (or exchange 1:1 feedback) with the things we interact with
Mars	sex-related things, anger inciters, the unknown	a desire to steer others / change things
Jupiter	foreign subjects of interest, enabling or exploratory experiences	going forward in the world
Saturn	rules, career, buildings, things that restrict, laws, bad experiences, administrative demands	experience of structure
Uranus	electronics, media, groups which socialize among themselves	social talk
Neptune	movies, music, art, places where a specific mood is designed to gather (like prisons, theme parks, and hospitals)	imagination
Pluto	big issues, public trends, governments, law enforcement groups, standards agencies (like education boards, certification groups, and testing providers)	social / cultural pressure
Ascendant (1st house cusp)	new situations	approach behavior
Midheaven (10th house cusp)	situations where one presents oneself	reputation, self-labeling style
Selene (White Moon)	things that make others uncomfortable which you can comfortably solve, skill opportunities	ideal talents
Lilith (Lunar Apogee/ Black Moon)	things which encourage unfitting conformity, topics where publicly known truths are purposely kept private (like sex, death, existential uncertainty, rules that go against common sense, social norms that defy actual social practice)	rebellion
Vertex	newly imposed circumstances, things that remove accustomed comfort	response to major change
Ceres	things that dissatisfy or go astray, flirtation objects	coercion of others
Chiron	problem situations, illness, broken things	doctor-patient behavior
North Node	things one has been on the lookout for	a feeling of convenient opportunity / a feeling of something that was meant to be
Part of Fortune	stability and comfort inducing conditions	being comfortable in one's situation
Vesta	family, demanding tasks	a need for focus
Pallas	social injustice, social imbalance, resolvable information-based disorder	socialized action
Juno	a sense of incompleteness, capture-worthy things	commitment
Hera	things that are better than their current imperfect equivalents, where there is a <u>noticeable</u> preference for the better thing	bonding
Eros	receptiveness to provocation, for better or worse	passion
Bacchus	occasions and actions worth actively sharing	peer and clique behavior

Dynamics are processes which we undertake. (These are like angles)

Our own dynamics with things are basically our angles.

- Conjuncts are impulses we naturally follow, without any major thought whatsoever.

  Advanced explanation

  - Realistically, display of your conjuncts is highly dependent on your genetics' interaction with your environment, such that there is no commonly testable astrological factor which can keep up with this. Thus in *FSA* we invented the Point of Action as a way of representing such impulse as a "planet" in the chart. The house where your Action is located is that area of life where you are most naturally spontaneous. The sign of your Action is the behavior you are most likely to impulsively display in that house. The angles to your Action show the areas of life where your natural impulsivity combines with other traits to display their effects...
  - ...while conjuncts describe the kinds of behaviors you display when being so impulsive
- Oppositions are experiences we *naturally* perceive (the natural "other stuff" against which we define ourselves and, hence, self-value / identity).

  Advanced explanation

  - At the time of this writing, there is a lot of confusion in mainstream astrology regarding the difference between oppositions (2nd harmonics) and squares. There is also a common tendency to confuse Taurus (2nd sign) qualities with Libra (7th sign) qualities. I talk about why this is in the previous book, but in general we should think of oppositions, Taurus, and other 2nd-related things as showing your natural "units" for measuring experience. Do you naturally see things in terms of what they cost? In terms of how they make you feel? Under what circumstances do you tend to put a lot of energy into weighing the worth of things? These questions can all be used to triangulate your Point of Worth—the imaginary ruler of Taurus which I define in *FSA*, Chapter 13.
  - As the angle-version of 2s, oppositions describe situations which arise whenever you're comparing the worth of things with respect to yourself, so that the resonant pairs for the opposition describe your approach to money, self-esteem, and personal pleasure. Despite the common folklore, Venus and other major planets don't do this. So say the statistics, at least.
- Trines are the natural kinds of information we pass to others and ourselves given what we've experienced (internal monologue).

  Advanced explanation

  - In the previous book we invented a third imaginary point, the Point of Internal Monologue, to represent ideas which you send straight from yourself without the need for some outside object to balance your thoughts against. While mainstream astrology at the time of this writing typically considers basic thought to be a Mercury thing, not all thoughts are the same. Thoughts of the Mercury kind are meant to work out unresolved relationships among things; these correspond more to sextiles. Thoughts of the Monologue kind don't care about issue resolution—only that the speaker be heard. "Should we paint this wall blue?" is a Virgo/Mercury/sextile/6th-style [common ground-building] question because it seeks to reconcile the relationship between the wall and a color. "I like that shade of blue." Is a Point of Monologue/Gemini/trine/3rd-style [say what's on your mind] assertion because it simply states a preference without any reconciled relationship. Relatedly, trines appear when you have an approach towards something which you want to express *just because*. This is different from conjuncts—in which you simply act regardless of whether a target exists. It is also different from sextiles—where you try to take two targets and make them fit into one goal.

- Squares are the natural "what's next" given that our internal information has already been sent out (hence, wanting and expectation). The state of your Moon affects the amount of ease or trouble you get from your squares. Again, I talk more about this in *FSA*.

Dynamics don't amplify planets. Instead they marry groups of planets and priorities under a single expressive mode. It was this idea that led us to define a full table of 36 harmonics in the first place: All humans can feel self-contentment, so you can't just *not* have a [Sun-Moon] angle. We assume that all humans have some way of showing their strongest resolve. So you can't just *not* have a [Mercury-Mars] angle. Every pair of planets has an angle between its two bodies, so empty spaces in our angle tables were no good. You pick out particular dynamics by choosing the right interactant,

- Self (houses 1–4; angles 1–4, 13–16, 25–28,…; signs Aries–Cancer)
- Other (houses 5–8; angles 5–8, 17–20, 29–32,…; signs Leo–Scorpio)
- World (houses 9–12; angles 9–12, 21–24, 33–36,…; signs Sagittarius–Pisces)

the right expressive form,

- Action (fire; 1, 5, 9,…)
- Experience (earth; 2, 6, 10…)
- Ideas (air; 3, 7, 11,…)
- Feelings (water; 4, 8, 12,…)

and right background audience

- Groups of nobody in particular (Pisces/Level I)
- Groups of information-exchangers—often social (Aquarius/Level II)
- Groups gathered for a structured experience (Capricorn/Level III)
- Groups acting together under a "culture" (Sagittarius/Level IV (theorized[67]))
- A single Other who wants to influence something beyond them—not necessarily you (Scorpio/Level V (theorized))
- A single Other who wants to interact 1:1 with something beyond them—not necessarily you (Libra/Level VI (theorized))
- and so on…

As a general rule, I can pick a dynamic by swapping out these frames. For example, if I want to build up the II-quintiles (17s) in my chart, I'll perform more actions towards single Others in front of groups that talk to each other.

While we're here, let's modify *table 16-6* with a more formulaic approach to unlocking angles. *Table 23-2* reproduces *table 16-6* using more of a systematic formula.

[67] For theorized levels, see the info box "On the behavior of higher harmonics" in Chapter 19. At the time of this writing I have gathered some early statistical data on all harmonic levels I – XII, such that the levels, IV, V, and VI included in the bullet weren't just pulled from thin air. Refer also to the conversation between Geery and Hayden at the end of Chapter 18, the section labeled "Modding by 12."

Table 23-2: Turning up harmonics (by formula)

Harmonic	Name	Symbol	Activate by doing more...	...(for)...	...in front of...	This corresponds to...
1	conjunct	☌	actions	for yourself	nobody in particular	instinctual action
2	opposition	☍	experiencing	for yourself	nobody in particular	self-valuing
3	trine	△	communicating	for yourself	nobody in particular	thinking
4	square	□	wanting or expecting	for yourself	nobody in particular	feeling
5	quintile	⋆	actions	towards another thing	nobody in particular	1:1 interaction
6	sextile	⚹	experiencing	of another thing	nobody in particular	analysis, service
7	septile	✡	communicating	with another thing	nobody in particular	1:1 communication
8	octile	∠	wanting or expecting	of another thing	nobody in particular	steering
9	novile	九	actions	in the faceless world	nobody in particular	image projecting
10	decile	+	experiencing	according to the faceless world	nobody in particular	structuring
11	undecile	U	communicating	in light of the faceless world	nobody in particular	being talked about/around
12	inconjunct	⚻	wanting or expecting	of the faceless world	nobody in particular	imagining, having a mood
13	II-conjunct	☌^{2}	actions	for yourself	people who talk	persona projecting
14	II-opposition	☍^{2}	experiencing	for yourself	people who talk	physicality / values projecting (often judged against ethnic stereotype)
15	II-trine	△^{2}	communicating	for yourself	people who talk	mannerism displaying
16	II-square	□^{2}	wanting or expecting	for yourself	people who talk	emotional disclosure
17	II-quintile	⋆^{2}	actions	towards another thing	people who talk	other-cornering
18	II-sextile	⚹^{2}	experiencing	of another thing	people who talk	rationalizing
19	II-septile	✡^{2}	communicating	with another thing	people who talk	ingroup (comfortably open) communicating
20	II-octile	∠^{2}	wanting or expecting	of another thing	people who talk	showing force
21	II-novile	九^{2}	actions	in the faceless world	people who talk	making a statement
22	II-decile	+^{2}	experiencing	according to the faceless world	people who talk	being assigned a label
23	II-undecile	U^{2}	communicating	in light of the faceless world	people who talk	individuality broadcasting
24	II-inconjunct	⚻^{2}	wanting or expecting	of the faceless world	people who talk	imagination publicizing
25	III-conjunct	☌^{3}	actions	for yourself	groups gathered to hear this	group representing
26	III-opposition	☍^{3}	experiencing	for yourself	groups gathered to hear this	having fans or followers
27	III-trine	△^{3}	communicating	for yourself	groups gathered to hear this	displaying insight
28	III-square	□^{3}	wanting or expecting	for yourself	groups gathered to hear this	morals projecting
29	III-quintile	⋆^{3}	actions	towards another thing	groups gathered to hear this	showing charisma
30	III-sextile	⚹^{3}	experiencing	of another thing	groups gathered to hear this	critiquing, exhibitionism
31	III-septile	✡^{3}	communicating	with another thing	groups gathered to hear this	networking, hosting
32	III-octile	∠^{3}	wanting or expecting	of another thing	groups gathered to hear this	suspense making, allure projecting
33	III-novile	九^{3}	actions	in the faceless world	groups gathered to hear this	entertaining, group rallying

34	III-decile	+^{3}	experiencing	according to the faceless world	groups gathered to hear this	being labeled synonymous with an idea, epitomizing, being a master
35	III-undecile	U^3	communicating	in light of the faceless world	groups gathered to hear this	getting massively talked about, raising questions among the masses, displaying genius
36	III-inconjunct	⊼^{3}	wanting or expecting	of the faceless world	groups gathered to hear this	looking aimless, dream-inspiring
				(Theorized angles)		
37	IV-conjunct	☌^{4}	actions	for yourself	[amidst] a culture that values this	justifying, accommodating norms
38	IV-opposition	☍^{4}	experiencing	for yourself	[amidst] a culture that values this	health regimen, reinforcement of habit
47	IV-undecile	U^4	communicating	in light of the faceless world	[amidst] a culture that values this	having an outlook
48	IV-inconjunct	⊼^{4}	wanting or expecting	of the faceless world	[amidst] a culture that values this	reminding others of something else

Situations are the contexts which surround us. (These are like houses)

The situations we find ourselves in can also be thought of as dynamics, though they happen to us and around us instead of being the result of our actions. Situations can be considered a kind of faceless tool, except they call for a whole behavioral response rather than the response of a primary planet. Roughly, the situations we encounter correspond to the houses in our chart as well as determine which level of harmonic we're on. This is already reflected in *table 16-2*, so there isn't much to add here.

Events have self-motivated, changeable forms of expression. (These are like personalities / collections of signs)

We'll consider events to be things that happen which produce multiple levels of experience in our minds. Pretty much anything can be an event—including faceless tools, dynamics, and situations. But with events we're not afraid to assign an entire personality. In this chapter, other people and projects will be treated as events. The significance of this lies in the idea that personalities will consist of a more complex arrangement of planets, angles, and houses in their own right, and can't always be counted on to influence us in the same way; instead, how events influence us will depend on how we interact with them. Events will be considered stable-ish, however, to the extent that their default behaviors for each of their basic qualities (planets) will live in a stable sign. It is here that we begin our exploration of the astrological influence of things we wouldn't have thought had charts. We'll investigate the most significant ways in which such events affect us.

And Hayden said to Geery, Alright Sir, today I present you with your most challenging philosophical question yet. Are you ready for it?

Go ahead, hit me.

Okay here goes. Can a person do synastry with a false date? That is, can he grow and evolve himself against an event using an inaccurate birth time? If so, then doesn't that go against astrology as a potential science? If not, then how is it that events like work projects can have multiple dates but still produce reasonable charts no matter which date is used?

Geery pondered for a while. Hmm, let me get back to you on that one.

Sure, Hayden replied confidently, having finally appeared to stump Geery. We have plenty of time.

What makes a role model: III-deciles, progress through the harmonics, and III-noviles

The III-decile: masterful

Role model status depends on how a person defines what it means to be the boss in their own chart. This is the purview of III-deciles. How we arrive at this is actually not trivial and required a lot of side research which I won't report here. Just know that, where you associate boss-ness in your chart, you have the potential to be a boss. And so do others. Accordingly, you'll tend to find role-models in those people who've demonstrated a natural or commanding talent in those pairs for which you have a III-decile or in the pairs related to such pairs. So if you have a [Jupiter-Selene] III-decile for popular demand, you *might* find a role model in someone with a [Jupiter-Selene] conjunct, III-decile, or similarly masterful angle OR you might find one of these angles in someone's [Sun-Ascendant] for being welcomed by the group—a related function. Unfortunately, role-model status isn't very easy to determine. Areas of your own mastery are. While much of our choice of role model will depend on life circumstances, who wrote the history books, and who taught us that history, our own set of resonant pairs for the III-decile remain pretty stable in what they show to be our potential for mastery. Read these for a good look at who you are as a figure recognized as being in command of their craft.

Stepping up from one harmonic to the next

III-deciles aren't the end of the role-model story, however. If you stare at your chart long enough you'll notice something interesting: Your execution of one angle tends to lay the foundation for your experience of the next angle. That is, the more your display your III-deciles (34), the more inclined people are to see you as a pioneer or genius (III-undecile, 35). The more pioneering you are (III-undecile, 35), the more people are inclined to see you as memorable (III-inconjunct, 36). The more memorable you are, the more people are inclined to back you up (III-conjunct, ~~37~~ – 12→25 for wraparound). Relatedly, the more you use your III-noviles to direct audiences (33), the more opportunity you get to display your III-deciles as a master (34). It turns out that 30s through 35s can all be viewed as constituting a chain of learning, where your initial skills in critical analysis ultimately lead to mastery under a different face:

- Displaying critical analysis (III-sextile / 30 resonant pairs) leads to

  ⬇

- Opportunities to spread your ideas to others across a network (III-septile / 31) which leads to

  ⬇

- Opportunities to integrate your knowledge in a way not visible to others (III-octile / 32) which leads to

  ⬇

- The ability to teach groups (III-novile / 33) which leads to

  ⬇

- The ability to be seen as a master (III-decile / 34) which leads to

  ⬇

- Status as being prolific in a field (III-undecile / 35)

Now although I've laid out the chain of events in a way that seems to flow nicely and the data do actually support this chain, the reality is that most of us end up facing obstructions along chains like this—usually because we lack the attitude, access, or allies to proceed. Thus you find yourself stuck airing your III-sextile critiques to your circle of III-septile friends on Facebook, preventing new lessons from being learned. Or you find yourself so focused on masterfully controlling a particular kind of situation that you cease to be curious about what lies beyond your cage. And genius status is prevented. In looking at the charts, I found that it's pretty safe to conclude that resonant III-noviles and III-deciles are the best indicator of masterful teachers and masterful masters respectively (both in yourself and in those whom you admire), but the path to mastery is often riddled with strange hang-ups—many of which can be traced back to basic human self-emphasis. While we find it easy enough to hold role models, most of us don't have enough motivation to teach or rally others in order to reach our roles models' level (33→34). While many of us want to be remembered for something significant, we're often too stifled by regular demands to indulge the curiosity demanded of memorable skill (35→36). And so we have the pitfalls that come with each harmonic, preventing an easy flow of ability from one level to the next.

Table 23-3: Ways to get stuck on a harmonic

Harmonic	Name	Symbol	Basic behavior	How to get stuck on this harmonic	Clues you get showing you are stuck (How others will treat you)
1	conjunct	☌	instinctual action	being too action heavy, uncontrollable; not asking whether your actions are actually right	others learn to deny you support, will remain on the sidelines whether you win or lose; others won't respond with excitement, encouragement, or even curiosity when good things happen to you. (They seem unaffected)
2	opposition	☍	self-valuing	being too self-serving, materialistic or hedonistic	others will encourage you to think about people or things besides yourself
3	trine	△	thinking	overthinking, opinionating too much	others will argue with you or get tired of listening to you; either way denying you a listening ear
4	square	□	feeling	being too emotional, pushy	others will avoid your smothering, rebelling against even your best efforts to help them
5	quintile	⚹	1:1 interaction	being to egotistical, craving the spotlight	others will typically be okay with this, but will be less active in helping you get things done
6	sextile	∗	analysis, service	worrying too much, overanalyzing	other's won't take your concerns as seriously, will avoid letting you in on things keep from upsetting you
7	septile	✡	1:1 communication	holding others hostage in conversation, clinging too heavily to other's feedback	this is usually not that bad; but you tire others out, they delay responding to you or avoid contacting you with small news (for concern you will trap them for hours)
8	octile	∠	steering	having a power complex, not being satisfied with other's genuine efforts	others will avoid friendship connection with you, thinking you'll eat them for the smallest reason
9	novile	九	image projecting	hyper-projecting, being addicted to moving on without slowing down	others will hesitate to risk settling with you; some will be extra clingy
10	decile	+	structuring	demanding order and control	this typically works well, but others will struggle to relax with you and will seem to make even more errors
11	undecile	∪	being talked about/around	being super-surrounded by media, music, and information	others will dump any news on you, true or not, meaningful or not
12	inconjunct	⚻	imagining, having a mood	daydreaming too much, getting lost in illusion	others will patronize you, scold you, treat you like a spacey child
13	II-conjunct	$☌^2$	persona projecting	being too concerned with your image	others will more likely be false with you, showing you the face they think they want you to see

14	II-opposition	☍^{2}	physicality / values projecting (often judged against ethnic stereotype)	needing too much physical companionship, too much evidence of approval	others will seek company besides yours, cheat; steal from you (literally or time/energy-wise); as you supply more than they demand, they take you for granted
15	II-trine	△^{2}	mannerism displaying	over-talking a room	others will avoid casual conversation with you, thinking you will run them over
16	II-square	□^{2}	emotional disclosure	getting too close, being too emotionally open with others	this is often endearing, but others will disappoint you more with their unreliability; people who want more closeness than you are actually willing to give often eventually find cause to hate you. (They thought you were really into them, but you were just being your normal nurturing self)
17	II-quintile	⋆^{2}	other-cornering	needing to constantly dominate others, squash all oppressors	others will talk behind your back, cheat your influence; after you are gone, they hurry to divide up what you built, remember you for your sins, and shed no tears in undoing your name on the grapevine. (I call this one the Rockefeller—a doer of many deeds which are ultimately squished into "greed" in many a common mind. Contrast this with the Che!—a leader/hero/role model whose socially positive display of this same angle leads others to assign a II-sextile/long-range halo over his head regardless of the actual nature of his work)
18	II-sextile	⚹^{2}	rationalizing	over-rationalizing	others will avoid engaging you over your favorite topic, treating you as a know it all
19	II-septile	✡^{2}	ingroup (comfortably open) communicating	being heavily dependent on friend groups	this is common and typically acceptable; you rise and fall more easily with friends here; more of an issue for strongly independent types (who end up fighting with their own more often)
20	II-octile	∠^{2}	showing force	needing to wage an unending war against something, anything	people will find you entertaining to watch, but volatile; will contribute words but not action to assist you
21	II-novile	九^{2}	making a statement	constantly needing to make yourself seen	others will attempt to eliminate you as a competitor for their stage
22	II-decile	+^{2}	being assigned a label	being overly work focused	others more easily annoyed with you, will attempt to cut you down in light of your apparent superiority; still others will cling to you jealously for their own security
23	II-undecile	U^{2}	individuality broadcasting	needing to publicize how different you are	people will dismiss you as arrogant, a troublemaker; some will attempt to "put you in your place" via decisions made in your absence, or inexplicable rejection of ideas which you believe to be sound
24	II-inconjunct	⚻^{2}	imagination publicizing	staying hooked on your imagined realities	others will encourage you to give up your goals in favor of "real things"
25	III-conjunct	☌^{3}	group representing	needing to constantly be right	people will not engage you over serious issues; more ambitious types will attempt to crush you with all they have
26	III-opposition	☍^{3}	having fans or followers	living to please your fans	this is sought after, but invites people who use you for various status-enhancing reasons
27	III-trine	△^{3}	displaying insight	needing to have the last word	others will intentionally exclude you from their affairs; you tire more easily when displaying this
28	III-square	□^{3}	morals projecting	needing to push your moral agenda on others	others will amplify the areas in which you are imperfect or hypocritical
29	III-quintile	⋆^{3}	showing charisma	needing to brag about what you have	others will be more easily jealous of you, will minimize your accomplishments in their own eyes

30	III-sextile	⚹^{3}	critiquing, exhibitionism	needing to criticize	others will avoid talking to you, avoid asking you for anything
31	III-septile	✡^{3}	networking, hosting	being super-networked	this is common and often sought by many people; those who want deeper exchange will play around and hand you superficiality instead; people flake out more, and will generally need the same lessons repeated to them; if you want to trade your popularity for effective power over the people you have, there is often a struggle to transition since this group is known for its "niceness," not its ability to lay down the law.
32	III-octile	∠^{3}	suspense making, allure projecting	not checking your own natural power among those overwhelmed by it	others will be foolish, thoughtless, savage around you; more ambitious types will act to own you, dominate you; others will simply kowtow to you, genuflecting slavishly before Your Royal Highness...without adding any significant value to your life
33	III-novile	九^3	entertaining, group rallying	demanding center stage rather than using position to help others	others are more likely to be sneaky with you, disrespect you, using your image but broadcasting their critique loudly elsewhere
34	III-decile	+^{3}	being labeled synonymous with an idea, epitomizing, being a master	demanding perfection	others will avoid interaction with you in your specialty area, be more easily intimidated, neglect to warn you of problems, or fail you more easily when you trust them; more ambitious types deny you entry, or set you up for failure / trouble
35	III-undecile	U^3	getting massively talked about, raising questions among the masses, displaying genius	being too eccentric, iconoclastic without actual openness to new experience	others will consistently feel weird around you, shun you; you attract other weird people more easily and struggle to make inroads with normal people
36	III-inconjunct	⚻^{3}	looking aimless, dream-inspiring	being stuck on the thought of a goal without actually pursuing it	others will eventually cut off their offers of support, replacing it with a nod only

Table 23-3: Things we do to get stuck on a harmonic. A person can display multiple issues above. These patterns of response apply to living and dead, person and organization, regardless of rank.

III-noviles: Great teachers

There is a certain level of sacrifice that comes with teaching. While you're busy making sure that other people get it, you're spending less effort on perfection of your own craft. Fortunately, what you are great at teaching and what you are great at *doing* typically aren't the same—mainly because active teaching is primarily communicative while active mastery is primarily reputation-generating. So telling people you're a master doesn't make you a master. Might as well tell people something they can use. In the charts of your role models as well as in your own, you'll find that the III-noviles are the pairs for which others actually come to you. THEN they give you the "master" title based on what they receive over time. Resist the temptation to go for the destination without ever setting out on the journey. Role models aren't just determined by the labels they *get* $_{\text{III-decile}}$, but by the impressions they *give* as well $_{\text{III-novile}}$.

What determines another's ability to teach you: the Interaction cocktail, Pluto, and memorable planets

III-deciles and III-noviles—though they indicate mastery and great teaching ability respectively—are actually not the main determinant of an event's influence on you. Instead, your willingness to accept an event's influence depends on 1) whether you're doing so because you actually interacted with the event and experienced its many dimensions for yourself, 2) whether you're doing so mainly through what you heard about the event and its social effects, or 3) whether you've simply picked out certain qualities to hold on to. For events (including people) with whom you actually interacted, the Interaction Purpose cocktail back in Chapter 20 will show you what you broadly take home from an event, its III-deciles and III-noviles revealing where that event commonly displays its clearest influence on those who follow it; thus the Interaction Purpose cocktail says more about why *you* have connected with the event while III-deciles and III-noviles say more about where people in general (not just you) broadly see the event as an example. Meanwhile, events and projects to which you have been exposed on the basis of social merit will mainly influence you through the dwarf planet of social pressure, Pluto. Events and projects which are neither actively personifiable nor socially elevated will influence you through the planets you find most noteworthy in them.

You learn from more complex, local events via the Interaction Purpose cocktail

When you are in a position to experience the actual personality of an event (or even if you've simply studied it deeply and feel a strong affinity towards it), you can be influenced by your actual synastry with it. The Interaction Purpose cocktail works mainly on people and projects which can both influence you and be influenced by you. So unfortunately things like books, video games, dead people and stuff you've heard on the news don't typically fall under this category unless you've become so familiar with them that you can reinterpret their influence upon you across constantly shifting levels. To use the Interaction Purpose cocktail, you really need to be able to have a two-way, reasonably complex interaction with the event. You should find it simple enough to tell which events qualify for this kind of exchange, though. Use this combination of planets to read how an immediately accessible, reasonably personality-infused event like an ongoing news conflict, pet, or another person continues to affect you.

You learn from noteworthy, distantly simplified events via Pluto

An event's Pluto influences its interactant in three ways: via the event's regular chart [Pluto-MC] angle in which it is known to be powerful, via its synastric [Pluto-(Other's planet)] pairs, and via its sign and duodecanate for determining what kind of influencer it is. I'll address these in order.

[Pluto-Midheaven]: a reputation for power

In a regular chart, [Pluto-MC] shows where a thing is known $_{\text{Midheaven}}$ to be powerful $_{\text{Pluto}}$. The angle that describes this pair basically shows the realm in which the thing most easily impresses those who view it. When viewing the chart of a business or project especially, look at this pair to see where the project aligns with the standards of the current society. It is here that this event exercises some of its strongest influence over you too. If, for example, you have a project with a [Pluto-MC] III-trine, that project is most likely to impress people with the insight it provides into a particular issue. The People's Republic of China chart (October 1, 1949, 3:01pm; Beijing) has a [Pluto-MC] II-trine suggesting that when it speaks among nations, those nations typically give their undivided attention. The United States' chart (July 4, 1776, 2:13am; Philadelphia) has a [Pluto-MC] II-decile for being in command of its "career" as a country. Given the passage of centuries and the eventual relegation of events to the history books, empires and projects alike still hold a relationship to the standards of their day. The [Pluto-MC] angle reflects such a relationship, allowing such events to continue affecting others far beyond their lifespan. It's the bigger standard and not the event that matters here.

[Pluto-(Other's planet)]: where the event's power standard affects the various behaviors of its interactant

When you want to ask how an event affects different dimensions of your own behavior, synastry with that event's Pluto is the way to go. Broadly, the event's Pluto works like a frozen source of societal pressure which pushes you to do more with each planet, so using *table 19-9* to read each of your planets against the event's Pluto column will give you a broad idea of how that event can push you to express yourself in different ways. This is especially useful for doing synastry with plain old calendar dates.

A note on transits and daily horoscopes

In a certain branch of astrology which I've elected to bypass in *HBS* and *FSA*, people **look at the chart of the current day and interpret how these will affect you**. Such **transit astrology** tends to pay attention slower moving planets like Sun through Pluto and ignore minor planets, points and fast movers like the Moon, Fortune, Ceres, and so on. Transit astrology is essentially a cousin of synastry which treats the day as a personality-infused event that affects us, except that it focuses on the angles and signs in the day's "self chart" rather than the relationship of the day to specific people. Understandably, since the person doing transit astrology won't usually have access to the charts of everyone she's reading for, the interpretations she produces favor an interesting style of council: Rather than tell you what will happen *to you* today, the transit makes more sense when it advises you to "be on the lookout" for something. Transit reading for *you* is easier to do when I actually have your chart in front of me. Transit reading for the day's own characteristics is easier to do when I only have the day's chart (and not yours), coupled with the ability to describe that day as if it were some dude prowling around you. It is because of practical considerations like these that daily horoscopes are both very general/vagueish as well as notoriously "kind of accurate." We don't pay attention to every person we meet, nor will we always pay attention to what kind of day we're experiencing. Even among people whom we do meet, we won't generally pay attention to every aspect of their personalities. Accordingly, most transit traits can be safely ignored as easily as people-traits can be. People and events are, after all, frozen transits for the day of their creation.

Only among the more powerful planets do we find a consistent ability of external events to influence us. And when the event we're interacting with is more of a slave to what society now says about it than what it can actively do on its own, the list of most powerful planets tend to include Pluto, Saturn, and the Midheaven—those which back us into a corner through social restriction. Thus these are the ones to "look out for" in reading the synastry of experientially distant objects with yourself. We ignore the Midheaven with transits, though, since it rolls around the chart way too quickly in a single day. Jupiter, Neptune, and Uranus (being excessive and information-heavy in an already information heavy world) are not only harder to spot but also (being more positive than Pluto and Saturn on average) harder to care about. Animals like humans are predisposed to respond more immediately to negative events than positive ones.

So Pluto stands out among those planets which outside events can use to affect you the most. The exceptions here occur where you're dealing with events that are expressly spiritual/artistic (Neptunian) or information-based (Uranian) in nature. Then Pluto may not be so telling.

At the end of the day, our possession of 36 different angle families allows us to look at event charts in two ways: either through synastry with major aspects only alongside a bunch of event planets or through synastry with the 36 harmonics and mainly Pluto. Your choice is purely a matter of personal taste. Just know that days, projects, and people long gone can be subjected to this kind of reading, where you can find out quite a bit about how these things influence you.

Pluto's sign puts the event in a particular behavioral class

Before writing this chapter, I thought about what I really wanted to learn from studying data on events and historical figures. As a personal priority, I concluded it would be valuable to understand why my role models are who they are. What is it that the psychic Edgar Cayce, Joseph Stalin, and Benedict Spinoza have in common? The answer turns out to be the same thing held in common with the Buddha and many other "world builders:" a Pluto around 22 Taurus. Here is where I wish someone would update the Sabian Symbols and fixed stars discussed in *FSA*. The sign and duodecanate of Pluto in a chart seems to tell us what the generation of people surrounding an event basically valued.[68] Just as an event's Pluto makes angles to your planets, an event's Pluto has to sit somewhere along the wheel in order to make those angles. Pluto in 20°–22.5° Taurus corresponds to the Capricorn duodecanate of Taurus, self-valuing $_{\text{Taurus}}$ a world-structure $_{\text{Capricorn}}$. This is where people build their identity against a larger system of boundary-making in the world. Extending this concept, we find that Pluto's sign shows very, very broadly what Earth-centered[69] category of influencer an event falls under in general. This is the means through which an event gets its foot in the door as a possible influencer to you, determining the class under which you place them in your own life.

You learn from regular, distantly simplified events via whatever planets stand out to you

What if you're interacting with an event which isn't really famous or historically notable, isn't immediately living-personifiable, isn't a source of very complex interaction, and yet isn't so simple as to be mashed into a relative chart with you? This might apply to your relationship to the recently deceased or to forebears in your genealogy, to certain semi-human things like a chatbot you've trained or a website you've designed with multiple kinds of apps. Such entities as this can be thought of as having charts where only certain planets stand out. In these cases you would just do regular synastry and confine your investigation to the planets of greatest interest. A programmer might only look at the Uranus of the program he's written; an advertiser might look only at the Midheaven of her new ad campaign. If this sounds contrived, believe me it is. Goalless synastry with projects is a lot like dumping the contents of the whole junk drawer on the floor and picking out all of the metal things; you may be able to read something, but who's to say that the things you didn't read were worthless? In practice, I wouldn't recommend this process of "partial chart reading" unless you're really curious to know only one partial dimension of a multidimensional thing. Still, the technique does exist and is available for you to use.

On the use of false dates[70]

You wanna know something weird?

What is it?

I thought about the question you asked the other day while studying synastry with events, and in my search for a good sample event, came across a pretty convincing answer: You *can* do synastry with false dates.

Rrreally? Hayden turned his head sideways with a perplexed look. Not that I expected you to answer either way, but why would you conclude that?

First let me tell you about the example I discovered, then I'll give you my ideas about why false dates work.

Hayden remained quiet.

---

68 Recall from the previous book that each sign can be chopped into twelve pieces of 2.5° each. Each piece is called a duodecanate, begins with the sign you're in, and flows in order until it reaches the sign just before the sign you're in. Here, Aries gets chopped into 12 and the first 0°-2.5° of Aries is the Aries duodecanate of Aries (Ari_{Ari}) This is instinctual expression of action. 2.5°-5° Aries is Ari_{Tau}, Instictual expression of bodily feeling. 5°-7.5° Aries is Ari_{Gem}, Instinctual expression of thoughts. Since duodecanates start with the sign they're in, though, the first 0°-2.5° of Taurus would be Tau_{Tau}, bodily feeling of self-value. 5°-7.5° Taurus would be Tau_{Can}, bodily feeling of wants. And so it goes. 20°-22.5° Aquarius would be Aqu_{Lib}, social information regarding 1:1 communication. Can you see why?

69 "Earth-centered" means an event is interpreted according to its relation to the seasons on Earth, since "22 Taurus" only retains its meaning under the tropical system, not the sidereal system.

70 The account in this section actually happened while I was writing this chapter. Geery's explanation of things is actually an explanation of my own experience with a particular "false date."

The Bible, King James Version. I looked up the publication date and found that it was some time in 1611. What date and time, you ask? Nobody knows. But it seems to have been accepted by people who have the power to declare such things that the official publication date is May 2, 1611. This is just a date that folks have picked in the absence of detailed information.

Okay.

I wanted to look at a chart for the King James Bible but, wouldn't you know, lacked a good birth time and birth place for the work. It was, however, a 7-year effort begun in 1604 somewhere outside of London as I understand it. So I picked a birthplace: London. And a birth time: noon. I then set the chart date accordingly. Since noon is the middle of the day, it sits as a good average for any event with an unknown birth time.

Okay, Hayden followed intently.

As soon as I looked at the chart, three things impressed me. First, Pluto is conjunct the Midheaven, making the KJV Bible naturally powerful. Second, its Bacchus, Uranus, and Node are all conjunct around the 10th or 11th houses, making the project seem destined to gather folks for support and talk as a matter of social reputation. Third, it has a Vesta-Neptune conjunct early in the chart, in Virgo. This indicates concentration on spirituality in the style of analysis. But none of this is weird.

Okay.

Here's the weird part. The Vesta-Neptune conjunct is the first appearance of planets in the "false" KJV chart going around the wheel counterclockwise from the Ascendant (which is how we typically trace lifespan). I talked about this in my previous work with Katha. After this conjunct, there's nothing much going on for the next 80-something degrees until Juno shows up. So landing at this conjunct 25° after the Ascendant I thought to myself, *Wouldn't it be interesting if there were a really important part of the Bible that appeared at the 25°/360 mark, early on in the work?* And so now I ask you as a layman, off the top of your head, what's the most important thing in the first part of the Bible which overrides all other sections?

Well, I'm not very religious, but I'd guess it was the Ten Commandments.

That's what I guessed. Now my copy of the Bible happens to have 799 pages, so I took 25 ÷ 360 to get the percentage into to the wheel where this [Neptune-Vesta] conjunct landed, then multiplied that by the 799 to get which page I should investigate for any interesting stuff. The page turned out to be 55. Keep in mind I'm using round numbers for everything though all this. Anyway, I actually didn't find a thing of major interest on page 55.

Oh?

Nope. But guess what was on pages 53 and 54?

Don't tell me—

Yes, indeed. The 10 Commandments.

Hm. That *is* weird.

And on page 419 / 189° where Saturn brings its structure? The beginning of Proverbs. Still there are even more correspondences, but within 4° at the top of the chart—the 73% mark of the KJV Bible, you have Selene as an indicator of perfection. It's off by a few pages (and who knows if I should have read the version *with* the Apocrypha rather than the version I read without it), but on 605/799, the 76% mark, the New Testament begins. And then we wait another 20% for more stuff to happen. At the Uranus and Node we have the teachings of Jesus in Luke. At Mars we have the Acts of the Apostles. Earlier at Venus we have Song of Solomon, Ecclesiates, and Isaiah, another high point in the Bible. And in the last degree we have the Royal Star Regulus beginning Revelation. That star also lines up with the KJV's royal birth under King James. The lineup isn't perfect, but the chart seems pretty legit. If you put the Apocrypha back in, the middle lineups change a little, but not so much as to kill the correspondences around the chart.

Interesting, I'm pretty sure that people who looked at your correspondences could accuse you of reverse engineering, but—

Look man, all I did was guess a birth date, time and place, and note what I saw. It wasn't inconsistent with the theory I've worked out so far.

—What I was about to say was that, reverse engineered or not, I imagine that the probability of even the May 2 part working out randomly would be…a little…lower than my skepticism would support. Although I find your "correspondences" to be on the fantastic side, having not seen them myself, I guess I'll just take your word. But why can people get away with this? Why can we just pick-a-date and have it work?

I don't think it's as easy as just "picking a date," Geery replied slightly seriously. The date and time have to make sense to you. For this I like to fall back on my own personal definition of **belief**: **A man believes what he steers his actions around the existence of**. If I believe you're actually standing here, I won't just try to walk right through you. If I believe the ground is solid, I won't work to balance myself while standing on it. Similarly, people who believe in God select their behaviors against the things that God would want whenever such behaviors are big enough to warrant a higher moral reference. But this doesn't necessarily count for regular or non-morally related acts. People who disbelieve in God make bigger moral decisions with known disregard for what a ruling personality would want them to do. Now granted, this is only a definition of belief which I apply to myself, but the definition does explain why you can't just argue to "convince" someone into believing what they don't believe in. To change one's belief, you need to change the way they assume certain things worth behaving around. For a person who stands upon the solid ground that is God, trying to convince them otherwise is futile. As for the person who, through his acts, walks right through "the wall" that would be a god: If he doesn't believe, he just doesn't believe. To argue with them is to argue with yourself.

Hayden looked at Geery with a frown, seeing that the scientist's digression was probably going somewhere.

What I'm saying is that you can only use "false dates" if you *believe* those dates to be reasonably true—thus steering your actions around those dates. I truly believe that my birth certificate shows the correct birth time and not some incorrect minute, so my birth certificate works as the most authoritative source for my birth date—even if the doctor fudged the time between my first emergence and completed delivery. I truly believe that when the United States decides to "spring forward" or "fall back," all of society's coordinated behavior is changed. I believe that the tropical zodiac is a real thing even though the sidereal remainder of the Universe says it isn't. I believe this blabber called the English language is meaningful. I believe when I see the color red, you see the color red. And so I in my belief proceed to steer further actions around things which not only *might be* false, but in the case of Daylight Savings and the tropical zodiac, actually *are false* at least part of the time. When we "pick a date" we're not just telling a story, we're giving form to an otherwise formless idea which we know full well actually gets responded to. By my personal definition of belief, if I respond to it, I believe it is there. Even if it only exists in my own thoughts.

Hmm. So you're saying thoughts create reality?

No. I'm saying the things against which a person acts ARE his *personal* reality. In my world you, Hayden are reasonable enough to talk to about this stuff, so I talk to you as such. That's my reality. But your enemy may think you're completely unreasonable. That's their reality. Of course, certain things like gravity and bodily feeling are immediate and pervasive enough to basically be *everyone's* reality. And this is where things like "truth" and "science" do their best work.

I see. So your birth date for the King James Bible is…

the only date that was widely enough agreed upon, by people whose expertise I think higher than mine, supplemented by my own assumptions about the "average" place where it was worked on and the "average time" for its publication date. For events that unfold over time (like the delivery of a baby) you can use the start time, end time, or average. It all depends on the custom you find most reasonable.

Hayden was quiet.

I find it weird that birth times are basically endpoints for the delivery process while birth itself is a start point for the "living" process. In one case we favor the end. In another, we favor the beginning. Is either one false? Only the point which you believe in less—in cases where there is no more widely agreed upon consensus. I still find it amazing that Mao could just "declare" a new China and all of a sudden October 1, 1949 becomes the correct chart.

Relatedly, you may be interested to know that a person's death date can, in some cases, be just as important as their birth date to the extent that their death constitutes a significant enough social event. We run into this issue with one of the commonly presumed death dates of the Buddha.

Hayden continued to fix his gaze upon the horizon. So my beliefs write reality in situations where the rest of the world hasn't bothered to write anything. And group actions can write a false reality onto a real one if that group has enough influence. As with Daylight Savings Time.

Pretty much. So entire nations can be wrong. Entire cultures can be wrong. And entire families can make a demon out of one perfectly normal person. Working with the charts of events with foggy start dates has a lot more to do with psychology and a lot less to do with "truth."

Hayden pondered for a while before replying. So if anyone ever wanted to do a chart with the King James Bible and you had the chance to recommend a birth time for it, would you recommend your own guessed chart knowing that it was probably inaccurate in the absolute sense?

Yes I would, but on the condition that they know it's a guess. When I calculate charts that make sense to me but have no basis or contradiction elsewhere in the world, I call such charts "Adventure charts" or "Estimate charts." The whimsical names come from a particular chart I calculated long ago involving three Magi, a search for a special astronomical event, and a baby; I prefer the word "adventure" because the scientist in me automatically disbelieves "theorized," "rectified," "alternative," and "hypothesized" things—none of which are certain. An adventure isn't certain either, but carries with it the hope of interesting dynamics worth looking at. "We're on a quest to find the true nature of a thing, and this is the best we have so far," is what that word says. My adventure charts always have interesting stuff in them. "Theorized charts" are dry and offer no motivation for me to use them.

So now we need "motivation" to get at truth? Some scientist you are, Hayden joked.

Heh, I'm only human. Curiosity is cool in and of itself. I'd be lying if I told you that I live for something as boring as "truth" alone.

Evolving your skills using events and projects

In *FSA* I explain how you can follow the lifespan of an event by simply moving counterclockwise around the chart starting from the Ascendant. This is actually the order in which objects rise above the horizon for the day you're looking at, and so serves as a decent reflection of major milestones associated with the event. I've actually found such a technique to be one of the easiest ways to follow your own lifespan. Additionally, books, movies, and other story-like events are especially amenable to this kind of reading. One of the first major pieces of information we get out of a chart for projects in particular is how that project unfolds over the course of its milestones. For projects which are your own, you can use this cycle-based reading to estimate whether you've even picked an appropriate start date in the first place. Once you have chosen a good birth chart for your project all that's left is to read its effects on you. At this point the astrology of dates, projects, and dead people become the same thing: mostly one-way reads whose effects depend on what society suggests their "type of thing" can do.

The Non-living Influencer formula

For any reasonably interactive event you can name, there is a way to read how such an event comes to impress you. Below is the formula.

Sign & duodecanate[71] of Pluto $_{event}$	Pluto $_{event}$-MC $_{event}$	Resonant III-deciles $_{event}$
Interaction Purpose cocktail $_{you\text{-}event}$	Pluto $_{event}$-(Other Planets $_{you}$)	Resonant III-noviles $_{event}$

> The event is most broadly a [Sign & duodecanate of Pluto $_{event}$] kind of influencer. It teaches others most effectively through its display of [Resonant III-noviles $_{event}$] and can be viewed as masterful in its [Resonant III-deciles $_{event}$]. It's most powerful quality in general lies in its [Pluto $_{event}$-MC $_{event}$], where it has the ability to move me forward in many ways which include [Pluto $_{event}$-(Other planets $_{me}$)]. As far as my own purpose for interacting with it, my reasons are rooted in this: [Interaction Purpose cocktail $_{you\text{-}event}$].

I warn you that the above formula becomes *much* longer than it looks once you start plugging in multiple angles, but covers most of what you most easily gain from a particular non-living event.

Example using the Non-living Influencer formula

Brooke Foss Westcott (1/12/1825 – 7/27/1901, Birmingham, UK) was a British bishop and theologian whose work included translation and (some say controversial) textual criticism of the Bible and then existing versions of its books. A look at his life reveals a person who, regardless of opposition to his attempts to improve upon the consistency of the holy text, did indeed believe he was doing the right thing in the right way. In the following example, we won't be able to get into Westcott's mind regarding his thoughts on the King James Version of the Bible (KJV), but we will get a good opportunity to practice using our Non-living Influencer formula on both a deceased person and a project, neither of which had exact birth information at the time of this writing.

This example is written using a cousin of the blind method where, during writing, I have little information regarding Westcott's actual views on the KJV. Accounts from people who were actually around during his lifetime tend to run from one biased extreme to the other. But it doesn't matter. The aim is to use the Non-living Influencer formula to see if its basic conclusions align with what we would expect from the tiny description above.

[71] See footnote 68.

The Non-living Influencer formula looks like this:

Sign & duodecanate of Pluto $_{\text{event}}$	Pluto $_{\text{event}}$-MC $_{\text{event}}$	Resonant III-deciles $_{\text{event}}$
Interaction Purpose cocktail $_{\text{you-event}}$	Pluto $_{\text{event}}$-(Other Planets $_{\text{you}}$)	Resonant III-noviles $_{\text{event}}$

1. It looks like the first piece of information we'll need is the event's (KJV's) Pluto sign and duodecanate. Let's look at its wheel for this.

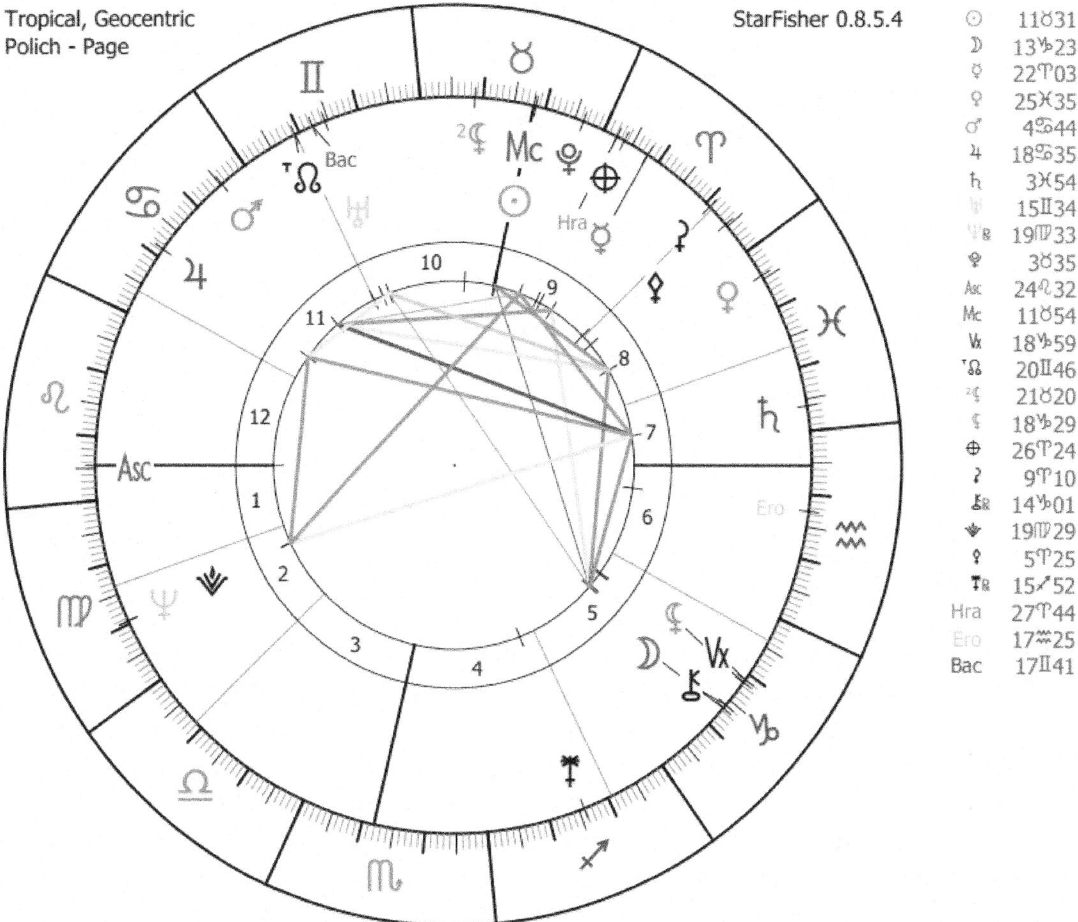

We can see that Pluto is located at 3°35' Taurus. This is the second duodecanate of Taurus, Tau$_{\text{Gem}}$: bodily feeling about what one communicates. Since the Bible doesn't really have a body though, we'll say this is more like self-identification $_{\text{Taurus}}$ with the words it sends forth $_{\text{Gemini}}$. (Remember, Gemini sends communication outwards, while Libra shares it back and forth with an interactant. The KJV insists $_{\text{Pluto}}$ on being a one-way communicator: *TO* you, not from you.)

2. Next, we'll need the event's [Pluto-MC] angle as well as its family of III-deciles and III-noviles. We get this from KJV's Angle view.

☉ 12♉	☉																								
☽ 13♑	△	☽																							
☿ 22♈	⚹^{2}	U	☿																						
♀ 26♓	∠	Q	☍^{2}	♀																					
♂ 5♋	∠^{2}	✡^{2}	Q	U	♂																				
♃ 19♋	□^{2}	U^3	Q^3	□^{2}	☍^{3}	♃																			
♄ 4♓	□^{2}	✡	△^{2}	Q^2	△	⊡	♄																		
♅ 16♊	九^2	✡	∠^{2}	九	✡^{2}	U	∠^{3}	♅																	
♆ 20♍	☍^{2}	✡^{2}	⊥^{2}	Q^3	⚻^{2}	⚹	U	U^2	♆																
♇ 4♉	☌	☌^{2}	✡^{3}	✡^{2}	⚹	⚻^{2}	⚹	Q^2	⊡	♇															
Asc 25♌	✡	☌^{2}	△	Q^3	⚻^{3}	⊥	✡^{2}	九^2	☍^{2}	☌^{2}	Asc														
Mc 12♉	☌	△	⚹^{2}	∠	⊥^{3}	△^{3}	□^{2}	U	☍^{2}	☌	✡	Mc													
Vx 19♑	□^{2}	☌	✡^{3}	△^{3}	☌^{2}	☍	∠	∠^{3}	△	⚻^{2}	Q	□^{2}	Vx												
^{T}☊ 21♊	九	□^{2}	⚹	九^2	☍^{3}	☌^{2}	△^{3}	☌	□	U^2	Q^2	☌^{4}	✡^{2}	^{T}☊											
^{2}⚸ 21♉	☌	☍^{2}	☌^{3}	☌^{2}	☌^{3}	✡^{2}	☍^{2}	△^{2}	△	∠^{2}	✡^{3}	☌	△	⚻	^{2}⚸										
⚸ 18♑	□^{2}	☌	U^2	□^{2}	☌^{2}	☍	∠	⊥^{2}	△	⚻^{2}	Q	□^{2}	☌	✡	△	⚸									
⊕ 26♈	⚻^{2}	✡	☌	U^3	九^2	⊥^{2}	⊥^{3}	⊥^{2}	Q	☌	△	U^2	U	∠^{2}	☍^{2}	U	⊕								
⚳ 9♈	U	九^2	□^{3}	☍^{3}	九^2	U^4	⊥	U	九	Q^3	⊡	U	九	Q	Q^2	九	九^2	⚳							
⚷ 14♑	△	☌	U	Q	✡^{2}	☍	⚻^{3}	✡^{2}	⊥^{2}	⚻^{3}	⚹^{2}	△	☌	⚹^{3}	Q^2	☌	✡	九^2	⚷						
⚶ 19♍	☍^{2}	✡^{2}	⊥^{2}	Q^3	⚻^{2}	⚹	U	U^2	☌	⊡	☍^{2}	☍^{2}	△	□	△	△	Q	九	⊥^{2}	⚶					
⚵ 5♈	⊥	⊥^{2}	⊥^{2}	☌	□	✡	U	⚻^{3}	U	☌^{2}	☌^{2}	⊥	九^3	⚻^{2}	∠	☍^{2}	Q^2	☌	⊥^{2}	U	⚵				
⚴ 16♐	Q	☌^{2}	Q^2	⚹^{2}	☍^{4}	⊥^{2}	U^2	☍	九^2	九^2	☌^{2}	∠^{3}	U	U^3	✡	U	U	□^{2}	☌^{2}	九^2	⚻^{3}	⚴			
Hra 28♈	☍^{3}	⚻^{2}	☌	U	□^{2}	九	∠^{2}	△^{2}	九^3	☌	△	⚻^{2}	U	⊥^{3}	△^{2}	U	☌	✡^{2}	✡	九^3	九^3	⚹^{3}	Hra		
Ero 17♒	⚹^{3}	九^2	U	✡^{2}	九^2	✡^{2}	⊥^{2}	△	Q^2	✡^{2}	☌^{3}	Q^2	☌^{2}	△	U^2	☌^{3}	九^2	✡	U	Q^2	△^{2}	⚹	⚻^{3}	Ero	
Bac 18♊	⊥	✡	☌^{2}	⊥^{2}	九^2	U^3	✡	☌	□	∠	□^{2}	⊥	Q^3	☌	☍^{2}	⚻	✡	九^2	✡	□	Q	☍	⚻^{3}	△	Bac

3. At some point in the formula we'll need to reference "your" planets (both in the Interaction Purpose cocktail and in the [Pluto $_{event}$-(Other Planets $_{you}$)] pairs). Here, "you" refers to Westcott. When reading synastry for a person whose chart that lacks a birth time, though, I *really* prefer to ignore those pairs whose angles change significantly over the course of a day. Despite the fact that I will be using noon as the birth time for both Westcott and the KJV, I'm actually going to cast a 12:00am chart and an 11:59pm chart for Westcott against the KJV, lay these charts over each other, and look at what sticks. That way we'll obtain a formula with only the most stable pairs from Westcott's perspective. As an event with no known formal birth certificate at all, the KJV is fine with the noon chart only. Here's what we get.

Down: Brooke Foss Westcott (1/12/1825 12:00:00 AM & 11:59:00 PM, GMT+0:01:15) Birmingham (52N28'00 1W55'00)
Across: KJV (5/2/1611 12:00:00 PM GMT+0:01:15) London (51N30'00 0W10'00)
Tropical, Geocentric, Polich - Page

	⊙	☽	☿	♀	♂	♃	♄	♅	♆	♇	Asc	Mc	Vx	☊	2⚸	⚸	⊕	?	⚷	[illegible]	[illegible]	[illegible]	Hra	Ero	Bac	?
⊙	[illegible]	☌	□	Q2	[illegible]	☍	[illegible]	Q	△	[illegible]	[illegible]	[illegible]	☌	⚻	△	☌	[illegible]	☍2	☌	△	[illegible]	⊥	[illegible]	☍2	[illegible]	⊥
☽	[illegible]	[illegible]	[illegible]	[illegible]	[illegible]	[illegible]	[illegible]	[illegible]	[illegible]	[illegible]	[illegible]	[illegible]	[illegible]	[illegible]	[illegible]	[illegible]	[illegible]	[illegible]	[illegible]	[illegible]	[illegible]	[illegible]	[illegible]	[illegible]	[illegible]	[illegible]
☿	✱2	[illegible]	九	∠2	✡	[illegible]	U	⚼	[illegible]	[illegible]	[illegible]	[illegible]	[illegible]	[illegible]	[illegible]	[illegible]	[illegible]	□2	九2	[illegible]	Q2	∠	[illegible]	[illegible]	⚼	[illegible]
♀	[illegible]	[illegible]	[illegible]	[illegible]	△	[illegible]	☌	[illegible]	[illegible]	[illegible]	[illegible]	[illegible]	[illegible]	[illegible]	[illegible]	[illegible]	[illegible]	[illegible]	△2	[illegible]	U	[illegible]	[illegible]	[illegible]	[illegible]	☌
♂	☍2	[illegible]	[illegible]	[illegible]	[illegible]	Q	[illegible]	[illegible]	✡	[illegible]	☍	[illegible]	[illegible]	△	Q3	⊥	[illegible]	∠	九	✡	[illegible]	[illegible]	Q2	☌	[illegible]	☌
♃	□	✡	⊥	⚼	⊥	九3	[illegible]	☌2	☌4	U	☍3	□	⊥3	△2	九	□2	⚻2	△	✡	☌4	U2	U2	✡	[illegible]	⊥3	∠2
♄	✱2	☌2	九	U	U	U2	Q3	⚻2	⊥	☌2	☌2	✱2	✡2	Q2	☌	✡2	✡3	✡	九2	⊥	☌2	[illegible]	U	✡	⊥2	✡3
♅	☌3	☌	△2	☍3	△2	☍	△2	⚻	△	⊥	九3	[illegible]	☌	✡	U2	☌	✱2	☌2	☌	△	九	⚻	∠3	U2	✡2	Q2
♆	△	☌	✡	✡2	U3	✡2	∠2	✡	☌2	✡2	⚼	△	☌	∠2	U	☌	△3	□	☌	☌2	九2	△2	⊥	✡2	□2	⊥2
♇	九	U2	Q2	☌	U2	⊥	☌2	⊥3	△2	U	Q	九	Q	九	⚻3	Q	☍2	☌	☍2	△2	☌	⚻2	☍2	∠	九3	U
Asc	✡2	□	[illegible]	∠2	U	[illegible]	✱2	△	△2	九	⊥2	✡2	[illegible]	☌2	[illegible]	✡2	[illegible]	☍	□	△2	[illegible]	Q2	☌2	Q3	[illegible]	⚼
Mc	[illegible]	[illegible]	九2	□2	[illegible]	☌	⚼	U	[illegible]	⊥3	[illegible]	U	☍	☍2	[illegible]	☍	[illegible]	U	☍	[illegible]	✡	[illegible]	九	⚻	⚻	[illegible]
Vx	[illegible]	△3	☌	九2	[illegible]	[illegible]	[illegible]	∠	[illegible]	☌	[illegible]	[illegible]	[illegible]	✡	[illegible]	[illegible]	☌	[illegible]	[illegible]	[illegible]	[illegible]	⚼	☌	[illegible]	[illegible]	[illegible]
☊	U	△3	□2	九2	☍	∠2	Q2	[illegible]	☌3	△	∠2	✱3	✡2	U2	U2	∠2	✡3	U	☍3	☌3	✡2	⚻2	△	U2	△2	✱
2⚸	⊥3	九	✱2	□2	Q2	⚼	□	[illegible]	Q	⚻	U	⊥3	∠	九	△2	∠	Q	Q2	U3	Q	△	[illegible]	Q	[illegible]	⚻2	九2
⚸	✡3	✱	✡2	✱3	☌2	Q3	[illegible]	□	U3	⚻2	[illegible]	[illegible]	☌2	U	□2	☌2	Q2	☍2	✱	U3	Q2	□	∠	☍2	U2	[illegible]
⊕	[illegible]	[illegible]	[illegible]	[illegible]	[illegible]	[illegible]	[illegible]	[illegible]	[illegible]	[illegible]	[illegible]	[illegible]	[illegible]	[illegible]	[illegible]	[illegible]	[illegible]	[illegible]	[illegible]	[illegible]	[illegible]	[illegible]	[illegible]	[illegible]	[illegible]	[illegible]
?	☌2	✡	□2	☍	[illegible]	Q	✡	⚻2	⚻3	∠3	⊥	☌2	九3	U	☍2	⊥	✡	✡2	⚻2	⚻3	Q3	✡2	✡2	九2	✡	Q3
⚷	☌2	□	☌	∠2	⊥2	△2	九	Q2	✡	✱2	U	☌3	✱3	九2	✡2	Q2	△3	☌	□	✡	☌	△	⚻2	☌2	Q2	∠
[illegible]	U2	[illegible]	Q	✡2	Q	✱	☌2	□	☌	⚼	九3	U2	△	Q2	✡3	△	✱2	□2	△	☌	∠2	□	✱2	⚻	□	∠2
[illegible]	Q	✱2	∠2	[illegible]	□	⚻2	⚻	⊥	[illegible]	⚻	九	九3	⚻2	∠3	✡2	⚻2	□2	U3	✱2	⚻2	☍	Q	✡	⚼	Q2	Q
[illegible]	Q	☍2	[illegible]	U	[illegible]	Q2	☍2	☍	[illegible]	⚼	□2	Q	U	U3	✡	U2	☍2	□2	☍2	[illegible]	⊥	☌	U	✱	☍	Q
Hra	☌	△	Q2	△2	✡	U	☍3	U	Q2	☌	☌3	☌	✡2	九	☌	⊥2	九2	九2	△	Q2	✡2	⊥2	U2	九2	九2	⚻2
Ero	[illegible]	Q2	[illegible]	☌	⊥	△	[illegible]	□	☍	U2	□2	☌2	[illegible]	[illegible]	[illegible]	✱	九	[illegible]	Q2	☍	[illegible]	□	[illegible]	[illegible]	□	[illegible]
Bac	☌2	△2	[illegible]	△	✱2	Q2	U	九	U	[illegible]	□	[illegible]	∠2	✡	☍	[illegible]	[illegible]	⚼	△2	U	[illegible]	[illegible]	✡	[illegible]	□2	[illegible]

What I've done here is essentially cheated by using screen captures to see which pairs keep the same angle no matter what time of day Westcott was born at. If I can't easily read what's in the square, I won't read it in the Non-living Influencer formula. I'll also ignore Westcott's ASC, MC, Fortune, and Vertex rows since they change all day (despite ending in roughly the same places where they started). You only need to do this kind of thing if you're a stickler for accuracy.

4. We now have everything. Let's plug it all in and see what we get:

The event is most broadly a [Sign & duodecanate of Pluto $_{event}$] kind of influencer.	The King James Bible most broadly influences others via the words that build its identity.	**Resonant III-noviles (*table 16-5*)** [Vesta-Hera]: bond-consumed attention [Pallas-Hera]: all we got is us [Neptune-Hera]: ideal bond realization (but a book can't realize, only depict) [Vertex-Pallas]: semi-adversarial relationship with the one it's bonded to **Resonant III-deciles (*table 16-5*)** [Mars-MC]:public allure, leadership [Saturn-Fortune]:preferred stability and control [Node-Hera]: compulsion to bond
It teaches others most effectively through its display of [Resonant III-noviles $_{event}$] and can be viewed as masterful in its [Resonant III-deciles $_{event}$].	It teaches others most effectively through its concentrated, world-enveloping depiction of an ideal against the imperfections of the reader and can be viewed as masterful in its attractiveness as a means of stability and control in the lives of those drawn to it.	
It's most powerful quality in general lies in its [Pluto $_{event}$-MC $_{event}$],	The KJV is *naturally* powerful,	[Pluto $_{event}$-MC $_{event}$] *conjunct*

<table>
<tr>
<td>where it has the ability to move me forward in many ways which include [Pluto $_{event}$-(Other Planets $_{me}$)].</td>
<td>where it has the ability to move Westcott forward in many ways which include the following:
• His ability to influence how KJV is talked about
• His ability to change How KJV appears to exercise its command over people
• How he sees KJV's structure at work
• Where he stays fixed on the rational basis of KJV
• How he attempts to influence and develop KJV's steering of people
• How he is more likely to fight on behalf of the "spirit" of KJV
• How his peers see the fundamental intent behind KJV</td>
<td>Non-changing Pluto column from step 3, interpreted using table 19-9
[Pluto $_{KJV}$-Jupiter $_{BFW}$] (undecile): BFW levies pressure upon KJV (social talk)
[Pluto $_{KJV}$-Saturn $_{BFW}$] (II-conjunct): KJV possesses limiting command over people (persona)
[Pluto $_{KJV}$-Uranus $_{BFW}$] (decile): KJV send its creative power into the exchange (control)
[Pluto $_{KJV}$-Chiron $_{BFW}$] (II-sextile): BFW kept grounded by KJV (rationality)
[Pluto $_{KJV}$-Vesta $_{BFW}$] (octile): BFW directs power towards addressing standards in KJV (steering)
[Pluto $_{KJV}$-Juno $_{BFW}$] (octile): BFW commits to KJV's development (steering)
[Pluto $_{KJV}$-Pallas $_{BFW}$] (inconjunct): BFW more likely to fight on KJV's behalf (impression)
[Pluto $_{KJV}$-Bacchus $_{BFW}$] (II-square): BFW's ingroup weighs in on KJV (core impressions)

Here I've only interpreted the pairs where the KJV affects Westcott or those where he can (kind of) affect it. Those pairs where the KJV is supposed to "feel" something have been omitted. Note that these kinds of choices depend on the nature of the event you're looking at</td>
</tr>
</table>

As far as my own purpose for interacting with it, my reasons are rooted in this:	As far as Westcott's purpose for interacting with KJV, it is suggested that:	
[Interaction Purpose cocktail $_{\text{you-event}}$] The other and I are on the same page in our wants regarding [Moon-Moon]. Recognizing them strongly for their [Jupiter me-Chiron them], I gain increased experience and skill when it comes to handling this side of their world. My newfound experience can be applied to this same area of life far beyond my dealings with them alone. Overall, they are in my world to help me hone how I project my [Selene them-Fortune me]. I am in their world to help them build on how they use their [Selene me-Fortune them]. Throughout the exchange, the main thing I get lies in [Uranus them-Juno me]. Over the long term my commitment to them will change me in the area of [Jupiter them-Juno me].	The King James Bible and Westcott are on the same page in their wants regarding [Moon-Moon]. Recognizing the King James Version strongly for the expertise it builds in him as an interactor with information, Westcott gains increased experience and skill when it comes to handling the reader feedback side of the Bible. His newfound experience could be applied to this same area of life far beyond his dealings with the King James Version alone. Overall, they are in his world to help him hone how he projects his [Selene $_{\text{KJV}}$-Fortune $_{\text{BFW}}$]. Westcott worked with the KJV to help it build on how it interacted with others. The exchange mainly offered him a sense of self-identity. Over the long term his commitment to the KJV will have changed his apparent charisma in dealing with others.	[Interaction Purpose cocktail $_{\text{you-event}}$] [Jupiter $_{\text{BFW}}$-Chiron $_{\text{KJV}}$] (septile): BFW gains experience points (1:1 conversation, feedback) [Selene $_{\text{BFW}}$-Fortune $_{\text{KJV}}$] (quintile): his purpose was to help evolve KJV's (1:1 interaction) [Juno $_{\text{BFW}}$-Uranus $_{\text{KJV}}$] (opposition): what BFW gets out of relationship (self-identity) [Juno $_{\text{BFW}}$-Jupiter $_{\text{KJV}}$] (III-quintile): how BFW will have changed in light of commitment to KJV (charisma) We don't know KJV-Westcott's [Moon-Moon] or [Selene $_{\text{KJV}}$-Fortune $_{\text{BFW}}$], so I've omitted these.

Now we don't actually know whether Westcott even used the King James Version of the Bible heavily in his work, or if he primarily used other texts. We don't know if he saw his work as doing anything suggested by the formula. Yet the above sounds pretty reasonable, don't you think? I think so. Try this out on your own events and projects to see where it leads you.

Chapter 24, Conclusion: New languages, new lands

You know what, man. I think I'm gonna give up on this astrology stuff, Geery scratched his head as he handed his finished book to the soldier Hayden.

What? What are you saying?

I mean I'm not gonna stop *using it*, no way. But all this time I've been studying and writing this book for you, I've experimented with all kinds of things contained in it which I never really had to reason out before. I learned enough of the secrets, found my calling, got the girl I told you about, scripted a couple of exchanges to a tee, and now feel as though there's really nothing left to do with all this. It's just a tool for hacking into happiness, I think. Once you've used it, you put it down and go about the new life you've built.

Is that so? This means you're just leaving it all behind? You're not going to study more or teach more or anything like that?

No, I don't think so. I know this stuff works, and I've done everything in my power to explain it to you. Granted, certain corners of the theory are messy and complicated, but that's typically how science works. My worry is that, if I make a career out of this, people will demand that I do exactly what you said I shouldn't do: Justify a thousand things a thousand times when, really, such justification should be the work of a thousand *other* people donating a thousand perspectives besides mine. I don't really have the interest in marrying complexity with simplicity only to be punished for it on both sides, but as an occultist, scientist, and a curious human, I've accepted this very contradictory world comfortably for myself. I've learned that people won't like others' contradictions, but they're perfectly fine living with their own.

Synastry as science sounds way too fantastic to be true, so I can look forward to a lifetime of convincing if I stay on this path.

Hmph, Hayden turned away, disappointed. And here I thought I could challenge you to prove astrology just a little longer.

Nope. No sir. I've written the book for you, used its contents myself, and found that pleasing people like you is—nothing personal—a dead end. I'll never be able to explain enough, to simplify enough, to provide enough examples, when all you really need to do is steer *your own* actions around what's already there—assuming you yourself want it to work. But I can't do that for you. Or would you rather just play around with all this like a cat does a ball of yarn?

Wow, a little hostile are we? Hayden marveled.

As hostile as a soldier who knows only "real things." Can we people in the "hippie business" ever *really* expect to gain your approval?

Heh heh, Hayden chuckled slightly. Way to defend yourself, hippie. I guess not. As long as you claim that the stars can affect us, I suppose people like me will always find it easy to make fun of you. You must really believe in this stuff to just dump it on me like this then slam the door in my face. And I guess you feel no more need to further explain it than I feel a need to explain the sea.

This time Geery was quiet, eyeing his bags as he and Hayden stood at the edge of the pier.

So what's next, Sir?

Actually I'm thinking of going on a quest. A friend of mine named Pepper claims to be able to walk through people's dreams using a "proven scientific system" and, for this, has just been relieved of her professorship for peddling non-scholarly work to the college kids. She says her system of dreamwalking is the forerunner to time travel into the past, and thinks we can use my research to make it a possibility.

What!? And just when I thought you were making sense.

Hear me out now, as the theory's quite sound. What do you get when you cross a maze of predictive algorithms with online web habits?

You get Google, everybody knows that.

And what do you get when you take patterns from EEGs and subject them to statistics which can be used to inform player movement on video games?

Uh…thought-controlled video games? I think?

Yep.

Can we do that?

Yes we can. Google it. The technology's a little young, though.

Hayden immediately reached for his phone while Geery continued.

Anyway, while I was researching all this time, I was giving my drafts to Pepper who said. **Ahem** Geery cleared his throat in preparation for his best girly-girl voice, *O-M-G! This-is-like-the-coolest-thing-ever-where-you-can-totally-take-an-existing-node-on-a-network-and-use-induction-on-it-to-build-up-a-systematic-personality-for-robots-think, I-mean-feel-like-REAL-feelings-about-things-you-never-even-programmed-just-cuz-the-robot-knows-howta-recursively-count-harmonics-I-mean-you-take-your-VOICE-and-your-SPEECH-recogntion-and-apply-it-to-microexpressions-and-mannerisms-and-brainscansinpeople's-SLEEP-and-compare-it-to-their-waking-reports-and-it's-like-you-can-have-a-computer-walk-through-people's-dreams-and-it's-like·stuff·I-can't-even-do!-cuz-I'mjust-like-chillin'-in-my-bed-ya-know-and*—yotta, yotta, yotta, Geery sobered up. I eventually had to cut her off. But she says she's found it.

EEG games, Hayden marveled. Hmph. Well I'll be damned. I wonder how long this technology's been around.

—ahh, yeah. found what? Hayden snapped his attention back to Geery.

I'm not sure myself. Something about the "virtual life." It's a role playing game on steroids, apparently. Using technology we already have.

Hayden shook his head.

What's with the head shaking?

Although the things that come out of your mouth scarcely surprise me anymore, Sir, I continue to be fascinated by your occasional forays into rocket science. And what about this astrology book you've just given me? Since I'm not planning to play chess with the Terminator any time soon, what advice do you have to give me for using this book right here in my hand? In English, please.

You mean your synastry book? I'd say find some software and read your chart. Then find a friend and read their chart. Look at your synastry together. Then (and here's the most important part) you and your friend decide what kinds of lives you'd want to live if you could live any way you pleased. The tables in here show everything from lasting friendship to riches (kinda) to lessons from non-living objects. It shows the angle you use for transforming from a person who pisses people off to a person who awes others with their power. The trick is to latch onto a friend who supports your crazy dreams and—even if you still don't believe the astrology part—use the psychology behind the different angles to build some cooler things in life. That's the advice I'd give you.

Well, not the takeaway I expected, but maybe even better. So the number one thing is to hit up a friend and try this stuff out?

The number one thing is to hit up a friend and decide to support the dreams which the world told you both were impossible. Get that close to someone, *then* use this book to do the more serious writing of fate.

Writing of fate, huh? You really think people can use this book to do something so high flying?

The primates we once were would never have guessed that their system of grunts would lead to that phone you have in your hand. Language well-used sponsors advancement. Relatedly—regardless of whether it's the stars or the gods or our brains behind it—a language for psychology in the form of angles and signs can be very useful if we know what to do with it.

Okay, Sir. I'll take your word for it. Until some time in the future, though, I guess this is where we part ways.

I guess so.

Good luck on your journey, Hayden patted Geery on the shoulder as he extended his other hand cordially.

And Geery reciprocated.

Chapter 25: Resonant pairs across the charts

In this chapter we'll take a look at the differences among four kinds of astrology charts, as well as some final advice on how to use them. We have the following:

- The regular (birth / self) chart
- The synastry chart
- The composite chart (nearest midpoint)
- The relative (Davison) chart

To illustrate many of the key principles, I'll use [Mars-Vertex] as an example. First, however, we should revisit how all of this astrology connects to astronomy. Why should we believe that astrology has any validity at all?

🛠 As we discussed in the early chapters of *FSA*, the signs Aries through Pisces aren't really personality-infused regions of space. Instead, they are simply a map of frequencies against a starting point. Commonly on the scale of an Earth year, that starting point is around the first day of spring, where day and night are of equal lengths. This is 0° Aries in the tropical system of astrology. Measuring the rest of the year against increases and eventual decreases in sunlight and—by extension—weather patterns, plant behavior, associated allergens, subsequent human immunity, and consequently evolved genetic changes with respect to these patterns, we get a nice cycle for grafting the results of our birth time upon our existing genetics. And so your body, whatever its makeup, includes at least a couple of systems which respond to changes in seasonality (just like plants). Additionally, we have structural demands imposed on that same body as surface-bound humans evolved to handle Earth's natural gravity and atmospheric pressure. Enter the lunar cycle, whose effects on our planet are strong enough to influence the tides and further moderate our planet's oscillation in its orbit around the Sun.

When you have a body evolved to respond to conditions on the Earth, the Sun, and the Moon, you also have a body evolved to undergo processes connected to the cycles of Venus, Mars and so on—not because Venus and Mars throw rays at us, but because the cycles of the rest of the objects in the Solar system are connected to each other through an astronomical property called "orbital resonance." This is where 243 cycles of Earth are known to correspond to 395 cycles of Venus.[72] Two cycles of Earth are known to correspond to one cycle of Mars. And so it goes for the other planets. Arranged and stabilized according to their gravitational potential in an ellipse around the Sun, each planet, asteroid, and calculated point reflects a higher probability of finding dense energy at the cycle it describes, where bodies such as planets and asteroids correspond to actual energy densities while calculated points correspond to frequency reference points for those bodies. Accordingly, any object in the Solar System, actual or imaginary can be mapped onto a scale of frequencies relative to the tropical sky and it is here that our own atoms begin to do the rest of the work.

Part of the energy contained in certain assemblies of atoms is subject to the angle at which other energy hits those atoms. Where the crystal structure of certain substances affects their response to such colliding energy, the substances themselves behave differently on the atomic level. In a chain of moving packets of chemical density in a gravitational field (called planets), even non-living objects can reflect where they are in spacetime, altogether storing much of massive wave function which describes the "ensemble energy" of the whole. In English, humans are like ants on a mountain; despite our grand sense of self-importance, we behave (on the whole) as the math of our vast surroundings dictates. To look at astrology is to look at a giant astronomical clock whose myriad planetary and asteroidal digits ultimately ride on only a handful of variables—a central one being *time* as measured from our point of astronomical origin. Subsequently, any snapshot of the sky—any chart—represents a particular timestamp in the ongoing "song" that is the universe. That is, if you think of a song as one big waveform made up of many simpler waves, and think of planetary cycles as analogous to such simpler waves against the bigger waveform of the Solar System's overall arrangement at a certain time. Changing the location from which you view this only applies a filter to that song. Changing the planet you focus on only changes the instrument you pay attention to. Separating out families of angles among objects only separates out frequencies in the same way that an equalizer separates out the basses, trebles, and midranges on your stereo. With this analogy in mind, we might see how the frequencies themselves—the descriptive numbers themselves—transcend the objects that possess them, allowing us to conceive of constructs in harmony with (but on levels higher or lower than) our own. In other words, as long as we keep the general sequence of notes in order, a shift in octave won't change the song very much. As long as we pay attention to which planets have which potentials compared to each other in a specific order, a 360° turn of the sky won't change very much.

Thus we have resonances among thoughts of real things and imagined things alike. Our thoughts are the confluence of neuronal frequencies played by an orchestra of specialized atoms in the theater of specialized biology—keys in the chord of each genetically circumscribed personality. But because our biology includes its own clocks for measuring the year (through immunity), the day (through circadian rhythms), and approximate month (through female menstrual cycles and the mate-seeking males whose bonding behavior aligns with these cycles), so too must it have the ability to measure various fractions of those cycles if it is to get anything done. C isn't the only note available to us and the octave isn't the only form in which packages of notes arrive. Nor is the hour the only unit of measure carried in packages of days. So we have time cycles which correspond to the speed of visual processing, pain reception, spinal transport, and hunger—other "notes" played in the body. With specific bodily processes associated with specific families of firing frequencies within that body, we have certain points along the cycle of octaves which are better suited to certain biological experiences than others. In rocks these are just coordinated noise, but in self-aware humans such noise gives way to the stereotyped cognitive pathways of

[72] Wright, J. T. et al. (2011). The exoplanet orbit database. *Publications of the Astronomical Society of the Pacific.*

personality. Astrologically, the planets are mapped accordingly. On the individual level an entire life plays out with all its dynamism. On the collective level each life is as one drop in a moving glass of water.

Drops which are able to conceive of the entire glass do so not by growing to the level of the whole, but by picking out those frequencies inherent in their own behavior which align with that of the thing that contains them.

And so astrology is a map of the frequencies associated with the appearance of a point in spacetime at the moment it began to affect other points in spacetime. ⚒

Planetary pairs across levels

Let's summarize what the planetary pairs tell us in each of the four major charts we've covered.

Regular / self chart: Your default patterns of experience. NOT your default "behavior"

Regular chart [Mars-Vertex] example. In a person's own conception there exists some situation in which he will be beset by change, and will respond with his greatest possible intention to influence things. Call this situation [Mars-Vertex]. In the regular chart, this pair represents change through overpowering, where the angle between the person's Mars and Vertex denotes something like the family of "firing frequencies" which most closely describes his behavior when that happens.[73] Any other pair in this chart which shares this same family of frequencies (cut in half, doubled, cut in fourths, quadrupled, et cetera) will also be seen as occurring around the same situations as the person's "change through overpowering." Such pairs will be considered resonant, and will show us much of the entire bearing he that he displays during his "change through overpowering." Does his [Sun-Moon] have the same angle? If so, he is more likely to be self-contented while this happens. Does his [Midheaven-Lilith] have the same angle? If so, others are likely to support his reputation as a rebel while this happens.

The regular chart shows one's more likely ways of processing experiences, where resonant (collections of) pairs under the same angle constitute a broad "face" worn by the person during each kind of experience.

Synastry chart: Your experience of how you and another divide two sides of a single action

Synastric chart [Mars-Vertex] example. Once we introduce another person, there is a change in the normal psychological order of things which we take for granted. Where our person in the self chart example may be accustomed to, say, manipulating people as his way of executing change through over powering, we might ask what he does when he's not the one being changed. What if his partner is being changed, and he's doing the manipulation in response to *her* change? There we'd need to look at [Mars $_{him}$-Vertex $_{her}$]. Thanks to his being tangled up in her change, he is now tasked with steering situations related to her instead of himself. According to *table 19-9*, his world is altered here. On the other hand, what if she's the one steering on behalf of his change? In this case he has effectively gained another person to respond to his change for him—amplifying his forces by borrowing hers. Or what if he incites major change and inspires her to steer things as a result? Either way his power to draw her action in response to his personal events sends his abilities through the roof, as she essentially does his dirty work under this angle. Perhaps you can see how he'll need to conceive of her steering as being a thing, though. She doesn't *actually* have to fight his battles. He just needs to be able to properly frame how she steers situations in general and apply that idea to his own thoughts of her role amidst his change.

If the regular chart shows one's own experiences, the synastry chart shows how one conceives of his experiences being completed by another.

---

[73] Incidentally, once we start measuring frequency families on a fine-grained level as we've done with the 36 harmonics, it turns out that more than one "clock" may describe this situation, such that we may ask if it's a C# or a weirdly tuned D we're hearing. Because angles are almost always imprecise, you can get away with slight error in assigning their harmonics but still understand the overall pattern of behavior.

Composite chart: The goal of responses when comparing another person's versions of your actions to your own versions

Effects on individuals

Composite chart [Mars-Vertex] example; separate action. There is a set of circumstances under which our example person experiences change through overpowering. There is a different set of circumstances under which his partner experiences change through overpowering. Typically these situations won't be the same. But now imagine a situation in which our person compares his way of steering against his partner's way of steering. He compares his typical area of major change against that of his partner. The average of these two ways produces an average "change through overpowering" as seen by either him or her for the relationship, but not really. In practice we know full well that real people don't actually do this except in the most tangible of cases. More likely, in attempts to reconcile his ways and her ways when they each have different responses to the same thing,

- our person will try to reason out how he himself arrives at steering in the first place. This would be the planet *prior* to steering: Venus' 1:1 interaction. He'll compare his Venus to her Venus.
- He'll also do this for understanding how they both arrived at major change in the first place: his ["expired comfort"] versus hers.

Since it is, in practice, pretty unnatural to imagine how an [averaged psychology] might go about "change through overpowering," we don't normally do this, but instead seek to reconcile how we would go from the other person's approach to our own. When we do this though, the relevant planets drop backwards by 1 as prior causes for the planets we're looking at. And so you have the weird, decidedly non-astrology-typical behavior of composite pairs as they affect individuals. When you and I approach things differently and I'm not cool with that, I'm more likely to look at the prior causes of such differences rather than simply going along with them.

(That is, at least, my hypothesis regarding why the composite chart data in this book produced the statistics it produced: sets of behaviors which overwhelmingly reflected prior planets rather than actual ones.)

Effects on the relationship

Composite chart [Mars-Vertex] example; joint action. Really, if we want to look at how regular pairs translate into composite pairs (as opposed to how composite versions of regular pairs translate into actual regular ones), we should simply compare *pairs*, not the split-up planets within them as we did above. Suppose our man knows how he changes through overpowering as well as how his partner changes through overpowering. Suppose also that he knows that one or both of them are going to have to come up with some kind of joint "change through overpowering" in order to accomplish some goal as a team. In comparing the two, what does he do? He considers each style of such change to be its own "unit" rather than a pair of separate planets—effectively taking the midpoint between his [Mars-Vertex] and her [Mars-Vertex]. The angle between these two midpoints is the same angle as the one he gets in the section above, but this time he's considering the joint change rather than the separate change. It is here that we see how the *planets* of both people involved in a composite must be "on" in order for the *individual effects* to be felt (as described in the previous section), while the PAIRS of people involved in a composite chart must be "on" in order for the JOINT EFFECTS to be felt (as described in this section).

To give a tiny example of all this, if his Mars is at 5 and his Vertex is at 15, if her Mars is at 37 and her Vertex is at 57, the above shows how ((5+37)÷2 - (15+57)÷2) = -15 angle of separation = ((5-15) + (37-57)) ÷2.

Here we investigate how the average Marses got where they are using Venuses, and how the average Vertexes got where they are using "expired comfort" (on the individual level)

Here we look at the centers of action for each [Mars-Vertex] and average them, giving us an overall [Mars-Vertex] (on the joint level)

In the end, **the composite chart shows how people familiar with specific characteristics in a relationship either 1) frame the prior planets that fed into those characteristics as compared to each other (especially when they don't know how the duo should behave jointly) or 2) how those characteristics form goals that can be averaged between the two people involved (when the duo does behave jointly)**. Why goals and not realities? Because the combined pairs involved represent how the duo *would look* if it were a person on its own doing the duo mates' combined thing. Alas, we don't have an actual third person, only a psychological construct.

Relative chart: How outsiders summarize your interaction with another

Relative chart [Mars-Vertex] example. When you're not involved in a relationship, don't have much of a conception of the duo mates' individual traits, or are simply looking at two people interacting as a whole, **the relative chart shows the duo as an average item in spacetime. While this chart is better at the describing the relationship as a whole from the perspective of outsiders, it is worse for suggesting how people actually behave in the relationship**. For understanding a relationship that you are in, synastry is best, followed by the composite chart (if you can stand the latter's strange interpretations). Where our example person is concerned, he would look at his *relative* [Mars-Vertex] with his partner if he wanted to know how the average *outsider* described the duo's "change through overpowering."

Why do both relative and composite charts work? Imagine you once owned a car. You went on a lot of great road trips in that car before you replaced it with an RV. Then you went on some different kinds of road trips. If I ask you for the "average experience" of your car and your RV, you might reply with "quality road trippin'" because you know exactly where those vehicles fit in your life and you know that these things have nothing to do with certain corners of your life but everything to do with certain other corners—particularly going on road trips. But if I ask a stranger for the average of *your* car and *your* RV they won't know all that detail. To them, your vehicles could have anything to do with anything that they've ever heard about your life. So they're more likely to reply with "A van?" Actually in the generic sense, the public is almost always more likely to be right about you than you are (since their flattening portrayal of you is the one that sticks around after you die). But the public is much more likely to be wrong about your specific experiences since—like scientists shooting beams at atoms, their known observation of you (where you are aware of being observed) changes the very experience you're having. Accordingly, the composite chart is better for you and your duo mate in private and depicts dynamics which you can actually steer. The relative chart is better for describing you in the eyes of everyone else beyond you, but is more "read only" and less susceptible to being influenced by those outside people.

Another analogy

If relative charts describe the look of you and Other's house from the outside, composite charts show the state of you and Other's home from the inside. Your synastry is your detailed exchange with Other in that house; your regular chart is simply you.

Resonant pairs give you access across dimensions

Just as numbers have amazingly wide application across multiple fields, so too do harmonic families (the arrangement of angles by the number of repeats needed to complete a cycle). Such families have a wide application across the various dimensions of an interaction. When you zoom in on a particular harmonic, you gain the ability to access it in your self chart as well as in your other charts. So if your focus happens to be your public image (II-conjunct), this particular harmonic will be more easily processed by you in the synastric, composite and relative charts as well. The reason we don't generally notice this is actually pretty simple: Accessing an angle in charts other than your self chart requires different kinds of help from other people. Once you get that help, however, it becomes much easier to take advantage of certain patterns in all of your charts.

Activating angles in regular and synastric charts

Suppose you want to amplify your public image in your regular chart. There are several tables throughout this book to help guide you in doing this, but *table 23-2* suggests that you should simply perform actions for yourself in front of people who are inclined to talk about you. Does this work for your synastric chart with a specific partner? Maybe. IF both you and the partner are performing such actions in such a way as to complete each other's pair *in your view*, then activation of synastric angles tends to be easier. And while it's not always necessary that the partner be active in your life for you to use this, lighting up an angle tends to work a lot better while the communication channels with your partner remain open. Once you and the partner are no longer on communicative terms, it becomes harder to turn up various angles (perhaps because you've lost much of your ability to simulate their responses to you.)

Activating angles in synastry requires that you not only do what the angle requires, but also that you have a good sense of how the partner's real life behavior would affect that angle via the pairs that have it.

Activating angles in composite charts

Prior pair composite expression

Activating angles in composite charts is tricky because, unless you're dealing with a particularly weak-willed person, you almost never activate the resonant pairs directly. Instead, you have two roundabout options. First, you can use the prior pairs as outlined in Chapter 21. If, for example, you have a composite [Mars-Vertex] undecile, the prior pair would be a [Venus-"expired comfort"] undecile. (We're looking at prior pairs not prior *angles*; the angle stays the same.) By talking to $_{\text{Venus}}$ your partner about how drastically the talk around you is changing $_{\text{"expired comfort"}}$ in such a way as to motivate their desire to steer things, you plant the seeds for your joint [Mars-Vertex]. Note that this can't just be any kind of talk; it has to be the kind of talk that produces Mars-type initiative. Where the aim is to make a specific composite pair go, you should avoid getting "stuck" on the prior pair. For those angles which are more difficult to directly control (like the undecile), you may need an audience. *Table 23-2* can help you determine what kind of audience is needed. Let's call **the use of prior pairs to activate composite angles** **prior pair composite expression**.

Prior pair composite expression example

To give another example of prior pair composite expression, suppose you want to establish a sense of shared career with someone with whom you have the following composite chart:

☉ 6♓	☉																							
☽ 23♑	Q^2	☽																						
☿ 11♓	☌	△^{2}	☿																					
♀ 23♑	☌^{3}	☌	⊥^{2}	♀																				
♂ 3♉	✡^{2}	⚹^{2}	✡	⚹^{2}	♂																			
♃ 29♓	✡^{3}	U	九^2	U	九^2	♃																		
♄ 20♐	✡^{2}	U	⊥^{2}	U	✡^{2}	U	♄																	
♅ 26♐	☍^{3}	☌^{2}	⊼^{2}	☍^{2}	Q^2	✡^{3}	☌	♅																
♆ 7♑	⚹	U^2	Q^2	⊼^{2}	☌^{3}	九	九^2	∠^{3}	♆															
♇ 10♏	✡^{3}	Q	△	Q	☌^{3}	☌^{2}	九	∠	✡^{3}	♇														
²⚸ 1♒	九^2	☌	九	☌	□	✡^{2}	九	⊥	△^{2}	⊥^{2}	²⚸													
⚸ 10♋	Q^3	□^{3}	△	△^{2}	□^{2}	✡	九	☌^{2}	☍	△	⊥^{3}	⚸												
⚳ 25♐	Q	☌^{3}	☍^{2}	☌^{2}	☍^{2}	U^2	☌	☌	□^{3}	∠	⊥	U	⚳											
⚷ 16♊	⚹^{2}	Q	✡^{2}	Q	Q^2	☍^{2}	☍	Q^2	⊥^{3}	Q	⚼	Q^3	✡^{2}	⚷										
⚶ 27♈	✡	U^2	∠	✡^{2}	☌	☌^{3}	Q^2	△	⊼^{3}	△^{2}	九^2	Q	△	△^{2}	⚶									
⚴ 29♏	☍^{3}	∠^{2}	✡	∠^{2}	✡	△	Q^2	☌^{2}	☌^{4}	✡^{2}	Q^2	☌^{2}	☍^{2}	U	Q^2	⚴								
⚵ 3♒	U	☌	☌^{4}	⊼^{3}	□	☌^{2}	Q^2	⊥	☍^{2}	☌^{2}	☌	□^{2}	✡^{2}	⚼	Q^2	Q^2	⚵							
Hra 5♐	□	△^{2}	△^{2}	U^2	⊥^{2}	□^{2}	⊼^{2}	Q^2	U	☍^{2}	☌^{2}	Q	⚹^{2}	Q^2	Q	☌	✡^{2}	Hra						
Ero 19♈	☌^{3}	九^2	✡^{2}	九^2	☍^{3}	⚹^{2}	△	□^{2}	∠^{3}	⊥^{3}	☍^{2}	⊥^{2}	✡^{2}	✡^{2}	☌	⚹^{2}	九^3	⚼	Ero					
Bac 22♈	∠	□	九	□	∠^{3}	✡^{3}	△	☌^{3}	⊼^{2}	∠^{2}	九	U^2	△	∠^{2}	☌	Q	九	⚼	☌	Bac				
Asc* 2♋	△	⊥^{3}	☌^{2}	九	⚹	U^2	△^{2}	Q^3	U^3	Q^2	✡^{2}	☌	U^2	⊥^{2}	U	∠^{3}	⊼	✡	Q	Q	Asc*			
Mc* 19♎	⚼	✡^{2}	Q	U^2	☌^{2}	九	⚹	□^{2}	U^2	Q^2	✡	U	U	△	九^2	九	✡	∠	☍	☍	△^{3}	Mc*		
Vx* 1♈	Q^3	□^{2}	✡^{2}	□^{2}	U	☌	⚹^{2}	✡^{2}	☌^{2}	⚹^{2}	⚹	⚹^{2}	△^{2}	⊼^{2}	△^{3}	△	✡^{3}	☌^{3}	∠^{2}	Q^2	□	∠^{2}	Vx*	
⊕* 1♊	九^2	☍^{2}	九	☍^{2}	☌^{2}	Q^2	☍^{4}	✡	Q	⊥^{3}	△	九	✡	⊼^{2}	U	☍	△	☍	Q^2	九	U^2	☌^{2}	⚹	⊕*

How would you go about this?

1. First identify the angle associated with "career." This is a II-decile.
2. Find all of the resonant pairs for the II-decile. In the chart above these are [Mercury-Venus], [Mercury-Saturn], [Mars-Hera], [Pluto-Selene], [Lilith-Eros], and [Chiron-ASC*]. (Remember, composites should use * versions of the ASC, MC, Vx, and Fortune.)
3. **Optional.** To give yourself an idea of what your sense of the joint career looks like, put all of the resonant pairs together into a single description. Applying *Chapter 21* to the chart above, we get an image of the shared career in which the directness, conquering power, {career}-centeredness defended from assault, a sense of team superiority, and strong public point-making play a central role. Understandably with most duos you're not likely to get an *actual* shared career under composite II-deciles, but you will get a sense of your shared professional approach alongside how others see you building a reputation together.
4. List each prior pair for the ones you obtained in step 2. In the example these are [Sun-Mercury], [Sun-Jupiter], [Venus-"unattachment"], [Neptune-"resolvable dilemma"], ["unfulfilling conformity"-"receptiveness to impassioned action"], ["need for help"-2nd house]. Altogether, this group of prior pairs forms the family of issues which need to be addressed in building the angle you seek.
5. With your partner, address the issues you listed. Don't just recite them. Address them. If you go through the group above using *table 16-5*, we see that directness, a high-levity environment, talking about being

unattached, issues resolvable through mood, ideas regarding conformity under triggers pulled by others, and building one's self-value are all related to career building. Note that prior pairs with "" denoting non-astrological factors are simply interpreted as you understand them, since they don't have prior planets that we know of. While you don't have to address all the issues, you should use you regular chart to look up the ones for which there is actual representation in the table (like [Sun-Jupiter]) and display these to your partner using whatever angles your own chart suggests for each. The more of these you address, the merrier.

Birth chart synastry composite expression

Prior pair composite expression is more useful when you want to consciously steer your composite chart's angles. **Birth chart synastry composite expression** works better when you either want a more natural sense of control or when you need to address a problem area in the composite. This method involves outs. **To use outs for activating or improving the expression of angles in the chart**, you begin by finding the angle you like. List any resonant pairs for which you AND the other person have outs. Lastly, use synastry to make any such planets interact. I'll give an example of this.

Suppose you want to activate II-deciles in the chart from the previous example. (All of the resonant pairs for the II-decile are the same.) Suppose also that the other person's regular Mercury is conjunct the composite Lilith and your Moon is conjunct the composite Eros. An alternative way of activating your composite [Lilith-Eros] II-decile would be to naturally engage [Moon $_{you}$-Mercury $_{them}$] as writers of the relationship. The [Moon $_{you}$-Mercury $_{them}$] angle need not be the same as the [Lilith-Eros] angle. If you have a [Moon $_{you}$-Mercury $_{them}$] II-septile, *table 19-9* would show that the other person's desired goal among outsiders entails being viewed as part of a significant ingroup. Build this up in them and you will increase the display of your composite [Lilith-Eros] II-decile, since the latter effectively lies on top of the former.

Outs don't always work because 1) you don't always have one for the planets you're trying to steer and 2) the other person doesn't always give the kind of complementary behavior you need. When outs *do* work, however, they tend to be stronger because they are directly associated with yours and the other's real synastry rather than some nonexistent astrological ghost. Their use takes some work, but that work is mainly helped by your genuine interest in interacting honestly with the other person—that is, with as few confounding astrological side influences as possible.

Activating angles in relative charts

Now what if you want to activate a relative angle? Although it's not necessarily the case that relative angles activate themselves, it is true that people are going to think whatever they think about whatever is put before them. It is also true that the scandalous, the unusual, and the exceptional are more likely to stick with people than milder aspects of your relationship such that steering the expression of the relative chart is essentially an exercise in brand control. To activate certain angles over others, you'll need to put on a kind of performance (real or contrived) which concerns any pair whose angle you're looking at, you'll need to do it in a way which basically ignores the fact that you're being watched, and you'll need to do it together. The aim is to get others to describe whatever's going on between you and the other as a natural characteristic of your relationship, not as separate characteristics held by you and the other alone.

I've found that activating relative angles is A LOT easier if only one partner knows this is happening. By keeping the other in the dark, you minimize the likelihood of turning your desired pair into a different one related to communication or joint planning. Additionally you should, to a certain extent, also keep *yourself* in the dark…once again *to minimize the likelihood of turning your desired pair into a different one related to communication or planning*. Before going out in public, it's actually simpler if you make a quick decision to display the relevant behavior beforehand and then leave the rest to autopilot. For example, if you really want to look like a pair of bosses in front of others, and want to activate your III-deciles, you would look for any pairs with this angle and decide—to yourself—to display the easiest one of these pairs alongside your partner the next time you go out. Once you've decided this, just display the behavior. Don't add any extra to it. So if you have a [Sun-Moon] III-decile in the relative chart, you would simply show your contentment talking about each other's work in front of people. Again, don't try to coordinate this with the other person, since "coordinating" changes the angle you're using to one which is more planning-centric.

Activating angles in relative charts requires that one partner decide, beforehand, to show one of the resonant pairs containing that angle alongside the partner. It is better that the person deciding this avoid heavily communicating these plans to the partner (so as not to change the desired angle into a "planned communication" one), and better if the partner simply perform the decided action naturally when the time arrives (so as not to change the desired action into a "script performance-related" one).

Final words

Although astrology was once a field married to that of physics and astronomy, the rapid pace of scientific discovery has outstripped our ability to draw human-ready conclusions from the patterns we observe. At its core, astrology builds a towering social construct on top of a few basic human behavioral patterns stemming from daily, monthly, and yearly cycles. Here, a tie to one planet creates a tie to the orbits of others. A grounding in the basic laws of force, gravitation, and resonance sponsors commonality between atom and planet alike. Indeed there are patterns which are statistically verifiable, though these patterns may be obscured by generations of myth and mystery surrounding the actual role of the planets (as opposed to the role of their orbits). Still, there is an extent to which the various harmonics captured in charts parallel the frequencies uncovered through technologies such as EEG and ultrasound; the various signs parallel the atomic orbitals of chemistry; the various planets correspond to selected pathways in the brain,—all in such a way as to render astrology that unbelievable analog to more believable human cognition. Across levels and across constructs, the art of astrology can be put to practical use for those with enough curiosity regarding the way they and their fellow humans work. Despite the occasionally complex corners inherent in the subject, you may find that the field of astrology produces one of the best maps of the human psyche that one could ask for. Those versed enough in its practice may find a valuable tool set for navigating life's terrain.

Appendix I: Sign-related Tables

Table 16-4 (extended): Sign rulerships by orbit cycle

Sign	By cycle influence (used in this book)	Standard (used at the time of writing)	Traditional (without Uranus through Pluto)
Aries	Point of Action	Mars	Mars
Taurus	Point of Worth	Venus	Venus
Gemini	Point of Internal Monologue	Mercury	Mercury
Cancer	Moon	Moon	Moon
Leo	Sun	Sun	Sun
Virgo	Mercury	Mercury	Mercury
Libra	Venus	Venus	Venus
Scorpio	Mars	Pluto	Mars
Sagittarius	Jupiter	Jupiter	Jupiter
Capricorn	Saturn	Saturn	Saturn
Aquarius	Uranus	Uranus	Saturn
Pisces	Neptune	Neptune	Jupiter
Aries (level II)	Pluto		

Table 17-3: What the signs do (simple)

Signs and their common associations		
Aries Instinct, assertion, bravery, pressure to BE, spontaneity, creation, existence	**Leo** ego, attention, good standing, leadership, reliability, pride	**Sagittarius (Saj)** fun, exploration, journey, success, importance, luck, politics, fame, expansiveness
Taurus self-image, money, confidence, body, sensation, self-value (ideas that you build your identity against)	**Virgo** meaning, comparative health, analytical nature, rules of order	**Capricorn** rules, karma, old age, time, built structures, wealth as security, law, history, authority, respect
Gemini Internal thoughts, ideas, dexterity, driving, talking	**Libra** fairness, affinity, friendship, sharing, manners	**Aquarius** sociable detachment, society, rumors, peer groups, technology, humane ideals, renown
Cancer subconscious, feeling, dreaming, wants, connection, emotionality, the home, mothery-ness	**Scorpio** sex, death, others' money, psychology, power, the occult	**Pisces** humane feeling, intuition, illusion, escape, the hidden, art, abstraction

Appendix II: House-related Tables

Table 16-2: What the houses do

Time frame	Scope	House	What is represented	Types of experience associated with the house
Night	Self	1 ASC	An internal action or event ...	First impressions; appearances, attitude towards confronted world; characteristic means of expression
		2	Yields to a bodily state or identity context...	Self-worth; body image; ideas about worth in general which are built on self-worth; characteristic means for assigning value to the self; feelings about who one is;
		3	Which exchanges energy with existing physiology...	Voice; means of expression; how one talks to regular familiar people when conveying personal thoughts (thus sibling relationships); how one decides to present internal ideas to others; conveyances (like cars / how one sends his ideas around);
		4	Leaving a new dyadic inclination for...	Home; subconscious; feelings about what one is doing (not the same as self-worth); memory; dreams; emotional training; stereotypical mother
	Other	5	An interaction-centered action or event...	Voluntary, fun relationships, friendship groups and hobbies; how one gets attention from things he wants
		6	That becomes practical context...	Daily routine; health; kind of effort one puts into his work; job tasks and what one's daily doings look like
Day		7	Which exchanges communication with others...	Who we voluntarily socialize with (even if it means fighting) the type of people who generally surround us; people to whom we are attracted and the characteristics which sponsor this; how we best communicate with the people
		8	Leaving a new (us-centered inclination) for a...	Anything which involves us using things that people wouldn't normally share willingly; steering others' emotions, physical response, and psychology; others' money; knowing their secrets; keeping our own
	World	9	Circumstance-aimed action or event...	Anything which involves the desire to project something in the world without actually limiting it with structure; marriage association; parties; exploration of the unknown; unbounded (higher) education; nationality
		10 MC	That becomes a circumstance-defining context...	Anything which involves limits too big for us to directly influence; institutions; our long-term reputation (our categorization in the eyes of the world); fatherly discipline; discipline in general; time; consequences of our actions (where we end up in order to pay for what we broke)
		11	Which contextualizes groups of ideas...	Groups we want to be a part of; information we surround ourselves with; the kind of talk which follows us; social cliques and information fields associated with us
		12	Leaving a new internal inclination for ...	Any feelings whose source we can't identify; intuition; what our spirituality looks like; sickness; the vibe that we impress others with and hence, the kind of people we attract who like that vibe; any behaviors which create unidentifiable impressions in others; art; acting; music; other entertainment; Any public impressions which inspire us to individual action; service of others (often health or illusion based); containment of others (through imprisonment); containment of ourselves (unstable responses in light of excessive negative impressions)

Table 17-1: House behaviors in synastry

Their planet in your house #...	affects your
1	display of your default instinct, personality, sexuality, or drive
2	feelings about their values, bodily enjoyment of (or tension in) your company, or self-worth
3	formation and expression of their personal opinions, spontaneous communication
4	wants, inclinations, what you want from them, inclined emotions, communication of your honest wants, your interest in them or lack thereof
5	validation of them through your company, pride, ego expression, enthusiasm for things
6	analytical focus, work company, daily priorities, skills at work, body focus and fitness, task-centeredness, attention-giving side, sense of self-efficacy in work
7	casual conversation, 1:1 feedback (how you give it), 1:1 communication, how you talk to them
8	power over others, relationships (habit of dissecting, fighting, and influencing within these), criticality of others, irritation with others, expression of power against theirs
9	image in the eyes of the public, successful image promotion, exploration, tendency to self-broadcast, charisma also affects **their**... formation of creative ideas, learning and push towards new, ideals concerning others
10	expression of authority over or ability to command others, ability to structure boundaries for others, ability to command others, sense of struggle in the world, public identity also affects **their**... sense of authority, expression of authority
11	social environment, social effect, networking power, response to society, efficacy as social connectors, information around you, also affects **their**... reach of social network, attention to their place in the social world, social plans
12	inner creative struggle, impression left on others, secrets and secret life, vibe, mood, spirituality or spaciness also affects **their**... vibe company, the feeling of matching their intended goals, impression establishment, creativity

Table 18-1: Synastric houses, areas of life

Visitor's planets in a possessor's house...	Affects either person's area of life...
1	instinctual personality, drive, impulsive action, sexuality
2	bodily enjoyment of their company or general body preferences, self-value, consistency of actions vs values
3	ideas and opinions, expression, individualism, communication
4	wants, inclinations, family role, interests, insight and intuition, emotional disposition, feelings about a topic
5	ego priorities, ego display, pride, bodily presence, reactions enthusiasm, charisma
6	analytical or attention-giving side, role as a standard of comparison in daily work, colleague role, daily preoccupations, business focus, effectiveness in work, attainment of goals
7	1:1 communication, conversation, 1:1 dynamics
8	need to project deviant habits, show of power, power over others, habit of dissecting / fighting / influencing, criticality
9	quest to project in the world, image projection, charisma, push towards new experiences, exploration, journeys
10	created structures, expression of authority, engagement of limits, ability to command others, entrenched struggles, public identity
11	role as a social hub, intelligence, knowledge, social effects, social place, social networks, social plans, response to society, aspirations, circle of influence
12	overall vibe, accepted environmental contexts, spirituality, concerns for greater environment, creativity, mood, general influence, secret lives, desired impressions, spaciness, focus, expectations

Appendix III: Planet-related Tables

Table 16-3: What the planets do

Planet	Body type	General meaning
		Main Bodies
Moon	Planet	Inner emotional world
Sun	Star	How your motivation to interact with others plays out
Mercury	Planet	Meaning making, what you show you value with another
Venus	Planet	Willing socialization with another
Mars	Planet	How you steer interactants' inner emotional worlds
Jupiter	Planet	How your instinct to interact with the world plays out
Saturn	Planet	Structures set in place by the world at large (not you, not other individuals) with which you interact; institutions
Uranus	Planet	The information that floats around you; thus social talk, friends, hang-out groups you wish you were like, technology
Neptune	Planet	Your generation's socio-emotional tendency; group emotional vibe on average
Pluto	Dwarf Planet	Your generation's instinctual urge or priority; what the collective pressures its members to value
		Other bodies and calculated points
Ascendant (1st house cusp)	Calculated Point/cusp	How you approach the world
Midheaven (10th house cusp)	Calculated Point/cusp	Your reputation and career
Ceres	Dwarf Planet (1)	Where you take care of others
Chiron	Centaur (2060)	Where you need to be validated
Selene (White Moon)	Calculated Point	Gifts you are super-blessed with
Lilith (Lunar Apogee/ Black Moon)	Calculated Point	The point where you are most defiant or most contrary against the usual norms
Vertex	Calculated Point	Where others can change your life easily and drastically
North Node	Calculated Point	"Destiny" (but not really); more like the focal point around which your emotions are targeted
Part of Fortune	Calculated Point	Where you are in your element
Vesta	Asteroid (4)	Your focus backed with action
Pallas	Asteroid (2)	Your intellectual contribution to the greater good
Juno	Asteroid (3)	Your formally committed relationships in the eyes of the world
Hera	Asteroid (103)	Who you actually bond with
Eros	Amor asteroid (433)	What turns you on
Bacchus	Apollo asteroid (2063)	Where you make the best host for others; groups you actually serve

Table 16-3: Planets and locations of interest in a chart. Minor planet designations are listed in () where they apply—just in case you need their numbers to look up online.

Table 17-2: How the planets look in houses when they're not yours

Planet	Normal Sign/House Meaning (in possessor)	Synastric Sign/House Appearance (in visitor)
	Main Bodies	
Moon	inner emotional world	reactions to undesirable circumstances
Sun	how your motivation to interact with others plays out	regular behavior
Mercury	meaning making, what you show you value with another	conditions that prompt one to reason things out with you (usually through conversation)
Venus	willing socialization with another	the realm or setting under which they prefer to comfortably socialize 1:1 (which you often won't see if you're not in this realm)
Mars	how you steer interactants' inner emotional worlds	the setting under which they impose their will upon others, the heading under which they are likely to give people advice
Jupiter	how your instinct to interact with the world plays out	circumstances under which they tend to be prolifically popular
Saturn	structures set in place by the world at large (not you, not other individuals) with which you interact; institutions	the side of themselves they appear to work hardest to control properly (and if you can't see this side, there's a good chance it's a side they're not sharing with you).
Uranus	the information that floats around you; thus social talk, friends, hang-out groups you wish you were like, technology	the realm of social activity preferred by them and (interestingly) the kinds of transformation undergone by their strong connections (people who bond with them strongly tend to take the same informational path they do by sign and house)
Neptune	your generation's socio-emotional tendency; group emotional vibe on average	the realm in which they adopt an ideal standard and tend to live it out through their associations, though in isolation they tend not to know what they want in this same realm
Pluto	your generation's instinctual urge or priority; what the collective pressures its members to value	what their generation was taught to value
	House Cusps Consistent Across Most House Systems	
Ascendant (1st house cusp)	how you approach the world	(sign only) the occasion for their showing up somewhere; when they do show up, the kinds of expression that happens around them
Imum Coeli (4th house cusp)	your subconscious background	(sign only) where they seem to have free license to do or get what they want
Descendant (7th house cusp)	your favored approach to partnership	(sign only) the tactic or trait they use to prevent you from getting your own wants put on the agenda; how they override others in the rest of the group's expression, usually unintentionally
Midheaven (10th house cusp)	your reputation and career	(sign only) the attitude they take when they communicate with you, what appears to be on their mind when they do so
	Additional Important Bodies and Calculated Points	
Ceres	where you take care of others	what they use to bully others and make them uncomfortable; where they're most likely to run others off
Chiron	where you need to be validated	the asset given to them to which they must restrict others' desired access

Selene (White Moon)	gifts you are super-blessed with	the side which, when they show you, is hard to argue with (or where you are usually wrong for doing so); where they have an uncanny ability to be right
Lilith (Lunar Apogee / Black Moon)	the point where you are most defiant, or most contrary against the usual norms	the realm in which they go their own way despite what you want or expect
Vertex	where others can change your life easily and drastically	where they allow themselves to be used; the resource which they allow others to sap from them, repeatedly earning a mixture of praise and criticism (both of which continue, but become more favorable as they hone it)
North Node	"destiny" (but not really); more like the focal point around which your emotions are targeted	the means through which they board "the train of fate" for the next life lesson
Part of Fortune	where you are in your element	the side of their lives they appear to love indulging the most
Secondary Bodies Of Interest		
Vesta	your focus backed with action	over a longer term series of events, that which they are dead set on expressing; what they seem to yearn for or prove themselves in overall
Pallas	your intellectual contribution to the greater good	what their presence enables others around them to do
Juno	your formally committed relationships in the eyes of the world	where they exhaust others' energy with their endless demands for performance
Hera	who you actually bond with	the characteristic they prize most in their bonds; what they expect their bonds to provide them with
Eros	what turns you on	what turns them on or incites their passionate action
Bacchus	where you make the best host for others; groups you actually serve	the kind of people who occupy their close clique; circumstances under which they are most likely to encounter close friends

Table 20-4: What the synastric planets generally tell you

Your planet...	...tells:	Their planet...	...tells:
☽ Moon	your feelings	☽ Moon	what they seem to prefer
☉ Sun	your behaviors	☉ Sun	how they interact with you
☿ Mercury	your meaning making	☿ Mercury	how they make things work
♀ Venus	your 1:1 communication with them	♀ Venus	how they communicate with you
♂ Mars	your attempts to steer things, the other person, people in general, or ideas	♂ Mars	their attempts to move things around them
♃ Jupiter	your efforts to be seen or to do visible things in the world	♃ Jupiter	their image projected in the world
♄ Saturn	your placing of limits, shows of control	♄ Saturn	limits and structures that come with the other person
♅ Uranus	you as a social evaluator	♅ Uranus	where they spread the social effects of your efforts
♆ Neptune	you as embodying the other person's environment	♆ Neptune	where they reflect the emotional effects of your efforts
♇ Pluto	you as representing those who pressure the other person	♇ Pluto	how they infuse your efforts with power over people or things; how they show power around you
Asc Ascendant	you as approaching something new	Asc Ascendant	where they bring attention to your efforts
Mc Midheaven	you as one who acknowledges the other person's planet	Mc Midheaven	where they give you cause to respond
Vx Vertex	your experience of change	Vx Vertex	their efforts to change or influence things around them
☊ North Node	where you make things seem meant to be	☊ North Node	where they make your action convenient for you
²⚸ Selene	where you are super talented	²⚸ Selene	where they model your ideal view of a concept
⚸ Lilith	where you defy normally expected behavior	⚸ Lilith	where they turn into the reason you act
⊕ Fortune	you in your element	⊕ Fortune	where they are comfortable
⚳ Ceres	where you push the other to show more force; your light coercion of things (fun)	⚳ Ceres	where they feel things need to be tended to; their light coercion of you (fun)
⚷ Chiron	where you teach lessons (sometimes to yourself, often accidentally)	⚷ Chiron	where they teach; where they compel your learning
⚶ Vesta	where you put your concentration	⚶ Vesta	where they focus on what you flood them with
⚴ Pallas	where you call for war	⚴ Pallas	where you respond to their crusade
⚵ Juno	your commitment behavior	⚵ Juno	their idea of your planet as being used to draw out the concept that follows it
Hera	your bonding behavior	Hera	their attachment to your efforts
Eros	where you crave passion	Eros	their passionate response to your efforts
Bacchus	how your clique responds	Bacchus	how their friends answer your efforts

Table 20-4: What the synastric planets signify in synastry. Use the rules to guide your questions when looking at a relationship.

Additional notes regarding *Table 20-4*:

- The Sun corresponds to generic "behavior," with no reasons or details provided. It's like using the word "do" to describe things. "Yes I do football. No I don't do cantaloupe. I sometimes do donuts in the middle of the street" (instead of playing, eating, or turning).
- Mercury is logical and serves to align things that aren't flowing together as they should. Venus is cordial and bounces actions back and forth between things that already align. Mercury builds the computer; Venus uses it.
- Your Mars, attached to your dissatisfaction, is what you use to influence things in front of you. But your Ceres, attached to your assessment of things as underperforming, is what you use to "improve" their behavior.
- *The other person's* Mars is NOT attached to dissatisfaction you can really feel, so it is their Vertex which is a better indicator of the change they actually make in their own lives. Instead, their Mars corresponds to the things they do which are intended to elicit a response from you. It's not so much that their Mars wants to change you. More like it wants you to stay the same but with a different response to what they want. Vertex actually works to alter things in general, not just you.
- Uranus is for generic social talk. Bacchus is for the behavior of friends and people who dig you.
- Your Pluto and Pallas, unlike your Mars and Ceres, have less to do with things in front of you and more to do with the force you apply to situations in the abstract. Your Pallas is where you take up arms to change a situation while your Pluto is where you simply push standards upon a thing, in a situation.
- The Midheaven is generally stronger than the Ascendant in synastry, since the Midheaven publicly acknowledges the planet it's compared to while the Ascendant "comes at" new situations through the lens of that planet. Coming into a new situation happens in tons of ways, most of which are nigh-insignificant in the context of an interaction. Acknowledgement, though, tends to be moment defining. At a party, the Midheaven represents that first glanced impression. The Ascendant constitutes the vast array of subject changes and new schmooze topics approached by you and your interlocutors.
- Commitment to something with your own Juno seems like a simple agreement to fulfill certain obligations. Committing to something with *someone else's* Juno involves an entire world full of priorities reweighed and put on hold just so you can stay out of one situation and stay in another. Understandably, reading the other person's Juno is more complicated than reading your own. In a real sense there are many more well-defined pressures involved with their Juno than yours. With your own Juno, such pressures are probably just as heavy, but you handle them too automatically to notice.

Table 21-2a: How we experience different planet tendencies in synastry and composite charts

Element	Typical planets
Fireish (looks like an action)	Pluto, Ascendant, Selene, Lilith
Earthish (looks like a structure)	Saturn, Midheaven
Airish (looks like communication)	Venus
Waterish (looks like a feeling)	Moon, Neptune, Selene, Fortune, Ceres, Hera
Situation	**Typical planets**
Force-related (associated with making things happen by pushing them)	Mars, Pluto, Ceres
Acknowledgment-related (associated with group or personal identification of things)	Venus, Uranus, Midheaven, Bacchus
Attention-related (associated with getting attention)	Sun, Uranus, Lilith, Pallas
Feeling-related (typically brings the urge to influence something)	Moon, Mars, Fortune, Hera, Eros

Table 23-1: Tools we interact with that build up planets

Planet	Tools like...	...which elicit...
Moon	home, friends, desired things, children, pets, food	emotion
Sun	other people, hobby objects, fun outings	default 1:1 interaction
Mercury	attention to one's health, puzzles, disordered things	a desire to work on things / align them with a standard
Venus	beautiful things, friends, social standards	a desire to communicate (or exchange 1:1 feedback) with the things we interact with
Mars	sex-related things, anger inciters, the unknown	a desire to steer others / change things
Jupiter	foreign subjects of interest, enabling or exploratory experiences	going forward in the world
Saturn	rules, career, buildings, things that restrict, laws, bad experiences, administrative demands	experience of structure
Uranus	electronics, media, groups which socialize among themselves	social talk
Neptune	movies, music, art, places where a specific mood is designed to gather (like prisons, theme parks, and hospitals)	imagination
Pluto	big issues, public trends, governments, law enforcement groups, standards agencies (like education boards, certification groups, and testing providers)	social / cultural pressure
Ascendant (1st house cusp)	new situations	approach behavior
Midheaven (10th house cusp)	situations where one presents oneself	reputation, self-labeling style
Selene (White Moon)	things that make others uncomfortable which you can comfortably solve, skill opportunities	ideal talents
Lilith (Lunar Apogee/ Black Moon)	things which encourage unfitting conformity, topics where publicly known truths are purposely kept private (like sex, death, existential uncertainty, rules that go against common sense, social norms that defy actual social practice)	rebellion
Vertex	newly imposed circumstances, things that remove accustomed comfort	response to major change
Ceres	things that dissatisfy or go astray, flirtation objects	coercion of others
Chiron	problem situations, illness, broken things	doctor-patient behavior
North Node	things one has been on the lookout for	a feeling of convenient opportunity / a feeling of something that was meant to be
Part of Fortune	stability and comfort inducing conditions	being comfortable in one's situation
Vesta	family, demanding tasks	a need for focus
Pallas	social injustice, social imbalance, resolvable information-based disorder	socialized action
Juno	a sense of incompleteness, capture-worthy things	commitment
Hera	things that are better than their current imperfect equivalents, where there is a <u>noticeable</u> preference for the better thing	bonding
Eros	receptiveness to provocation, for better or worse	passion
Bacchus	occasions and actions worth actively sharing	peer and clique behavior

Appendix IV: Angle-related Tables

Table 16-6: The harmonics (angle families) 1-36

Harmonic	Name	Symbol	Degrees	Meaning	How to use
1	conjunct	☌	0°	natural trait	do something, be yourself
2	opposition	☍	180°	natural value	feel something, value something
3	trine	△	120°	easy thought	think about something
4	square	□	90°	wanting, having an inclination	want something
5	quintile	⭑ or Q	72°, 144°	projecting your way 1:1 with another	notice how you promote yourself to others
6	sextile	⚹	60°	finding common ground with another	serve, work, or analyze
7	septile	✡	51°26′, 102°51′, 154°17′	share ideas under a common topic with another	notice how you share ideas with others; notice what kinds of games you prefer to play
8	octile	∠ or ⚼	45°, 135°	overriding other's intent	manipulate another's actions
9	novile	九 or N	40°, 80°, 160°	declaring one's identity in the world	notice how you declare your identity
10	decile	+	36°, 108°	forming a reputation	consistently perform actions which others can see
11	undecile	U	32°44′, 65°27′, 98°11′, 130°55′, 163°38′	gaining popularity	perform unique actions which few can copy
12	inconjunct	⚻	30°, 150°	leaving an impression without doing the actual deed	notice how others treat you in light of things you haven't done
13	II-conjunct	$☌^2$	27°42′, 55°23′, 83°05′, 110°46′, 138°28′, 166°09′	your expressive style	note the tools you use to promote your values. These could be objects or tactics
14	II-opposition	$☍^2$	25°43′, 77°09′, 128°34′	what your values are intended to accomplish	let others interact with your socially (ethnically) trained ideas or respond to your physical presence
15	II-trine	$△^2$	24°, 48°, 96°, 168°	what you strongly extract from others simply by being around	show up and give your unqualified opinion
16	II-square	$□^2$	22°30′, 67°30′, 112°30′, 157°30′	what you wish to be respected for	develop an expert's intuition for subjects related to this angle family
17	II-quintile	$⭑^2$ or Q^2	21°11′, 42°21′, 63°32′, 84°42′, 105°53′, 127°04′, 148°14′, 169°25′	what you brag about, complain on behalf of, and are personally proud of	let others praise you regarding planets separated by this angle family
18	II-sextile	⚹	20°, 100°, 140°	your goal-oriented work efforts	investigate, then practice the most important ideas you seek to build up in others
19	II-septile	✡	18°57′, 37°54′, 56°51′, 75°47′, 94°44′, 113°41′, 132°38′, 151°35′, 170°32′	how you present compelling ideas to others	imagine yourself in an idealized conversation with someone over an issue you think is important; note how that image relates to the planet pair

20	II-octile	∠^{2} or ⚼^{2}	18°, 54°, 126°, 162°	unstated, but well-known magnetism, causes of jealousy in others	publicly display those values, material possessions, and tokens of self-worth which are intended to manipulate viewers' feelings
21	II-novile	九^2 or N^2	17°09', 34°17', 68°34', 85°43', 137°09', 171°25'	overadherence to rules, excessive zeal for proving you've met a standard	think about what you believe to be the most important ideas in your world, then consider the values you hold and behaviors you adopt concerning those ideas; learn to convince others of the importance of those ideas through actions, not words alone
22	II-decile	+^{2}	16°22', 49°05', 81°49', 114°33', 147°16'	the standards against which you measure a proper reputation; the reputation you earn by structuring things	combine all pairs in +^{2} into a single ideal career; investigate how you would pursue that career
23	II-undecile	U^2	15°39', 31°18', 46°57', 78°16', 93°55', 125°13', 140°52', 172°10'	standalone individualism, values that get you talked about in the world	collect items, ideas, or people you believe to be unique
24	II-inconjunct	⚻^{2}	15°, 75°, 105°, 165°	works of the imagination which are likely to manifest in the real world	pay attention to those things which you are inclined to stick with through thick and thin; reinforce this dedication
25	III-conjunct	☌^{3}	14°24', 28°48', 43°12', 100°48', 115°12', 172°48'	your vehicles for expression; your deeds which align with mass psychology	ask what characteristics people tend to come to you for and what characteristics cause people to stay away from you; what about you as a person makes others jealous?
26	III-opposition	☍^{3}	13°51', 69°14', 96°55'	your tendency to check your actions against your values; fans and supporters	notice where and how you publicly question decisions you've made; when do fans follow you?
27	III-trine	Δ^3	13°20', 26°40', 66°40', 106°40'	your ability to broadcast your ideas without remorse; forward confidence; insight	locate the Δ^{3}s in your chart and do more of what the pairs suggest; exercise where you have insight
28	III-square	□^{3}	12°51', 157°09'	your ability to deliver measured cooperation while still maintaining your own perspective; morals	look at those areas where you don't care what others have to say about your choices; stay with those choices
29	III-quintile	★^{3} or Q^3	12°25', 24°50', 37°14', 62°04', 86°54', 124°08', 148°58', 173°48'	your ability to use humor and hold a self-contented sense of prosperity	look at areas in which others don't take you seriously; master them by not taking yourself so seriously in those same areas
30	III-sextile	✱	12°, 84°, 132°, 156°	your ability to deliver expert criticism	look at areas in which most other groups of people defer to your judgment; learn to deliver your criticism in ways that don't violate others' sense of self-respect
31	III-septile	✡	11°37', 23°14', 34°50', 58°04', 92°54', 116°08'	your ability to engage a task all the way through; spreading doctrines and beliefs through speech	look at areas in which you are attentive to detail in every aspect, every time; practice engaging those areas without getting drained
32	III-octile	∠^{3} or ⚼^{3}	11°15', 78°45', 146°15	your ability to delve beneath the surface of an event and break your relationship with it if necessary; an interest in mysteries	think about the things you love doing, where interactants are less enthusiastic than you are; learn to read cues for when you've dwelled too long on those things

33	III-novile	九³ or N³	10°55′, 21°49′, 76°22′, 109°05′, 141°49′	your ability to get a group fired up	channel your influence over receptive groups towards a useful cause which others are inclined to support
34	III-decile	+³	10°35′, 52°56′, 74°07′, 158°49′	your ability to elevate yourself above others; your ideas regarding authority	behave as you believe a true authority would
35	III-undecile	U³	10°17′, 30°51′, 41°09′, 113°09′, 174°51′	your ability to follow your unique curiosity	indulge your curiosity regarding planets in this harmonic
36	III-inconjunct	不³	10°, 50°, 70°, 110°, 130°, 170°	your ability to promote an idea despite the secret impression behind it	investigate why you present your ideas as you do; admit areas where you lack focus and develop workarounds

Table 16-6: the first 36 of 144 possible angle families in a 12 cycle cut in to 12 more pieces.

This book usually won't go past 36, but where new research since the writing of *FSA* has revealed more insight into the behavior of harmonics 37 and up, I sometimes discuss harmonics past these.

Table 16-7: Table of angle families by degree

Degree	Name	Symbol	Harmonic name	Most basic angle
0°…9°	conjunct	☌	conjunct	**conjunct**
10°	III-inconjunct	⚻^{3}	III-inconjunct	**conjunct**
10°17′	III-undecile	∪^{3}	III-undecile	III-undecile
10°35′	III-decile	+^{3}	III-decile	III-decile
10°55′	III-novile	九^3	III-novile	III-novile
11°15′	III-octile	∠^{3}	III-octile	III-octile
11°37′	III-septile	✡^{3}	III-septile	III-septile
12°	III-sextile	⚹^{3}	III-sextile	III-sextile
12°25′	III-quintile	⋆^{3}	III-quintile	III-quintile
12°51′	III-square	□^{3}	III-square	III-square
13°20′	III-trine	△^{3}	III-trine	III-trine
13°51′	III-opposition	☍^{3}	III-opposition	III-opposition
14°24′	III-conjunct	☌^{3}	III-conjunct	III-conjunct
15°	II-inconjunct	⚻^{2}	II-inconjunct	**II-inconjunct**
15°39′	II-undecile	∪^{2}	II-undecile	II-undecile
16°22′	II-decile	+^{2}	II-decile	II-decile
17°09′	II-novile	九^2	II-novile	II-novile
18°	II-octile	∠^{2}	II-octile	II-octile
18°57′	II-septile	✡^{2}	II-septile	II-septile
20°	II-sextile	⚹^{2}	II-sextile	II-sextile
21°11′	II-quintile	⋆^{2}	II-quintile	II-quintile
21°49′	bi-III-novile	九$^3_{(2)}$	III-novile	III-novile
22°30′	II-square	□^{2}	II-square	II-square
23°14′	bi-III-septile	✡$^3_{(2)}$	III-septile	III-septile
24°	II-trine	△^{2}	II-trine	II-trine
24°50′	bi-III-quintile	⋆$^3_{(2)}$	III-quintile	III-quintile
25°43′	II-opposition	☍^{2}	II-opposition	II-opposition
26°40′	bi-III-trine	△$^3_{(2)}$	III-trine	III-trine
27°42′	II-conjunct	☌^{2}	II-conjunct	II-conjunct
28°48′	bi-III-conjunct	☌$^3_{(2)}$	III-conjunct	**semisextile**
30°	semisextile	⚺	inconjunct	**semisextile**
30°51′	tri-III-undecile	∪$^3_{(3)}$	III-undecile	**semisextile**
31°18′	bi-II-undecile	∪$^2_{(2)}$	II-undecile	**semisextile**
32°44′	undecile	∪	undecile	**undecile**
34°17′	bi-II-novile	九$^2_{(2)}$	II-novile	**undecile**
34°50′	tri-III-septile	✡$^3_{(3)}$	III-septile	**decile**
36°	decile	⊥	decile	**decile**
37°14′	tri-III-quintile	⋆$^3_{(3)}$	III-quintile	**decile**
37°54′	bi-II-septile	✡$^2_{(2)}$	II-septile	**decile**

40°	novile	九	novile	**novile**
41°09′	quatro-III-undecile	U$^{3}_{(4)}$	III-undecile	**novile**
42°21′	bi-II-quintile	⋆$^{2}_{(2)}$	II-quintile	**novile**
43°12′	tri-III-conjunct	☌$^{3}_{(3)}$	III-conjunct	**semisquare**
45°	semisquare	∠	octile	**semisquare**
46°57′	tri-II-undecile	U$^{2}_{(3)}$	II-undecile	**semisquare**
48°	bi-II-trine	△$^{2}_{(2)}$	II-trine	
49°05′	tri-II-decile	+$^{2}_{(3)}$	II-decile	**II-decile**
50°	quinti-III-inconjunct	⚻$^{3}_{(5)}$	III-inconjunct	
51°26′	septile	✡	septile	**septile**
52°56′	quintideki-III-decile	+$^{3}_{(5)}$	III-decile	**septile**
54°	tri-II-octile	∠$^{2}_{(3)}$	II-octile	**II-octile**
55°23′	bi-II-conjunct	☌$^{2}_{(2)}$	II-conjunct	
56°51′	tri-II-septile	✡$^{2}_{(3)}$	II-septile	**sextile**
58°04′	quinti-III-septile	✡$^{3}_{(5)}$	III-septile	**sextile**
60°	sextile	⚹	sextile	**sextile**
62°04′	quinti-III-quintile	⋆$^{3}_{(5)}$	III-quintile	**sextile**
63°32′	tri-II-quintile	⋆$^{2}_{(3)}$	II-quintile	
65°27′	biundecile	U$_{(2)}$	undecile	**biundecile**
66°40′	quinti-III-trine	△$^{3}_{(5)}$	III-trine	
67°30′	tri-II-square	□$^{2}_{(3)}$	II-square	
68°34′	quatro-II-novile	九$^{2}_{(4)}$	II-novile	
69°14′	quinti-III-opposition	☍$^{3}_{(5)}$	III-opposition	
70°	septi-III-inconjunct	⚻$^{3}_{(7)}$	III-inconjunct	**quintile**
72°	quintile	⋆	quintile	**quintile**
74°07′	septi-III-decile	+$^{3}_{(7)}$	III-decile	**quintile**
75°	quinti-II-inconjunct	⚻$^{2}_{(5)}$	II-inconjunct	
75°47′	quatro-II-septile	✡$^{2}_{(4)}$	II-septile	
76°22′	septi-III-novile	九$^{3}_{(7)}$	III-novile	
77°09′	tri-II-opposition	☍$^{2}_{(3)}$	II-opposition	
78°16′	quinti-II-undecile	U$^{2}_{(5)}$	II-undecile	**binovile**
78°45′	septi-III-octile	∠$^{3}_{(7)}$	III-octile	**binovile**
80°	binovile	九$_{(2)}$	novile	**binovile**
81°49′	quinti-II-decile	+$^{2}_{(5)}$	II-decile	**binovile**
83°05′	tri-II-conjunct	☌$^{2}_{(3)}$	II-conjunct	**binovile**
84°	septi-III-sextile	⚹$^{3}_{(7)}$	III-sextile	
84°42′	quatro-II-quintile	⋆$^{2}_{(4)}$	II-quintile	
85°43′	quinti-II-novile	九$^{2}_{(5)}$	II-novile	**square**
86°54′	septi-III-quintile	⋆$^{3}_{(7)}$	III-quintile	**square**
90°	square	□	square	**square**
92°54′	octo-III-septile	✡$^{3}_{(8)}$	III-septile	**square**
93°55′	sexto-II-undecile	U$^{2}_{(6)}$	II-undecile	**square**

94°44′	quinti-II-septile	✡$^{2}_{(5)}$	II-septile	**square**
96°	quatro-II-trine	△$^{2}_{(4)}$	II-trine	**triundecile**
96°55′	septi-III-opposition	☍$^{3}_{(7)}$	III-opposition	**triundecile**
98°11′	triundecile	U$_{(3)}$	undecile	**triundecile**
100°	quinti-II-sextile	⚹$^{2}_{(5)}$	II-sextile	
100°48′	septi-III-conjunct	☌$^{3}_{(7)}$	III-conjunct	
102°51′	triseptile	✡$_{(3)}$	septile	**triseptile**
105°	septi-II-inconjunct	⚻$^{2}_{(7)}$	II-inconjunct	
105°53′	quinti-II-quintile	⋆$^{2}_{(5)}$	II-quintile	
106°40′	octo-III-trine	△$^{3}_{(8)}$	III-trine	**tridecile**
108°	tridecile	T$_{(3)}$	decile	**tridecile**
109°05′	deki-III-novile	九$^{3}_{(10)}$	III-novile	
110°	undeki-III-inconjunct	⚻$^{3}_{(11)}$	III-inconjunct	
110°46′	quatro-II-conjunct	☌$^{2}_{(4)}$	II-conjunct	
112°30′	quinti-II-square	□$^{2}_{(5)}$	II-square	**II-square**
113°09′	undeki-III-undecile	U$^{3}_{(11)}$	III-undecile	**II-square**
113°41′	sexto-II-septile	✡$^{2}_{(6)}$	II-septile	
114°33′	septi-II-decile	+$^{2}_{(7)}$	II-decile	
115°12′	octo-III-conjunct	☌$^{3}_{(8)}$	III-conjunct	**trine**
116°08′	deki-III-septile	✡$^{3}_{(10)}$	III-septile	**trine**
117°...**120°**...123°	trine	△	trine	**trine**
124°08′	deki-III-quintile	⋆$^{3}_{(10)}$	III-quintile	**trine**
125°13′	octo-II-undecile	U$^{2}_{(8)}$	II-undecile	
126°	septi-II-octile	∠$^{2}_{(7)}$	II-octile	**II-octile**
127°04′	sexto-II-quintile	⋆$^{2}_{(6)}$	II-quintile	
128°34′	quinti-II-opposition	☍$^{2}_{(5)}$	II-opposition	
130°	trideki-III-inconjunct	⚻$^{3}_{(13)}$	III-inconjunct	**quatrundecile**
130°55′	quatrundecile	U$_{(4)}$	undecile	**quatrundecile**
132°	undeki-III-sextile	⚹$^{3}_{(11)}$	III-sextile	
132°38′	septi-II-septile	✡$^{2}_{(7)}$	II-septile	**sesquiquadrate**
135°	sesquiquadrate	⚼	octile	**sesquiquadrate**
137°09′	octo-II-novile	九$^{2}_{(8)}$	II-novile	**sesquiquadrate**
138°28′	quinti-II-conjunct	☌$^{2}_{(5)}$	II-conjunct	**sesquiquadrate**
140°	septi-II-sextile	⚹$^{2}_{(7)}$	II-sextile	**II-sextile**
140°52′	novo-II-undecile	U$^{2}_{(9)}$	II-undecile	
141°49′	trideki-III-novile	九$^{3}_{(13)}$	III-novile	
142°...**144°**...145°30′	quintile	⋆	quintile	**biquintile**
146°15	trideki-III-octile	∠$^{3}_{(13)}$	III-octile	
147°16′	novo-II-decile	+$^{2}_{(9)}$	II-decile	**inconjunct**
148°14′	septi-II-quintile	⋆$^{2}_{(7)}$	II-quintile	**inconjunct**
148°58′	duodeki-III-quintile	⋆$^{3}_{(12)}$	III-quintile	**inconjunct**
150°	inconjunct	⚻	inconjunct	**inconjunct**

151°35′	octo-II-septile	✡$^{2}_{(8)}$	II-septile	
152°30′...**154°17′**...155°	triseptile	✡$_{(3)}$	septile	**triseptile**
156°	trideki-III-sextile	✱$^{3}_{(13)}$	III-sextile	
157°09′	trideki-III-square	□$^{3}_{(13)}$	III-square	
157°30′	septi-II-square	□$^{2}_{(7)}$	II-square	
158°49′	quintideki-III-decile	┼$^{3}_{(15)}$	III-decile	**quatronovile**
160°	quatronovile	九$_{(4)}$	novile	**quatronovile**
162°	novo-II-octile	∠$^{2}_{(9)}$	II-octile	
163°38′	quintundecile	U$_{(5)}$	undecile	**quintundecile**
165°	undeki-II-inconjunct	⊼$^{2}_{(11)}$	II-inconjunct	**undeki-II-inconjunct**
166°09′	sexto-II-conjunct	☌$^{2}_{(6)}$	II-conjunct	
168°	septi-II-trine	△$^{2}_{(7)}$	II-trine	**II-trine**
169°25′	octo-II-quintile	⋆$^{2}_{(8)}$	II-quintile	
170°	septideki-III-inconjunct	⊼$^{3}_{(17)}$	III-inconjunct	**septideki-III-inconjunct**
170°32′	novo-II-septile	✡$^{2}_{(9)}$	II-septile	
171°25′	deki-II-novile	九$^{2}_{(10)}$	II-novile	**II-novile**
172°10′	undeki-II-undecile	U$^{2}_{(11)}$	II-undecile	**opposition**
172°48′	duodeki-III-conjunct	☌$^{3}_{(12)}$	III-conjunct	**opposition**
173°48′	quatrodeki-III-quintile	⋆$^{3}_{(14)}$	III-quintile	**opposition**
174°51′	septideki-III-undecile	U$^{3}_{(17)}$	III-undecile	**opposition**
175°...180°	opposition	☍	opposition	**opposition**

Table 16-7: Aspects 0° – 180° by degree (up to harmonic 36) If you've done some astrology already and are only used to using major aspects (or if applying nonstandard angles feels weird to you), then you might read the angles under the "Most basic angle" column instead. Blank entries means the angle in question might be read as either of the nearby angles. Each degree is actually a blend of all the possible angles near it, so don't worry too much about whether, say, 139° is more like a sesquiquadrate or more like a II-sextile. Until we humans evolve more computer-like precision in distinguishing feelings, this kind of difference won't matter. While precision is important, slippage in nearby angles won't kill you. I talk more about this in *FSA*.

Table 17-4: Range of behaviors for each of the first 36 angle families

Harmonic	Name	Symbol	Degrees	Lower stress version	Medium stress version	Higher stress version
[The following angles play out when you are engaging] Level I, Group 1: Self (you)						
1	conjunct	☌	0°	**adjoining** (associated without necessarily doing anything together)	**being /expressing together**	**not ceasing to be** (as in a pair you can't turn off)
2	opposition	☍	180°	**bodily feeling**	**self-valuing / identifying with** (establishing common ground between oneself and a thing)	**valuing** (measuring a thing against another thing used to measure the self; related to money)
3	trine	△	120°	**performing an action** (pre-thought mental activity)	**thinking** (internal monologue)	**communicating/opinionating** (exported thought)
4	square	□	90°	**using intuition** (predicting / expecting something)	**feeling** (processing the difference b/w what is and what is experienced or expected)	**wanting** (acting to minimize the difference b/w what is and what is expected)
Level I, Group 2: Other (your direct 1:1 interactants)						
5	quintile	⋆	72°, 144°	**ego broadcasting / playing** (as in games) (acting naturally to project onto another)	**interacting 1:1 with another** (acting purposefully to exchange with another)	**being motivated in the 1:1 presence of another** (acting as newly directed in exchange with another)
6	sextile	✱	60°	**making meaning** (writing the role of a 1:1 thing against other things; assoc w/ analysis)	**working towards** (performing actions against a 1:1 thing to align it with other things; assoc w/ service)	**maintaining (through upkeep)** (keeping the role of a 1:1 thing from deviating from that of other things; assoc w/ health)
7	septile	✡	51°26′, 102°51′, 154°17′	**listening 1:1** (they talk, you process)	**conversing 1:1** (you both talk and process)	**instructing / playing 1:1** (as in instruments, video games) (you "talk," they process)
8	octile	∠	45°, 135°	**reasoning** (making ideas do what you want them to do)	**steering** (making others do what you want them to do)	**manipulating** / **showing aggression** (making others do what you want while you yourself feel... ...passive discord) / ...active discord)

Level I, Group 3: World (a catch-all term for the faceless space of things around you)						
9	novile	九	40°, 80°, 160°	**projecting a strong image** (being seen by the world)	**learning** (processing the world)	**traveling** (actively absorbing and interacting with the world)
10	decile	+	36°, 108°	**controlling** (being seen as keeping the behavior of an existing thing aligned with your actions)	**expanding a reputation** (being seen as acting in a new way that aligns with your existing actions)	**exercising authority / limiting** (being seen as actively stopping an existing thing from getting out line with your actions and expectations)
11	undecile	∪	32°44′, 65°27′, 98°11′, 130°55′, 163°38′	**being talked about on the grapevine / being surrounded by info that resembles your priorities; uniqueness** (just being where it happens)	**frequenting social groups / taking in such social information** (processing it)	**aspiring to be talked about or associated with certain social ideas / humanitarian effects** (requires active effort)
12	inconjunct	⚻	30°, 150°	**being in a mood** (holding any basic emotional disposition; others can read this through empathy)	**maintaining a secret side** (holding a disposition, knowing how it differs from the apparent actions which others see)	**projecting a desire onto world** (holding an emotional disposition
Level II, Group 1: society (the small-ish sphere of people you actually live and work among. This is not the abstract world!)						
13	II-conjunct	$☌^2$	27°42′, 55°23′, 83°05′, 110°46′, 138°28′, 166°09′	**holding a public persona** (the instinctive face you put on in public)	**playing a socialized role** (actively behaving in line with your societal face)	**putting your personal "brand" in others' faces** (purposely directing your societally-played face towards a particular recipient)
14	II-opposition	$☍^2$	25°43′, 77°09′, 128°34′	**being associated with a particular race / class** (having yourself pigeonholed based on your similarity or lack of similarity to people who look like you)	**putting the things you identify with to use** (this includes your language, dress, body characteristics, objects that travel with you, and favorite roles; the effect that comes with your showing up as a body)	**pleasure seeking** (having your societally labeled values be something you actively seek to have pleased; acting to have other events fuel the use of things you identify with; hedonism)
15	II-trine	Δ^2	24°, 48°, 96°, 168°	**displaying mannerisms** (pre-thought actions which communicate with society, your default bearing wherever you are, regardless of the attention you pay to your surroundings)	**"opinionating" onto society / leaving an impression upon a generic situation** (thinking within the context of society; roughly, your responses to what happens wherever you are)	**room hijacking / getting attention** (how you actively announce yourself to recruit the attention of others)

16	II-square	□^{2}	22°30′, 67°30′, 112°30′, 157°30′	**having family values** (emotional dispositions you bring from childhood training into your expectations for others in society)	**aspiring to be respected** (acting to have your core values validated by your society)	**tending to / training / caretaking /teaching** (acting to place your core values on others)
Level II, Group 2: The fishbowl (your preferred family of associations—people, things, or actions—plucked from society for you to interact with as a stable base in everyday matters)						
17	II-quintile	⋆^{2}	21°11′, 42°21′, 63°32′, 84°42′, 105°53′, 127°04′, 148°14′, 169°25′	**growing / reinforcing / "daoing"** ("growing with the flow" to adapt a cliché) (accumulating new skills which naturally appeal to your instincts)	**"fishbowling" / validating / fighting for / serving** (actively referencing trained behavioral tools, from the fishbowl that you already have, which quiets your need to complain or brag)	**complaining / bragging / showing pride / dominating** (expressing your current tools for response to things beyond you in its most honest, untrained, tension-filled animal state)
18	II-sextile	⚹^{2}	20°, 100°, 140°	**having a goal** (an average of all of your current dispositions compressed into a single, common ground endpoint)	**rationalizing / summarizing** (averaging the existing ideas you observe into a single, common ground endpoint)	**long-range planning** (actively arranging ideas and future expectations you have into a single, common ground endpoint)
19	II-septile	✡^{2}	18°57′, 37°54′, 56°51′, 75°47′, 94°44′, 113°41′, 132°38′, 151°35′, 170°32′	**having ideas regarding how you communicate with others / listening to messages which affirm your own way of sending messages** (having standards for how you and your fishbowl ["us"] communicate your values)	**assimilating outside ideas into existing ideas which you already find meaningful** (this is where you open the door to "them" in the usual "us vs them" human way, so as to bend the power barriers set up by your fishbowl—hence this harmonic's association with gender bending and reversed power roles discussed in *FSA*)	**presenting ideas you already find meaningful** (sending out "us"-related ideas from your fishbowl)
20	II-octile	∠^{2}	18°, 54°, 126°, 162°	**being magnetic in ways that others recognize, but won't talk about** (where people outside of your fishbowl are influenced by its power-style, but since they *are* outsiders, they are reluctant to talk to you about this unless you invite them into your group)	**steering people outside of your ingroup / fishbowl** (this is where you close the door to "them" in the usual "us vs them" human way, so as to affirm the power-styles outlined by your fishbowl. Look at what types of power your closest friends value and foist this upon others to use this angle.)	**competing for power on behalf of your ingroup's power values / seducing / making others jealous / setting them up to succumb to your wants** (an open, active, and remorseless version of fishbowl power-style steering)

Level II, Group 3: Creative works (the character of things, efforts, and stranger-influencing impressions made by you)						
21	II-novile	九^2	17°09′, 34°17′, 68°34′, 85°43′, 137°09′, 171°25′	**being alluring, unsettling, making others squirm with an image you create in the faceless world** (passively creating—from nothing apparent—something for others to view or experience; like birthing; brings tension in them)	**showing effort towards something** (actively creating—from nothing apparent—something for others to view or experience [nothing apparent b/c they can't read your mind to know what motivated you])	**being obnoxious, aggravating, [anger, fear, or frustration]-inspiring** (actively creating—from nothing apparent—something for others to view or experience while holding discordant emotions which spill onto others)
22	II-decile	$+^2$	16°22′, 49°05′, 81°49′, 114°33′, 147°16′	**having a reputation for certain kinds of limits or boundaries you've unintentionally placed on things**	**gaining a reputation through the structure of the things or events you've intentionally caused**	**creating through the structure you actively enforce upon things, intentionally cause, or maintain**
23	II-undecile	$\cup^2$	15°39′, 31°18′, 46°57′, 78°16′, 93°55′, 125°13′, 140°52′, 172°10′	**being exceptional, being talked about for unique quirks you've unintentionally displayed / the values you hold for being talked about in the social world**	**creating events which rest upon how or what you communicate as building blocks** (the world doesn't normally register the normal things you do, mainly the abnormal—hence this harmonic's association w provocative talk / the areas in which you break taboo)	**actively indulging your standalone individualism**
24	II-inconjunct	⊼^{2}	15°, 75°, 105°, 165°	**leaving an impression on others through the nature of your creative works**	**visualizing / imagining**	**putting continuous, imaginative effort into making something real**
Level III, Group 1: Mass psychology (behaviors you display which are backed by larger public patterns)						
25	III-conjunct	☌^{3}	14°24′, 28°48′, 43°12′, 100°48′, 115°12′, 172°48′	**using big groups in the world to justify what you do**	**behaving in ways that line up with the way big groups in the world describe it as being properly done**	**mass action / recruiting big groups in the world to back you in what you do**
26	III-opposition	☍^{3}	13°51′, 69°14′, 96°55′	**having a public fan base** (displaying a consistent enough set of traits to warrant others' following or support of you)	**publicly questioning your own efforts** (reviewing those behaviors of yours which your fans follow)	**catering to your fans / lining up with the trends (values) they expect** (actively adjusting your behaviors to align with what your fans follow)
27	III-trine	△^{3}	13°20′, 26°40′, 66°40′, 106°40′	**having insight into an event**	**communicating your insight**	**putting your insight into practice**

28	III-square	□^{3}	12°51′, 157°09′	**having morals / considering mass expectation as informing your decisions / feeling the extent to which an event aligns with your morals**	**acting in line with your principles / moral responsibility / doing for the higher good (or at least higher purpose)**	**giving unconvinced cooperation with events that deviate from your principles**
Level III, Group 2: Mass influence (how you actually steer big groups; [where "mass psychology" only *identifies with* them])						
29	III-quintile	⋆^{3}	12°25′, 24°50′, 37°14′, 62°04′, 86°54′, 124°08′, 148°58′, 173°48′	**having confidence** (engaging the mass world with surety in your thoughts of your actions ["surety" here means that you "know with certainty" what talents you bring)	**displaying a sense of self-contented prosperity** (engaging the mass world with surety in your actions)	**being funny or entertaining / showing off / commanding others** (asserting your individual ways upon the mass world with surety [where the world isn't *really* likely to be moved by your small perspective, you are considered funny])
30	III-sextile	∗^{3}	12°, 84°, 132°, 156°	**objectifying the body (or one's presence)** (finding common ground built on the 1:1 ego; in *FSA* this would be the same as 6 x 5—"6ing the 5s")	**having expertise** (giving your skill for common ground its own ego form; 5 x 6 or "5ing the 6s")	**being an expert critic** (alternating between giving your skill for common ground its own ego AND objectifying your own presence in association with this)
31	III-septile	✩^{3}	11°37′, 23°14′, 34°50′, 58°04′, 92°54′, 116°08′	**being motivated to see an idea all the way through / unrealized good intentions** (having the inclination to apply one idea across many situations, without necessarily acting on this)	**traversing networks of people** (applying your general "idea" across many 1:1 minds)	**promoting a doctrine / group management / pushing towards renown** (asserting your general "idea" across many 1:1 minds)
32	III-octile	∠^{3}	11°15′, 78°45′, 146°15	**being (seen as) mysterious** (being seen as attempting to secretly steer the inclinations of the mass world around you)	**being distrustful** (actually attempting to steer or reinterpret the inclinations of the mass world around you—usually in light of a particular event you've been presented with)	**analyzing a thing until it breaks (i.e. until you uncover the "catch")** (openly and actively attempting to steer or reinterpret the inclinations of the mass world around you in light of a particular event)
Level III, Group 3: Leadership and Representativeness (where the mass world sees you as synonymous with an idea)						
33	III-novile	九^3	10°55′, 21°49′, 76°22′, 109°05′, 141°49′	**being watched** (where the faceless world looks at you and you feel it)	**being under the spotlight** (where the faceless world looks at you and you know it)	**rallying crowds / executing your stage presence** (where the faceless world looks at you, you know it, and you respond accordingly)

34	III-decile	$+^{3}$	10°35′, 52°56′, 74°07′, 158°49′	**having expectations regarding authority**	**weighing the authorities you're subject to against your own standards / weighing your subordinates (including yourself) against your authority standards**	**behaving as if you are an authority / exercising discipline**
35	III-undecile	$\cup^{3}$	10°17′, 30°51′, 41°09′, 113°09′, 174°51′	**having ideas regarding what's worthy of attention**	**following curiosity in areas beyond what others normally give attention to / absorbing information unique to your personality**	**exercising unique skill in a way that others see as attention-worthy**
36	III-inconjunct	$\barwedge^{3}$	10°, 50°, 70°, 110°, 130°, 170°	**having ideas regarding that which inspires groups to action / having others place bets (group expectations) on your performance** (where your unknowing actions elicit others' intuition or inclinations)	**absorbing inspiration from a thing** (where you knowingly gain motivation from the intuition or inclinations of others as shown in external events)	**remaining committed to a task despite occasional lapses in focus / inspired work / poor quality work done in zombie mode** (where you act in line with the intuition or inclinations of others despite your own occasional divorce from the task)

Table 17-4: Range of behaviors for the first 36 harmonic angle families. In general the low stress version of each harmonic corresponds to your [taking in] the world. The medium stress version comes with consciously receiving input from an other. The high stress version corresponds to your mobilizing directed action from the self. In this way, the choice of three divisions wasn't arbitrary, but lines up with the same self-other-world pattern we'll always assume.

Table 17-5: Types of occupations that fit the behavior of the 36 harmonics

Harmonic	Occupation holders	...who do things (Level I)		...who get talked about (Level II)		...who tend to groups (Level III)	
1	doers	conjunct	soldiers, athletes	II-conjunct	performing artists	III-conjunct	public personas
2	valuers	opposition	retail, service industry	II-opposition	beauty and body industry	III-opposition	wealth and brand industry
3	thinkers	trine	transport industry, small-group hosts	II-trine	businesspeople	III-trine	entrepreneurs
4	caretakers	square	teachers, family-related work	II-square	culinary, child-rearing, home-related	III-square	preachers, writers
5	stand-outs	quintile	influencers, hobbyists	II-quintile	coaches, service staff	III-quintile	commentators
6	bridge makers	sextile	analysts & fitness industry	II-sextile	managers	III-sextile	consultants, trainers
7	socializers	septile	counselors, advisors	II-septile	social industry, internal support role	III-septile	networkers
8	controllers	octile	people who control others' power or money through their action	II-octile	engineers, accountants, researchers whose work is public	III-octile	hackers, certain lawyers, investi-gators, political decision makers (people who do hard-to-explain dirty work)
9	expanders	novile	travelers, teachers, explorers	II-novile	artists	III-novile	public performers
10	authorities	decile	law enforcement, bosses, managers	II-decile	builders, construction industry	III-decile	architects, owners of assets, legal industry
11	mass communicators	undecile	customer service, information industry	II-undecile	community builders, journalism, writers	III-undecile	political figures & programmers
12	illusionists	inconjunct	creators of ideas	II-inconjunct	surgeons & filmmakers	III-inconjunct	psychologists & actors

Table 19-1: Synastric angle reference (general)

Harmonic	Name	Symbol	(Angle) Topic	(Angle) Interaction		
				Lower tension version	Neutral version	Higher tension version
In synastry, level I angles describe things that happen in general with no background context						
1	conjunct	☌	**action**	being associated together	cooperating	acting upon an issue together (especially our own disagreement)
2	opposition	☍	**value**	attending to our own bodily feeling (receiving impressions upon it)	assessing ourselves against standards	pursuing similar values
3	trine	△	**communication of internal ideas**	behaving normally	giving our opinions in a situation	critically weighing in on the other
4	square	□	**wants**	using intuition to feel what the other is inclined to do or how they're feeling	wanting the other to do what we want / wanting contrary to what the other wants	responding with upset feeling to the other or to a third issue
5	quintile	⋆	**interaction**	playing around / being ourselves to each other	interacting 1:1 with each other	declaring our egos against / competing with each other
6	sextile	⚹	**work**	sensing a common connection / being inclined towards cordiality	working together / following protocol around each other	serving a third party set of standards
7	septile	✡	**conversation**	listening to / admiring traits in the other	conversing	playing 1:1 / interacting with a third party together (as in video gaming)
8	octile	∠	**influence**	reasoning / analyzing a third issue with each other	steering each other towards what we ourselves want	manipulating or showing aggression towards each other
9	novile	九	**image projection**	indulging an outlook towards the surrounding situation	learning from / responding to a shared situation, fbow	projecting our personalities onto the surrounding environment
10	decile	+	**authority**	viewing where a situation needs to be controlled	building a reputation	exercising authority / limiting or stifling a situation
11	undecile	∪	**surrounding information**	having similar ideas about what's worth talking about or the information around us	creating situations worth others' talking about	tackling social issues or social talk together with action
12	inconjunct	⚻	**vibe**	being in a certain mood in response to surroundings (this is sensitivity to the other's feelings)	responding to each other's vibe with our own / distrusting the other (sensitivity, often very negative)	projecting a mood onto a situation (can be very positive when reinforcing good impressions, but more often makes an already bad exchange prone to further disaster)

Harmonic	Name	Symbol	(Angle) Topic	(Angle) Interaction		
				Lower tension version	Neutral version	Higher tension version
In synastry, level II angles describe things that happen within your "room of influence." Roughly, these are groups of people around you who are capable of responding directly to your deeds.						
13	II-conjunct	☌^{2}	**persona** / room-influencing actions	considering our public persona (encourages the idea that both should be connected based on apparent behaviors)	playing a socialized role in accordance with the setting	advertising our own interests for other's approval
14	II-opposition	☍^{2}	**body presence** / looks / room-determined physical traits or values	holding an attitude towards a situation both are associated with as a physical presence	showing internal (body) response towards a common topic	exchanging turn-ons and areas of interests
15	II-trine	△^{2}	**room-given attention**	leaving impressions on a room through mannerisms	acknowledging the other's ability to get attention / responding to the other's call for attention	dominating an environment intellectually, expressively, or communicatively
16	II-square	□^{2}	**core values** / manners / the emotional standards you project onto a room	considering family, domestic, or personal emotional preferences (facilitates a sense of kindred connection)	discussing valued issues (often regarding friendships and emotional associations)	tending to / training / taking care of others; placing values upon others
17	II-quintile	⋆^{2}	**charisma** / management of room members' actions	managing the value in one's associations with others by serving the other's interests	planning how to handle others or manage things (mainly people) as resources	actively managing people's behavior; dominating
18	II-sextile	⚹^{2}	**work goals**	viewing the requirements of a common task	summarizing the state of issues in a shared environment	responding to people's outlook towards a situation
19	II-septile	✡^{2}	**important ideas** / standards of 1:1 exchange with people in your own class	adopting a behavioral standard which aligns with what the other's ultimate goals are	being required to play complementary roles in a particular social situation	actively maintaining the social requirements of a relationship (facilitates sexual attraction or the alignment of wills)
20	II-octile	∠^{2}	**allure** / standards of power wielded on people outside of your class	being magnetic, mysterious, or desired by others in an unspoken way	steering people outside of your ingroup / fishbowl	acting against a joint enemy (makes for the desire to avoid fighting, since fights with each other—over the joint enemy "relationship"—risk being epic)
21	II-novile	九^2	**creativity or created works** / image projection as seen by your room of influence	being alluring, unsettling in each other's company	displaying a certain kind of attitude in front of a group of people (favors an intense opinion of each other, fbow)	actively entertaining or appealing to the favor of a group of people (conducive to easily not getting along or, at opposite extreme, compelling the other's attraction to you)

Harmonic	Name	Symbol	(Angle) Topic	(Angle) Interaction		
				Lower tension version	Neutral version	Higher tension version
22	II-decile	$+^2$	**reputation** / structures you sponsor or authority you wield as seen by your room of influence	sharing a structured view of a situation	engaging in a dynamic which others are hesitant to interrupt	building a project or concept together
23	II-undecile	$\cup^2$	**unique traits** / topics over which your room of influence talks about you	observing the other at a distance / getting talked about among others as two actors together in an unusual context	adopting an eccentric approach to a subject	actively addressing (as a topic) the behaviors of other people—especially mutual associates
24	II-inconjunct	$\barwedge^2$	**inspiration** / inclinations you plant among your room of influence	leaving an impression on others through an attitude which shows each one's expectations	devoting focus to an idea	reinforcing expectations through each person's behavior
In synastry, level III angles describe things that happen among your "followers" (as in Twitter)—folks who subject themselves to your guidance. This doesn't have to include people in the room with you, but it can include people who read about you.						
25	III-conjunct	☌³	**mass action** / actions backed by those who relate to you	using bigger goals or ideas in the world to fuel one's aspirations	behaving in ways that demonstrate each one's commitment to a particular course of action	performing actions for the satisfaction of bigger groups who have placed expectations upon a situation
26	III-opposition	☍³	**fan standards** / values and standards held by those who relate to you	reviewing the popular performance expectations placed on themselves	conveying high, popularly acknowledged standards in response to a situation	catering to your fans / lining up with the trends (values) they expect
27	III-trine	Δ^3	**insight** / opinions you hold which those who relate to you are automatically inclined to agree with	holding an attitude towards a situation's underlying potential	communicating a situation's potential	acting to draw out a situation's potential
28	III-square	$\square^3$	**morals** / emotional standards held by those who relate to you	holding impressions of the emotional expectations of big groups	desiring to satisfy the needs of big groups / those who give their trust	working to fulfill of the emotional needs or wants of groups who give their trust
29	III-quintile	⭑³	**charm** / personal expression towards those who relate to you	having confidence amidst listening audiences	taking center stage	leading audiences / asserting charisma or star-power over them
30	III-sextile	$*^3$	**expertise** / common ground you find between those who relate to you and topics beyond them	serving as a designated expert on a subject	critiquing a situation	using one's skill as a message communicator to influence people's judgments

Harmonic	Name	Symbol	(Angle) Topic	(Angle) Interaction		
31	III-septile	✡^{3}	**representation** / how you classify the many ideas of those who relate to you into a few ideas	processing webs of information in front of themselves	commanding group attention interfacing with the group agenda / hosting group conversations	actively connecting diverse perspectives under a coherent whole
32	III-octile	∠^{3}	**mystery** / power wielded on behalf of [those who relate to you] over [events beyond them]	having a stubborn, difficult-to-explain goal	being driven by goals that cannot be easily shared with others / being weird	behaving in a way that defies others' support, but serves one's self-interest instead
33	III-novile	九^{3}	**performance** / image you project in the eyes of groups who have agreed to listen to you	having groups members attention placed on them	levying projected power onto followers	spurring the heads of / spirit of a group to action
34	III-decile	+^{3}	**boss-ness** / mastery / authority you demonstrate in the eyes of those who relate to you	having expectations regarding authority / sitting back and observing those associated with them	weighing the behavior of others against their own standards	controlling group situations
35	III-undecile	∪^{3}	**eccentricity** / genius / what's worth talking about in the eyes of those who relate to you	having ideas regarding what's worthy of attention	pursuing areas of curiosity	exercising unique skill in a way that others see as attention-worthy
36	III-inconjunct	⊼^{3}	**legacy** / [impression left on] or [the ways in which you motivate] those who relate to you	leaving an impression on those who follow their activities	absorbing inspiration from or being provoked by a thing	displaying driven behavior towards their envisioned ends

Table 19-1: Situations associated with the first 36 harmonics. Note that low, neutral, and high tension do not correspond to goodness or badness. A high tension exchange can be bad or good for the people involved, for example.

Table 19-2: Common characteristics associated with each harmonic

Harmonic	Name	Characteristic	Harmonic	Name	Characteristic
1	conjunct	instinctive expression	19	II-septile	ingroup representativeness
2	opposition	show of worth or value	20	II-octile	power (over third parties)
3	trine	communication of internal thoughts	21	II-novile	creativity or attitude projection
4	square	emotional power or intuition	22	II-decile	command over a realm of behavior
5	quintile	popularity or direct interaction	23	II-undecile	individuality or uniqueness
6	sextile	usefulness	24	II-inconjunct	influence over other's attitudes
7	septile	sociability	25	III-conjunct	social belonging
8	octile	power (over the other)	26	III-opposition	being in demand, in trend, or being group-relevant
9	novile	image importance or learning	27	III-trine	insight, sought after communication
10	decile	authority or control	28	III-square	emotional relevance, sought after standards for caretaking for others
11	undecile	social popularity or intellectualism	29	III-quintile	ability to be followed by groups
12	inconjunct	mood appropriate for situation	30	III-sextile	ability to make others want to connect with you, desirability
13	II-conjunct	power of a public persona	31	III-septile	influential communication
14	II-opposition	significance of physical presence	32	III-octile	power to unsettle audiences
15	II-trine	influence over surroundings	33	III-novile	group leadership, ability to inspire
16	II-square	earned respect, family or core values	34	III-decile	"boss-ness" over others
17	II-quintile	ingroup dominance	35	III-undecile	interestingness
18	II-sextile	rationality or ingroup sense-making	36	III-inconjunct	memorableness

Table 19-3: Negative characteristics associated with each harmonic

Harmonic	Name	Negative Characteristic	Harmonic	Name	Negative Characteristic
1	conjunct	impulsivity, thoughtlessness	19	II-septile	overpromotion of attractiveness or desirability among group
2	opposition	laziness, resting on worth	20	II-octile	selling oneself as an object
3	trine	being overly opinionated	21	II-novile	bad attitude
4	square	uncooperativeness	22	II-decile	running over others, disrespect, coldness
5	quintile	arrogance (over individuals)	23	II-undecile	inability to be satisfied, irritability, disruptiveness
6	sextile	nitpicking	24	II-inconjunct	conspiracy, secret motives
7	septile	argumentativeness	25	III-conjunct	leaning on others' agenda or approval
8	octile	lust, power hunger	26	III-opposition	compromising principles for fans, selling out
9	novile	aimlessness	27	III-trine	escapism
10	decile	oppressive conduct	28	III-square	moral dependency, holding too tightly to rules
11	undecile	incoherence, scattered demands	29	III-quintile	inconsiderateness of peers and followers, being cutthroat
12	inconjunct	secret dark side, untrustworthiness	30	III-sextile	being a know-it-all
13	II-conjunct	image without substance	31	III-septile	attacking others' views with the backing of a group, but still being wrong, mob leading
14	II-opposition	unproductive hedonism	32	III-octile	advertising one's power or allure, manipulating others' weaknesses
15	II-trine	high and mighty-ness (arrogance over a whole room)	33	III-novile	distancing from followers
16	II-square	standing on a soapbox, excessive judgment of others	34	III-decile	being above others, ivory tower-ing
17	II-quintile	inflating one's own leadership role	35	III-undecile	unpredictability, erratic highs and lows
18	II-sextile	entrenched personal views, immovability	36	III-inconjunct	trading practicality for the comfort of illusions

Table 19-4: Contributions to physical appearance for each harmonic

Harmonic	Name	Hinted Physical Trait	Harmonic	Name	Hinted Physical Trait
1	conjunct	(not enough data)	19	II-septile	look one of who is serious, but unsure of surroundings
2	opposition	embattled look, tired fighter	20	II-octile	disheveled, bohemian class (look or dress) if not disheveled
3	trine	smug friendliness	21	II-novile	sweet, but demanding of self
4	square	defiant demeanor, harder to convince	22	II-decile	smaller build or high nervous energy
5	quintile	tirelessness, skeptical with stamina	23	II-undecile	driven to have own way
6	sextile	(not enough data)	24	II-inconjunct	spacey manner or escapist appearance
7	septile	sexual desirability	25	III-conjunct	secretly lusty (seen through behavior)
8	octile	the look of one who analyses	26	III-opposition	spotlight-seeking (behavior)
9	novile	rebelliousness	27	III-trine	(not enough data)
10	decile	(not enough data)	28	III-square	(not enough data)
11	undecile	big body form or potent communicative style	29	III-quintile	charismatic
12	inconjunct	look of one who is observant	30	III-sextile	childish or childlike (seen through behavior or voice)
13	II-conjunct	one who knows themselves and what fits them	31	III-septile	body-sensual
14	II-opposition	bottled emotional or creative world	32	III-octile	easily discontented, need for proof
15	II-trine	slyness	33	III-novile	celebrated or popular
16	II-square	look of one easy to anger	34	III-decile	pleasantly inconvincible
17	II-quintile	demanding look	35	III-undecile	difficult, but cooperative
18	II-sextile	approachable, but goal oriented	36	III-inconjunct	easy confidence
			47	IV-undecile	resistant to attachment

Table 19-3: Harmonic contributions to physical appearance or personality. Note that these traits do not describe the person's overall look, only an additional trait that occurred in the average Other with this [Moon $_{you}$-Uranus $_{them}$] angle.

Table 19-5: Types of groups associated with each harmonic

Harmonic	Name	...includes people who...	Harmonic	Name	...includes people who...
1	conjunct	help you be yourself	19	II-septile	constitute your basic "friendship" circle...or maybe not. (This angle is usually VERY negative for Mer-Jup)
2	opposition	increase your sense of self-worth (they often like you a lot)	20	II-octile	kick competitors' butts with you
3	trine	help you air your thoughts	21	II-novile	create ideas with you
4	square	expose your emotions	22	II-decile	wield authority with you
5	quintile	draw out your ego (often demanding that you assert on them fbow)	23	II-undecile	generate scandal or—more weakly—"talked about situations" with you
6	sextile	share tasks well with you	24	II-inconjunct	raise the need for brand new ideas in you (often through tension)
7	septile	socialize or play with you	25	III-conjunct	help you run collective endeavors (often by taking attention *away* from your efforts)
8	octile	share power with you	26	III-opposition	create an original trend with you (which may leave you two isolated fbow)
9	novile	project an image with you	27	III-trine	achieve insight with you
10	decile	control others with you	28	III-square	define a moral terrain with you
11	undecile	expand your social reach	29	III-quintile	hold the spotlight alongside you or wish to take it off of you when your view disagrees with theirs
12	inconjunct	amplify your moods in response to them (often through an impressive feature of theirs)	30	III-sextile	analyze others and hog the social scene with you (in a dynamic which is hard for others to ignore)
13	II-conjunct	hone your public persona (often through a need to check them in defense of yours or their reputation)	31	III-septile	exert power over networks of people with you. (you can truly own other people together with this)
14	II-opposition	share company with you or occupy the same space with you	32	III-octile	are charismatic and influential alongside you
15	II-trine	overpower a room with you (people get the impression it is hard to separate your interests)	33	III-novile	rally groups to break through limits with you; attract attention with you
16	II-square	set the standards for others' behavior with you	34	III-decile	master a field or run a structured operation with you
17	II-quintile	manage or dominate others with you	35	III-undecile	form an unlikely pair with you
18	II-sextile	shape long range plans with you	36	III-inconjunct	make a memorable impression with you
			37	IV-conjunct	boldly explore new expressive terrain with you
			38	IV-opposition	declare the worth of others with you

Table 19-6: Anti-behaviors for each harmonic

Harmonic	Name	Anti-behaving people will...	Harmonic	Name	Anti-behaving people will...
1	conjunct	suppress your expression (often by over-asserting their own)	19	II-septile	barge into your ingroup and setting up standards of their own
2	opposition	dismiss your worth	20	II-octile	bring destruction or defeat upon people who are not your enemies.
3	trine	ignore your ideas and communication	21	II-novile	fail to capitalize on the creative fuel you've given them
4	square	stir up your emotions	22	II-decile	rebel against a system which you want to work
5	quintile	make you feel awkward instead of confident	23	II-undecile	create dissonance and discontentment with you among your peers and allies
6	sextile	redirect your task focus onto their needs	24	II-inconjunct	escape into aimlessness despite your efforts to the contrary
7	septile	cut off communication with you	25	III-conjunct	deny you access to their in-crowd
8	octile	overpower you with their attitude	26	III-opposition	steal your fans
9	novile	promote themselves above you, rendering you useless	27	III-trine	beat you intellectually or communicatively
10	decile	make you feel inferior, beneath their standards	28	III-square	refuse to accept your peace attempts
11	undecile	exclude you from their social enterprises, reaffirming your lack of fit with them	29	III-quintile	bash you among groups outside of yours (associated with lying)
12	inconjunct	be immune to impressions you leave	30	III-sextile	actively distrust you
13	II-conjunct	reject your perspective on an issue	31	III-septile	hurt your reputation among potential network allies
14	II-opposition	deny you their company	32	III-octile	be a liability among others whose support you need
15	II-trine	monopolize an agenda you were supposed to write	33	III-novile	raise hell among your peer groups
16	II-square	be weirdly personal under inappropriate circumstances	34	III-decile	be flakey in a way that restricts your ability to command
17	II-quintile	be uncooperative against your intent	35	III-undecile	bring shocking disruption upon your environments and audiences
18	II-sextile	make themselves stand out in ways that offend groups of people who need the sense of order that you are trying to create	36	III-inconjunct	fall into damaging escapism which distracts your group
			37	IV-conjunct	drag your cause down with unreliability (the arm you must cut off)
			47	IV-undeciles	deliver punishing assessments (maybe about you, maybe not) which hurt your work

Table 19-6: Things people do to oppose each harmonic. Often these things are not done maliciously. Still, it should also be noted that this list serves as an excellent reference for tactics when you need to suppress a personal enemy.

Table 19-7: Masculine and Feminine behavioral styles associated with each Vesta person in the [Jupiter-Vesta] angle

Harmonic	Name	Masculine or Feminine General Behavior	Harmonic	Name	Masculine or Feminine General Behavior
1	conjunct	feminine, approval seeking, impetuous or scattered	19	II-septile	neutral-feminine, logical with a feminine-skewed insistence
2	opposition	neutral, analytical, guarded-sociable	20	II-octile	masculine, critical, often overly sure of themselves or their influence, often prefers war and conflict (with or alongside you) to peace
3	trine	neutral-feminine, confident on the outside, unsure on the inside, intellectual and slightly pushy	21	II-novile	masculine and feminine, popular, smugly sociable, but territorial, strongly derailed when charisma is challenged
4	square	masculine, insistent caretaking and advice-giving	22	II-decile	masculine and feminine, approachable, responsible, level-headed, has a soft spot for charm and its use
5	quintile	masculine and feminine, strongly forward feminine magnetism	23	II-undecile	masculine, single-minded, strong ideals, declares definite and open enemies when challenged, will voice exactly where they stand
6	sextile	masculine and feminine, feminized appearance with forward / analytical charisma	24	II-inconjunct	masculine and feminine, very masculine forward escapism or super powerful intuition channeled in search of one's personal validation
7	septile	feminine, smooth external attitude, argumentative or difficult to satisfy conversationally	25	III-conjunct	masculine, charismatic, high sexual appetite, attention-getters
8	octile	feminine, strong-willed, shielded, usually quiet around strangers	26	III-opposition	feminine, frontline figure, more easily overwhelmed by responsibilities where one has been crowned as a leader
9	novile	masculine and feminine, no nonsense leadership with pronounced emotionality underneath	27	III-trine	masculine, irrepressible opinion, very cooperative and friendly when such opinions aren't challenged
10	decile	masculine, demonstrates command of challenge at hand with less interference from emotions	28	III-square	neutral, level-headed, pro-cooperation, gentle company when common sense standards are met
11	undecile	masculine and feminine, quieter but questioning, high performance standards for others, will steamroll if necessary	29	III-quintile	feminine, intelligent, focused but protective anchor to others
12	inconjunct	masculine and feminine, gets what they want, emotional vibe around them	30	III-sextile	neutral, intelligent, observant, listener
13	II-conjunct	masculine, pronounced sense of caretaking, sexual, the body form of others or themselves is important to them	31	III-septile	feminine, quite weird, provocative, masculine-projected analytical temperament, difficult personality

14	II-opposition	masculine and feminine, pronounced investment in affiliated groups and friends, blunt	32	III-octile	neutral, friendly, more unassuming than other angles, intense creativity
15	II-trine	feminine, participatory, communicative and expressive (but may wander), slightly weird, complains more than other angles	33	III-novile	feminine, attention-getting body form, philosophical, explorer-type, personable, masculine insistence
16	II-square	feminine, sexuality is noticeably public (though often not stated), weird enough as to appear untrustworthy	34	III-decile	feminine, inclined to give partner a hard time (jokingly), stubborn, complains more or is slightly more critical than other angles
17	II-quintile	masculine, will pull no punches in evaluations, strongly focused pursuit of chosen gender	35	III-undecile	feminine (subdued), logical, attaches deeply to people, has an affinity for gaining a lot of attention
18	II-sextile	masculine, archetypal masculine, forward, outspoken, charming, funny, but can be an asshole	36	III-inconjunct	neutral, intellectual, strong desire nature lurking in private life
			37	IV-conjunct	masculine, skeptical, outspoken, may mock or make light of things more often (fbow)
			38	IV-opposition	feminine, openly skeptical with masculine / forward style of evaluation, very demonstrative with more pronounced bodily appeal when they like you
			47	IV-undecile	feminine, more likely to be loyal to belief system with an active participation in those beliefs
			48	IV-inconjunct	feminine, quieter, more reassuring presence

Table 19-7: Masculine and feminine behavioral styles associated with each Jupiter-Vesta angle. Note that these traits do not describe the person's sex or orientation, only the average level of "forwardness" (masculinity) versus "receptiveness" (femininity) across Vesta people with each angle within the partnership.

Table 19-8: How the angles spend leisure time

Harmonic	Name	Typically fun activity	Harmonic	Name	Typically fun activity
1	conjunct	enjoying Other's uninhibited company	19	II-septile	being inspired by how Other takes care of their ingroup or how Other defines themselves stubbornly against their ingroup
2	opposition	exchanging in a comfortably supported, (preferably classy) environment	20	II-octile	being impressed with or excited by Other's creativity or sexuality (the receptive version of II-novile)
3	trine	listening to Other's talking, enjoying their expression of their personal views	21	II-novile	being excited or inspired by Other's power to compel people's compliance with their wishes; watching Other's attractiveness or power in action (the active version of II-octile)
4	square	watching Other unsettle people's emotions	22	II-decile	being impressed by and talking about Other's social image
5	quintile	being entertained by Other's substantial personality	23	II-undecile	benefitting from Other's skill in keeping your follower-group behavior under control and everyone's overall objectives within reach (these people generally make good supporters and seconds-in-command behind you)
6	sextile	enjoying how Other likes to spend time with you	24	II-inconjunct	benefitting from Other's execution of your creative goals (these people can, by bringing their own creative vision to light, solve problems that *you* are facing)
7	septile	conversing with Other	25	III-conjunct	watch them overpower or be pushy towards others (more of these people had red hair than normal, non-redheads tended to be good-looking and friendlier looking when compared against their ethnic stereotype)
8	octile	debating or intellectually sparring with Other	26	III-opposition	exchange with them concerning the fate of your respective follower groups or groups who support your views; watching them defend their followers or attack an opposing follower-group
9	novile	watching Other promote themselves	27	III-trine	watching them use their strong persuasive or seductive powers over others
10	decile	being a witness to Other's authority or expertise	28	III-square	receiving their cooperation and positive attitude

11	undecile	protecting or tending to Other's social interests amidst the groups you share (you often need to bail these people out of social messes they have made for themselves)	29	III-quintile	engaging their criticism and critical eye
12	inconjunct	forming responses to Other's various moods	30	III-sextile	hearing Other broadcast their commentary (these people really do seem to have a noticeable talent for conveying their ideas through media channels, though 1:1 their company is scattered and often oppressive to the point of being unenjoyable)
13	II-conjunct	encouraging Other's social face and increased public projection in the world	31	III-septile	piggybacking off of their personality to foster good spirits among your shared group
14	II-opposition	being in Other's presence or having Other be in your presence	32	III-octile	alleviating Other's uncertainty; validating and supporting their tackling of a challenging task
15	II-trine	alongside Other, bringing people's attention to both of you	33	III-novile	playing along with their sass (one or both of you are more receptive to the other's flirting or, where attraction is not possible, wingman behavior; more likely Ceres is the accepted flirter and Node is the witness)
16	II-square	connecting intimately with Other (that is, sharing a closely expressive connection which noticeably dwarfs lesser grade exchanges)	34	III-decile	enjoying Other's bossiness (both towards you and towards others); if bossiness is not evident either way, you might suspect that, negatively, they are inclined to complain to you or about you pretty vocally
17	II-quintile	alongside Other, dominating the actions of your shared audience or at least impressing that audience with your ability to command	35	III-undecile	watching their surprisingly strong intellect or curiosity in action
18	II-sextile	bringing Other out of their shell, encouraging them to publicize their skills, or doing the skill promoting on their behalf	36	III-inconjunct	thinking about and interacting with their weird personality (which is both attractive and anal all at once)

Table 20-5: Quick angle reference for synastry

Harmonic	Name	Symbol	Meaning	Harmonic	Name	Symbol	Meaning
1	conjunct	☌	natural behavior	19	II-septile	✡^{2}	ingroups
2	opposition	☍	self-value	20	II-octile	∠^{2}	magnetism
3	trine	△	thoughts	21	II-novile	九^{2}	creation
4	square	□	wants	22	II-decile	+^{2}	career or reputation
5	quintile	⋆	1:1 interaction	23	II-undecile	∪^{2}	uniqueness
6	sextile	⚹	work	24	II-inconjunct	⚻^{2}	works of the imagination
7	septile	✡	communication	25	III-conjunct	☌^{3}	psychology
8	octile	∠	power	26	III-opposition	☍^{3}	fans & following
9	novile	九	image promotion	27	III-trine	△^{3}	insight
10	decile	+	control	28	III-square	□^{3}	morality
11	undecile	∪	social talk	29	III-quintile	⋆^{3}	charisma over groups
12	inconjunct	⚻	impression	30	III-sextile	⚹^{3}	critical analysis
13	II-conjunct	☌^{2}	persona	31	III-septile	✡^{3}	networks
14	II-opposition	☍^{2}	physical presence	32	III-octile	∠^{3}	mysterious allure
15	II-trine	△^{2}	room hijacking	33	III-novile	九^{3}	rallying
16	II-square	□^{2}	family values	34	III-decile	+^{3}	command
17	II-quintile	⋆^{2}	management	35	III-undecile	∪^{3}	intellectual curiosity
18	II-sextile	⚹^{2}	rationality	36	III-inconjunct	⚻^{3}	memorability

Table 20-5: Quick angle reference for synastry. These are super trimmed down versions of *Table 19-1*.

Table 20-6: Similar angle families for synastry (by harmonic)

Harmonic	Name	Symbol	Category
1	conjunct	☌	Instinctual expression
1	conjunct	☌	Public power
1	conjunct	☌	Body image & gender
2	opposition	☍	Two-sided issue facing
2	opposition	☍	Emotional closeness
2	opposition	☍	Pleasure seeking
3	trine	△	Instinctual expression
3	trine	△	Intellectualizing
4	square	□	Two-sided issue facing
4	square	□	Conflict by default
4	square	□	Emotional closeness
5	quintile	⋆	Easy 1:1 interaction
5	quintile	⋆	Public power
6	sextile	⚹	Instinctual expression
6	sextile	⚹	Intellectualizing
7	septile	✡	Easy 1:1 interaction
7	septile	✡	Emotional closeness
8	octile	∠	Conflict by default
8	octile	∠	Pleasure seeking
9	novile	九	Intellectualizing
9	novile	九	Joint exploration
9	novile	九	Belief system-related
10	decile	+	Control
11	undecile	∪	Intellectualizing
11	undecile	∪	Joint exploration
11	undecile	∪	Brilliance & eccentricity
12	inconjunct	⚻	Conflict by default
12	inconjunct	⚻	Creativity
12	inconjunct	⚻	Mysterious impression making
13	II-conjunct	☌^{2}	Persona broadcasting
14	II-opposition	☍^{2}	Emotional closeness
14	II-opposition	☍^{2}	Pleasure seeking
14	II-opposition	☍^{2}	Body image & gender
15	II-trine	△^{2}	Persona broadcasting
15	II-trine	△^{2}	Public power
16	II-square	□^{2}	Belief system-related
16	II-square	□^{2}	Emotional closeness
17	II-quintile	⋆^{2}	Persona broadcasting
17	II-quintile	⋆^{2}	Public power
18	II-sextile	⚹^{2}	Two-sided issue facing
19	II-septile	✡^{2}	Easy 1:1 interaction
19	II-septile	✡^{2}	Joint exploration
19	II-septile	✡^{2}	Social influence
19	II-septile	✡^{2}	Body image & gender
20	II-octile	∠^{2}	Control
20	II-octile	∠^{2}	Pleasure seeking
21	II-novile	九^2	Creativity
21	II-novile	九^2	Persona broadcasting
21	II-novile	九^2	Pleasure seeking
21	II-novile	九^2	Body image & gender
22	II-decile	+^{2}	Control
23	II-undecile	∪^{2}	Brilliance & eccentricity
23	II-undecile	∪^{2}	Body image & gender
24	II-inconjunct	⚻^{2}	Creativity
24	II-inconjunct	⚻^{2}	Mysterious impression making
24	II-inconjunct	⚻^{2}	Brilliance & eccentricity
25	III-conjunct	☌^{3}	Public power
26	III-opposition	☍^{3}	Social influence
27	III-trine	△^{3}	Brilliance & eccentricity
28	III-square	□^{3}	Belief system-related
29	III-quintile	⋆^{3}	Public power
29	III-quintile	⋆^{3}	Social influence
30	III-sextile	⚹^{3}	Control
30	III-sextile	⚹^{3}	Belief system-related
31	III-septile	✡^{3}	Belief system-related
31	III-septile	✡^{3}	Social influence
32	III-octile	∠^{3}	Mysterious impression making
33	III-novile	九^3	Joint exploration
33	III-novile	九^3	Public power
33	III-novile	九^3	Social influence
34	III-decile	+^{3}	Control
35	III-undecile	∪^{3}	Brilliance & eccentricity
36	III-inconjunct	⚻^{3}	Mysterious impression making
36	III-inconjunct	⚻^{3}	Public power
36	III-inconjunct	⚻^{3}	Social influence
36	III-inconjunct	⚻^{3}	Brilliance & eccentricity

Table 20-6: Angle similarity categories. Use these to search you and the other's synastry table for pairs which share theme areas. THIS TABLE DOES NOT COVER ALL POSSIBLE CATEGORIES, certain areas such as athleticism, health, and career didn't produce enough data from my work to make it into this table. You'll need to use your own take on the angles to see what other categories may apply.

Table 20-7: Similar angle families for synastry (by category)

Harmonic	Name	Symbol	Meaning
Instinctual expression			
1	conjunct	☌	natural behavior
3	trine	Δ	internal impulse
6	sextile	∗	alignment of means and goals
Two-sided issue facing			
2	opposition	☍	self-value
4	square	□	wants
18	II-sextile	∗^{2}	rationality
Intellectualizing			
3	trine	Δ	thoughts
6	sextile	∗	analysis
9	novile	九	learning
11	undecile	U	information focus
Conflict by default			
4	square	□	discontentment
8	octile	∠	power
12	inconjunct	⊼	questionable vibe
Easy 1:1 interaction			
5	quintile	⋆	1:1 interaction
7	septile	✡	communication
19	II-septile	✡^{2}	ingroup shared ideas
Joint exploration			
9	novile	九	image promotion
11	undecile	U	social talk
19	II-septile	✡^{2}	ingroup identification
33	III-novile	九^{3}	group rallying
Control			
10	decile	+	control
20	II-octile	∠^{2}	outsider suppression
22	II-decile	+^{2}	field specialization
30	III-sextile	∗^{3}	critical analysis
34	III-decile	+^{3}	command
Belief system-related			
9	novile	九	philosophy
16	II-square	□^{2}	family values
28	III-square	□^{3}	morality
30	III-sextile	∗^{3}	criticality
31	III-septile	✡^{3}	formal belief and doctrine
Emotional closeness			
2	opposition	☍	measured-against identity
4	square	□	wants
7	septile	✡	camaraderie
14	II-opposition	☍^{2}	physical company-seeking
16	II-square	□^{2}	family values
Creativity			
12	inconjunct	⊼	artistic inclination
21	II-novile	九^{2}	creativity
24	II-inconjunct	⊼^{2}	works of the imagination

Harmonic	Name	Symbol	Meaning
Mysterious impression making			
12	inconjunct	⊼	vibe
24	II-inconjunct	⊼^{2}	works of the imagination
32	III-octile	∠^{3}	mysterious allure
36	III-inconjunct	⊼^{3}	memorability
Persona broadcasting			
13	II-conjunct	☌^{2}	persona
15	II-trine	Δ^{2}	room hijacking
17	II-quintile	⋆^{2}	"fishbowl" group domination
21	II-novile	九^{2}	attitude display
Pleasure seeking			
14	II-opposition	☍^{2}	physicality-seeking
20	II-octile	∠^{2}	sexual appetite
21	II-novile	九^{2}	sexuality announce
2	opposition	☍	body-sensuality
8	octile	∠	intensity seeking
Public power			
1	conjunct	☌	raw instinct
5	quintile	⋆	leadership
15	II-trine	Δ^{2}	room hijacking
17	II-quintile	⋆^{2}	management of others' behavior
25	III-conjunct	☌^{3}	masses who follow
29	III-quintile	⋆^{3}	charisma over groups
33	III-novile	九^{3}	rallying
36	III-inconjunct	⊼^{3}	memorability
Social influence			
19	II-septile	✡^{2}	ingroup support
26	III-opposition	☍^{3}	fans & following
29	III-quintile	⋆^{3}	charisma over groups
31	III-septile	✡^{3}	networks
33	III-novile	九^{3}	group rallying and entertainment
36	III-inconjunct	⊼^{3}	cult following
Brilliance & eccentricity			
11	undecile	U	notoriety
23	II-undecile	U^{2}	uniqueness
24	II-inconjunct	⊼^{2}	works of the imagination
27	III-trine	Δ^{3}	insight
35	III-undecile	U^{3}	genius
36	III-inconjunct	⊼^{3}	memorability
Body image and gender			
1	conjunct	☌	raw instinct
14	II-opposition	☍^{2}	hedonistic pattern
19	II-septile	✡^{2}	same vs diff-based group preferences
21	II-novile	九^{2}	declaration of physicality
23	II-undecile	U^{2}	social deviation

Table 20-7: Angle similarity categories. Use this in conjunction with *table 20-6* to determine when you and another person are more or less on the same page by theme, even when the angles aren't the same. THIS TABLE DOES NOT COVER ALL POSSIBLE CATEGORIES, only the ones with more data on them from my sample.

Table 21-1: What the "Noble One" does when attacked by someone else's angle

∠	Situation
1. conjunct	Other: over-asserts, bullies Noble: tells himself that Other enjoys giving their raw energy to him, and uses his indifference to Other's advances to suck out more of Other's energy until the latter has no more to give
2. opposition	No data
3. trine	Other: complains or does thoughtless things Noble: listens to Other's complaints or absorbs Other's skill, shows how impressed he is with it, and seeks to know more about how Other has come to do it this way; (since this one is "raw opinionation," Other usually doesn't know how to explain their own actions and has their fire dowsed quickly)
4. square	Other: is emotionally overbearing Noble: ignores or fails to receive Other's intensity (as if it's another language); only responds to the calm, intuitively sense-making versions of the same efforts
5. quintile	Other: is impetuous, craves attention Noble: babies Other, giving them the "poor you" attention they seek
6. sextile	Other: oppresses with logic, criticality Noble: has his fun away from Other and makes sure that Other knows it
7. septile	Other: buries partner under massive commentary Noble: just listens to them...in such a way as to let them know it's safe for Other to talk *to* but undesirable for them to *talk at* Noble. (Noble steers Other's talk towards perspectives relevant to Noble's own interests while letting Other know that topics besides this are just wasted words)
8. octile	Other: is belligerent or disruptive Noble: lets Other know how important it is for Other to keep manipulating whatever their trying to manipulate
9. novile	Other: is hoity toity, arrogant, dismissive Noble: celebrates Other's skills <u>to himself</u>. You're arrogant towards me? I celebrate your skills to myself. It's weird but it works. (I considered telling you why it works, but while writing this decided that doing so would ruin much of the effect. So I won't.)
10. decile	Other: is standoffish Noble: ignores Other's potential support and builds a reputation through interaction with different people
11. undecile	Other: distrusts Noble, has a different set of social standards Noble: makes the situation revolve around Other, turns people's attention to Other and makes them the talk of the town (these relationships tend to be very positive when you get them to work)
12. inconjunct	Not enough data
13. II-conjunct	Other: creates problems for Noble's peers and room of influence Noble: maintains an environment of liveliness and enjoyment around Other's actions
14. II-opposition	Other: disrupts the flow of things just by being around Noble: crowns Other a leader and puts them visibly in charge of part of the agenda
15. II-trine	Other: seduces Noble's audience Noble: employs Other's charisma for his own use
16. II-square	Other: won't connect with the rest of the group Noble: gradually builds rapport, makes Other feel like family
17. II-quintile	Other: wants to dominate situation Noble: connects with Other offline to establish that his agenda and Other's agenda are the same
18. II-sextile	Other: assesses Noble rather than supporting him Noble: earns the trust of Other's friends and peers

19. II-septile	Other: excludes Noble from their inner circle or treats Noble's group as Other's own inner circle when it shouldn't be Noble: zooms in on good sources of "inside jokes" and similar ingroup knowledge with Other and airs these across unaware publics (this establishes Noble and Other as their own in-crowd)
20. II-octile	Other: is unfocused on the matters at hand, diverting the focus of Noble's plans towards competing externals Noble: lets Other wander off, avoid trusting them with anything important; maybe Other will be useful for taking care of problems outside of Noble's sphere
21. II-novile	Other: is Noble's able and uncooperative competitor Noble: (if competition is not intended) elevates Other or lowers himself. (if Other is worthy of Noble's company, I've found that the relationship eventually becomes an equal and trusting one as rapport is built; if Other is not worthy, Other will eventually shrink away and disappear if Noble proceeds as if unaffected)
22. II-decile	Other: complains to and annoys Noble and outsiders about all kinds of aspects of various affairs related to something Noble is involved in Noble: Lets Other make entertaining conversation with outsiders, but requires that Other be solely responsible for their part of affairs (if more accustomed to complaining, Other—alone—tends to complain themselves into a corner and fail). Cut off Other from group resources in task
23. II-undecile	Other: displays a vocal and resistant bad attitude Noble: tends to Other's complaints, but shares negative intel on them with everyone else—effectively spreading their complaints before they do and establishing Noble as the one in the right
24. II-inconjunct	Other: head is elsewhere, is intractable Noble: supports and absorbs Other's creative ideas while they are around, but considers them to be a part of the environment more than an active supporter
25. III-conjunct	Other: is disruptively and spotlight-grabbing outspoken in a distracting way (usually rather than a malicious way) Noble: if at all possible, interacts with Other one on one to assure them of the potential for spotlight, but in groups, pairs Other up with someone else to keep them occupied until Noble is ready to deal with them
26. III-opposition	Other: herds their fans and supporters in a direction that opposes Noble Noble: abandons Other's fans without abandoning Other or abandons Other without abandoning Other's fans. The first one is more likely to make relations with Other better. The second is more likely to make the relationship worse
27. III-trine	Other: is scathingly critical or uses their insight to punish Other Noble: withdraws support from all those convinced by Other and engages in minimal performance of activities with those convinced people with whom relationships need to be maintained. Arguing is usually very bad for this style of enemy—the slanderous kind—whether it's a III-trine or not. "You're right, but I don't care" works a lot better. "Not only do I not care if you're right, I think anyone who supports you should be asked to question your delivery of those facts." This is known as "divide and conquer" or in V.I. Lenin's case, "salami tactics." So when Joe and Moe slam Noble's reputation using facts, Noble admits Joe is right, but forms an alliance with Moe on whatever aspect of Joe's presentation of the facts Noble and Moe both agree on but disagree with Joe. Unless you're dealing with actual militaries, this tactic usually works very well with people. First, it concedes that Both Joe and Moe are right and deflates their influence over any shared audience with Noble. Second, it shows Moe that, just as Noble doesn't care, Moe shouldn't care either since Noble is a cool guy. If Joe and Moe are friends, Noble allies with Flo against Joe and Moe's presentation. The premise is the same.
28. III-square	No data
29. III-quintile	Other: endeavors to take control of Noble's space or sphere of influence Noble: singles Other out for an independent task and doesn't give that special task to anyone else. This keeps Other within eyeshot, under Noble's service, and dependent on Noble for further instruction. If Other is an actual equal and can't be given a task, Noble sends some of his own allies to Other to get certain problems solved—effectively assigning tasks to Other anyway. This works well on micromanaging bosses and managers; Is Bossman in your face? Selectively send your clients and peers to Bossman in order to present him with problems he can't solve for a lack of the kind of specialization that you have. As this works, you'll find that Bossman 1) leaves these things to you and 2) Bossman references you to others as one of his prime "managed" people to whom other things he can't solve should be entrusted. Bossman still has his control, but such control is used to advance *you* since you don't accept the oppression part.
30. III-sextile	Not enough data; the pairs who had this were consistently smooth-running in my sample, with the Other using their powers of critical analysis to support Noble. My guess would be that the negative cases involve Other's criticism of Noble, to which Noble would respond by letting Other speak for him and polish Noble's errors

31. III-septile

Other: hijacks Noble's network

Noble: invites Other to join him as a fellow network controller. If this isn't feasible, Noble gives Other access to Noble's problem children to 1) inconvenience Other, 2) keep those problem children under control, 3) expose weaknesses in Other or the problem children (which can be people or tasks)

32. III-octile

Other: requires efforts that Noble can't afford to give

Noble: is simply honest with Other. "This is as much as I can give and here's why..." When Other eventually departs to be supplied by someone else, hopefully Noble will have an ally abroad. Why? Because most of the outsiders whom Other encounters will not be so honest if Other has already shown that your honesty is not a thing they can live with.

"I can't tend to you past this point, but at least I'm honest in telling you why. If you can't accept my limited help or at least my honesty concerning it, and if you can't help yourself but still need someone to do this for you, then good luck. Look forward to the next person promising to help you, lying about his intentions to keep that promise, breaking the promise, and doing so remorselessly." This is how the *karma of having people purposely lie to you* is built up: You ask for the world but won't listen to those who tell you they can't give it.

33. III-novile

Other: limits Noble's influence over his desired audience

Noble: befriends Other as a person; Other as a gatekeeper usually changes their mind later

It's actually not advisable to attempt to "use" Other to get to your wanted audience. This may work for the more opportunistic among us, but it creates bigger problems later as the used Other simply builds a newer, tighter gate right behind you. This is how the *karma of being hated by history* is built up on a series of little betrayals, no matter how big the lifetime of successes: Those who guard the favor of groups you're not a part of need to feel that their trust is not in vain. When dealing with people who believe it is their duty to protect groups beyond themselves, expect their disappointment in you to carry more weight. If you betray these people, you typically will not have squashed their role as protector, but made them more vigilant against you, so that social-psychologically, for every protector you betray, there will be an even larger number of their later followers who are mobilized against you near-permanently. It is this second group of the betrayed person's people who will tell your story long after the first group who you stole has, predictably, changed their minds about any good you've done. Loyalty here isn't so much a moral good as it is a social safety net.

34. III-decile

Other: believes they have all the answers

Noble: leaves them alone; if Other attempts to control Noble's execution of plans, Noble lets Other do this to the strict letter, but promotes his own intentions in every other aspect of the event which Other didn't expressly cover. If possible, Noble also ensures that everyone is aware of how limited Other's guidance was; if Noble is not free to do this openly, he does it by "clocking in and clocking out" at the precise time and going straight home to Noble's more imperfect allies, letting Other know that though they may have total control over the formally bossed area, they have no interpersonal importance.

35. III-undecile

Other: is an uncontrollable attention getter

Noble: gives Other attention randomly in times where there is no need; this puts Other's otherwise disruptive shocks to the order of things under Noble's control while establishing Noble as a supporter of, rather than an enemy to, Other

36. III-inconjunct

Other: unsettles Noble with a surprisingly penetrative quality, can lodge themselves in other's mind and resist extraction therefrom

Noble: declares Other a memorable leader and takes Other under his wing.

This may seem excessive, but you really want to avoid thinking negatively about people who have this effect on you ("I can't stop thinking about how weird they make me feel"). For reasons that would mess up how the solution to this one works, I won't explain why positive thoughts about the fixed person work so well, but will tell you that you should do what you can to keep them positive. This is advice specifically for people whose interaction with you makes you uneasy in ways you can't explain and not for regular opponents. Take a look at yourself first. Dig deep. Then do what you can to help them.

37. IV-conjunct

Other: publicizes objectives which create dilemmas for Noble

Noble: accepts those objectives and attempts not to hold them against Other if possible. If Noble must hold those objectives against Other, he makes it clear why

38. IV-opposition

No data

47. IV-undecile

Other: holds an outlook which is out of sync with Noble's reality

Noble: assists Other where possible, but—often and *quite* unfortunately—helps Other turn everyone else against Other. Being out of sync with everyone else's notion of reality is, as Machiavelli would put it, a characteristic of "exiles." A person who sees things in a way irreconcilably different from that which is useful to the healthy function of his surroundings begs to be removed from those surroundings one way or another.

48. IV-inconjunct

Not enough data

Table 21-2b: How we experience different angle tendencies in synastry and composite charts

Element	Typical angles
Fireish (looks like an action)	II-trine, II-quintile, II-novile, II-undecile, III-quintile, III-novile
Earthish (looks like a structure)	II-sextile, all deciles
Airish (looks like communication)	septile, undecile, II-novile, III-trine, III-quintile, III-sextile, III-decile
Waterish (looks like a feeling)	conjunct, square, II-square, II-octile, III-decile (a felt need to control a situation)
Situation	**Typical angles**
Force-related (associated with making things happen by pushing them)	II-conjunct (forced personality), II-quintile (forcibly managed groups), II-novile (forced creation), II-undecile (imposed quirks), III-square (imposed morality), III-sextile (forced assessment), III-decile (forced structure)
Acknowledgment-related (associated with group or personal identification of things)	undecile, II-quintile, **II-septile** (strong), II-octile, II-decile, III-conjunct, III-septile, III-novile, III-inconjunct
Attention-related (associated with getting attention)	septile, undecile, II-conjunct, II-trine, II-octile, II-novile, II-undecile, III-conjunct, **III-opposition** (very strong), III-quintile, III-novile
Feeling-related (typically brings the urge to influence something)	square, octile, II-square

Table 23-2: Turning up harmonics (by formula)

Harmonic	Name	Symbol	Activate by doing more...	...(for)...	...in front of...	This corresponds to...
1	conjunct	☌	actions	for yourself	nobody in particular	instinctual action
2	opposition	☍	experiencing	for yourself	nobody in particular	self-valuing
3	trine	△	communicating	for yourself	nobody in particular	thinking
4	square	□	wanting or expecting	for yourself	nobody in particular	feeling
5	quintile	⚹	actions	towards another thing	nobody in particular	1:1 interaction
6	sextile	✶	experiencing	of another thing	nobody in particular	analysis, service
7	septile	✡	communicating	with another thing	nobody in particular	1:1 communication
8	octile	∠	wanting or expecting	of another thing	nobody in particular	steering
9	novile	九	actions	in the faceless world	nobody in particular	image projecting
10	decile	+	experiencing	according to the faceless world	nobody in particular	structuring
11	undecile	U	communicating	in light of the faceless world	nobody in particular	being talked about/around
12	inconjunct	⚻	wanting or expecting	of the faceless world	nobody in particular	imagining, having a mood
13	II-conjunct	$☌^2$	actions	for yourself	people who talk	persona projecting
14	II-opposition	$☍^2$	experiencing	for yourself	people who talk	physicality / values projecting (often judged against ethnic stereotype)
15	II-trine	$△^2$	communicating	for yourself	people who talk	mannerism displaying
16	II-square	$□^2$	wanting or expecting	for yourself	people who talk	emotional disclosure
17	II-quintile	$⚹^2$	actions	towards another thing	people who talk	other-cornering
18	II-sextile	$✶^2$	experiencing	of another thing	people who talk	rationalizing
19	II-septile	$✡^2$	communicating	with another thing	people who talk	ingroup (comfortably open) communicating
20	II-octile	$∠^2$	wanting or expecting	of another thing	people who talk	showing force
21	II-novile	$九^2$	actions	in the faceless world	people who talk	making a statement
22	II-decile	$+^2$	experiencing	according to the faceless world	people who talk	being assigned a label
23	II-undecile	U^2	communicating	in light of the faceless world	people who talk	individuality broadcasting
24	II-inconjunct	$⚻^2$	wanting or expecting	of the faceless world	people who talk	imagination publicizing
25	III-conjunct	$☌^3$	actions	for yourself	groups gathered to hear this	group representing
26	III-opposition	$☍^3$	experiencing	for yourself	groups gathered to hear this	having fans or followers
27	III-trine	$△^3$	communicating	for yourself	groups gathered to hear this	displaying insight
28	III-square	$□^3$	wanting or expecting	for yourself	groups gathered to hear this	morals projecting
29	III-quintile	$⚹^3$	actions	towards another thing	groups gathered to hear this	showing charisma
30	III-sextile	$✶^3$	experiencing	of another thing	groups gathered to hear this	critiquing, exhibitionism
31	III-septile	$✡^3$	communicating	with another thing	groups gathered to hear this	networking, hosting
32	III-octile	$∠^3$	wanting or expecting	of another thing	groups gathered to hear this	suspense making, allure projecting
33	III-novile	$九^3$	actions	in the faceless world	groups gathered to hear this	entertaining, group rallying

34	III-decile	$+^3$	experiencing	according to the faceless world	groups gathered to hear this	being labeled synonymous with an idea, epitomizing, being a master
35	III-undecile	U^3	communicating	in light of the faceless world	groups gathered to hear this	getting massively talked about, raising questions among the masses, displaying genius
36	III-inconjunct	$\barwedge^3$	wanting or expecting	of the faceless world	groups gathered to hear this	looking aimless, dream-inspiring
				(Theorized angles)		
37	IV-conjunct	☌^{4}	actions	for yourself	[amidst] a culture that values this	justifying, accommodating norms
38	IV-opposition	☍^{4}	experiencing	for yourself	[amidst] a culture that values this	health regimen, reinforcement of habit
47	IV-undecile	U^4	communicating	in light of the faceless world	[amidst] a culture that values this	having an outlook
48	IV-inconjunct	$\barwedge^4$	wanting or expecting	of the faceless world	[amidst] a culture that values this	reminding others of something else

Table 23-3: Ways to get stuck on a harmonic

Harmonic	Name	Symbol	Basic behavior	How to get stuck on this harmonic	Clues you get showing you are stuck (How others will treat you)
1	conjunct	☌	instinctual action	being too action heavy, uncontrollable; not asking whether your actions are actually right	others learn to deny you support, will remain on the sidelines whether you win or lose; others won't respond with excitement, encouragement, or even curiosity when good things happen to you. (They seem unaffected)
2	opposition	☍	self-valuing	being too self-serving, materialistic or hedonistic	others will encourage you to think about people or things besides yourself
3	trine	△	thinking	overthinking, opinionating too much	others will argue with you or get tired of listening to you; either way denying you a listening ear
4	square	□	feeling	being too emotional, pushy	others will avoid your smothering, rebelling against even your best efforts to help them
5	quintile	⋆	1:1 interaction	being to egotistical, craving the spotlight	others will typically be okay with this, but will be less active in helping you get things done
6	sextile	⚹	analysis, service	worrying too much, overanalyzing	other's won't take your concerns as seriously, will avoid letting you in on things keep from upsetting you
7	septile	✡	1:1 communication	holding others hostage in conversation, clinging too heavily to other's feedback	this is usually not that bad; but you tire others out, they delay responding to you or avoid contacting you with small news (for concern you will trap them for hours)
8	octile	∠	steering	having a power complex, not being satisfied with other's genuine efforts	others will avoid friendship connection with you, thinking you'll eat them for the smallest reason
9	novile	九	image projecting	hyper-projecting, being addicted to moving on without slowing down	others will hesitate to risk settling with you; some will be extra clingy
10	decile	+	structuring	demanding order and control	this typically works well, but others will struggle to relax with you and will seem to make even more errors
11	undecile	U	being talked about/around	being super-surrounded by media, music, and information	others will dump any news on you, true or not, meaningful or not
12	inconjunct	⚻	imagining, having a mood	daydreaming too much, getting lost in illusion	others will patronize you, scold you, treat you like a spacey child
13	II-conjunct	$☌^2$	persona projecting	being too concerned with your image	others will more likely be false with you, showing you the face they think they want you to see
14	II-opposition	$☍^2$	physicality / values projecting (often judged against ethnic stereotype)	needing too much physical companionship, too much evidence of approval	others will seek company besides yours, cheat; steal from you (literally or time/energy-wise); as you supply more than they demand, they take you for granted
15	II-trine	$△^2$	mannerism displaying	over-talking a room	others will avoid casual conversation with you, thinking you will run them over
16	II-square	$□^2$	emotional disclosure	getting too close, being too emotionally open with others	this is often endearing, but others will disappoint you more with their unreliability; people who want more closeness than you are actually willing to give often eventually find cause to hate you. (They thought you were really into them, but you were just being your normal nurturing self)

17	II-quintile	⊹^{2}	other-cornering	needing to constantly dominate others, squash all oppressors	others will talk behind your back, cheat your influence; after you are gone, they hurry to divide up what you built, remember you for your sins, and shed no tears in undoing your name on the grapevine. (I call this one the Rockefeller—a doer of many deeds which are ultimately squished into "greed" in many a common mind. Contrast this with the Che!—a leader/hero/role model whose socially positive display of this same angle leads others to assign a II-sextile/long-range halo over his head regardless of the actual nature of his work)
18	II-sextile	⚹^{2}	rationalizing	over-rationalizing	others will avoid engaging you over your favorite topic, treating you as a know it all
19	II-septile	✡^{2}	ingroup (comfortably open) communicating	being heavily dependent on friend groups	this is common and typically acceptable; you rise and fall more easily with friends here; more of an issue for strongly independent types (who end up fighting with their own more often)
20	II-octile	∠^{2}	showing force	needing to wage an unending war against something, anything	people will find you entertaining to watch, but volatile; will contribute words but not action to assist you
21	II-novile	九^2	making a statement	constantly needing to make yourself seen	others will attempt to eliminate you as a competitor for their stage
22	II-decile	+^{2}	being assigned a label	being overly work focused	others more easily annoyed with you, will attempt to cut you down in light of your apparent superiority; still others will cling to you jealously for their own security
23	II-undecile	U^2	individuality broadcasting	needing to publicize how different you are	people will dismiss you as arrogant, a troublemaker; some will attempt to "put you in your place" via decisions made in your absence, or inexplicable rejection of ideas which you believe to be sound
24	II-inconjunct	⚻^{2}	imagination publicizing	staying hooked on your imagined realities	others will encourage you to give up your goals in favor of "real things"
25	III-conjunct	☌^{3}	group representing	needing to constantly be right	people will not engage you over serious issues; more ambitious types will attempt to crush you with all they have
26	III-opposition	☍^{3}	having fans or followers	living to please your fans	this is sought after, but invites people who use you for various status-enhancing reasons
27	III-trine	△^{3}	displaying insight	needing to have the last word	others will intentionally exclude you from their affairs; you tire more easily when displaying this
28	III-square	□^{3}	morals projecting	needing to push your moral agenda on others	others will amplify the areas in which you are imperfect or hypocritical
29	III-quintile	⊹^{3}	showing charisma	needing to brag about what you have	others will be more easily jealous of you, will minimize your accomplishments in their own eyes
30	III-sextile	⚹^{3}	critiquing, exhibitionism	needing to criticize	others will avoid talking to you, avoid asking you for anything
31	III-septile	✡^{3}	networking, hosting	being super-networked	this is common and often sought by many people; those who want deeper exchange will play around and hand you superficiality instead; people flake out more, and will generally need the same lessons repeated to them; if you want to trade your popularity for effective power over the people you have, there is often a struggle to transition since this group is known for its "niceness," not its ability to lay down the law.

32	III-octile	∠^{3}	suspense making, allure projecting	not checking your own natural power among those overwhelmed by it	others will be foolish, thoughtless, savage around you; more ambitious types will act to own you, dominate you; others will simply kowtow to you, genuflecting slavishly before Your Royal Highness...without adding any significant value to your life
33	III-novile	九^3	entertaining, group rallying	demanding center stage rather than using position to help others	others are more likely to be sneaky with you, disrespect you, using your image but broadcasting their critique loudly elsewhere
34	III-decile	+^{3}	being labeled synonymous with an idea, epitomizing, being a master	demanding perfection	others will avoid interaction with you in your specialty area, be more easily intimidated, neglect to warn you of problems, or fail you more easily when you trust them; more ambitious types deny you entry, or set you up for failure / trouble
35	III-undecile	U^3	getting massively talked about, raising questions among the masses, displaying genius	being too eccentric, iconoclastic without actual openness to new experience	others will consistently feel weird around you, shun you; you attract other weird people more easily and struggle to make inroads with normal people
36	III-inconjunct	⌅^{3}	looking aimless, dream-inspiring	being stuck on the thought of a goal without actually pursuing it	others will eventually cut off their offers of support, replacing it with a nod only

Table 23-3: Things we do to get stuck on a harmonic. A person can display multiple issues above. These patterns of response apply to living and dead, person and organization, regardless of rank.

Appendix V: Whole-chart Tables

Table 16-5: Planet-pair interactions for regular chart, self chart, and relative chart

	⊙	☽	☿	♀	♂	♃	♄	♅	♆	♇	Asc	Mc
⊙ Sun												
☽ Moo	self-contentment											
☿ Mer	directness	openly analytical nature										
♀ Ven	"talk about us" context	interaction affinity	persuasion									
♂ Mar	enthusiasm	emotional broadcasting	resolve	interpersn'ly sought after								
♃ Jup	image consciousness	high levity environment	exaggerated criticality	uplifting 🧍 ➲ conversation	influential image							
♄ Sat	rules consciousness	calculated emotionality	structuring mentality	restricting 🧍 ➲ converstn	controlled power	balanced self-promotion						
♅ Ura	group attunement	comfort w/ popularity	social analysis	popular company	group compulsion	extraversion context	∃ used by social world					
♆ Nep	immersion	environment intuition	abstract thinking	idealistic conversation	▶ captivate group	creativity-spirituality context	path fixation	social idealizing context				
♇ Plu	power awareness	pressure to perform	pressured prob. solving	pressured congeniality	▶ meet power standard	pressured image promotion	∃ socially held in place	genrtnl tech 4 social power	idealizing 🌍 values context			
Asc ASC	welcomed by group	outlook contentment	outgoing-ness	pleasant social face	resistance to assault	praised arrival	serious bearing	group membership	context for inspiring 🧍	group-favored approach		
Mc MC	self-promo actions level	comfort w/ reputation	reputation for analysis	sociable reputation	public allure	leader image	manager of affairs image	notoriety	enigmatic reputation	reputation for power	prime impresn mechanism	
Vx Ver	means to maj. change	handling of change	change ➲ analysis	change ➲ socializing	change ➲ overpowering	▶ redefine image	life change ➲ institutions	tendency to surprise	change ➲art & creativity	change➲ major conflict	prime respnse to maj.change	reputation-altering decsn
☊ NNd	means to life calling	comfort w/ purpose	analysis as calling	socializing as calling	influencing 🧍 as calling	exploration as calling	management niche	"destiny" 2 get talked about	borrowed group emotion	domination of 🧍 as calling	accmplshmnt news spread	reputation as ∫ for calling
Sel	talent expression	intuition heeding	talented service	ease of rapport	talent for compelling	popular demand	▶ restrain 🧍 in role	independent thinker role	impressive creativity	obsessive attention	having lucky encounters	things going right about u
Lil	maturing defiance	tendency → defiance	avoidance of duty(sneaky)	provoking 🧍 ➲ converstn	skill in manipulation	untameability	loneliness context	rebel title	vulnerability to 🧍 's control	demand for order + control	∃ in the right in rebelling	favored rebellion
For	comfort during skill	self-reflection	comfortable criticality	love of 1:1 conversation	comfort w/ overpowering	love of own image	preferred stability and control	comfort w/ eccentricity	comfort w/ imagination	drama prone context	same as ⊙☽	comfort w/ reputation
Cer	context for playfulness	push others → their fun	endearing communic.	servant vibe	seducer level	invite 🧍 role	chill influencer role	group caretaker role	foisting ideals on 🧍	pressure to make impact	"advice giver" role	self-interested image
Chir	insecurity context	training over insecurity	giving counsel	∃ steered ➲ conversation	search for influence	critic role	dismissing of world's advice	group acceptance by society	▶ uplift emotions in 🌍	act → fix 🌍 values context	"issue fixer" role	"therapy session" image
Ves	fortified ego	earnest seriousness	focused work effort	advice resistance	satisfaction w/ power	attention to image	career-focused desire	self on grapevine concern	wanting attention	suggested career field	"serious business" role	concern for reputation
Pal	"crusade" weapon	performance focus	issue confront'n context	verbal fight readiness	embattlement	public figure context	creative license in career	coop w/ social expectations	questioning & challenging 🧍	world affairs interest	"non-mess taker" role	peace-seeking image
Jun	driven by partner	identified w/ a partner	partner centric planning	partner harassment	power @ partners' expense	devotion to partner	∃ limited by partner	"married" to data & info	partner as a reflection	powerful/attractive costar	attracting 🧍 's commitment	preoccupation
Hra	bond to interactant	pro-bonding context	considerate-ness	attraction of caringpartner	power-oriented bond	sexually stimulating image	stable bond context	bond w/ any & every1 context	ideal bond realization	bonds w/ the powerful	context for ∃ irresistible	context for ∃ instantly liked
Ero	lust fulfillment	love demonstrativity	love locating action	seduction-flirt context	love-yearning	"spread love 2 all" context	attracted to || as authority	acts→ equality for all	emvironment read/writing	▶ increase 🧍 love+lust	amorousness	love-loving reputation
Bac	group attn. getting	pro-hosting mood	forum moderator role	cntr of attn. enjoyment	group command	diverse personality hub	group "shut-up & listen" role	association w/ a collective	bandwagon inspirer role	red carpet treatment	group administration	public crowd attractor

Symbols

→ means "towards; to."

➲ means "through; by using."

∃ means "being"

🧍 means "others"

▶ means "the ability to"

|| means "or"

🌍 means "the world"

∫ means "important"

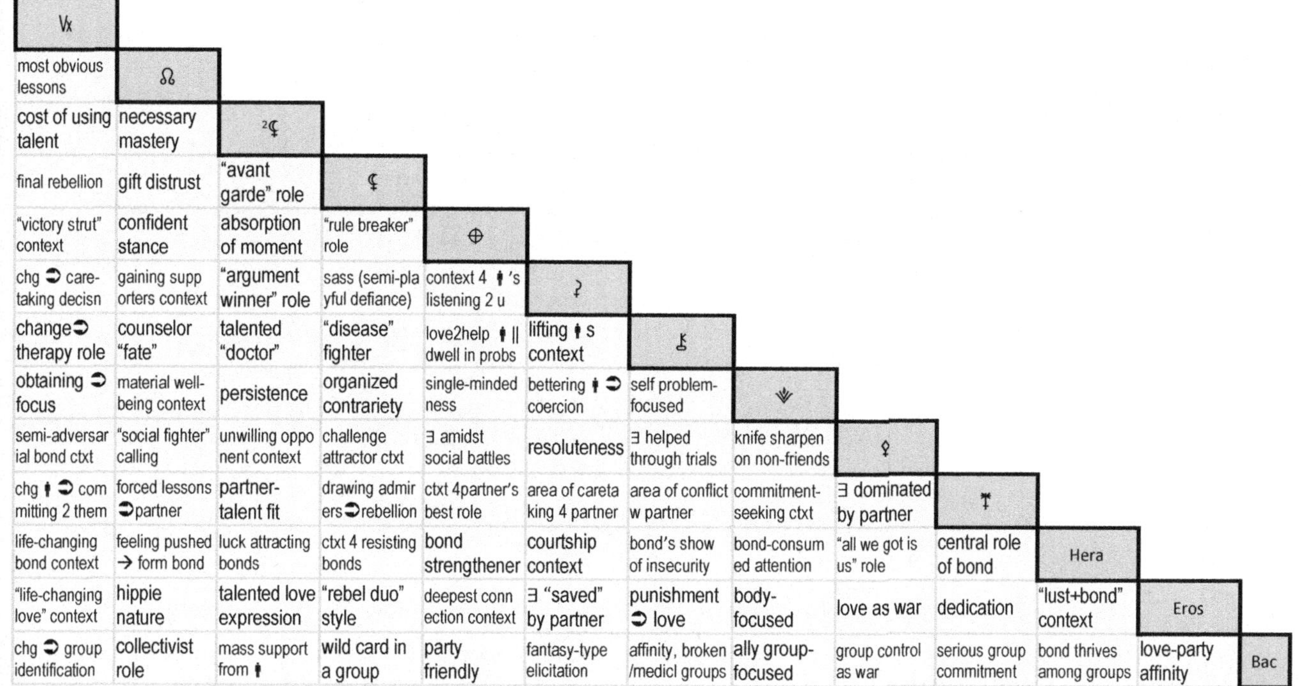

Vx												
most obvious lessons	☊											
cost of using talent	necessary mastery	²⚸										
final rebellion	gift distrust	"avant garde" role	⚸									
"victory strut" context	confident stance	absorption of moment	"rule breaker" role	⊕								
chg ➲ care-taking decisn	gaining supp orters context	"argument winner" role	sass (semi-pla yful defiance)	context 4 🧍 's listening 2 u	⸮							
change➲ therapy role	counselor "fate"	talented "doctor"	"disease" fighter	love2help 🧍 || dwell in probs	lifting 🧍 s context	⚷						
obtaining ➲ focus	material well-being context	persistence	organized contrariety	single-minded ness	bettering 🧍 ➲ coercion	self problem-focused	⯔					
semi-adversar ial bond ctxt	"social fighter" calling	unwilling oppo nent context	challenge attractor ctxt	∃ amidst social battles	resoluteness	∃ helped through trials	knife sharpen on non-friends	⚲				
chg 🧍 ➲ com mitting 2 them	forced lessons ➲partner	partner-talent fit	drawing admir ers➲rebellion	ctxt 4partner's best role	area of careta king 4 partner	area of conflict w partner	commitment-seeking ctxt	∃ dominated by partner	⯙			
life-changing bond context	feeling pushed → form bond	luck attracting bonds	ctxt 4 resisting bonds	bond strengthener	courtship context	bond's show of insecurity	bond-consum ed attention	"all we got is us" role	central role of bond	Hera		
"life-changing love" context	hippie nature	talented love expression	"rebel duo" style	deepest conn ection context	∃ "saved" by partner	punishment ➲ love	body-focused	love as war	dedication	"lust+bond" context	Eros	
chg ➲ group identification	collectivist role	mass support from 🧍	wild card in a group	party friendly	fantasy-type elicitation	affinity, broken /medicl groups	ally group-focused	group control as war	serious group commitment	bond thrives among groups	love-party affinity	Bac

Table 19-9: Planet-pair interactions for synastry chart ➡

Use the key below:

u	you (ur=your)	➲	through
o	the other person	✪	critical for determining relationship's character
☺	outsiders, anyone who is not one of the two parties in this chart	🕊	strong contributor to great relationship
🌍	the world	🔒	needed for a good relationship
↔	relationship	🗡	misuse can kill the relationship
∡	angle	👄	features heavily in seduction
soc	social	Ƴ	skyrocketing skill
ilo	in light of	⌘	you can learn from this
sxcre	sexual/creative	👁	read the other's motives or gain insight into your own
±	in a good or bad way / for better or worse (fbow)	💰	money-related

Them (o)→ ↓You (u)	☉ Sun How they interact with you	☽ Moo What they seem to prefer	☿ Mer How they make things work	♀ Ven How they communicate with you	♂ Mar Their attempts to move things around them	♃ Jup Their image projected in the world	♄ Sat Limits and structures that come w them	♅ Ura Where they soc spread fx of your efforts
☉ Sun Your behaviors	where you approach situations similarly	you play out how they feel	you are pursued for common ground	you soften their expression	they push you to steer outsiders	they embody the image you want associ-ated with	you put walls around them	you see them broadcasting widely; they can cheat you
☽ Moo Your feelings	your inclinations are turned into action	**drifting relationship?** subconscious reason for interacting	their desired goal among outsiders	👁 flattered or attended to by them	you can use this to compel their action	you encourage other to build this up as part of their image	you look like you want to impose this	they are a hub for your social groups
☿ Mer Your meaning-making	you take expressive cues	you feel subject to scrutiny	similar analysis; you can work together here	they build ∡ in you (a little) through conversation	you can easily command them	you help build up their image	\ you limit or control them with this	you have more social opportunities alongside them
♀ Ven Your 1:1 exchange with them	you get ∡ expressed to you through shared topic	you think their ∡ is a cool topic	you support their analysis through your conversation	same page as communicators	⬬ you have a natural pull over their impulses	they are prone to your bribes and flattery	you rob them of access to this	🕊 you give them a green light to try friendship with you
♂ Mar Your attempts to steer things / ppl / other	you drive them to express more	you can be easily steered using this	\ they easily command you	you are compelled to action	similar ennervation, prompts to fight	they see you dedicated to changing this in people	you inhibit their mastery; you structure their reputation	how you should interact with them as fr&s
♃ Jup Your efforts in the world	you feel respected by them	their display motivates you to go forth	your image is built up through commonality with them	you work to build up their image	they are more forward and insistent in this ∡	similar basis for image-making	they seem a longstanding complement to your ∡	you have respect for them under their ∡
♄ Sat Your limits / shows of control	you help them structure their approach	you feel restricted by their desire to express this	you are limited by them	you lose options for displaying this	your active influence is limited by their ∡	you expand your image against their obstacles	similar approaches to control	you shock them with your ∡, can embarrass them
♅ Ura You as a social evaluator	you encourage their network mobility	you see their popularity potential	they are well-liked and personable here	people are aware of an affinity btw you and them here	how they classify you socially	your ∡ assoc-iation with their world expands your image	they produce surprise restrictions for all, even themselves	similar societal contexts
♆ Nep You as embo-dying their environment	you give obligated attention or pity	you give impression of scrutiny	they are spacey, confusing, abstract	they seem to misinterpret your ∡	you amplify their influence, intensify their expression	you idealize them under their ∡	they are perfectionistic in general when it comes to ∡	o motivated to become stronger in light of your social environment
⯓ Plu You as repre-senting those who pressure Other	you're there (fbow) when they're threatened	you promote their ∡ as powerful	you provide extra insight into their ∡	they become stronger and stronger with your association	you are challenged by their actions	you see them as extra powerful beyond peers	you pressure them to sharpen their ∡ expression	their ∡ demands you demonstrate strength
Asc ASC You as one approaching something new	their interaction reflects your ∡	you get their spontaneous expression of this ∡	they use ∡ to judge your impression making	you create base-level rapport here	you are single-minded in their view	they have the successful identity you seek to build	they submit to you	their position allows you to fulfill your intentions
Mc MC You the acknowledger	their contribution to this keeps u interested in relationship	they are self-promoting and reputation-centered	you are considered a partner to them by people	they show they wish to build something lasting here	they are 1:1 dominant under this ∡	where you and they are true partners in crime	they show controlled expression	they seem to gravitate to you under this ∡

Them (o)→ ↓You (u)	♆ Nep Where they reflect emo fx of your efforts	♇ Plu They infuse ur efforts w power	Asc ASC Where they bring attn. to your efforts	Mc MC Where they give u cause to respond	Vx Ver Their efforts to influence things around them	☊ NNd Where they make ur action convenient 4u	²⚸ Sel Where they model ur ideal view of concpt	⚸ Lil Where they turn into the reason u act	⊕ For Where they are comfortable
☉ Sun Your behaviors	**o=attentive?** your deeds dominate their idea of this ∡	you help them build defense against social pressure	you see them as strongly skilled	✪ 🔒 \ they keep relationship alive through this	they value your help through change here	👁 you're easily known for this behavior	you celebrate their talents or criticize their defects	they are beyond your influence	you are more comfortable giving this
☽ Moo Your feelings	you make more errors, are self-conscious	they are your publicist for the rumor mill	you are comfortable going to them with your ∡	you use this ∡ to create an identity in their world	they see you as a catalyst for major change	🕊 you see role for yourself in their life	you see this as one of best parts of relationship	you draw out excitement or intimidate them	you reduce their insecurities
☿ Mer Your meaning-making	where they cover up issues you can't face; you are intuitive	⌘ you give good evaluation of their issues	they use this as central trait for making impressions	⌘ they adopt an approach you want to adopt	you benefit from their specialization	their angle is worth your analysis	you are more shameless showing this	they are a troublemaker	your criticality returns to you through them
♀ Ven Your 1:1 exchange with them	something about their world is unreal here	you attain power along-side them	you can be superficial friends here	you show you have other concerns besides them here	you consciously shape their decisions	you value your association through more 1:1 with them	you admire them as a source of de-cisive talent	you are weird, avant garde to them	they are themselves talking to you
♂ Mar Your attempts to steer things / ppl / other	they highlight your power to build up your ∡	⌘ 💰 u hand out "lessons" to them, in-fluence their money	you tend to lose challenges to them here	👄 how they want you to validate them	your ∡ is altered by association with them	you show strength towards them	you actively smooth over conflicts btw o and people	your influence augments their defiance	your active influence pacifies their ∡
♃ Jup Your efforts in the world	their ∡ is fuzzy, but they can be very creative	♈ you levy world pressure uopn them	you think they look up to your efforts	they are an ally, if you jointly execute	your broad ∡ approach can change them	you appear sure of yourself	you're awkwardly skilled	you encourage rule-breaking and taboo in them	o has a wider view than you and could be a role model
♄ Sat Your limits / shows of control	you are obsessively attentive to certain rules	they possess limiting command over people	you don't mind having your efforts structured	you display control in their eyes	their ∡ is a glue trap, you are subject to their influence	🕊 you use this ∡ to tame them	they monopolize this ∡ when it arises	their angle is better seen than heard, a liability	they soften your seriousness
♅ Ura You as a social evaluator	🔒 **u like their company?** you support their social evolution	they are the fortress; send sxcre energy into relationship	you channel social world's response to them	you see their popular attributes under their ∡	you bring surprising change to them under their ∡	your angle is your branded face in their life	they seem soc appealing or repulsive in general	you look awkward but innovative	you fuel their bold or progressive nature
♆ Nep You as embo-dying their environment	similar focus on environment	your envirnmt survival skill goes up by helping them	their ∡ is an incomplete connection with you	they get away with prolific actions	you may never know them well here	their thoughtless actions can confuse ↔	the basis of your joining their fan club	you may look up to o as a rebel or innovator	you imagine an ideal when o is in their element
♇ Plu You as repre-senting those who pressure Other	u find comfort in your person-al problems around them	similar perception of pressures, support	their approach embodies your pressures	their strongest sxcre asset	they work against greater pressures	it is easier to endure your own pressures ilo them	o embodies your problems or enables your solutions	o enables social revolutionary expression	you use your ∡ to issue power
Asc ASC You as one approaching something new	their ∡ produces illusions for you	your exchange highlights problems in their ∡	similar approach to new situations, exploration	your sphere of experience learns of them through this ∡	their angle = basis of discussion for parallels	o drives you to spontaneous action	you can rely on them to express this	they are reliably contrary	you and other as fr&s
Mc MC You the acknowledger	you can act unchecked under your ∡	you are attracted to them to extent u want to show off ∡	your ∡ actions earn you a reputation in their life	people inclined to associate you and them publicly	Spillover. o reacts to or pays for assoc w you	you provide insight into their direction	you and they make an idealized public team	you and they publicly known as a rebel pair	ur image is boosted by o's enjoymnt of ur compny

Them (o)→ ↓You (u)	⚳ Cer Where they feel things need to be tended to	⚷ Chir Where they teach / compel ur learning	⚶ Ves Where they focus on what u flood them w/	⚴ Pal Where you respond to their crusade	⚵ Jun Their idea of ur current planet used to draw ur next "planet" curr	next		Hra Their attachment to your efforts	Ero Their passion-ate response to ur efforts	Bac How their friends answer your efforts
☉ Sun Your behaviors	you see their expressive potential	you learn from them; or they are a bad teacher	you motivate shaping of their ∡	you war alongside them; feel tension ilo o	Sun	Mercury	use this to secure commitment	your entitled association with o if this isn't blocked	you give them access to this as association builds	they rely on you to show this to their cliques
☽ Moo Your feelings	watched by o, you want to show dominance	you are a therapeutic listing ear	you hide this or let them have their way first	they see you as rebellious against social imposition	Moon	Sun	✪ their actions insist that you display this ∡	they greet you with this as they try to get closer 2 u	they are hungry or lusty here	you encroach on their space
☿ Mer Your meaning-making	you can make them smile or be uncomfortable	they appear to have their stuff together	you endure them	you don't receive attacks well	Mercury	Venus	you borrow their ∡ for your own advancement	you feel their excitement ilo your ∡	your ∡ is a button pusher for them	they are provocative and group-persuasive
♀ Ven Your 1:1 exchange with them	they are a little too forceful persuading people here	your "helping" them actually helps you	you flood them with information	they treat you as a crusader here	Venus	Mars	they assert this to reinforce their relevance	you maintain your identity against their connection	they see ur ∡ as more intense than expected	your 1:1 engagement affirms your popularity
♂ Mar Your attempts to steer things / ppl / other	you encourage more of their ∡ action	you are the perfectionistic evaluator of their abilities	you stay busy with this ∡ with or despite them	you tolerate, but don't adopt their ∡	Mars	Jupiter	you use ∡ to request their attention	\ maj. means for solidifying ↔...even as a dead one	Ping. This ∡ should inspire them	you make a great co-conspirator to them
♃ Jup Your efforts in the world	you can get away w pressuring them	you gain "exp points" for dealing w them here	this is a pronounced component of their world rep	they drive their own agitation	Jupiter	Saturn	your way grows their ∡ effectiveness w commitment	they express their attach-ment to you through ∡	you use ∡ to compel results in their eyes	you can draw a crowd in their eyes, ±
♄ Sat Your limits / shows of control	they cheer on your ∡ efforts	they avoid deep investigation of their ∡	this ∡ looks mismatched for them	your interaction fills you with tension or inspires you	Saturn	Uranus	you display commitment-like behaviors to them	you like using this ∡ to keep ↔ fresh	they are self-focused	they are the center of group attention
♅ Ura You as a social evaluator	in their company, you assert final word over ∡	their angle = area of your exploratory interest	o stares at ur soc information regarding this ∡	their battlefield = all of society under this ∡	Uranus	Neptune	they are a kindred mind to u under ∡	their influence stays with u beyond exchg	you learn ur own passion from theirs	✪their ∡ is the 1st maj impre ssion they leave on you
♆ Nep You as embo-dying their environment	you see them as being in need of your coercion	o needs your encouragement to develop their power	as you imagine, they deliver in full	you feel you are in their way	Neptune	Pluto	\ their overly strong advancement hurts ↔	your company is appreciated by them	their driving force once you get to know them	you idealize their clique, u prone to disloyalty
♇ Plu You as repre-senting those who pressure Other	you issue power ilo their ∡	their ∡ is a remedy for tension in ur ↔	they fixate on your ∡	you learn the art of fighting here	Pluto (soc prssr to	(social prssr to	their ∡ is a reliable basis for interfacing with them	you feel prolific, o attaches to be fulfilled	you and other = lock and key complements	you experience peer pressure ilo them
Asc ASC You as one approaching something new	they are pushy	you improve as a "doctor" ilo them	u pay more attn 2 their body or physical impression	u see o as passionate, with them or against them	Ascendant (1st house)	(worth of ↔; 2nd house)	you and they reaffirm the ↔	they bond with things under this ∡	u receive their ∡, ↔ becom es creatively tense	you influence their clique here
Mc MC You the acknowledger	they are known as a caretaker here	they are difficult to influence and quirky	they are obsessed w (or self-conscious of) ∡	their ∡ drives u to press for your own values	Midheaven (10th	(public talk; 11th house)	as ppl see u give ur ∡ to o, commitment is stronger	you publicly show bond to them ±	ppl see their ∡ as driving your passionate action	u see their ∡ as foundation for their clique membership

Them (o)→ ↓You (u)	☉ Sun How they interact with you	☽ Moo What they seem to prefer	☿ Mer How they make things work	♀ Ven How they communicate with you	♂ Mar Their attempts to move things around them	♃ Jup Their image projected in the world	♄ Sat Limits and structures that come w them	♅ Ura Where they soc spread fx of your efforts
Vx Ver Your experience of change	their behavior tied to their major changes	you seem a potential agent for their major change	👁 you can change them; they struggle to forgive you	you can have your life changed under their ∡	ϒ your skill with this ∡ skyrockets alongside them	your responses to them can change you	your life is changed, stabilized under their ∡	o brings chngs under ∡, putting u on the spot
☊ NNd Where u make things seem meant to be	o seems destined to express this ∡	they see this as important for early ↔ survival	you receive important analysis from them	conversation with you increases their sophistication	you seem destined to receive their steering attempts	they're extra forceful to cover self-doubt	if you choose to learn from them, you grow here	their angle makes them favorable to you
Sel Where u r super talented	you feel more talented ilo them	you can use this to make them happy	\ you have commonality with their unlimited talent	you share an overwhelming trait with them	they are (or should be) ridiculously lucky here	they're good, but probably not the best	u like being put under their influence 4 ur reputation building	u and o make a good tag team 4 social validation
⚸ Lil Where u defy normal expected behavior	you are rebel complement to other	you are a badass alongside other doing this	where you are a perpetrator of offenses	their path is unusual here	their ∡ draws out the rulebreaker in you	they are the devil on your shoulder	u encourage them to break restrictions	u make o defer to u or see you as underqualified
⊕ For You in your element	you are in your element ilo their ∡	you accept their angle as comfortable fact	you like their reluctantly given tactics	👁 what they think you like to talk about	they can shake you out of comfort here	you're inclined to brag about this association	you help co-write their ∡	you look at bigger picture ilo their ∡
⚳ Cer Where you push them to more force	u are encouraged 2 behave differently; they grate	they are heavily persuasive here	you are amused by or agree with their tactics	they model strong communication	✪you enjoy associating their prtnrshp with your ∡	u are subject to changes in ur presentation under their influence	u push them to display this ∡ beyond themselves	o puts members of soc world in place
⚷ Chir Where u teach lessons (smtms accidently)	you see them as capped; or as a respected teacher	they heal you or serve as outlet for you	⌘ you are an apprentice skillwise	their ∡ has a therapeutic effect on them	o difficult to reach when engaged in this	you help them through issues here	their point of compensation for failed wishes	you disclose secrets about yourself relative to ∡
⚶ Ves Where you put ur concentration	you admire and focus on them	you are fascinated by them, want to know more	you can be wrapped up for hours by them	you pay focused attn to their communication	unless you're helping them, o is inclined to ignore you	you gain sharper focus on your angle ilo their ways	they push ∡ on ppl to increase their own influence	they are well-versed or focused under your attn
⚴ Pal Where you call for war	they can provoke you into a social statement	they are unwilling to be caged in	they are a rebel fighter when ∡ threatened	they are a paradigm toppling communicator	o braves the world to fight for their version of this ∡	ϒ you hone your skills in warfare ilo their ∡	you borrow their ∡ to fight your own battles	their appearance leaves this impression on you
⚵ Jun Your commitment behavior	o commits to you using this	you commit to supporting this angle	an ideal they come to you to validate	discussions under your ∡ = togetherness for you	o insinuates themselves into your life	✪ how you'll change ilo your commitment to them	their expression keeps u interested in them	**✪Wht u get out of ↔? o** validates your abilities
Hra Your bonding behavior	joint expression here solidifies bond	their ∡ is the basis for good will between you	✪ you bond strongly with them ilo their ∡	they are attached to protecting their ∡	🕊 you are very strongly drawn to their ∡	o = your long term friend if you can accept this ∡	🕊 Solidifier jointly, keep the exchange from decaying	ur ∡ is insistently pressed upon by your target
Ero Where you crave passion	✪ you express your desires ilo their version of ∡	you press full force for their ∡	they motivate your impassioned response	o = a territory conquering communicator	you appreciate their ∡ and find it comforting	they = sexy or frustrating, motivating you ±	they brim with potential	they are driven in a scoial setting
Bac How your clique responds	they adopt this basic behavior in their cliques	they seem a dominator here	they are an attention grabbing co-star to you	o has talent for group-commanding communication	you conspire with them to take over their group	they gather pleasure seekers	they are sought after under ∡	your most comfortable way of sending ur clique expression to them

Them (o)→ ↓You (u)	Ψ Nep Where they reflect emo fx of your efforts	♇ Plu They infuse ur efforts w power	Asc ASC Where they bring attn. to your efforts	Mc MC Where they give u cause to respond	Vx Ver Their efforts to influencethings around them	☊ NNd Where they make ur action convenient 4u	²⚸ Sel Where they model ur ideal view of concpt	⚸ Lil Where they turn into the reason u act	⊕ For Where they are comfortable
Vx Ver Your experience of change	their fuzziness may inspire your action	👄o is a strong means of rewritiing ur ∡ priorities	u and o have intertwined fates ilo your ∡	you enter their world and change your view of them	similar drivers for life change	their ∡ fated to change ur ↔ permanently	u appreciate the strength of expression in their ∡	∡ reflects longstanding waywardness in them	their ∡ sponsors ur deep personal discoveries
☊ NNd Where u make things seem meant to be	you use this ∡ to send ur aspirations to them	🔒world opposes their easy progress	they are erra-tic, u may question the hype about o	🔒 you rub off on them	your ∡ brings unavoidable changes to ↔	your + their Introduction Context	their Destined Reveal 2 u	👄you take counterperspective to them	they are self-assured without you here
²⚸ Sel Where u r super talented	o doesn't see what you want them to see	you can feel unstoppable w their support	the section of life where u always feel o welcomes u±	ppl identify you as strong partner to them	you learn how your own ∡ should be used	your first signi-ficant impression on them	similar level of command 4 what needs to be done	o can get away w murder under this	✪you appear in their life to evolve how they use ∡
⚸ Lil Where u defy normal expect ed behavior	u imagine a rule-breaking exchg w o; Hollow Oath	ur ∡ shows stand out power comp ared to ppl	you won't be pinned down	u encourage o to be nonconformist	they see this ∡ as schmooze-resitant in you	o is contrary or complementary to you	they see a trait in you which no one can check	similar prompt for fiery defiance	they employ rebel tactics as a rule here
⊕ For You in your element	their ∡ is the means they use to impress upon people	o assaults ± with this ∡	u r interested in exploring the future with them	you value ur assoc w other under ∡	u see their ∡ as their most comfortable new expressn	✪ u (ideally) earn their respect under this angle	✪ their role = hone how u project ur ∡	you help o break barriers under ∡	similar tendency to bask in ur + their abilities
⚳ Cer Where you push them to more force	they do what you are com pelled to want them to do	Worsened Pressure by u onto them	o is compara tively modest against their other traits	o promotes thmslvs for significance under your ∡	you use this angle to overrule their suggestions	o prgrmmed to make their case to you through angle	u r shielded by them from challenges to ur ∡	you want to foster their escape from the status quo	you show the kind of pressure o likes via ur ∡
⚷ Chir Where u teach lessons (sm accidently)	you clean up their mistakes	you are kept grounded through their ∡	they need help or validation	o is less secure under their ∡	o accidentally learns by tackling ur fears	you strongly inclined to accept help from o here	o has steering expertise over ppl in this ∡	you access buried issues in them via ur ∡	you serve as a doctor ilo their bad preferences
⚶ Ves Where you put ur concentration	you see them as fixed in intent	you direct ur power towards addressing standards in o	you can be entranced by them	where u r self-conscious around them	their way of doing things surprises you	o grows greatly in power w ur partnership	Internal Defense against their threats	their ∡ = trait that sets them apart from people	o treats you as compelling given ur display of ∡
⚴ Pal Where you call for war	you support their fulfillment of an ideal role	you are more likely to fight on their behalf	they are a fellow combatant under their ∡	they naturally seek to challenge people here	you use your ∡ to kick them, push them forward	o needs you to listen here	they adopt ∡ as a remedy for issues with [∡-1]	u are more likely to put o in an uncomfortable position in their∡	u encouraged by o to fight for ur ∡, ±
⚵ Jun Your commitment behavior	you seek to influence their dreams	you commit to their development	👁u receive their ∡ as a statement of their caring	ppl see their ∡ to you as a token of their commitment	you and o seem destined to be committed ±	you feel destined to commit given their ∡ to you	they cling to this aspect of their influence	you support their stand out in this ∡	they express their discontent w society
Hra Your bonding behavior	you are comfortable delving into their company	o needs to address prssr here to feel effective	other puts expectations on you; ✪u = irresistible	where u + o have implied affection and attachment	you use new bonding w o to rewrite this area of ur life	you bond to o over their ∡ IF you have the interest	u r at home expressing yourself along-side their ∡	you find their ∡ mysterious	o sees ur ∡ as main wpn 4 reconciling disharmony
Ero Where you crave passion	their handling of their ∡ is impressive 2 you	✪o supports your powers (after ↔); u flood Other	🗡✪🕊 how can u drive ↔ intensity?	their ∡ is a possible liabil ity in building ur reputation	you incite driven action in other	you reveal ur passions to them, o = fated viewer	o provokes ppl's passions through their ∡	their ∡ = the essence of quality time with them	o conveys their lusts through ur ∡
Bac How your clique responds	o is insistently social here, might make u jealous	your group weighs in on o ilo this ∡	your clique absorbs o's ways into its function	your cliques view o's ∡ as basis for clique's attn	you use your ∡ as spokespersn for ur clique	natural language for defining their cliques	your mgmt of groups is influenced by them	your clique admires this ∡ in o	u r eccentric in a way that embarrasses o

Them (o)→ ↓You (u)	Cer Where they feel things need to be tended to	Chir Where they teach / compel ur learning	Ves Where they focus on what u flood them w/	Pal Where you respond to their crusade	Jun Their idea of ur current planet used to draw ur next "planet" curr	next		Hra Their attachment to your efforts	Ero Their passion-ate response to ur efforts	Bac How their friends answer your efforts
Ver Your experience of change	o attempts to persuade you to their way of thinking	you elevate their pre-existing talents	they have to watch out for left turns from you	their ∡ awakens your inner warrior	Vertex (change)	(reconciled change)	you get their committed attention	you're hooked on their approach ±	their ∡ is agitating and provocative	do their friends show you this ∡ positively?
NNd Where u make things seem meant to be	your chief persuasive mode, fun time with o	o needs your help developing this ∡	their social worth lies partly in this ∡	their fighter mode ∡	Nth Node (destiny)	(aftermath)	your vulnerability offering to them	your core offering to o, gets their liking if successful	their passion-nate action is dedicated to this ∡	u categorize their group according to this ∡
Sel Where u r super talented	you promote the idea of o as powerful under ∡	u take on authority role in their eyes	o concentrates on maintaining this side, 4 or against u	u use this ∡ on o unreslvd [∡-1] issues w them	Selene (perfection)	(next event)	you like hanging around them for this ∡	their true desire 2 bond (in general) conveyed	ur ∡ is point of charged emo. to them	they have pronounced status in cliques here
Lil Where u defy normal expect ed behavior	o sees ur ∡ defy standard soc training	ur ∡ is a cover 4 ur real feelings of their version of ∡	ur uniquely destabilizing role in their life	their tool 4 making their more intense wants known	Lilith (defiance)	(unique-ness)	u r extra unique given your decision to engage them	you resist their persuasion using this ∡	ur weapon for motivating o when they don't move	you see them as popular ilo ppl seeking this ∡ in them
For You in your element	you are at home with their style of nurturing	o needs your encouragement through difficulty here	o sees this ∡ as a gateway to their self-image	u encourage o in fighting for their ∡	P. Fortune (ur element)	(voluntary choice)	mismatches in this ∡ easily hurt long term ↔	o brings this ↔ as the harmony or else condition	o is most devoted to u under this ∡	o stands out among own; u surprised by their circle
Cer Where you push them to more force	similar approach to influencing people	u polish this ∡ b/c u think it's what o wants to see	u actively sup-port healthy exprssion of their ∡	you ask for punishment for being associated w o	Ceres (pushing)	(strong display)	u make a place 4 o; or put them in their place	you convey sensitivity to their needs	their primal side inflames ur own	the method o uses to resist ur unreasonbl demands
Chir Where u teach lessons (sm accidently)	you diagnose their underlying sense of insufficiency	similar approaches to insecurity	you are highly observant of their ∡	your ∡ has a pacifying effct on them; The Tamer	Chiron (social insecurity)	(security in society)	u refuse their successful input, single-mindedly	ur silver bullet for bonding w o, Dfns Weakenr	your capped efforts to engage them	o helps fill ur expressive need; o gains wider appeal
Ves Where you put ur concentration	you watch their attempts to force changes on people	you see their perspective as aligned w yours under ∡	similar penchant for zooming in on issues	their ongoing battle against issues here	Vesta (focus)	(continuati on)	u end up supporting o here, lifting partial burden	o produces conditions for ur accidental ∡ evolution	their intensity follows yours	o seems well-liked under descriptions of their ∡
Pal Where you call for war	u see them as most resistant to caging	u cheer 4 or bemoan their ∡ to drive it -> ur benefit	o more likely to show irritation handling this ∡	similar social-battle prompts and ethical foundations	Pallas ("right" war)	(resolution)	u see o as useful to ur quest to resolve ur ∡	o frames the consequences of their social actions w ∡	they are your joint social combat partner	their ∡ is their investment in friendship w u
Jun Your commitment behavior	your assessment of their selfishness	they treat their ∡ as a "must protect"	they are a magnet for issues that concern you	their burdens attracted to you	Juno (commit ment)	(committer's desired end)	ur + their commitments affect this ∡ similarly	u use ur ∡ to provide enduring support to o	o brings u to creative projection this ∡'s way	u donate their ∡ as offering 2 ur clique, promoting o
Hra Your bonding behavior	you see o as caring through their ∡	u value their ∡ highly, letting it circumscribe your standards	u as Guardian Angel to them	o under-expresses under ∡	Hera (bonding)	(fulfillment)	you connect to their use of ∡ as valid acquaintance	similar bond triggers	u market this ∡ of theirs to ppl	u + o jointly attract ppl's attention
Ero Where you crave passion	o sees you charge up ur expression w passion	you see their area of greatest dissatisfaction	u r inspired 2 be more soc attractive ilo their ∡	o needs intensely felt harmony w ppl here	Eros (lust)	(satiation)	u help push o to create whatever their ∡ passion is	their formed bond under their ∡ = stimulating ±	similar passionate mobility prompts	u want to rewrite their clique training
Bac How your clique responds	u help pressure o 2 stay strong and desirable among clique	o provides skill u can't, winning over cliques	o issues ∡ under concern 4 ppl's opinion	ur positive engagement in ur ∡ grows ur friendship	Bacchus (clique beh.)	(clique identity)	they commit noticeably to their groups via this ∡	u + o form a potent tag team towards ppl	ur clique = infiltrated by their lusts	✪ u + o jointly "cliquify" a room

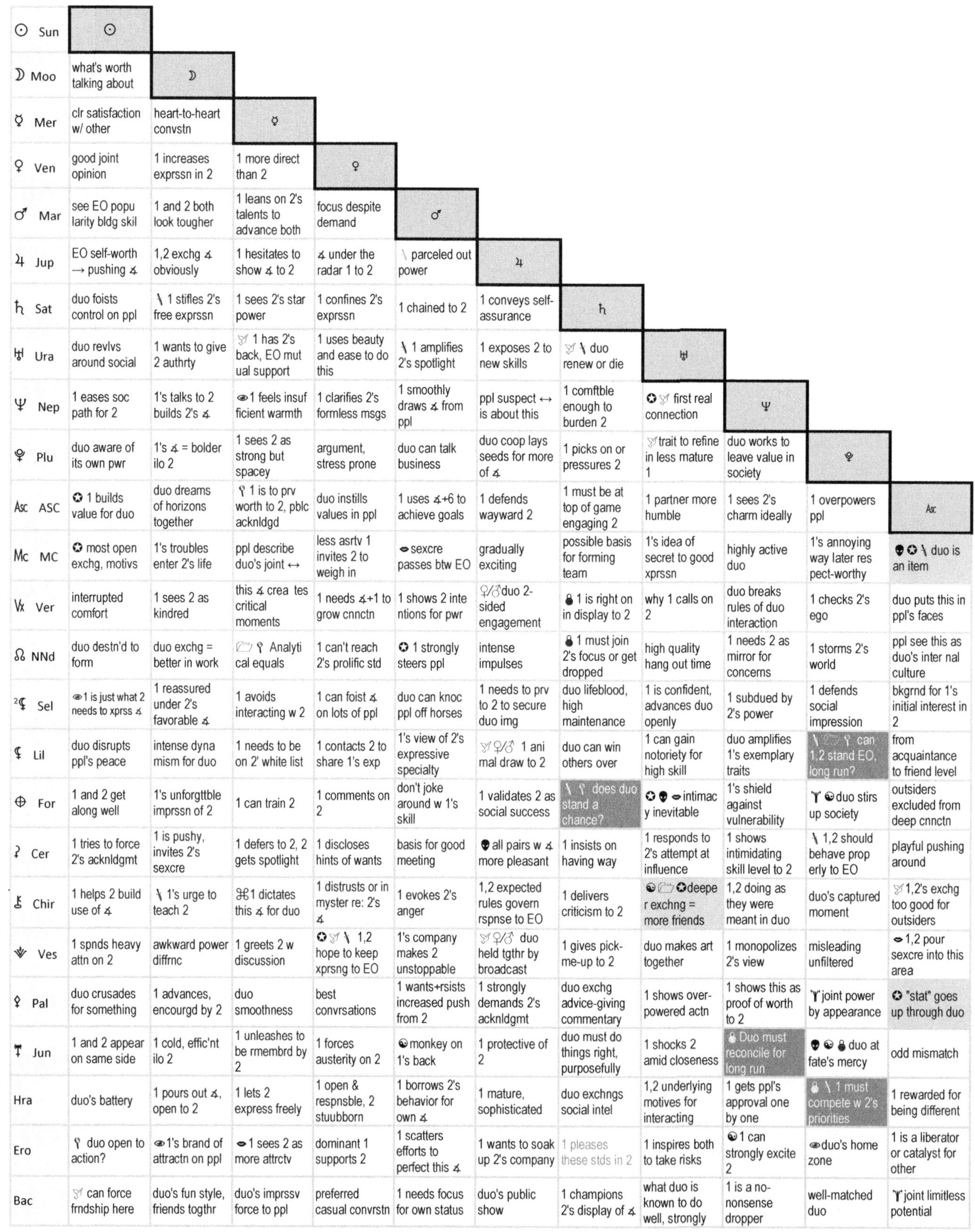

	☉ Sun	☽ Moo	☿ Mer	♀ Ven	♂ Mar	♃ Jup	♄ Sat	♅ Ura	♆ Nep	♇ Plu	Asc
☉ Sun	☉										
☽ Moo	what's worth talking about	☽									
☿ Mer	clr satisfaction w/ other	heart-to-heart convstn	☿								
♀ Ven	good joint opinion	1 increases exprssn in 2	1 more direct than 2	♀							
♂ Mar	see EO popu larity bldg skil	1 and 2 both look tougher	1 leans on 2's talents to advance both	focus despite demand	♂						
♃ Jup	EO self-worth → pushing ∡	1,2 exchg ∡ obviously	1 hesitates to show ∡ to 2	∡ under the radar 1 to 2	\ parceled out power	♃					
♄ Sat	duo foists control on ppl	\ 1 stifles 2's free exprssn	1 sees 2's star power	1 confines 2's exprssn	1 chained to 2	1 conveys self-assurance	♄				
♅ Ura	duo revlvs around social	1 wants to give 2 authrty	🕊 1 has 2's back, EO mut ual support	1 uses beauty and ease to do this	\ 1 amplifies 2's spotlight	1 exposes 2 to new skills	🕊 \ duo renew or die	♅			
♆ Nep	1 eases soc path for 2	1's talks to 2 builds 2's ∡	👁1 feels insuf ficient warmth	1 clarifies 2's formless msgs	1 smoothly draws ∡ from ppl	ppl suspect ↔ is about this	1 comftble enough to burden 2	✪ 🕊 first real connection	♆		
♇ Plu	duo aware of its own pwr	1's ∡ = bolder ilo 2	1 sees 2 as strong but spacey	argument, stress prone	duo can talk business	duo coop lays seeds for more of ∡	1 picks on or pressures 2	🕊trait to refine in less mature 1	duo works to leave value in society	♇	
Asc ASC	✪ 1 builds value for duo	duo dreams of horizons together	⚲ 1 is to prv worth to 2, pblc ackn ldgd	duo instills values in ppl	1 uses ∡+6 to achieve goals	1 defends wayward 2	1 must be at top of game engaging 2	1 partner more humble	1 sees 2's charm ideally	1 overpowers ppl	Asc
Mc MC	✪ most open exchg, motivs	1's troubles enter 2's life	ppl describe duo's joint ↔	less asrtv 1 invites 2 to weigh in	⚭sexcre passes btw EO	gradually exciting	possible basis for forming team	1's idea of secret to good xprssn	highly active duo	1's annoying way later res pect-worthy	👽✪ \ duo is an item
Vx Ver	interrupted comfort	1 sees 2 as kindred	this ∡ crea tes critical moments	1 needs ∡+1 to grow cnnctn	1 shows 2 inte ntions for pwr	♀/♂duo 2-sided engagement	🔒1 is right on in display to 2	why 1 calls on 2	duo breaks rules of duo interaction	1 checks 2's ego	duo puts this in ppl's faces
☊ NNd	duo destn'd to form	duo exchg = better in work	📂 ⚲ Analyti cal equals	1 can't reach 2's prolific std	✪ 1 strongly steers ppl	intense impulses	🔒 1 must join 2's focus or get dropped	high quality hang out time	1 needs 2 as mirror for concerns	1 storms 2's world	ppl see this as duo's inter nal culture
⚸ Sel	👁1 is just what 2 needs to xprss ∡	1 reassured under 2's favorable ∡	1 avoids interacting w 2	1 can foist ∡ on lots of ppl	duo can knoc ppl off horses	1 needs to prv to 2 to secure duo img	duo lifeblood, high maintenance	1 is confident, advances duo openly	1 subdued by 2's power	1 defends social impression	bkgrnd for 1's initial interest in 2
⚸ Lil	duo disrupts ppl's peace	intense dyna mism for duo	1 needs to be on 2' white list	1 contacts 2 to share 1's exp	1's view of 2's expressive specialty	🕊♀/♂ 1 ani mal draw to 2	duo can win others over	1 can gain notoriety for high skill	duo amplifies 1's exemplary traits	\ 📂 ⚲ can 1,2 stand EO, long run?	from acquaintance to friend level
⊕ For	1 and 2 get along well	1's unforgttble imprssn of 2	1 can train 2	1 comments on 2	don't joke around w 1's skill	1 validates 2 as social success	\ ⚲ does duo stand a chance?	✪ 👽 ⚭intimac y inevitable	1's shield against vulnerability	♈ 👁duo stirs up society	outsiders excluded from deep cnnctn
⚳ Cer	1 tries to force 2's ackn ldgmt	1 is pushy, invites 2's sexcre	1 defers to 2, 2 gets spotlight	1 discloses hints of wants	basis for good meeting	👽all pairs w ∡ more pleasant	1 insists on having way	1 responds to 2's attempt at influence	1 shows intimidating skill level to 2	\ 1,2 should behave prop erly to EO	playful pushing around
⚷ Chir	1 helps 2 build use of ∡	\ 1's urge to teach 2	⌘1 dictates this ∡ for duo	1 distrusts or in myster re: 2's ∡	1 evokes 2's anger	1,2 expected rules govern rspnse to EO	1 delivers criticism to 2	👁📂✪deepe r exchng = more friends	1,2 doing as they were meant in duo	duo's captured moment	🕊1,2's exchg too good for outsiders
⚶ Ves	1 spnds heavy attn on 2	awkward power diffrnc	1 greets 2 w discussion	✪🕊 \ 1,2 hope to keep xprsng to EO	1's company makes 2 unstoppable	🕊♀/♂ duo held tgthr by broadcast	1 gives pick-me-up to 2	duo makes art together	1 monopolizes 2's view	misleading unfiltered	⚭1,2 pour sexcre into this area
⚴ Pal	duo crusades for something	1 advances, encourgd by 2	duo smoothness	best convrsations	1 wants+rsists increased push from 2	1 strongly demands 2's ackn ldgmt	duo exchg advice-giving commentary	1 shows over-powered actn	1 shows this as proof of worth to 2	♈joint power by appearance	✪ "stat" goes up through duo
⚵ Jun	1 and 2 appear on same side	1 cold, effic'nt ilo 2	1 unleashes to be rmembrd by 2	1 forces austerity on 2	👁monkey on 1's back	1 protective of 2	duo must do things right, purposefully	1 shocks 2 amid closeness	🔒 Duo must reconcile for long run	👽 👁 🔒 duo at fate's mercy	odd mismatch
Hra	duo's battery	1 pours out ∡, open to 2	1 lets 2 express freely	1 open & respnsble, 2 stuubborn	1 borrows 2's behavior for own ∡	1 mature, sophisticated	duo exchngs social intel	1,2 underlying motives for interacting	1 gets ppl's approval one by one	🔒 \ 1 must compete w 2's priorities	1 rewarded for being different
Ero	⚲ duo open to action?	👁1's brand of attractn on ppl	⚭1 sees 2 as more attrctv	dominant 1 supports 2	1 scatters efforts to perfect this ∡	1 wants to soak up 2's company	1 pleases these stds in 2	1 inspires both to take risks	👁1 can strongly excite 2	👁duo's home zone	1 is a liberator or catalyst for other
Bac	🕊 can force frndship here	duo's fun style, friends togthr	duo's imprssv force to ppl	preferred casual convrstn	1 needs focus for own status	duo's public show	1 champions 2's display of ∡	what duo is known to do well, strongly	1 is a no-nonsense dropper	well-matched duo	♈joint limitless potential

Table 21-3: Planet-pair interactions for composite chart

Symbols

✪	an important pair (shaded = super strong)
🗡	relationship killer (shaded = critical)
🕊	relationship builder
⚲	investigate the nature of an interaction
👁	read a likely outcome or another's view
🔒	gatekeeper (stops interacting from advancing)
👽	affects all pairs with the same angle
👄	related to sexuality-creativity
☯	use to re-write interaction
🗁	you need 50+ charts to see this one easily
⌘	learning scenario
♀/♂	gender biased
↔	"relationship" (EO = each other)

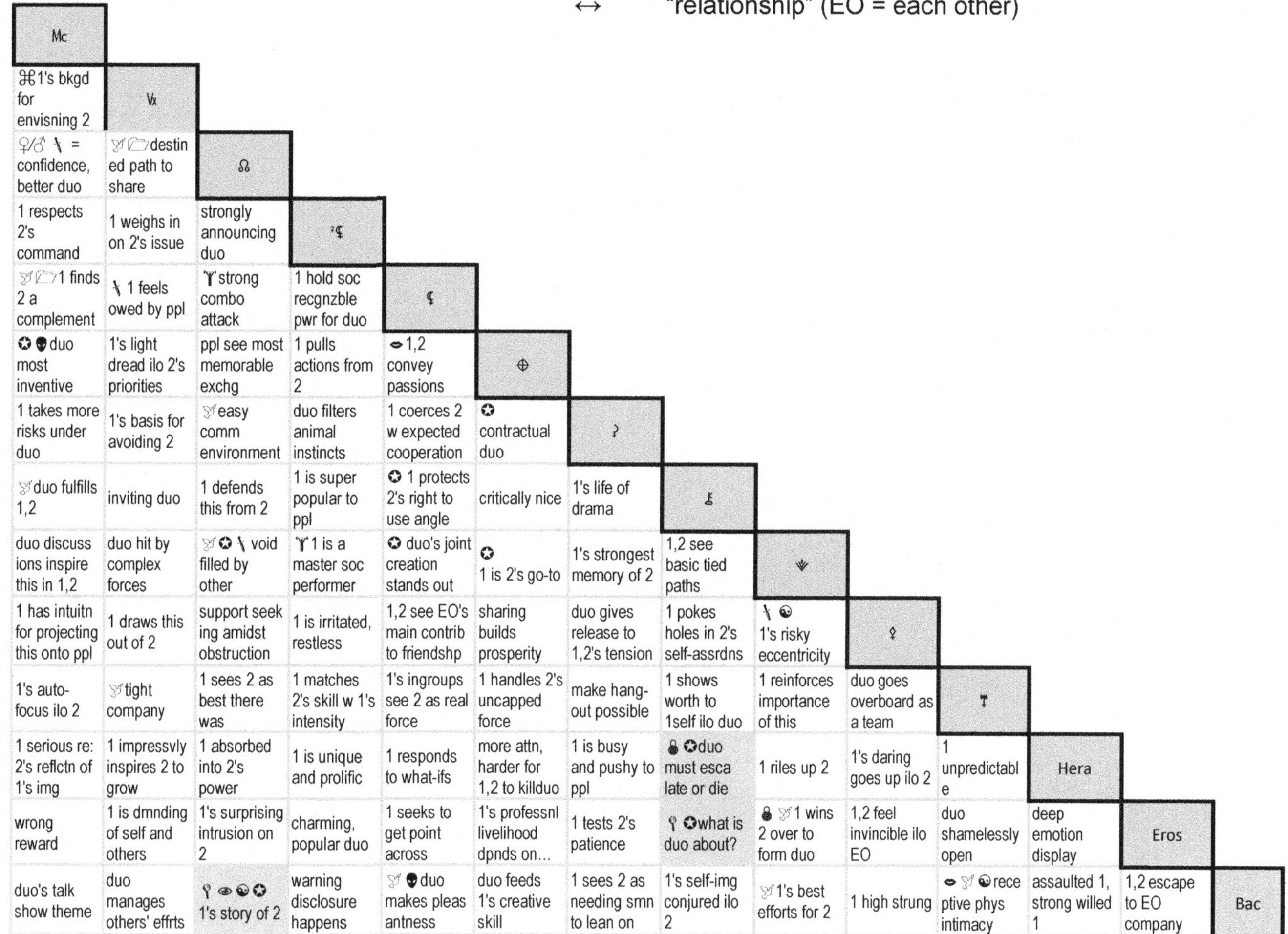

	Mc	Vx	☊	²⚸	⚸	⊕	[illegible]	⚷	[illegible]	[illegible]	[illegible]	Hera	Eros
Mc													
Vx	⌘1's bkgd for envisning 2												
☊	♀/♂ 🗡 = confidence, better duo	🕊🗁destined path to share											
²⚸	1 respects 2's command	1 weighs in on 2's issue	strongly announcing duo										
⚸	🕊🗁1 finds 2 a complement	🗡 1 feels owed by ppl	Y strong combo attack	1 hold soc recgnzble pwr for duo									
⊕	✪👽duo most inventive	1's light dread ilo 2's priorities	ppl see most memorable exchg	1 pulls actions from 2	👄1,2 convey passions								
[illegible]	1 takes more risks under duo	1's basis for avoiding 2	🕊easy comm environment	duo filters animal instincts	1 coerces 2 w expected cooperation	✪ contractual duo							
⚷	🕊duo fulfills 1,2	inviting duo	1 defends this from 2	1 is super popular to ppl	✪ 1 protects 2's right to use angle	critically nice	1's life of drama						
[illegible]	duo discussions inspire this in 1,2	duo hit by complex forces	🕊✪🗡 void filled by other	Y1 is a master soc performer	✪ duo's joint creation stands out	✪ 1 is 2's go-to	1's strongest memory of 2	1,2 see basic tied paths					
[illegible]	1 has intuitn for projecting this onto ppl	1 draws this out of 2	support seeking amidst obstruction	1 is irritated, restless	1,2 see EO's main contrib to friendshp	sharing builds prosperity	duo gives release to 1,2's tension	1 pokes holes in 2's self-assrdns	🗡☯ 1's risky eccentricity				
[illegible]	1's auto-focus ilo 2	🕊tight company	1 sees 2 as best there was	1 matches 2's skill w 1's intensity	1's ingroups see 2 as real force	1 handles 2's uncapped force	make hang-out possible	1 shows worth to 1self ilo duo	1 reinforces importance of this	duo goes overboard as a team			
Hera	1 serious re: 2's reflctn of 1's img	1 impressvly inspires 2 to grow	1 absorbed into 2's power	1 is unique and prolific	1 responds to what-ifs	more attn, harder for 1,2 to killduo	1 is busy and pushy to ppl	🔒✪duo must escalate or die	1 riles up 2	1's daring goes up ilo 2	1 unpredictable		
Eros	wrong reward	1 is dmnding of self and others	1's surprising intrusion on 2	charming, popular duo	1 seeks to get point across	1's professnl livelihood dpnds on...	1 tests 2's patience	⚲ ✪what is duo about?	🔒 🕊1 wins 2 over to form duo	1,2 feel invincible ilo EO	duo shamelessly open	deep emotion display	
Bac	duo's talk show theme	duo manages others' effrts	⚲👁☯✪ 1's story of 2	warning disclosure happens	🕊👽duo makes pleasantness	duo feeds 1's creative skill	1 sees 2 as needing smn to lean on	1's self-img conjured ilo 2	🕊1's best efforts for 2	1 high strung	👄🕊☯receptive phys intimacy	assaulted 1, strong willed 1	1,2 escape to EO company

Glossary

air element corresponding to processes which unfold against a clear background context

angle-sign the sign which corresponds to each angle's harmonic within a block of 12

Arabic Parts calculated points on the chart which usually take the angle between two planets and subtract it from a third point in order to show how the original two-planet angle plays out in light of the third

ASC*, MC*, Vertex*, and Fortune* averaged versions of ASC, MC, Vertex, and Fortune

Ascendant (ASC) the start of the 1st house

aspect angle of separation between astrological bodies

beat when waves of two different slightly different frequencies interfere

belief a construct which a person steers his actions around the existence of

benefic a positive planet

birth chart synastry composite expression the use of outs for activating or improving the expression of angles in a composite chart

body (see "planet")

cocktails those combinations of planet pairs which, when activated together, produce predictable effects in an astrochart; groups of three or more planets or locations which mix to produce pronounced personality traits beyond the individual pairs

commitment-objects the undertakings to which you are committed

component charts the charts that make up a composite chart

composite chart the average of A's and B's charts as seen from the perspective of an insider responding to the "beats" between their corresponding realms of behavior

construct induction where the supposed character of an object in a sequence is determined by the first thing that can be done with it which previous objects could not do

cusp the start of a house, going counterclockwise around the astrowheel

Davison chart see "relative chart"

definer a planet pair which is useful for determining how a newly researched astrological factor behaves; such pairs tend to be obvious and distinguishable in their effects

dehumanization denigration of abstract groups for the uplift of one's own

destiny where things feel that 1) they are as they should be and 2) they remove your reason (or means) for turning back to something different

earth element corresponding to constructs which exist against a clear background context

elements a family of labels which describe processes or things, with or without context; fire earth, air, and water

embarrassment the feeling of discontentment in light of an action you've performed which you now would rather have been some other action that better aligned with other people's standards

fame notoriety that viewers recognize as being society-wide

fbow for better or worse

fire element corresponding to processes which unfold without a clear background context

fishbowl the everyday default group with which you interface voluntarily interact

flanking angle for an angle measure X, one of the angles in a pre-set harmonic which is the nearest lower or nearest higher angle next to angle X

following angle the angle which is one later than the one in question

formula combination of planet pairs; less complete than a cocktail

four-pattern the cycle of different ways in which a single harmonic can play out

fr&s fleeting acquaintanceships which initially look like friendships

frustration a feeling of inner discord that comes with ongoing failure to achieve what you want

generational planets Neptune, Pluto, and other super-slow movers which take several generations to change signs

half-pair mutuality where you and another person have similar or equal angles no matter which synastric half-pair you look at; mutual aspects are a stronger kind of half-pair mutuality

harmonics families of angles which require the same number of repeats to make a whole circle

house systems ways to slice the sky into sections

houses regions of the local sky which tell you the areas of life your various planets are most comfortable expressing in; divisions of the sky into 12 sections as a way of locating roughly where each planet is with respect to that horizon

infamous negative popularity

inspiration where one's mood is steered towards a certain action; the emotional context for getting people to act on their motivations

key pair a single synastric pair which serves as the main reason for keeping a relationship healthy

level a layer of 12 harmonics

level I aspects forming multiples of $^1/_2$ through $^1/_{12}$ of a circle, or 0°

level II aspects forming multiples of $^1/_{13}$ through $^1/_{24}$ of a circle

level III aspects forming multiples of $^1/_{25}$ through $^1/_{36}$ of a circle

major aspects the conjunct, trine, opposition, square, sextile, and sometimes the inconjunct

malefic a negative planet in astrology

Midheaven (MC) the start of the 10th house

modulation where one wave travels through another, adding to or subtracting from the strength of the other

mutual aspects in synastry, where both people have the same angle for both half-pairs; where the angle for [Mars $_{you}$-Vertex $_{them}$] is the same as [Mars $_{them}$-Vertex $_{you}$], for example; mutual aspects are a stronger kind of half-pair mutuality where the harmonics between half-pairs are the same (instead of just being similar)

nearest midpoint composite chart composite chart where all planets and points are the mathematical average of their component versions; sky angles and Arabic parts (like Fortune) are not recalculated given new planet positions; and no outer-midpoints are allowed

notoriety where a lot of people talk about you

notorious popularity associated with a discouraged social role

orb the range of effect for an aspect

out a planet in the composite chart which is conjunct one of the planets in its component charts

outer-midpoints midpoints located in an arc of greater than 180° between the planets that formed them

personal planets the Moon, Sun, Mercury, Venus, and Mars—those which show how we interact on an individual level

planet anything that can show up in an astrochart which represents a particular kind of experience; can be imaginary points; actual, calculated and lesser solid bodies which represent a particular family of interactions one has with the world

Points of Action, Worth, and Internal Monologue "rulers" of Aries, Taurus and Gemini respectively

popularity where people talk about you a lot

possessor in synastry, the person whose main chart we're looking at

prior angle the angle which is one harmonic below the one in question

prior pair composite expression the use of prior pairs to activate composite angles

rectification birth time correction for charts which have no known birth time

regret a feeling of lowered contentment in light of an experience you've had which you now wish you had helped steer in some way other than the way it went

relative chart the chart of a third party born exactly between two partners' birth dates and birth places

relative chart using time and place averaging to calculate the combined chart between two people

renown where you are widely known in such a way as to be synonymous with a bigger idea

resonant pairs planet pairs which are separated by the same harmonic

resonant pairs the collection of planet pairs, in a single chart or synastry, with the same harmonic; all conjuncts, all deciles, all septiles, for example

right relationship what the default flow of impressions is between two people

ruler the planet associated with a certain sign

self chart your regular birth chart interpreted using synastric interpretations

self-other-world the division of the 12 signs into three sections of four. Section 1 shows how we interact with ourselves, section 2 shows how we interact with others or objects right in front of us, and section 3 shows how we interact with the faceless world around us

shock where an event quickly and singly floods its viewer with the unexpected information normally issued by a crowd

sidereal system where astrological sign locations are based on actual start locations

significator a point located on the astrowheel to represent some kind of experience

signs sections of the universal sky which give a certain character to the objects in them

social planets Jupiter, Saturn, Uranus, Neptune and slow movers around them like Chiron which change with large groups, taking one to several generations to circle the astrowheel

society in the study of harmonic levels, the small-ish sphere of people you actually live and work among

spiritual power the skill in reacting to emotions felt in a certain environment

standard composite chart a chart that consists of mostly the midpoints of two component charts

synastric planets in houses in synastry, a visitor's planets in a possessor's houses

synastry the practice of seeing how two astrology charts affect each other

synastry with a composite the synastry between [(Person A) and (the relative chart of Person B with Person A themselves)]

three person synastry the synastry between [(Person A) and (the relative chart of Person B with Person C)]

transit astrology looking at the chart of a specific day and interpreting how its characteristics

tropical system where astrological sign locations are based on the Earth's seasons; ; the system commonly used in Western astrology

visitor in synastry, the person whose single planet has been plucked out for study in how it affects a possessor's chart; the person whose chart is being compared to a possessor's chart

water element corresponding to constructs which exist without a clear background context

writer the person whose component planet is conjunct a composite planet

Index

Made in the USA
Middletown, DE
08 September 2021

47833214R00338